Marian Anderson

A SINGER'S JOURNEY

Allan Keiler

A LISA DREW BOOK

SCRIBNER

NEW YORK LONDON SYDNEY SINGAPORE

A LISA DREW BOOK/SCRIBNER
1230 Avenue of the Americas
New York, NY 10020

SCRIBNER and design are trademarks of
Macmillan Library Reference USA, Inc., used under license by
Simon & Schuster, the publisher of this work.
A LISA DREW BOOK is a trademark of Simon & Schuster, Inc.

Set in Bembo

Designed by Colin Joh

Manufacturued in the United States of America

1 3 5 7 9 10 8 6 4 2

Library of Congress Cataloging-in-Publication Data

Keiler, Allan
Marian Anderson: a singer's journey/Allan Keiler
p.   cm.
"A Lisa Drew Book"
Includes discography, bibliographical references, and index
1. Anderson, Marian, 1897–1993.
2. Contraltos—United States Biography.
3. Afro-American women singers Biography. I. Title.

782.1'092—dc21   99–43319
[B]   CIP

ISBN 0-684-80711-4

Photo permissions appear on the last page of the photo insert.

In memory of my mother, Pearl Keiler

Acknowledgments

In May 1992, I wrote to James DePreist, conductor of the Oregon Symphony Orchestra and Marian Anderson's nephew, telling him of my desire to write a biography of Miss Anderson and asking him for his support. I explained to Jimmy—as I gradually came to call him—that I felt that the legend of Marian Anderson was now so deeply anchored in our social consciousness that it has thrown a long shadow over her achievements as an artist, and that I wanted to write a biography in which Miss Anderson's art would remain at the center of her legacy. Jimmy promised to help in any way he could, and to encourage his aunt to participate. In December, I traveled to Portland, where Miss Anderson was then living with Jimmy and his wife, Ginette. I was able to meet twice with Miss Anderson. The first time was an informal, impromptu visit in which we talked a great deal about Roland Hayes, who acted as a mentor to Miss Anderson during her high school years and whom she idolized, and her grandfather, Benjamin Anderson, whose religion—he was a black Jew—I wanted to know more about. The second visit, the following day, was a much longer session of several hours. Miss Anderson was ninety-five at the time yet she responded to my questions with patience and remarkable concentration, in one instance, during a discussion of her student days in Berlin, gently correcting my less than perfect German. I remain, as I no doubt always will, grateful for the hours of conversation I had with Miss Anderson, and for the hospitality of Jimmy and his wife and their kindness in making my visit—and later visits as well—possible.

In general, my debt to Jimmy is enormous. Through the years of my research and writing in which interviews, phone calls, requests for more information and more clarification, and gentle reminders of promises to make available to me private material must have seemed to him endless, Jimmy's patience and encouragement never wavered. And more than anything, I think, I am grateful for his readiness to discuss with me personal matters of considerable delicacy, matters that required trust as well as time and patience. Hardly less am I indebted to other family members, whose help I hope is apparent, directly and indirectly, throughout the text and notes. I must mention here Ginette DePreist; Sandra Grymes and Lillian Bass, both cousins of Miss Anderson; Brenda Anderson, the grandniece of Queenie and Grace Anderson, whose father, William

Acknowledgments

Anderson, was the brother of John Berkley Anderson, Marian Anderson's father; George Fisher, a nephew of Miss Anderson's husband, Orpheus Fisher; and James Fischer, Orpheus Fisher's son by his first marriage, all of whose help I found invaluable. I owe as well an enormous debt to Sylvia Rupp and June Goodman, both of whom have helped me with extraordinary dedication in innumerable ways.

I must express my appreciation to the extraordinary staff of the Walter H. and Leonore Annenberg Rare Book and Manuscript Library of the University of Pennsylvania, where the Marian Anderson Papers are housed, and particularly to Nancy M. Shawcross (Curator of Manuscripts), Marjorie Hassen (Head of the Otto E. Albrecht Music Library), Maggie Kruesi (Manuscripts Cataloguer), and Adam Corson-Finnerty (Director of Library Development). My debt to them—for their encouragement, unfailing patience, and resourcefulness in dealing with my relentless questions and calls for help—goes well beyond the usual. Indeed, my work with them constitutes what can only be thought of as an ongoing, seven-year-long partnership.

I would like to acknowledge the generous assistance of the following archivists and librarians in my research: Alice Adamswzyk (Schomburg Center for Research and Black Culture, New York Public Library), JoAnne Barry (Philadelphia Orchestra Archives), Johan Bielke (Swedish Broadcasting Company), Thomas Boltenstern (Konsertbolaget, Stockholm), Beverly Carlson (American Baptist Association, Valley Forge, Pennsylvania), Bryan Cornell (Library of Congress), Birgitta Dahl (Musikmuseet, Stockholm),Sonita Cox (EMI Music Archives), Claudia Depkin (BMG Archives), Ruth Edge (EMI Music Archives). Laverne Hill Flanagan (Office of the Registrar, Howard University), Gino Francesconi (Carnegie Hall Archives), Sid Grolin (Music Division, Free Library of Philadelphia), Barbara Haws (New York Philharmonic Symphony Orchestra Archives), Louisa Hegedus (Library of Congress), Walter B. Hill, Jr. (National Archives at College Park, Maryland), Margaret Jessup (Sophia Smith Collection and College Archives, Smith College), Agatha Pfeiffer Kalkanis (Music and Performing Arts Department, Detroit Public Library), Phil Lapansky (Library Company of Philadelphia), Roger Lindberg (Fazer Artists' Management Inc., Helsinki), Don McCormick (Rogers and Hammerstein Archives of Recorded Sound, New York Public Library), Bernadette Moore (BMG Archives), Mary C. Ordway (Danbury Scott-Fanton Museum and Historical Society, Inc.), Dede Puma (San Francisco Performing Arts Library and Museum), Roswitha Rash (Lynchburg Virginia Museum System), the Reference Division of the *Danbury News Times,* Wayne Rhodes (Jones Memorial

Library, Lynchburg, Virginia), Simon Rooks (BBC Information and Archives), April Smith (University Musical Society, University of Michigan), Jessie Smith (Special Collections Archives, Fisk University), Tom Tierney (BMG Archives), Robert W. Tissing, Jr. (Lyndon Baines Johnson Library), and the archival staff of the Wigmore Hall, London.

In connection with research on Marian Anderson's commercial as well as unpublished and private recordings, I wish to thank the following people for their help: Maria Fernandez (Corporación Artes Escénico-Musicales, San Juan, Puerto Rico), Ernie Gilbert (VAI Recordings), Daniel Guss (BMG), Niels Høirup (BMG, Germany), Lawrence Holdridge, Ward Marston, Mark Obert-Thorn, Anibal Ramirez (General Archives, Museo Pablo Casals, Santurce, Puerto Rico), and William H. Scheide.

Several scholars were kind enough to give me the benefit of their ongoing research: Murray Dubin, who talked to me about his research on the history of South Philadelphia; Harlow Robinson, who allowed me to read an early version of his chapter on Marian Anderson and Sol Hurok from his book *The Last Impressario*; and Scott A. Sandage, who, with extraordinary generosity, shared with me not only archival material but his ideas about Anderson's concert at the Lincoln Memorial.

For their skill and assistance in translations I am grateful to Ani Chamakhian-Hovsepian (Russian), Shachar Gilad (Hebrew), Paulina Girsen (Finnish and Swedish), Hinda Gutoff (Czech), Ole Jensen (Norwegian and Danish), Alex Spivakovsky (Russian), Maria Virkkunen (Finnish and Swedish), and Antonina Zebedeva-Emelina (Russian).

I have had a number of research assistants, both here and abroad, whose dedication and thoroughness was in every case remarkable: Ned Bloom, Danielle Anctil, Ani Chamakhian-Hovsepian, Joe Darby, Jonothan Douglas, David Ferris, Caroline Johns, Kevin Karnes, Tom Licata, Eric Marshall, Daniel Page, Luann Rosenthal-Erickson, Pia Rothstein, Stephanie Schlagel, Simon Sinek, Donovan Stokes, and Antonina Zebedeva-Emelina. Kevin Karnes deserves credit not only for his work as a research assistant, but for organizing and putting together virtually the entire discography.

I am also grateful to many people who gave generously of their time in ways too numerous to mention: Jay Axelbank, David Cohen, Bill Esher, Robert Etherington, Patrick Fairfield, Victor Ford, Michal Glover, Patrick Hayes, Carol Keiler, James Kloppenberg, David Kopp, Rebecca Kowals, Carla Lane, Blanche Burton Lyles, Neal Marcus, Robert Marshall, Dr. Robert Mehlman, Donald Polzella, Dorothy Potter, Nancy Redgate, Bonnie Rowan, David Saint George, Sol Saporta, Michael Schiano,

Acknowledgments

Andrew Seplow, Richard Sylvester, Steven Watson, Dr. Samuel Williams, Pamela Wolf, Rachel Worby, and Jed Wyrick.

Brandeis University has been generous with its support, providing me with leave time in the fall of 1993, sabbatical leave in the fall of 1996, and a Mazer Grant for Faculty Research and Creative Projects in the summer of 1998. I am indebted to Northeastern University Press for its encouragement and support during the initial stage of work on the present biography. I am very grateful to Jeffrey Masson, from whose encouragement and advice I have profited in many ways.

I am very grateful to Leontyne Price for allowing me to quote from one of her letters to Marian Anderson.

A number of people have read parts of the manuscript at various stages, providing me with advice and criticism that I cannot imagine now having done without: Scott Burnham, Sheila Brachfeld-Child, Peter Child, David Cohen, Kevin Karnes, David Kopp, Jeffrey Masson, Edward Nowacki, Daniel Page, Donald Polzella, and Anne Tyson. I owe a special debt of gratitude to Marion Wasserman, who read the entire manuscript with extraordinary care and dedication. Her wisdom and experience as a writer have left their mark on virtually every page of my book.

I am grateful for the dedicated work of Jake Klisivitch, assistant editor at Scribner and Charles Naylor, my copyeditor.

Finally, I wish to thank my agent, Elaine Markson, and my editor at Scribner, Lisa Drew. They have been my twin pillars of support and encouragement, Elaine constantly urging me on, and Lisa holding me to the highest standards of accuracy and conception.

Contents

Marian Anderson

CHAPTER ONE

Childhood in South Philadelphia (1897–1915)

"Come and hear the baby contralto, ten years old."

Catching sight of a small handbill lying on the ground, the young girl noticed something curiously familiar about it. When she picked it up, she saw her picture in the corner and then, beneath the picture, her name, Marian Anderson. Only then did she notice the words of invitation. Her excitement was so great that, returning home from the grocer's, she discovered she had bought potatoes and not bread, as her mother had asked. On her way back to the grocer's, she held fast to the handbill which had so unexpectedly made her aware of her fame. In later years, thinking about her childhood in South Philadelphia, she recalled that handbill far more vividly than her actual singing.[1]

Benjamin Anderson, Marian Anderson's grandfather, was the first of the Andersons to settle in South Philadelphia. He was born in 1848, in King William County, Virginia, part of the Middle Peninsula in the Tidewater.[2] Like many freed blacks in the fertile lands of eastern Virginia, he earned his living farming. Benjamin was a small man. For someone who worked outdoors in the fields all day, he did not seem in the least robust. Quiet, rarely raising his voice at all, he was kindly and sensitive. In 1869 he married Mary Holmes. She too had grown up in the Tidewater of eastern Virginia, in King and Queen County. To many they must have seemed an unlikely couple. Mary, or Isabella, as everyone knew her, was tall, easily a head taller than Benjamin, and temperamentally as outspoken and fiercely determined, even imperious, as Benjamin was soft-spoken and tolerant. As far as Isabella was concerned, her self-reliance came from her Native American heritage, which she exhibited prominently in her high cheekbones and her large, almond-shaped eyes with their thick, perfectly arched eyebrows. In twelve years of marriage, Isabella gave birth to eight children, five of whom—four sons and a daughter—survived infancy.[3]

Virginia suffered more physical destruction than any state during the Civil War, causing a vast exodus of blacks to the large industrial cities of the North after the war. Near the end of the century Benjamin Anderson and his family joined the exodus north, not only to escape the clutches of Jim Crow but to seek more opportunites for work and better schools.[4] They settled in South Philadelphia, in a large house on Fitzwater Street, among the blacks, Jews, Italians and Irish who made up one of the oldest ethnically and racially diverse neighborhoods in the country.[5] Like most streets in South Philadelphia, Fitzwater was lined with row houses, many of them with the green shutters and white marble stoops typical of the neighborhood. Benjamin found work as a laborer. Isabella took in boarders, some of them children whose parents were not able to keep their families together. On occasion, she also acted as midwife for neighborhood doctors.

John Berkley Anderson, the oldest of Benjamin and Isabella's children, was only nineteen when, in 1895, he met Annie Delilah Rucker. Annie Delilah's parents, Robert and Ellen Rucker, had grown up in Boonsboro, in Bedford County, Virginia, just west of Lynchburg. Both parents believed in the value of education and encouraged their four children to aim high. Robert himself was resourceful, with good business instincts and a clear eye toward the economic advantages offered by the growing city of Lynchburg after Reconstruction. With John T. Wilkinson, another merchant, Robert opened a livery stable on Sixth Street, in downtown Lynchburg, where they sold feed, boarded stock, and transported passengers to and from the train station. Annie's brother, William Henry, like her sister Elnora, remained in Lynchburg. Alice, another sister, left Lynchburg for Philadelphia, where she married Grant Ward. It was an illness of Alice's that first brought Annie, who was then twenty-one, to Philadelphia, and it was Grant Ward who brought Annie and John Berkley together.[6]

John and Annie must have had a whirlwind romance, to judge from Marian's version of their first meeting, which she wrote down many years later in a notebook filled with concert engagements and everyday domestic reminders: "On a summer vacation visit to her older sister, my Mother, a Virginian by birth, came to Philadelphia from Lynchburg where she was a school teacher. . . . It was Mother's brother-in-law who introduced her to his friend, the unusual young man who neither drank, smoked nor chewed, was an active Christian, a steady worker and maintained his own room in the home of his parents. And so it is little wonder that she should become Mrs. John Berkley Anderson." [7] They married that same year and moved into the house of one of John's friends, on Webster Street, where they rented a room on the second floor.

John and Annie, like John's parents, formed a study in contrast. Annie was short and rather plumpish. John, well over six feet tall, towered above her. As Marian often recalled in later years, John liked to tease Annie about how much shorter she was: "I remember once when she was helping Father put on his tie and she was reaching up on tiptoe. He laughed heartily and told her to get a newspaper to stand on to make herself a little taller."[8] Annie was modest and retiring. John was a man of considerable charm, outgoing, even flirtatious. Like all the Andersons, he had Isabella's features, the same high cheekbones and piercing eyes. Like his mother and most of the Andersons, John Berkley was Baptist and attended Union Baptist Church, where he was a special officer, helping to seat people and to keep the children out of the balcony. For him religion was in large measure a social and neighborly activity. Annie was a Methodist, worshipping at the old Bainbridge Street Methodist Church, later the Tindley Temple. With an unquestioning belief in the church and its teachings, Annie was guided by a dutiful yet compassionate spirituality.

John and Annie both worked hard during their first year of marriage, hoping to earn enough to raise a family. John worked in downtown Philadelphia at the Reading Terminal, where he sold ice and coal. Eventually he had a small liquor business as well, which Marian always chose to forget. Annie had attended the Virginia Seminary and College in Lynchburg for a short time, which had allowed her to teach in the Virginia schools even without the full credentials of a teacher's college. In Philadelphia, however, no black teacher could teach without full credentials, and even with them could teach only in schools attended primarily by black students. Few blacks were able to attend high school in those years, so only the elementary schools in predominantly black neighborhoods held any promise for black teachers. Eventually Annie might have been able to teach in one of these, but even this would have required further accreditation and considerable good fortune. She settled instead, until her first child was born, for looking after small children.[9]

Marian was born on February 27, 1897, the first of three daughters.[10] When she was about two years old, the family, having outgrown the small room on Webster Street, went to live with Benjamin and Isabella. Marian's two sisters were born there, Alyse in 1900, Ethel May in 1902. Years later, Marian would recall Alyse's arrival as the first event of consequence in her grandparents' house: "My earliest recollection is that of the third-story room my parents occupied in that house. Somehow I was in that room—I had crawled under the bed when the doctor had arrived and perhaps had fallen asleep there. I heard a cry. It was the first cry of my new sister, Alyse. I peeked out. There was the doctor and there was his black bag. Long after I should have known better, I believed that Alyse had been fetched in that black bag."[11]

After Ethel was born, John Berkley and Annie rented a small house of their own, on Colorado Street, near the corner of Seventeenth Street, only a few blocks from John's parents. Marian always carried vivid memories of the house on Colorado Street: "The house did not have a real bathroom, but Mother was undaunted. We were lathered and rinsed at least once a day, and on Saturday a huge wooden tub was set in the center of the kitchen floor. After sufficiently warm water was poured in, we were lifted inside. Mother would kneel and give us a good scrubbing with ivory soap. Then we were put to bed."[12] But more than anything, it was the powerful bond between mother and daughter that Marian remembered most vividly: "Mother spent a lot of time in the kitchen. Because I was the eldest I was soon allowed to remain with her when my sisters were tucked into bed. Sometimes I would try to help with little things, although I don't know how much use I really was to Mother."[13] For the most part Marian was content to be near her mother, often sitting alone, quietly self-absorbed. Later, Marian liked to recall an incident when her mother found her sitting in a little chair in the living room, laughing. When her mother asked her why she was laughing, Marian explained that she had been watching the flower-decorated border around the room, the walls becoming alive with people laughing and waving.

As an adult Marian claimed to have a clear memory of her father, but her portrait of him is anything but distinct: "We do not have any photograph of him, but I have a picture in my mind of a man, dark, handsome, tall, and neither too stout nor too thin. I cannot say how tall, but he was well over six feet and stood very erect."[14] Mostly she remembered her father's pride in his daughters, and his delight in showing them off: "Easter was another big day. Father made it a point to provide us with new bonnets, and he would go to a shop, and select them himself. When we were very young he would bring each of us one of the sailor hats then in fashion, with a gay ribbon trailing down the back. Later on he chose different bonnets for each of us, and he always insisted that they be trimmed with flowers."[15]

Even before the family moved to Colorado Street, Marian's musical talent was apparent to everyone. Her mother remembered that, "even before the age of two years, [Marian] would sit at her toy piano, and play and sing original ditties, sometimes in a loud voice, then, in subdued tones, sincere and always highly delighted. Thus she would entertain herself for more than an hour at a time."[16] When she was three, her mother told a friend years later: "She had a toy which was made of metal strips mounted on two small blocks of wood. When the metal strips were hit with the little hammer, they produced music. This was her great pleasure from the first thing in the morning to the last thing before bed. In time the little eight note toy could no longer do all the things she wanted it to do, so by a great stretch of the imagination, a stair step became her instrument. The bottom step was her piano stool while the step above was her piano. She would sit there and play and sing by the hour."

When she was six—the family had already moved to Colorado Street—Marian enjoyed a brief period of excitement with a violin. As she later recalled: "Somebody took me to a concert and this was a Negro orchestra and the violinist came forward and played a solo, and I thought, that's for me. The big thing then for making money was scrubbing steps, so I scrubbed steps and would get five cents or ten cents, or whatever. I did steps for four or five different people. Finally I saw a violin in a pawn shop and my aunt went with me and I think it cost all of three dollars or a little more."[17] There was no money for lessons, so she had to make do with the frustrating help of a family friend who gave her some rudimentary instruction. Her interest may very well have outlasted the violin, for gradually, string by string, it gave out.

A few years later Marian's father bought the family a piano from his brother Walter. Although there was no money for lessons, she and her sisters learned to play the scales and some melodies in the key of C. They liked to sit on their father's knee as he sat at the piano, trying to teach him what they had learned on their own: "He would almost always manage to strike two keys at a time in order to let us feel that we were so much better at piano-playing than he was. He could easily have struck one key, you know, but generally, when we were guiding his finger, it went on two keys at a time. We were so thrilled that we were able to teach him."[18] One day Marian discovered in a powerful way that she could excel at playing the piano if she wanted to: "I was walking along the street one day, carrying a basket of laundry that I was delivering for my mother, when I heard the sound of the piano. I set down my basket, went up the steps, and looked into the window. I knew it was wrong to peep, but I could not resist the temptation. I saw a woman seated at a piano, playing ever so beautifully. Her skin was dark, like mine. I realized that if she could, I could."[19]

At home Marian threw herself into every musical opportunity that presented itself. At school there were few such opportunities. In 1906, after four years of primary school, she entered the Stanton Grammar School. Like the neighborhood, the Stanton school was mixed, with white and black students, but, reflecting the school board's policy not to place black teachers in all-white or mixed schools, it had only white teachers. Not until the twenties did the school have good musicians among the faculty and offer regular music classes as part of the curriculum. When she went to Stanton, there was music at morning assemblies where the children sang hymns or heard recordings—often Scottish ballads or records of David Bispham, a Philadelphia-born baritone who had a distinguished career in opera. Otherwise, the children would have only occasional opportunities to sing in the classroom.[20] If a room in which there happened to be singing was close by, Marian was there with the students singing. "I was as completely in that other room," she recalled years later, "as one could be while one's body was elsewhere. When the day came for our class to go there for singing, I was the happiest child in the school. I knew every song—at least I thought I did. I remember that when my favorite song was passed out to the children I just put back my head and sang as loudly as I could." Marian's mother too remembered how much music dominated her attention in school: "While she was studious in school, no lessons came easy to her. Taking a part in devotionals in school, the teacher soon noticed Marian's voice, and when a class play was given, Marian was always assigned a singing part. She not only learned her part, but invariably learned all of the other parts, and taught the song to her two younger sisters at home."[21]

In South Philadelphia's black community, musical talent was fostered and encouraged in church. Gifted black musicians who could not teach in the schools or were ignored by the white musical establishment of the city found jobs in black churches as choir directors. By the turn of the century, Philadelphia had the largest black population of any city in the North, more than half living in South Philadelphia, so many of the black churches had large enough congregations to be able to hire well-trained musicians and to support a large program of musical activities. Union Baptist Church, founded in 1832 during the presidency of Andrew Jackson, is one of the oldest and most important black churches in South

Philadelphia. The original church building was on Minster Street between Sixth and Seventh, in one of the densest and liveliest black neighborhoods. In less than a decade there was a membership of 200; by the end of the Civil War, the congregation had doubled, and only Shiloh Baptist Church was larger. In 1888, the cornerstone for a new church building was laid on Twelfth Street below Bainbridge. There, in the church where Isabella and all of her children worshipped, Marian's musical talent developed.[22]

Even before Marian was six she would go with her grandmother and the other Andersons to Union Baptist every Sunday, first to Sunday school and, when she was older, to the main service. When she was six she joined the junior choir, which was then directed by Alexander Robinson, an experienced choir director and assistant director of the Arion Glee Club, one of the largest and most important black choral groups in Philadelphia. Robinson was the first professional musician to recognize her extraordinary voice, with its well-developed lower range that extended upward nearly three octaves, unusual in a young child. He also recognized how consumed she was with the desire to learn and to perform. In later years, she always gave Robinson credit for his generosity and his musical knowledge. He was a person, she later said, "who, out of sheer love for the church and out of a spirit of service, gave his time freely to help others. It gave him pleasure to work with those young voices, and since he loved music and understood enough to communicate his feeling to us, he was able to do something with us. It was not long before the group was singing so well that it was invited to appear before the older children's Sunday school, which convened in the afternoon."[23]

As part of the choir, Marian was entrusted with duets and eventually solos. With a friend who lived across the street, she performed the hymn "Dear to the Heart of the Shepherd," first for her Sunday school class, then for the main service. Later on, she sang the alto part in a quartet of young girls, and with her Aunt Mary—John Berkley's sister—who sang with the senior choir, she would get to sing duets, one of their numbers being "Sing Me to Sleep, the Shadows Fall." Before long she had opportunities to sing in neighborhood churches. On one such occasion, her Aunt Mary, wanting to do something for the building fund of a new storefront church, made sure that she would take part in a concert she helped arrange. Handbills were printed up with her picture, promising the unusual pleasure of hearing a ten-year-old singer who was a real contralto.

It was Aunt Mary more than anyone in the family who encouraged

Marian's love of singing, taking her to concerts in the local churches and encouraging her to take part. From the time she was six or seven, Aunt Mary would take her to church functions, YMCA or YWCA events, or social gatherings arranged by women's groups devoted to the cause of a black charity, where Marian would perform one or two songs and earn twenty-five or fifty cents. "Are you her mother?" Mary would invariably be asked. "No, I'm her aunt!" she would respond, and off they would go to another church.[24] The twenty-five or fifty cents soon became several dollars, sometimes as much as five dollars. As Marian liked to recall, with a certain amount of pride, one dollar would go to each of her sisters, one dollar to herself, and two dollars to her mother.

Eventually Marian's abilities brought her to the attention of professional musicians in Philadelphia's black community. One of these was Emma Aza-lia Hackley, an accomplished singer and a teacher of tireless energy and strong musical convictions, who had come to Philadelphia at the start of the century. At the request of the Reverend Phillips of the Church of the Cruci-fixion, which had become since its modest beginning half a century earlier one of the great cultural and spiritual forces among black Episcopalians in South Philadelphia, Hackley undertook to develop the best choir in the city. In 1904, in addition to her work at the Church of the Crucifixion, she founded the People's Chorus, composed of a hundred voices recruited from the various church choirs of the city.[25] Marian's triumphs at Union Baptist were so celebrated that Hackley accepted her among the younger members of the People's Chorus. Before long, she gave her a solo to sing—"to inspire the other members to higher things," she liked to say. At the time, she was only ten or eleven. Hackley had her stand on a chair as she sang. "I want her to feel elevated," Hackley told the man arranging the stage properties, "and, too, I want no one in the back of the hall to have the slightest difficulty in seeing her."[26]

In 1909, a few weeks before Christmas, John Berkley was accidentally struck on the head while at work at the Reading Terminal. He lay ill for weeks before he died, of heart failure, a month later. He was thirty-four years old. As she did with most painful experiences, Marian later spoke about the loss of her father obliquely, her memories of his illness, and of her attendant fear and sense of deprivation, intertwined with that Christ-mas season. "A woman who lived in our neighborhood," she recalled many years later, "met me on the street a few days before Christmas and asked me what I wanted to find under the tree. She was married, and had no children, and was very well off. Perhaps I hoped she could help with our Christmas, although I had not thought much about the fact that

Father's illness would affect our celebration of the holiday. In any event, I told her what I wanted from Santa Claus and she replied, 'Well, you're not going to get it. I'm ashamed of you, a girl as old as you who doesn't know there is no Santa Claus.' I was old enough to know, of course, but I had been told at home that there was a Santa Claus and that was it for me. My eyes filled with tears. I could not speak about it to Mother. We did get some gifts at Christmas time, but they were things that Mother knew we needed, and the woman's thoughtlessness clung to me and spoiled that Christmas."[27]

Mrs. Anderson thought she could keep her children together best by going back to Virginia, where most of her family still lived, but Isabella, who wanted a say in raising her son's children, was willing to take them all in and would have none of it. It was Ethel, Marian's younger sister, who later recalled the move back to Fitzwater Street: "The day John Berkley was buried, in the middle of the night, Aunt Mary and some of the men in the family took down the beds and took them around the corner to Fitzwater Street."[28] The house at 1617 Fitzwater was a small, shallow three-story row house that now had to accommodate not only Mrs. Anderson and the three girls, but Isabella and Benjamin, two of their children, Mary and Walter, and two other grandchildren, Queenie and Grace. Robert William, one of Isabella and Benjamin's sons, who had died while still young, had left his wife with four children, two of whom—Queenie and Grace—Isabella was helping to raise. As always, there were also boarders.

Mrs. Anderson kept her children together, but the years under Isabella's watchful eye were difficult for her and the children both economically and emotionally. Mrs. Anderson found a job at Newman and Mayer, a tobacco factory on Second Street. Later, she took in laundry and, after some years, worked for Wanamaker's scrubbing floors. Marian, who was thirteen, and Alyse, ten, were old enough to help. In addition to scrubbing steps, they often traveled to different homes in Philadelphia, sometimes taking the trolley car, to deliver laundry their mother had done. On one such occasion, Mrs. Anderson, in need of money, had hurried through a batch of laundry so that it could be delivered before the weekend. Marian delivered the laundry alone, taking it to a small apartment in a private house. As she later described the experience:

No one answered. I called out again and again; then I went into the next room and caught a glimpse of the young woman whose laundry I was delivering. She was sitting as quietly as a mouse, a book in her hands. I suspect she knew who was calling, and I can only guess that she did not answer because she did not have the money to pay. I could not bring myself to let her know that I knew she was there. I left the laundry and went home without the money. Mother did not scold me; somehow she managed that weekend.[29]

Marian said in later years: "We learned how to share a home with others, how to understand their ways and respect their rights and privileges."[30] Certainly sharing could not have been easy in a household so large and with such complicated and conflicting loyalties. Queenie and Grace, unlike Marian and her sisters, could see their mother only infrequently and unpredictably, and this in turn created a bond between the two girls and Isabella that Marian and her sisters did not always share. Mrs. Anderson needed all the patience and tactfulness she was fortunate to have in order to do her share in a household in which she was more isolated by background and relationship than Isabella's only daughter, Mary, who was committed to remaining in her mother's house and taking care of her.

After her father's death, Marian's attachment to her grandfather, Benjamin, grew significantly, his gentle presence helping to soften the sense of loss. Later she remembered with no small measure of satisfaction the times when Benjamin, usually so quiet and meek, would say to his wife when she had finally gone too far: "Isabella, that's enough!"[31] She also seems to have been drawn, perhaps more than the other Andersons, to her grandfather's unusual religion and his determination to practice it among a household of zealous Baptists. As she later recalled: "In his religion he observed Saturday as his Sabbath, spent the whole day at the Temple, and referred to himself as a Black Jew. The words 'Passover' and 'unleavened bread' I heard first from his lips."[32] Benjamin attended a small storefront church on Rosewood Street, behind Fitzwater, between Fifteenth and Broad. The congregation, which often called themselves Hebrews or Israelites, kept the Sabbath on Saturday and observed the Passover and other important Jewish holidays. The women of the congregation wore long white gowns that covered their heads, the men wore the traditional skullcaps. During the service, members of the congregation practiced the ritual of foot washing, in which they actually washed each others' feet, a ritual that led to the derogatory term of "foot washers" often attached to the church's followers.[33]

William Saunders Crowdy, the founder of the church, came to Philadelphia at the turn of the century. At first he preached on a box on Broad and Rodman Streets, taking away members from other black congregations, as his followers liked to tell it, until a delegation of black ministers went to the mayor and asked that he be run out of town. He nonetheless persisted, inspiring his followers with his extraordinary confidence and charisma, and the hope that they would one day find means to escape their state of oppression. The Old Testament story of the Exodus; the Jewish conception of the Kingdom of God; and a strong sense of family and community, drawing on the figure of Abraham, the original patriarch—these were themes Bishop Crowdy incorporated into his religious doctrine, and they appealed to Benjamin and other blacks seeking a sense of pride and self-esteem.[34]

Benjamin Anderson died only a year after Marian's father. His death not only cut off a warm and supportive relationship that had existed for Mrs. Anderson and her daughters, but also changed the complexion of relationships for Marian and her sisters in a crucial way, for now they were to spend their adolescent years in a household of strong-minded and purposeful women, each one in her own way making her life productive without the presence of husband or father.

After Benjamin's death, the family moved often, always in the same neighborhood, like many black families, having to contend with the balancing act of finding a house small enough that they could afford to rent it, yet large enough to provide decent comfort and enough room for boarders, who contributed an important share of the rent and expenses. From Fitzwater Street, the family moved to Christian Street, where Aunt Mary found them a bigger house to rent, one with more bedrooms and a beautiful bay window. Most of the families on Christian Street, white and black, were wealthy enough to own their own homes, and many of the black residents had achieved a level of success and prominence in the city. John C. Asberry, a well-known judge and civic leader, lived on the other side of Christian, two doors from the black YMCA, and William Dorsey, who had a successful catering business, lived nearby. The house was comfortable but the neighbors, observing young children under Isabella's care coming and going every day, not to mention a brood of teenage girls and their friends, made them feel uncomfortably unwelcome. As Ethel put it years later, "We didn't have any business there. When there were people on a block who didn't belong, they are ignored. We didn't have enough sense to be insulted."[35] But eventually they did, and moved again, first to a house on Eighteenth Street, and again to the Twentieth block of Carpenter.

The most difficult time for Mrs. Anderson after the death of her husband came in the summer of 1912, when Marian graduated from the Stanton School. In the fall, Marian would be ready to attend high school, but the expenses required—for clothes, books, and social gatherings—were considerable, and would put an intolerable strain on the family's income. Moreover, her return to school would deprive the family of income that she was now old enough to earn, not only from domestic work but from singing. Isabella's authority must have contributed to the final decision. If Queenie and Grace were working, then why should not Marian, who was fifteen and only two years younger than Grace, shoulder a full share of work? With what must have been aching disappointment, Mrs. Anderson acceded to the decision that, at least for the present, she could not attend high school. When she was older, Marian avoided any mention of the interruption to her education and the circumstances necessitating it, going so far, in fact, as literally to expunge those years from memory. At the time, however, she no doubt saw advantages. For her, school was not only drudgery but a distraction from music. Moreover, she had by then a powerful sense of responsibility toward her mother and younger sisters, which she could now exercise in a more mature way.[36]

Marian's teenage years, even without high school, brought many opportunities for social events. She joined the Baptists' Young People's Union, whose activities included not only music but religious discussions, and competitions such as speech making. Her attraction to the stage, an inevitable extension of her love of singing, was satisfied by membership in the Camp Fire Girls, a group that gave her opportunities for acting as well as singing. "There was a big affair," she recalled in later years, "with specialty acts, comedy skits, and singing and dancing numbers for which special music was written. There must have been about forty of us taking part. My assignment was to go on alone and sing a song at certain intervals in the entertainment, and these appearances served as introductions to what was to follow. Although my acting was confined to a few gestures here and there, I was immeasurably happy about the whole venture."[37]

In the senior choir at Union Baptist—she had joined the more advanced group a few years earlier, when she was thirteen—Marian had frequent opportunities for solos, and occasions to learn difficult and more varied music. Although naturally a contralto, with the rich, dark timbre of a lower voice, she had the range to sing soprano parts with ease. The director of the senior choir, Mr. Williams, had already discovered that she could sing any part in the choir, and was more than willing to do so when a soloist or choir member failed to appear. Marian always longed to replace Mrs. Buford, the contralto soloist in Union Baptist, but it was the absence of the soprano soloist that gave her an unexpected challenge she was to recall years later: "One of the choir's show pieces was 'Inflammatus,' which had a series of high C's for the soprano soloist. Mr. Williams, the choir leader, liked to spring pieces on us without advance warning. One Sunday morning he motioned to me to take the seat of the absent first soprano. He handed out 'Inflammatus,' and we began to sing. The high C's did not daunt me at all. I was happy to have a chance to sing them, and they came out with no effort. They may not have been perfect, but they certainly were uninhibited."[38]

Both of Marian's sisters sang in the choir at Union Baptist, and both had beautiful voices. Alyse was a soprano and Ethel had the same kind of deep, richly textured voice as Marian. Yet neither had her passion for music, nor her seriousness of purpose. More often than not they preferred to combine music with companionship, forming a trio with another young singer, Leila Fisher. The trio would sing at local churches and other events sponsored by the black community, their sense of adventure challenged on occasion as much as their musical abilities. Ethel loved to tell about one such occasion: "Reverend Jordan from the Foreign Mission Board had us sing and we gave the concert and he said he was going to pay us but Jordan slipped out and didn't give us anything. He was staying at the YMCA on Christian Street. The three of us marched to the Y and asked him where the money was. We had got him on the phone. He said he would get us some money but now he was going to bed."[39]

Marian's appearances brought her more and more into contact with other performers as well as local leaders interested in fostering talent within the black community. The resulting friendships helped to give her confidence in her abilities, and deepened her desire to have a professional career as a singer, a desire that had formed itself in her mind with little effort or much conscious awareness. Many in the black community, aware of her talent and believing that her chances for a career rested on education, were dismayed that her family could not afford to send her to high school or to provide singing lessons. One of them was the Reverend Wesley Parks, the dynamic pastor of Union Baptist, who had a special love for music. After the service one Sunday morning, the Reverend Parks took up a special collection for Marian; he wanted, as she later remembered, "to do something for our Marian."[40] The collection, amounting to $17.02, was turned over to Mrs. Anderson, to be used for whatever Marian needed most. The Buster Brown shoes she wanted, and the white silk dress she had seen at Wanamaker's, were too expensive, so they settled on making a satin evening dress that she could wear for one of her appearances, with "a five-and-ten-cent store 'gold' braid decorated with miniature blooms and leaves."[41]

Prepared to do their part, the People's Chorus organized a concert for the evening of March 26, 1914, a month past Marian's seventeenth birthday. The concert was designed to demonstrate the great diversity of talent of Philadelphia's black musicians. Music by Harry T. Burleigh, Hall Johnson, and Coleridge Taylor was performed; the performers included singers as well as instrumentalists. Marian joined the chorus in Rosamond Johnson's "Since You Went Away." Her part was noticed by the reviewer of the *Philadelphia Tribune,* who remarked on "the singularly rare contralto voice of Miss Marion E. Anderson."[42]

The sad contradiction of the seventeen-year-old contralto of immense promise who for several years had done without formal education continued to trouble the directors of the People's Chorus. In a few years, joining with other members of the black community, they would raise the money needed to further Marian's education.

CHAPTER TWO

The Struggle for Education
(1915–1921)

After Marian's appearance with the People's Chorus, a full year would go by before she was able to begin high school. Her musical education would begin sooner, but not without disappointment and humiliation. Philadelphia was still very much a southern city when it came to providing blacks opportunities for serious musical study. Most of the music conservatories had all-white faculty and accepted only white students. Any opportunities for blacks to study with white teachers were limited and unpredictable. Many black teachers, instrumentalists as well as singers, had left Philadelphia by the time of the First World War in search of better economic and artistic conditions. Emma Azalia Hackley, who had contributed so much to the musical life of Philadelphia, had chosen to open her Normal Vocal Institute in Chicago, where graduates from high school would be able to find well-trained musical instructors at a moderate cost. Carl Diton, a distinguished pianist and educator who spent a full decade in Philadelphia as a music teacher after holding a number of teaching positions in southern colleges, had settled in New York City.[1]

Only rarely was a black student accepted by a white teacher, and in every case there was the risk of unpleasantness. Agnes Reifsnyder, an experienced voice teacher whom many found utterly free of prejudice and sympathetic to the needs of black students, felt constrained to ask Agnes Pitts, a talented young black contralto, to go around to the back door on Saturdays when she came for her lesson. Only in this way could Reifsnyder hope to keep her white students. Malcolm Poindexter, because he was fair-skinned enough to pass for white, was accepted as a student by Ed Lippy, a teacher with a strong sense of fairness about racial matters. In later years, Poindexter always remembered seeing his teacher flailing his arms and yelling aloud that he had been called a renegade and a turncoat for taking him as a student.[2]

Like most talented black students ambitious for a musical career, Marian knew that a white teacher could give her more advantages than a black teacher. White teachers had the benefit of better training and wider experience as performers. Many had connections with other musicians and music conservatories enabling them to better promote the careers of their students. Most white voice teachers had their studios in those years in the Presser Building, on Chestnut Street. Marian went from one teacher to another, only to be consistently turned away.[3]

For the members of Union Baptist Church, Marian's need to have formal voice lessons became a church cause. Learning that she wanted to attend a certain music school not far from her own neighborhood, the church members assured her they could guarantee tuition. She went to the school to ask for an application. When her request was refused, she experienced a sense of rejection that she would always remember "as the most painful realization of what it meant to be a Negro."[4] "That day there was a line of people in front of the window," Anderson recalled many years later, "where applications and information were given out. There was a young girl behind the window. She was blond, very pretty, and had a way of tossing her head that was pert but cute, I thought. I had time to notice all these things, because she didn't seem to notice me. She looked over my head when it came to be my turn, and took care of one after another of the ones behind me until I was the only one left. She spoke to me then, but in a different tone of voice from the one she'd used to the other people. 'What do *you* want?' was what she said. I told her an application blank. She tossed her head, and this was still pert but wasn't cute. Her face wasn't even pretty, because she raised her upper lip as if she smelled something bad and said to me, 'We don't take colored.' I promise you I was as sick as if she'd hit me with her fist right in the middle of my stomach, and I mean really, physically sick. I wonder I didn't throw up right there, but I didn't. I don't know how I got out of the place and home. All I could think of was how anybody who was as pretty as that, and had a chance to listen to music all day long, could act that way and say such a terrible thing. And then I'd think, 'Can't I sing, can't I be a singer because I'm colored?'"[5]

Knowing her Aunt Mary would make a scene, Marian wouldn't allow herself to tell her what had happened, but confided in her mother, who reassuringly told her what she had said countless times before—that there would be others "raised up" sufficiently to act with understanding, and that, consequently, she would find other ways to achieve the same ends. As Marian understood from a very young age, her mother's philosophy was not one of passivity or weakness, but of pride and a belief in the natural goodness of most people.

As it turned out, the woman who would become Marian's first voice teacher lived only a few blocks away from her, on Fitzgerald Street. They were brought together by John Thomas Butler, an elocutionist and dramatic reader who often performed for local churches and black community groups and who had had occasion to hear her sing. Butler might never have taken an interest in her were it not for his job on a mail car whose route took him along Eighteenth Street, where the Andersons were then living. Butler would often see Marian sitting on the front steps of her house and would wave to her as the mail car went by. Gradually, Butler befriended the Andersons, sometimes visiting them on Sundays and eventually inviting Marian to appear with him on musical and dramatic programs. When Butler realized that she had never had formal voice lessons, he gathered his courage and asked her grandmother, Isabella, if Marian might sing for one of his friends, Mary Saunders Patterson, a singer and voice teacher in the neighborhood.

Patterson was the most energetic black voice teacher in Philadelphia. In addition to teaching, Patterson opened her home to visiting black artists—Harry T. Burleigh and Roland Hayes among them—who, because adequate public accommodations were unavailable to blacks, needed a private home to stay in while performing. Patterson, a light coloratura soprano, had been a student of Emma Azalia Hackley. Although Patterson appeared as an assisting artist in concerts with other black musicians and on charity concerts until after the First World War, she had realized from the early days of her career that her true calling was teaching, not performing. With some of her students, she formed a chorus, and with the more talented ones, small vocal ensembles. Her spring concerts at the Musical Fund Hall, in which all her students appeared, were always eagerly anticipated by the community. When Butler offered to pay for Marian's lessons, Patterson offered, instead, to teach her without charge until Marian herself could afford to pay. Young people, Patterson said, "just starting on what might be long careers should not have obligations or strings attached to them, no matter how unselfish or noble the offer of help might be."[6] Patterson's generosity to students went well beyond teaching. In later years, Marian recalled: "As for the evening gown that she gave me, I wore it many times in succeeding months and still cherish pieces of it that I have saved through the years."[7]

To judge from Marian's recollections of her studies, she was introduced to vocal technique in a fairly systematic way by Patterson. Never having thought consciously about how she sang, Marian had to learn how important it was "to realize that the voice could be controlled and channeled." Recognizing that Anderson had no difficulty with breathing, Patterson worked mostly on voice placement and projection. As she later recalled, "Mrs. Patterson insisted that I begin thinking about how I sang a tone. She taught me to throw the voice toward a corner of the ceiling, high up where two walls joined, and she said that I must seek to direct the voice toward one point. She did not use the word 'focus,' which I heard a great deal about later on with other teachers."[8]

Patterson also worked on repertoire. So far, Marian had had little opportunity to build a varied repertory of songs, nor any opportunity at all to sing in a foreign language. Apart from spirituals, she knew the music she had learned in church, songs her Aunt Mary had taught her, and a few songs by popular American composers such as Stephen Foster and Ethelbert Nevin. With Patterson, Marian began to learn songs from the traditional stylistic categories that constitute most recital programs—Italian songs of the seventeenth and eighteenth centuries, French mélodies, and German lieder.

Marian's ability to communicate with an audience was as much the result of the clarity and vividness of her diction as the individual beauty and unique range of her voice. Indeed, the congregation of Union Baptist Church liked to say that, while they appreciated Roland Hayes's artistry, it was Marian they could always understand, not only because she sang in English, but because of the expressiveness with which she projected the words she sang. Unlike many in the congregation, Marian was drawn to Hayes's performances of French and Italian songs, and especially German lieder, so to be unable to understand the words he sang was an unending source of frustration to her. To heighten her enjoyment of the German lieder she heard Hayes sing, and to compensate for her ignorance of the language, Marian tried to imagine a concrete scene or group of characters for each of them. Not until Marian began to study abroad did she finally begin to acquire the linguistic skill and knowledge to transfer her extraordinary verbal gifts to languages other than English. In the meantime, she did learn how to pronounce a few non-English songs with Patterson—for example, "Serenata," by Tosti, "L'été," by Chaminade, and her first song in German, Schumann's "Die Rose, die Lilie, die Taube, die Sonne," from *Dichterliebe*—although some of Patterson's choices seem strangely inappropriate. The Schumann song, for example, is relentlessly fast, delicate, and breathless at the same time and with mouthfuls of German words that go by at breakneck speed—an unlikely choice for a student without any knowledge of German.

Marian studied with Patterson for about a year, taking part, in May, 1915, in the annual spring concert of Patterson's students. "The Awakening of Spring," as the concert was called, provided the theme for the music. One of two advanced students, Marian was given two songs to perform—"Under the Rose," by Fisher and "Spring Tide," by Becker. After the intermission, the students took part in *Flower Queen,* a short operetta by George F. Root, in which Marian played the role of the Recluse. Mrs. Pearl Battey, the reviewer for the *Philadelphia Tribune,* called attention to "the Misses Frederica Draper and Marion Anderson, whose voices show indications of a very bright future,"[9] although the most applause went to Miss Evelyn Crawford, who played Dandelion.

G. Grant Williams, the editor of the *Tribune,* was one of Philadelphia's most successful black promoters of cultural events, helping to give black performers and cultural leaders opportunities to appear in Philadelphia. During the next few years, for example, Williams would sell out the Academy of Music six times to black performers, often weeks in advance. Because of Williams's enterprise, audiences heard, for example, W. E. B. Du Bois, the Williams Singers, and the New York Clef Club.[10] Like other prominent members of the black community, Williams felt concern that Marian was still not able to attend high school. In June, 1915, when the People's Chorus decided to give a benefit concert to raise money for her education, Williams joined forces with them, appealing to his readers for their support. "The People's Chorus, Prof. Al Hill, director," he informed his readers, "has arranged to give a testimonial concert for Miss Marion Anderson our young contralto. Miss Anderson, without a doubt, possesses one of the best contralto voices ever heard in this city for one of her years. The object of this testimonial is to raise some funds to give her a better musical education. Every citizen of color should subscribe and help the People's Chorus in this worthy movement. . . ."[11]

The concert took place on June 23, in the Musical Fund Hall, Marian's appearance coming near the end of the program. Although many in the audience could not stay to hear her, those who did were enthusiastic.[12] About $250 was collected for her education, and a committee of Philadelphia Negroes was formed, with the president of the People's Chorus as chairman, and Dr. Algernon B. Jackson, the head of Mercy Hospital, as treasurer. The money collected was deposited into an account for Marian, and Agnes Reifsnyder was chosen to be her voice teacher. The choice was a felicitous one. Reifsnyder was well-trained as a pianist as well as a singer. Like Marian, a contralto, Reifsnyder was still active as a performer, singing the kind of repertoire especially suitable for Marian's voice.[13]

Marian studied with Reifsnyder for two years. "She spent a lot of time," Anderson later recalled, "working on my medium and low tones. She was not interested in fireworks or vocal gymnastics, but she concentrated a great deal on breathing and gave me exercises further to set the voice. She introduced me to the songs of Brahms, among others, and helped me to prepare whole programs for the concerts I was beginning to give out of town."[14] Gradually their relationship changed into something more than one of teacher and student. The catalyst was Alfred J. Hill, the director of the People's Chorus, whose energy and success as a choral director had an enormous impact on the black community. Eager to train beginning singers not advanced enough to sing in the People's Chorus, Hill started a sight-singing class, with Reifsnyder as the vocal coach and Marian as her assistant. The students met twice a week and after eight months' of work were able to sing with the People's Chorus. The concert, a performance of "The Rose Maiden," earned the chorus and its teachers enthusiastic praise. As one critic wrote, "for tonal quality, balance, and all that goes to make up a first class chorus they were truly wonderful. The solo work by various members of the chorus was truly marvelous, each one singing his or her part with excellent voice, fine expression and artistic feeling." Marian's work with Reifsnyder in training the sight-singing class was acknowledged at the end of the performance, when, as the *Tribune* reported, "the class presented a huge bouquet of American Beauty Roses to Miss Agnes Reifsnyder, the teacher in vocal culture, [and] a huge bunch of pink roses to Miss Marion Anderson, the demonstrator and assistant teacher."[15]

The $250 collected by the People's Chorus had been intended to help the Anderson family not only pay for Marian's lessons with Reifsnyder, but enable her to begin her high school education. The committee formed at the time of her appearance with the People's Chorus believed strongly that, aside from vocal instruction, Anderson needed to be sent through high school to have the proper education. Each year, in fact, the committee would make an appeal to the black community for additional funds so that her schooling would not be interrupted.[16] Well past her eighteenth birthday, Marian started high school in the fall of 1915. For Mrs. Anderson, Marian's return to school meant more hardships and Marian felt keenly the need, as she later said, "to be able to get a job as soon as possible—both to help Mother and to have some money for music studies."[17] After her father died, she had begun to help support her sisters by singing as often as she could, earning as much as five or ten dollars an appearance. As she got older, she had begun to assume something of a parental role, sharing her earnings with her sisters and helping her mother care for them. Although she had lost none of her convictions about wanting a career as a singer, she was realistic enough to believe that, upon graduation, it was essential that she be able to support herself. When a friend of the family promised to find Marian an office job if she could type and take dictation, it must have seemed a welcome road to security. Indeed, everyone thought it best that she attend William Penn, a business-oriented high school that provided students with a commercial curriculum.

Marian's years at William Penn were difficult and unsatisfying. She was not good in bookkeeping, worse in shorthand. The few black students attending William Penn were often treated badly. She at least was lucky enough to enjoy the music teacher's encouragement and to participate in the assemblies, but the widening reach of her appearances as an assisting artist was interfering more and more with her progress in school. Her teachers were not always understanding when it came to her absences and were rarely willing to help her make up work. She struggled along at William Penn High School for three years.

Even before Marian entered William Penn, she had met Roland Hayes, soon to be recognized as the foremost black singer of his time.[18] Hayes was born in 1887, in Curryville, Georgia, the son of ex-slaves and, like Marian, had lost his father when he was still young. After her husband died, Fannie Hayes, a strong-willed and resolute woman, had taken the family to Chattanooga, Tennessee, where she hoped her children would have more opportunities for education. Hayes sang there in the choir of the Monumental Baptist Church, where his love for music was encouraged. His mother wanted him to become a minister, but when he was nineteen he left Chattanooga for Nashville, to enter Fisk University. Hayes was accepted as a student in the Fisk music department and, although he didn't graduate, remained at Fisk for four years.

While still a student, Hayes joined the Fisk Jubilee Singers. The original group had banded together in 1866, only a year after the university's founding, to perform black folk music as a way to raise money for the school's building fund. In 1911, he joined a quartet of young men, all former students of Fisk, who toured the eastern part of the country. Beginning in New England, they reached Philadelphia in the fall of that year, where they were heard in a number of churches, including Union Baptist Church, where Marian heard Hayes sing for the first time. Two years later, as a member of the People's Chorus, she heard Hayes again when he was one of the soloists in Mendelssohn's *Elijah* .

During Marian's years at William Penn, Hayes began to sing in black colleges and churches in the South, his career progressing through the circumscribed series of stages that every talented black singer faced in the racially discordant climate of the country. In 1916, he gambled all of his savings in order to rent Boston's Jordan Hall, hoping to achieve a measure of artistic success in one of the important musical centers in the East. Later, he was forced to go to Europe, hoping to earn the success as a singer denied him at home. He sang at London's Wigmore Hall, and the next day was summoned by the king and queen to perform. His fame grew, first in England and then in France and Russia, although he met with hostility and prejudice in Berlin in the Fall of 1924, when his appearance at the Beethovensaal evoked angry protest. Only Hayes's calm and noble demeanor finally quieted an audience that was not prepared to accept a Negro tenor singing the music of Schubert and Beethoven.

Hayes's influence on Marian was profound and many-sided. He became for her, as he would for countless aspiring black singers in the early part of the century, a figure of immense dignity, who, through unusual talent and quiet persistence, achieved acceptance and eventually international success as a performer, in repertory that was not limited to the spirituals and folk songs of the Negro. For Marian, he set the important example of a singer who held true to his own experience and to the natural qualities of his voice in the repertory of European art songs, in which he could be, within his own style and imagination, as moving and insightful as he was in the music of his own people.

Hayes visited Union Baptist Church many times. Eventually Marian was given an opportunity to sing a song or two on one of his programs. Their first important appearance together was during the Easter weekend of 1916, when she was invited by the People's Chorus to be the contralto soloist in a performance of Handel's *Messiah.*[19] Fortunately, she had the benefit of Reifsnyder's experience, who had sung the contralto part in *Messiah* herself many times. The *Tribune* devoted its praise to the accomplishments of the chorus and its director Alfred Hill—their performance of Handel's oratorio was only the second in the eleven years of the chorus's existence. "It is rather doubtful," wrote the reviewer, " if any city in the country can produce such a well-trained chorus of Negro voices." It had less to say about the soloists.[20] Du Bois's journal, *Crisis,* on the other hand, initiated its recognition of Marian's career by describing little else but her performance: "But most exquisite was the dark, sweet, full-blossomed contralto—Marion Anderson, who felt with her soft, strong voice the sorrows of God. Few voices have ever sung 'He was despised and rejected of men' with so deep feeling and significance. It brought a sob to the throats of two thousand."[21]

Marian's accomplished singing in *Messiah* prompted Hayes to recommend her for a performance of Mendelssohn's *Elijah* , in Boston, the following Easter, 1917, with Hayes himself, and Harry T. Burleigh as the Evangelist. The performance, presented by a chorus of black singers conducted by Dr. Walter O. Taylor, was Marian's first appearance in Boston. The *Crisis* again commented on Marian's performance, noting that "her singing was the sensation of the evening."[22] Marian did not sing with Hayes very often. She had appeared with him some months before her appearance in Boston at an autumn musicale at the Good Shepherd Episcopal Parish House in Rosemont, Pennsylvania, and, together with Harry T. Burleigh she appeared with Hayes at the Philadelphia Academy of Music, in the spring of 1920, only a month before Hayes left the States for his first trip to Europe.

Although still only as an assisting artist, Marian began to sing more frequently while at William Penn, enabling her to establish friendships with other young artists, many of them long-lasting. In the fall of 1916, she sang at a concert at St. Thomas P.E. Church, where she was accompanied for the first time by William King, a young church choir director and pianist who would before long become her first regular accompanist. On occasion, she performed with another young contralto of great promise, Emmaline Tindley, one of Charles Albert Tindley's eight children. Tindley had come to Philadelphia in 1902, as minister of the Bainbridge Street Methodist Episcopal Church. All of his children exhibited a fondness for musical performance, and Tindley himself was one of the earliest composers of songs that were part of a tradition eventually known as gospel music. Although Emmaline and Marian were considered friendly rivals for a time, they remained good friends, Emmaline even accompanying Marian at the piano on occasion.

Marian's first opportunity to sing in the South came during the Christmas season of 1917, the invitation coming only four days before the actual concert, in a gala concert of black folk music by the Glee Club of the Georgia State Industrial College and the chorus of the Cuyler Street School. Her parents had come from Virginia and the family had friends from the deep South, so she knew about the humiliations routinely suffered by blacks under Jim Crow, but, as she later said, "meeting it bit deeply into the soul."[23] She traveled with her mother to Washington, where they had to change trains. Their bags were taken onto the first coach, the Jim Crow car, which was dirty and without proper ventilation. When the car became too stuffy and the windows were raised, smoke and soot from the train's engine entered the car along with the fresh air. Throughout the night Marian kept thinking of stories she had heard of whites forcing their way into the Jim Crow car to take the Negroes off the train. She got through the night with little sleep, remembering later that she felt safe only when the window blinds were lowered.[24]

In Savannah, Marian and Mrs. Anderson experienced the gracious hospitality of the South. "Our bedroom was quite large," she later remembered, "with a fireplace and an adjoining bath. In the morning a girl came in and lit the fire so that the room was most comfortable when we arose."[25] Because she had been engaged only four days before the concert, it became known only after the festival programs were printed that a young high school girl from Philadelphia, already reputed to be "a second Schumann-Heink," would appear as soloist.[26] Marian's part on the program, in addition to the encores she was compelled to sing, included Tosti's "La serenata," "The Owl," by Wells, "Danny Boy," Coleridge-Taylor's "Island of Gardens," and Burleigh's arrangements of "Deep River" and "Go Down, Moses." The concert was held in the new Municipal Auditorium, inaugurated only a few years earlier when President Wilson's daughter had performed there. A mixed audience of nearly a thousand people turned out on December 28 for the concert, whites sitting in the boxes and dress circle, blacks in orchestra or gallery seats. The critics were full of praise for Marian:

> Mary [*sic*] Anderson, the soloist, has one of the most remarkable voices ever heard in Savannah. A contralto, its range is amazing and the upper notes as perfect and full as the lower, with a lovely middle register. Something unusual in its quality, difficult to analyze, made it sound more like an exquisite wind instrument than like the human voice, the tones ringing out like a clarionet. It was interesting that she happened to sing two songs that Miss Wilson sang here recently, one the Irish ballad, "Danny Boy," which was most beautifully given, and the other, the Negro spiritual "Deep River." This and her singing of another spiritual, "Go Down, Moses," were most impressive, although her interpretation of music that was not the traditional music of her own people was quite as successful. She was particularly happy in some imitative or echo songs, one, "The Cookoo," with a touch of humor in the interpretation, being most effective.[27]

Another milestone for the young singer was her first appearance in Philadelphia's prestigious Academy of Music, the following April 22, as soloist with the visiting New York Clef Club Syncopated Orchestra, one of the best-known black dance bands in New York. G. Grant Williams, the *Tribune* editor, always ready to help further Marian's career, and alert to the possibility of another sold-out house at the Academy, encouraged readers of the *Tribune* to make contributions for the huge bouquet of flowers to be given to Marian at the end of the concert. Preparations for Marian's debut at the Academy were very much a family affair, all the Andersons turning out for the concert. Marian's cousin, Lillian Bass, would later always remember the white satin dress Marian wore at the concert and how the whole family gathered in the Anderson home to help stitch decorative rose buds to the satin.[28]

The program was a skillfully heterogeneous affair. In addition to Marian's numbers, there were duets for violin and cello and performances by the Right Quintette. "Deacon" Johnson, the president of the Clef Club, sang "He Draws No Color Line," and the orchestra, conducted by Frederick M. Bryan, played their usual vocal and instrumental numbers. Somehow there was time for a short address by a member of the banking firm of Brown & Stevens, who urged the audience to buy Liberty Bonds; nearly $5,000 was subscribed within minutes.

Mrs. Anderson spoke for her whole family a few weeks later when she wrote to Williams: "I wish to apologize for my seeming ingratitude on Monday evening. Your presentation of Marian on the Academy stage was more unique than any one could have anticipated. Then when the two men brought in the enormous basket of flowers I was filled through and through. I sat motionless, and it was with much difficulty that I suppressed my tears. No one in that vast audience had an idea of the war that was waging within my breast, when within a few seconds possibly a thousand thoughts rushed through my mind. I wondered if Marian's father could have seen her how he would have expressed his appreciation. . . ."[29]

Marian's debut at the Academy exposed her to a wider critical perspective, bringing with it a disturbing note of caution. Until then her talent and accomplishments had been judged predominantly by black audiences and by the reviewers of black newspapers, based on appearances rarely far from Philadelphia. Her appearance with the Clef Club Orchestra invited a more cosmopolitan response. Lester A. Walton, the manager and drama critic of the *New York Age,* praising Marian's singing, nevertheless wrote soberly about her future:

She is only eighteen years old and gives promise of creating a sensation in the musical world if she continues to improve. Miss Anderson is now at the critical stage of her career. Her future will largely depend on her decision to continue to study; for if she enters the professional field at this time she will never rise above the level of mediocrity.[30]

At an assembly at William Penn, Marian met a Mr. Rohrer, one of the guests the school's principal had invited to hear her sing. Rohrer strongly urged her to abandon commercial courses for a college preparatory course, and to do as much as she could in music. In the fall of 1918, already twenty-one, having completed three hard years at William Penn, Marian transferred as a sophomore to the South Philadelphia High School for Girls. Only three years before, the Philadelphia Board of Education had asked Lucy Langdon Wilson, a University of Pennsylvania graduate in the sciences and one of the most creative pioneers in secondary education in the country, to establish a high school for girls in South Philadelphia, a neighborhood populated largely by newly arrived immigrants and black families. Her development of the "Dalton Plan," in which students were encouraged to work independently according to their own ability and potential, helped contribute to the original character of the newly opened high school.[31]

Marian could not have found a more sympathetic principal and friend than Wilson. Recognizing both her musical talent and her slower record of academic achievement, Wilson encouraged her in the one and patiently guided her in the other. Wilson was also responsive to the awkwardness and insecurity she knew Marian would feel in a school where she was not only five or six years older than the other students, but one of a small number of black students in an atmosphere in which high academic performance was expected and usually achieved. When Marian arrived, Wilson introduced her to the girls in her class, informing them about Marian's singing. Fortunately, Wilson's thoughtfulness was shared by the school's teachers, many of whom made a considerable effort to help Marian make up the work she missed while away from school for performances. Although her singing in the morning assemblies made her a school celebrity, her classmates remembered her keeping very much to herself, shy and often self-conscious. One of her classmates, Lily Venning, who lived in Marian's neighborhood and sometimes played for Patterson's students, remembered her as a serious and hardworking student, "interested in pretty much nothing else but singing, not taking part in dances or things like that."[32]

Marian's transfer to South Philadelphia came none too soon, for her appearances were taking her away more and more from her studies. In her first year at the new school, her appearances included a benefit concert for the Mercy Hospital and School for Nurses, a concert of the Broad Street Station Protective League at the Parkway Auditorium, and another benefit for the Hotel Hanover Employees' Beneficial Association, in addition to concerts in local churches. In the spring of 1919, Marian appeared a second time at the Academy of Music, in an all-star concert with Emmaline Tindley and other singers, and on May 21, she sang for the second time with the New York Clef Club Orchestra.

Even as the benefits of a sound high school education, under Wilson's pedagogy, now seemed assured to Marian, the problem of her vocal studies raised by the critic of the *New York Age* remained. The immediate problem for her was to advance strategically beyond her vocal studies with Reifsnyder, which had ended several years before. Since then she had had to endure well-meaning advice and frequent auditions. Hayes had suggested that Marian study with Arthur Hubbard, a distinguished Boston teacher, with whom he himself had studied for nearly a decade. Hayes had, in fact, taken her to Hubbard's studio when they had appeared together in Mendelssohn's *Elijah* during the Easter season of 1917, so that Marian could sing for him.[33] Hubbard had agreed to take Marian as a student and Hayes had suggested that she work in Hubbard's house to cover the cost of her lessons, but Marian's grandmother Isabella made the final decision. "Grandmother told Mr. Hayes," she later recalled, "that we had no money to pay for lessons, and Mr. Hayes replied that Mr. Hubbard was willing to let me earn my way by working in his home. Grandmother was not impressed. So far as she was concerned, I could sing and what was the need of lessons? There were discussions pro and con. Mother would not oppose Grandmother, and Grandmother decided that a young girl should not be sent away from home."[34]

In the summer of 1919, new opportunities for both concerts and study came her way. In June, presenting complete programs for the first time, Marian gave a week of concerts in Tennessee—at Fisk University, in Nashville, and at other black universities and churches. In effect, these concerts were the prototype for the longer and more strenuous southern tours that Marian was to give for nearly a decade after her graduation from high school.

Although not solving the problem of a permanent voice teacher, an unusual and unexpected opportunity for advanced musical training occurred when Carl Diton recommended to Marian that she study with

Oscar Saenger in Chicago later that summer. An important New York voice teacher and coach, Saenger taught each summer at the Chicago Conservatory of Music, where he offered a six-week course in operatic literature and performance. She shared a scholarship with the soprano Florence Cole Talbert, both singers traveling to Chicago near the end of June in time for a meeting with Saenger and the other students. Marian had private lessons two days a week with Saenger and attended his repertoire class. For his private lessons with students, Saenger used the exercises and vocalises of Panofka, Cancone, and Marchesi, and, as an introduction to operatic repertory, he chose ten of the most popular operatic roles for each voice range, with specific arias drawn from each of the roles for the students to work on. Marian's included the title roles in *Samson et Dalila, Mignon,* and *Carmen,* Fidès in Meyerbeer's *Le Prophète,* Amneris *(Aida)* and Azucena *(Il Trovatore)* of Verdi, and Ortrud in Wagner's *Lohengrin.*[35]

Marian often said in later years that she didn't feel ready to study with Saenger, that his emphasis on operatic literature threatened her self-confidence. Moreover, the other students in Saenger's class were more advanced, some having had considerable experience with foreign languages. But those weeks of study, whatever their consequences for her development as a singer, proved unexpectedly fortunate, for the last days of the summer course coincided with the establishment of the National Association of Negro Musicians (NANM), providing Marian with an opportunity to be heard by many black musicians and teachers who gathered in Chicago to participate in their first national conference.[36]

The initial efforts to establish a formal organization of black musicians on a national scale had begun in 1906, when Harriet Gibbs Marshall, a music teacher in Washington, DC, decided to send out letters to some of the leading black musicians in the country—Harry T. Burleigh and Emma Azalia Hackley among them—in order to gain support for the creation of a national organization. Not much came of Gibbs's work, and although there were similar efforts in successive years, the involvement of the United States in the First World War and the devastating influenza epidemic of 1918 impeded their success.

The feeling of hope imparted to the country by the ending of the war acted as a stimulus to the formation of a national organization. The long-standing interest in such an organization on the part of black musicians in Washington was shared by performers and teachers from Chicago, who a few years earlier had created the Chicago Music Association. Other important black musicians in the country had similar ideas, including Clarence Cameron White and the composer R. Nathaniel

Dett. An organizational meeting took place in Washington on May 1–3 at the Dunbar High School, as part of the school's annual music festival. Among those taking part were Henry Grant, Carl Diton, the violinist Clarence Cameron White, who was then director of music at West Virginia Collegiate Institute, R. Nathaniel Dett, and Mrs. Nora Douglas Holt, the music writer for the *Chicago Defender*. The aims of the proposed organization, reported widely in the black press, included the encouragement of musical composition by black composers and the creation of a market for it, the promotion of better economic conditions for black musicians, and the promotion and guidance of talented young black artists.

The choice of Chicago for the first national meeting was a natural one. Black musicians in Chicago enjoyed relative freedom and tolerance compared with musicians in other industrial cities of the East and Midwest, and the Chicago Music Association agreed to handle the arrangements. Unfortunately, the relaxed and friendly atmosphere the delegates anticipated was thwarted by circumstances no one could have foreseen. Even as prospective members began arriving in Chicago, during the last days of July, the city was about to witness the worst eruption of racial hatred and violence in the history of Illinois.[37]

On Sunday afternoon, July 27, Eugene Williams, a black youth of seventeen, was struck by a stone while riding a raft on Lake Michigan at the 29th Street Bathing Beach on Chicago's South Side. Apparently knocked unconscious, William fell from the raft into the lake and drowned. George Stauber, a twenty-two-year-old white man, not used to seeing blacks on that part of the beach, had thrown the rock, but it was the action of Officer Callahan, a white policeman, who presumably kept expert swimmers from reaching Williams and failed to make any arrest, that set off the rioting. The patrolman's negligence so enraged the black bathers at the beach that they began beating him. When whites took the policeman's part, a battle began within minutes. The news of Williams's death spread quickly, and by that evening the whole of the South Side was embroiled in violence.

By Wednesday, the rioting had quieted and was nearly under control, but in those four days over forty people were killed and nearly 500 wounded. Delegates to the NANM had already arrived by midweek, while there were still unmistakable reminders of the rioting that had reached as far north as sections of the Loop. The next Monday evening, a meeting of Divisions 241 and 308 of the Surface and Elevated Railway Employees was held at the Ashland Boulevard Auditorium, in an attempt to avert a strike of all surface and elevated transportation. The strike came on Tuesday morning and a settlement was not reached until Friday night. With the transportation strike in full force, black musicians from ten states gathered in the old YMCA building on Wabash Avenue.

Somehow the work of the first NANM was accomplished. The constitution for honorary, charter, and local organization membership was established and educational possibilities for talented black musicians were discussed. Because of the chaotic conditions of the city and the complete suspension of transportation service, the concert scheduled for Wednesday evening at Grace Presbyterian Church had to be postponed until Friday morning, when it was held within the relative safety of the small assembly hall of the Y. Those able to attend heard an extraordinary range of talent that helped foster a sense of pride in the newly formed organization: singers from Chicago and Hillsdale, Michigan, from New York and Kansas City; the violinist Sidney Woodward from New York; and Marian Anderson and the soprano Florence Cole Talbert. Nora Douglas Holt, the first secretary of the organization, described the excitement of that initial concert in the *Chicago Defender* a week later:

> A wave of intense enthusiasm swept the audience as each of these artists demonstrated what years of training has done for them. The greatest height was reached when Marion Anderson, a high school girl, exhibited a voice equal to that of Rosa Raisa, the wonderful contralto of the Chicago Grand Opera Company, and everyone stood and acclaimed her with cries of bravo and bis, while tears of joy were in the eyes of many of the musicians who felt that a new era in music has arisen for our people.[38]

Many of the delegates attending the conference expressed genuine concern over Marian's musical education. Maud Roberts George, a music writer for the *Chicago Defender,* took Marian to sing for Herman Devries, an important music critic and vocal coach, although nothing came of the meeting. Alice Carter Simmons, who later became the NANM's secretary, left an account of Marian's singing and the first steps taken by the members to help further her education:

> Every number on this occasion was creditably performed. The interpretation of the Gray Wolf, by Burleigh, sung by Cleota Collins Lacey, is well stamped in the memory of those present and will linger long. Following Tschaikovsky's Adieu Forêts, by Marion Anderson, who possesses a contralto voice of rare quality, came a chorus of Bravos from all parts of the house. So intense was the

enthusiasm, that to the response of President Grant's appeal for contributions to a scholarship fund, with Marion Anderson as its first beneficiary, one hundred and sixty five dollars was pledged and a cash collection of twenty three dollars was realized.[39]

Some members believed strongly that Marian should apply to the Yale School of Music after her graduation from high school. Eventually she applied to the school, but the amount of pledges was not nearly enough to cover the tuition and other costs. Not until 1922, at the fourth meeting of the association in Columbus, was a scholarship finally awarded to Marian.[40]

In the fall of 1919, Marian began her junior year at South Philadelphia. The following spring, with the help of Wilson and other Philadelphia musicians, more auditions for her were arranged. Sarah Stein, a friend of Wilson's, suggested she sing for the baritone David Bispham, with whom she had studied, and an audition was arranged. Sensing immediately Marian's promise, Bispham was willing to accept her as a student. Unfortunately, his death some months later robbed her of the chance to study with a brilliantly accomplished musician. Later, the soprano Lisa Roma, another of Wilson's friends, visited the school to hear her sing in one of the morning assemblies. Wilson and Roma met with Marian after the assembly and decided to arrange an audition for her with Giuseppe Boghetti, who had been one of Roma's teachers.

Of Russian-Jewish descent, Joe Bogash was born in 1896, in Philadelphia. Hoping for an operatic career as a tenor, he studied at the Royal Conservatory in Milan. Later he sang in several European cities, along the way becoming Giuseppe Boghetti. His career never flourished in Europe and after the First World War he returned to the United States, where he opened vocal studios in New York and his native Philadelphia. Roma and Wilson accompanied Marian to Boghetti's studio, then located at Seventeenth and Chestnut Streets. Both Marian and Boghetti have left recollections of their first meeting, the accounts as much reflecting their personalities as accurate descriptions of what took place.[41] She remembered she was nervous and intimidated. Boghetti said he was much too busy but he listened to her sing "Deep River," which she sang without once looking at him. He was overwhelmed by her promise and said he would make room for her immediately. "Two years is all he would need and she would be able to go anywhere and sing for anybody," is what Marian remembered Boghetti saying. Yet in an interview long after the event, Boghetti talked about how unformed Marian's voice was and how much work would be required to make a success of her. In these comments, he ignored the fact that Marian had already had good training and had sung to some acclaim. It suited Boghetti's temperament, fitted with his flamboyant posturing to exaggerate the challenge Marian presented to his pedagogical virtuosity.

Boghetti was no more than five-foot-six in height, stocky and vigorous; he enjoyed exercise, spending most weekends on his boat on the Hudson River. In the studio, he was dynamic and full of energy, very much the showman. He had a vast store of knowledge and opinion about vocal technique, which he communicated to his students more than they would have chosen. There was always a blackboard in his studio and he liked to draw pictures to illustrate important points. He was demanding and could be stern, expecting his students to respect his teaching and to follow his advice without question. More than one left a lesson in tears.

Although Boghetti accepted Marian as a student, she could not afford the cost of lessons. While her fees as a singer had continued to grow, much of what she earned went toward helping Mrs. Anderson keep three teenage girls in school. Again Union Baptist Church came to the rescue. With the help of Ida Asbury, the wife of a prominent black lawyer and civic leader, John C. Asbury, a gala performance of the song cycle, *In a Persian Garden,* was organized by the church for May 14. In addition to Marian, the soloists invited were Florence Cole Talbert, Harry Delmore, and Arthur Brown, all prominent young black musicians in Philadelphia. To help ensure the concert's success, the *Philadelphia Tribune* carried an announcement on May 1, encouraging readers to attend: "A committee of public spirited ladies have organized for the purpose of providing a scholarship to enable Miss Marian Anderson to complete her musical education. She is a native Philadelphian of whom the race in this city should be proud. She has great possibilities, with a natural contralto voice that has yet to be equaled by any singer in America. She does not think she knows it all, but is modest almost to the point of self-depreciation. She is a diligent student and wants the support of all who believe in her."[42] The $566 raised that evening enabled Marian to begin her studies with Boghetti. There were times in the years to come when she could not pay for lessons; Boghetti never asked for money, and she always managed to pay him eventually.

Boghetti immediately began work on technique. He gave Marian exercises to help place the voice properly, initially limiting her to humming alone, so she could concentrate on exactly where the vibrations and resonance were located. Next came work on evenness of scale. He determined first that Marian's best tone was the E-flat above middle C, providing exercises to enable her to produce all the tones throughout her range in the same way. Boghetti also worked on vocal agility, constructing exercises that had to be done lightly and rapidly in each register. As for her range, he took special pains with the top, enabling her to push up to A, then B and even high C, explaining to her that the highest tones were for insurance. One didn't need to sing them often, he said, but one needed the security they provided.

There were periods when Marian fell into the self-conscious worry that always marked the beginning stages of work with a new teacher, and these periods brought out insecurity and self-doubt. On these occasions, she would avoid practicing for most of the week before a lesson. As the day of the lesson approached, she later recalled, she would snatch a look at the music whenever she could during school hours, concentrating even more on the way to the lesson. Boghetti was always impressed at these sessions, remarking on how much Marian had applied herself that week. There were also moments of conflict. Marian could be stubborn—in later years she would often say that she always knew enough about her voice so that no teacher could do her any real harm—and Boghetti did not like challenge. Once, she expressed a strong desire to learn the aria "Care selve," from Handel's *Atalanta*. From the time she had heard Roland Hayes sing "Care selve," she had always wanted to learn it. She had been particularly struck by the subtle and delicate pianissimo of Hayes's singing and wanted to match its softness. Boghetti did not like the idea, asking her if she wanted to be the "pianissimo contralto." With his flair and background in Italian opera, Boghetti was unimpressed by Hayes's small voice and refined timbre. He ended the discussion, finally, with "I am the teacher."[43]

Boghetti's professionalism enriched Marian's studies considerably. He made sure he had the most competent accompanist in the studio. As for foreign languages, he was himself a knowledgeable coach in Italian. In the case of French, he felt less secure and for some years employed a Miss Janny, who taught in the Philadelphia schools, to teach the necessary amount of French to his students. Gradually he worked on the arrangement of entire recital programs with Marian.

The loss of satisfaction a career would have brought Boghetti seemed only to broaden his enthusiasm for teaching. He often allowed his students to remain in the studio after a lesson in order to hear a more advanced singer. When Boghetti felt more compelled to sing than to teach, he would go through one operatic scene or another with a student. With Marian he often did the scene between Amneris and Radames from the last act of Verdi's *Aida*. Boghetti took these read-throughs seriously, and although she often remarked in later years how amusing these interludes seemed to her at the time, she admitted as well how much they made her aware of her desire to sing in opera. In addition to studio recitals, Boghetti often arranged musical evenings that brought together lecturers and performers—lecture demonstrations in which some of his pupils were invited to take part. After Boghetti had moved his studio to St. James Place, he organized a series of informal talks each year; one of these was a lecture demonstration led by Samuel L. Laciar, the music editor of the *Philadelphia Public Ledger.* Laciar spoke on "The Life and Works of Giuseppe Verdi," whose music Marian and a group of students that included a young soprano, Reba Patton, performed. The lively activity of Boghetti's studio made possible warm friendships for Marian. She met Blanche Thebom, the distinguished American mezzo-soprano, for example, during the years when Thebom worked for Boghetti as an appointments secretary in order to pay for her lessons.

In later years, Boghetti may have exaggerated his accomplishments in regard to Marian's career, but there is little doubt that their relationship was artistically and professionally decisive not only for Marian but also for Boghetti. Boghetti was only in his mid-twenties when Marian came to study with him, only a few years older than Marian. He had opened his studios only a few years before and his career as a vocal teacher was almost entirely before him. The good fortune that brought them together offered Boghetti the opportunity to foster the talent of a singer who would in less than a decade become famous throughout Europe, if not yet in the United States. His enthusiasm and enterprise were as yet not fully tapped; both singer and teacher grew enormously in confidence and in accomplishment from their relationship. How ironic that a young black singer refused by one white teacher after another only a few years before would soon inspire other singers to seek out Boghetti as a teacher.[44]

The start of Marian's lessons with Boghetti came, fortunately enough, on the eve of her graduation from high school. Most of her work with him still lay ahead, when the demands of school would no longer take attention and energy away from working toward a full-time career as a singer. The kindness and generosity of Wilson and of many others who had contributed to Marian's education were not far from her mind on the evening of June 20, 1921, when she graduated from South Philadelphia High School for Girls with the other students of the seventh commencement class. There were many addresses by students reflecting the themes Wilson had so painstakingly emphasized: "We Train Our Bodies," "We Prepare for Business," "We Learn New Languages," "We Learn to Know the World." Celia H. Barkin, graduating with distinction, spoke on "We Have Music and Marian Anderson," one of the first grateful testimonies on record of the affection Marian could inspire in people who shared some part of their lives with her.

Touring with Billy King
(1921–1928)

Throughout her life, Marian acknowledged only a single intimate romantic relationship. If she had others, she never spoke of them. As she always remembered it, her romantic coming of age began and ended with Orpheus Fisher. A young architecture student from Wilmington, Delaware, Orpheus met Marian while both were still in high school, during a reception following Marian's first appearance in Wilmington. After the concert, Marian was escorted by Mrs. Banton, a woman prominent in civic affairs, to a reception at the home of George Fisher, Orpheus's father, who was entertaining some of his Washington friends. "Mrs. Banton preceded me up the high front steps of the Fisher house and entered," Marian later recalled. "I happened to be walking slowly. When I reached the entrance the fine-looking young man at the door stretched his arm across my path. I tried to move past him at the side, and he barred the way with his body. All through this performance he kept laughing as though it were a huge joke."[1] The young man at the door was Orpheus Fisher, the youngest of George Fisher's children. Once inside the house Marian met Leon, another of Fisher's five sons, and later Robert, yet another. She did not stay at the reception very long, taking the train back to Philadelphia after meeting the host and his family, and some of his guests.

The impression Marian made on three of George Fisher's sons lasted well beyond the reception. In the coming months, in fact, all three boys called on her, the trip to and from Philadelphia from Wilmington, some twenty-five miles to the south of Philadelphia, easily accomplished in one day. Robert always said that he, and not his brother Leon, first dated Marian, but the real contest was between Leon and Orpheus. Visiting

Marian after she had finished school for the day, Orpheus, "sitting on the same divan as I," she recalled, "moved his hand across the back of the seat, touched my shoulder, and, when I looked to see why, slipped me a folded piece of paper that lay under his fingertips. When I could do so without drawing attention, I opened the paper, which bore this message: 'This affair between you and my brother has got to stop.' "[2]

Orpheus Fisher was born in 1900, in Oxford, Pennsylvania, near Lincoln University, the son of George Alfred Fisher and Pauline Conklin. Of mixed race and European origin, both parents were light-complexioned, Pauline more so than her husband. Pauline Conklin was born in Santo Domingo, her parents having settled in Baltimore during the nineteenth century. Her grandmother had come from Martinique, the family having made its way there, perhaps from Corsica, by the time of the War of 1812. George's ancestors had come from Scotland or Ireland, emigrating to the United States near the beginning of the nineteenth century. Orpheus's parents had met when still young in Baltimore, where George was born. Soon after their marriage, George and Pauline moved to Chester County, Pennsylvania, to the area around Lincoln University, where they began to raise a family.[3]

Responding to the need for black clergyman during Reconstruction, George Fisher entered the preparatory school of Lincoln University in 1881. After only a year of study he was ready for the freshman class. In three years he finished the English course in the Department of Theology, a course designed for students with no knowledge of Greek or Hebrew who wanted to learn scripture and become preachers. After graduation, Fisher entered the university's seminary and in 1888 received a bachelor's degree in sacred theology, which qualified him for the Presbyterian ministry. For a time he served as the university's chaplain. When his wife died, well before the First World War, he took his large family of five sons and three daughters to Wilmington, settling into a comfortable but modest house on Walnut Street, on the edge of the rougher, working-class neighborhood. He went to work for the Dupont family, whom he impressed with his seriousness and dedication.[4]

In raising his children, George Fisher always gave careful consideration to their education. Orpheus attended the Central Friends School in downtown Philadelphia, traveling there each day by bus from Wilmington until the ninth grade, when he began to attend Wilmington Central High School. After high school, he came to Philadelphia to study architecture, beginning to court Marian more seriously and, gradually, to think of marriage. Orpheus and Leon shared an apartment in those years in Philadelphia. Light-skinned enough to pass for white—Orpheus more so than Leon—and immensely popular with women, both men dated white women as often as black. For a time, their feeling of rivalry for Marian's affections was intense, but the situation changed that afternoon when Orpheus playfully but no less determinedly demanded that Marian rebuff his brother's advances.[5]

To those who knew them, Marian and Orpheus seemed an unlikely couple for each other's affection. The Andersons were Baptist, Orpheus's family was Presbyterian. Marian was quiet, even shy, an attentive and sympathetic listener. Orpheus was outgoing, full of charm, and quick to act. Marian, however, was impressed with Orpheus's sense of determination, his tall, rather aristocratic bearing, and his education and strong professional aspirations. Also, she could identify with his resolve about career, and this must have strengthened her own resolve, especially during a period in which she had to face the difficulties of striking out on her own. Physically, it was not surprising that Marian had caught the attention of more than one Fisher. She was rather tall and looked older than other women her age, and a gentle wisdom and dignity shone in her huge, sparkling eyes.

When Marian and Orpheus were still in high school, Orpheus had already suggested they run off together to be married. As Marian later recalled, the thought had terrified her. When they were out walking one afternoon, Orpheus suggested they stop to pay a call on a Mrs. Roberts. Marian did not like visiting people whom she didn't know, nor did she see for the moment what Orpheus was leading up to. She asked him what the visit was all about. "I'm going to see if she has a little place that we can stay when we're married," Orpheus told her. "You never saw anyone get off those steps as fast as I," she recalled.[6]

Orpheus was a shrewd strategist when it came to courting Marian, but she was not to be deflected from her plans for a career. Although Orpheus too was devoted to his work and anxious about career opportuninites, he needed and depended on the company of women. In a few years' time, impatient with Marian's resistance to the idea of marriage, he began to see others.

While in high school Marian met another young man, William King (known to everyone as Billy), a Philadelphia pianist and choir director. Her recollection of their first meeting is full of the excitement she felt in being noticed by a musician further along than she: "On one of those busy evenings when I was singing in several different places, I arrived at the Y. W. C. A., ready to do a few songs. I sat down at the piano and sang my first number. When I finished and looked up, there was a young man standing beside me. 'May I?' he whispered, and took my place on the piano bench. It was Billy King. I don't know how I got through the next number, I was so excited that Billy King had offered to play for me."[7] At the time, Billy was the accompanist for Lydia McClane, a beautiful young soprano who often sang in Philadelphia. Marian was in awe of Lydia's popularity, and this only added to her admiration for Billy.

Billy King was born in Philadelphia in 1897, Marian's junior by only half a year. His parents had come from the eastern shore of Maryland, settling on the west side of Philadelphia. His father, Eben King, who died when Billy was still a young boy, had worked as a messenger for the Pennsylvania railroad. Although Billy's mother liked to play the zither, his parents were not musical. Billy's musical talents were revealed at an early age, when he began to study piano. His career as a musician progressed rapidly and in many directions. He was active as both pianist and organist, and he taught piano as well as coached young singers. He was only eighteen when he presented a concert of his vocal students. Two years later he acted as Roland Hayes's accompanist for a tour of western states. The beginning of Billy's commanding presence as a musician in Philadelphia came with his appointment as organist and choirmaster of the Church of the Crucifixion, which had been recognized for its musical excellence since the start of the century when Emma Azalia Hackley established its choir.

Billy was much shorter than Marian, a bit stooped, olive-complexioned, and with small, delicate features. Malcolm Poindexter thought he looked more like a Hindu than a Negro. He was immediately likable and gregarious, enjoying more than anything else other people's company and a glass of his favorite Chivas Regal whiskey. No doubt his outgoing personality encouraged him to seek so many outlets as a musician. He was unwaveringly optimistic and rarely suffered from self-doubt about his career, yet he was easily distracted, usually by an amorous interest or a social occasion. Most of his sexual liaisons were homosexual, although he was known to have had more than one serious affair with an older woman.

To Billy's parents it seemed that Marian was much more focused about her career than Billy, and they encouraged him not to let Marian get ahead. "Don't let Marian pass you, she might come up and pass you," Marian remembered Billy's mother saying to her husband.[8] Billy never really lacked focus—he was simply unable to channel his musical interests in a single direction. Although Marian could grow impatient with the ease with which Billy became distracted from his work, it was Billy who often lost patience with Marian, finding her hesitant and unconfident, not willing to be pushed too quickly. Poindexter remembered one occasion, related to him by Billy, who arrived at his house all "riled up" about Marian. Billy explained to Poindexter that Marian had a habit of hiding invitations to sing when she felt overwhelmed. Having just discovered several of them hidden under a pile of things on her dresser, he had "raised a huge fuss with her about them."[9] To Billy, Marian's behavior showed a singular lack of ambition. Billy's way was to charge ahead. For Marian, the weight of her professional responsibilities was heavier, the struggle harder.

Billy accompanied Marian for the first time in October 1916, at a concert at the St. Thomas P. E. Church in Philadelphia that included Nannie Burden, a young soprano, and Thomas Shackelford, a well-known Philadelphia reciter. In the following years, except for a brief period of service in France, in the Medical Corps, Billy frequently accompanied Marian, eventually becoming her regular accompanist. During the early 1920s, after Marian graduated from high school, both assumed the responsibilties of self-management, Billy taking advantage of the contacts he had made while on tour with Roland Hayes, and he and Marian writing to concert managers and to black colleges and churches in order to secure commitments and the promise of return appearances. In February 1922, they arranged a small tour of three concerts that included Charleston, West Virginia; Indianapolis, Indiana; and Fisk University, in Nashville; their traveling costs for concerts at such distances from each other no doubt exceeded the fees they earned.

In her concerts before predominantly black audiences, generally in black churches and colleges in the South, Marian's accomplishments as a black singer and the sense of pride she engendered helped to ensure an enthusiastic response to her singing. When she sang for predominantly white audiences in the more cosmopolitan centers of the Northeast and Midwest, the lack of full emotional maturity in her singing and her unfamiliarity with foreign languages were often mentioned by critics. In response to a concert in Philadelphia's Witherspoon Hall, in May 1922, for example, Marian received genuine praise, the critic of the *Philadelphia Public Ledger* noting that "her program contained nothing weak nor unworthy, and she brought to it a serious and conscientious disposition as well as a voice of exceptional resonance and richness in its lower register." But this same critic went on to say that "what the youthful artist most needs is to develop enlivening passion, and an emotional accent of warmth and color in her remarkable voice."[10] The critic of the *New York Age* had much the same response: "As it is now, this young girl stands and sings with a voice of power and purity, charming and entrancing her audience by the sheer beauty of her tonal production. But when she 'wakes up,' injecting life's passion into her vocal outpourings, she will indeed have become a great singer."[11]

The effect of these reviews on Marian was dispelled for a while by the growing interest that Charles Hirsch, a Philadelphia physician and music lover, took in her career. Generous in encouraging young performers, Hirsch often welcomed them to his home, a large and inviting row house on the corner of Ninth and Pine Streets, where, in an atmosphere of friendly informality, they were frequently encouraged to perform. Marian was a frequent guest, as was Joseph Pasternack, the conductor of the Philharmonic Society of Philadelphia, who often heard Marian sing in Hirsch's home. As an accompanist for singers and instrumentalists, Pasternack had already made a number of recordings for the Victor Talking Machine Company. Eventually he discussed with Marian the possibility of her making some recordings of Negro spirituals, one of which, "Heav'n, Heav'n," Marian had sung for him and the other guests. At one of Hirsch's gatherings, thinking ahead to the difficulties she might face in the studio, as Marian had had no experience in making records, Pasternack asked her to sing "Heav'n, Heav'n" a number of times, wanting to find out the extent to which her interpretationss would change from one performance to another.

Pasternack raised the question of records with Marian for several reasons. Like many who heard her sing, Pasternack was moved by the intensity of her interpretations of Negro sprituals and wanted to help preserve them for a wider public. Aware of the increasing popularity of spirituals among singers and audiences following the First World War as well as the near absence of recordings of spirituals by black artists, Pasternack was also acting in the interest of the Victor company by helping to secure a contract for Marian. Although Hayes had made a few private recordings of spirituals for a small company, Marian was about to become the first black concert artist to record spirituals for an important American recording company.

All the spirituals Marian recorded for Victor were arrangements by Harry T. Burleigh, the first black composer to publish concert arrangements of spirituals for solo voice. Burleigh's first collection of spirituals appeared in 1917 and included "Deep River" and "Go Down Moses," two of his most popular arrangements. From then until 1924, Ricordi published nearly fifty Burleigh arrangements, many of which were immediately embraced by white and black singers alike. Marian had sung two of Burleigh's arrangements for the first time in 1917 at the folk song festival in Savannah and, during her high school years, continued to learn other Burleigh arrangements and to include at least one or two on every program.

Because of Marian's inexperience with recording and her strongly self-critical instinct, sixteen sessions were required over the course of an entire year before six spirituals were successfully recorded. As the sessions progressed, Marian was assigned a Victor studio pianist as well as several conductors, including Rosario Bourdon. After the first sessions in December 1923, with Bourdon as the conductor, Marian approved "Deep River" and "My Way's Cloudy," which were issued in March 1924. More sessions were scheduled in March, April, and May, and again in November and December. Only when Pasternack took over as conductor in November were takes of the remaining four spirituals eventually approved. The last session took place on December 30, 1924, when a successful take of "Nobody Knows de Trouble I've Seen," was achieved. Marian could not have known at the start how appropriate the final spiritual would turn out to be.[12]

Another important step in her professional development came later in the year, when Pasternack invited Marian to appear as a soloist with the Philharmonic Society. An organization of both talented amateur and professional musicians—some of the members came from the more prestigious Philadelphia Orchestra—the Philharmonic Society had been formed soon after the First World War, its founding encouraged by Leopold Stokowski, who often appeared as a guest conductor. Although a number of celebrated soloists appeared with the orchestra, including Pablo Casals, Alexander Siloti, Olga Samaroff, and Florence Easton, the Philharmonic Society was dedicated to furthering the careers of young and talented Philadelphia musicians, at least one of whom was engaged each season.[13]

Marian's debut with the Philharmonic Society, on December 23, at the Academy of Music, made her the first black artist invited to appear as a soloist with the society. The concert attracted an audience of three thousand, until then the largest ever to attend a Philharmonic Society performance. She shared the program with the Polish pianist, Mieczyslaw Munz, who played Rachmaninoff's Second Piano Concerto. Marian sang the recitative and aria, "O mio Fernando," from Donizetti's *La Favorita,* which she had been studying with Boghetti, a difficult aria often chosen by contraltos and mezzo-sopranos to demonstrate both slow and sustained legato singing and the agility required for the more florid section, including the long and demanding cadenza toward the end of the aria. On the second part of the program, she sang two spirituals, with piano accompaniment, "My Lord, What a Mornin'" and "Heav'n,

Heav'n." The critic of the *Public Ledger* was cautious in his praise: "It is too much to say that Miss Anderson is as yet a great artist. There is much that she still has to learn in the intellectual and dramatic values of singing. But it is not too much to say that she has one of the most superb contralto voices that has been heard in Philadelphia for a very long time."[14] There was, however, universal agreement about her remarkable performances of the two Burleigh spirituals, which caused her to be brought back to the stage repeatedly.

As the first black musician to have appeared with the society, Marian's debut with the orchestra attracted a certain amount of attention. Unfortunately, owing to the less than front rank status of the orchestra, her appearance inspired only local and, in the end, temporary interest. The biggest disappointment, for both Marian and Pasternack, was that her appearance did not lead to other orchestral invitations. For the moment it was left to Roland Hayes to open the doors of symphony orchestras for other black artists. A week or so before Marian's appearance with the Philharmonic Society, in fact, Hayes's debut with the Boston Symphony had marked the first appearance by a black artist with a leading American orchestra. The success of Hayes's Boston debut was such that, a month later, he was engaged by the Detroit Symphony Orchestra. His stay in Detroit, however, brought home to him the limits of his achievements. When arranging for Hayes's accommodations, the Detroit Symphony's business management was informed that three of Detroit's hotels—the Salter, the Wolverine, and the Fort Shelby—would not accept him as a guest. Marian was fortunate to have enjoyed her more modest success in her hometown, where such indignities were often avoidable.

Pasternack and Hirsch did what they could to advance Marian's career, but they could do little to lessen the burden of self-management with which she and Billy struggled. Trying to put the most formal face on their enterprise, they had begun to use printed business cards and stationery advertising the Marian Anderson Management, with Marian's little studio on Martin Street serving as an office. In order to help pay expenses, she made the first of a number of attempts at teaching, usually of young black students who wanted vocal instruction and could afford her small fee. Although Poindexter, who took over some of her students when she was away from Philadelphia, thought her attempts at teaching halfhearted, more than one voice student wrote to Marian in later years, expressing gratitude not only for her help but her patience and encouragement.[15]

Eventually G. Grant Williams, the *Tribune* editor and entrepreneur, took over Marian's management, paying her thirty-five dollars for two or three numbers as assisting artist. When Williams became ill and had to retire, a young Harlem promoter anxious to introduce her to New York audiences arranged a contract for her with the Donald Musical Bureau. So far her New York appearances had been limited to black churches and other black organizations. As a teenager she had sung at Reverend Adam Clayton Powell's Abyssinian Baptist Church, at the National Baptist Convention, and at national meetings of the NAACP. She had also sung in Carnegie Hall as an assisting artist, once during her last year in high school, at the annual concert of the Martin-Smith Music School, and a second time the following winter at a gala farewell concert organized by the black tenor, Sidney Woodward, to celebrate his thirty-first anniversary as a singer.[16]

With far more ambitious plans in mind, Marian's new management booked a concert for February 18, 1924, in the Renaissance Casino, one of the most popular dance halls in Harlem. Because recitals of serious concert music by black singers were still a rarity there, the Donald Musical Bureau expected to generate considerable excitement with Marian's appearance.[17] To meet the challenge, she put together as varied a program as she was then able, including an opening group of Italian *arie antiche* (by Giordani and Scarlatti), a group of German lieder (Strauss's "Morgen" and Schubert's "Heidenröslein" and "Aufenthalt"), and the aria "Mon coeur s'ouvre à ta voix," from Saint-Saëns's *Samson et Dalila,* as well as a French group (Massenet's "Crépuscule" and "À toi" by Bemberg), two songs in English translation (Dvorak's "Songs My Mother Taught Me" and Rachmaninoff's "O Thou Billowy Harvest Field"), and Dett's "Zion Hallelujah." The large and appreciative audience that greeted her at the Renaissance Casino was enough to persuade the Donald Musical Bureau that she would enjoy the same success downtown as she had in Harlem, and a second recital, in Town Hall, was booked for April 10.

The months following Marian's concert at the Renassiance Casino were a period of great emotional turmoil for her. In addition to working with Boghetti on the Town Hall program, Marian was trying as best she could to contribute to the work and the cost of refurbishing a small house Mrs. Anderson had bought earlier that winter. Even though Marian and her mother and sisters were only moving across the street, they were feeling sad and regretful for breakng up a household in which they had lived since the death of Marian's father. "It may seem that this was a chancy thing for us to do," Marian later recalled. "We had stayed with grandmother and my aunt for a number of years, moving with them from Fitzwater Street to other houses on Seventeenth and Christian, on Carpenter Street, on Eighteenth Street, and on South Martin Street.

Grandmother and my aunt had been kind and loving, but nothing could take the place of a home of one's own."[18] Aunt Mary, who was particularly close to Mrs. Anderson and her daughters, found it difficult to accept Mrs. Anderson's decision to move. Marian later recalled how often Aunt Mary would repeat, "I can't understand it, we've lived together so long."[19] Then in the middle of February, with work on the new house underway, Aunt Mary, who had gradually adjusted to Mrs. Anderson's decision, died unexpectedly of a cerebral hemorrhage. She was only forty-seven years old.

Adding to Marian's emotional turmoil during those months was the news that Orpheus had decided to marry a young medical student. Even though she had made it clear to him that she would only consider marriage once she felt secure about her career, they had shared a tacit understanding that eventually they would be married. Only recently, in fact, Orpheus had proposed marriage in a way that Marian was to remember for years to come: "Marian I surely do miss you terrible," he wrote to her while she was on tour, "and when you return I will have to ask you if our laundry can be sent to the Laundry in the same basket. I hope that this little phrase is not too deep for you dear."[20]

Marian's single-minded focus on her career was difficult for Orpheus, and he had begun spending more and more time with other women, some of them white. Recently, in fact, he had developed a wide circle of white friends, all of them caught up, like himself, in the optimism of the years following the First World War and hopeful of career opportunities. Aware of the hardships he knew lay ahead for blacks in his profession, and hesitant to threaten the camaraderie he was enjoying, he had fallen easily into the pattern of passing for white. His circle of friends included Morrell Jacobs, Ida Gould, and her sister Myrtle, all in professional schools at the University of Pennsylvania. Ida and Myrtle came from a large family of nine children. Their parents were well-to-do Dutch Methodists. Their father owned a number of bakeries around the city. Although Orpheus dated Myrtle for a while, he was eventually attracted to Ida, a charming, tall, auburn-haired woman, outgoing and energetic. Their affair became more serious and later that year they were married. Ida worked in the medical field and Orpheus took a job with the Department of Public Education. The couple set up housekeeping in North Philadelphia, and a year after they were married, their only child, James Fischer, was born.[21] Their marriage was not easy. Because both Orpheus and Ida worked, Ida's mother, Kathryn, who did not like Orpheus, had to take care of the baby. When the marriage ended, a few years later, Orpheus left his son to be raised by Ida and her mother.[22]

Through those months of emotional strain Marian somehow managed to work steadily on the program for her Town Hall concert. Knowing that a recital in Town Hall, where young artists were traditionally presented to New York audiences for the first time, would be seized on by critics as Marian's official debut as a concert artist, Boghetti encouraged her to work on a program even more ambitious than the one she had presented at the Renaissance Casino. The works finally chosen included a group of Italian *arie antiche* by Scarlatti and Pergolesi, "Ombra mai fu," from Handel's *Xerxes,* a German group with the long and dramatically challenging "Von ewiger Liebe" of Brahms, Strauss's "Morgen," Schubert's "Aufenthalt" and "Wohin?," "O mio Fernando" from Donizetti's *La Favorita,* songs by Dvorak and Rachmaninoff, a group of songs including "The Awakening," by Rosamond Johnson, "You May Lay So Still," by Coleridge-Taylor, the spirituals "Deep River" and "Heav'n Heav'n," and a final group of English songs by Douty, Becker, and Quilter. Although the program contained a variety of interpretive challenges, the German group presented the greatest risks, requiring that Marian bring out the dark torment of "Aufenthalt" as well as the deep and quiet rapture of "Morgen," a song in which even experienced and accomplished lieder singers slip into sentimentality.

Marian had prepared for months for her Town hall debut, but, as she remembered the concert years later, she lost courage the very moment she stepped onto the stage. Although the concert was scheduled to begin at 8:15, she was not called by the signal man to appear on stage until nearly 9:00. Boghetti had told her the house was sold out, yet when she and Billy King finally walked onto the stage, the house was no more than a third full. To make matters worse, the mutual support they might have given each other during the first number was denied them because it had been decided that Billy would accompany her on the organ for Handel's "Largo," requiring that he sit far to the side of the stage.

The New York critics had kind things to say so far as Marian's voice and technique were concerned. "Miss Anderson possesses one of the best contralto voices heard in this town in many moons," the critic of the *Sun* wrote. "It is a pure contralto, of even quality, imposing in its freely produced and resonant lower register, which is without the forced opacity often heard in contraltos, and velvety in the medium." No one questioned Marian's sincerity or her pleasing personality, but neither did anyone disagree with the final verdict of the *Sun,* that "till she broadens her imagination and acquires a knowledge of the art of color she will probably not realize all her ambitions." As for the German lieder, there was near unanimous agreement that, in the words of one critic, "Miss

Anderson betrayed a sad want of understanding of the deeper meanings of her lyrics and of lied interpretation."[23] Of all the critics, Lucien H. White was the most direct, advising that she "should devote more time to earnest, consistent study and less to the concert stage."[24]

The Town Hall experience brought about a period of disillusionment and reflection for Marian that was bound to come sooner or later. As she often said in later years, the harshness of the critics' judgment made it difficult for her to ignore what other reviewers had already begun pointing out. Demoralized by her Town Hall performance, Marian was troubled during the months that followed not only by doubts about her singing but also by serious self-recrimination. She was afraid she had deceived the people who came to hear her. She felt embarrassed and guilty, prompting her to question retrospectively even those times when critics and audiences had received her with unequivocal approval.[25]

For months Marian did not think about singing. Eventually Walter White, who counted on her admiration for Roland Hayes to coax her out of her depression, persuaded her to sing again. When it was announced, in July, that Hayes would receive the Spingarn Medal, awarded each year by the NAACP to a black person making a significant contribution to some field of endeavor, White, the NAACP's secretary, invited Marian to sing at the ceremonies in Philadelphia and to accept the medal for Hayes, who would be away giving concerts in Germany. Marian had to be asked a number of times before she felt ready to accept.[26]

In the fall of 1924, Marian and Billy began touring again. In early November they returned to Winston-Salem to perform at a conference sponsored by the State Music Teachers' Association and the Southern Music Supervisors' Conference, and a few days later they presented a concert at the court house in Chambersburg, Pennsylvania. With the new year came the annual Emancipation Celebration at the Academy of Music and in the spring, a recital at Witherspoon Hall.

Early in the new year, without her knowledge, Boghetti entered Marian's name in a contest sponsored by New York's Lewisohn Stadium in conjunction with the National Music League. The contest was open to both instrumentalists and vocalists. The winners from both categories would be invited to appear as soloists with the New York Philharmonic during its summer concert season at the stadium.[27] Although Boghetti saw the contest as an opportunity to demonstrate his acumen, the prospect terrified Marian, raising all her fears about her interpretive shortcomings. In keeping with the requirements of the contest, Boghetti asked her to prepare the Donizetti aria "O mio Fernando," as well as two songs in English. The first auditions were held at the end of June at New

York's Aeolian Hall, where she would be judged together with some 300 vocal contestants. On the day of the trials Marian and Reba Patton, another Boghetti student and contestant, took the train to New York in the morning. After a short rehearsal with Boghetti at his Park Avenue studio, the three drove to the auditorium, where the contestants were given numbers. Although Marian's was 44A, she remembered that she had to wait for at least sixty people to perform before she was called.

Sitting at the back of the balcony, the judges sounded a noisy clicker whenever they finished with a contestant. Boghetti knew that the judges, who were required to hear as many as a hundred contestants a day, would not listen to more than a minute or two of anyone's performance, but he didn't waver in his advice to Marian. "As my turn approached," Marian later recalled, "Mr. Boghetti whispered that no matter what happened I must continue to the end of my aria and to be sure to sing the trill. It was lovely of him to refuse to be intimidated by the clicker, but I had been sitting there listening to the other singers, and at least six of them had launched into 'O mio Fernando' and had been interrupted before they reached the middle. I made up my mind that I would not defy the rules of the contest. I would stop when the implacable clicker sounded."[28] Marian was not stopped. She was, in fact, applauded after the aria, which also went against the rules, and the judges asked for an additional song. By the end of the first round of auditions, Marian was chosen as one of the sixty contestants to appear in the semifinals the following week.

The summer heat in New York was uncomfortably muggy for the next round of performances. On the way to Aeolian Hall, Marian confessed to Boghetti that she was bothered by some discomfort in one of her ears. She had been taking swimming lessons, and, as she later learned, had caused a bad abscess by stuffing cotton and earplugs in her ears to keep the water out. She insisted the pain did not affect her hearing, and she was able to perform her aria and two songs. When Boghetti and Marian left the hall later that day, they still had no idea which contestants had been chosen to participate in the next round. Normally a total of fifteen semifinalists were chosen from the two categories— singers and instrumentalists—to compete in the finals, where four soloists were then chosen as winners. Back at the studio, Boghetti was informed by telephone that Marian had been chosen as the sole winner among the vocal entrants. By then in considerable pain, Marian took the seven o'clock train back to Philadelphia. She stopped at home for a minute, but only to tell her mother that she needed to see Dr. Taylor. It was Boghetti, in fact, who told Marian's family that she had won, having called them while she was still at the doctor.[29] Still surprised and overjoyed at having won, Marian told an interviewer from the *Philadelphia Tribune* a few days later: "Of course I am happy, very happy. I regard this as a victory for our group rather than for myself. While I was singing I seemed to feel the 'urge' of all of those who have been so kind as to make it possible for me to become their representative at an occasion of this character. I feel obligation to my teacher, Mr. Giuseppe Boghetti for entering me in the contest."[30]

Marian appeared as a soloist at Lewisohn Stadium on Wednesday evening, August 26. Willem von Hoogstraten conducted the New York Philharmonic and she sang "O mio Fernando" and, later in the program, accompanied by Billy King, three spirituals, "Deep River," "Heav'n, Heav'n," and J. Rosamond Johnson's "Song of the Heart." An audience of 7,500, the third largest of the summer, filled the stadium. The experience could not have been more different from her last appearance in New York. At Town Hall she had had to face the dispiriting prospect of a hall more empty than full, with a program that was bound to uncover weaknesses of style and of interpretation. At the stadium, concentrating her efforts on a single aria and a group of spirituals, she sang before an audience already looking forward to hearing her. Their enthusiasm gave her courage. The difference in accomplishment was not lost on the reviewers. F. D. Perkins, for example, writing in the *Herald Tribune,* said that "last night's was not her first appearance here. She had given a recital on April 25, 1924, but that had hinted little at the astonishing vocal powers displayed by the young singer last night. The present reviewer, on that occasion, had animadverted on a powerful voice of true contralto quality, in need of some further development, but it had hardly seemed then the voice in a thousand—or shall we try ten thousand or a hundred thousand?—that it appeared to be last night."[31]

Edward Henry, a prominent Philadelphia civic leader, called for a public demonstration by Philadelphia civic organizations to help celebrate Marian's triumph in New York. On a Thursday evening in late October, a crowd of 1,000 filled University Hall of the John Wanamaker store for a reception. There were performances by the band of the Robert Curtis Ogden Association, which had helped to sponsor the reception, and by two young singers, Alice Dorsey and Mozelle Neal. The speeches included one by Boghetti, "who graphically related the story of [Marian's] recent achievement in the realm of music."[32]

During the years following her stadium appearance, Marian and Billy were able to establish a more or less uniform pattern of touring that included a tour of southern states after Christmas and a midwestern tour around Easter. By 1927, the southern tour had grown to as many as twenty concerts in nine states, including Virginia, the Carolinas, Georgia, and Florida. The midwestern tour that year included Cleveland, Cincinnati, Dayton, Akron, Minneapolis, and Chicago. Marian generated the greatest enthusiasm at black colleges and universities throughout the South, where the halls were invariably filled to capacity. Her concert in Dayton in the spring of 1926 was typical. Sponsored by the National Cash Register Company for the benefit of blacks, the concert attracted a capacity audience to the 2,300 seat auditorium. The previous December, at the Agricultural and Technical College in Greensboro, North Carolina, the huge dining room of the college had to be converted into a concert hall, and the following season, in the spring of 1927, at the First Baptist Church in Norfolk, Virginia, in a concert presented by the Girl Reserves Committee of the YWCA, she was the only artist in years to draw a capacity audience.[33]

Marian's popularity in the South gradually grew among white as well as black audiences, especially on the campuses of black colleges and universities, where there were often generous seating arrangements for white patrons, arrangements strictly in keeping with the practices dictated by segregation. Often segregation was so strict that black and white patrons were not permitted to attend the same concert. The concert would have to be repeated for a white audience. Marian's concert at the teachers' college in Winston-Salem was attended by both blacks and whites. When she sang in Greensboro, the college dining room accomodated both white and black patrons, including a large delegation of students and faculty from the white North Carolina College for Women. At the city auditorium in Charlotte, the main floor of the hall was given over to white patrons, black patrons taking seats in the balcony.[34] Throughout the decade of the 1920s college freshmen across the campuses of black universities could count on hearing Marian at least once before graduating. In addition to Fisk University, Howard University, Tuskegee Institute, and Morehouse College—colleges and universities where Marian had sung since her high school years—black colleges in North and South Carolina, Virginia, Alabama, and Florida had begun to invite Marian and Billy on a regular basis. By the end of 1928, they had assembled a file of over 200 names of churches and colleges where they had performed, and of local managers who had shown interest in them.

When Marian and Billy first began to tour, during the early twenties, she had been earning $100 for an appearance. Her fee then gradually increased until, by the end of the decade, she was earning $250 or $300. Local managers covered rental fees for the concert hall or auditorium; her expenses included, in addition to the 25 percent accompanist's fee, travel for herself as well as Billy. Because they could not stay in hotels, accommodations were generally covered by local managers, who arranged for them to stay on college campuses—Billy in a men's dormitory and Marian in a guest house or the home economics visitors' suite. When they performed at a church, Marian stayed at the home of a member of the church's congregation and Billy at a YMCA.

Travel was a constant source of humiliation and frustration. During the early years of touring, Marian bought her own tickets. Sometimes she was told there were none available; other times she was given berth 13, which she learned soon enough was not a typical passenger car, but a lounge converted into a passenger car for blacks. Most of the time Marian and Billy had to sit in the Jim Crow car, where the bathrooms were so filthy as to be unuseable. Whatever their accommodations, it was never an easy matter to arrange for a hot meal. During one trip in the Jim Crow car, they were allowed to eat in the dining car, behind a drawn curtain and at tables where the porters and waiters ate, only when the car was empty of other passengers. Eventually a Mr. Ross, a Philadelphia music lover, having learned of Marian's difficulties in managing her career, took over the problem of her train reservations, trying to arrange her itinerary in the most comfortable way.

Traveling with Billy was often a mixed blessing for Marian. She respected him as a musician and valued his enthusiasm and his devotion to furthering her career, but she did not want their lives entwined in more personal ways. His easy familiarity and possessiveness grew to annoy and even embarass her. Although many of Billy's friends knew him to be homosexual, some of them were aware that he also enjoyed intimate relationships with women. More than one believed that he may very well have thought about marrying Marian. To judge from the erotically suggestive language and sexual innuendo of Billy's letters to her, as well as Orpheus's warnings to her that she "be careful of Billy," Billy did not share Marian's sense of where the line between them should be drawn. One can imagine how often he stepped over the line in ways she found inappropriate. Offended by his behavior, concerned that it was interfering with their professional work, she eventually insisted that local managers provide a chaperon for her.[35]

Hampered by the grim realities of segregation, forced back into self-management after the Town Hall recital, Marian became increasingly restless and dissatisfied professionally. Even the recent interest that Arthur Judson, one of New York's most influential managers, had shown in her career led to disappointment. Judson had heard her sing with the Hall Johnson Choir as soloist in Nathaniel Dett's "Listen to the

Lambs." Impressed with her performance, Judson had come back to talk with her after the concert, asking her to come and see him. A few days later, Marian went to Judson's office with Boghetti to discuss the possibility of a contract. Realizing it would take him considerable time to adjust to the problems of managing a young black singer, Judson was unwilling for the moment to make any guarantees.

The most damaging restriction to Marian's professional satisfaction was artistic. The fervert desire to study German lieder remained unfulfilled while she continued to study with Boghetti. Her repertoire did grow to some extent during the years of touring, but she made hardly any progress with German lieder; during her first tours after high school, she had known no more than five. Eventually she added Brahms's "Die Mainacht," and, in 1927, after more than six years of touring, three new songs of Schubert—"Lachen und Weinen," "Der Erlkönig," and "Im Abendroth."

Only concern about her family's welfare could keep Marian from leaving home to study abroad, but on that score she had begun to feel a certain peace of mind. Her rising concert fees and her sisters' steady income—Alyse was working at Wanamaker's, Ethel, at a printing company—had significantly improved the family's finances. Indeed, Marian had arrived at the point of trying to persuade Mrs. Anderson to retire from Wanamaker's, where she was still cleaning and scrubbing floors. The right moment came when Mrs. Anderson, having suffered a bad cold and periods of fatigue, was encouraged by her doctor to stay at home a while longer. As Marian later recalled: "I went to the telephone and called Wanamaker's. I asked to speak to the supervisor, and as I waited for her to come to the phone I felt, I must say, a glowing satisfaction. I was primed for the lady. She was a big person on her job, and maybe she had a heart, but it remained at home when she went to work. It was a good and happy moment when she came to the phone and I could say, after identifying myself, 'I just wanted to tell you that Mother will not be coming back to work.' "[36]

Gradually Marian began to think more and more seriously about going to Europe. As she understood only too well, an American singer who did not study and perform successfully abroad could not hope to have a significant career at home. A decade earlier, Rosa Ponselle, without any experience abroad, had made a successful debut at the Metropolitan Opera in Verdi's *La Forza del destino,* but that was a unique accomplishment, not to be duplicated again for decades. For black singers, success in Europe was even more imperative. "I was going stale," she later said. "I had to get away from my old haunts for a while; progress was at a standstill; repeating the same engagements each year, even if programs varied a little, was becoming routine; my career needed a fresh impetus, and perhaps a European stamp would help."[37]

CHAPTER FOUR

London
(1928)

On a Saturday afternoon in late October 1927, Anderson sailed for England on the *Ile de France*. "I wish you would have listened to me," Boghetti wrote her a few days after her arrival in London, "and not gone to Europe alone, however, I know that you have good sense and that you will not suffer any interference." Arthur Judson, too, had voiced strong disapproval of her decision. Seeing themselves now as the principal overseers of Marian's artistic future, they did not want her professional career or training falling into the wrong hands. To them, her sudden independence was worrisome.

Marian had come to envision London more and more as a welcoming place for study. A number of black musicians had begun to arrive in the British capital after the First World War, to find work in what they hoped would be an environment free of segregation and hostility. Many had stayed on to study and establish careers, and more than one had promised to help her if she came to England.[1] The triumph of Roland Hayes not many years before, when he was summoned to sing for the king and queen, stood as a striking example of what a black concert artist could achieve in London.

Once Marian had decided to study in London, friends came forward with advice and offers of recommendation. By the time she was ready to leave, she had letters of introduction to the English composer, Roger Quilter, to Ira Amanda Aldrich, a famous black vocal teacher, and, most importantly, Raimund von Zur Mühlen, the foremost teacher of the German lied in England. John Payne, who had gone to England in 1919 as the baritone soloist of a popular male quartet, promised her a home.

So she set out for the British capital, taking with her the encouragement of friends, all the money she had managed to save—$1,000 in a letter of credit drawn on Brown Brothers, $500 in travelers' checks, and $50 in English pounds. She felt terribly lonesome even before the ship left the harbor, but hopeful of opportunity.[2]

Arriving in Southampton, Marian took a late-evening train to Paddington Station. She telephoned Roger Quilter, who was expecting her, and learned that the composer was ill and for the time being in a nursing home. She then turned to John Payne, who responded cordially to her telephone call and immediately gave her directions to his home. "After gathering up my things," she later recalled,

> I walked out of the booth to get a cab, and I felt relieved and oddly buoyant. It must have been eleven-thirty P.M.; when I got into the taxi I was eager to catch sight of some of the famous landmarks, but I could see little of anything in the dark, and I noticed, too, that there was no window in the back of the cab. We pulled up at 17 Regents Park Road, and John Payne was there at the door to greet me before I got out of the cab. He was warm in his welcome, and we sat around and talked for two hours.[3]

The house at 17 Regents Park Road, an elegant three-story building surrounded by some of London's more stylish and aristocratic homes, was given to John Payne by Lady Mary Cook, the wife of Sir Hubert Cook, a wealthy businessman and art historian. Lady Cook had a fondness for blacks and was devoted to Payne and his guests, mostly visiting black artists and students who needed a home.

In a few days Anderson was able to reach Quilter. As a young man, Quilter had suffered from an ulcer, from which he later developed physical complications that left him frail and often debilitated for long periods. He was a man of exquisite sensibility and refinement, with a profound knowledge of poetry and of painting, and he was wealthy enough to possess a remarkable collection of books and paintings. As a composer, Quilter felt most comfortable with smaller vocal and instrumental forms, especially songs, for which he became known to the British public early in the century. Personally he was compassionate and of nearly inexhaustible generosity. His friendship with Marian, about whom he had heard much from Roland Hayes and Billy King, lasted many years. As Anderson remembered him from her first meeting, "he was a tall, thin, sensitive man, an English-looking Englishman, as I put it to myself. He had a fine home, always open to musicians. It was not uncommon to go there and find his music room occupied by someone who needed a quiet place to work and study."[4]

From the time of her arrival in London, Marian was content to think of herself as a student. She enrolled in the Hugo Institute, where she took courses in German and French, and made plans to travel to Steyning, in Sussex, where the aged Zur Mühlen had settled some years after coming to England. Zur Mühlen was one of the greatest interpreters of German lieder during the late nineteenth century. He studied in Berlin and Frankfurt, and then Paris, but it was his personal connection with Brahms, for whom he sang, and Clara Schumann, in whose master classes he studied the lieder of Schubert and Schumann, that helped to give him his authoritative understanding of the German song repertory. In 1925 he settled at Wiston Old Rectory, near Steyning, in the Sussex countryside, where he taught until the last years of his life, when illness finally overtook his efforts.

A few days after she arrived in London, Anderson traveled by train to Steyning, making arrangements to stay with a young printer, Vicky Newburg, and his wife, who gave her a small room on the second floor of their house. It was a rather cold November that year, and Anderson later remembered having to ask for a pay-as-you-go heater, which she fed with shillings. The Newburgs did not have a piano, so she made plans to rent one in nearby Brighton. At Zur Mühlen's home, she was taken into a large room with the piano at the far end. The old man sat in a big chair, his knees covered by a red plush blanket hanging down to the floor, his cane nearby. During her first meeting with him, she sang Schubert's "Im Abendroth," which she had learned only that year, and the memory of her first lesson was dominated by the embarrassment she suffered when she could not tell Zur Mühlen what the song meant word for word. It was not enough to know in general what a song meant, he told her, and if that was the extent of it, then one should not sing it. As she was reminded some twenty years later, however, she had nonetheless made a favorable impression on Zur Mühlen. On the eve of a concert that she gave in London in June 1949, she received a letter from Daniel Kelly, who had been Zur Mühlen's accompanist during that first lesson. Kelly recalled the initial impression that she had made on the aged teacher: "The first song I played for you was Gluck's 'O del mio dolce ardor,' and I remember I nearly fell off the stool at the first notes! Mühlen said—'A voice of gold!'—which was far more to the point."[5]

Zur Mühlen was by then suffering from thrombosis and could not sit up for long periods, but he was able to talk with her for a while, and lent her a volume of songs by Schubert, asking that she learn the first one in the volume, "Nähe des Geliebten." No doubt Zur Mühlen chose it with some care. It requires the same kind of slow and sustained legato singing demanded by the Gluck song Anderson sang for him. Moreover, its strophic character (each of the four verses is sung to the same music) would force her to think carefully about the meaning of the text, because each verse would have to be inflected in a way that suited its meaning, without the help of a different accompaniment. Goethe's text proved too much for Anderson and Vicky, who worked on a translation together, and Vicky resorted finally to calling in a friend who also knew some German.

Anderson worked with Zur Mühlen until a week or so before Christmas, when his health became so precarious that he was forced to abandon teaching altogether. She moved back to Payne's home at 17 Regent's Park, where the winter months were full of activity. Two black American students were already living there, F. H. Robb, who was studying law, and Errington Kerr, a violinist who was studying medicine. Anderson was given a large room on the third floor. Near the end of January the room next to hers was taken over by Alberta Hunter, one of the great popular black performers who was just then having a huge success in Paris and on the Riviera.

The severe flooding of the Thames that winter had led to the establishment of a Flood Relief Fund by the mayor of Westminster, and Noble Sissle, who had formed his own orchestra and was touring Europe, was helping to organize "the greatest all-star colored show ever staged" in England to raise money for the victims of the flooding. The show was to take place on Sunday afternoon, January 29, at the London Pavilion in Piccadilly Circus. The list of performers included Layton and Johnson, the Four Harmony Kings, Leslie Hutchinson, and James B. Lowe. Josephine Baker boarded a plane in Paris on the morning of the twenty-ninth, after working all night in her nightclub, and arrived just in time to perform. Alberta Hunter arrived in London on the Friday before, after a telegram from Noble Sissle reached her on the Riviera. She went to work at the Florida Club on Bond Street immediately after the show at the London Pavilion and later that night took up residence on the third floor of John Payne's house.[6]

Anderson did not want for companionship. Payne's guests felt very much like a family. She took her meals at Payne's house and went to concerts and the theater with Payne and some of his guests, the tickets often provided by Lady Cook. In later years she remembered hearing the Spanish mezzo-soprano Conchita Supervia and the pianist Artur Rubinstein. A friendship developed between Anderson and Alberta Hunter, who would often ride for hours on the top level of the double-decker buses, going to the end of the line and back in order to see the sights of the city. But the friendship was an uneasy one, as Anderson was uncomfortable with Hunter's uninhibited frankness, and Hunter often found Anderson cold and passionless.[7] In April, when rehearsals for the London production of *Showboat* began at the Drury Lane Theatre, Anderson met Paul and Essie Robeson. Paul, who was to star in the production, arrived in London in mid-month, his wife several weeks later. There was always music at Payne's home on Sunday afternoons, and Roger Quilter often invited Marian to his house, where she was usually asked to sing. At Quilter's home she met the composer Cyril Scott and the baritone Mark Raphael, who was one of the most important interpreters of Quilter's songs.

In spite of her socializing, Anderson was rather lonely at first, although the excitement of the city and her studies helped to "take off the edge" of some of the loneliness. For the most part she did not go out alone. When she did—to have tea at the Lyon's Corner House, near Regent's Park, or to take walks around the city—she was often ill at ease. Anderson was tall, nearly five foot ten, very slim and quite beautiful, and often people would stare at her when she walked down the street. She would nervously look down, to see if perhaps something was wrong with how she was dressed. Eventually she acquired more self-confidence, taking for granted the kind of freedom she had rarely known so unequivocally in her own country.

The stream of letters from home, especially from Mrs. Anderson and Billy, helped too. Back home, Marian's absence was particularly hard on Mrs. Anderson, who until now had not spent a holiday season without her. Managing to earn some money by singing in private homes, she was able to send some home for Christmas. "Dear I am so much afraid," her mother wrote to her on Christmas day, "you can not spare the $25 you sent me. I have not words to express my joy and appreciation for the kind and loving remembrance. After having left me so very well fixed, I was indeed surprised that you could send me any thing. I thank God that He gave me you, and placed within you the make up He has. It is indeed a blessing and a God send."[8]

Orpheus wrote too. To judge from his letters, his marriage to Ida Gould, the birth of his son, and his separation from them was an unhappy interlude he wanted only to forget. He was living on Long Island now, closer to New York and hoping to find work there, although for two months nothing had turned up. Without work, away from his circle of friends in Philadelphia, tormented by Marian's infrequent letters and coolness, he wanted more than anything to feel a spark of hope that they would have a future together. "This is my fifth letter to you," he wrote Marian, "and I shall write until you answer my letter. Why is it that you don't write? . . . I miss you so much, I love you so much, I am always thinking of you wishing and hoping you were home and with me, I am only happy when I think of you. . . . I have [been] a very good boy, I mean it, I only get a thrill from my Marian."[9]

Anderson did not let her disappointment over Zur Mühlen's illness dampen her determination to study. She sought out several other teachers, each one of differing background and appeal. Roger Quilter advised her to study with Mark Raphael, who had himself worked with Zur Mühlen and become one of Quilter's closest friends and most important interpreters. Raphael was a high baritone, with a small voice and intensely expressive interpretive gift. Raphael's voice, with its pure, slightly dry and reedy quality, and its unshowy interpretive manner, were similar to Roland Hayes's voice, as was his style of singing, and these similarites were no doubt evident to Anderson. Raphael's dedication to the music of Schubert, which intensified during the Schubert centenary celebrations of the new year 1928, created a special bond between them. Raphael's contribution to the performance of Schubert's music throughout the year included several recitals of his songs, and a performance of *Die schöne Müllerin* cycle, at the Wigmore Hall.[10]

Just after Thanksgiving, a month or so after her arrival in London, Marian was given her first opportunity to meet Amanda Ira Aldrich at a party given by Payne in honor of some Washington friends. Some of the musicians among the guests were asked to perform, including Aldrich, who accompanied Hattie King Reavis in one of her own songs. Amanda Aldrich was the daughter of the famous black actor Ira Aldrich. Both she and her sister, Irene Luranah, were very musical at an early age. Irene had an important career as a contralto, singing operatic roles in Europe and participating in the Bayreuth Festival performances of 1896, until a serious illness left her an invalid for the last twenty years of her life. Amanda attended the Royal College of Music in London, studying voice with Jenny Lind and George Henschel and elocution with Madge Kendal. It was her teacher Jenny Lind who advised her to adopt her father's name: "Amanda, you must not drop your father's name; you must always call yourself Ira. Your father was the greatest Othello of them all. I am proud to have been his friend."[11] The two sisters lived together at 2 Bedford Gardens, in Kensington, where Amanda Aldrich became well known as a teacher of voice and elocution. She had taught Roland Hayes and John Payne, at whose home she was a welcome visitor, and she would soon coach Paul Robeson in the part of Othello when he performed the role in London in 1930. Anderson was drawn to Aldrich not only because of their common vocal range—both were contraltos—but because of Aldrich's emphasis on the importance of a song's text and its proper declamation.

Later that winter Anderson came to hear of Louis Drysdale, a voice teacher who was having great success in training young singers in London. She began lessons with him in February. Drysdale was born in Kingston, Jamaica, and came to London at the invitation of Sir Alfred Jones, through whose efforts Drysdale entered the Royal College of Music. There he became a pupil of Clerici and Lenghi-Cellini, Italian masters of the bel canto tradition. However, it was Gustave Garcia, another of his teachers at the Royal College, who was the most important transmitter of that tradition to Drysdale. Gustave Garcia was the son of Manuel Garcia the younger, the most famous singing teacher of the nineteenth century. Gustave Garcia's grandfather, Manuel Garcia the older, had created the role of Count Almaviva in Rossini's *Il Barbiere di Siviglia.* Indeed, the whole of the later nineteenth-century Italian school of singing was descended from the Garcia family; in addition to Manuel the younger, there were his sisters Maria Malibran and Pauline Viardot, both of whom had sung first performances of many of the important roles in operas by Bellini, Donizetti, and Verdi.[12]

Drysdale had to work as a tailor to guarantee himself a steady income. Gradually he began to attract students, at first mostly black students, to his home in Forest Hill (South London), where he hoped to pass on to his pupils his knowledge of the art of bel canto, a tradition of vocal technique and performance that emphasized beauty of sound, correct tone placement, and breath control. His reputation began to flourish the year before Anderson's arrival in London, when the entertainer Florence Mills, who was starring in Lew Leslie's *Blackbirds of 1926,* went to Drysdale for lessons. She was enthusiastic enough about Drysdale to write a letter to the editor of the *New York Age.* The following year brought many black artists to his studio, among them Ethel Waters and Nell Hunter.[13] Even before Marian arrived in London, Drysdale had enough pupils to open a studio in the West End, at Grotian Hall, and to pay regular visits to music studios in Regent Street and in Margate (southeast London). In later years Anderson talked about her lessons with Mark Raphael and Amanda Aldrich, but in the interviews she gave after her return to the United States, she spoke mostly about Louis Drysdale and the remarkable benefits of his method.[14]

The beginning months of 1928 were filled with study and lessons and occasional invitations to sing in the private homes of those who heard about her singing from Lady Cook and her husband, or Roger Quilter and his circle. Anderson attended concerts of visiting singers whenever she could, Lily Pons, Elisabeth Schumann, and Conchita Supervia among them, although it was Elena Gerhardt's performance of *Die Win-terreise* at Queen's Hall that had the profoundest effect on her. Although Schubert's *Die Winterreise* was originally intended to be sung by a tenor, many female singers, sopranos (Lotte Lehmann and Mitsuko Shirai), as well as mezzo-sopranos (Christa Ludwig and Brigitte Fassbaender), have performed the cycle. Gerhardt had first sung *Die Winterreise* in London soon after the First World War. She became immersed in the cycle again during the spring of 1928, singing it in London and other cities on the continent to mark the centenary of Schubert's birth. During those months in London, Gerhardt recorded eight of the twenty-four songs of Schubert's cycle. Desmond Shawe-Taylor, who attended Gerhardt's performance of *Die Winterreise* at Queen's Hall that spring, has left a vivid testimony of the singer's interpretation:

> Speaking for myself, I do not remember to have been more strongly affected by any other concert; nor can I recall another performance of Schubert's cycle which, in the controlled intensity of passionate grief, came within measurable distance of hers. It is in these songs, above all, that we remember the strong, often deliberately harsh, chest notes of her mature voice: it seemed as though sorrow and bitterness had etched themselves into the very timbre, so that (among other consequences) one had no impression of incongruity of a woman's voice in the tragic story of a man's broken heart.[15]

Gerhardt, whose career began before the First World War and lasted some four decades, was one of the supreme lieder singers of her generation. She impressed the conductor Arthur Nikisch so profoundly while a student at the Leipzig Conservatory that he accompanied the young singer at her debut recital when she was only twenty. After having sung the roles of Mignon and Charlotte at the Leipzig Opera, she took the unprecedented step early in her career of devoting herself entirely to the performance of lieder. Gerhardt began her career as a soprano but made the change to mezzo-soprano very early.[16]

Marian was fortunate to have drawn inspiration from more than one important contralto or mezzo-soprano while still relatively young. While in high school she had heard Schumann-Heink at the Academy of

Music. Although her performance of Schubert's "Die Erlkönig" impressed Marian, she did not want "her low tones to sound like that." Later on Sigrid Onegin had made a powerful impression with her coloratura facility, especially in Mozart's "Alleluja," which Marian could not resist working on with Billy soon after they heard her. The influence of these singers on Marian was superficial, however, compared with the influence of Gerhardt. With Gerhardt there came a shock of recognition. Here was a mezzo-soprano who had long before given up the world of opera for the more austere and less glamorous one of German lieder, and with whose quality of voice, of timbre and of dramatic intensity Marian could immediately identify. That evening in Queen's Hall was something of an artistic epiphany for Marian, as she listened to the more mature singer whose whole being became absorbed in song.[17]

The powerful impression Gerhardt's singing made on Marian was reason enough for her to hope that she might be able to study with her one day. The idea took practical form when Marian became aware of the success Gerhardt was then enjoying in London as a teacher of lieder. It was in London, where Gerhardt's concerts had kept her during February and March of 1927, that Harold Holt, her London manager, suggested she give some lessons in lieder interpretation. She was then only in her forties—she would, in fact, continue to sing for several decades—so the idea of teaching seemed premature to her. Curious about how many applications would actually appear, she was persuaded to allow Holt to announce a course of study. As it turned out, there were over a hundred. Gerhardt found her involvement in teaching so satisfying that she offered a second course during the spring season of 1928, when she again found herself in London. Busy with her studies and happy with her teachers for the time being, Anderson did not yet feel ready to approach Gerhardt. That would come later.

That spring, Raphael and Quilter decided Anderson was ready to give a public concert, which they scheduled for the afternoon of June 15, at the Wigmore Hall, a small and intimate hall ideal for instrumental and vocal recitals. The audiences there were generally sophisticated about music and used to hearing not only the greatest European and American artists but also younger performers at the start of their careers. The concert was to be Anderson's European debut.

By the end of the twenties black performers, at least in jazz and vaudeville, as members of vocal quartets, dance bands, musical theater, and music revues, were finding enthusiastic audiences in Europe. Payne had come to England in 1919 as one of the singers with the New York Syncopated Orchestra and as baritone sololist in the male quartet known as the Exposition Four. By 1921, the group had severed its connection with the orchestra and changed its name to the Royal Southern Singers. Having gotten themselves an agent, and with Payne acting now as the quartet manager, they were performing regularly in the dance halls, "where we are still knocking them a twister," as he liked to say. Later in the decade, another vocal group, the Four Harmony Kings, who had built their reputation in America in the musical *Shuffle Along,* were even more popular in London.

The success of black musicians in the British capital and the influx of ever greater numbers in the early 1920s created racial tension.[18] That tension came to a head in May of 1923, when the Plantation Revue, which included Florence Mills and a company of black players and musicians, opened at the London Pavilion. On opening night, a writer for several London newspapers who was presumably responsible for much of the antagonistic propaganda directed against black performers, was refused a pass, taken politely yet firmly by the hand by the Revue's producer and asked to leave. Several months before that, Paul Whiteman and his orchestra of white jazz musicians had caused a public stir when the conductor appeared in a revue at the London Hippodrome with a company of black players led by Harper and Blanks. The revue's popularity helped to focus attention on the dissatisfaction and frustration felt among the 4,000 variety artists and musicians without jobs at a time when large numbers of black performers could receive a work permit without difficulty.[19]

When a troupe of black artists was engaged to stage a cabaret show at the Empire Theatre after regular theater hours, the Variety Artists Confederation officially protested the engagement. As the London County Council proceeded to rule on the licensing of the all-black cabaret, it became clear that the real fear was the possibility that black artists might actually mix with the audience. The license was granted only when the proprietor of the Empire, Sir Alfred Butt, assured the board that a rail would be put up around that part of the room where the show was to be staged. With each controversy it became more difficult for black performers to gain a work permit. In 1928, Alberta Hunter, after appearing in the revue organized by Noble Sissle, tried several times to acquire one before she was allowed to remain in England.[20]

In opera or on the recital stage, the appearance of black performers abroad was still uncommon even after the First World War; usually their success was determined by the kind of repertoire they performed. The sopranos Lillian Evanti and Catarina Jarboro made some headway in opera, but only in roles that could be considered appropriate for black performers. Evanti sang the Indian princess in Délibes's *Lakmé* in the mid-twenties, first in Nice and then at the Trianon Lyrique in Paris, while Jarboro sang the title role in Verdi's *Aida* at the Puccini Theater in Milan in 1930. For the most part, black performers tended to sing the music of their own people, generally spirituals. Lawrence Brown, the accompanist for Roland Hayes and later Paul Robeson, settled in England for several years during the twenties, studying music at Trinity College and voice with Amanda Aldrich. He appeared in a number of concerts, but always in performances of spirituals.[21]

When it came to the traditional repertory of the European concert artist—German lieder, French and Italian songs—European audiences and critics could be expected to demonstrate their natural reserve and proprietary feeling toward any singer from America, especially toward those who were not trained in Europe. The challenge to black artists in this repertoire was even greater, for European audiences still had little contact with them in any context other than black musical idioms. At his London debut in 1920, Roland Hayes attempted a program of lieder and French and Italian songs, together with spirituals, in the Aeolian Hall, but he was met with considerable reserve in the traditional groups of songs. Slowly the thoughtfulness of his interpretations won over his audiences and a month later he enjoyed a great success at Wigmore Hall. A few years later, he suffered the same test in Berlin, in the Beethovensaal, when he sang in Germany for the first time.

Anderson had come to Europe to study and had found teachers steeped in the central European tradition of the art song, but she, like Hayes before her, would be forced to earn her right to interpret that repertory.[22] As the plans for her first concert began early in April, she was nervous and circumspect about the outcome. She wrote to her sister Alyse, excited yet still anxious enough to want to keep the concert a secret for the time being: "I must ask you not to say anything about the recital just yet, because there may be something interesting to write you in connection with the affair. The only thing that has been done is the hall taken. Nobody in this house knows a thing about it. So you see how I'm keeping it."[23] She did not, in fact, look much beyond the concert, planning to return home should Boghetti inform her of any possibility of appearances during the summer.

Boghetti and Alyse were on her mind a good deal during those months. Boghetti was still disgruntled about Marian's decision to study abroad, hurt that she would prefer to study with another teacher. She was uneasy, therefore, asking for his help when Alyse wrote to her about being asked to sing in the operetta, *A Night in the Harem,* and wanting to study the part with a teacher. Alyse had always found it difficult to settle for long on a course of study or a job. Encouraged that she now showed such enthusiasm for her singing, Marian wrote to Alyse:

> You can't know how happy I am that you see the need of study. You must try to realize the marvelous opportunities you have had to do things that other girls would give anything and work night and day to prepare for it. Go to Mrs. Patterson to have your voice trained— while you work on the Opera or else go to Mr. Boghetti to have him teach it to you. Whether or not he has taught it before I don't know. Find out his lowest price and let me know, or would you rather I would find out? I shall help you all I can.[24]

As for her own concert, Anderson had the help of both Raphael and Quilter. As the day approached, Quilter invited her to stay at his home in Montague Street. Raphael lived nearby and the three could work together more easily, especially on the songs that Anderson was just then learning. One group consisted of Schubert's "Wiegenlied" and "Nähe des Geliebten," which Zur Mühlen had given her during her first lesson with him. Another group included two songs by Schumann, whose music Anderson had not yet sung: the first and last songs of the Eichendorff *Liederkreis,* op. 39—"In der Fremde" and "Frühlingsnacht." Quilter also worked with her on a group of six of his own songs (only one, "Love's Philosophy, " with a text by Shelley, had she sung before), planning to accompany her in them himself. The rest of the program was devoted to music that she had sung before: arias from Purcell's *Dido and Aeneas* and Debussy's *L'Enfant prodigue,* and a group of spirituals, including "Deep River," "Ev'ry time I Feel the Spirit," "I Stood on the Ribber ob Jordon," and "Weepin Mary." To mark the occasion, Quilter provided her with a new arrangement of Burleigh's "Heav'n, Heav'n," which he titled "I Got a Robe."

The critics took only casual notice of the concert, a few lines in the *Observer,* a routine paragraph in the *Times* and the *Daily Telegraph,* the final judgments rather cool. One critic mentioned Anderson's very warm and rich tone,[25] another, "a certain naive appeal in her readings that compensated for occasional lack of subtlety."[26] They were also proving to be far from comfortable with how different Anderson's voice was from the traditional European lieder singers of their experience. One critic pointed out that "her voice has the peculiar timbre common to colored vocalists,"[27] while the writer for the *Times* was more severe: "The 'scoop' is evidently a racial fault, for it fell into place as the natural thing in some Negro spirituals."[28]

Although the criticisms could not have pleased Marian, she was not disappointed, considering the concert all of a piece with her studies and knowing better than others what she could expect. Indeed, excited and gratifed by what she had so far achieved, she sent cables to her family and to Boghetti, portraying the whole experience as a grand success. Nor was she unaware of her own contribution to the achievements of "our folks" that summer. In this sense, too, she took a broad view of her accomplishment, seeing it in context. Paul Robeson, who with his wife attended Marian's concert—Essie pronounced her voice "glorious"—had opened in *Show Boat* in May and, together with Lawrence Brown, was about to give the first of two concerts devoted entirely to Negro spirituals at the Drury Lane Theatre.[29] The cantata *Hiawatha,* by Coleridge-Taylor, another of "our folks," was attracting huge crowds at the Royal Albert Hall, where it had opened on June 11 for two weeks.

Thanks to Quilter, another appearance was arranged at the Proms for August 16. That summer the Proms were extended from six to eight weeks, with concerts every night but Sundays, a "sweet boon," in Artemus Ward's phrase, for the great working-class population of London. The programs were more popular and eclectic than the weekly symphony orchestra concerts. At least one soloist was engaged for each concert. There was less elitism to the audiences at the Promenade concerts than elsewhere, and they were always eager to welcome the young, often relatively unknown, soloists that appeared.

At her Proms debut Anderson was joined by a young tenor, Francis Russell, who sang Lohengrin's "Farewell to the Swan," and the pianist, Victor Hely-Hutchinson, who gave the first English performance of Alexandre Tansman's First Piano Concerto. The program included De Falla's *The Three-Cornered Hat* dances, several overtures, and Mendelssohn's "Italian" Symphony. Anderson sang "O don fatale," Eboli's aria from Verdi's *Don Carlo,* as well as the four spirituals from her Wigmore Hall recital. Her long familiarity with her part of the program, and the typical Proms excitement and enthusiasm all had their effect. This time the reviews took particular notice of her performance, praising her without reservation.[30] The next morning the *Daily Mail* sent photographers to Regent's Park Road, where she posed in the beautiful garden at the back of the house. In the next few days she received inquiries from the HMV, Columbia, and Metropolis record companies, as well as an invitation to give a BBC recital. On the Tuesday following the concert, she wrote to her mother:

Darling little mother,
There is no doubt that you are rooting for me all the time and you've no idea how it helps. When Sir Henry Wood led me by the hand on the stage, and a fine ovation was received, I felt extremely happy and at ease. We got on so well together.
Attention—all eyes, were those who stood with up turned faces,—masses, hundreds.
These—were they who yelled more More, while those in the balcony and circle yelled Bravo and stomped the floor after spirituals. There were lots of bows and two encores. Roger was extremely pleased and at the banquet which followed he was fine.[31]

Anderson had been away from home nearly a year. She did receive offers to perform and not a few entreaties to remain through the following spring, but with little savings left, she could hardly remain indifferent to what Judson might be planning for her. She booked passage on the *Aquitania* for the end of September. In the meantime she was given her second opportunity to make recordings, this time for the Gramophone Company. In the next several weeks she recorded her first operatic arias, "Amour! Viens aider ma faiblesse," from *Samson et Dalila,* and Eboli's aria from *Don Carlo,* as well as some Negro spirituals.[32] The time before her departure on the twenty-second was filled with more plans and activity. Her hope of visiting Paris for several days before leaving England had to be given up in order to appear on the BBC for a farewell program. On the eve of her departure, John Payne hosted a farewell party for her. The guests began arriving early and by midday the house was already crowded. The main feature was a musicale in which Anderson herself sang, Beatrice Lillie performed comical readings and sayings from her repertoire, and the American Duncan Sisters and the Southern Trio sang some of their numbers. Friends and well-wishers included the dancer Anton Dolin, Mabel Mercer, Alberta Hunter, and King Wools, the director of the BBC.[33]

The *Aquitania,* with its 1,400 passengers, arrived in New York Harbor several hours behind schedule, at 1:30 in the afternoon on the twenty-eighth of September. There was a large crowd waiting to welcome Marian, including her mother and sisters, Harry T. Burleigh, and Billy King.

The official Philadelphia welcome took place a week or so later at the home of Mr. and Mrs. Weaver. Among palms, cut roses and subdued rose-colored lights, Marian, with her two sisters and many friends, stood in the receiving line to greet the more than 200 guests who filed past. Heading the line was the hostess, Mrs. Weaver, "in a robe of sequin and crystals, over green crepe and silver cloth." Marian wore an evening wrap of black satin, gold cloth and Chinese hand painting, lined with the satin black crepe that she had bought in London, an extravagance encouraged by her warm reception at the Promenade concerts and the thought of returning home.[34]

CHAPTER FIVE

The Judson Years
(1929–1930)

A brilliantly calculating empire builder, Arthur Judson was the most powerful concert manager in America for more than four decades. As a manager of orchestras—he managed both the New York Philharmonic and the Philadelphia Orchestra for many years—as well as concert artists, Judson was able to control a significant segment of American concert life. In 1928, Judson bought the Wolfson Musical Bureau, proposing at the same time a merger with four other concert bureaus. Two years later, accepting Judson's terms, six of the largest New York concert agencies were brought together as the Columbia Concerts Corporation. As chairman of the board of the new corporation, Judson directly managed orchestral organizations and more established and well-known concert artists. Less experienced artists were assigned to the recital bureau headed by George Leyden Colledge, one of the divisions within Columbia Concerts Management. In 1930, for example, Judson's roster of artists—he managed more than fifty himself during most years—included the sopranos Claire Dux, Florence Easton, Maria Kurenko, the mezzo-soprano Madeleine Grey, the contraltos Sophie Breslau and Kathryn Meisle, and, among male singers, Dino Borgioli, Giovanni Martinelli, Richard Bonelli, Nelson Eddy, and Ezio Pinza. Judson's instrumentalists included the pianists Vladimir Horowitz, Robert Casadesus, Edwin Fischer, Ossip Gabrilowitsch, and José Iturbi, and the string players Adolph Busch, Jascha Heifetz, Nathan Milstein, Albert Spalding, Joseph Szigeti, Jacques Thibaud, and Gregor Piatigorsky. Colledge's list of artists was smaller, though rarely comprising fewer than twenty or thirty artists.[1]

Judson offered Anderson a contract for one year, for 1929, and assigned her to Colledge's bureau. She had hopes that the prestige and influence of the Judson organization would eventually mean more work, higher fees, and less dependence on black auspices. It did not take long, however, for her to see that her connection with Judson would be neither entirely comfortable nor unequivocally beneficial. Judson had spoken casually at their first meeting about fees of $750 a concert. When the terms of the contract were finally drawn up, Anderson was offered $500, commensurate with the lower status of the artists under Colledge's management. Out of the $500 she had to pay the 20 percent commission due the Judson agency, and, as she had always done, her expenses for publicity, traveling, and accompanist. Her fee was an advance over the $350 Anderson had usually earned for her concerts before the Judson years, but she was still dissatisfied. As it turned out, she also faced the reluctance of many local managers to accept so substantial an increase. In many cases it was a struggle to negotiate an acceptable fee, the negotiations growing even more difficult with the economic hardships of the Depression years.[2]

Anderson also hoped for a greater number of concerts than she and Billy had been able to give on their own, but here, too, she was disappointed. In any single year under Judson she would be only one of at least six contraltos for whom recital dates had to be arranged, and Anderson could not depend, as did Sophie Breslau or Katherine Meisle, for example, on a regular European season or operatic engagements to supplement recital appearances. It was to Judson's credit that he was willing, for the first time, to engage a black singer, but he was nervous about the difficulties involved. He had little experience with black universities and churches and the local musical organizations and concert series that traditionally accounted for the largest number of Anderson's concerts. In order to organize the first season of appearances, Colledge and his staff depended on the nearly 200 references Anderson and Billy had collected.

Although Judson had agreed to manage a black artist, he was hardly ever willing to take a bold path that would transcend the issue of color. On occasion, Judson apparently even discouraged opportunities that presented themselves to Anderson.[3] In many ways, Judson's agency was less effective than Anderson and Billy had been in finding new audiences. For them, each addition to the growing collection of references had been the result of some act of personal involvement—friendships were established, old friends were recalled, a new note of pride was struck within the self-nurturing world of the black community. For Judson, all this was replaced with business and the detachment that invariably accompanies bureaucratic efficiency.

On Friday evening, October 12, at the Philadelphia Academy of Music, Anderson sang for the first time since her return from Europe. The concert, sponsored by the Phi Beta Sigma fraternity, was her first concert under Judson's management. Her welcome on this occasion was not unlike the welcome she had received at the Weavers' a week earlier. There she had been joined by her family and many friends. At the Academy of Music, she was received by an audience filling every seat in the hall, including the several hundred stage seats. And in a parquet box could be seen the diminutive figure of Mrs. Anderson, dressed in black and wearing a single string of pearls. Anderson herself wore a gown of gold tulle and lace, with a corsage at the shoulder.

To judge from her program that evening, Anderson's devotion to German lieder had not abated. Her recital contained the familiar groups of songs by early Italian masters, English and American composers (on this occasion, Griffes, Quilter, and La Forge), and Negro spirituals, all of which she had sung many times before. But the challenge in her program were the four songs of Schubert and Schumann which she was singing for the first time in America: Schubert's "Wiegenlied," "Die junge Nonne," and "Die Allmacht," and Schumann's "Frühlingsnacht." She had studied them with Mark Raphael, although her Wigmore Hall recital had not included "Die junge Nonne" or "Die Allmacht." For the critics as well as the audience, Anderson's concert was a long-anticipated homecoming. The black community especially felt a renewed sense of pride in her accomplishments, which Eva Lynn expressed eloquently in the *Philadelphia Tribune*:

> To think of one of our own, a young colored woman bringing two thousand people, nearly all of our group, together to hear her sing a repertoire of songs in French and German and English. Each person in that audience must have had a sense of pride to hear that small figure pour forth such golden notes. It will take such artists as Marian Anderson, Florence Cole Talbert, and Roland Hayes to help tear down racial prejudices thru their message in song.[4]

The one note of criticism was reserved for Anderson's interpretation of the German songs. No doubt she was nervous about them. She had had only two weeks to rehearse with Billy after her return from Europe, and he had had even less time to learn the songs. "A lack of ardor of spirit" was noted in Anderson's interpretation of Schubert's "Die junge Nonne," and a lack of "something of real majesty," in his "Die Allmacht."[5]

Anderson struggled tenaciously with German lieder during the first months under Judson's management in spite of continued criticism. Her year abroad had been important to her artistic and emotional growth, but she had been unable to become immersed in the study of German lieder in the way she had wanted. Mark Raphael, Amanda Aldrich, and Louis Drysdale had all encouraged her efforts and taught her what they could, but they were not Zur Mühlen. Nor had her German improved much during her year in London. Once back in America, she and Billy were again very much on their own. The thought of returning to Europe to study—this time, to Germany—was never very far from her mind.

Anderson had chosen wisely, in her Academy of Music concert, when she included Schubert's "Wiegenlied" and Schumann's "Frühlingsnacht" in the German group. She had worked on these songs with Raphael and Quilter. Both are psychologically direct in their sentiment, without complicated emotional detours. "Wiegenlied" is a quiet, gentle lullaby; "Frühlingsnacht," a rapturous outpouring at the thought of spring and of love. By contrast, Schubert's "Die Allmacht" and "Die junge Nonne" are far more complex. These two songs had no doubt been suggested by Aldrich, a contralto herself, who had urged Anderson to work on songs requiring reserves of power and greater intensity. "Die junge Nonne" a poignant and introspective song, portrays the emotional journey of a young nun. For a moment thrown into turmoil by a raging storm, she is overcome by the doubts of her earlier years, but as the music shifts from minor to major, her religious serenity returns. "Die Allmacht," a song of praise to the Almighty, requires a voice capable of both power and majestic radiance. With these two songs, Anderson's ambition went far beyond her abilities.

For her concert at the Municipal Auditorium in Savannah, before Thanksgiving, Anderson eliminated "Die junge Nonne," replacing it with a song of Brahms, "Das Mädchen spricht." The year ended with a concert at Carnegie Hall, on December 30, the most formidable challenge of the season. Except for a concert in the spring of 1926 at the Salem M. E. Church in Harlem, on behalf of the Empire State Federation of Colored Women's Clubs, Anderson had not sung in New York since her triumph at Lewisohn Stadium. Persistent as ever, she met the considerable expectations of the evening not with the simpler and more direct song of Brahms, but with yet another of Schubert's most complex and dramatic lieder, "Der Zwerg," another song Raphael had introduced her to. "Der Zwerg" is an eerie ballad in which a narrator, the queen, and her dwarf are all given individual roles. The appeal of the song for Anderson was the dramatic narrative and the challenge of presenting all three voices, with the queen and the dwarf etched in two extremes of register. The same challenge of creating multiple roles as part of a compelling narrative later drew Anderson to Schubert's "Der Erlkönig," a song which was to become a hallmark of her repertoire.

The audience at Carnegie Hall was large and receptive. The strongest impression was created by the songs with English texts, especially the Negro spirituals, where Anderson's clear and vivid enunciation and powerful interpretations were noted by the critics. As for the German group, here Anderson was judged out of her depth.[6]

The remaining six concerts that season came to an end by Easter, having taken her from Massachusetts one week to Indiana and West Virginia the next. With few engagements to look forward to in the summer of 1929, she began to think about how to advance her musical education. In high school, Anderson had studied piano with Carl Diton, who helped prepare her to play her own accompaniments when the need arose. During the mid-1920s, when Diton's career centered more on composition, he had suggested that Anderson study piano with his cousin, the composer Harvey Hebron, which she had continued to do as time allowed. Because her lack of any formal study of music history or theory weighed heavily on Marian, she used her studies with Hebron to try to acquire as much as she could of a more academic musical education, working out exercises in four-part harmony and reading dictionary articles on music history. Her work with Hebron was intermittent and unsystematic, but it increased her courage to seek out voice students again in a few years, to help supplement her earnings when concert dates from Judson all but disappeared.[7]

Anderson also resumed her lessons with Boghetti. His irritation at her temporary desertion did not last, although he was aware of her determination to study in Germany. That summer, she went into action. In June 1929, she wrote to Elena Gerhardt, who had so impressed her in London with her performance of *Die Winterreise*. Marian sent her press clippings, asking if she might work with her, thinking that if Gerhardt agreed, then she would somehow find a way to go abroad again. Gerhardt answered promptly, inviting her to Tupper Lake in upstate New York, during the month of August, near the estate of some American friends on the Upper Saranac, with whom she had been spending part of each summer since the end of the First World War. Whatever the reason—no doubt Anderson felt she needed those weeks to work with Billy on the coming season's concerts—she did not accept Gerhardt's invitation. Thinking also about when she might work with Anderson later in the year, Gerhardt suggested that she try to come to Leipzig at the beginning of September, when Gerhardt would begin her teaching duties at the Leipzig Conservatory.[8] Although excited by the offer, Marian was not prepared to give up what she was earning with Judson for a prolonged period of study abroad, where there was no promise of concerts at all. Another possibility for study in Germany came that summer. In New York, Marian and Billy had recently met a German manager, Eric Simon. Impressed with Anderson, Simon told her he was prepared to help book concerts for her in Berlin and on the continent. The possibility of singing in one of the great European musical centers began to seem more enticing than the invitation to study with Gerhardt. There were, after all, teachers in Berlin too, she felt, and once in Germany she would manage to find one.[9]

In early June, in the midst of trying to weigh Gerhardt's and Simon's proposals, Anderson was invited to appear as soloist with the American Philharmonic Orchestra, in the opening concerts of the annual summer music festival held at the University of Washington, in Seattle. The knowledge that she was being invited virtually at the last minute to fill in for an indisposed singer did not interfere with her readiness to accept the invitation—her first opportunity to sing with an orchestra since her appearance with the Philharmonic Society six years earlier.

Anderson arrived in Seattle by train on Friday morning, June 7, in time for rehearsals with the orchestra, with whom she was scheduled to appear on Sunday evening and the following Wednesday. The annual festival, held each summer in the University of Washington Stadium, was a highlight of the tourist season; city officials put their weight behind the concerts to make them a success. The Street Railway Department had agreed to allow all of Seattle to ride the streetcars free to the University of Washington Stadium on Sunday evening, from 7:15 until the start of the concert. For the intermission a huge display of fireworks was planned.[10]

The opening concert was a great success, in spite of the weather. The audience no sooner stood for the national anthem than a fine mist began to fall. The rain increased steadily during Elgar's "Pomp and Circumstance" and the *Tannhäuser Overture,* and the concert was moved to the nearby pavilion. The rest of the program included orchestral works by Liszt and Saint-Saëns, and a group of popular songs of 1928 arranged by the conductor of the concerts, Francesco Longo. Anderson sang "O don fatale" and "Amour! Viens aider." At the end of the concert, she received a long and enthusiastic ovation; with Myron Jacobsen, a young Seattle pianist and composer acting as her accompanist, she was called back again and again for encores.[11] At the second concert, on Wednesday,

Anderson sang Lia's aria from Debussy's *L'Enfant prodigue* and "O mio Fernando," once again receiving a long ovation. Less than two months later she was invited back to Seattle for more appearances with the orchestra.[12]

The extraordinary success Anderson enjoyed in Seattle resulted not only from the arias she sang with the orchestra, but from her encores, which she sang only with piano accompaniment. The audience could thus experience both the grand dimensions of "O mio Fernando" or "O don fatale" and, in the more intimate setting with piano, the simplicity of "Danny Boy," the exuberant coloratura of Chaminade's "Été," and the dramatic urgency of the spiritual "Gospel Train." For her return engagement in August, beside Thomas's "O My Heart Is Weary" ("Me voilà seule, hélas!") from *Mignon,* and Tchaikovsky's "Adieu, forêts," Anderson again sang a group of encores with piano that included Cyril Scott's "Blackbird's Song," the spiritual "Sometimes I Feel Like a Motherless Child," and, to show her gratitude to her accompanist, Myron Jacobsen, "Last Love," one of his own compositions.

Anderson's first season with Judson had been a disappointment. On their own, during the year before Anderson studied in London, she and Billy had managed to give over thirty concerts; the tour of southern states alone had included twenty in nine states and was followed by a tour of the Midwest including Cleveland, Cincinnati, Dayton, Akron, Columbus, Minneapolis, and Chicago. Judson, in his first season representing Anderson, had offered sixteen concerts, all of them, save one in Boston at the end of March, return engagements. The new season, to begin in the fall of 1929, was no improvement. Although Colledge managed to add five concerts to the sixteen of the previous year, some of his scheduling was absurdly impractical and costly. Anderson rightfully complained that a lone date in Prairie View, Texas, between one a week earlier at home and one a week after, in Greensboro, North Carolina, with all of the attendant expenses for travel and publicity, was both unreasonable and unprofitable.[13]

The season, which began on October 11, opened once again with a concert at the Philadelphia Academy of Music sponsored by the Phi Beta Sigma fraternity. Anderson instituted her custom of including songs by lesser-known contemporary composers; for the concert at the Academy she chose Erich Wolff's "Faden," "Last Love," by Myron Jacobsen, and "At the Spinning Wheel," by Saar. The audience at the Academy included many of Anderson's friends, as it had the previous year, and she was able to greet them after the concert at a reception and banquet held in her honor.[14]

For her concert in Chicago, in mid-November, Colledge had risked booking Orchestra Hall, the spacious and prestigious home of the Chicago Symphony Orchestra. Marian drew a large and enthusiastic audience. Herman Devries, reviewing the Orchestra Hall concert for the *Chicago Evening American,* reacted to her singing with a mixture of lavish praise and the prediction of greater achievement to come:

> Anderson , colored contralto in recital at Orchestra Hall last night, began her well-arranged program with [Donaudy's] "O del mio amato ben," and had she sung nothing but that our story today would be a sheer hymn of unreserved praise. Here she reached near perfection in every requirement of vocal art, —the tone was of superb timbre, the phrasing of utmost refinement, the style pure, discreet, musicianly. But after this there was a letdown, and we took away the impression of a talent still unripe, but certainly a talent of potential growth. There was also proof of fine schooling in the exhibition of coloratura in Mozart's "Alleluia," usually sung by a soprano, and of course transposed for Miss Anderson's range. The Brahms "Schmied" lacked the rich flavor of its mellow, vigorous character. This is perhaps Miss Anderson's greatest lack—temperamental abandon and swing.[15]

The large audience was wildly enthusiastic. So were Ray Field and George Arthur, both representatives of the Rosenwald Fund, an organization established by Julius Rosenwald, the Chicago financier and philanthropist, to grant fellowships for study abroad to a selected number of blacks who showed promise of leadership or accomplishment in the arts. George Arthur, the Associate for Negro Welfare on the Fund committee, and Ray Field asked to see Anderson at the end of the concert. They showed interest in her plans to study in Germany and encouraged her to apply for a Rosenwald fellowship. A week later, she submitted her application. In the questions it asked, the application form placed what she considered an unrealistic emphasis on a candidate's prior success. Anderson did her best with the required questions and essay, putting the strongest face on her year in London.[16] She also adjusted her high school record (eliminating the years at William Penn) as well as her age, giving 1903 (not 1897) as the year of her birth. Anderson was only too happy to bury the humiliating years when she had been unable to attend high school. For some time now she had adjusted her age to eliminate those years.[17]

During the months of December and January, Anderson struggled to meet her professional obligations while waiting anxiously for the Fund's decision. After the New Year, she could not refrain from reminding the committee that she had submitted an application and hoped for a reply. On January 9, the Fund informed her that she would not have a response before the middle of February. The weeks of February were taken up with the usual tour of southern states. In West Virginia when the Fund's decision arrived, she did not learn until the end of February that she had been granted an award of fifteen hundred dollars for one year of study in Berlin.

Preoccupied with preparing for her Carnegie Hall recital, scheduled for March 2, Marian put off responding to the Fund's offer. More careful about her program than she had been the previous year, Anderson decided to include only one new German song, Schubert's "Die Krähe," of which she had become confident during the season. To this she added Schubert's "Wohin," as well as Brahms's "Von ewiger Liebe" and Strauss's "Zueignung," songs she knew well. Feeling obliged to offer her Carnegie Hall audience more in the way of novelty, perhaps for the moment feeling more at home in French than German, she tried out Fauré's "Les berceaux" and the card scene from Bizet's *Carmen*, "Voyons que j'essaie à mon tour," with its foreboding prediction of imminent death, and its call upon the darker timbre of Anderson's lower register.

The audience that Sunday afternoon was "regretfully small," as Herbert Peyser noted in the *New York Telegram*. Peyser's review of Anderson's performance was mixed:

Miss Anderson has one of the rarest voices of the time—a noble contralto, spontaneous in utterance, amazingly rich in timbre and, except for some hard and faultily produced high notes, smooth as satin in texture. There is a welcome absence of coarse or exaggerated chest tones, of "registers" of perceptible transitions in its ample and remarkably even scale. It lends itself most beautifully to sustained, long-breathed cantilena. Indeed, a ravishingly supple and jointless legato, flowing like oil, is probably the chief glory of Miss Anderson's singing.

When his review shifted from voice to interpretation, he was less kind:

If the young woman's voice is in itself of an emotional timbre, at moments almost capable of coaxing tears to the listener's eyes, one is repeatedly conscious, nevertheless, of a want of ingrained emotional temperament behind her singing.

The German songs elicited the harshest judgment, for they still appeared "to lie considerably beyond Miss Anderson's imaginative and emotional scope."[18]

If these judgments, echoed by the other critics, disappointed her, there was no sign of it in her reply to the Rosenwald Fund. She sent her reply a few days after her Carnegie Hall concert, her thoughts turned toward the future with characteristic modesty and idealism:

My dear Mr. Arthur,

Your letter of February 21st has been received, and I am lost for words to express my delight over the outcome of the Rosenwald Contribution to my studies.

This work or vocation that I have chosen or rather, was chosen for me, seems to be filled with ups and downs. At first things went very well and I was able to save a few dollars, but, now as more publicity piles up, more songs to learn—and living expenses to consider,—this business of singing looms up with magnitude.

What I did save, was used for eleven months study in England before returning to America. I found that I had only scratched the surface. Now I wish to return and get more.

It is my true ambition to become a great artist and a credit to my race in every way possible. I do not feel that the voice is my personal property, it belongs to everybody. I do feel that I should make every effort to present it to the public in the best form possible. It is also my sincere wish to, in the future, help some talented Negro boy or girl who has ambitions to become a great singer. It is my earnest prayer that some day my financial position will permit me to do this.

Please extend my sincere thanks to all who helped to secure this contribution for me.

Just now I am not sure as to my sailing date but trust to have definite plans completed and passage booked at my next writing. New York recital over, much of interest to tell you.[19]

By mid-May, Anderson had formed a clear idea of what she wanted to accomplish in Berlin. Concerned about finances—this time she had only $500 of savings to take with her—and mindful of her contract with Judson, she arrived at a plan to study in Berlin for six months, using half of the $1,500 of her Rosenwald fellowship. She was prepared to use her $500 of savings for transportation, and the award money on her studies. She could then return to the States by Christmas, in time to fulfill her obligations to Judson. The second half of the $1,500 from the fellowship would be used the following year in the same way. Whatever funds were required for concerts would somehow come out of her own pocket. Confident that the Rosenwald committee would agree to her proposal, she booked passage on the Bremen, scheduled to leave at midnight on June 11.

Anderson wrote to the Rosenwald committee toward the end of May, outlining her plans. The committee was dissatisfied with her proposal, both because she was asking to split the award and because she wanted to take time away from her studies in order to give concerts. A flurry of telegrams ensued. Only a few days before Anderson was to leave for Germany, the committee finally agreed to her proposition, and Anderson received the first payment.[20] On the twelfth of June, she set sail for Europe from New York, her spirits buoyed by the support of the Rosenwald committee, a growing sense of purpose, and a deep belief in herself.

CHAPTER SIX

𝒱

Berlin and Scandinavia
(1930–1931)

Anderson arrived in Berlin in mid-June, 1930, not knowing who her teacher would be or whether any concert offers would materialize. Max Walter, a partner in a small Berlin concert bureau, having been informed by Colledge of Anderson's impending arrival, had found her accommodations in the home of Matthias and Gertrud Von Erdberg, a middle-aged couple with a large and comfortable apartment at No. 34 Geisberg Strasse, in the eastern part of Charlottenburg, an elegant suburb to the west of the city's center. A Russian by birth, fiercely aristocratic looking with a Van Dyke beard and large piercing eyes, Matthias Von Erdberg had been prominent as an actor and reciter. Although he was now retired, Matthias accepted occasional pupils while Gerturd took charge of their rooms and meals. For the time being the only guest, Anderson was given a large room on the second floor that looked out onto the street.[1]

The Von Erdbergs were only too happy to help Anderson with German, a necessity in any case, since they spoke very little English. Gertrud, whose daughter Sosie was no longer living at home, was glad to have a young woman in the house again to talk to. Anderson thought she had made considerable progress in German when she was eventually able to console Gertrud on those occasions when Matthias, having angrily yelled at his wife about one thing or another, "stormed out of the house, his shoulders indignantly thrown back, every inch the Recitator."[2] Matthias, who made a career of the art of declamation, relished the opportunity to help Anderson with German. He was able to do much more than correct mistakes or provide appropriate words or expressions. As she later recalled: "Herr von Erdberg took the trouble to coach me in

German. I bought a primer, and we poured over it together. He read to me, and I read to him. He would not let me look at the side of the page that contained English translations, forcing me to plow my way through the German. It was an effective method; when I turned to the German songs I found myself more comfortable with them, and I began to detect nuances of expression in the German that quickened my grasp of the music."[3]

News from home arrived regularly.[4] Orpheus was visiting Martin Street more often now that Marian was abroad, talking with friends and neighbors in the hope of receiving news of her.[5] Ethel had begun a secretarial course in night school and was away several evenings during the week working toward a diploma. Although Alyse still received invitations to sing, politics was becoming her enduring passion, especially with the approach of the fall elections. She had become drawn to politics while in high school and her interest had been encouraged by Ed Henry, a lawyer who was later to become the first black judge in Philadelphia. Henry offered not only encouragement but the promise of a job to anyone willing to join his entourage, although so far he had not been able to find a job for Alyse. The news from Billy was troubling. Billy felt isolated from Anderson now, threatened by her chance to study in Germany. He feared that her eventual progress would make it difficult for him to accompany her when she returned to the States. He had made up his mind, in fact, to come to Berlin in order to study along with her. Anderson had expressed concern about Billy's decision to her mother, enough so that Mrs. Anderson felt obliged to offer counsel. "Now love," she wrote to Marian, "just do the best you can with B. there and don't let him inconvenience you."[6]

July and August were taken up with studying German and a month-long visit to London, where Anderson made two appearances at the Proms, on August 19 and September 16. Not used to her frequent habit of not writing, the Von Erdbergs grew concerned and tried writing her in English. Gertrud took on the task of actually composing the letter: "Deare Miss Anderson, Why have we yet not letter? Please writing you soon once. I should like writing but it comes to me fearfulness hard. We are hard sorry not of you to heard. Many kind regards and hearty greetings."[7]

Anderson returned to Germany during the third week of September, in time for Billy's arrival. At the beginning of October they left Berlin for Prague, where Walter had arranged two concerts for them. They left early on the morning of the second, journeyed for seven hours, enthralled by the magnificent scenery, much of it along the Elbe, arriving in Prague in time for a rehearsal and radio broadcast that evening. There was one day of rest before the second concert, on the fourth, which Marian devoted to learning a little folk song in Czech, complaining of how difficult the language was, but determined to sing at least one song in the language of her audience.[8]

Only after the trip to Prague was Anderson finally able to begin vocal studies. Having given up the idea of studying with Elena Gerhardt, she had put her trust in Max Walter, who suggested she study with Kurt Johnen, one of the most active and experienced teachers in the city. It was an unusual and at the same time imaginative suggestion.[9]

Johnen, a native of Aachen, had come to Berlin when he was twenty to study musicology at the university. He remained there the rest of his life, playing an important role in the musical life of the city. Before the First World War, he studied composition as well as musicology at the Hochschule für Musik, as well as piano with Robert Kahn and Egon Petri, the latter a pupil of Busoni. After the war, he made his living accompanying and teaching. In the decade before Anderson's arrival in Berlin, he had begun a second career in the psychology of music, studying first at the psychotechnical laboratory of the Technische Hochschule in Charlottenburg, then with Carl Stumpf, the leading psychoacoustician in Germany and the founder of the Psychological Institute at the University of Berlin, where Johnen was given a position as independent researcher.

Johnen's work in the field of psychology was concerned with the relationship of musical rhythm and phrasing to the performer's breathing and pulse. He wanted his students to learn to avoid tension and any concentration of energy that didn't conform to the precise pulse and rhythm of the music. Johnen was no inflexible scientist but a brilliantly well-rounded musician whose pedagogical method was joined to a thorough knowledge not only of the art song, but the entire literature of Western music.

Anderson took her musical studies with Johnen seriously, but she never lost sight of the advantages to be gained from European concerts and good notices. Indeed, she was counting on the offers she had received, even before leaving the States, from more than one European manager. Walter had asked for a monthly contribution of 250 marks to cover concert expenses, assuring Anderson she would gain it all back from actual appearances.[10] There had also been a proposal from the French manager Arnold Meckel, for concerts in Europe outside of Germany. Meckel wanted Anderson to make her operatic debut at the Paris Opera, and he suggested the role of Amneris in Verdi's *Aida*.[11] Walter and

Meckel were well-intentioned, but their proposals were extravagant enticements rather than bona fide offers. Both men calculated their inducements to impress a young singer of great promise who they genuinely believed to be a good prospect. As it turned out, none of the offers materialized.

In the end, it was Anderson's own impatience that led to her debut in the German capital. She was eager to present a full-length concert in Berlin and had mentioned the idea to Walter. He was not opposed but had refused to provide sufficient backing for it. "Accordingly," she later said, "I did what I had never done before and have not done since—I put up the money myself. I handed five hundred dollars' worth of American Express checks to the manager, parting with them with the greatest reluctance. . . ."[12] The concert was scheduled for later in October, and Michael Raucheisen, the foremost accompanist in Europe, whom both Walter and Johnen had recommended, agreed to accompany Anderson. Raucheisen had studied with the conductor Felix Mottl in Munich and had played viola and violin in the court orchestra before the First World War. After 1911, he had become increasingly active as a pianist and accompanist, settling in Berlin in 1920. He did not limit his work as an accompanist to singers, who invariably held the greatest respect for his musical abilities and knowledge, but acted also as accompanist to some of the most important instrumentalists of the time.

Raucheisen shared a small apartment with his mother, where he and Anderson began working together, the two often joined by Johnen. The work was not always smooth going. Like two benevolent Svengalis intoxicated by her ability and willingness to absorb everything they had to teach, Johnen and Raucheisen would often argue, in the excitement of preparation, about differences of interpretation.[13] Because he enjoyed exploring the less frequently trod byways of German lieder, Raucheisen had chosen, for the first half of the program, some songs of Beethoven, the last two Wesendonck lieder of Wagner, and songs by Grieg and Liszt for Anderson to learn. To judge from Raucheisen's choices, he thought Anderson capable of songs with greater dramatic weight and rhetorical intensity than the Schubert and Schumann songs she was used to singing. One of Raucheisen's choices, for example, Grieg's "Vom Monte Pincio" ("Fra Monte Pincio"), is a shifting panorama of images of Rome's famous Monte Pinchio, from the dazzling splendor of evening to the sounds and colors of Rome's ancient past. Still a more challenging choice was Liszt's dramatic ballad, "Die drei Zigeuner," a character study of three Gypsies—a fiddler, a smoker, and a sleeper—in which the singer, in recitative style, has to impersonate each of the characters.

In the final days of preparation, everyone was so tense that Anderson decided she could ill afford to be nervous herself, her calm alarming everyone else. The last rehearsal, as she remembered it later, was "shamefully poor." Billy was present, as he was at many of Anderson's lessons. His reaction to the rehearsal was typical of him: "Well," he told her, "if we had worked more together I think the program would go better."[14] The concert, Anderson's Berlin debut, took place on October 10, 1930, in the Bachsaal. Berlin's concert season was already in full swing—that same evening there were concerts by Emil von Sauer, who was celebrating the fiftieth anniversary of his debut as a pianist at the Philharmonie, and by Winfried Wolf and Emil Frey. But Anderson had a large audience nonetheless. Raucheisen's presence and the featuring of a young black contralto, a rarity in German concert life, attracted the merely curious as well as the genuine music lover. Among the important musical celebrities in the audience were Artur Schnabel; his wife, Therese Behr-Schnabel; their son Karl Ulrich; and the contralto Madame Charles Cahier, with whom Anderson would enjoy a long and warm friendship.[15]

The first review to appear, a few days later, was the *Vossische Zeitungs*:

Marian Anderson, Negro contralto, tall, slim, elegant in appearance, obviously used to appearing on the stage, enjoyed a tremendous success yesterday in the Bachsaal. Her complexion is not altogether black, but she has a dark, blue-black dark voice, which she handles with artistic accomplishment and taste. She sang lieder and songs in German, then the aria of Eboli from 'Don Carlos', which our contraltos have become so attached to, in Italian, then a series of Negro spirituals in English. Marian Anderson is very musical, and she gives, without any posing, strong and genuine expression and is a mistress of the styles of performance. In sound her voice sounds somewhat unusual to our ears, exotic: but we readily take a fancy to its appeal. The ballad "The three Gypsies" by Franz Liszt is one of her showpieces: she can sing it twice without tiring the attention of her enthusiastic listeners.. . She is successful with gradations and nuances [of tone], acquired from brilliant perceptions which enthrall [the listener] spontaneously. Interesting women concert singers are few and far between. Here we have one who will continue to engage our attention.[16]

Only on the 14th, in Prague for a concert, did Anderson find time to write to her mother about her debut:

From the very beginning the applause was—good. The German songs, ten in number, proved quite a success [and] one of them I had to repeat. The accompanist was so tickled, he almost had a—I don't know what. And the manager rushed back and said, "I did not know I had such an artist. You are marvelous."

The great climax came at the end of the program when the audience refused to leave until they heard more music. Feet were stomped, men said "more more" and applause went on and on. We bowed several times together but it was no good and yet—after two more songs the people crowded around the stage in an effort to get more—and they only left when the lights were put out and the entire hall in almost absolute darkness. It was truly a marvelous demonstration one which the Germans themselves say has not been witnessed in many years, some say never (but that's a long day). The press notices I've seen are wonderful and one critic says I should sing again soon and he hopes Berlin may hear me many years to come. I've been photographed and sketched and now on the return your child is to be painted. A great world this.

You know mother dear, the Lord is so good to me. The success of last week could not have been bought for ten thousand dollars. My great surprise came when the ushers handed me a huge bouquet of chrysanthemums and you couldn't imagine from whom they came. Quaker City #720 Phila. Mother dear you can't imagine my thrill. You know I seldom have them but the flowers were the largest of their kind I've ever seen. They were too bad. . . . You know I would be quite satisfied to stay if you were here.

Well any way it won't be as long as it has been.

Lots of love to you mother darling hellow to the kids.

Always
Marian[17]

Reviews of Anderson's debut, remarkably uniform in their praise, continued to appear in German newspapers for several weeks. She must have been particularly pleased with the words of the *Berliner Tageblatt:* "Her command of our language and of our world of feeling was amazing"; and she must have been moved by the comparison with Roland Hayes in the *Signale:* "We are already acquainted with the high development of the vocal and musically spiritual art of the Negro race from Roland Hayes, who unfortunately has not sung in Berlin for several years. It was Marian Anderson who recalled this for us, whose first appearance in the Bachsaal caused a sensation."[18]

Anderson's debut made her a figure of interest and curiosity in Berlin society. During the last days of October, Marie von Bülow, the daughter of Hans von Bülow, the conductor and pianist who had been Liszt's son-in-law and a friend of Wagner, invited a small group of friends to hear Anderson sing. The next day, at an afternoon tea at Hause Joel, the home of Madame Charles Cahier in Grünewald, Anderson, who had been asked to sing a group of spirituals, gave a small, private concert. Billy not only accompanied her but saw to it that a photograph was taken of her with Cahier. Retired after a distinguished career, first in opera and then as a lieder singer, Cahier was now teaching. In her years as a performer, she had gained particular renown as an interpreter of Mahler's music, having been chosen by the composer as the contralto soloist in the premiere of *Das Lied von der Erde.* Cahier had numerous prominent and glamorous friends, many of whom she invited to hear Anderson sing. Her guests included the Metropolitan Opera soprano Johanna Gadski; the Swedish ambassador, Wirsen and his wife; Lorenz Adlon, the great restauranteur and founder of the hotel which bore his name, and his wife, Hedda; and the banker Otto Hallstrom. Cahier had given some practical thought to Anderson's career, inviting as well both the concert manager Louise Wolff, widow of Hermann Wolff, who had started the firm of Wolff and Sachs, the oldest and most prestigious concert bureau in Berlin, and Professor Orlik, who sponsored younger artists and musical organizations.[19]

The aftermath of Anderson's Berlin debut was something of a letdown for her. In the weeks following, her homesickness increased to the point that she began to think seriously of returning home. As always, her most loving thoughts were for her mother, whom she longed to have by her side in Europe, a plan that grew more urgent with each European separation. For the moment, she wrote to Ida Browne, one of her oldest Philadelphia friends, asking if she would bring her mother to New York when Anderson arrived home: "We could spend the night at the Y, take in a good show and come to Phila[delphia] the next afternoon. At the moment it is difficult to know when the boat will arrive so I should not suggest that we have tickets for a show that night but rather take a chance on getting in if we are in time. My tickets already arranged for Dec. 16 Bremen to arrive the 21st. Let me know how you feel on this point. If not we can show mother a little of Broadway."[20]

Anderson reserved for Ida news of two young men she had recently met. Her charm, her easy and unaffected manner, and her singular beauty had always attracted hopeful young suitors. While Anderson was not encouraging enough for most of them, her sense of fun and her enjoyment of attention were easily stimulated. As she wrote to Ida,

Now then, read carefully. I have had a most wonderful time. Two men made violent love to me in one night—each ignorant of the other's interest. It was too much. I must tell you about it in detail. They were both foreigners but one is dark. The one A is quite fine looking, quite tall, clever, a good dresser and marvelous company. In a room of many men, he is usually picked out by the women as being the one they would like to meet. He is therefore a bit conceited and what have you. The women have almost ruined him. It never occurred to me to fall over myself about him but that is just what he had been used to. That's how it all started. His voice like the deep rumble of the distant sea, has a force which arrests you. He is attending college and takes his final exams in December. We saw quite a lot of each other and tho one had intimated his growing interest, I took no stock in it. So when the other one B came, and I prepared to go for a walk with him, A who was at that time on the scene rushed to me and said "Are you going out"? The right girl could have capitalized that moment but all I could do was giggle. He had just declined an invitation to a party too. Well B and I talked for a long time and promised and asked a lot of silly things. I had known B before you know. Now then A was not to be outdone, so he waited until I returned and B had to go home. Then we talked until 1:30 AM. Well girl I must tell you, when I went to bed that nite I could not sleep. Too much I tell you, too much. I poor head. The next night he waited again but when I returned from the theatre I simply said I was tired and went to bed. Having a firm will he was determined to talk again and we were invited out and he naturally brought me home and told me in so many words how he felt, asked me if I was in love with anyone and heaps of things among them if I cared. [He] told me he had no interest in his work now etc it was awful for a minute.[21]

The months before Anderson's departure were taken up with concerts in Scandinavia. Although the interest of the Berlin public and the enthusiasm of the critics did not lead to more concerts in Germany, Max Walter turned out to be more helpful than he could have imagined. Walter, in fact, had already told Rule Rasmussen, an important Norwegian manager, and Kosti Vehanen, the Finnish accompanist, about Anderson.

When Rasmussen and Vehanen, traveling together in search of talented performers, arrived in Berlin, Walter had encouraged them to visit Raucheisen. They went to Raucheisen's apartment while he was working with Anderson in preparation for her Berlin debut, and although they had never met Raucheisen, his mother allowed them to sit quietly and listen while he and Anderson finished their work.[22] Johnen had arranged a small concert for Anderson that evening at the Technishe Hochschule, where he was then teaching, and the two visitors were invited to attend. Rasmussen had been impressed enough with her to invite her to give some concerts in Norway.

Anderson no doubt breathed a sigh of relief when the details of Rasmussen's offer arrived, for the political situation in Germany had been growing steadily worse. The autumn and winter months of 1930, in fact, were the most anxious and threatening period of a nearly two-year decline in economic prosperity and political stability that had begun early in 1929, with the Wall Street crash in the United States. By the autumn of 1930, NSDAP (Nationalsozialistische Deutsche Arbeiterpartei, the Nazi Party) membership had risen to 1 million. "A black day for Germany. . . , " Harry Kessler wrote in his diary. "The Nazis have increased their representation almost tenfold, rising from twelve seats to 107. The impression made abroad must be catastrophic. . . ."[23] The poet Stephen Spender, who was in Berlin during those difficult months, left a chilling portrait of the city:

> There was a sensation of doom to be felt in the Berlin streets. For years the newspapers contained little news but of growing unemployment and increased taxation necessary to pay reparations and doles. The Nazis at the one extreme, and the communists at the other, with their meetings, their declamatory newspapers, their uniformed armies of youths, their violence against the Republic and against one another, did all in their power to exacerbate the situation.[24]

In the Von Erdberg household, located in a prosperous residential district near the Kurfürstendamm, Anderson lived in relative safety. Although she was not one to become absorbed in the political discussions going on around her, she was aware of the dangers, the poverty, and the worsening situation enough to confide her anxiety to a friend in the States:

> Though outwardly everything looks calm here, there is liable to be a demonstration at any moment. Things are far from being settled

and tomorrow has been set aside for [a] big demonstration. It may or may not happen. Of course the police know, and will try to prevent any trouble. The economic situation with the poorer classes is steadily growing worse. . . .[25]

By the start of November, with conditions in Germany worsening, Anderson turned her thoughts to Rasmussen's offer. Rasmussen had proposed a tentative schedule of concerts—perhaps six in all—with pairs of concerts in Oslo, Stockholm, and Helsinki, and the possibility for extra concerts in additional cities, should the tour prove successful. Sverre Jordan had agreed to accompany Anderson for her concerts in Oslo. A native of Bergen, Jordan had been trained as a pianist in Bergen and in Berlin. At the start of the First World War, he had settled in Bergen as a piano teacher, accompanist, and critic, becoming one of the leading musicians in Norway and gradually forming relationships with many of the leading musical institutions there. Rasmussen was counting on Jordan's prestige in Norway to draw the public's attention to Anderson's concerts. For the rest of the tour, Kosti Vehanen had agreed to act as her accompanist.

There was a frantic, improvisatory character to Anderson's tour. Indeed, she was forced to travel back and forth to the same place more than once as new concerts were added in the wake of continued success. At one point she complained to Walter that she had to leave and come back to Norway three times during the tour.[26] Rasmussen and Jordan, in spite of their enthusiasm for her singing, were nonetheless cautious. Jordan agreed with Rasmussen that she should appear first as a soloist with the Bergen Symphony. On Thursday evening, November 6, the audience had to listen first to Berlioz's *Harold in Italy,* and only after the intermission, Anderson made her appearance, for the first time in Scandinavia, singing arias from Donizetti's *La Favorita,* Debussy's *L'Enfant prodigue,* and Tchaikovsky's *Jeanne d'Arc.* She returned for the Sunday afternoon concert of the series, singing arias from Handel's *Serse,* Rossi's *Mitrane,* and Arthur Goring Thomas's *Nadeshda.*

Her success with the Bergen Symphony was genuine, even brilliant.[27] Even before appearances in Oslo could be planned, a solo recital had to be arranged in Bergen before she was able to continue her tour. Of course there was more to her success than her singing. No black singer had ever sung in Scandinavia, nor did the public know much about Negro spirituals, which Anderson included in her first orchestral concert. In fact, few American singers had sung in Scandinavia at all. Richard Crooks had sung in Norway with success, as did Madame

Charles Cahier, but at the time both were already successful in Europe.

As Anderson was later to recall, "there could be no getting around the mixture of open-mindedness and curiosity" that greeted her appearances.[28] She was approached casually in the streets, there were visitors and phone calls to her hotel, people came with presents, and newspaper interviews were arranged. Anderson sang her first Scandinavian recital on November 12. The program was not in any way unusual for her—*arie antiche* by Scarlatti and Cesti, and lieder by Liszt and Grieg. For the Norwegian public, however, it was the group of Negro spirituals that held the greatest interest, the program drawing attention to them by the inclusion of some explanation about the music by Anderson herself.[29]

From Norway, she continued on to Stockholm, where her appearances came under the management of Helmar Enwall, whose concert bureau, Koncertbolaget, was the largest in Scandinavia. Enwall, encouraged by Anderson's success in Norway, was willing to take the risk of extending the tour. As she remembered him, he had "vigor, enthusiasm and vision. He felt that the name Anderson would be an asset in his country as well as in the other Scandinavian countries, particularly since I did not look in the least like a Scandinavian."[30] Anderson arrived in the Swedish capital on the fifteenth, in time to attend a concert by Yvette Guilbert. Following Rasmussen's lead, Enwall arranged that she would appear first as soloist with the Norrköping orchestra, conducted by Tord Benner. Two days later a solo recital followed at Stockholm's Royal Academy of Music. The concert was enough of a success that a second was arranged for the twenty-eighth. In the meantime, Anderson had to return to Norway for a recital in Oslo with only one day's rest.

She arrived there at the beginning of winter, and the cold finally caught up with her. The ground was frozen, with a light layer of snow everywhere. Nevertheless, the unexpected cold did not prevent her from having a day of sightseeing. In later years she recalled in particular a visit to Drammen—she had already heard of the famous Drammen cakes—one of a group of picturesque towns lining the western side of the Oslo Fjord. Although the town reminded her of Niagara Falls, the line of hills surrounding the city made her feel hemmed in.[31]

Anderson's introduction to Finnish audiences came with two concerts at University Hall, in Helsinki, on November 24 and 26. Again the exotic appeal of a young, relatively unknown black singer helped to attract large audiences. Anderson found herself more nervous and tired than usual for the first concert. The critics found her interpretations too studied, too deliberately accurate in style.[32] The single day of rest she had been allowed between concerts and the constant traveling were beginning to take their toll. Before coming to Finland, in fact, she had written to Walter, one of her German managers: "I am trying ever so hard to keep in good health for the concerts but the arrangement is such as to make it very difficult and tiring . . . tomorrow again I must spend the whole day on train going over the same road I've just come. It is very very difficult."[33]

The second Helsinki concert was a decided improvement, and the review in *Suomenmaa* the most encouraging so far:

> Perhaps even more obviously than the last time Anderson proved to be in her concert yesterday a singer of the first rank. Anderson's performance, the splendid program—broad and varied—showed her to be a singer of both magnificent voice and an interpreter of high artistry. Anderson sings with such self-confidence as far as the stylistic side of the performance goes that one cannot talk about a more cultivated art of singing. But there is, in addition, the singer's sincere and ardent inner relationship to what she is performing, such a genuine dedication that one cannot really tell if she actually expects any applause for herself. But experience shows that it is only these kinds of occasions that music really has its effect on the audience for whom singing is seldom about technical matters. It is true that Anderson has, for example, a thick vibrato. But what does it mean in this case! Kosti Vehanen also accompanied this time very well, in a concert that belongs to the most enjoyable song recitals that have taken place here in a long time. The delighted audience once again filled the hall to capacity.[34]

A few days later, again in Stockholm, Anderson gave what was scheduled to be her final concert of the tour before returning to Berlin. Enwall wanted more concerts. So did Walter, telling Anderson that "in the first season, you must catch all you can and where and when you can."[35] Accordingly, two Oslo concerts were scheduled, for November 29 and December 6 and, at the last minute a third Copenhagen concert was added, on the eighth, before Anderson was ready to return to Berlin. Less than a week now remained before she was to leave for the United States.

By the end of the tour, Anderson had given more than twice the number of concerts originally planned, over a dozen appearances in Scandinavia during the course of three weeks. In spite of the relatively good notices, however, she received no more than the equivalent of seventy-five dollars a concert. Although some news of her achievements did reach the States, she had little expectation that successful appearances in Scandinavia would have the same effect as triumphs in Paris or Vienna. Nevertheless, in a relatively brief period, she had earned the loyalty and admiration not only of Enwall, one of the most prominent managers in Europe, but Scandinavian audiences as well. Indeed, the extraordinary friendliness and unqualified acceptance Anderson had felt while in Scandinavia made it a haven of equality for her that would remain for many years a constant source of encouragement. As she later wrote,

> the acceptance by these audiences may have done something for me in another way. It may be that they made me feel that I need not be cautious with such things as Lieder, and it is possible that I sang with a freedom I had not had before. I know I felt that this acceptance provided the basis for daring to pour out reserves of feeling I had not called upon.[36]

Anderson arrived home a few days before Christmas, her second season under Judson's management scheduled to begin the second week of January 1931. While she was in Germany, it had been left to Billy to deal with the Judson Agency. Once back from Berlin, in fact, encouraged both by her upcoming tour of Scandinavia and Walter's promises that next year she would enjoy the success in Germany that had thus far eluded her, he lost no time in meeting with Colledge, urging him to take more risks during the coming season. In his turn encouraged by Billy's enthusiastic reports of Anderson's recent successes abroad, Colledge organized a tour of nearly forty concerts in the States, twice as many as the previous year. Many of the dates were in the South, in black colleges and universities that had been regular subscribers to Anderson's concerts for years. Others were arranged nearer to home, where she was well-known—towns in Pennsylvania, at Swarthmore College, in Baltimore, Atlantic City, and Washington, DC. For the first time, a small tour of West Coast cities as well as a group of concerts in Texas were arranged. Believing a successful Carnegie Hall concert was now possible, Colledge was even willing to risk losing the rental fee for Carnegie Hall if the amount should fail to be covered by box office receipts.[37]

The tour was an advance over previous seasons, not only in the number of concerts, but in Anderson's greater artistic assurance, many critics commenting in particular on her command of German. Along with the increased number of concerts, however, came the usual problems. Because many local managers were now trying to reduce costs due to deteriorating economic conditions, Anderson could not count on the previous season's fees. Another problem was the cost of publicity. Responsible for paying both the accompanist's and her manager's fee, Anderson had always been more cautious than Billy about how much she was willing to spend on publicity. Having built up the potential for large audiences in cities in the South through years of regular appearances, she was able to sing to full houses in her second season with Judson without having to increase the amount of publicity over previous years. But in cities where she had not sung before—and even in some, like Chicago, where she had performed a number of times—the embarrassingly small audiences during the tour made it clear how much publicity was a key factor in attracting large audiences.[38]

Claude Barnett, director of the Associated Negro Press, disappointed with the small turnout for Anderson's concert in Chicago, especially after having heard Paul Robeson's sold-out concert there a few days later, was concerned enough to write to her offering advice: "I hesitate to suggest the expenditure of any sum of money which might seem to you considerable, and yet if it aids in the securing of larger audiences, it might be considered justified."[39] Barnett had other suggestions to make, their irony hardly lost on Anderson or Billy. He argued, for example, that it would be helpful for them to meet personally with important figures in the world of promotion in cities along the tour, or to cultivate the leading critics by asking for interviews or conferences. To Anderson and Billy, it seemed as if Barnett were asking them to undertake the same tedious and time-consuming tasks of self-management they had been burdened with for nearly a decade. She was beginning to see that the impersonally bureaucratic machinery of the Judson agency was never going to advance significantly her career in America.

In May, near the end of the season's tour, Anderson resumed discussion with the Rosenwald committee, hoping she would be awarded the balance of her fellowship in order to study in Berlin for the remainder of the year. The committee agreed to Anderson's plan, promising that the first installment of $250 would reach her sometime after her arrival in Berlin.[40]

Orpheus came down from Philadelphia to Atlantic City to hear Anderson's last concert there, on the fourteenth, four days before she was to leave the States for Germany. The leave-taking was unhappy for both. Orpheus had planned to remain in Atlantic City after the concert, hoping she would stay overnight with him before returning to Philadelphia, but she was unwilling to disappoint her family. The next morning Orpheus wrote to Marian, unable to hide his bitterness: "Dearest Marian, I am so sorry that you couldn't stay over and permit me to see you but as usual you must go to mother. Marian, sometimes darling I don't understand you, you are old enough to be a woman, but sometimes you act as a girl of 16. Of course you just couldn't go home to a better person than your mother, but darling I wanted to see you and talk with you. I hope someday you will come out of it. . . ."[41]

Anderson was ambivalent about whether or not to live with the Von Erdbergs again. Grateful for their warmth and concern about her welfare, she had in the end found them annoyingly overprotective. As she learned from Johnen, things had become more difficult for the aged couple. They had even asked Johnen to see if she might be willing to sing for them and a few guests in their home, so that they could charge a small fee. As the Von Erdbergs eventually confessed to Anderson themselves, they had even consulted a fortune teller about whether they would ever see her again. In the end, she moved back into her old room. She felt comfortable there, and sorry for the Von Erdbergs. In spite of their tactlessness, she even consented to sing, counting the days until the whole thing was over.

As far as prospective concerts were concerned, she had more to look forward to than the previous year. Because of her successful Berlin debut and concerts in Scandinavia, Wolff and Sachs, Berlin's most prestigious concert bureau, agreed to manage her concerts outside of Scandinavia. Since the death of Hermann Wolff, who founded Wolff and Sachs, the firm was managed by his son, and his widow, Louise Wolff, who had become acquainted with Anderson after her Berlin debut the previous year. Enwall promised a longer and better organized Scandinavian tour. Again the Rosenwald Committee was unhappy about Anderson's plans for concerts, but they agreed in the end not to hold up her stipend.[42]

Anderson was, in fact, studying three times a week with Johnen, intending to add a fourth lesson each week as soon as the second payment of $375 arrived from the committee. And Johnen was demanding more of her, giving her the Brahms *Vier ernste Gesänge* (*Four Serious Songs*) and a group of Wolf lieder to learn. Because she had a strong predilection for songs that were melodically direct and strongly characterized, or songs that had a realistic narrative with individually drawn characters, the Brahms and Wolf songs were a departure for her. The *Vier ernste Gesänge* are one of the great challenges of the lieder singer's art. Drawn from Ecclesiasties, Ecclesiasticus, and St. Paul's First Epistle to the Corinthians, the texts are bleak and harsh, the last two songs only slightly more consoling. Taken together, the songs offer a sobering view of man's lot, with little promise of comfort. In these bleak meditations on man's faith, Brahms forged a vocal style very much at odds with the lyrical richness and vivid melodic character of much of his song writing, the vocal part here more angular and declamatory. Only in the last two songs, in keeping with the more consoling nature of the texts, are there moments of impassioned lyricism.

Anderson was thus faced with a group of songs with little beguiling melody to draw the interest, and a setting of texts largely philosophical in their abstractness. Of course, she had much to offer in the cycle. Written to be sung by a bass, the four songs gave Anderson plenty of opportunity to exploit her rich and powerful lower register. The words too would have a strongly personal meaning for anyone with Anderson's deep faith. Not inclined to identify with the harsh words of an Old Testament teacher, she would find a way to extract the last measure of hope and consolation in the songs.

Johnen was satisfied enough with Anderson's progress in the Brahms songs to arrange a concert at the Psychological Institute of the University of Berlin during the first week of August, giving her only six weeks to prepare. In his letter to the Rosenwald Committee several months later, Johnen described her performance of the Brahms songs, not in his own words, but in those of Professor Max Friedländer, emeritus professor at the university, who attended the concert at the institute. Friedländer was then nearly eighty, a scholar whose work on the history of German song, especially the songs of Schubert, was only a small part of his distinguished contribution to musicology. He had been a close friend of Brahms and this no doubt helped attract him to the young singer's concert. As he later told Johnen about Anderson's interpretation of the *Vier ernste Gesänge,* "this is the very greatest miracle which I ever heard in the long years of my life."[43]

Although Anderson sang, in addition to the Brahms songs, a group of spirituals and Eboli's aria from Verdi's *Don Carlo,* the Berlin critics lavished their praise on the Brahms. The critic of the *Deutsche Allgemeine Zeitung,* for example, wrote: "As an introduction, she had selected for herself nothing less modest that the 'Serious Songs' of Brahms, a work that poses the highest demands in the severity of expression and the harsh Low Country character of its style, a work rightly feared as a touchstone of ability. Remarkable how the singer succeeded in a rendering both musical and artistic, remarkable the extent to which she accommodated herself to the characteristic emotional outlook of this typical North German world of feeling."[44]

In spite of all her hopes, Anderson did not sing in Berlin again that year. With less than a month before her first concerts outside of Germany, she permitted herself a small Paris holiday, early in October, with the Johnens and their niece. On October 14, after a seven-hour journey by train, she arrived in Prague for the first of four concerts in Czechoslovakia—a broadcast for Prager Radiojournal that evening, an appearance in the Smetana Hall on the sixteenth, and two concerts in the Czech provinces. For these concerts she was fortunate to have László Halász as her accompanist. Near the beginning of his career as a conductor, working as an assistant to George Szell, who was then principal conductor of the German Opera in Prague, Halász was already well-known as an accompanist. During the four or five days of the tour, working on programs, traveling together, and eating in the best restaurants and hotels, they formed an enduring friendship. Halász found her ravishingly beautiful, soft-spoken yet willing to talk openly about racial matters in the States. As he recalled in later years, Halász was amazed to learn, for example, that conditions in America would rarely have allowed them to travel or eat together so freely.[45]

Halász has preserved the most vivid memories of working with Anderson into his eighth decade. He thought her German—the only language they had in common—perfect, her voice as even as possible throughout its three octaves. Whenever he would suggest anything in rehearsal, she would always wait a moment before answering, giving herself time to reflect before making up her mind. She never came with music to rehearsals, everything was always thoroughly prepared. He also remembered she didn't have perfect pitch, which he determined by playing his usual trick of transposing some music to see what would happen. Anderson, he recalled, just sang naturally without taking much notice of the key.

Anderson's concerts in Prague brought her to the attention of Szell, who invited her to return as a guest at the Prague German Opera, mentioning the title role of Meyerbeer's *L' Africaine* and Amneris in Verdi's *Aida* as possible roles for her. She was enthusiastic enough about the possibility to mention it a month later to an interviewer in Stockholm: "At home in America it is difficult for people of my race to get to perform in opera. I believe I have some dramatic capabilities; in any case I have a strong desire to try."[46] Less than two weeks remained before the start of her second Scandinavian tour, which was scheduled to begin on October 30, with an orchestral concert in Göteborg, Sweden. Anderson and Enwall had already agreed on terms—a decided improvement over the previous year. Enwall had promised at least twenty concerts—the final arrangements not yet completed—and a fee of 500 Swedish kronor (about $150) a concert. Anderson would have to pay for travel and visa, and, of course, the 10 percent manager's fees, but now Enwall was willing to pay the income tax earned on fees and for the accompanist.

In the final weeks of preparation before she was to leave for Scandinavia, Johnen concentrated on the Wolf lieder with her. Johnen had chosen three songs from the Mörike lieder ("Er ists," "Das verlassene Mägdlein," and "Fussreise") as well as "Auch kleine Dinge" (*Italienisches Liederbuch*) and "Anacreon's Grab" (Goethe). The Wolf songs proved no less of a challenge for her than the Brahms *Vier ernste Gesänge*. Indeed, the songs of Wolf—the vocal line unerringly faithful to the thoughts and feelings of the characters and the rhythm of the words, the harmonic language complex and highly chromatic, and the poetic content often dense with nuance—make considerable interpretive demands on the singer. "Fussreise," for example, is simple and direct at first, more rapturous with each climax; "Das verlassene Mägdlein," is a bleak and desolate song in which a young girl remembers her faithless lover; and "Auch kleine Dinge," requiring delicacy and restraint, provides challenges of a high order.

As Enwall had promised, the tour turned out to be organized with a minimum of travel back and forth. Between October 30 and December 8, Anderson gave twenty-two concerts. In Sweden there were appearances in Uppsala and Linköping in addition to Stockholm. In November, she sang in Wiborg as well as Helsinki. The scheduled part of the tour (extra concerts had to be added in Sweden) ended in Norway, with six concerts. Even at the start of the tour there was much praise for her interpretations of the Wolf songs. After the first Stockholm concert, for example, the critic of *Dagens Nyheter* wrote: "What shall one say, for example, about this young foreigner's performance of Hugo Wolf's "Anacreon's Grab," with its atmosphere of Goethe-like yearning for the antique and musical romance? It was not charming, as some ladies sitting next to me sighed; it was touching, beautiful, splendid. And "Fussreise!" Quite extravagantly sung, with fine, well-balanced proportions and behind everything a shy delight, which somehow rippled forward between the words—without the regular tricks of the diva, with eyes blinking and head shaking."[47] The *Vier ernste Gesänge* made an even more striking impression, her interpretation compared more than once to Emmi Leisner's, an important German contralto particularly known for her performances of Schubert's *Winterreise* and the *Vier ernste Gesänge*.

For both Vehanen and Anderson, the high point of the tour occurred in Helsinki, a few days before their first concert there on November 12. Like all Scandinavian, especially Finnish musicians, Vehanen believed

ardently in the music of his countryman, Jean Sibelius. He also understood that Finnish musicians had little chance of performing Sibelius's
music outside their native country, that only musicians of international
reputation could make Sibelius's music known throughout the world.
As far as Sibelius's symphonies were concerned, Beecham in England
and Koussevitzky, who came to American to conduct the Boston Symphony Orchestra in 1924, were already performing his music. Although
Sibelius's international prestige rests primarily with his seven symphonies, included among his smaller forms are nearly a hundred songs,
written throughout the composer's creative life, which show a remarkable variety of form and style. Partly because of the language, however
(most are written to Swedish texts), partly because of their often cold
and darkly mysterious world rooted in the northern landscape, they have
made little progress on the international scene.

Vehanen was always eager to interest singers in Sibelius's songs. He
had once arranged for a meeting between the American tenor Richard
Crooks, whom he was accompanying, and the Finnish composer Yrjö
Kilpinen, one of the most important Scandinavian song composers, but
very little came of the meeting. Knowing how important it was for
Anderson to sing in the language of her audience, and believing her voice
appropriate for many of Sibelius's songs, he suggested they work on
some of them as well as folk-song arrangements in Swedish and Finnish.
Anderson found herself immediately drawn to Sibelius's songs, but she
found the music difficult. As she later recalled, "Norden" in particular
was one she found beautiful in a strange way, but difficult to grasp.[48]

By the time they reached Helsinki, Vehanen was more than eager for
Anderson to meet Sibelius, and to try out some of his songs for the composer. A telephone call from Vehanen was enough for Sibelius to offer an
invitation. The next afternoon, the thirteenth, the two of them drove
from Helsinki to Järvenpää, where Sibelius and his wife lived. As Vehanen
later remembered, he and Anderson entered from a small hall into the
salon, the walls decorated with paintings by the Finnish artist Gallen-
Kallela; in the corner was a Steinway piano with a photograph of Queen
Victoria of Sweden on it. The salon looked out over forests and fields,
with a large lake clearly visible in the distance. As Sibelius and his wife
came to greet them, Anderson was struck by Sibelius's presence—"the
whole head," as she later recalled, "looked like something chiseled out of
marble."[49]

They were offered coffee, but Vehanen, who did not think that coffee
was good for singing, suggested they perform first and enjoy coffee after.

Anderson sang four songs for Sibelius that evening—"Aus banger Brust," "En Slända," "Norden," and "Im Wald ein Mädchen singt." Vehanen and Sibelius conversed in Finnish, after each song Sibelius coming to the piano to speak to Vehanen. Sibelius was full of praise for Anderson, insisting on champagne as they walked into the dining room. Anderson spoke about her mother and sisters, and Sibelius, as Vehanen remembered, "smoking his big, strong cigar, told many amusing episodes of his life in a way that only he can do."[50]

At her first concert in Helsinki on the twelfth, Anderson did not feel ready to include any Sibelius songs, but she did hazard the folk song "Läksin minä kesäyönä käymään," ("One summer's night I went walking") that Palmgren had arranged. It was a popular song known to almost everyone in Finland, mournful and bleak, about someone who goes walking on a summer's night seeking calm and repose as the sleepless birds sing and the grouse squawk, only to find a young girl who sits and weeps, her heart full of sorrow. Coached carefully by Kosti, Anderson sang the folk song in Finnish. No reviewer the next day failed to mention the extraordinary impression she had made. "Enthusiasm rose to its highest," wrote the critic of the *Helsingin Sanomat,* "when the artist, endowed with the infallibility of instinct, sang as an encore 'Läksin minä. . . .' in authentic sounding Finnish and with beautiful feeling that went directly to the heart."[51]

Vehanen left his own version of that evening:

As I played the first few bars of the music, the audience, recognizing the song, sank back in their chairs. They were filled with eagerness and great expectation, waiting to hear how this singer from a race and a land so far away from Finland would render the song we all loved. The silence was so tense that Anderson's knees began to shake, and only with great will power could she begin to sing. However, she rendered the song admirably; only in the last phrase her breath became short, and she took a breath in the middle of the sentence. The song had never been done this way before, but it happened that the pause came at just the right place; it gave to the meaning of the words a greater degree of beauty. I felt big tears rolling down my cheeks and could scarcely see the music. The last tone vanished; no one moved; and after a stillness as of a closing prayer of gratitude, the applause broke out—applause so powerful that I am sure that we have never before or since heard such an expression of deep and sincere appreciation.[52]

After the last scheduled concerts in Finland—in Wiborg on the thirteenth and Helsinki on the fourteenth—Anderson was asked to sing an additional concert in Helsinki's Conservatory. Encouraged by the audience's reaction to the Finnish folk song she had sung a few days earlier, she repeated it at her concert in the conservatory, together with Sibelius's "Auf dem Balcon am Meer" and "War es ein Traum?" Her courage failed her only to the extent that she chose, for the time being, to sing the two Sibelius songs in German translation rather than Swedish. Sibelius himself came to the concert, and was kind enough to come to the artists' room during intermission to greet her and Vehanen. As the critics were quick to realize, the concert was a prophetic one in the musical life of Finland. The critic of *Suomenmaa,* for example, put it thus:

> Her program is imbued with the spirit of internationality and in that way points to the future. Exceptional, but in this case not surprising was the name of Sibelius on the program, and with even such demanding songs as 'På verandan vid hamet' ["Auf dem Balcon am Meer"] and 'Var det en dröm?' ["War es ein Traum?"]. What other visiting singer would have dared to step onto the stage in Helsinki to perform these songs and in front of the master himself. This was one of the greatest artistic victories achieved here by the singer. We wish that she would take with her the abundant catch of this most valuable treasure of our music to Europe and across the ocean. Since our country does not give importance to cultural propaganda anymore than it does. . . . we must put our hope in just the kind of international artist as Marian Anderson who is not bound by necessity to promote any one particular nationality.[53]

Only a few weeks remained after the final concert of the tour, in Copenhagen, before Anderson was to leave Germany. The Rosenwald fellowship having run its course, there was now little certainty of returning to Germany. In less than two years, Hitler's rise to power would make her unwelcome there. In 1935, presumably because of some stupid bureaucratic mix-up about Anderson's racial origin, Enwall received an inquiry about whether she was free to sing in Germany. There were renewed requests when it was noticed that she was scheduled to sing in Warsaw. Anderson was not eager to sing in the Germany of those days, but the opportunity to appear in Berlin under different circumstances than those of her student days persuaded her to accept the single date Enwall had found. Inquiry was made as to whether she was 100 percent Aryan. Enwall responded that she was not. There was no further correspondence.[54]

CHAPTER SEVEN

"Marian Fever"
(1932–1934)

Anderson returned to America on the eve of 1932, the beginning of the bleakest period of the Great Depression. Without plans for further study abroad or definite offers for concerts from Enwall, she was once again dependent on the unpredictable and often tentative offerings of Judson.

The new season under Judson began in mid-January in Quebec, reduced now to twenty concerts spread over a period of nearly five months, with long periods of inactivity. In March there was a single concert at the Hampton Institute, in May a single concert near the end of the month in Albany. When a small group of concerts were scheduled together, their distance one from the other required long and expensive periods of travel. The three concerts scheduled in January, for example, each less than a week apart, took Anderson from Quebec to Norwalk, Connecticut and then to Wheeling, West Virginia.[1]

Caught in the usual trap in which no concert could be turned down, however much it defied convenience or logic, both Anderson and Billy felt the old desperation return. Now there were signs of attrition that could only be attributed to the country's worsening economic pressures. No concerts had come through on the West Coast, even though she had made a good impression in California the previous year. In an effort to cut costs, a merger between CBS and Columbia Management was created for the West Coast and a committee was formed to decide on those artists who would be invited to appear. As a result, Judson lost much of the influence he once had there. The South as well, once the bedrock of Anderson's concert seasons, was all but disappearing from the geographical makeup of the tour. Funding for state colleges was being reduced and private colleges were at the mercy of whatever generosity northern philanthropists could offer. Of the four or five southern colleges normally included in Anderson's schedule, only West Virginia Institute of Technology and the prestigious Hampton Institute, where Nathaniel Dett still preserved the high standards of musical education, could afford to invite her.

There were good notices and demonstrations of enthusiasm during the tour. There were also disappointments and near disasters that mirrored the insecurity of the times. In Columbus, in early February, for example, a "meager handful of people" sat patiently in Memorial Hall until nine o'clock, when Anderson was finally forced to announce that the concert would have to be cancelled.[2] In mid-April, in Boston's Symphony Hall, the largely black audience in attendance left so many empty seats that the local manager paid Anderson only half of the agreed-upon fee of $500, refusing to turn over the rest. She thought the concert a "wretched one;"[3] according to one Boston critic, she seemed apathetic, her singing having little variety or enthusiasm.[4]

Difficult as the season was, it led to an important and enduring friendship. In April, with her first appearances with the Hall Johnson Negro Choir, she came to know Hall Johnson, the choir's director, one of the most significant composers and arrangers of spirituals. Johnson gained his musical education at Allen University, in South Carolina, and in Philadelphia, where he attended the Hahn School of Music. His last two years of study were completed at the University of Pennsylvania, where he graduated in 1910. He was trained primarily as a violinist, although he found time to study composition. He spent his early years in the orchestra of James Reese Europe and Will Marion Cook. Cook, a black composer of extraordinary originality, especially in the area of musical comedy, stimulated Johnson's interest in the theater. A turning point in Johnson's musical career came in 1921, when he joined the orchestra of the famous revue *Shuffle Along,* the first all-black show to appear on Broadway in more than a decade. Written by Eubie Blake and Noble Sissle, *Shuffle Along* was something of a revolution in Broadway theater, breaking away from the stereotypical blackface minstrel show and introducing ragtime and jazz in the context of black folk humor.[5]

In addition to his work as an instrumentalist, Johnson developed a profound interest in black choral music. He felt that the work and folk songs of his people and their spirituals offered a rich and untapped field and he wanted the world to know that music. Johnson's originality as an arranger of spirituals lay in his differing attitudes from those of Harry T.

Burleigh and the original Jubilee singers. Burleigh viewed the concert spiritual as a form of art song, not as an opportunity to convey through musical and interpretive means its original singing style. As a boy growing up in Georgia, Johnson heard the slave songs sung by family and church members who had themselves been slaves. When he came to form his own choir, during the 1920s, he wanted to reproduce the authentic spirit and fervor of the camp meeting, where many of the songs had been created as part of an oral tradition. He settled on a mixed group of twenty singers, arranging all of the spirituals for the choir. By 1930 the fame of the Hall Johnson Negro Choir was such that Johnson was engaged as the musical director for the Broadway production of *The Green Pastures,* a drama written by Marc Connelly and hailed by one critic as "one of the loftiest achievements of the American theater." The spirituals Johnson wrote for *The Green Pastures,* sung by the "Celestial Choir" during the course of the play, struck a new note, becoming enormously popular with black performers.

In her appearances with the Hall Johnson Negro Choir, in Philadelphia on the fifth of April and in New York on the twenty-fifth, she sang several groups of art songs, joining the choir at the end of the concert in two Johnson arrangements, "Fix me, Jesus" and "Deep River." Gradually, a warm friendship developed, and over the years Anderson sang many of Johnson's arrangements. Some of them, "Certn'y Lord," "Dere's No Hidin' Place Down Dere," and "Roll, Jerd'n Roll," became a permanent part of her repertoire. The most important collaboration between Anderson and Johnson was still more than thirty years away—a recording of spirituals in which Johnson succeeded to a surprising degree in winning Anderson over to his own views about the interpretation of spirituals.[6]

By the summer of 1932, Judson could not escape the realization that something had to be done to infuse new life into Anderson's dwindling career, yet he could do nothing more than recommend measures that placed the full burden on Anderson and King. He tried first to convince her to become a soprano. Whatever reasons lay behind Judson's advice, they were ill-judged and thoughtless. If sopranos were more glamorous than contraltos, it was primarily the world of opera that made them so. Certainly success in opera would have enhanced the public's appreciation of Anderson, but for a black singer to accomplish such a feat in the 1930s presented difficulties more extreme than those that were already a constant feature of the career of any black singer. Anderson, in any event, knew that she was naturally a contralto and not a soprano, that any such change would before too long put a virtual end to her career as a singer. Even the possibility of one day singing the role of Aida, which Judson and others frequently held out to her, did not change her thinking.

Another suggestion from Judson was that Anderson study with Frank La Forge, an important New York vocal coach and accompanist. Perhaps La Forge would share his view about her becoming a soprano. If not, then at least he might interest one of the American recording companies in her. Anderson had made some recordings in Europe, but except for those and a series of spirituals that she had recorded in 1924 at the beginning of her career for the Victor Talking Machine Company, American recording companies had shown little interest in her. La Forge worked with many of the most important operatic and lieder singers of the day, accompanying many whom Judson managed, and a number of these collaborations had made their way onto recordings. Moreover, La Forge had connections in New York—one of his close friends was Olin Downes, the dean of New York music critics—and he had a long-standing association with RCA Victor, for whom he had made recordings with Lily Pons, Marcella Sembrich, and Richard Crooks.

Although there was more than one obstacle to studying with La Forge, Anderson liked the idea. She always found the prospect of studying with an accomplished and sympathetic teacher exciting and self-renewing. As usual there were Boghetti's feelings to worry about, but Anderson could usually harden herself against his angry outbursts when it came to furthering her career artistically. Hurt and offended, Boghetti refused to teach Anderson so long as she remained with La Forge. There was also the problem of La Forge's fee, much higher than Boghetti's. La Forge was understanding, agreeing to give her an hour's time for his usual half-hour fee if she could manage to get to New York early enough to be in his studio by nine in the morning. She could manage that but still not La Forge's fee. In April, Judson informed her that there was a half scholarship available for study with La Forge, and this allowed her finally to begin studies with him in the summer.[7]

The summer months were an occasion primarily for study, but there were distractions as well. Orpheus began once again to urge Marian to think of marriage. After the 1929 crash, which had put an end to the holding company he had formed with a bank executive and builder, Orpheus had decided, with $1.37 in capital, to try his luck as an architect in New York. He worked for a time for the New York Civil Service, organizing the maintenace of school buildings, and in 1932, he landed a job with the American Cottonpicker Corporation. He was rarely away from the company of women, many of them white, and he was often seen with them in Atlantic City, where he enjoyed relaxing. He visited Marian when he could manage the trip to Philadelphia, hoping to see her more often now that he was no farther away than New York. "You are always on my mind," he wrote to her that summer. "I don't know what I am going to do—things are all upset. Can't make plans from day to day. I love you darling, that is all I know."[8] Anderson knew that she was not ready for marriage—not in such difficult economic times, and with her career in America virtually at a standstill.

For Alyse and Ethel it was an exciting summer in spite of the hard times. An avid Democrat and supporter of Roosevelt, Alyse had begun to involve herself in local political work, and was feeling a new sense of purpose. The family was even beginning to feel encouraged that Alyse might eventually land a job through the many contacts coming her way. Unlike Alyse, Ethel was never in doubt about what she wanted most out of life. For her it was a family and children. For nearly a year now the family had looked forward to Ethel's marriage to James DePreist, a young man whom she had met at the Church of the Crucifixion, where both served as soloists, singing with Billy King's chorus on Sundays and holidays. Their attraction and affection for each other was immediate. Kenneth Goodman—one of the first black organists to have an important career, both in the United States and abroad, and a frequent soloist in Billy King's church—knew the young couple well, often accompanying Ethel and Alyse when they performed. Goodman recalled that it was Ethel's voice that brought her and DePreist together. Ethel had the same extraordinary range as Marian, with a low register of power and beauty that many thought comparable. James DePreist was distinctive looking, with an olive complexion and features that reflected his partly Native American ancestry. The couple were married near the end of June 1932. Charles Tindley, the minister of Tindley Temple, performed the ceremony at the Andersons' home on Martin Street. For entertainment, there were solos by Alyse and William Smith, another of the singers at the Church of the Crucifixion, who sang "I Love You Truly."[9]

Anderson continued to study with La Forge throughout the summer and fall of 1932 and well into the following year. That summer, arriving early for a lesson one morning, she overheard one of La Forge's students—at the time she had no idea it was the great contralto Margarete Matzenauer—rehearsing a song that produced one of those moments of spellbinding intensity. "I remember sitting downstairs one afternoon," she later wrote, "waiting to see him, when I heard a magnificent voice singing a song in German. I was unfamiliar with this song, but I thought it was by Schubert. I could hear how perfectly the singer was enunciating the German, making the words so completely a part of song. To sing a song like that in that way, I thought, I would be the happiest person in the world."[10] Much later, when she brought the incident up with La Forge, she learned that Matzenauer had been rehearsing "Er, der Herrlichste von allen," the second song of Schumann's *Frauenliebe und -leben* cycle. He agreed to work on the songs with Anderson, and later in the summer they performed the entire cycle in La Forge's studio to an invited audience that included her friend Harry T. Burleigh. During the performance she forgot some of the text of the songs and had to improvise some words to get through it, reminded yet again how insecure she felt singing in German.

By the fall, nearly one quarter of the country was out of work, and Philadelphia, with its large black population, suffered acutely from unemployment. The Anderson home felt the strain. Alyse enjoyed the competitiveness and the camaraderie of political work, but neither brought her any wages. Ethel managed to keep her job with a neighborhood printing business where she had worked since her high school days, but her husband, who was a skilled contractor, had to contend with the miserable conditions felt everywhere in the building profession. Fortunately, in the first years of the Depression, in spite of the uncertainties and diminishing opportunities, Marian had been able to earn more than many skilled workers. For the period from April 1931 to February 1932, her fees from Judson came to $7,799. After expenses—for Judson's commission, her accompanist, travel, and advertising—her earnings for that period were about $1,600, enough to support herself and her mother.[11]

As the time for Anderson's fall season under Judson approached, Adele Cooper, in charge of the Booking Department, informed Billy King that she had few definite prospects to offer, and those, she told him, "all write in the same vein about the limited budget."[12] The security that black colleges provided each season had slipped away. "Unfortunately the colored colleges throughout the country," Cooper wrote to Billy, "seem to be very fearful of making any contracts . . . though some of them write that after they have their student enrollment they may be able to engage Miss Anderson. Most of them have a sob story to tell and I am not very sanguine about the prospects."[13] By the first of December, with the exception of a single date in Kitchener, Ontario, the story had not changed. Cooper's letters sounded desperate: "I want you to know that I have been writing and writing to the following towns, but as yet without result, except that most of them are so pressed for funds as to be postponing activities this year or giving up altogether."[14]

The situation failed to improve, and Anderson sang less after the Christmas holidays than she had since before her high school days. Judson managed to secure only four concerts and a single radio performance in Chicago before the start of the summer. Fortunately only one of the concerts—on the Community Concert Course in Battle Creek, Michigan, on May 4—required much travel.

Late that summer, Anderson was asked to make a test recording for RCA, with La Forge as accompanist. It was the first hopeful sign in months. Anderson wanted to try "Er, der Herrlichste von allen." Toward the end of July they traveled down to Camden, New Jersey, for the test, the first time Anderson had recorded anything in German. Surprisingly, La Forge gave her no more than the most understated of accompaniments, but her contribution was in many ways impressive. One is struck first by the sheer beauty and opulent fullness of her voice, from top to bottom. Her German sounds accurate and natural. If there are any shortcomings they are interpretive. Although Anderson already has the emotional shape of the song clearly in mind, and manages the modulation from rapturous excitement to humility and sadness in a natural and convincing way, there is a certain squareness to the rhythm, the whole lacking some of the subtle refinements of expression that she would acquire in later years. The Victor company rejected the test. Years later, La Forge recalled being told by Victor that "they had so many contraltos that they would have no use for her at that time."[15] Anderson remained with La Forge a few more months. She found him cordial and generously supportive. Although he gave her frequent opportunites to sing to small audiences in his studio, inviting critics and musicians whom he thought it might be useful for her to know, he did not have the decisive impact on her career that Judson had hoped for.

Anderson had already begun to think of ways to break free of Judson. In mid-April, she had told one interviewer about her plans to open a vocal studio, hoping to turn an occasional and casual interest in teaching into something more serious and productive. Not even bothering to hide her dissatisfaction with Judson, she had told another interviewer in June that, rather than signing a new contract with him, she preferred to think about a career in radio.[16] Such constructive ideas may have eased Anderson's sense of helpnessness in the face of a failing career, but her interest in them was halfhearted. Those who knew her saw easily how little interest she had in teaching. As for radio, the few opportunities that existed for black classical performers during the 1920s all but disappeared during the Depression.

Billy King's advice was to keep faith with Judson. Billy always believed that Judson would come through in the end. But Billy had less to lose than Anderson. He had his position as choir director at the Church of the Crucifixion; and he had whatever real estate business came his way—not much for the moment but at least a possibility for the future. There was hardly a time when he did not have more than one iron in the fire. Anderson was more single-minded of purpose; she wanted to sing, and if she could not manage it one way she would try another. The oppportunity came at the beginning of July, when Enwall reasserted his belief in her, offering her a contract for twenty concerts in Scandinavia for October and November.[17] She did not hestitate. Without even bothering to inform Judson of her plans, she accepted Enwall's offer. In the middle of October she set sail for Sweden.

Anderson was not obsessed with the possibility of fame. With the exception of Paul Robeson, whose fame was the result of a multiplicity of talents and an outspoken charisma not shared by Anderson, fame was still out of reach for black concert singers. What she worked for was artistic accomplishment. What she expected, and felt she deserved, were the same opportunities that white concert artists enjoyed. In Germany, in the early 1930s, when the promise of concerts in the great European capitals had been held out to her, she had allowed herself to imagine more than mere accomplishment. But her most enduring successes had come, not on the Continent, but in Scandinavia. Even someone more disposed than she to dream of the impossible would have stopped short of imagining that the great turning point would come just there, in the cities and provinces of Scandinavia.

The first two of the twenty concerts promised by Enwall were scheduled for the first and fourth of October, in Helsinki. Apart for nearly two years, Anderson and Kosti had less than two weeks to prepare before beginning the tour. Always willing to listen to him about matters of repertoire, open to the stimulus that his wide knowledge of repertoire provided, she followed his advice and prepared Brahms's *Zigeunerlieder* and Fidès's aria "Ah! mon fils" from Meyerbeer's *Le Prophète,* for the Helsinki concerts. The aria, from the second act of Meyerbeer's opera, is Fidès's great outburst of gratitude to her son after he sacrifices his bride to save her. The noble and intense aria, rising to high drama at the end, suited Anderson well. The American impresario Sol Hurok, who heard her sing the aria the following spring in Paris, remarked often that the effect Anderson had made on him with "Ah! mon fils" was overwhelming. So it was for the reviewers that first evening in Helsinki: "The singer," wrote one of them, "completely conquered her audience with the aria from *Le Prophète* by Meyerbeer, in which the strange beauty of her voice—the brilliancy of the high notes and the sonorous ring of a cello in the deep part —produced a magnificent effect, whilst her interpretation was filled with deep feeling and warm expression."[18]

Anderson's performance of the Brahms songs, on the other hand, did not please the critics.[19] In the *Zigeunerlieder,* Brahms sought to convey his love of the Gypsy temperament with songs that are direct and earthy, and capture the exuberance of the Gypsy character, requiring the kind of abandon that was not a natural part of Anderson's temperament. Marian never sang the *Zigeunerlieder* again. For the concert on the fourth, having decided that familiarity was the better part of virtue, she chose five songs from Schumann's *Frauenliebe und -leben* and Lia's air from Debussy's *L'Enfant prodigue.* The critics were kinder, altogether charmed by her simplicity, emotional directness, and technical brilliance.

The two concerts in Helsinki (there was a third in Turku on October 5) were only a prelude. The fall of 1933 and winter of 1934 proved to be a different kind of artistic journey from any Anderson had experienced. The concerts Enwall had scheduled—nearly every two days—were creating a swell of unprecedented interest. Word and excitment spread. By the time she reached Sweden, on October 20, all seats to her recital in Stockholm were sold out long in advance. Even the Swedish king was intrigued enough by all the publicity to attend.[20]

Enwall was encouraged as much by Anderson's stamina as by her continuing success. Eager to capitalize on her popularity in the smaller towns in Sweden, he frequently filled her free days with additional concerts in the provinces. This scheduling rested on that fact that Sweden is small by American standards—no larger than California. Anderson could reach most of the smaller towns and provinces in the southern half of Sweden by train in less than half a day's journey, some in three or four hours. In October, she gave sixteen concerts, four of them—in Linköping, Orebro, Stockholm and Uppsala—in a single week. She was beginning to feel the strain, although she kept it back for a time from Enwall, too afraid to risk disappointing him. She could not hide her growing exhaustion in her letters to her mother, who, by the end of the month, began to express concern: "Just now I am listening to the strains of the 'Old Rugged Cross,' . . . Maud is singing soprano, Jimmy tenor, and Ethel has given way to Lena, singing contralto. You should hear them. My dear, I was so glad to hear from you, but my precious, I am sore afraid the four concerts a week will work you too hard. It is well you do not mind it, yet I am asking God's blessings on you, that you may feel no ill effect from it."[21]

Blessed with good health, her spirits buoyed by having constant work and by the exhilarating acclaim of audiences, Anderson was able to meet the demands that Enwall made on her in spite of the grueling schedule and the toll it was taking. In November she gave eighteen concerts. During one week she sang on five successive evenings in Finland (two in Helsinki between concerts in Tamerfors and Wasa). On November 30, she reached Copenhagen in preparation for her first concert in Denmark, scheduled for the following evening. The first disappointment of the tour, unsettling as it was unpredictable, awaited her in the Danish capital. The concert on the first was a brilliant success. Anderson sang a group of old Italian songs and a series of Schubert lieder ("Aufenthalt," "Wohin," and "Die Allmacht"), then Verdi's "O Don fatale," songs of Rachmaninoff, Tcherepnin, and Chaminade, and a group of spirituals, beginning with Burleigh's "Deep River." Once again she tried out Schubert's "Die Allmacht," its grand and majestic tone ideally suited to her now. When she began with the words "Great is Jehovah, the Lord, for heaven and earth proclaim his power," there was no mistaking the deep spiritual conviction guiding her interpretation. Concerts followed in Copenhagen, Aarhus, and Odense, but on the morning of December 2 the Danish papers carried the news that the minister of justice was forbidding Anderson to give further concerts in Denmark. In view of the difficult economic times, he explained, foreign artists who earned considerable fees in Denmark could not be allowed to take large amounts of Danish currency out of the country.[22]

Unbeknownst to Anderson and Kosti, in fact, there had been a flurry of activity during the days preceding her concert on December 1, leaving it uncertain until an hour before the concert whether she would be allowed to sing. It was the local manager, Freede Skaarup, who, innocently enough, made the first blunder. He was required to apply to the state police for a working permit for visiting artists; the police would then pass the request on to the minister of justice. Skaarup made the request only after the event had been advertised and tickets sold, and on Friday morning, the day of the concert, Skaarup was notified that the working permit was denied. Later that day, Max Rothenburg, Skaarups's legal adviser, appealed to Zahle, the minister of justice, explaining to Zahle how embarassing the affair had become. Rothenburg was told that it was the National Bank of Denmark that was responsible for the refusal, "maintaining that such big amounts as were given to foreign artists as fees could not be allowed to pass out of the country."[23] By early evening, Zahle relented somewhat. In order to demonstrate that the real obstacle was the economic concerns of the National Bank and not Rothenburg's late application for a working permit, he allowed Anderson's performance that evening to take place.

Skaarup had kept the whole affair from Anderson and Kosti so as not to cause them unnecessary anxiety before the concert. They both learned of the minister's decision the next morning. Kosti learned of it first, from Enwall, who phoned him after reading about it in the newspapers. At breakfast, Kosti gave Anderson the news. She hid as best she could how she felt, but experience told her that racial prejudice, not national economy, lay at the bottom of the decision. "Marian Anderson's expression hardly changed," Kosti later recalled. "Perhaps she frowned a little: it was as if I read in her face: again the white man's slap at the face of the black—but all she said was: then we cannot sing our new Sibelius songs here! But I will sing in the charity concert—or maybe they will prohibit it as well with police force."[24] By then nearly everyone else in Copenhagen knew about the ban on her concerts. An extra edition had already appeared on the streets, proclaiming on the front cover in thick letters: "Marian Anderson's concerts prohibited! Minister of Justice has banned the concerts on the recommendation of the central bank so that Danish money would not go overseas."[25] Before the day's end, flowers were delivered to Anderson's hotel, letters arrived, poems were written in defense of the singer, delegations came to protest the treatment she had suffered. There were further appeals to the minister, but the National Bank would not relent.

Enwall had made sure that Anderson's appearances in Denmark would receive sufficient publicity. The publicity turned into a small furor when the newspapers took up her defense, fearing that if she were prevented from singing by such a ruling, "it would look too much like prejudice against Negroes, and Denmark must not be guilty of even the appearance of such a thing."[26] In spite of the growing tide of sentiment in her favor, the bank's officials remained firm in their ruling, refusing to respond to public pressure. Their only concession was to allow Anderson to offer her services, without pay, for a charity concert for indigent children in the Town Hall on Sunday afternoon. Anderson was to be only one of a number of performers, and her contribution amounted to three or four songs, but as soon as the rumor spread that she would appear at the Town Hall, there was a run on the booking office. By ten o'clock, one hour after its opening, every seat had been sold. The American flag hung that evening alongside the Danish flag in the hall. There was a near demonstration when she appeared, and at the end of the concert, one newspaper recounted, "people jumped up on their chairs cheering and crying 'Long live Marian!' "[27]

The sense of personal rejection Anderson experienced at the hands of the Danish authorities was quelled by the gratitude and affection she felt toward the Danish public. Not drawn to speechmaking, she wanted nevertheless to show her appreciation to the throngs of people who had transformed the decision of the authorities into a small cause célèbre. After many attempts to find the right words, she settled on a brief speech:

> My dear friends and well wishers. I have since my first visit here had a very warm spot in my heart for the people of Denmark and knew of no better way to express it than by singing to them. That it is now impossible to continue naturally makes me quite sad, but please understand that I shall always think of you and thank you for your enthusiasm in my concerts and kind words through the press. And I hope my dear friends that you shall not forget me. As my farewell to Denmark I have the honor of singing this afternoon for the benefit of the poor children, an honor which gives me very great pleasure.[28]

Anderson and Kosti left Copenhagen on the fourth, crossing by ferry to the southwestern coast of Sweden for a series of seven concerts that Enwall had arranged for the first half of December, taking Anderson, for the first time, to Hälsingborg, Lund, Göteborg and Malmö. Ironically, the first part of the tour ended in Copenhagen, where she was allowed to give only a single charity concert for the poor, this time a Christmas concert with orchestra. Anderson expected to conclude her tour of Scandinavia and return to America in December, wanting to spend the holidays with her family. Encouraged, however, by the steady increase in enthusiasm which greeted each of her concerts (a veritable "Marian fever," the newspapers reported), Enwall offered to extend her contract to cover twenty more concerts in Scandinavia for the months of January and February. She did not hesitate to accept.

Anderson spent the Christmas holidays in Sweden with the Enwalls, her first of many opportunities to enjoy the country setting and peacefulness of their summer house in Vattershaga, in the archipelago north of Stockholm. Like Burleigh before him and eventually Hurok, Enwall fell easily into the role of a kindly paternalistic figure. Like them, he was important to the development of Anderson's professionalism at a decisive moment in her career. By the end of the first part of what would become a concert tour of almost unprecedented achievement, Enwall already glimpsed far better than did Anderson the fame that lay within her reach. He also saw how little prepared she was to think of herself in the role of a glamorous concert singer. Before long, he told her, everyone—audiences, the press, interviewers—would become fascinated with the image she created. There would be more interviews, questions about her private life, curiosity about how she dressed and the gowns she wore. Anderson liked to dress simply, still used to saving a penny whenever she could, but her innate good taste and sense of style, and her natural desire for fine clothes, made prolonged encouragement on the part of the Enwalls unnecessary.[29]

Kosti gave advice freely, having an eye for fashion and enjoying the fun of making Anderson glamorous. "The first really elegant gowns," Kosti later wrote, "that Miss Anderson purchased were from the N.K., an exclusive and beautiful store in Stockholm where the latest Paris models were to be found. One of the most attractive gowns was a brilliant black lace entirely embroidered with black pearls."[30] Later on, with advice from Madame Cahier, she sought out the Viennese designer Ladislav Czettel, who began to design gowns and dresses for her. When she got around to writing to Alyse about the success of the charity concert in Copenhagen, she could not help mentioning her modest first steps in what she still thought of as self-indulgence: "The publicity has been colossal, and I fear that I am not nearly elegant enough to carry it thru. We return in two or three days to Copenhagen and perhaps one might be tempted to purchase something there since if we make the film, on which idea I'm not completely sold, one must be quite fine."[31]

Alyse was much in her thoughts those days. Marian was finding it difficult, in fact, to hide her impatience with Alyse's inability to channel her interests in a single direction:

There is a Negro girl studying race relations at an institution near Copenhagen in Denmark. I find it such a pity that you are satisfied to sit around and get along any way you can. You have talent which you should put to work. Think sometimes, and think deeply, it shant always be as now. Ask yourself what about you five or ten years from now. If I'd had someone to depend on as you have me, I think that I would have spent my time a bit better. I don't lose sight of the fact that you may not be able to work at what you most desire but we must not let everything go on that account. I didn't want to be forced to come up here, but it was that or unpaid bills and I <u>had</u> to come, for I've no one to go to and it's sad when you think of it.[32]

Of course it was not only Alyse's perpetual floundering that was on her mind. Working harder than she ever had, even worried about her ability to keep to the pace that Enwall had set, she was for the moment feeling resentful and angry that so much of the burden of the family was falling on her shoulders.

The post-Christmas part of the tour began on January 14, 1934. With Marian's success and sold-out houses in the principal cities assured, Enwall was intrepid enough to arrange concerts in the smaller coastal and inland towns of Sweden. Traveling north along the Swedish coast, she sang for the first time in Falun, Gävle, Hundisvall, Sundsvall and Härnösand, enjoying almost daily the changing folk customs and crafts, the native cuisine, and breathtaking scenery of the Swedish coastal towns. In the second half of January, Anderson gave twelve concerts in Sweden and Norway, with six concerts on successive evenings before she was allowed a single day's break, during which she traveled across Sweden and Norway for a concert in Trondheim, near the western coast of Norway, on the twenty-third.

The National Bank of Denmark finally decided to allow Anderson to give one additional concert in Denmark. Enwall lost no time in scheduling two concerts in Copenhagen, the first on the eighteenth and a charity concert on the twentieth of February. The weeks preceding her return to the Danish capital saw Anderson make her way gradually south from Stockholm to Hälsingborg. From there, she had only to make the short trip by ferry across the narrow channel to Copenhagen. She reached the inland town of Jönköping, at the southern tip of Lake Vattern, on the seventh of February, where a telegram from Enwall awaited her. He was now prepared to extend her tour through April, offering her thirty additional concerts.[33] When Enwall's offer reached her, she had already given sixty concerts since the fall of 1932. For the moment, however, she felt invigorated. The growing warmth of her friendship with the Enwalls and her relaxation with them during the holidays had helped to remove some of the worries plaguing her during the fall. Emboldened by her growing reputation and the confidence Enwall placed in her, she took only a few days to respond to his offer: She was willing to sing as many as fifty concerts by the end of April, asking for an increase from

500 to 600 kroner per concert.[34] Enwall agreed. Before her first concert in Copenhagen, on the eighteenth, Anderson wrote to Judson, asking him to cancel her concerts in America during March and April.[35]

Anderson's concert in Copenhagen on the eighteenth of February proved to be a joyous homecoming: "Once more the slim dark singer Marian Anderson appeared on our concert course," one of the reviewers reported,

> and the moment she stepped onto the stage, she was greeted with a demonstration of enthusiasm that rose and rose, whilst the singer smiled and bowed in acknowledgement to the heavy welcome the audience gave her. This applause did not diminsh during the course of the evening. Marian Anderson's wonderfully beautiful voice, ranging from night's dusky depths to the sparkling clearness of the heights exercised its irresistible charms, whether in Veracini's fascinating "Pastorale," in Brahms's "Schmied," in the momentous "Von ewiger Liebe," or whether she played and toyed with coloratura, warm and rich in tone and yet as light as dancing sunbeams. Finally she sang some of her negro spirituals—and now the applause grew beyond all bounds. The audience, who had already asked for and been given two or three encores, received many more—and tomorrow the grand lamps will again light the Grand Hall.[36]

All of the reviews of her two concerts in Copenhagen were ecstatic. Although she was on occasion still dogged by criticism of her interpretation of lieder (one Copenhagen critic mentioned Brahms and Sibelius), those who felt dissatisfaction with her lieder singing were beginning to soften their comments. What were once considered flaws needing to be corrected were now seen as occasional blemishes in a technique and style that were otherwise nearly flawless.[37] Anderson had more to celebrate in Copenhagen than her renewed successes there. Taking another important step in advancing her career, Enwall opened discussions with concert managers in Paris, Milan, and Vienna. During February, he was able to promise her a Paris debut as soon as the Scandinavian tour ended. The promise of debuts on the Continent gave her a degree of confidence she had rarely, if ever, experienced. "Regret disappointing you," she had telegrammed to her family on the fifteenth of February, "Remaining some months longer. London and Paris recitals in May." She promised to write, but a week later, on the twenty-fourth, a few days from her thirty-seventh birthday, she managed only: "My letter delayed. Great success Copenhagen. Send twelve pairs stockings shades brown. Had screen test. Much love."[38]

Ever since her student days in Berlin, Anderson had talked about having her mother with her in Europe. Enwall's news about London and Paris was the impetus she needed to broach the subject with her mother. To her surprise, Mrs. Anderson expressed no hestitation at making the long sea journey. She was even willing to make the voyage alone, but Marian would not hear of her going abroad without an escort. In the end, it was Alyse who proved the main obstacle. During the middle of March, Mrs. Anderson reported the first signs of trouble: "When I read that you really wish to make arrangements for me to make the trip abroad, I really could not keep back some tears . . . Not taking time to put the letter away, [Alyse] was in the room and immediately picked up the letter, and began reading. When she read what you said about her [not] accompanying me, she said aloud (for my benefit): 'If any body goes with you, I am going.' . . . You know that Maud is in no means ready to make the trip, I mean as far as her clothes are concerned, neither is she deserving . . . Jimmy says that he is willing to send Ethel over with me, but you know Maud's disposition."[39]

Alyse finally found the courage to write to Marian on the twenty-fifth, pulling out all the stops: "Now about Europe, you know Ethel has a husband and if Mother goes and leaves me it is sort of leaving me alone. You know I went with Mother to attend to all the bills and she is not so steady in the street or walking around because she doesn't get out often. They are telling Mother to go alone but I am sure you would not want that. . . . It would be so lovely if I could come to you with Mother. Won't you please consider it and let me come? Please."[40]

During March, the problems surrounding her mother's trip not yet resolved, Anderson found time for only a few telegrams home. March, in fact, was turning out to be the most relentlessly intense period of the tour so far. In thirty-one days, Anderson gave twenty-four concerts, with several stretches of four and even five concerts on successive days. Anderson and Kosti traveled to twenty-one cities and towns across Sweden that month, eighteen of them for the first time—from Boden and Lulea in the north, less than seventy miles from the Arctic Circle, to Karlskrona and Kalmar along the southern coast at the tip of Sweden. On April 11, with a concert that evening in Borås, an inland town near Göteborg on the western coast, Anderson finally wrote to Alyse, direct and firm, trying hard to be supportive but allowing her impatience with Alyse to get the better of her:

Dearest Al

Your letter was a peach, although it was about five and a half months late. You must have <u>forgotten</u> that I was over here until Mother's invitation came. Yes, you are quite right, I never had any intention of having mother make the trip alone, but preferred that her companion should be one who had made the trip before and understood what to do. At this time it is quite impossible to bring you here because aside from your transportation, your board and keep here for a month or two would be too expensive for me. I thot however that if you were a good girl I might suggest something of interest to you. . . .I wondered if you had given up entirely your interest in Community or Recreational work. Is there a summer course offered this year—and would you be interested in taking it. I must have your <u>frankest</u> opinion. I would be more happy than I could tell you, when, for your own good, you get on the proper road to be self supporting and independent. I find it a bit disgusting, your reference to clothes for a trip to Europe. At your age and with your intelligence,—well—you should be in a better position. Let me know what you would like to do this summer."[41]

In the end, Marian asked Billy King to make the trip with Mrs. Anderson, offering to pay his fare. Billy agreed but hoped for more. Irritated by Anderson's failure to communicate with Judson, and sensing that his own relationship as accompanist was in jeopardy, he made it clear that he expected to accompany all of her recitals until her return to America. She did not encourage Billy's demands, offering him only the role of companion to Mrs. Anderson: "Expect to remain a year longer. Do not advise giving up business there for engagements here. Will send fare if you can stay six weeks to accompany mother and remain Paris debut May 30."[42] True to his word, Billy prepared to leave with Mrs. Anderson on the *Europa* on the twenty-eighth of April.

Anderson's tour of Scandinavia bears comparison with the tour of America, more than eighty years earlier, of the great Swedish singer Jenny Lind, known affectionately as the "Swedish Nightingale." It was Phineas Barnum, the American entrepreneur and museum owner, who brought Lind to America. Having heard of the furor her singing had caused in Europe, he conceived a plan for an American tour. Unlike Anderson's tour of the Scandinavian countries, which grew from a modest beginning, Lind's tour was conceived at the outset on the grandest scale. Barnum offered to pay Lind up to $1,000 a night per concert, for up to 150 nights, and allowed her to choose up to three musical assistants who would accompany her on the tour.[43]

On the morning of August 28, 1850, Lind, the conductor Julius Benedict and the baritone Giovanni Belletti left Liverpool on the steamship *Atlantic* for New York City. After two preliminary concerts in New York, the official start of the tour took place on September 11, 1850, in Castle Garden at the tip of Manhattan Island. With her servants and secretary (all paid for by Barnum) and her two musical colleagues, Lind set out from New York on September 27 on a tour that would become part of musical legend. By the time of the last concert, in Philadelphia, Lind and her entourage had travelled by train, steamship, and paddlewheel boat as far west as St. Louis and as far south as New Orleans; they had sung to audiences in eighteen cities in the East, Midwest, and South. Altogether, Lind gave ninety-five concerts in six months—on the average, one concert every three days.

While Lind is not a singer who comes generally to mind in any comparison with Anderson, either with respect to voice or repertoire—Lind was a light coloratura soprano who gained her reputation in the bel canto works of Bellini and Donizetti, and the operas of Meyerbeer—the historical connection created by their tours, nearly a century apart, is both irresistible and illuminating. In her tour of Scandinavia, Anderson did not travel the great distances that Lind did, nor did she face the primitive conditions that Lind faced. Yet Anderson's accomplishment was no less daunting. In seven months' time Anderson sang 116 concerts—on the average, one concert every two days. She sang in over sixty cities and towns. All of this grew out of the original modest proposal of twenty concerts. While Lind was already famous in Europe when she arrived in America, Anderson was not really famous anywhere at the time her Scandinavian tour began. Yet, by the end of her tour, she had become the most beloved singer to the Scandinavian people since Jenny Lind herself, gaining enormously in self-confidence and artistic maturity. Her Paris debut, now fixed for the second of May in the Salle Gaveau, Anderson felt ready to conquer the greater European stage.

CHAPTER EIGHT

Fame in Europe
(1934–1935)

Only a small audience attended Anderson's Paris debut. Fritz Horowitz, the French manager whom Enwall had engaged to promote her concerts, had not had sufficient time to publicize the debut of a singer not yet well known outside of Scandinavia. The concert, as Anderson later recalled, "was sold to a woman's club. When I came out with Kosti, some women were seated on the stage. I was a little surprised. There were only a few hundred people in the hall, and there were enough unoccupied seats to accommodate these ladies."[1] It was one of the busiest times of the season. Only two nights before, at the Paris Opera, the dancer Ida Rubinstein had performed in the premiere of Stravinsky's *Perséphone,* a work Rubinstein commissioned from the composer. Aware of her status as a newcomer to the Paris scene, Anderson and Kosti chose not to tempt fate with music that was untried; instead, they emphasized variety of expression: the simple and folksy "Wohin" alongside the grandeur of "Die Allmacht" for the Schubert group; the lyric intensity of Rachmaninoff's "O thou billowy harvest field" in the same group as Chaminade's "L'été," with its sparkling coloratura.

Two days after the concert, *Le Jour,* with the first review to appear, proclaimed the event a triumph:

MARIAN ANDERSON. Don't forget this name, it will be famous before very long in Paris. When I will have told you that Marian Anderson, a black singer, possesses one of the most beautiful contralto voices at present, wonderfully steady, of a timbre both fullbodied and agile, of an astonishing expertness of diction that brings her interpretations intensely to life, it would only remain for me to try to define the indefinable, that is, this strange charm and this succession of fascinations that are radiated by her extraordinary personality . . . The first contact of this young black artist with Paris constitutes a dazzling victory, one that calls for an even greater effect.[2]

Reviews continued to appear for the next several weeks, none less enthusiastic.

Anderson left Paris for London a day or so after the concert. She was unaware of the praise her singing had earned from the Parisian press. Her mother and Billy arrived in London from Dover on the fourth. Five days later, in the Aeolian Hall, Anderson gave her first London recital in five years. Her next concert, a second Paris recital, was not scheduled until May 30, leaving her plenty of time to enjoy a reunion that she had been planning since the Christmas holidays.

The London concert was a joyous occasion for Mrs. Anderson, but frustrating and unsettling for Billy, who was forced to hear Marian and Kosti perform together for the first time. Anderson enjoyed few of the superlatives she had earned in Paris less than two weeks before. The response of the London critics, typically condescending toward artists who strayed in any way from tradition, was, with but one exception, cool and reserved. The *Morning Post,* for example, reported: "This lady—a contralto of coloured extraction, proved herself . . . a singer of merit distinctly above the average. By no means confining herself to the conventional Spirituals, she ventured into the deeper waters of Schubert, Brahms, and Sibelius, the higher classicism of Handel and Scarlatti. As an interpreter she is in no ways remarkable, though quite up to the average, and her sense of color could be developed with advantage. But her breath-control is admirable and her phrasing excellent."[3]

Constant Lambert, writing in the *Sunday Referee,* was the one critic who wrote about Anderson's concert with genuine enthusiasm: "Were I asked to mention the two most outstanding pieces of singing I have heard in recent years I think I should say Conchita Supervia's singing of Joaquin Nin's 'Elegiac Song,' at the Queen Charlotte's Hospital concert on Tuesday and Marian Anderson's singing of Sibelius' 'Die Libelle.' "[4] Lambert, a music journalist of considerable standing, was also a composer of no small repute in Britain, having earned attention in the field of ballet music. Open to a wide range of musical styles, Lambert was naturally enough drawn to Sibelius's music, little of which had yet been heard in Europe. "Die Libelle" ("En slända"), with a text by Oscar Levertin, portrays the bewitching power of the dragonfly's beauty, elusive and impermanent. The vocal line attempts to imitate the sound of the dragonfly at each repetition of the word *slända* ("dragonfly"), broadening melismatically in an effort to portray the flickering of the insect's wings. In its haunting, elusive strangeness it is a difficult song to sing with conviction. Supervia impressed Lambert in a musical style that was part of the Spanish's singer's tradition. Anderson achieved her effect in a style few singers not Scandinavian-born have attempted.

Anderson spent most of May with her mother and Billy in France, acting as guide to the sights around Paris, all three anticipating her second Paris concert on the thirtieth. Happy and encouraged over the success of her debut earlier in the month, she regretted not being able to offer French audiences a group of songs in their own language. In addition to the French arias (from *Samson et Dalila, L'Enfant prodigue,* and *Jeanne D'Arc*) that she had mastered in her student days, and Meyerbeer's "Ah! mon fils," from *Le Prophète,* which she had worked on with Vehanen, Martini's "Plaisir d'amour" and Chaminade's "L'été" were the only French songs she knew. Having suffered the barbs of critics for years over her inexperience in German, she was reluctant to sing any more of the French repertory without serious and sustained work with the right teacher. For the moment, in addition to Handel ("Ombra mai fu," from *Serse*), Mozart (the "Alleluja"), and pairs of songs by Beethoven, Schubert, Strauss, and Sibelius, she decided on Meyerbeer's "Ah! mon fils," which had so thrilled the Scandinavian critics. It proved a fortunate choice, for it had the same powerful effect on Sol Hurok, the American impresario, who was in the audience that evening in the Salle Gaveau.

In later years Hurok loved to tell of his first encounter with Anderson. "In Paris one evening," he later wrote, "I was sitting at a sidewalk café on the Champs-Elysées with my wife—she had begged me to take a night off and sit in the fresh air, instead of going to the concert of a young American contralto I had never heard of. But something told me I should hear that voice, and so I dropped in at the concert, and after the first few notes . . . I knew. . . . After the first part of the concert, I hurried backstage and introduced myself to a young Negro woman . . . who was quite excited when she heard I was coming backstage to see her. Her name? Marian Anderson."[5] Revealing little of how he felt to Anderson, he asked to see her and Vehanen the next day in Horowitz's office.

The truth is that Hurok was not unaware of Anderson. During the early thirties, disillusioned with Judson, Anderson and Billy King had made several unsuccessful attempts to see him. At the time, Hurok was involved in bringing the great European dance companies to America. Not having managed a singer since the early days of his career, he showed little interest in a Judson artist who was then at the low point of her career in the States. Obviously things had changed. How could Hurok fail to be intrigued by this same American singer, now enjoying a sensational success in Paris? Anderson later recalled her meeting with Hurok: "With Kosti I went to Mr. Horowitz's office the next day. I still have a vivid picture of the scene in my mind. Mr. Horowitz sat at one side of his big desk, while Mr. Hurok occupied the chair behind it. Kosti and I took seats in front of it. In those days Mr. Hurok was built along generous lines. . . . I cannot tell you how big and important he seemed to me; Kosti and I felt inadequate in his presence. As Mr. Hurok slowly lifted his cane, which he held at his side, and placed it before him on the desk, his shoulders seemed to broaden. I think that I would have run away if I had dared."[6]

Hurok spoke cautiously at first. He wanted to know how many concerts Judson had been able to offer, and what fees Anderson had received for them. "I might be able to do something for you," he finally said.[7] Then came Hurok's offer. He was willing to guarantee her fifteen concerts with a fee of five hundred dollars per concert. Disappointed for the moment, she eventually took heart, becoming convinced in the end that "he could do something unusual for a performer if he took a notion to do so."[8] Kosti was elated at the offer. "Marian," he said as they reached the street, "the only thing to do now is to have a schnapps and come to life once more."[9] Anderson was still under contract to Judson. For the moment the matter rested.

The excitement of Hurok's offer was muted during the first week of June, a sad week of goodbyes, as Mrs. Anderson and Billy prepared to return to America. As a farewell celebration, Anderson entertained them at Bricktop's café, in the rue Pigalle, the newest and one of the smartest clubs in all of Montmartre.

Anderson gave her third recital in the Salle Gaveau on June 14 to an overflowing audience. Having had more than a month to reconsider their initial verdicts, the Parisian critics were as excited as ever. It was an American writer, the music historian Gilbert Chase, at the time the Paris correspondent for the *London Daily Mail,* frankly astonished at the rapidity and sureness with which Anderson secured her popularity with Parisian audiences, who left the most eloquent account of Marian's first concerts in Paris. "I think it can be safely said," he wrote,

> that Marian Anderson has triumphed through sheer artistry. . . . If genius can be associated with the interpretive, as well as the creative faculty, then Marian Anderson certainly possesses this quality. How

else can one account for the fact that this young coloured singer should be able to give such wonderfully convincing and intensely artistic expression to the sublimest lyrical thoughts of such composers as Beethoven, Schumann and Schubert. When all tangible factors have been taken into consideration, such as the beautiful quality of the voice, with its uniquely moving timbre in the lower register, the perfect steadiness and control of the tone, with its . . . extraordinary range of dynamic shading, the absolute homogeneous nature of the voice . . . and the consummate artistry of the phrasing, there still remain the intangible spiritual factors which make Marian Anderson's singing so utterly satisfying.[10]

Anderson decided not to return home during the summer of 1934. Beginning to feel more secure professionally, feeling less dependent on Judson, she saw more of her future as an artist now under her control. She now had the choice between the businesslike and distant Judson and the flamboyant and imposing Hurok. Because of her European successes and Enwall's plans for the coming year, she was finally able to worry less about her earnings. There had never been a time when Anderson did not keep a detailed record of expenditures and income, unsure of her ability to earn enough money to support herself and her family. Now she felt that she could permit herself the occasional thrill of reckless shopping, for clothes, presents, jewelry, and decorations for her home. "My total earnings were the highest of my career," she later wrote. "I sent money home to my family. I bought new evening dresses and clothes for street wear. I purchased a great deal of music, and for the first time I could indulge in the luxury of having it bound in leather. I bought luggage, and gifts for friends, including Mr. and Mrs. Enwall."[11]

By the middle of June, Anderson had resolved to end her relationship with Judson and to sign with Hurok. On June 20, three weeks after her meeting with Hurok, she wrote to Judson, telling him "it is impossible for me to continue working under our former conditions."[12] Judson, thinking the matter over carefully, wrote to Anderson in mid-July that "it will be impossible for us to offer you a different contract than the one we have with you. . . ." Furthermore, Judson explained, ". . . if you have any thought about our offering a guarantee, that would be entirely out of the question, as we are not offering guarantees to our artists."[13] Taking Judson's response as tantamount to a release from her contract, she wrote him a few days later that she "must accept other propositions."[14]

Acting quickly and without advice, ignoring possible legal problems in obtaining a release from her contract with Judson, Anderson was following her instincts. In haste to free herself from the Judson agency, she had not consulted Billy about her decision. Learning about it from the Judson people, Billy began to realize how little say he now had in Anderson's future. Hurt, suspicious, angry at the influence that others, especially Kosti, might be having on her, he urged her to reconsider. "A wrong step at this time," he wrote to her in early July, "will spoil everything. I have noted what you said about the letter to Judson asking what he could offer, if you will remember that is just the thing I asked you not to do for the present time. . . . For God's sake Marian please be a woman and be stable in mind and realize that none of these people who surround you know conditions in America like you do."[15] Having always had more faith in Judson than Anderson, he still believed that Judson was the lifeline connecting him to Anderson's future. For once, she was acting more boldly than Billy and this frightened him. "Suppose by any chance," he wrote to her, "you should jump over to another Management then Concert Management Arthur Judson step in and collect a twenty per cent commission on all those concerts that you sing in America in that period. Be careful Marian you are on dangerous ground. This can be done. I know that much about law."[16] As it turned out Judson did not place any barriers on Anderson's signing with another management. Only days before the start of the fall season, Anderson instructed her attorney, Hubert Delany, to prepare a legally binding contract with Hurok.

To judge from her letters home, Anderson became more positive and encouraging to her family now that the decision to sign with Hurok had been made. Although still concerned about Alyse's future, she was less carping, less likely to treat her as a disappointing child. Trusting in education, as always, she suggested to Alyse that she enroll in a social service course at the University of Pennsylvania, agreeing to pay for the tuition if Alyse would make another attempt in the fall to find a job. Reflecting on how she herself had, perhaps, contributed to some of Alyse's problems, she shared her thoughts with Mrs. Anderson: "About Maude and school, I felt that if she could be awakened somehow, contact other people who were trying to become somebody, perhaps she might get the bug. Her letter was very interesting and I am not surprised that she received an E in her exams. With her brain it is an absolute sin, that she lets it sleep so long. Some of her failure is my fault because in my effort to be fair, she was indulged. . . ."[17] Feeling grateful about how much easier her own life was becoming, Anderson wanted nothing more than to ease the way for her family. Ethel, too, was on her mind. "I wondered," she wrote to her mother, "if Ethel would have the time to study with Harvey [Harvey Hebron, who had taught Anderson piano] again. When you wrote that she was studying [voice], I said (Well—how fine.) Now then I'd like to help her a bit with her lesson fees, but I'll write her about it later."[18]

In the end it was her mother who caused Marian the greatest concern. Having decided to remain in Europe indefinitely, for the first time without any clear idea when she would see her mother again, Anderson felt a desperate need to retain control of her welfare. "The thing that I am most interested in," she wrote to her mother, "is—how quiet and still are you keeping in this hot weather. . . . All washing, all ironing, all cooking <u>must</u> be taken out of your program until the weather is cool: then you may resume cooking, but not washing and ironing. Do you understand Mother dear, that I <u>do not want you to do these things</u>. . . . <u>Don't under any circumstances do this yourself.</u> I know you—that's why I write this way. You used to do such things when my back was turned."[19]

It was hard after so long a period away from home for Anderson to feel satisfied that she was doing enough where her family was concerned. Nonetheless, she allowed herself a period of relaxation, spending the whole of July on holiday—the first weeks in Stockholm, which had become a second home for her, the last weeks with the Enwalls at their summer home. As she reported to her mother in August, those weeks with the Enwalls went a long way in giving her needed rest and relaxation: "It was marvelous including hay rides, picnics, motor boat racing—fishing—auto tours, crab suppers and killing snake—<u>too</u> bad it was."[20]

In August, looking ahead to the long fall tour, Anderson began to think about ways of enlarging her repertoire. Opera was on her mind, especially the role of Amneris. She went so far as to take some lessons with Tullio Voghera in Stockholm. Voghera, who had studied in Bologna and Padua, spent his entire career in the field of opera, acting first as an assistant to Toscanini at the Metropolitan Opera. He spent most of his career at the Stockholm Opera, first as conductor and later as chorus master and *répétiteur.* Over the years he accompanied and coached many singers, including Caruso and Björling. She also wrote to her friend Madame Cahier. They arranged for Anderson to travel to Germany during the second half of August, when Cahier would be able to work with her. With Cahier she worked on songs from Mahler's Rückert lieder ("Liebst du um Schönheit"), the *Knaben Wunderhorn* ("Urlicht" and "Rheinlegendchen"), and the whole of the *Kindertotenlieder.*

The new season began on the fifth of September, with a pair of concerts in Göteborg. September and October followed the pattern of the previous year, with concerts in all four of the Scandinavian countries, in the capitals as well as smaller towns. The schedule was again strenuous, with fifteen concerts in September and twenty concerts in October, although Anderson and Kosti, this time, began to travel by plane between engagements. Although air travel became more and more frequent in Europe during the early thirties, Anderson had never been very eager to fly. She had flown for the first time, in fact, only the previous November, from Stockholm to Helsinki. The flight had made her slightly airsick, but the sight of the clouds beneath the plane as it rose higher up into the sky, the dark shadow of the plane visible against the white clouds, moved her deeply. Kosti remembered her words at the sight of the small shadow as it darkened the clouds: "Now I understand, if the good Lord doesn't like to behold the misery on the earth, he takes the clouds and covers it from His sight; but where human beings dwell there is always a dark shadow."[21]

September was spent for the most part in Norway, where Anderson sang in Oslo, Bergen, Fredrikstad, Drammen, Hamar and Trondheim. She wrote to her mother soon after the Norwegian tour with new instructions, still compulsively managerial:

> For every so many years I have been wanting eiderdown comforts for us but found them much too expensive for my purse. When Ethel received two as wedding gifts, and Maude shortly before or after, made herself a present of one, you and I were the only members of the family without. In Norway, a centre for such things, one finds comforts very, very reasonable: so I bot four and had them sent to you. The duty will be less than fifty dollars and I shall send you the money as soon as you let me know how much the cost was. As for directions, I will ask you to buy also an inexpensive box or suitcase where these comforts may be kept without being too tightly pressed together. At the beginning of the cold weather, you <u>must</u> take one out for your bed. Measure the comfort and then buy some washable material and have Ethel make a cover for it: a sort of bag or sack sewed up on three sides. There should be at least two washable covers and one rather swanky one made of a better material. That is left entirely to you. The other three comforts I want kept stored away until I come home.[22]

In October there were concerts in Sweden, Finland, and Denmark, including two in Copenhagen. The weeks in Sweden and Finland especially were a veritable homecoming, with visits to old friends. Sibelius himself came to Anderson's first concert in Helsinki, on October 7, in many ways the artistic highlight of the season. She sang a group of four Sibelius songs, including "Schwarze Rosen," "Die stille Stadt," and, for the first time in Swedish, "En slända" and "Norden." Anderson's heightened identification with Sibelius's music was not lost on the critics. "A still greater interest," one of the Finnish critics wrote, "was called forth by the four Sibelius songs, the singer giving two of them in the original language. . . . It is surprising and praiseworthy in a singer coming from altogether different worlds, so to say, that she can go so deep into the compositions of a Finnish composer, so familiarize herself with them and make their musical style her own. Even from our own point of view these interpretations left not the least thing to be desired; they were ideal. And yet there were among the songs some of the most difficult, and therefore so seldom sung ones. The quiet feeling of longing in the German song "Die stille Stadt" I have never heard with such a warm and natural interpretation."[23]

The weeks in Finland proved to be the most exciting ones of the entire Scandinavian season for Anderson. She was especially charmed and intrigued by life in the Finnish countryside. From Viborg, she wrote to her mother: "The women come with their carts of vegetables, fruit, fish, clothing and what not. They remain to sell their wares from eight in the morning until noon and during those four hours the town square belongs to them. They are dressed alike in white Hoover aprons and white scarves tied around their heads. Most of them have high yellow boots with a funny hook in the front. . . . It was to me, of course, rather strange to see women struggling with these huge push carts."[24] In Jyvaskila, in the heart of Finland, Anderson gave a concert in the largest church in the town. While rehearsing there, Anderson and Kosti were told that Svinhufvud, the president of Finland, and his party, inspecting munitions plants nearby, had been attracted to the sound of singing and had come into the church to listen. Embarrassed that she was wearing only a rehearsal dress, Anderson refused at first to meet the president. Aware of the publicity such a meeting would provide, Kosti was adamant. A few days later, back again in Helsinki, Kosti saw another opportunity for publicity. The newly elected Miss Europe, a Finnish girl, was being honored with a dance in the hotel where Anderson and Kosti were staying. "Kosti wanted to telephone to a newspaper," Anderson later recalled, "and arrange that we be photographed together, and only gave up the idea when I threatened to go to my room."[25]

Only Billy's letters, now more frequent and emotionally charged than ever, threw a shadow over the sold-out houses and enthusiastic audiences greeting her everywhere. By October, the full impact of Anderson's signing with Hurok was weighing heavily on Billy. A contract with Hurok, he now realized, meant that Kosti would continue as Anderson's accompanist in America. What Hurok wanted, in fact, was the partnership that he had heard in Paris. Anderson was still thinking it feasible to use Billy as her accompanist for concerts in the South under Negro auspices, but both must have realized how impractical such a division of labor would become. Full of hurt and wounded pride, Billy wrote to her on the eleventh: "I want to share the success you are having in those wonderful places. I want the experience. You owe nothing to Kosti, they all owe everything to you. Can you imagine how I felt when I saw him at the piano in London and in Paris, then read of the wonderful success you had in Geneva. Does that all belong to him? If so why?"[26]

Believing he was about to lose a relationship whose emotional satisfactions had always been as important as artistic ones, he took on the role of spurned lover, a characteristic role for him in periods of emotional crisis with her: "I do not like to be neglected and no one knows that better than you, and why sometimes you seem to forget that I live, I cannot understand. Remember I still hold the same feeling for you whether we are three feet apart or whether we are three thousand miles apart. Get wise to yourself, the only way to keep a fire burning is to keep putting fuel on it, this distance between us is about getting my goat and if you put this much space between us again for any length of time I shall be convinced that you no longer care. . . ." [27] And more in the same vein: "Went down to your home Sunday night after church and had quite a chat with Mrs. Anderson, she seemed so pleased that I had heard directly from you. Oh, if you only cared as much as she. I think in the long run I shall propose to Mrs. Anderson. I feel I will get far more consideration than if I proposed to you, then I will be your Father, and would turn you up and spank your bottom whenever you needed it."[28]

Fanning the flames of Billy's emotional ordeal was the fact that Anderson sent him only the briefest occasional word of her plans. She too saw that her partnership with Kosti would cause a rupture in their relationship that might never be repaired. Kosti was the more experienced musician. They had worked together in hundreds of concerts, building up an artistic understanding and repertory that exceeded Billy's competence. What she might have accomplished by writing openly and honestly to Billy about her plans to bring Kosti back to America with her is hard to say. In the midst of concerts that stretched months into the future, backing away from emotional confrontations, she kept Billy in the dark about her plans.

In November, Anderson left Finland for concerts in the Hague and Amsterdam as well as three recitals in Paris, the first of the season outside of Scandinavia. During the weeks before Christmas, there were concerts in Holland, Switzerland, France and Belgium. While in Scandinavia, Anderson had had few opportunities to work with important conductors; on the Continent, she appeared for the first time with some of the leading European maestros of the day. In Geneva and Lausanne she sang with Ansermet; in Paris, with Monteux; and in Monte Carlo, with Emil Cooper. Although excited by the artistic prospects of such collaborations, Anderson did not find the shift from recitalist to orchestral soloist an easy one. Artistically, she felt most secure with the mutual artistic understanding built up over years of work with the same accompanist. As Kosti later wrote:

> Anderson dislikes working with people new to her, because she is hesitant about explaining to others how she wants to interpret a song and is reluctant to insist that a song shall be interpreted in her way. Often, in singing with orchestras, Miss Anderson has found that the conductor's idea of the interpretation differs considerably from hers. Because of the short time available for rehearsals, it has not always been easy for her to make clear to him her conception, and for that reason she has not always been satisfied with the results.[29]

Among those conductors with whom she sang, her experiences with Monteux were the most satisfying. His return to America a few years later to conduct the San Francisco Symphony Orchestra would coincide with Anderson's, giving them years of opportunity to forge a strong musical relationship.

Anderson sang her last concert before Christmas in the Hague. She had only ten days of holiday, which she spent with the Enwalls in Stockholm, where she gave a single concert on January 5. The following day, Anderson and Kosti left Finland for the Soviet Union, on a journey that both felt would be one of their great European adventures. They entered the Soviet Union by train, bound for Leningrad, across "a small river," as Kosti remembered, "over which was thrown a narrow bridge with a single railroad track. The first half of the bridge that belonged to Finland was painted white; the other half was painted red—the first sign of soviet Russia."[30] Both Anderson and Kosti were excited, though with some trepidation, to see a country that was, in Kosti's words, "to the outside world a big question mark."[31] Kosti had, in fact, visited Leningrad and

Moscow on concert tours in prerevolutionary days, and was particularly anxious "to see the change that had taken place in this huge, mysterious, half-Oriental country under the soviets."[32]

They had their first experience of the new regime at the border, at the custom house, where the train was held up for half an hour while the two were questioned exhaustively about the small phonograph and records which the authorities had found among Anderson's baggage. She liked to travel with these, which she enjoyed listening to in her hotel room. Unknown to her, only a few days before her arrival in the Soviet Union, a number of prominent Soviet radio officials and announcers had been removed from their posts for allowing the broadcast of a recording of the spiritual "Steal Away to Jesus," by Paul Robeson, who was then near the end of his two-week visit to the Soviet Union. Kerzhertseff, chairman of the All-Soviet Broadcasting Committee, had been forced to publish a public apology for allowing the broadcast of a song with obvious religious content. According to Kosti, the border guards, apparently suspicious of a black singer traveling with recordings of her own, went so far as to listen to them before allowing the train to continue.

In Leningrad, Anderson and Kosti stayed at the Europa, a large and luxurious hotel built during the time of the czars. "Silk draperies were much in evidence," Kosti remembered, "and large vases of French and German origin were everywhere. After a few days, several of the valuable, pretty vases and other things disappeared, probably to be used to adorn the suite of a new guest. The plumbing, alas, was in direct contrast to these lavish appointments. Bathroom facilities were seldom in working order."[33]

The first recital, on the seventh, was entirely sold out. Anderson made sure to include a group of songs by Russian composers: "If I had only known," by Tchaikovsky, Tcherepnin's "A Kiss," and Rachmaninoff's "O thou billowy harvest field." On making her way onto the stage, Anderson noticed a microphone near where she was to stand. Remembering that her contract stated that none of her concerts in Russia was to be broadcast, she was concerned enough to ask Kosti, while they stood offstage after the first group of songs, what to do about the microphone. "The woman interpreter," as Kosti recalled, "hearing what she said, wrinkled her brow and said in a decisive tone, 'In Russia, one does not ask questions.' "[34]

The four concerts in Leningrad, one an appearance with orchestra, were all sold out. Anderson and Kosti took advantage of the days between concerts to see as much of the city as they could before leaving for Moscow. Many of the sights that Kosti remembered from his travels during the czarist years—Tsarskoe-Selo, for example, the former czar's palace—had been turned into vehicles of propaganda by the Bolsheviks. The greatest disappointment for Kosti was the Isaac Cathedral, the largest in Leningrad. Under the high cupola there had been hung, as Kosti recorded, "paintings of Russian homes before and after the revolution, comparing the prerevolutionary squalor and drunkenness with the improvements of the new age, comforts such as books, luxurious chairs, and, of course, the steaming samovar instead of vodka bottles."[35] Only the enormous palace of Catherine the Great retained a portion of its original splendor; there, for example, visitors could still see the tiny bedroom of the last czar and czarina, with its countless icons, some of them gifts from Rasputin.

On January 15, Anderson and Kosti left by train for Moscow, where the first of three concerts in the Russian capital was scheduled for that evening in the Great Hall of the Moscow Conservatory. Excitement ran high after Anderson's four sold-out concerts in Leningrad, especially among Russian musicians and singers who, aside from recordings, had had little opportunity to hear Western singers. Within the black community, a small but close-knit group in Moscow, Anderson's visit had aroused extraordinary anticipation. Indeed, some in the black community had formed a small welcoming committee, ready to greet Anderson as her train pulled into the station. The group included Wayland Rudd, a black actor who had come to the Soviet Union in 1932 to take part in *Black and White,* a motion picture dramatizing the American race problem. Another was the singer Coretta Arli-Titz. Unlike Rudd, Arli-Titz was one of the few blacks in the American colony in Moscow who had come to Russia not after the revolution but during czarist times. She was married to Boris Arli-Titz, another musician, whom she had met while a student at the Imperial Conservatory in St. Petersburg. The couple remained in the Soviet Union, with Coretta, along with Ella Ross, another expatriate black singer, both helping to keep the music of black Americans before the Russian public.[36]

Anderson sang three recitals in Moscow, on the fifteenth, nineteenth, and twentieth. She had been warned before leaving for Russia that she could expect trouble if she insisted on singing spirituals—indeed, any music with religious content. She was, however, determined not to alter the character of her programs, which meant keeping groups of spirituals on every program, and occasionally Schubert's "Ave Maria" as well. Nor was she inclined to set judicious limits on those spirituals which she chose to sing. She did not restrict herself to work songs like Boatner's

"Trampin'" or Robinson's "Water Boy," spirituals usually interpreted as protest songs against the treatment of the Negro race, or as songs extolling the character and virtues of the slaves. In her first Moscow concert, Anderson sang Burleigh's "Heav'n, Heav'n" and Hayes's "Lord, I Can't Stay Away," and on the nineteenth, she sang Payne's "Crucifixion." To sing "Crucifixion" took more than a small amount of courage. In the entire repertory of spirituals, there is hardly a more vivid and moving musical depiction of the death of Christ than Payne's celebrated arrangement.

Audiences had always responded enthusiastically and spontaneously to Anderson's performances of spirituals. In Russia, from the first concert in Leningrad, the response took on an intensity bordering on frenzy. As Anderson recalled later: "Half the audience—the half that had sat in the rear of the house—had rushed down the aisles and had formed a thick phalanx around the stage. Those nearest the stage were pounding on the board floor with their fists. Deep voices were roaring in Russian accents, 'Deep River' and 'Heaven, Heaven.' " We did several encores with the throng almost underfoot. It was disconcerting for a few moments, but how could one resist such enthusiasm?"[37] There were similar demonstrations at every concert. It mattered little whether the Russian interpreter present for each concert could capture the full meaning of the words of the spirituals. Once the audiences heard Anderson sing, they could not fail to be moved by these songs of an oppressed people. The first of Stalin's purges had begun the previous year, and had intensified in December with the assassination of the Leningrad dictator Alexander Kirov. Stalin was, for the moment, concentrating his terror among technicians, factory workers, and scientists. Fear and suspicion were already widespread. Russian audiences heard in Anderson's singing the struggles of their own lives.

Anderson's performances brought no official reprisals, in contrast to the reaction to Robeson's broadcast. The explanation for the difference in the official response lies, ironically, in Robeson's sympathies with the Soviet state. These sympathies were well-known to the Soviets. Indeed, on his arrival in the Soviet Union, Robeson told interviewers that he had come there "to study the national minority policy as it operates among the peoples of Central Asia."[38] As a black man of international prestige sympathetic to Soviet ideology, Robeson was a figure of considerable propagandistic importance to the Soviets. The ideological confusion created by his singing of a Negro spiritual with as strong a religious character as "Steal Away to Jesus" could prove awkward and embarrassing. Unlike Robeson, Anderson had no ideological purpose in coming to the

Soviet Union. Robeson was outspoken, ideologically engaged, ready to take a strong position whatever the consequences. Anderson was not. She remained moderate and self-composed, expressing sympathy without censure, hopefulness without blame. Anderson's performances of spirituals were the expression of a woman with strong religious beliefs, of a singer expressing the feelings and aspirations of her people. References to Anderson as a distinctly black singer began and ended for the most part with her art, not her politics.

Robeson moved like a colossus around Moscow, interested in everything and everyone. He sought out members of the black community eager to hear about how they were treated; he met with members of other minorities; he visited schools and factories; and all the time he talked, discussed, and argued—with Eisenstein, with the theater director Alexander Tairov, with the film director Pudovkin.[39] With Anderson it was altogether different. Her singing was her focus, and it was the unique character of her singing that made her an object of curiosity and intense interest. Shostakovitch came to meet her during the intermission of one of her recitals. The composer Ippolitov-Ivanov, only days away from the end of his life, invited Anderson and Kosti to a huge banquet at his home. The great coloratura soprano Nezhdanova, intrigued with the unusual range and timbre of Anderson's voice and style of singing, so different from the quality of Russian altos, came to all of her recitals in Moscow. Even Stalin, so the rumor went, hidden behind a curtain in one of the boxes of the theater, attended one of Anderson's recitals.

On the afternoon of the twenty-first, Anderson and Kosti were invited by Stanislavsky, the renowned theater director, to visit his studio, in those years part of Stanislavsky's apartment on L. Street. The two, as Kosti later remembered, "were ushered into his dimly lighted dining room, where tea was served in typical Russian fashion from the large samovar. At first [they] sat talking with his two sisters. Suddenly a side door opened, and the famous man entered."[40] Stanislavsky was then seventy-two years old. In spite of declining health—he had only three years to live—he was then embarked on the formation of the Opera-Dramatic Studio, his last attempt to create a milieu designed for the transmission of his artistic legacy. Kosti remembered Stanislavsky's first appearance as he entered the dining room of his house: "I have not often seen such an aristocratic-looking gentleman. He was elderly, very tall, and his whole being showed great refinement. He had a clear voice, and his French was as good as a Parisian's."[41] Stanislavsky had arranged for some of his students to present a small scene for his visitors, and Anderson and Kosti were asked to perform for the assembled group, which contained, as

Anderson later remembered, "many important people in Russia's artistic life."[42]

As the evening progressed, Stanislavsky drew Anderson aside and, with the help of an interpreter, asked her if she had any interest in singing in opera, and whether or not she would be interested in studying Carmen with him. It was an unusual request. When Anderson began to think about the proposal, she felt herself inadequate to the dramatic demands of the role, doubting whether she was up to the required dancing. Anderson did have the card scene, in the last act of Bizet's opera, in her repertoire but that aria requires a concentrated and nearly motionless intensity as Carmen begins to read her own fate in the cards to her Gypsy friends. No one acquainted with Anderson or her singing would easily have imagined her capable of the erotic allure of the opera's first act.

Carmen was, in fact, much on Stanislavsky's mind at that time. He had been working for months on a production of the opera, experiencing great frustration and difficulty with his students.[43] No doubt the idea of a black Carmen intrigued him. He could develop the theme of Carmen as social outcast, as a woman scorned, as a figure barely tolerated in a social milieu to which she could not hope to belong. Stanislavsky must have been struck by the powerfully vivid attention Anderson gave to the texts of everything she sang, a skill that he never tired of trying to instill in his students. Stanislavsky was above all a shrewd and perceptive judge of character. He must have sensed Anderson's iron will and singleness of purpose beneath her self-composed and gentle exterior. He must have felt the mystery and fascination engendered by Anderson's emotional restraint. It remained a collaboration for the imagination alone. "I told Stanislavsky," Anderson later wrote, "that I would be interested, but time passed too quickly. I did not return to Russia. Stanislavsky died. I lost an invaluable opportunity, and I have so regretted it. It would have been wise to grasp that opportunity even at the expense of postponing the tour."[44]

On the twenty-second, Anderson left by train for Riga, where she was to give three concerts. Stanislavsky had the last word of farewell. In her sleeping car, he had had placed a basket of white lilacs. The tour continued unabated throughout the winter and spring. In February, there were concerts throughout Eastern Europe, with debuts in Warsaw, Vienna, Prague, and Budapest. In early April, Anderson sang for the first time with the conductor Dimitri Mitropoulos in Monte Carlo. Mitropoulos had not yet conducted in America, but his permanent move there in 1937, when he took up the leadership of the Minneapolis Symphony Orchestra, coincided with the beginning of Anderson's fame in the

States. Mitropoulos, together with Monteux, understood and admired Anderson's singing perhaps more so than any other American conductors, and they encouraged her and performed with her for most of her American career.

Later in the month Anderson gave a series of concerts in Italy, including performances in Turin, Rome, Trieste, Venice, and Milan. In Rome the Crown Princess Marie José and her party attended Marian's recital on the thirteenth in the Santa Cecilia Hall, and invited her and Kosti to a tea the following afternoon in the Quirinal Palace, where they were asked to perform for the crown princess along with her family and guests.

A second tour of the Soviet Union began on the sixteenth of May, extended this time to five concerts in Leningrad and six in Moscow, the latter including three appearances with the Moscow Philharmonic Orchestra. The unique qualities of Anderson's voice and art continued to fascinate the Russians. They even considered it important to preserve a record of her singing, especially (as at least one Soviet writer pointed out) as an example for the young people of the Soviet Union. In propagandistic terms, Anderson was an American Negro artist who, in the face of racial prejudice and injustice, had cultivated the art of singing in ways that never compromised her cultural or racial identity. Anderson agreed to record four sides for the state gramophone company, including two songs that she often sang as encores, "The Cuckoo" and Chaminade's "L'été," and two spirituals, surprisingly enough approved by the arts board of the factory, Robinson's "Watercarrier" and Burleigh's "Trampin.'" During the few days off in Moscow before leaving for Leningrad, Anderson and Kosti went to the recording studio in October Hall for the first session on the twenty-third.[45]

Anderson sang her last recital in the Soviet Union in Leningrad, on June 5. in gratitude for her concerts, she was invited by the Soviet government to spend several weeks' vacation in July in the resort town of Kislovodsk. In the meantime there were concert engagements in the Ukraine, Georgia, and Azerbaijan. The long journey southward, which would take them as faraway as Baku, grew into one of the unforgettable adventures of Anderson's life. In Moscow, which was to be the start of the journey, Anderson and Kosti were joined by the Enwalls, who had planned to accompany them part of the way, and a Mr. Tolchinsky, "a small, friendly man who spoke a kind of German-Jewish dialect,"[46] who was to act as a guide for the travelers. They set out by train for Kharkov, crossing the Russian frontier into eastern Ukraine from the border town of Belgorod. There was a single concert in Kharkov on the eighth, and from there the party traveled across the Ukraine to Odessa, passing through "a land of fertile fields and golden wheat."[47] As they neared the Black Sea the weather became warmer, and the train seemed to pass through a dark cloud of dust. Anderson gave two recitals in Odessa before the Enwalls had to return home to Sweden. With the ever-vigilant Mr. Toll (Tolchinsky) in attendance (his name was progressively shortened as the party traveled south), Anderson and Kosti spent several days as tourists, attending the Odessa Opera one evening and, another evening, listening to a jazz orchestra that played in the dining room of their hotel.

The concerts in Kharkov and Odessa drew large and enthusiastic audiences, but they became nearly incidental to the breathtaking scenery and days of magnificent warm weather—June had marked the official opening of the bathing season in the famous resorts along the Black Sea—as Anderson and Kosti enjoyed a much needed period of rest. They were approaching the end of ten months of concerts, the longest and most arduous tour Anderson was ever to make in Europe, having sung, by the end of June, 123 concerts in fifteen countries. The journey by steamer across the Black Sea to Tiflis was leisurely enough to provide a few additional days of restfulness and quiet.

In Odessa their steamer had been delayed for several hours waiting for the arrival of Postichov, the dictator of the Ukraine, who was to make the journey with the other passengers as far as Yalta. Postichov was said to be the most feared man in the Soviet Union after Stalin. On board, Anderson and Kosti were informed by Toll that Postichov would like to hear Anderson sing, and that arrangements had already been made for her to sing a short program of songs in the salon of the steamer. There was no thought of refusing. Anderson and Kosti were ushered into the large salon where Postichov and his staff were waiting. Postichov's "blond hair was standing straight up," Kosti remembered, "his lips were thin and cruel-looking, his blue eyes seemed to bore through us."[48] The short concert over, Postichov seemed bored and tired, leaving the salon without saying anything. Later in the day, after he had left the steamer at Yalta, Anderson received a telegram from Postichov thanking her for singing for him.

Anderson and Kosti remained the entire day in the harbor at Yalta, sitting out on the quiet deck, watching the dolphins as they played around the steamer, and enjoying the famous Crimean wines. From Yalta, the steamer made its way south along the eastern rim of the Black Sea, passing the snow-covered Caucasus that divided Europe from Asia. For Anderson and Kosti, the steamer journey ended in Batum, where they stepped down onto Asian soil, rested and ready once again for strenuous traveling. They could not have known how strenuous those last days would be.

The difficulties began once Toll was forced to return to Moscow and a second guide failed to show up. Without the benefit of an interpreter, Anderson and Kosti were forced to travel alone to Tiflis, where two concerts were scheduled. When the concerts were postponed for two days, they took the time to enjoy the famous sulfur baths and the gray caviar. The end of the tour was scheduled for the famous oil city of Baku, near the eastern coast of Azerbaijan, on the Caspian Sea. To reach Baku, Anderson and Kosti continued their journey by plane. "Once more we had a nerve-racking experience," Kosti remembered, "when a bad storm broke and forced us to make an emergency landing. Marian and I sat on the ground of the desert for hours until our plane was able to fly again. We had to go through still another storm before we caught a glimpse of the Caspian Sea, with its rough waves dashing high."[49] They landed in deep mud, which came up to their knees as they struggled to reach the tiny waiting room that they found dirty and infested with flies.

The journey to Kislovodsk was another nightmare. There was no car to be had, Anderson and Kosti having to travel in a large truck overcrowded with passengers, all making their way northward across the Caucasus. By evening they reached the city of Vladikavskas, still without a guide. The plane that was to take them to Kislovodsk the next morning did not arrive. The roads, lacking proper drainage, were in a terrible condition after three days of steady rain. Anderson and Kosti were finally able to make arrangements for a private plane, which they shared with another passenger, who ruined the inspiring view of the Caucasus by asking the pilot to entertain the passengers with stunts in the air. By the time the plane arrived, Anderson was so sick she could barely walk. The only conveyance that could take them to Kislovodsk was, as Kosti recalled, "a horse-drawn wagon with a flat bottom and no springs. We put our luggage in the center of the wagon, and Anderson and I sat on either side, with our feet dangling down."[50] "By the time we reached our destination," Anderson recalled in later years, "I wished we had never started; in fact, I wished by then that I had never journeyed so far from home."[51]

Kislovodsk is one of five towns in the region of the central Caucasus, its landscape studded with mineral springs whose carbonic waters have attracted visitors since the end of the eighteenth century. The towns are dotted with sanatoria where the healthy have always outnumbered the ailing. For Russians and foreign travelers alike, the Caucasian Mineral

Waters, as the area is known in Russian, has always been a favorite resort area. The atmosphere is relaxed and friendly, the air fresh, the parks and mountainous areas perfect for walks and hiking. Kislovodsk is the farthest east of the five towns, hillier, greener and higher than Piatigorsk, the capital of the spa region. In their remote yet idyllic atmosphere, away from the turmoil of city life, the resorts have always inspired romance. The formally elegant parks and gracious spa buildings recall the time when, in the nineteenth century, fashionable Moscow and St. Petersburg society trekked to the spa region to be seen, to attend balls, and to preside over anticipated courtships.

Anderson and Kosti spent nearly two weeks in the serenity of Kislovodsk. Judging from their recollections, they seem to have been strangely unmoved by the famous resort town. About her "fantastic trip to Kislovodsk," Anderson mentioned nothing more than the nerve-racking journey and the confusion and annoyance over accommodations. Curiously detached, no more than brusquely informative, Kosti later reported that the two did some hiking and took the baths "in the Narzan mineral water, which seems to have curative values and which gave [Anderson] renewed energy for continuing her concerts when we returned to Moscow."[52] Both choosing discretion, neither mentioned another of the vacationers, Emanuel Kaminka, who was also on holiday in Kislovodsk. Already well-known in Russia as a reciter, Kaminka, a Russian Jew, was born in the Ukraine. He had trained as an actor in Kharkov, in the studio attached to the Theater Sinelnikov, where he earned his living for several years as an actor. In 1930 he gave up acting altogether and concentrated on solo readings, giving his first performance as a reciter in the small hall of the Moscow Conservatory. Excelling in the satiric genre, Kaminka included among his favorite authors Gogol, Chekhov, Twain, Pushkin, and Sholom Aleichem. He was one of the first artists to introduce the works of the great Yiddish writer to Russian audiences.[53]

Enjoying a brief respite from the demands of career, together in an enchanted world where love affairs blossomed easily, Anderson and Kaminka were immediately drawn to each other. They had much in common. There was nothing about Kaminka's appearance or personality that suggested in the least the flamboyant man of the theater. He was short and slight in size, always wore glasses, and was always elegantly dressed. His shyness, his kind and attentive interest in people, and genuine compassion for those who suffered, which everyone who knew him remarked on, made him sympathetic to Anderson. So did his artistic beliefs. On the stage Kaminka's gestures were economical yet expressive. Without artifice, without false rhetoric or overplaying, Kaminka drew his characters as if he himself were experiencing their emotions. Near enough in age (Kaminka was Anderson's junior by five years), both having recently earned a certain measure of fame after years of difficult apprenticeship, they could understand each other (though they could converse only in German), confide in each other, and discuss their aspirations.

For Kaminka their time together was all too brief, circumscribed by Anderson's determination not to allow amorous entanglements to interfere with her professional ambitions. Anderson left Kislovodsk for Moscow on the thirteenth. Kaminka wrote to her the next morning, then nearly every day, sometimes two and three times a day, until the end of the month, when he too returned to Moscow. Kaminka's letters form an emotional curve—from recollection, to painful acknowledgment of loss, to bitterness and finally acceptance. They are as rhetorically effective as one of the stories Kaminka might have read, yet the pleading, frustrated discontent that fills their pages stikes one as sincere—the brief record of a man desperately in love with Anderson, holding on to the hope they would one day see each other again.[54]

On July 14, the day after her departure, Kaminka wrote: "My love, sweet, good, beautiful Marian! Last night I came back from [my] concert and I was so sad, so sad. . . . I went out onto the balcony, I wanted to tap at your window (as I always did) I wanted so strongly to see you, but . . . but you have gone off, and I am alone. . . . You cannot imagine how sad it was for me. Twelve hours after we last spoke I said to myself a thousand times: 'Love, sweet, good [Marian], near yet far. Marian! How much I love you!' . . . . The whole night I dreamed: 'Marian!' Everything that once was has once again passed me by."

Sure of his own feelings, he was less sure of hers. "Where are you now my love?" he wrote to her on the fifteenth, "How do you feel? Do you remember everything that happened between us? . . . . Do you feel me as I feel you? My sweet! Do you remember how we were together all day long, and now I am alone. . . . What will I do today? Go to breakfast without Marian? Go off to the Narzan baths without Marian? Is this life? No, no, no! . . . ." Again on the eighteenth, with still no word from Anderson: "Have you no desire to write to me? Have you forgotten those sweet kisses? Did you not say to me the words " 'My love.' " Reiterating a plan he must have urged on Anderson many times while they were together, he wrote a few days later: "My love, if you love me, come to me. You will have a vacation. It is not so expensive, not so much money. Come to me. Come to Russia to spend your vacation. . . ." Her future as a singer more secure now than any time in the past, Anderson was still not ready for personal matters to take precedence over professional ones. In one of his last letters to Anderson, Kaminka found it difficult to suppress the bitterness he felt over her coldhearted dedication to professional concerns: "I will have a holiday soon, one or two months . . . and I will be better off spending it with my love! What is money without happiness. No! I will not write more about this. Every child knows it. . . . Only Marian doesn't."

With no word from Anderson, Kaminka gave up writing to her toward the end of July. Anderson returned to the Soviet Union the following year for another series of concerts but there is no record of them having seen each other again. Kaminka died in 1972, from all accounts having lived an artistically satisfying life. In spite of his Jewish background, he somehow survived Stalin's purges and, in the 1950s, he was honored as an Artist of the People. Did Anderson ever speak about Kaminka, confide to anyone about him? In her recollections, interviews, and letters, his name never appears. There are only his letters, which Anderson kept all of her life, and some slips of paper on which Kaminka's name is written out, in large, Cyrillic characters.

In the weeks that followed her departure from Kislovodsk, Anderson's thoughts turned to the Salzburg Festival concert scheduled for August 28, which so far had been banned by the festival authorities. The idea that Anderson appear as part of the prestigious Salzburg Festival had come from Dr. Waitz, the archbishop of Salzburg. Moved by Anderson's singing during a concert in Vienna, he came back after the concert to meet her and to suggest that she give a charity concert in the Salzburg Cathedral as part of the festival concerts. Did Waitz think that such an idea would actually be accepted by festival authorities? No one living in Austria during those times could have been unaware of the growing Nazi menace and the response that would greet the idea of inviting a black artist to the festival. Only miles across the border from Bavaria, Salzburg was a hotbed of fascist sentiment. The writer Stephan Zweig as well as other Jewish intellectuals had found Salzburg no longer livable as early as 1933. Toscanini, making his first appearances at the festival that summer of 1935, would resign in protest two years later.

No doubt encouraged by the archbishop's invitation, Enwall had attempted to secure a date for the concert through the Viennese manager Wilhelm Stein. The answer from the authorities came on May 21: "According to your wish I hereby answer your two letters of March 29 and April 24 as well as that of Dr. Hohenberg that there can be no question of Marian Anderson [singing in the festival] since earlier experiences firmly speak against it."[55] Outraged at the response, Enwall wrote to Stein the same day:

> When every summer, singers of different nationalities appear in Salzburg, and when Marian Anderson is known throughout the world as one of the finest and most distinguished lieder singers and interpreters of Schubert, Mahler, Brahms, and others, all the more must we be given a reason why permission has not been granted. [I wonder] whether it is perhaps her dark complexion? Will you please send me the original document from Salzburg; once I have it I shall speak, among others, with the Austrian ambassador here, Baron Sommaruga, whom I know quite well.[56]

By early July, news of the ban on Anderson's concert began to appear in the New York press, where it was learned that "a projected concert in Graz also was frowned on by city authorities."[57] From the festival authorities there was only a show of surprise and denial: "Baron Puthon, president of the Salzburg Festival committee, said it was not possible for his organization to have Miss Anderson's concert scheduled within the Festival program because it had been prepared months ago. He said the concert had not been barred and that he knew no reason for Miss Anderson's complaint."[58] Although Enwall had kept her informed about the festival's actions from the very beginning, it is unlikely that Anderson herself voiced any complaint. She would have responded only with feelings of discomfort and sadness that the incident had been publicized at all. Such was her reaction four years later, when the very same drama, with different players, was carried out in Washington, DC, on a scale much larger and with consequences far more complex. Now it was Enwall who did the protesting, just as Hurok was to do later. In early August, concerned about the negative publicity, the festival authorities relented, giving permission for the concert to take place in the Mozarteum, one of the festival concert halls, with the understanding that the concert would not be included as an official part of the Salzburg Festival that summer.[59]

Anderson sang in the Mozarteum on August 28. The audience was small at first—Bruno Walter was conducting *Don Giovanni* at the Festspielhaus that evening—but word managed to circulate of an extraordinary American singer, enough so that a bigger crowd assembled after the intermission. The concert included lieder of Schubert, Mahler, and Sibelius. Although impressed with Anderson's singing, the critic of the

Salzburger Volksblatt devoted much of his review the next day to the usual racial musings of German critics: "Without letting oneself become enticed by the exotic, the song recital by the Negro singer Marian Anderson—actually she is a Mulatto, who has most recently studied with Madame Cahier in Vienna—was a great surprise. Of medium build, slender, amply brown, the lady is, in so far as a white person is entitled to a judgment of taste, a charming, lively figure with pitch raven-black hair, beautiful intelligent eyes and mobile play of features. In a long, white, low-necked silk dress, on her neck a giant, pale-red flower, she looks as if she has for far too long bathed in the sun of Africa."[60]

The distinguished musicians gathered in Salzburg that summer would remain unaware of Anderson a few days more. Kleiber, Toscanini, Walter, and Weingartner were all conducting that summer. During the last week of August, Lotte Lehmann sang the Marshallin (*Rosenkavalier*) under Krips, the role of Leonore in Beethoven's *Fidelio* under Toscanini, and a song recital with Walter as accompanist. After Anderson's first appearance, some of the Americans attending the festival took up Anderson's cause. Madame Cahier introduced her to Mrs. Gertrude Moulton, an arts patron and lover of music, who arranged for a private recital a few nights later in the ballroom of the Hôtel de l'Europe, where Anderson sang for some three hundred guests that included, in addition to many of the leading artists of the festival, government officials, church dignitaries and members of the diplomatic corps. Walter and Toscanini came back to greet Anderson after the concert. Words of praise that would follow Anderson for the rest of her career were spoken by Toscanini to her and Madame Cahier: "What I heard today one is privileged to hear only once in a hundred years." Nervous and distracted in front of Toscanini, she heard little of what he said to her, merely mumbling a few words of thanks. It was left to Madame Cahier to tell Anderson what Toscanini had said.[61]

Vincent Sheean, who later reported on his visit to the festival, left a moving portrait of Anderson's singing in the Hôtel de l'Europe: "Her superb voice commanded the closest attention of that audience from the first note. The Archbishop was sitting in the front row, and at his insistence she repeated the Schubert 'Ave Maria.' In the last group she sang a spiritual, 'They Crucified My Lord and He Never Said a Mumblin' Word.' Hardly anybody in the audience understood English well enough to follow what she was saying, and yet the immense sorrow—something more than the sorrow of a single person—that weighted her tones and lay over her dusky and angular face was enough. At the end of the spiritual there was no applause at all—a silence instinctive, natural and intense, so that you were afraid to breathe."[62]

Toscanini's words were for Anderson the emotional culmination of two years of concerts in Europe. Her return to the States, now planned for the middle of December, was still four months of concerts away. In September and October there was the usual tour of Scandinavia; in November and December, concerts in many of the European capitals, including Zurich, Vienna, Budapest, Paris, and Brussels. The season was to end with a concert in the Hague on December 14, giving Anderson and Kosti sufficient time to return to the States, where Hurok had already scheduled her first concert in America, in New York's Town Hall, for December 31.

Anderson's anticipation of returning to America, after more than two years, under Hurok's management was marred only by the steady stream of letters from Billy.[63] By the end of the summer, Anderson and Hurok had given up the idea of a separate series of concerts in which Billy and Anderson might perform together. Billy seems to have learned this from Hurok, the knowledge precipitating the final stages of an emotional crisis that continued through the fall. "My Mother is heart sick," he wrote to Anderson in August, "to think that you would turn so against me, when she knows our financial plight and how dependent we both were on this coming American tour. . . . You will remember I borrowed Nine Hundred Dollars and came to Berlin to work with you. . . . Then you know we returned and made the American tour. Now Marian I am saying that to say this, that was the beginning of my downfall financially. Later you know my Father died, he left a little money and for a time I felt a little secure knowing at least my Mother would not want in case I became ill, now this is gone. . . ."[64]

Alongside Billy's feelings of betrayal was his very real belief that the American public was not ready to accept the racially mixed partnership Anderson was contemplating. The idea was certainly unprecedented. Neither Robeson nor Hayes had thus far performed with other than black accompanists. The recent appearance of Anne Brown in Philadelphia with a white accompanist had created a considerable stir. Billy tried to make his case, his own hurt hovering over the surface of his arguments: "Don't you feel that you are making the mistake of your life in attempting to force a proposition of this kind down the throats of the American people? Don't you realize that unless you intend to make Europe your home, you are in a fair way to have both the whites and the blacks down on you. What do you think the reaction in Philadelphia will be? What do you think the reaction all over the United States will be? What do you think the Negro Press will do to you? . . . After all could you have the heart to bring another accompanist to Philadelphia to play for you and especially a white man. Marian where are your senses? Do you feel that even your home town would support you if you do a thing of this kind? . . . Should you bring Kosti to America or allow Hurok to engage him for your American tour I don't ever want to see you again."[65]

Without any word from Anderson, Billy looked for allies everywhere. He arranged a meeting with Hurok to plead his case. He poured out his feelings to Anderson's family. Stirred up and fearful of the consequences that Billy convinced them awaited Anderson upon her return, Mrs. Anderson, Ethel and Alyse all urged her to reconsider her plan.[66] Near the end of September, nervous about her family's reactions and annoyed at what she considered intrigue on the part of Billy, she wrote to Burleigh for advice. Her sole concern, she argued, was artistic: "Unfortunately Billy has been doing almost no accompanying in the meantime—and his suggestion that I return to America a month earlier to work out the program with him, was neither expedient nor possible. The plan to bring him here a month before my return, is also unpractical since I do not wish anymore to work out our struggles before my European audiences than those audiences in America."[67] Burleigh told her unequivocally what he thought: "Now Billy King has written me a long letter about your accompanist, hoping and asking me to write you with a view to altering the arrangement. Billy doesn't know that I heartily approve of Hurok's plans. I never felt that King was a good accompanist. He lacked poetry and imagination and technique too; and now, since you have such an extended repertoire he would be quite impossible. Of course, I shan't tell him this but will surely try to assure him that everything that Hurok has done for you is for the best."[68]

Encouraged by Burleigh's response, Anderson kept her resolve. She trusted Kosti and Hurok; for the time being, she felt them to be the best guardians of her future. Perhaps Billy would come around. Indeed, resilient as ever, he wrote her a few weeks later, more resigned now, even hopeful about his own career. Anderson, who had sung a nearly disastrous concert in Town Hall ten years before, would, in a few weeks time, sing there again, this time a Hurok artist.

CHAPTER NINE

A Hurok Artist
(1935–1939)

O n December 30, 1935, Sol Hurok presented Anderson in New
York's Town Hall. She had been away from the States for nearly
two and a half years and Hurok, uncertain of the audience she would
draw, chose the smaller theater for her homecoming rather than the
more prestigious Carnegie Hall. Beyond his original proposal to present
her in fifteen concerts, and the necessary arrangements for the Town
Hall recital, Hurok could not have given much thought to Anderson
during the months before her return. Not inclined to think ahead for
more than a season or two, his energies were taken up during much of
1935 with the difficulties of managing the American tour of the Monte
Carlo Ballets Russes. One can only wonder whether he foresaw the
extraordinary potential of the contralto whom he had agreed to manage,
or the remarkable relationship they would enjoy.

Hurok was a unique figure in America's cultural life—a man who
often performed the impossible. Born Solomon Izraelevitch Gurkov—
only in America did he become Sol Hurok—he arrived in the United
States in 1906 from his native Pogar, a small village at the extreme southern tip of Russia, a few miles from the northern border of what is now
Ukraine. About eighteen years old when he arrived in the States, he
came first to Philadelphia, where he bundled newspapers and served as a
streetcar conductor. That same year he moved to New York, where he
worked as a stockboy in a hardware store and peddled notions, settling in
the Brownsville section of Brooklyn. In those years before the First
World War, Brownsville was a veritable hotbed of socialist activity, which
Hurok entered into with enthusiasm. In Brownsville, Hurok's special
entrepreneurial talents asserted themselves, as he became involved in the

endless debates and rallies, meetings and fund raisings that were a constant part of the political and social scene. In a closely knit neighborhood made up almost exclusively of Jewish immigrants, there was endless intellectual stimulation and political debate. "In meeting rooms above the crowded stores," Hurok later reminisced, "the air shook with furiously happy argument, spiced with the odors from the delicatessen downstairs—a peculiarly fortunate arrangement considering how intellectual activity always sharpens the appetite. And the argument continued through the adjournment for a hot pastrami sandwich with dill pickle and unnumbered glasses of tea."[1]

In a few years time, with no training in music or artistic management, Hurok began to supply labor organizations and clubs with musical talent. For the benefit of the Socialist party, Hurok engaged the famous violinist Efrem Zimbalist, the first artist of international significance to appear under his management. Eventually Hurok presented concerts at the Brooklyn Academy of Music, for a series called "Music for the Masses," and a successful series of Sunday evening concerts at "popular prices" at the Hippodrome Theater in Manhattan. After failed attempts, he was able to bring Chaliapin to America and manage a highly successful tour by the dancer Anna Pavlova. There were failures along the way, and more than once Hurok lost more money than he made. In 1926, more out of personal interest than managerial acumen, he presented the Habima Theatre, a small group of Jewish players who had come from the same background as Hurok and who had managed, with the support of Stanislavsky, to remain successful in Moscow theatrical life. He lost $55,000 on the venture, deciding in the end to put his energies into the field of dance, where there was less competition than in theater.

In the early 1930s, already one of the foremost impresarios in New York, Hurok strengthened his financial and managerial position by a unique arrangement which capitalized on the growing centralization of concert management in America. The presentation of high culture was then controlled by two corporate giants. One was the Columbia Concerts Corporation, for which Arthur Judson managed two of the agencies merged as part of Columbia. The other was the National Broadcasting and Concert Bureau, under the aegis of NBC. By virtue of his entrepreneurial shrewdness and well-placed contacts in the artistic world, Hurok was able to enter into a relationship with NBC, keeping control of his hard-working and devoted business staff while continuing to promote his own artists. He paid NBC a small percentage of his artists' fees, in return acquiring a rent-free office in Rockefeller Center. By the mid-thirties Hurok could not have been in a stronger position,

1. Marian Anderson, 1898, one year old.
(Strawbridge and Clothier Photographic Studios)

2. John Berkley Anderson, 1890s.

3. Isabella Anderson (left) and
Mary Anderson, ca. 1900.

4. Billy King, 1918. *(The Bailey Studios)*

5. Front row, from left: Alyse Anderson, Marian Anderson, Ethel Anderson; back row: Anna Anderson, ca. 1910.

6. Marian Anderson in 1918.

7. Philadelphia High School for Girls, June 1921 class portrait. Marian Anderson is in the
second row from the back, second from the left. *(Slutsky Studio)*

8. Matthias and Gertrud von Erdberg,
Berlin, 1930.

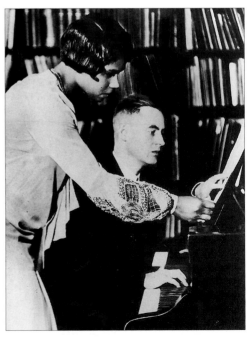

9. Marian Anderson and Kurt Johnen,
Berlin, 1931.

Městská dvorana v Náchodě.

V. členský koncert
Komorní hudby v Náchodě.

U pondělí 19. října 1931.
Začátek
přesně o 7. hodině večerní.

Marian Andersonová,
americká koncert. zpěvačka, největší soudobá kontraaltistka.

U klavíru
László Halász.

Koncertní křídlo fy. Ant. Petrof
zapůjčil Jan Boura, obchod klavírů
v Náchodě.

POŘAD:

I.
1. D o n a u d y : O, del Mio Amato Ben. (Kouzlo mého pokladu.). — 2. S c a r l a t t i : Gia il sole. (Již slunce.). — 3. C e s t i : Tu mancavi a tormentarmi. (Nezdařilo se ti mé zmučit.) — 4. M o z a r t : Alleluia.

II.
1. Q u i l t e r : It was a lover. (Byl to milenec.). — 2. S a a r : At the spinning wheel. (U kolovratu.) — 3. C a d m a n : Call me no more. (Nevolej mne zpět.). — 4. D v o ř á k : Když mne stará matka (česky).

III.
V e r d i : O, don fatale. (Arie z opery Don Carlos.). (Neblahý dar.).

IV.
Negro spirituals. (Černošské duchovní písně.).
1. B u r l e i g h : By and by. (Pozvolna.). — 2. B o a t n e r : Tramping. (Toulám se.). — 3. B r o w n : Going to ride up in the chariot. (Jízda kočárem.).— 4. B u r l e i g h : Deep river. (Hluboká řeka). — 5. B r o w n : Every time I feel the spirit. (Vždy cítím Boha.). — 6. B u r l e i g h : My Lord, what a morning. (Bože můj, jak krásné ráno!). — 7. B u r l e i g h : The Gospel Train. (Boží vlak.).

Členové Komorní hudby vstup na legitimace. Při přednesu jednotlivých čísel budou vchody uzavřeny.
Ceny míst: Sedadlo v přízemí Kč 16.—, 13.—, 9.—, k stání Kč 3.—, na studentskou a dělnickou legitimaci Kč 2.—, galerie Kč 2.—. — Předprodej vstupenek laskavě převzala sl. A. Fritschová.

MARIAN ANDERSON-OVA, mladá, sympatická mulatská zpěvačka, vystoupila v Praze poprvé r. 1930 v Mozarteu. Její koncert měl tak pronikavý úspěch, že krátce na to uspořádala druhý koncert ve Smetanově síni, která byla úplně vyprodána. Letošního roku zpívá uměleckyně v Čechách pouze v Praze, Pardubicích a Náchodě.

Z hlasů kritik uvádíme :
»České Slovo« 6. X. 1930: Marian Andersonovou, mulatskou pěvkyni, předcházela pověst hlasového fenoména, která sobotním výkonem pěvkyně v Mozarteu byla po mnohých stránkách výkonu také potvrzena. Nádherný tento alt jest přímo příkladně zvládnut technicky a jeho výrazová mnohotvárnost poukazuje na hluboké fondy citu, ukázněného jemnou kulturou hudební.

»Telegraf« 6. X. 1930: Nádherný její hlas prošel návodem italské školy. Delikátním půvabem obestřela písně starých mistrů italských, Mozartovi a Beethovenovi dala ušlechtilost stylovou a jímavě přednesla duchovní písně černošské. Vedle umění známé altistky Emy Leisnerové příklad vskutku vzorný a pro naše pěvce i poučný. Sympatický zjev znásobil její úspěch.

»Berliner Tageblatt« 4. XI. 1930: Již zevně působí její štíhlá postava neobyčejně sympaticky. V barvě pleti není více než tmavá, kdežto její nádherný kontraalt s hlubokým, zvučným prsním rejstříkem, jest tím černější. Její hlas je pln lesku ve forte, měkký a zvonivý v pianu, nesen bez námahy dechem, který výborně funguje. Ovládání naší řeči a citového světa jest prostě ohromující. Večer stal se svým úspěchem sensací.

Knihtiskárna V. Rydlo, Náchod.

10. Concert program, with László Halász as accompanist,
Czechoslovakia, 1931.

11. Marian Anderson, Vienna, 1934.
(Lotte Meitner-Graf)

12. Marian Anderson, Helmer
and Terese Enwall, May 1934,
at the London Zoo.

13. Konstantin Stanislavski (far left, with monocle). listening to Marian Anderson, January 1935, Moscow.

14. Kosti Vehanen and Marian Anderson, January 15, 1935, first concert in Moscow.

15. From left: Madame Charles Cahier, Kosti Vehanen, Marian Anderson, August 1935, Salzburg. (Erika Gast)

16. Center column front, from left: Marian Anderson and Anna Anderson; behind them: Alyse Anderson and Ethel Anderson, Philadelphia, 1930s.

(Brown Studio)

17. Marian Anderson at the Lincoln Memorial, Easter Sunday, 1939.
(AP/Wide World Photos)

18. Marian Anderson receiving the Spingarn Medal from Eleanor
Roosevelt, July 2, 1939. (Corbis-Bettmann)

19. From left: Franz Rupp, Marian Anderson, Guiseppe Boghetti, 1940. (Noël Boghetti)

20. Franz Rupp and Marian Anderson, 1940s.

21. Wedding photograph of Marian Anderson and Orpheus Fisher, July 1943, Danbury, Connecticut.

22. Orpheus Fisher, Marian Anderson, Pauline Milbourne, 1940s, Marianna.

23. Steffi Rupp and Marian Anderson, 1940s.

24. Marian Anderson at Marianna, 1940s

25. Marian Anderson at Marianna, 1940s.

26. Front, from left: Anna Anderson, Alyse Anderson; back: James DePreist, Ethel Anderson DePreist, ca. 1955, Philadelphia.

27. Marian Anderson, 1955, at concert in Goshen, Indiana. (Gordon D. Rapp)

28. Marian Anderson, 1953, in Tokyo, during concert tour of Japan.

29. Marian Anderson, 1953, in Rome.

30. Marian Anderson's debut, in Verdi's *Un Ballo in maschera,* at New York's
Metropolitan Opera, January 7, 1955, with Zinka Milanov. (Sedge LeBlanc)

31. Marian Anderson at the Gandhi Memorial, India, 1957, during a concert
tour of the Far East.

32. Marian Anderson during a discussion about the Cameroons in the Fourth Committee of the United Nations, November 12, 1958. (United Nations Photo Library)

Photo permissions: 1–6, 8–17, 21, 22, 26 and 27 courtesy of the Marian Anderson Collection, Rare Book and Manuscript Library, University of Pennsylvania; 7 courtesy of the Library Company of Philadelphia; 19 courtesy of Ethel K. Boghetti; 20, 23–25, 28–31 courtesy of Sylvia Rupp.

both financially and in terms of prestige, to take on the management of a black singer who, nearing the age of forty, was about to face her first season in America after nearly two and a half years abroad, and a New York audience for the first time in nearly six years.

The nervousness and anxiety Anderson had felt at her first Town Hall recital a decade earlier was replaced on the evening of her first concert under Hurok by a different kind of nervousness. Returning to America on the *Ile de France* only a few weeks before, she had fallen on a stairway of the ship as she was making her way from a practice room the captain had put at her disposal. "One afternoon about four-thirty," she explained later, "just after tea had been served, I left the practice room to descend to my own deck. My heel caught in the brass rim which held the carpet in place and suddenly I felt myself falling. A vast panorama flashed through my mind during the next second or two, as I envisioned myself falling on my face and realized that if I could throw my foot forward as I fell the two remaining steps, it might save more serious injury. This I did and although I experienced great pain momentarily, I did not realize that the accident was as severe as it proved to be."[2] The ship's doctor bandaged Anderson's foot, but only after arriving in Philadelphia and undergoing an examination in the Post Graduate Hospital was it determined that she had broken her ankle. With a full cast still on her leg at the time of the concert, Anderson had to walk onto the stage with crutches while the curtain was still down. Once standing securely in the curve of the piano, the crutches hidden, she was able to sing. She needed only to remember to stand motionless, the cast well hidden by her gown.

Word that a remarkable American singer had returned from Europe after considerable success traveled quickly, enough to provide a capacity audience. "To show whatever [she] was capable of doing, including low notes and high,"[3] Anderson chose a varied program, in both style and language: a group of Handel arias; Schubert's "Der Tod und das Mädchen," "Die Allmacht," and "Liebesbotschaft"; some Finnish songs, including Sibelius's "Die Libelle"; Verdi's "O Don fatale," from *Don Carlo*; and a group of spirituals including "Crucifixion," arranged by John Payne. Howard Taubman, writing in the *Times* the next day, judged Anderson's concert an occasion of historic significance: "Let it be said at the outset: Marian Anderson has returned to her native land one of the great singers of our time. The Negro contralto who has been abroad for four years established herself in her concert at the Town Hall last night as the possessor of an excelling voice and art. Her singing enchanted an audience that included singers. There was no doubt of it, she was mistress of all she surveyed."[4]

In recalling the concert some years later, Anderson confessed that she herself had felt her singing that evening to be unusually compelling, and that she was exhilarated the next day by the flattering reviews. Characteristically, she did not let it go at that. It was as if the very absence of criticism left her troubled, only that much more aware of the "weight of greater responsibility" she had to face in the weeks ahead. She later commented:

> When I returned to Philadelphia, and several days had passed, taking the keen edge off the excitement, I got out my music. I studied the songs I had sung in Town Hall, examining my singing in retrospect to check where I had not done as I would have liked and where a point had been exaggerated or undervalued. Here was a song that should have begun more softly and ended more powerfully. There was another that had not been all of a piece. I thought back to the spirituals, and I felt that in some places I had touched too lightly on the essential feeling, missing its depth. Had I given passages in them the character of art songs, which is not their nature at all? I feared that I might have. I resolved to be more careful.[5]

Whether from self-doubt or the harshest self-criticism, Anderson could not remain sanguine for long about any achievement. It was not simply a matter of aspiring to the highest artistic standards. She knew that in the arena Hurok had opened to her, she would be compared with white artists, and as a black singer she would have to achieve much more than they in order to hold her ground.

Hurok's strategy from the beginning was to present Anderson in her first American appearance outside of her native Philadelphia, where she was bound to have a great success, but in New York, where the critics had not once in the past been unequivocally positive about her singing. As it turned out, the demand for tickets for the Town Hall recital was such that Hurok felt encouraged to arrange a second New York recital, this time in Carnegie Hall, for January 20. In the meantime, Anderson's true emotional homecoming took place in Philadelphia on the sixteenth, at the Academy of Music. The concert was sponsored by her own Alpha Kappa Alpha sorority, an organization one of whose aims was to present at least one outstanding Negro artist each year. The program included arias from Handel's *Siroe* and *Amadigi,* and Verdi's "O don fatale," and, in addition to spirituals, a group of Schubert lieder ("Die Forelle," "Ave Maria," "Der Tod und das Mädchen," and "Liebesbotschaft") and four

Scandinavian songs, including Kilpinen's "Die Fusswaschung," and Sibelius's "Die Libelle" and "War es ein Traum?," as well as his "Säv, säv, susa," which she sang in Swedish.

Although the Academy audience still looked patchy at 8:20, with bare spots over the entire main floor, by 8:30 most of the hall was filled, with many people still scurrying frantically to their seats. The audience roared its approval after each group of songs, reaching a level of near frenzy when, after many encores, Anderson sang "Home, Sweet Home." As the *Philadelphia Tribune* recounted the next day, "following the recital, hundreds of newspapermen, photographers, and autograph seekers blocked the passage from the dressing room of the star whom they remembered as a little girl in a local church choir."[6]

In the days following the concert, writers for the black press were exultant with pride. Pictures of Anderson, and headlines about her homecoming, filled the front pages in Philadelphia and along the eastern seaboard. Orrin C. Evans wrote in the *Philadelphia Tribune :* "The 'opera feathers' of the ritziest Main Line dowager were plucked by the humble maid in her kitchen . . . racial distinction melted away . . . prominent Negro civic figures rubbed shoulders with their domestic employees. Marian Anderson, a product of South Philadelphia, who has achieved the pinnacle in the field of art, was relating a chronicle of victory and courage in the sibilant notes that rolled from her lips. The Academy of Music, last Thursday night, was the scene of the triumphal return to her kin folk and community sisters."[7] And Eva Jay, in the *Pittsburgh Courier:* "The audience composed of all walks of life applauded the lovely Miss Anderson. Swathed in shimmering white satin with a scarf draped over her shoulders, kerchief style in front and held in place by a diamond brooch at the back of the neck, she made an adorable picture . . . so far removed from one night in 1919, a shy, retiring little girl [who] sang a solo in a musical play at Music Fund Hall directed by Madame Saunders Patterson."[8]

Four days later, at Carnegie Hall, came the second of Anderson's New York concerts within a month. She sang arias of Bach, lieder by Brahms and Strauss, and spirituals; the novelty was a group of Italian folk songs that her teacher Geni Sadero had arranged for her. Reports of Anderson's accomplishments in Europe and Taubman's review in the *Times* had aroused so much excitement among New York society that the audience that Monday evening was as glamorous as any the city could offer. Living in New York at the time and working for the New York World's Fair Commission, Orpheus Fisher, who had had almost no communication with Anderson in more than two years, was in the audience that night.[9] He wrote to her the next evening, still in thrall to the glamor of the occasion:

> So I just had to hear the "grand" lady sing—for standing room. But much I was not alone. I want you to know that I stood with Miss Gloria Swanson on one side and Katharine Hepburn on the other sharing my precious program with both. I pretended that I did not recognize either of them, so I thought that they got a big kick out of it. They went into ecstasy about your voice. . . . I stood in the lobby during intermission and child you had the cream of New York there. The Astors, Morgans, Warburgs, just too too many to mention. I'm a telling ya!!! Marion my darling you really don't know how thrilled I was last evening. Without a doubt I think your concert last night was the "nuts" the finest you have had and I am wishing for many more. . . . Your dress, stage appearance was just too devine!!! . . . What happened to your 140 pounds on the stage you look like Lily Pons.[10]

Marriage was still not a priority for Anderson. She had told an interviewer a few days after her return to America that, engrossed as she now was in her career at home, she was not interested in marriage. Although marriage was very much on Orpheus's mind, he tried hard not to seem overly eager: "I wanted to come back stage to see you but I knew that there would be so many more important people than I to see you, that I decided to wait for the day when I could have you all alone, when you can arrange to give me one just one whole day and evening all to myself, sounds like me doesn't it?? I shall come over to Phila for that day maybe a week end—I sort of thought that you would have called me, but I was wrong. I have been wrong so many times in these last few years, it is getting to be natural for me. . . . If by chance that you are in New York or care to come over do so and come by for supper or dinner or breakfast."[11]

With Anderson's recent successes, first in Europe and now America, came new interest from record companies. Encouraged by the furor of acclaim that greeted her in Europe, His Master's Voice (HMV) had brought her back to the studio with a new contract the previous winter, a few months before her return to America. In January, after her first New York recital, the Victor company followed suit, arranging for sessions through the first week of February. The HMV sessions, devoted to spirituals, some German lieder, and Sibelius songs, had gone badly, with Anderson rejecting all of the takes. The Victor sessions she found much more to her liking, approving all but one. In addition to spirituals and two Schubert songs ("Ave Maria" and "Aufenthalt"), she approved the first two of what would eventually become a historic series of Sibelius recordings.

An important test for Anderson and for Hurok came on February 18, when Anderson was scheduled to sing in Washington. With Washington, as with New York, Anderson had enjoyed a long history before going off to Europe, one that extended back to her high school days. But Washington had a special character because the color line there was sharply drawn—by law and custom. In terms of race relations, Washington was a southern city. In New York and Philadelphia, Marian had sung to mixed audiences from a very early age. As her career advanced, the doors of Carnegie Hall and the Academy of Music opened to her. In Washington, segregation placed limits on Anderson's opportunities to appear, in addition to determining the racial makeup of her audiences. At the start, Anderson was welcomed primarily by the large and enthusiastic black population of the city. While still in high school she sang in black churches; in the twenties, she appeared at the Lincoln Theater, one of the small number of black-operated theaters where vaudeville shows and other presentations featuring black performers could be seen. When larger, mixed audiences had to be accommodated, she sang in the auditoriums of black high schools—for example, the Paul Dunbar High School, which dedicated a great deal of its resources and energy to fostering the arts among black performers. In the early thirties, her local concerts were a part of the Howard University Lyceum Concert Course, an annual concert series established at Howard in 1933 under the direction of Charles Cohen, a pianist and member of the music faculty.

For Anderson's concert in Washington on the eighteenth, Hurok again presented her as part of the Howard University Lyceum series. In the past, her recitals at Howard were held on the university's campus, in the Edward Rankin Chapel, too small now to satisfy the anticipated demand for tickets. For a white artist with Anderson's prestige, Constitution Hall, owned by the Daughters of the American Revolution, would have been the only appropriate hall. Because black artists were barred from appearing there, Howard decided to use Armstrong High School, one of the larger black high schools with a much larger auditorium that the Rankin Chapel. A large, mixed audience greeted Anderson the evening of the eighteenth; the reviews, serious in tone and lavish in praise, were no less enthusiastic than they had been in New York and Philadelphia.

The White House, too, was aware of Anderson's sensational homecoming. Taking advantage of her presence on the Washington scene, the president and Mrs. Roosevelt invited her to sing at the White House a few evenings after her concert at Armstrong High School, at a small dinner party for Circuit Court of Appeals Judge William Denman and his wife, who were San Francisco friends of the Roosevelts. On occasion, black artists had appeared at the White House during previous administrations. Marie Selika had sung for the Harrisons during Reconstruction days, and Siserietta Jones had sung for Presidents Hayes, Cleveland, and Theodore Roosevelt. While both FDR and Mrs. Roosevelt were eager to broaden the variety of musical entertainment heard in the White House, it was Mrs. Roosevelt who tried hard to break down racial and ethnic constraints in the preparation of musical programs, going to considerable effort to invite black performers. During Roosevelt's first administration, the Sedalia Quartet, from South Carolina, Lillian Evanti, a young black lyric soprano, and Dorothy Maynor and Todd Duncan had all been guests in the White House.[12]

For the White House concert, Anderson was asked to sing a group of spirituals, but she preferred a more varied program, one more representative of her repertoire as a whole. Robeson or Hayes would have welcomed the opportunity to display the emotional range of Negro spirituals on so opportune an occasion. Both had a missionary spirit about black folk music, eager to learn about its origins and to demonstrate its variety. Anderson's interests and sense of purpose were different from theirs. Indeed, she went so far as to object when exclusive attention to her singing of spirituals diverted interest from lieder and other art songs. For the Roosevelts she decided on three Schubert songs, ending the short program with two spirituals.

In addition to Kosti, who would accompany Anderson, Mrs. Roosevelt was gracious enough to invite Mrs. Anderson. On entering the White House, they waited downstairs, walking about in the official reception rooms until the president and his guests had finished dinner. Anderson sang for the official party in the Monroe Drawing Room, which had been converted in FDR's time into a charming and intimate room for visiting musical artists.[13] As Kosti remembered his appearance a few years later, FDR was sitting on a large, comfortable sofa at one side of the great fireplace, enjoying the fire. "His sure and strong handshake," Kosti recalled, "gives one a feeling of confidence, and his friendly, warm glance is good for the heart. That we were in the presence of a big personality no one could doubt."[14] Kosti appears not to have been intimidated in the least. For her part, as she later recalled, Anderson felt "a bit of fear—awe is a better word—even though there was such warmth in the atmosphere."[15] The next day, in her "My Day" column, Mrs. Roosevelt took special notice of Anderson's visit to the White House: "My husband and I had a rare treat last night in listening to Marion Anderson, a colored contralto, who has made a great success in Europe and this country. She has sung before all the crowned heads, and deserves her great success for I have rarely heard a more beautiful and moving voice, or a more finished artist."[16]

In the end, it was Mrs. Roosevelt, not the President, who made the deeper impression, not only on Marian and Mrs. Anderson, but on Kosti too. "After she sang," Kosti wrote, "there was a very touching scene. Mrs. Roosevelt, our charming hostess, took Marian's Mother by the hand, and led her over and introduced her to the President. I shall never forget seeing these two ladies enter the room. Mrs. Roosevelt's manner was sure and free, as becomes a woman of the world, happy to welcome the mother of America's best-known singer. In all of Mrs. Anderson's being, there was evident the feeling that this was one of the greatest moments in her life. Her face reflected her gratitude and the pride she felt."[17] Kosti had traveled widely and was always at ease with the great figures of the world whom he encountered. Anderson was more timid, at the outset almost awestruck, when coming face to face with people of great accomplishment and fame. On such occasions, she could be awkward in speech and manner. She was able to feel truly comfortable with these personages only after finding ways to make them seem less grand and lofty. And she was generally successful at this, for she had a remarkable intuitive understanding of people, sensing quickly what lay under the surface. In Mrs. Roosevelt, as she told an interviewer some years later, there "radiated a beauty as big as life itself. And with all of this one was aware that she was shy—there was always a sadness in her eyes."[18] In spite of their differences in background, Anderson and Mrs. Roosevelt sensed in each other a common experience of disappointment and struggle, the shared understanding of women seeking, each in her own way, her rightful place in an often hostile world, a place in which to find both self-approval and public approval. It was a bond that would draw them together in the years ahead as their lives continued to touch.

Anderson's first season under Hurok's management came to an end in early March, with a group of concerts in Quebec and Montreal. In looking back at the first months of their relationship, Hurok liked to emphasize the foolhardy daring of his decision to rebuild the American career of a nearly forgotten black singer. Anderson herself often added fuel to the legend of Hurok's genius: "I have since learned from another source, not from Mr. Hurok, that when he returned to America and reported that he had signed me a person who knew the concert business had told him, 'You won't be able to give her away.' "[19]

Anderson was self-effacing, diminishing her own contribution to the extraordinary success of her return to America. She went far in the opposite direction from Hurok's braggadocio. "As events developed," Anderson later recalled, "the fifteen concerts Mr. Hurok had hoped for did not pan out, but this did not worry him. . . . Mr. Hurok was not disturbed. He had faith in his own judgment, and he did not hesitate to take big risks in support of them. The normal thing in the music world is for the performer to defray the costs of a New York concert, but Mr. Hurok did not follow routine. He met all the expenses himself. He never bothered to tell me how he made out of the event, but I learned later that the gross receipts at the box office were about nine hundred dollars, a good deal less than the amount he spent."[20] Ironically, the truth appears only in the scrupulous records kept by Anderson herself during that first season. All fifteen of the concerts Hurok promised were, in fact, given, with additional concerts in New York, Philadelphia, and Montreal, where already-scheduled appearances could not satisfy the demand for tickets. Anderson's fees came to $6800—she was paid $400 a concert—out of which she, and not Hurok, covered the $2200 of expenses for accompanist, transportation, advertising, and hotels. During the course of the tour, Anderson sang to sold-out houses in every city except Utica. How much Hurok earned from Anderson's concerts that first season is not known, but he could not have been displeased with the results.[21]

To everyone's surprise, Anderson's decision to bring Kosti to America as her permanent accompanist caused hardly a ripple of comment in the press. Even in the black press there was no more than mild curiosity over Billy King's absence. It was Kosti, in fact, in whom the press was interested. The private drama that had continued for months while Anderson was still in Europe was successfully hidden by the official position which Hurok lost no time in presenting to the press. The Philadelphia *Afro-American* carried the story a few days after Anderson's return to America:

> Anderson, at the insistence of her management, is bringing to America as her accompanist, the famous Finnish pianist, Kosti Vehanen. Mr. Vehanen, an artist of distinction, has accompanied her during her tours since 1933. Critics abroad have been enthusiastic in their praise of the combination and Mr. Hurok predicated the handling of her American tour upon the importing of Mr.

Vehanen to play for her as he wished America to hear the same performance he heard in Europe. There has been a tendency on the
part of some zealous persons to question her change in America
from William King, Philadelphia pianist, who formerly served as
her accompanist. There is no diminution of Miss Anderson's
appreciation of the ability of her old co-worker although it is true
that too brief a time was left from her landing until her December
30 concert for Mr. King even to begin to surmount the technical
difficulties which would face him.[22]

Hurok had fashioned a skillful explanation designed to cater to the
snobbish preference of American concert audiences for European artists,
with Kosti portrayed as the embodiment of European musical culture, a
useful reminder of the now-international status of Anderson's career.
His wry mannerisms, his slightly stooped appearance, his stateliness and
fatherly manner so intrigued concertgoers that the question of race was
defused. Kosti was accepted by blacks and whites alike. For blacks, acceptance of Kosti was motivated by special concerns. Most blacks during the
1930s believed that some form of accommodation was necessary to the
advancement of one's career. Studying with a white teacher, performing
in Europe—these were inevitable challenges for Anderson as for other
black musicians. Many blacks shared Mrs. Anderson's view of Kosti.
Once she saw that racial protest was unlikely, as Burleigh had predicted
when Anderson sought his advice, Mrs. Anderson viewed Kosti as
Anderson's best choice for a career in America. In the end, it may have
been Anderson's character more than anything else that made possible
so easy a transition. Not out to challenge, she felt not the slightest unease
with Kosti. She was too disarmingly earnest to invite protest.

Anderson's first season back in America was in every way a success. Its
brief duration—not much more than five weeks—had from the start
been dictated by her commitments in Europe. Her return to Europe was
postponed, however, in order for her to take part in the United Campaign, held that year in Philadelphia. The Campaign, made up that year
of 141 charitable organizations, was hoping to attract as many artists and
entertainers with a Philadelphia background as possible. Campaign officials felt that Anderson's appearance on the program would give a substantial boost to the response of the colored agencies represented in the
Campaign, and Hurok favored Anderson's participation. He prevailed
over her reluctance, and Anderson postponed her departure until mid-
March, intending to remain in Europe for the rest of the year. Eager for
her to consolidate her reputation in the European capitals, Enwall had

arranged her schedule so that she would sing in Scandinavia only in the fall, and then only in Sweden and Denmark. The first series of concerts was scheduled for Italy, Spain, London, Paris, Belgium, Holland, and in May the Soviet Union. In June, Anderson was scheduled to sing in Austria, with Bruno Walter, and in the fall and winter, following Scandinavian concerts, Paris and London, Geneva, Budapest, and Prague.

Anderson returned to a Europe in turmoil, and closer to war than a year before. Following a wildly enthusiastic tour of Italy in April, Anderson and Kosti performed in Spain, where they could feel the disintegrating political atmosphere. They arrived in Barcelona a few days before May 1, when the country celebrated Labor Day. Only two months before the leftist "popular front," composed of parties made up of socialists, communists, syndicalists, and anarchists, had won the February elections, with violence breaking out as soon as the results were announced. "There was much confusion and excitement in the streets," Kosti later recalled, "which were crowded with people. I could see the dark expression in many faces and a frantic look in many eyes."[23] On Labor Day, Anderson and Kosti were invited to the home of the Spanish singer and disciple of Enrique Granados, Conchita Badia; they were able to reach their destination only with the help of a government official and escort.

The next day they left Barcelona for Valencia. "There were no trains running," Kosti later wrote, "so we were forced to obtain a private motorcar to drive us to our destination. Since the chauffeur did not dare to leave Barcelona in the daytime, we pulled out from the city just before dawn. . . . In Valencia, the excitement was again evident, with nervous-looking people surging around as though expecting a terrible thunderstorm. Policemen were numerous and strongly on the watch. In Madrid, the uprising had already reached great heights."[24] At the railroad station people were carrying their belongings through the streets, the cries of women and children filling the air. Kosti remained in a continuous state of alarm. Not easily given to panic, trusting in God to do her worrying for her, Anderson remained at least outwardly calm. Having braved the Caucasus in order to fulfill a contract, she was not going to allow impending civil war to deter her from giving her recital in Bilbao. She decided to go on.

Anderson and Kosti breathed a sigh of relief when, in a few days, they started out for the Spanish border near San Sebastian. At the border, the customs officials ordered a search of their luggage, where one of the first things they found was an elegant evening cape of dark red velvet that she had bought in Moscow. Only after Kosti had dug out some pictures taken the previous year in Stockholm of her actually wearing the cape did the custom officials allow them to go on. "As we came over the border into France," Kosti later recalled, "we both looked sadly back, thinking of poor, beautiful Spain and the terrible future she was facing."[25] Less than three months later, after an army mutiny in Spanish Morocco led by Franco, civil war was declared.

Germany was closed to Anderson, but she was still able to sing in Austria, which, although by no means free of ideological unrest, had become a temporary refuge for musicians, writers and artists who had been driven out of Germany. In the summer months, tourists and musical enthusiasts flocked to Salzburg and Vienna for the annual music festivals. Anderson sang twice in Salzburg during the summer. Once again the Salzburg Festival authorities denied their official recognition to Anderson's concerts. During the Vienna Festival Weeks—the *Festwochen in Wien*—held that year from the seventh to the twenty-first of June, the situation was different in the extreme. As Herbert Peyser reported to readers of the *New York Times:* "In Vienna these past weeks every whipper-snapper who felt like squawking Brahms or scraping a fiddle preempted space in the Musikverein, the Konzerthaus or elsewhere and made hideous the long Summer twilights within the frame of the festival weeks." One such performer, "the most outrageous exhibition of the lot," was "an American matron resident here, who desecrated a long list of classic Lieder in particularly shocking fashion and seemed to glory in her shame."[26]

As Peyser was quick to assure his readers, not everything that happened to fit within the framework of the festival weeks was bad. Indeed, three of the greatest German conductors of the interwar years came to Vienna that summer. One was Weingartner, who traveled from Switzerland to conduct, during the opening days of the festival, a new version of Millöcker's operetta, *The Beggar Student,* garishly costumed by Czettel and inflated with half a dozen pieces from other works by the composer.

Furtwängler was the most eagerly anticipated musician invited to the festival that summer. Because Furtwängler had resigned in 1934 from the musical posts he held in Germany, many believed he had been forced into at least temporary retirement by the Nazis. The truth was that the illustrious conductor, hounded by Hitler and Goebbels, had finally made an agreement with them. In return for his acknowledging Hitler's power to determine cultural policy in Germany, Furtwängler was allowed to remain a nonpolitical musician, not required, in other words, to accept any official artistic position nor called upon to perform at state functions. Exhausted from endless negotiations and worry, Furtwängler decided in 1935 to withdraw for a year from public performances in order to work on a series of compositions he hoped would reflect more truthfully his stand against totalitarianism than the portrait of him the Nazis had created for the outside world. His performance of Wagner's *Tannhäuser* that summer, with Lotte Lehmann, during the second week of the festival, was one of only five performances of opera conducted by him in Vienna that year.[27]

Only months before the festival, Bruno Walter, hounded out of Germany after Hitler came to power, had reentered Viennese musical life as director of the Vienna State Opera. During one of his performances of *Tristan und Isolde* prior to the festival, stink bombs were dropped from aloft in the theater. The Isolde, Anni Konetzi, was so nauseated by the odors that she did not even attempt to sing the Liebestod, "but just rested, voiceless and procumbent on Tristan's corpse,"[28] as Walter later recalled. Apparently the stink-pots were not meant for Walter personally for, as he recalled in later years, "at the same time that evening, at eight-thirty, they befouled the air in all theatres and a number of cinemas in Vienna. The performance at the Burgtheatre was stopped. I did not care to give the Nazis the satisfaction of having disrupted our performance, and kept on conducting, though a number of frightened or indignant people left the theater."[29]

During the festival weeks, Walter conducted two orchestral concerts. About the first of them, with the Vienna Philharmonic, Walter later wrote: "I even received a much-signed letter conveying a threat of death. I handed the message over to the police, who seemed to take it seriously, for a number of stalwart men in shag suits and with chamois brushes on their hats . . . surrounded me as a bodyguard on that evening."[30] It was not Walter's program—music of the Viennese composers Haydn, Schubert, Mozart, and Johann Strauss—that drew so extreme a response. The true irritant was the announcement that, for Walter's second concert, with the Vienna Symphony, the Negro contralto Marian Anderson was to be the soloist in the Brahms *Alto Rhapsody*. To Nazi sympathizers, the choice of Anderson was an act of defiance of Nazi cultural policy by a Jewish musician.

Audiences in Germany and Austria had long since accepted Anderson as a significant interpreter of the German classics. As Peyser noted in the *New York Times,* Anderson was loved by Viennese audiences, who had "reached the point of accepting practically without challenge her sovereign interpretations of Schubert, of Wolf, of Mahler—in short, of masters whom they usually concede to foreigners only with all manner of hair-splittings and reservations."[31] Recitalists who challenge ethnic or racial feelings, especially within the framework of long-standing cultural institutions, stir up deep feelings of proprietorship in their audiences. For all of Anderson's acceptance as a recitalist by German-speaking audiences, her appearance that evening was unprecedented. A daring sense of community was created as Anderson stood not only with Walter, but the Vienna Symphony musicians and the chorus of the *Gesellschaft der Musikfreunde,* as the soloist in one of Brahms's most popular and emotionally direct works, with a text taken from Goethe, the national poet of Germany.

The critics were more than kind to Anderson. They were also aware of what had been done to Viennese concert life. One writer remarked in amazement, "What would Brahms have said if he could have known that his rhapsody would be sung by a Negress?"[32] If Anderson was aware of the unprecedented step she would take as she walked onto the stage of the *Grosser Musikverein,* it was not what she recalled in later years. What stayed in her mind was the rather cold and unsatisfying reception she got from Walter at the first rehearsal. In the past, when appearing with orchestras, Anderson had always been able to determine herself what she would perform. For the concert with the Vienna Symphony, Walter had asked her to prepare a work new to her. She had begun to work on it, in fact, only a few days before the first rehearsal, when she still needed to have the music before her. Walter admonished her for her apparent lack of preparation, insisting that a soloist was expected to perform without music. At the next day's rehearsal, Anderson knew the part from memory. The critics, aware that she had learned the part in a surprisingly short time, spoke with great admiration of her performance. Peyser reflected the feelings of his Viennese colleagues when, writing in the *Times* a few weeks later, he extolled Anderson's performance, remarking "with what intuitive grasp of its poignantly human message, with what spiritual elevation, with what noble contempt of effect and outward show, with what complete subordination of herself to the ends of the composition,"[33] Anderson delivered her part.

Anderson's experience with the *Alto Rhapsody* was much as it had been with the *Four Serious Songs.* After a process of assimilation both brief and intense, guided by musicians steeped in the German tradition, Anderson embraced both works with undaunted enthusiasm and dedication. A few years later she made her first recording of the *Alto Rhapsody* with Eugene Ormandy and the Philadelphia Orchestra, recording it twice more in subsequent decades in keeping with technological changes in the recording process. Anderson hesitated many years, however, before facing the challenge of the *Four Serious Songs* in the studio, a successful performance eluding her through repeated attempts.

Between concerts, there were sessions for HMV. Although a few lieder of Schubert and Schumann were included, Sibelius remained the consistent focus. Anderson approved only five of the ten Sibelius songs she recorded, but the achievement was nonetheless without precedent for an American singer. At the time, apart from recordings that were not meant for distribution outside of Scandinavia, only Florence Wiese and Aulikke Rautawaara had made recordings of Sibelius songs. Set mostly to Swedish texts, barely known outside of Scandinavia, Sibelius's songs were naturally enough considered a risky investment by record companies. When the Finnish soprano Aulikki Rautawaara recorded "Den första kyssen" and "Flickan kom ifrån sin älsklings möte," in 1935, for the German Telefunken company, she, of course, recorded them in German rather than Swedish. By contrast, Anderson, with her newly won reputation on both sides of the Atlantic, was allowed by the HMV and Victor companies to record Sibelius's songs in Swedish. Once released, the recordings were received with unrestrained enthusiasm, Sibelius himself later remarking that Anderson's recording of "Come away, death" was the most satisfying recording, by any singer, of any of his songs.[34]

Concerts and recording sessions kept Anderson in Europe until well into January 1937. More than a little homesick after having had only three months in the States, the news from home as the time for her departure neared increased her impatience to join her family. There was Alyse's excitement and pride over her recent successes in state Democratic politics. Eagerly looking forward to the Democratic Convention in Philadelphia, in June, and the meeting of the National Negro Congress a few months later, Alyse felt more enthusiastic about politics than ever. Her dedication was finally rewarded when, as Marian learned from her mother in the fall, Alyse was made director of Democratic Negro women's activities for eastern Pennsylvania. More hopeful than usual about Alyse's future, Mrs. Anderson reported that she had been given an office on South Broad Street, and was "travel[ing] to places like Buck's County, Upper Darby and the like, speaking."[35]

The news of Ethel's pregnancy had reached Anderson only after she had left the States for Europe. Her husband, James de Preist, was reported to be ecstatic, "nearly wild with joy. Ethel says he is crazy."[36] Anderson expressed her own joy at the news in a note to John Payne a month or so before her return to America, while on vacation in Vienna:

"My family was terribly disappointed that I was not at home for Christmas and I had looked forward to becoming acquainted with my little nephew. O yes, I became an aunt on Nov. 21st. and what a relief, ha ha. They've told me very little about him other than he is lovely and my excitement is almost uncontrollable. Well it won't be long now."[37] The little nephew, named for his father, quickly became the family's adored "Jimmy," spoiled relentlessly by a doting household of four women. Jimmy would, in short order, become the child Marian never had.

Anderson's second season under Hurok began on January 26, 1937. She gave forty-four concerts that season—a coast-to-coast tour in little more than three months. Minneapolis, Milwaukee, Oklahoma City, Houston, Des Moines, Pittsburgh, and Salt Lake City were added for the first time. The third season, in 1938, included sixty concerts, beginning shortly after the new year and lasting to the end of May. During the fourth season, forced to begin as early as Thanksgiving and continuing until the middle of June 1939, Anderson sang nearly eighty concerts, one of the longest and most strenuous tours ever undertaken by an American concert artist. Just as in Europe, the pace had become relentless, with concerts every two days for long periods, and with little or no rest after days of traveling.

Hurok, like Enwall, had discovered that a great deal of money could be made with Anderson. Indeed, ever the shrewd businessman and promoter, Hurok reported to the press in January 1939 that Anderson had earned $238,000 during 1938, an astonishing record for a concert singer in those years.[38] For her part, Anderson complained about the exhausting schedule, but Hurok, arguing that such schedules were necessary in order to "build up" her career in America, did nothing to address her complaints. Finally, in January 1939, after Hurok's boast to the press of her phenomenal earnings, Anderson drew the line, sending Hurok the following letter:

> My experience from this tournee has already shown me that the concerts with the long trips in between are too strenuously booked for me. Last year I said to your bureau, and seriously too, that it was a physical impossibility for me to properly sing a recital immediately after having spent two days in travel. This is exactly what happened last week in the dash from Grand Forks ND to Pittsburgh where we arrived the evening preceding the afternoon concert. (I enclose a criticism from Pittsburgh which unfortunately is true due to exhaustion.)

Further I begged an easier arrangement for California this year in order that I might have a breathing spell before the following strenuous months, but against my wish two concerts on the heels of each other have been booked at the very beginning of the coast tour (February 9th and 10th). It is imperative as I said last year and as we understood upon the signing of the contract, that I have one day of rest between each concert and a good rest after a strenuous trip.

I implore you Mr. Hurok, to inform your bureau that in the coming season if similar arrangements continue I will be forced to give up such engagements. It is very evident that with an all too strenuous program of concerts, my future career can not be "built up."

I regret the necessity of writing you such a letter but honestly feel that it is the only right thing to do under the circumstances.[39]

A great deal of the success of those first seasons in America must be credited to the ingenuity and persistence of Hurok. He worked slowly and logically, building each year on the previous year's accomplishments. During Anderson's second season with Hurok, he increased her fee to $600, $200 more than her fee the first season, and more than she had ever earned with Judson. Judson had always thought of Anderson as a black singer who would have to bend to local tradition and policy. Only when sure that no risk was involved was he willing to raise her fee. Hurok did not parry and thrust with local concert managers, willing to take less when he could not get more. A skilled salesman, Hurok showed no weakness in negotiation. Local managers would have to pay to have Anderson, just as for any other artist, or they would not have her at all. Of course, the economy was on Hurok's side. During the latter months of 1936, managers could risk more and concertgoers could afford more, as America experienced a long-awaited improvement in economic conditions.

Hurok had on his side as well the bureaucratic machinery of the National Broadcasting and Concert Bureau, under the aegis of NBC, where it was now the usual custom to offer, often in advance by subscription, a series of concerts with a diversity of performers. Feeling strongly that Anderson should appear wherever other great artists appeared, he could now group her with a wide variety of well-known and glamorous performers, conveying to local managers and the musical public that she was in every way the equal of the others.

Hurok rarely hesitated to add to the number of Anderson's concerts in any given season when the opportunity for her to appear at a prestigious musical event occurred. In early 1937, for example, he wrote to her: "The Ann Arbor committee telephoned me yesterday long distance and I accepted the date without hesitation for several reasons. Firstly, it is one of the finest musical cities in the country; their yearly May Music Festivals attract international attention and this May both Flagstad and Melchior are appearing there. When the opportunity presented itself, I naturally felt that this type of audience should hear you."[40] Anderson agreed to sing, and Hurok could not have been more right. She not only appeared along with Flagstad and Melchior but sang for the first time with Eugene Ormandy, the new conductor of the Philadelphia Orchestra. He invited her to appear with him at the May Festival the following year, a reunion leading to one of Anderson's longest and most fruitful artistic relationships. In 1939, Anderson and Ormandy collaborated in a recording of Brahms's *Alto Rhapsody,* Anderson's first recording with orchestra.

Hurok, in his practice of offering concerts as parts of a series, was more inventive and, some would say, more ruthless than anyone else. When local managers were reluctant to accept Anderson, Hurok told them that without Anderson they would not get another artist they wanted. In a few years' time, she was enough in demand in many sections of the country for Hurok to use her as the means by which less well-known artists or groups were forced upon managers. Anderson always cringed when she recalled that the Hampton Institute, one of the prestigious black colleges in the South where she had performed regularly for years, had been subjected to Hurok's arm- twisting tactics: "I do hope we shall secure the rest of your business, as we have worked so cooperatively with you in regard to ANDERSON, and I am lining up, as I previously stated to you, the BALLET RUSSE, ENGEL LUND and the COMEDIAN HAR-MONISTS."[41] The Musical Art Committee at Hampton, forced to retrench because of financial problems, felt that they could not afford the Ballets Russes; moreover, they did not approve of the Comedian Harmonists. In order to have Anderson, they would accept only Engel Lund. Hurok's response was swift and firm: "In view of what you say, we regret to advise you that we have no date available for MARIAN ANDERSON in Hampton, Virginia next year."[42] The Musical Art Committee then wrote to Anderson herself, that "they would go to considerable trouble and expense to bring this [an appearance by Anderson] to pass,"[43] explaining that they did not think it was necessary, in order to have Anderson at Hampton, to book the Ballet Russe and Comedian Harmonists as well.

The Hampton Institute was representative of black colleges and churches throughout the South. The same institutions that had provided most of the opportunities for Anderson in the twenties had suffered during the Depression years, enjoying only limited economic recovery in the thirties. Anderson could have continued to sing in places like the Hampton Institute, but Hurok, not wanting her to be identified as essentially a black artist, preferred that she appear on the same prestigious and well paying concert series in the South as in the rest of the country. In many cities, especially in the deep South, however, segregation created obstacles for Hurok. Whether by statute or tradition, some theaters excluded blacks, while others set aside only small groups of seats for blacks. Many managers were wary of presenting Anderson, whose presence they feared would encourage blacks to challenge local traditions. The dilemma for Hurok was to decide how far to push local managers into challenging existing conditions. For Anderson, obstacles posed by segregation were far more burdensome. She had to deal with the disappointment of having much of the South closed off to her. By the late thirties, after four seasons under Hurok, there was little progress. In 1937, when the season had already grown to forty concerts, Houston was the only southern city on the tour. Texas, with its long activist tradition on behalf of civil rights, was the only southern state where Hurok could make significant inroads. The next year, in addition to Houston, Anderson sang in San Antonio, Fort Worth, and Dallas.

Radio helped introduce Anderson's voice across America. With the waning of the economic hardships left behind by the Depression, radio opportunities for classical artists, including black artists, increased significantly. Radio benefited black artists like Anderson, especially in the South, where it helped to neutralize the inequalities caused by segregation. During the late thirties, her voice could be heard on such programs as the General Motors Hour, the Magic Key program and the Ford Hour. Her striking voice, never more opulent than in those years; the range of her programs, which included, in addition to spirituals, more popular numbers than she normally sang on concert programs; and the charm and radiance of her personality, so intimately bound up with her singing, made her an extraordinarily popular radio performer. Some of her most fervent fans were those who heard her on the radio, and they began to write to her in great numbers. After one of her first radio broadcasts, on the General Motors Hour, in March 1937, James Weldon Johnson, the distinguished black writer of spirituals and musical comedies, and his wife, fired off a telegram: "Listening tonight in Nashville you are glorious perfectly superb."[44]

By 1939, after only five seasons, Anderson had more than duplicated in America what she had achieved in Europe. In America, her fees had risen from $400 to as much as $2,000 for most performances. With more engagements for Anderson than she could comfortably fulfill, Hurok's job was now "not to seek dates for Marian, but to winnow out the most attractive ones each season."[45] To meet the repertoire needs of constantly expanding seasons, which included yearly appearances in many cities, she had to change programs more rapidly. In developing her repertoire, she had the help of a network of teachers on both sides of the Atlantic— Boghetti on the East Coast; on the West Coast, Madame Cahier, who had settled in California; and in Europe, Madame de Castro and Geni Sadero. She added an abundance of new material to her repertoire, exploring the more unusual, even esoteric byways of the vocal literature. Her programs had a striking cosmopolitanism, which she liked to emphasize particularly in her Carnegie Hall recitals. For her first recital there in 1939, she chose music by Spanish composers ("El Luto de garrido," by Pablo Esteve, "Menuet chanté," by José Bassa, "Del cabello más sutil" of Obradors, and Granados's "Elegie eterna"); a group of French chansons ("La cloche," by Saint-Saëns, "Chère nuit" of Bachelet, and Fauré's "Au bord de l'eau" and "Après un rêve"); Pauline's aria from Tchaikovsky's *Queen of Spades,* music by American composers (Horatio Parker, Herbert Bedford, Florence Price and Samuel Barber), and spirituals.

In only five seasons with Hurok, Anderson had become an indelible part of the American musical scene. Occasionally a critic preferred to maintain some appearance of sobriety in response to an Anderson concert. Olin Downes, for example, never comfortable with extravagant praise, held to his gravity of manner in reviewing Anderson's first New York recital in 1939: "Miss Anderson sings music by classic masters, not as a lesson learned, or a duty carefully performed, but as an interpreter who has fully grasped and deeply felt the import of the song."[46] For the rest, critics threw caution to the winds, outdoing each other in their efforts to capture the excitement generated by Anderson's appearances. From New York ("Outside the hall were twenty policemen, waiting for possible demonstrations; but the demonstration was confined within the walls of Carnegie Hall and all was peaceful on fifty-seventh Street"),[47] to Buffalo ("Anderson aroused an audience to a demonstration of ecstatic enthusiasm such as is seldom seen in this city. . . ."),[48] to Milwaukee ("It was a night of soaring, inspiring song—a combination of such melody, skill, power, warmth and graciousness as to make the hearers stare at each other in startled disbelief and ecstasy"),[49] Anderson was rewarded with a triumphal chorus of brilliant reviews.

Of course, there was much more to Anderson's success than voice and art. In her every appearance, the unique qualities of her character and personality made themselves felt just as strongly as her technique and interpretations. Perhaps, in the end, what touched audiences most deeply was the provocative contradiction between the effortless warmth, sincerity, and dignity Anderson radiated and the quality of aloofness that was always present. The critic Glenn Dillard Gunn, after one of her Washington recitals, provided a moving portrait of Anderson's compelling hold on the imagination of her audiences: "Miss Anderson's power to move her listeners as can no other singer of her generation is not made less by the simple, almost unsmiling dignity which clothes her like a garment. She holds herself aloof and doubtless with intention. Her eyes closed, her face expressionless, she retires into her world of song, inviting us to enter it, but remaining remote, nor sharing her personality. Even in her moment of triumph the barrier is there."[50]

In the black community, Anderson's accomplishments as a singer and the sense of pride and purpose she inspired brought her the first of many honors. In June 1938, Howard University awarded her an honorary doctorate of music. At the commencement ceremonies, the nearly 700 well-wishers created a near riot as they mobbed the singer at the end of the exercises. The following January, the NAACP announced that it would award Anderson the Spingarn Medal, given annually by its president, Joel Spingarn, "for the highest or noblest achievement by an American Negro during the preceding year or years." The Spingarn award was an honor that carried more prestige than any other in the black community. Since the inception of the Spingarn award in 1915, only two other musicians, Roland Hayes and Harry T. Burleigh, had been so honored. By the time the Spingarn committee's selection was announced to the public, officials at Howard University and the NAACP had already joined forces in a battle with the D.A.R. over Anderson's right to sing in Constitution Hall—a battle that would prove to be one of the great milestones in the struggle for racial equality in America.

CHAPTER TEN

The Concert at the Lincoln Memorial (Easter Sunday, 1939)

The Daughters of the American Revolution (D.A.R.) dedicated Constitution Hall in April 1929, during the fortieth Continental Congress, the annual gathering of delegates to their national headquarters in Washington. The last of the buildings conceived and brought to completion by the Daughters, Constitution Hall was designed to hold both a library and spacious auditorium, forming part of a complex of buildings that stands at the center of many of the most important symbols of democratic government in the nation's capital. A block or two northeast is the White House; directly south, and separated only by spacious Constitution Avenue, is the reflecting pool and mall which extend east from the Lincoln Memorial to the Washington Monument. Although Constitution Hall was built to accommodate the increased numbers of delegates who wished to attend the annual Continental Congresses, it was anticipated from the start that the hall would "open its doors to Washington as a part of that city's daily life."[1] At the formal opening of the Hall, the Right Reverend James E. Freeman, the Episcopal bishop of Washington, in his consecration address, spoke in lofty terms about those ideals in whose name the building was erected:

Proudly we affirm that the basic law of the land is the Constitution. We look to it as unto the rock whence we are hewn. By it we measure our privileges and weigh our obligations. It is the polar star by which the ship of state determines its course. Unfamiliar as our people might be with its specific language, nevertheless they believe that in its unfailing recognition and maintenance resides all that contributes to life, liberty and the pursuit of happiness.[2]

Constitution Hall promised much for the city of Washington, but its completion could not have come at a more troubling period for the Daughters. For the D.A.R., the Red Scare had persisted for nearly two decades as a dangerous threat, affecting its attitudes and policies on education, immigration, national defense, and the peace movement. The reformist impulses that still remained during the early 1920s were gradually swept away as the D.A.R.'s fears of subversive groups and their possible effects on American society broadened into a fear of liberal ideas generally. In 1923 and again in 1926, with Mrs. Alfred Brousseau's election as president-general of the society, the new leadership introduced an ever more reactionary and unflinchingly authoritarian rule. The organization now became outspoken in its opposition to persons and groups promoting disarmament and world peace, and with connections to economic reform movements such as women's rights and organized labor.[3]

Ultra-conservative groups such as the American Legion, as well as self-appointed super patriots and subversive hunters such as Captain George L. Darte found Mrs. Brousseau and Mrs. Walker, chairman of the Committee on National Defense, willing supporters of their efforts to target subversive groups and individuals. At the Continental Congress of 1928, a year before the completion and dedication of Constitution Hall, D.A.R. leadership formally approved the circulation to the various state regents and local chapters of a pamphlet entitled "The Common Enemy," blacklisting hundreds of organizations and individuals that were considered radical and dangerous to the patriotic ideals of the D.A.R. Chapters were urged not to allow the blacklisted individuals, or any associated with blacklisted organizations, to address local chapters. The list included such organizations as the YMCA, YWCA, NAACP, Federal Council of Churches, U.S. Department of Labor, National Catholic Welfare Council, National Child Labor Committee, American Civil Liberties Union—more than ninety in all. Among the individuals on the list were distinguished clergy, presidents of universities (among them Vassar, Smith, and Mount Holyoke); Roscoe Pound, dean of the Harvard Law School; W. E. B DuBois, the distinguished black leader and editor of *Crisis;* Will Durant, Carrie Chapman Catt, Jane Addams, and three U.S. senators (LaFollette, Norris, and Borah).[4]

There was certainly opposition to the new leadership and its views, but for many D.A.R. members it was the repressive tactics behind the blacklist and the curtailing of free speech that it entailed that drove members to open revolt. Indeed, the blacklist program blew up in the D.A.R.'s face and embroiled them in scandal that made national news. In May 1928, eleven members from two New Haven, Connecticut chapters resigned in protest. Two of the members signed a joint statement, carried in the *New York Times,* that read, in part: "The United States has grown in power and influence for 150 years by carrying out the principles of our fathers of free discussion of public questions. For this the present policy of the Daughters of the American Revolution substitutes a face about to tyrannical suppression of all who differ with the present national officers on the questions of the day. If such efforts should succeed, the result would be to crush the initiative and creative energy of the American people."[5]

The most embarrassing opposition from within came from Mrs. Helen Tufts Bailie, a D.A.R. member from Cambridge, Massachusetts, who, as part of a committee of protest, authored a pamphlet entitled "Our Threatened Heritage," prepared as an open letter to the D.A.R. In her pamphlet, Mrs. Baillie traced the history of the influence on the D.A.R. that resulted in the adoption of a blacklist and the opposition that it caused within the organization, urging members to reject the humiliating and wrongheaded position of the organization and the authoritarian manner of its leadership. When speaking to the press about "those upstart women from Massachusetts,"[6] Mrs. Brousseau, the president-general, in typical high-handed terms, argued that "Not one of the women of this 'committee' is known to me personally. Therefore, their combined judgment could hardly be said to be reliable. . . ."[7] Mrs. Baillie's behavior was eventually examined by the Board of Management, which voted with little opposition to expel her from the organization.

From outside the organization criticism ranged in tone from mild amusement and satiric dismissal to outrage and anger. Having found himself on the D.A.R.'s blacklist, given to him by an Emporia D.A.R. regent, William Allen White, the distinguished journalist, thought it best to resort to ridicule: "Within two years the D.A.R. has fallen from its high estate and its leaders are taking program from a lot of hard, arrogant, vain, old lady snobs and brass buttoned mannikins around Washington who have nothing to do but draw their pay and whisper 'Fee, Fo, Fi, Fum, raw head and bloody bones,' into the ears of the timid and idle rich."[8]

The more serious and sustained opposition came from progressive leaders among women's liberal organizations. For years the D.A.R. had positioned itself against the leading women's liberal social organizations and its more prominent members. Carrie Chapman Catt, Jane Addams,

Florence Kelly, and Rose Schneiderman were all eventually blacklisted. Catt, a tireless worker for women's suffrage and international peace, led the attack on the D.A.R. When she discovered in early 1927 that the D.A.R. blacklist, "The Common Enemy," had been widely circulated together with reprints of pages of the Congressional Record that contained arguments against important pieces of social legislation, Catt went into action. In an article published in the *Woman Citizen,* she lashed out at the D.A.R.'s attacks on liberal women's organizations, refuting their arguments and defending Jane Addams and others who were blacklisted. Mrs. Roosevelt, herself critical of the shift in policy of the D.A.R., wrote with enthusiasm about Catt's article, encouraging all progressive leaders to read and to circulate it.[9]

By the time Mrs. Lowell F. Hobart succeeded Mrs. Brousseau as president-general in April 1929, amid the Daughters' jubilation over the dedication of Constitution Hall, many members who were openly critical of the blacklist had resigned or been expelled. Mrs. Hobart brought little change in ideology to the organization. During the early thirties, criticism of the D.A.R. centered around its openly militaristic ideology. The resignation of prominent and dedicated members continued. Valeria H. Parker, honorary president of the National Council of Women, resigned in protest at the organization's condemnation of any groups and individuals interested in promoting international understanding, world peace, and disarmament. The following year, half of the membership of the Stanford University chapter withdrew after years of frustration, protesting against "the high-handed methods of administration by which member chapters have no effective voice in the determination of the national policies of the association."[10]

During the three years of leadership under President-General Hobart, much of the policy regarding the renting of Constitution Hall was established. For the most part, there was little change from the policy that had existed before its completion—the D.A.R. leadership simply denied use of the hall to those whom they considered ideologically inimical to their stands on social and political issues. In 1931, the Daughters refused to allow the author Sinclair Lewis to deliver his lecture "American Literature Comes of Age" in the hall. Inquiries as to the reason elicited merely that "the D.A.R. did not care to rent the hall for that purpose."[11] Later on in the decade, the biennial convention of the United Mine Workers had to meet in the cramped Rialto Theatre because the D.A.R., which had promised them the use of the hall, reneged on the arrangement. The United Mine Workers published a report in their journal on their conflict with the D.A.R. that would have earned the approval of William Allen White: "Everyone knows that the DAR is an aristocratic high-hat institution whose members parade around like peafowls in silks and sealskins and imagine themselves as the elect of the human race. They turn up their individual and collective noses at the prospect of another gathering of working people in their hall, and the result was that it became necessary to select another meeting place."[12]

It was the use of Constitution Hall as a much sought-after concert hall that would soon embroil the D.A.R. in another scandal of far greater magnitude than the blacklist affair. Its 4,000-seat capacity (the largest of any auditorium in Washington) and the excellent acoustics and reception areas for performers and other visitors, made it an ideal place for the presentation of concerts. Even before the official opening of the hall, in October 1929, the D.A.R. anticipated that there would be many such events and plans for them were immediately begun. As Edna Scott Magna, the national chairwoman of finance, informed D.A.R. members with obvious pride: "Mrs. Wilson-Greene's delightful concerts, which will be given in the early autumn, are social, as well as musical events. The Philadelphia Orchestra and the Philharmonic-Orchestra of New York, under T. Arthur Smith's management, will each give a series of concerts. With such outstanding attractions certain, and many others probable, it is anticipated that Constitution Hall will be the musical center of the Capital."[13]

Exciting prospects, but not equally for all of the citizens of Washington. The black population of the city stood at 600,000 near the end of the decade, roughly 27 percent of the total. Only four other American cities—New York, Chicago, Philadelphia, and Baltimore—had a larger black population. But by law and custom Washington was a segregated city, and those provisions that the D.A.R. established for the use of the hall by blacks reflected that division. No local ordinance existed to separate blacks and whites in places of entertainment, but it was customary to request that blacks occupy assigned and separate sections when attending white theaters. In keeping with local policy, D.A.R. officials, meeting in October 1929, passed a ruling "that a special request of any lessee of Constitution Hall to set aside a small group of seats for Negroes be granted."[14] Accordingly, two sections, H and O, in the curve of the rear balcony, were set aside for black patrons.

As for black performers, there seems to have been no fixed policy to exclude them from appearing when the hall opened. During the years of blacklisting, the D.A.R. had never gone so far as to exclude blacks as a group from renting the old Continental Memorial Hall, although there were many black organizations as well as prominent black leaders on the blacklist. In the first years of Constitution Hall's existence, some black artists and managers did apply to the hall for its use. Shortly after the hall opened, the D.A.R. hired Fred Hand, a former actor, to run its daily affairs, and it is from Hand's own report about the use of Constitution Hall, written some years later, that much of the D.A.R.'s behavior with respect to black performers is known. Because the Daughters themselves had no experience of running a theater and concert hall, they depended in large measure on Hand and his recommendations. Apparently Hand was a typical proponent of southern attitudes toward segregation, never hesitant in enforcing those customs which relegated blacks to marginal status. At least one of his colleagues, in fact, Patrick Hayes, a concert manager who followed the Washington scene closely following his arrival in the capital in 1938, found Hand to be outspokenly racist.[15]

It is unlikely that, at the start, the D.A.R. gave much thought to the use of the hall by blacks, either as performers or as patrons. They simply had no experience of their own to guide them in their decisions. But during the first several years of the hall's existence such occasions did present themselves. During the summer of 1930, the D.A.R. gave Mrs. Wilson-Greene, a Washington concert manager, a contract to provide for a series of concerts in the hall. It was left to her to decide on the artists who would make up the series—no names, at least, appeared on the contract that she signed for the coming season. One of the artists that she planned to present was the tenor Roland Hayes. Even before Hayes was given his contract, the Metropolitan Musical Bureau of New York had applied for the use of the hall for a concert by Paul Robeson. Hand indicated in later years that "On December 10, 1930, the Executive Committee refused this request."[16] Early in 1931, however, the D.A.R. did agree to allow the black Hampton Institute Choir to present a benefit concert, "in honor of the Negro's contribution to America and his achievement along all lines."[17]

In these early years the D.A.R. appears to have decided in each case whether or not to rent the hall to a black performer. Because of their contract with Mrs. Wilson-Greene, they were not given any choice about Roland Hayes's concert, an oversight that they would later regret. Hand apparently did not indicate the reasons for denying Robeson the use of the hall, so one can only guess at them. In 1930, Robeson was not yet the passionate and outspoken defender of racial equality that he would become in a few years, but his stormy personal life, which was already beginning to make news, and his performances of Othello, celebrated but not uncontroversial, were no doubt enough to make the D.A.R. wary of him. As for the Hampton Choir, it was an educational institution, and its plan to erect a national memorial building in the capital represented a benefit to the Washington community that obviously appealed to the Daughters.

Roland Hayes sang in Constitution Hall on January 31, 1931, the Hampton Choir on March 21. The D.A.R.'s policy with regard to segregated seating alone caused enough commotion at these concerts to set Fred Hand and the Daughters on a path with respect to black performers that lasted nearly twenty years. In the spring of 1942, Hand, in telling Patrick Hayes about the hall's policy toward black performers, recounted the events of Hayes's 1931 concert. As Hayes later remembered that conversation,

> Roland Hayes came on stage to observe a large group of black men and women seated together on one side of the orchestra. It was a "group sale," purchased by a social club or alumni group. Hayes saw it as segregation and announced that he would not sing until the audience was properly mingled. He then left the stage. There was a long delay, during which the ushers stood still. Hand stood with his arms folded in the middle of the aisle facing the stage, and the black patrons remained silent in their seats, not venturing to move. Roland Hayes finally did appear and sang the recital. But the incident so infuriated Hand that he vowed, he told me, that no black artist would ever appear in the hall while he was manager. He did not tell me, nor did I ask, whether this was the policy of the DAR or merely his own policy, to which the DAR acquiesced. . . .[18]

There are differing accounts of what happened at Constitution Hall the night of March 21, when the Hampton Choir appeared. Hand summarized the occasion years later in his notes: "So much pressure was brought to bear upon the committee sponsoring this concert that the Daughters of the American Revolution waived its contractual rights in the matter and permitted the sale of tickets to Negroes in any part of the auditorium."[19] But an editorial in the *Washington Daily News* after the concert recorded the events differently: "The DAR management ruled that only two blocks of seats, those on the corners of the surrounding tiers, might be sold to colored people. After these were disposed of, hundreds of colored people were turned away with the information that the seats were sold out. It being a Saturday night concert, the turn-out of Washington's regular concertgoers was small, although the boxes were filled, consequently the Hall was two-thirds empty. The seats assigned to colored people were packed; beside them were empty blocks. Here and there through the hall, a few other colored people sat, doubtless in seats sold personally by members of the memorial association."[20] A few days after the *Daily News* editorial, the matter was taken up again in the *New York Herald Tribune,* where an open letter appeared signed by Walter White, secretary of the NAACP, protesting the D.A.R.'s lack of coopera- tion with Negroes.[21]

In later years, the Daughters stated that, as far as they knew, the Hampton Choir concert was the first time in which blacks and whites sat together in a Washington auditorium since Reconstruction. The same could be said about Roland Hayes's concert, but in neither case was it the D.A.R.'s doing. Indeed, what motivated the D.A.R.'s response to each of those events was the "unwillingness of the original sponsors of the con- cert to restrict the sale of tickets as per their contract."[22] What Hand and the Daughters learned from these early appearances of black performers was that they could not entirely prevent blacks from sitting in sections not designated for them, and thereby sitting alongside white patrons. Group sales, or any sale of tickets that did not come through the hall, but through sponsors and managers, could result in mixed seating. In 1932, the D.A.R. achieved the control that they desired, voting to include in all rental contracts beginning with March 23 a clause specifying "white artists only."

D.A.R. leaders would argue for years that their decision to insert the "white artists only" clause was motivated by the necessity of bringing the policy regarding the use of Constitution Hall into line with established Washington custom. But established custom in Washington was varied. Although blacks were customarily required to sit in separate sections in white theaters, many exceptions were made during the late 1920s and 1930s for meetings and musical and charitable events. These included concerts at the Library of Congress, services at the Washington Cathe- dral, and the Community Chest dinners at the Willard Hotel. Paul Robeson and Roland Hayes sang to interracial audiences in Washington Auditorium, and so did Anderson at the Armstrong High School and the Rialto and Belasco theaters. As for black performers, there was hardly a theater in Washington that did not allow them onto the stage. Ethel Waters and Abby Mitchell as well as Anderson appeared at the Belasco Theatre. In the National Theatre there were performances of *Green Pas- tures* in February 1933; in March 1936, Todd Duncan appeared in *Porgy and Bess,* and a year later Ethel Waters starred in *As Thousands Cheer.*[23]

In truth, the D.A.R.'s decision to insert a "white artists only" clause and to continue to maintain strictly separate sections for blacks in the Hall was not at all compelled by local custom. The exclusion of black performers was an extreme measure for the city of Washington. As for segregated seating, although the usual custom, it was nonetheless frequently abandoned in favor of mixed seating. The D.A.R. settled on an exclusionary policy because they wished to achieve a certain result in the running of the Hall and found it expedient to justify their behavior by invoking long-established custom. If artists such as Roland Hayes could cause confusion and embarrassment in the hall, if whites were finding themselves sitting next to blacks when concerts or artists proved to be popular with the black community, what would happen when such controversial artists as Paul Robeson, or such popular and beloved figures as Marian Anderson were allowed to perform?

In 1936, after Anderson had given two sold-out concerts in New York in less than a month's time, officials at Howard University, who normally sponsored her concerts in Washington, were encouraged enough to approach the D.A.R. for the use of Constitution Hall for Anderson's first concert in Washington under Hurok. V. D. Johnston, the university's treasurer, requested the use of the hall from Fred Hand. Johnson's request could hardly have been routine. University officials knew well enough what response they were going to receive from the D.A.R. Every contract issued for the use of Constitution Hall carried the "white artists only" clause, and every local manager and concert promoter was well aware of the policy. Did they believe that the D.A.R. could hardly refuse to make an exception to their exclusionary policy for Anderson, whose status as one of the foremost singers in the world was now recognized as much in America as it was across Europe? If Howard University was testing the D.A.R.'s resolve, they received no encouragement from Hand, who reminded Johnson of the "white artists only" clause, advising him to apply for permission to the D.A.R.'s National Board of Management, the governing body that included national officers and all state regents, if he wanted to pursue the matter.[24]

Not yet prepared to fight, Johnston did not follow Hand's suggestion and let the matter drop, turning instead to the Washington School Board for the use of the black Armstrong High School Auditorium. For Anderson's appearance the next year, the university again settled for the Armstrong High School. In 1938, with the demand for tickets continuing to grow, the university booked the larger, downtown Rialto Theatre.[25]

In 1939 Hurok again included Washington in Anderson's American tour, an appearance that would prove to be a watershed in the racial history of the country. Preparations for Anderson's 1939 concert, as Hurok related in his memoirs, "included a perfectly routine request from Howard University in Washington, D.C., for a concert by Marian

Anderson under the University's auspices. Arrangements were made in June 1938 for a concert to take place in Washington the next season."[26] Howard University accepted the afternoon of April 9, Easter Sunday, for Anderson's concert. In early January 1939, as plans for the concert series developed, university officials had once again to decide which hall to book. They might very well have settled for the Rialto Theatre, but the theater was then in receivership, and the receiver refused to enter into a binding contract for a single event.

On January 6, for the second time in three years, Howard University applied for the use of Constitution Hall.[27] Charles Cohen, chairman of the university's concert series, asked Fred Hand to reserve the date of April 9 for a concert by Marian Anderson. Three days later Hand informed Cohen that the date in question had already been booked by the National Symphony Orchestra, reminding him of the long-standing clause that barred blacks from appearing. Confronted with the same refusal as in 1936, university officials could well have acted as they had earlier and explored other possibilities. There were the Belasco and the National theaters, for example, or the larger of the white high school auditoriums, possibilities which officials did attempt to explore later, when little time remained to find a suitable concert hall. But Constitution Hall, even more so than earlier in the decade, was the appropriate place for Anderson's concert, and this time Howard University officials were prepared to take a firm stand against the D.A.R.

There were many reasons for the new sense of purpose and resolve on the part of university officials. For one thing they shared in the growing optimism felt by blacks across the land during the New Deal years. In many areas of race relations it was a time of gradually awakening understanding and awareness on the part of whites, and a slowly increasing, albeit cautious, hopefulness on the part of blacks.

On the Washington scene, Mrs. Roosevelt worked tirelessly for racial equality, bringing constant encouragement to blacks. As first lady, she opened the doors of the White House to black groups and civil rights leaders and regularly invited black entertainers to perform. As the New Deal years advanced, her commitment to racial justice became more political, both publicly and behind the scenes. She attended national civil rights conventions, wrote more openly about civil rights in her articles and newspaper column, and forged sympathetic and fruitful alliances with important leaders in the black community. Especially important were her friendships with Mary McLeod Bethune, head of the National Youth Administration, and Walter White, the executive secretary of the NAACP.[28]

Improvements in interracial good will and cooperation in Washington, although hampered by the dual school system and the mores of public segregation, were frequent enough during the thirties to provide encouragement to black leaders. By the end of the decade, buses, trolleys, and taxicabs were open to the public regardless of race. So were the dining rooms and waiting rooms of railroad stations. Blacks could use public libraries of the District of Columbia as well as attend lectures, meetings, and concerts in all government halls and in the Library of Congress. And there was black representation on the Board of Education and the Board of Public Welfare, as well as in such agencies as the Community Chest and the Washington Housing Association.[29]

Younger black Washingtonians especially felt a great urgency to bring about change, for example in the area of jobs. A group of black leaders that included William Hastie, Charles Houston, who later became special counsel to the NAACP, and Robert C. Weaver, aided by NAACP officials, formed the New Negro Alliance in 1933, which began to devote its energies to the picketing and boycotting of local business establishments. In two years there were nearly 300 jobs filled by blacks in businesses that had been held exclusively by whites. There were changes as well in graduate education in Washington that inspired some measure of hope in all of the black universities there and beyond. In 1936, the first black was admitted to the school of social work at Catholic University, and several months later the graduate school faculty of American University voted unanimously to admit black students.[30]

The decade of the thirties was a period of great change for Howard University. Since 1926, when the first black president, Mordecai Johnson, took office, race became more and more of an issue in the university. During the New Deal years the university found a great friend and advocate in Interior Secretary Harold Ickes, a strong proponent of racial justice and equality. The expenditures for Howard came under the jurisdiction of the Interior Department, and Ickes, together with Mrs. Roosevelt, fought hard over the years to push a recalcitrant Budget Department into giving Howard sufficient funds for expansion and development. They rarely succeeded, but their committed advocacy gave the university a feeling of much needed support and encouragement.

Charles Houston, the young Harvard-trained black lawyer who became dean of the Howard University Law School in 1924, was another of those who helped to create a new order at Howard. Houston's vision for the Law School was to provide "superior professional training and extraordinary motivation . . . to prepare the professional cadres needed to lead successful litigation against racism as practiced by government and sanctioned by law."[31] By the end of 1931, full accreditation and approval were granted the Law School. During his years at Howard, Houston taught many students who were later to gain prominence in the area of civil rights, among them Oliver W. Hill, Edward P. Lovett, William Bryant, and Thurgood Marshall. From the early thirties, in addition to his duties at Howard, Houston became more and more involved with the activities of the NAACP, working as a member of its National Legal Committee on racial discrimination in the areas of public accommodation, education, and jobs. In 1935 he resigned from the University to become Special Counsel to the NAACP, working with its executive secretary, Walter White.

By the end of the thirties, having begun as a biracial institution, Howard was on its way to becoming a black university of prestige and leadership in the nation's capital. It could look to New Deal leaders for support. Its Law School had become a training ground for young lawyers prepared and eager to take up the fight for blacks on many fronts. It felt prepared, indeed, morally responsible, for taking a stand on issues of concern to the black community. When Hand, speaking for the D.A.R., refused the request of V. D. Johnson, the university's treasurer, for the use of Constitution Hall for a concert by Marian Anderson, Howard University was not prepared to back down. On January 12, an open letter from Johnson appeared in the *Washington Times-Herald,* criticizing the D.A.R.'s decision: "The question arises . . . whether there are not a sufficient number of persons in Washington and vicinity interested in hearing Miss Anderson and what she represents to impress upon the D.A.R. that this restriction may not represent public opinion in Washington."[32] Three days later the *Washington Times-Herald* published an editorial castigating the D.A.R.: "It stands almost in the shadow of the Lincoln Memorial, but the Great Emancipator's sentiments about 'race, creed or previous condition of servitude' are not shared by the Daughters, for contracts of a commercial nature, the use of these halls contains a clause banning any member of the Negro race. Prejudice rules to make the Capital of the Nation ridiculous in the eyes of all cultured people and to comfort Fuehrer Hitler and the members of our Nazibund."[33] The *Times-Herald* would not be the first to point to the Lincoln Memorial as a symbol of importance, so close in its physical presence to Constitution Hall yet so distant from the D.A.R. in the political and social ideals it represented.

What Howard lacked was strategy, and a large enough base of support. Realizing this, they went first to Sol Hurok for help. Cohen wrote to him on the nineteenth about the university's difficulty in obtaining the hall for Anderson's concert. Hurok wasted little time in acting. He wrote to Hand himself on the twenty-third: "Without attempting to discuss the justification of such a policy, we are asking whether you would waive that restriction in the case of Miss Anderson. It need not be pointed out to you, we hope, that Marian Anderson is one of the greatest living singers and the application of such a restriction would be to deny a great musical experience to the people of your city, since it is impossible to present her in any other hall in Washington. Would you, or a possible board of managers whom you might represent, take up this request as soon as possible and advise us of your decision."[34] Clearly Hurok was outraged, yet he managed to control his feelings, hoping that Hand and the D.A.R. would listen to reason. Hand also wanted to avoid unnecessary confrontation. His response to Hurok, written on the twenty-fifth, refers only indirectly to the "white artists only" restriction. He still hoped that if he stressed the conflict of date long enough (neither Hurok nor anyone else had yet requested alternate dates) the problem might go away: "I beg to advise you that Constitution Hall is not available on April 9th, 1939, because of prior commitments. In the matter of policy under which Constitution Hall operates, I would recommend that you address a letter to Mrs. Henry Robert, Jr., President General of the National Society, DAR."[35]

In later years Hurok took a great deal of credit for fanning the flames of public opinion on behalf of Anderson. In 1974 he issued perhaps the most extravagant statement of all: "I took over the Washington Hotel, a whole floor upstairs, and I brought in my press agent and all to start to bombard the whole country, you know—artists, actors and so on and so on. A big campaign, we made. It was to protest that the D.A.R. are not allowing Marian Anderson to perform there. The whole thing was just a question of mass protest. I raised the sentiment all over the country, as a matter of fact. The world protested."[36] Of course Hurok felt very deeply the outrage done to Anderson. An immigrant Russian Jew, having faced his own share of hard times and discriminatory behavior, he was able to identify with Anderson. Nevertheless, there is no evidence that Hurok engaged in any campaign from the headquarters in the Washington Hotel to marshall public support. Write-in protests were organized by Hurok weeks after Walter White and others would initiate such efforts. Later on, taking advantage of what was to become for him the "marketing opportunity of a lifetime,"[37] Hurok did act more decisively. In the meantime, however much as he may have huffed and puffed to friends and associates, he did very little.

It was to the NAACP, an organization alert to infractions of individual liberty and gaining in ability to marshall public opinion, that Howard could look for help. The university's ties to the NAACP were by then especially close. Houston, the former dean of the Law School and William Hastie, who had served on the school's faculty, were both NAACP lawyers, with Houston now serving as special counsel. Houston would have been particularly rankled by the D.A.R.'s refusal to rent Constitution Hall for Anderson's concert; earlier in the thirties the D.A.R. had gone after his teacher and mentor, Felix Frankfurter, when they grew alarmed that Frankfurter might be appointed solicitor general.[38] Anderson too had personal ties to NAACP officials. Walter White, NAACP executive secretary, had known Anderson for years, watching closely as her career blossomed.[39] It was White who had coaxed her back to the stage after her disappointing Town Hall recital fifteen years earlier. Her lawyer, Hubert Delany, was acting as council for the NAACP and sat on its executive committee.

By the middle of January, a small cadre of friends and associates, in or close to the Washington scene, used to working together in the interest of blacks and already alerted to the D.A.R.'s refusal, began to talk and to plan. They included, in addition to Howard University officials, Mrs. Roosevelt, Interior Secretary Ickes, and NAACP officials White and Houston. Indeed, Mrs. Roosevelt and White were already conferring about how they might show their support for Anderson in view of the D.A.R.'s refusal. On January 16, the Spingarn Committee of the NAACP voted to award Anderson its medal. White wanted very much for Mrs. Roosevelt to present it to her during the ceremonies in July. Mrs. Roosevelt was only too happy to agree, glad of the opportunity to honor Anderson publicly in a way that could hardly be politicized to her or her husband's disadvantage.

In the weeks following the Spingarn Committee meeting, ideas were exchanged and some plans outlined, yet there was little clear focus. The D.A.R., in fact, was not an easy target. As a private organization, it could act independently in ways that made public scrutiny difficult. In its long history, the only systematic and organized criticism, during the blacklisting scandal, came from inside the D.A.R. and not from without. Many people refused to take the organization all that seriously. Others felt that as a private organization, one that had done considerable good during all of its history, the Daughters had the right to rent their hall to whomever they chose. Indeed, in a *Washington Post* editorial that appeared as late as February 21, just such a position was voiced: "But as a private organization the D.A.R. have the same unquestionable right as a private school, or church, or club, to decide when their auditorium shall be made available, and when withheld, for purposes of public assemblage."[40]

Walter White took the lead. Only days after the Spingarn Committee meeting, he, together with Mary Johnson, a reporter for *Time* who was indignant over the D.A.R.'s action and wanted to do a story on them, worked out a plan to gather support for Anderson among her colleagues in the artistic community. On the nineteenth they sent out the following telegram: "Marian Anderson has been denied use of Constitution Hall in Washington, D.C., by Daughters of the American Revolution account clause limiting Hall to white artists only. National Association for Advancement of Colored People invites expression your opinion on this ban by telegraph collect."[41] The telegram went to Lawrence Tibbett, Giovanni Martinelli, Lily Pons, Elisabeth Rethberg, Nelson Eddy, Geraldine Farrar, Kirsten Flagstad, Sigrid Onegin, Leopold Stokowski, Arturo Toscanini, Walter Damrosch, and José Iturbi. Farrar and Tibbett responded the next day, Flagstad, Stokowski, and others by the end of the month. Flagstad expressed the thoughts of many who had received wires: "As a foreigner in America, I have always been impressed by the freedom and democracy in this country. I therefore am greatly surprised to learn from you that the use of Constitution Hall in Washington has been refused for a concert to my fellow-artist, Marian Anderson."[42] In the meantime, while responses to White's telegram were still coming in, Hurok, following Hand's suggestion, wrote to Mrs. Robert on January 27, "that the cultured people of America would be gravely offended by your decision to exercise the restriction above-mentioned."[43] Three days later Secretary Ickes, informed about Hand's decision by Howard President Mordecai Johnson, wrote to Mrs. Robert himself: "This is such an astounding discrimination against equal rights that I am loath to believe that the Daughters of the American Revolution should invoke such a rule. I am writing you to inquire whether Doctor Johnson was correctly informed."[44]

Mary Johnson's enthusiasm was infectious, and she, together with White, Houston, and Dr. Elizabeth Yates Webb, spent many hours talking about Mary's planned attack on the D.A.R. Johnson and White were concerned about timing: when to release to the press the telegrams of protest from artists. Yates suggested that they try to get the box holders at Constitution Hall to protest Anderson's exclusion, and that they try to convince artists who were going to appear in the hall to refuse to perform until the Daughters lifted the ban on Anderson. Houston and White, having determined that the D.A.R. was tax exempt, thought that the Hall should be attacked on the grounds that it was a public institution, where, as in government buildings, segregation was generally not practiced.[45]

But these ideas were long shots, and they would require considerable time in which to gather public support. No artist, in fact, refused to play in Constitution Hall. A month later, when the controversy had grown considerably, Heifetz, in his dressing room at Constitution Hall after a concert, remarked that "I was really uncomfortable on that platform, uncomfortable to think that this very hall in which I played has been barred to a great singer because of her race; it made me feel ashamed. I protest, as the entire musical profession protests, against such a sad and deplorable attitude."[46] Heifetz did not refuse to play on that stage, and he took care to voice his protest only after a sell-out audience had paid to hear him play.

Not until January 27 did White feel he had enough protests from artists to issue a press release. Not a single paper responded. On the thirty-first he added his voice, as secretary of the NAACP, to the protests that went to President-General Robert: "May we respectfully urge revocation of the ban on other than white artists appearing in Constitution Hall. Specifically, the refusal to permit Miss Marian Anderson, distinguished Negro contralto, to sing there in April, has shocked musicians, music-lovers and fair-minded Americans generally. Barring a world famed artist because of color from a building named by the Daughters of the American Revolution 'Constitution Hall' violates the very spirit and purpose of the immortal document after which the Hall is named."[47]

Finally, on February 4, the *Pittsburgh Courier,* so far an isolated voice in the black press and, as it turned out, too late to exert any influence on the D.A.R., ran a story about the protest by opera stars against the action of the D.A.R. As White and others, waiting patiently for telegrams of protest, entertained one idea after another, it was Mrs. Robert who acted decisively, a veritable general mobilizing her troops. She understood well that it was what happened inside the organization that she needed to be concerned about. She had to appear strong and decisive to D.A.R. leadership and state regents, and to assure them with enough conviction that her actions were appropriate and for the good of the organization. The experience of predecessors had shown her that strength within was the best safeguard against criticism from without. If public sentiment grew against the D.A.R. she needed to be ready for it, and that required discipline and credibility. She did not respond immediately to Hurok, or to Ickes, or to White. On February 1 she convened the Board of Management, persuaded them, with Hand's collusion, that no exception could be made for Anderson as far as the "white artists only" clause was concerned, and won a victory of 39 to 1.

Only then, having gained the support she needed, did she write to Hurok and to Ickes. She kept her remarks brief, circumscribed (again the conflict of date) and vague, a policy she followed relentlessly with the outside world. To Ickes she wrote:

> In reply to your letter of January 30, Constitution Hall had already been engaged for Easter Sunday for use by another musical organization.
>
> Dr. Johnson was informed of the existence of a policy of several years' standing, limiting the use of Constitution Hall to white artists.
>
> The artistic and musical standing of Miss Marian Anderson is not involved in any way. In view of the existence of provisions in prevailing agreements with other organizations and concert bureaus, and the policy which has been adopted in the past, an exception cannot be made in this instance.[48]

She waited until February 13, the day before she was to leave Washington for her spring tour of state D.A.R. conferences that would keep her away for nearly two months, to issue a press release: "The rules governing the use of Constitution Hall are in accordance with the policy of theaters, auditoriums, hotels and public schools of the District of Columbia."[49] As any keen observer of the color line in Washington could have pointed out at the time, Mrs. Robert's statement made claim to a uniformity that did not exist. Public schools were segregated by law, although there was provision for mixed use after school hours; hotels stuck relentlessly by tradition to the color line; as for theatres and auditoriums, the practice was more complicated and exceptions to standard provisions or custom were frequent.

In light of the D.A.R.'s history throughout the late 1920s and most of the 1930s, these explanations on the part of the president-general seem like high comedy. Here was an organization that was portraying itself as helplessly restricted by prevailing policy, swallowed up by social and political forces over which they could hardly be expected to have any control or impact. Yet here was an organization whose leadership had for years circulated a blacklist of all those who opposed the D.A.R.'s views, that had testified before congressional committees in support of anti-liberal legislation, that had summarily expelled members who disagreed openly with D.A.R. policy. Can there be much doubt that the D.A.R.

banned Anderson because she was black, and what's more because her concert was sponsored by the prestigious black Howard University, and because she was defended by officials of the NAACP, an organization that had been included in the infamous blacklist? Hand, who always spoke his mind, had presumably told the D.A.R. at the time the "white artists clause" was adopted, that the more prestigious theaters in Washington do not rent to Negroes. For the D.A.R. nothing had changed.

By February 1 Howard and NAACP officials realized that there was little advantage, at least for the time being, in trying to rent Constitution Hall from the D.A.R. Only Hurok held out, still enticed by the D.A.R.'s continual reminder that April 9 was not available. As Hurok related years later in his memoirs: "Mark Levine, my good friend, of National Concert and Artists Corporation, wrote to Mr. Hand at about this time asking for available dates for a concert by Ignacz Paderewski in Constitution Hall. Hand replied with a list of dates which did not include the 9th, but did mention the 8th and 10th as open. I wired the University's concert manager that the 8th and 10th were open and he promptly applied to Hand for either date."[50] On February 15, Cohen received Hand's reply, that "the Hall is not available for a concert by Miss Anderson."[51]

Now Hurok had to accept what White, Ickes, and others had already realized, that the D.A.R. would not reverse its ruling for Anderson. In the meantime, concerned that time was running out, Howard University applied to the Community Center Department of the Washington Board of Education for the use of the Central High School Auditorium, one of the city's largest white high school auditoriums, for Anderson's concert on the ninth. The terrain of battle had shifted.

Howard's application to the Washington School Board was not without precedent. For Anderson's 1936 and 1937 Washington recitals, Howard had applied to the Board of Education for the use of the black Armstrong High School, and both times permission for its use was granted. Howard's request to use the Armstrong High auditorium was allowed under the "Community Center Use of Buildings," a 1915 act of Congress that allowed for the supplementary use of public school buildings and grounds in Washington for educational purposes—civic meetings, social centers, and centers of recreation. It was up to the Board of Education to establish the rules under which such community use of schools was carried out. Accordingly the board set up a Community Center Department and structured it in keeping with the segregated use of public schools in Washington, with separate individuals in charge of all matters of community use for white and black facilities. Furthermore it had been determined by the board that "the use of school facilities will not be granted to any organization for any purpose which will result in a financial profit accruing to the organization to which such school facilities have been granted."[52]

A policy of understanding and good will between the public schools and the colleges and universities in Washington developed over the years as a result of the School Board's willingness to interpret generously the original statute's provision that community use had to be directly connected with the primary educational functions of the public school system. In the school year 1939, for example, the Community Center Department approved the use of school gymnasiums and auditoriums for sports events, recitals, and the presentation of plays. Whether the School Board, in setting up the Community Center Department, had in mind that performers of Anderson's reputation, used to earning large fees for their concerts, would request the use of high school auditoriums is hard to say, but Howard got around the restriction on profit by agreeing to turn over any proceeds to its scholarship fund.

With only two months to go before Anderson's concert, Cohen had turned to the School Board as a last resort. From his point of view it may have been a routine request, but strategically its wording was unwise, giving undue prominence to what the School Board might easily consider a question of profit: "The first two years [1936 and 1937] she was presented at Armstrong High School auditorium. Last year, due to the increase in fee, it was necessary for us to secure a larger auditorium which resulted in our success in getting the Rialto Theatre."[53] But the Rialto had closed, and the National and Belasco theaters could not give Cohen a definite statement about April 9 until two weeks before the concert. For the School Board, however, the request was anything but routine, since the racial division of the Community Center Department's staff made it impossible for Elizabeth Peeples, the director of the Community Center Department, or Dr. Garnet C. Wilkinson, who assisted the superintendent in matters of community use of school facilities in black schools, to rule on the request for the use of a white facility by a black organization. It was sent to School Superintendent Frank Balou, who rejected it. Balou's response to Cohen came on February 3, with the most perfunctory of explanations: "In the opinion of the school officers, it is not possible under the law for the Community Center Department to grant your request for the use of Central High School auditorium to present Miss Marian Anderson."[54]

Although two weeks of relative standstill followed Superintendent Ballou's refusal, it was not, at least for Howard University, a period of retrenchment. Indeed, the university reached out to its own community,

and to Mrs. Roosevelt, thereby setting in motion a series of jolts to biracial consciousness that by the end of the month would be felt throughout Washington and eventually across the country. The first of those jolts
involved the school system. This time Howard enlisted the help of Dr.
Doxie Wilkerson, a professor of education in the university, whose strategy was to present a second application for the use of Central High
School to the School Board, a biracial committee. Wilkerson himself
appeared before the Board of Education at its February 15 meeting, on
behalf of a group of citizens, hoping to convince them to override the
earlier decision by Superintendent Ballou. Wilkerson made it clear that
the request "is made to meet a specific emergency situation. We do not
raise with you any question of continuing policy."[55] Wilkerson acted in
good faith when he assured the board that he wished in no way to establish precedent, but his arguments did not prevail, and the Board upheld
Ballou's refusal. Before long, the issue of precedent would cause unexpected conflict and disagreement. What the D.A.R. said and did within
its own executive sessions was private. How the School Board acted was
not, and its decision to deprive the people of Washington, white and
black alike, of hearing Anderson sing, was potentially incendiary in a city
in which, in spite of the excellence of it's black schools, the economic
advantages enjoyed by white schools was a fact known to black teachers,
administrators, and parents.

Three days later the citizens of Washington began to react. Teachers
were among the first to become indignant over the School Board's decision. On the eighteenth, the local chapter of the American Federation of
Teachers met at the YWCA to protest the racial ban against Anderson.
The next day, Charles Edward Russell, a liberal white attorney, then
president of the Inter-Racial Committee, held a meeting that resulted in
the formation of the Marian Anderson Citizens' Committee (MACC).
The following day, February 20, they picketed the Board of Education, a
form of interracial protest that had not been used against the board in
nearly two decades. A steering committee of MACC was quickly formed
by representatives of twenty-four local and national organizations, and
its interim officers began to collect signatures for a petition of protest
they planned to present on March 1, the next meeting of the School
Board.[56]

Before the end of the month the MACC, an independent coalition of
teachers, clergymen, and representatives of civic and fraternal organizations had set up its headquarters at 615 F Street, Northwest, Houston's
law firm, with Houston as chairman of the committee, John Lovell, Jr.,

as secretary, and Bertha Blair as vice-chairman. An informal alliance between the committee and the NAACP was quickly established, with Houston and White conferring regularly on strategy. Houston especially was in his element. A few years back he had served two frustrating years on the School Board, fighting for equal appropriations for black schools, protesting the restrictions on free speech, and arguing for the nonsegregated use of school buildings after school hours and in the summer. Houston and his colleagues and supporters in the NAACP appreciated well the significant impact they might have in Washington with the MACC. Here was a cause that did not require lengthy and costly legal battles, nor long and strenuous hours of boycotting, with its demands of personal sacrifice and of potential danger. Many felt what John Lovell later wrote, that "Washington is a giant awakened."[57]

The MACC called its first protest meeting for the twenty-sixth, at the Mt. Pleasant Congregational Church. Fliers for the meeting were circulated, inviting the public to "defend our democratic right to hear Marian Anderson sing." As the handbill proclaimed, the public had a right to hear Anderson in the semi-public, tax-exempt Constitution Hall, and in the publicly owned Central High School. The fliers and mass protest were meant to stir the public to outrage and shame on the widest possible front. Again the comparison with Nazi Germany was raised: "Marian Anderson is a Negro. Thus, even as in Naziland, superb art is here crucified upon the altar of racial bigotry. Shall we permit the DAR and the Board of Education to impose this unwholesome policy upon our community? Shall the people of Washington dictate, or be dictated to?"[58]

In two days time the conflict in Washington grew to national proportions. Mrs. Roosevelt had debated for many weeks in what way she could best demonstrate her support of Anderson and her feelings about the actions of the D.A.R. and the Board. She was active behind the scenes but hesitant to add her voice publicly to the growing controversy. A month earlier she had agreed to present the Spingarn Medal to Anderson at the ceremonies in July, met with White about the broadcast of the ceremonies and made plans to invite Anderson to the White House in June to perform for the British royal couple. In early February, however, she refused Howard treasurer V. D. Johnston's request to rebuke the D.A.R. publicly for its ban on Anderson, concerned about the kind of impact any public statement from her might have.[59] She was a beloved friend to blacks, yet she had to worry about steering a careful course around her husband's opponents and others who found her position on civil rights and social issues too extreme. What good would a public statement from her to the D.A.R. do, she asked Johnston, when the organization already found her too extreme?

Mrs. Roosevelt understood well that the target of any public action on her part must be the D.A.R. and not the Washington School Board, a local issue that could not possibly resonate successfully on a national scale. By February twenty-sixth she was ready to act. As plans continued for the first protest meeting of the MACC that evening, Mrs. Roosevelt wrote to D.A.R. President-General Robert that she was resigning from the organization, explaining that she was "in complete disagreement with the attitude" that the D.A.R. represented in banning Anderson from the stage of Constitution Hall. "You had an opportunity to lead in an enlightened way," she told Mrs. Robert, "and it seems to me that your organization has failed. . . ." For her there was no other alternative but to no longer "continue to be a member of your organization."[60]

On February 27, Mrs. Roosevelt used her "My Day" column to inform her readers across the country of her resignation from the D.A.R. No one can fail to see the skill with which she told the public of her feelings. Understated, not even mentioning the organization by name, she focused rather on the soul-searching that the decision required of her. In those paragraphs Mrs. Roosevelt, almost thinking out loud, was not a political activist, nor a champion of causes, but a concerned citizen who was trying to do what was right.

> The question is, if you belong to an organization and disapprove of an action which is typical of a policy, shall you resign or is it better to work for a changed point of view within the organization? In the past when I was able to work actively in any organization to which I belonged, I have usually stayed in until I had at least made a fight and been defeated. Even then I have as a rule usually accepted my defeat and decided either that I was wrong or that I was perhaps a little too far ahead of the thinking of the majority of that time. I belong to an organization in which I can do no active work. They have taken action which has been widely talked on in the press. To remain a member implies approval of that action, and therefore I am resigning.[61]

During the next week, news of Mrs. Roosevelt's resignation could be read in newspapers across the country. In the court of public opinion her action was generally approved of. In a national survey reported in the press in mid-March, 67 percent of the country as a whole supported Mrs. Roosevelt's resignation. Only in the South was there a majority of opposition. As the *Washington Post* reported, "Southerners dissented by an average vote of 57 per cent, but even some of the dissenters declared they had no objection to Marian Anderson's singing as a paid performer. It was Mrs. Roosevelt's 'making a fuss about it' that they disliked."[62]

How did Anderson herself feel about what was going on? What did she want to see happen? On the basis of her recollections, her own awareness of the controversy began only with Mrs. Roosevelt's resignation. "Negotiations for the renting of the hall," she said later, "were begun while I was touring, and I recall that the first intimation I had that there were difficulties came by accident. . . . I was in San Francisco, I recall, when I passed a newsstand, and my eye caught a headline: MRS. ROOSEVELT TAKES STAND. Under this was another line, in bold print just a bit smaller: RESIGNS FROM D.A.R., etc. I was on my way to the concert hall for my performance and could not stop to buy a paper. I did not get one until after the concert, and I honestly could not conceive that things had gone so far."[63]

If Anderson learned about how far things had gone from the headlines of a San Francisco newspaper, she learned as much, and more, from a telegram she received that same day from Hurok. He too was pleased with Mrs. Roosevelt's resignation, aware of its publicity value. Indeed, he was already full of plans about a huge outdoor concert, plans that he had never bothered to discuss with Anderson. "For details of the case," he wrote her, "please refer to my manager in New York who is arranging an outdoor concert in Washington on April ninth free to the public."[64] In the meantime, Anderson could speak to the press, "but with only the briefest possible statement in this vein. . . ."[65] Anderson did speak to the press that day, her first public statement about the controversy that now involved not only the D.A.R. but the Washington School Board, delivering verbatim the words that Hurok had suggested in his telegram: "I am not surprised at Mrs. Roosevelt's action because she seemed to me to be one who really comprehended the true meaning of democracy. I'm shocked beyond words to be barred from the Capital of my own country after having appeared in almost every other capital in the world."[66]

Whatever emotional turmoil Anderson may have suffered over the actions of the D.A.R. and the Washington School Board, and the nationwide controversy in which she was embroiled, outwardly she remained self-possessed and dignified in all of her public statements. Eventually hounded by newsmen wherever she appeared, she continued to maintain that she knew little of what was happening. Of course, it was not like her to become involved in controversy. And no doubt she found it expedient to maintain, when asked for interviews, that she knew little of what was going on. One has the impression, however, that, on this occasion, Anderson's reticence to speak out was the outcome of an inner battle that was unlike anything she had experienced before.

Was she entirely candid in her continued avowals that she knew nothing of the controversy until that fateful day in San Francisco, a position from which she never wavered? Had not a single person—family, the Hurok agency, or her old friend Walter White —told her what was happening, asked her advice about how to proceed, warned her of possible consequences of the growing controversy that by late February had become nationwide? In fact she knew what was happening from the very beginning. In the weeks before Mrs. Roosevelt's resignation, mail began to pile up for her at home from individuals and organizations who wanted to express their support. Some mail, at least, was duly forwarded to her. Alyse especially could hardly contain her excitement over what was happening when she wrote to Marian, sometimes letting her know of events just as they were broadcast on the radio. As early as the last weeks of January, Walter White wrote to Anderson about the Spingarn Medal, telling her of his and Mary Johnson's plan to elicit telegrams from leading musical artists criticizing the D.A.R. During the following weeks, he continued to keep her informed by mail.[67]

For Anderson, the controversy brewing in Washington and around the country was frightening, a burden that made her feel threatened, even pursued. "It seemed to increase and to follow me wherever I went,"[68] she confessed in later years. The symbol that she was being made to represent was not of her own choosing and this made her feel ashamed and unworthy, even defensive that she might herself have caused some of the unpleasantness. Given her background and upbringing, it is no wonder that her reactions were very often much like those of a frightened and confused child. She sought desperately to humanize the controversy, to reduce it to everyday proportion, to find a way to deal with events on the level of people—good and bad people alike—rather than attempt to follow the issues, evaluate arguments and understand the political implications of what was happening. "I was sorry for the people who had precipitated the affair. I felt that their behavior stemmed from a lack of understanding,"[69] is how she put it in later years. In Mrs. Roosevelt she found a lifeline of reality to the controversy, and she held on to that support. Here was a woman of great courage and liberal spirit, a woman with whom she had met and felt a great kinship. Mrs. Roosevelt became her savior, her defender in a swirl of ugly events that she did not want to think about or even entirely acknowledge.

As news of Mrs. Roosevelt's resignation made headlines across the country, Houston and the MACC, feeling that they had now reached a state of embarrassing emergency—there were only five weeks left before Anderson's scheduled appearance—counted on reversing the School Board's ban. Armed with a petition bearing 3,000 names, Houston appeared before a crowded and tense board in the Franklin School on March 1, declaring that the School Board's decision against Anderson was a "travesty on democracy."[70] Sidney Katz, the secretary-treasurer of the Washington CIO, appearing on behalf of the MACC, compared the action of the school board to "the treatment of Jewish artists in Nazi Germany and Fascist Italy."[71] To the School Board's review of its decision of two weeks earlier, based on arguments over profit and the legal requirement of maintaining a dual system in the schools, Houston responded eloquently. He reminded the board that both the New York Philharmonic and Rachmaninoff had appeared at Central High School for a profit, that the tennis stars Tilden and Vines had played in McKinley gymnasium, with tickets selling for only $1.65. Applicants in the past, in fact, were not even required to present any statement about expenditures and ticket prices. Anderson, he explained, had reduced her fee so that the ticket prices could remain virtually as they had in previous years.

In the end it was decided to turn the controversy over to the Committee on the Community Use of Schools, scheduled in two days' time. Houston had high hopes as he made his way to the committee that Friday afternoon, March 3. As he told White and Hubert Delany after the meeting, "I had expected Friday a real hearing by the Committee, and had obtained thru the Committee [MACC] new signatures on the petition, a file of newspaper comments, letters and telegrams of endorsement, resolutions, and Canon Anson Phelps Stokes was present to speak pro permission."[72] The committee was biracial and passions ran high. Houston could see that the argument over profit was a sham. In the end what mattered was race. In order to quell the unprecedented outrage against the School Board's earlier decisions, the committee was prepared, as a proof of good will to Anderson and the black citizens of Washington, and to remove the conflict from public scrutiny, to grant Anderson the use of Central High School. There would have to be assurance, however, that the concession would not be taken as a precedent, and that in the future no further applications would be submitted. When people on the committee tried to speak out against the proposal they were ruled out of order. One of the white members insisted that the black members state individually that he or she unequivocally supported the resolution. As Houston reported to White and Delany the next day, the black members on the committee "were somewhat afraid that the report was deliberately provocative, and that some elements in the school administration really hoped the Negroes would indignantly reject it, so that these elements could go to the public and say: see, the radicals don't want Marian Anderson particularly, they are just using her concert as an opening to attack segregation."[73]

The Board of Education upheld the committee's decision, voting six to two for its acceptance. For Houston it was a hollow victory. He wanted Anderson to sing at Central High School, but not at the cost of having to make concessions to the Board. Significantly, no one thought to ask Anderson herself how she felt about the School Board's decision. Of course the pattern had been set from the very beginning of the controversy. Anderson was certainly regularly informed, but there is little reason to believe that she was ever consulted seriously about decisions. Those who knew her well, Hurok and White certainly, feeling instinctively that her first impulse was to avoid unpleasantness and friction when she could, simply treated her as a compliant figure rather than as an equal partner as events transpired. Is it possible that Anderson felt on some level hurt and angry that she was being used for motives and purposes for which she had little say, no matter how much sympathy she would have expressed? At fundamental moments of decision she was, in fact, ignored. In the case of the School Board's offer, even with the proviso that her appearance could not be seen as a precedent, she would have been strongly inclined to accept. In such dilemmas her thinking was always clear: accept graciously any show of support and compromise from your opponents, even with strings attached, for that is the only way that people make progress in social understanding. If it was up to Anderson, she would have agreed to sing at the Central High School auditorium even in the face of the Board's stipulation that no future applications be submitted.

During the first weeks of March, in the immediate aftermath of the School Board's decision, the differing motives and individual concerns of the participants revealed themselves. Houston wanted to drive as big a wedge as possible into the armor of segregation in the school system. White and NAACP officials were content to denounce the implications against free speech inherent in the School Board's reversal. Cohen, who desperately needed the Central High School auditorium for Anderson's concert, notified the school board on the ninth that he would accept the offer to use the auditorium, but not the conditions imposed on it. For Ballou things had gone too far. If a black performer of Anderson's stature, backed up by a biracial coalition that had already stirred up so much opposition to the school board, were allowed to perform to a mixed audience in a white high school in Washington, what might he expect next? On March 17, Ballou withdrew the School Board's offer. As for Hurok, he had already, weeks before, begun to entertain an idea that would grow into a solution of unprecedented significance.[74]

On February 24, as the MACC was anxiously gathering signatures for a petition that they would present to the School Board on March 1, Hurok, in a telephone conversation from his home, told the NAACP that Anderson would keep her April 9 engagement in Washington, when she will sing "out in the open air in the park immediately in front of Constitution Hall. She will sing for the people of Washington and there will be no charge, because the concert will be held out in the open. Our only stage decoration will be two American flags."[75] Did Hurok really mean to act on the idea then, or was it merely a showman's daydream born of frustration and anger? Could he have gotten the idea from Lulu V. Childers, Howard University's director of music, who had said to the press a month earlier that "She"ll sing here—even if we have to build a tent for her."[76] The idea of an outdoor concert was in the air. So was the image of the Lincoln Memorial and the spirit of democracy that graced its columns. Indeed, the very first editorial to appear in the Washington press about Anderson and the D.A.R. controversy, in the middle of January, made just such a reference: "They [the D.A.R.] stand almost in the shadow of the Lincoln Memorial, but the Great Emancipator's sentiments about 'race, creed, or previous condition of servitude,' are not shared by the Daughters, for every contract for the use of these halls contains a clause banning any member of the Negro race."[77]

By the first of March the two ideas—an open air concert, and the symbolic significance of the Lincoln Memorial—had not yet come together. Hurok persisted in his idea about a concert in the small park across the street from Constitution Hall, but White disliked the idea: "I think it would be undignified and too much like a small boy thumbing his nose at the back of a larger boy who has beaten him up."[78] In the end, it was Walter White who joined the two ideas into one, who had the imagination to see that an open air concert, with Anderson singing on the steps of the Lincoln Memorial, would create a powerful statement of defiance against bigotry and the evils of segregation. The possibility grew stronger in his mind as he began to discuss it with black colleagues in Washington. At the end of the first week of March he wrote to Houston that Cohen and Johnston of Howard University had already mentioned the idea to Hurok.[79]

The others needed persuading, for other options were not yet decisively closed off. The possibility that a way could be found to use Central
High School ended only on the seventeenth when Ballou withdrew the
offer. During the following week Cohen was prepared to rent the
Belasco Theatre when word was received that it would be available.
Cohen's decision made another round of conferring necessary. White
told Howard officials that it "would be a let-down since the Belasco is a
dilapidated old theater which is not highly regarded in Washington,"[80]
but Cohen and Johnston seemed reluctant to give up on the theater. At
the March 13 meeting of the board of directors of the NAACP, a formal
resolution was passed that Anderson should give her concert at the Lincoln Memorial. White wrote to Hurok the same day: "I would like to
offer the suggestion that should an open-air concert by Miss Anderson
be held in Washington the possibility of holding it at the Lincoln Memorial be considered. This would have a particular significance, which you
will readily see."[81] Hurok did more than consider White's proposal.
Quick to see both the symbolic potency of the suggestion and the enormous publicity that would be gained from such an event, he appropri-
ated it for himself. On March 21, Hurok announced to the *New York
Times* that Anderson would sing at the Lincoln Memorial. Perhaps a little
peeved at Hurok's intrusion White informed Anderson himself on the
twenty-fourth—she was in Waco, Texas, for a concert—that he had suggested to Hurok that she sing at the Lincoln Memorial, that the formal
resolution, in fact, had been introduced to NAACP board members by
her old friend and lawyer, Hubert Delany.[82]

There was no turning back. Before the end of the month the leading
voices of a coalition that had worked tirelessly for nearly three months
were in agreement that Anderson should sing at the Lincoln Memorial.
White did not get around to writing Anderson again about plans until
April 4, when he was able to tell her about the enthusiasm over the idea
in the Interior Department and the White House.

> When I telephoned Oscar Chapman, Assistant Secretary of the
> Interior, who happens to have been a friend of mine for a good
> many years and who is a protege of one of the greatest human
> beings who ever lived—the late Senator Costigan who introduced
> the anti-lynching bill—Chapman was ecstatic about the idea of the
> Lincoln Memorial. This was more important than just an individ-
> ual reaction since the Lincoln Memorial is under the control of the
> Department of the Interior.

Chapman immediately talked over the idea with Secretary Ickes and he in turn went over to the White House to talk with the President who, Chapman informs me, was as excited as the rest of us were. I understand the president told Mr. Ickes to make all the resources of his Department available to insure success.[83]

On March 30, Ickes announced publicly that permission had been granted for Anderson to sing at the Lincoln Memorial. With only a week left before Easter Sunday, Hurok, White, and Houston, putting differences aside, joined together in a harmonious attempt to arrange for a concert that was expected to attract one of the largest assemblages in Washington since Lindberg's return from Paris a decade before.

The NAACP urged organizations able to reach Washington easily by train to send large delegations to the concert. Houston called a special meeting of the MACC to find ways to coordinate activities with White and others. Gerald Goode, Hurok's head of publicity, traveled down to Washington to meet with White, Chapman, and Mike Straus, head of publicity for the Interior Department, where arrangements were made for the Park Service to handle the special needs of the huge crowd that was expected. Goode spent a week in the capital arranging for sound amplification and press coverage.

White was in his own way as much a strategist as Hurok and knew the benefit that the NAACP would derive from the publicity surrounding the concert. Nonetheless, as he later wrote in his autobiography, "Because the NAACP is known as a fighting propaganda agency, its sponsorship of the concert might have created the impression that propaganda for the Negro was the objective instead of the emphasizing of a principle."[84] He suggested to Hurok that a committee of prominent people in civic and political life be assembled to act as cosponsors for the concert. Although Mrs. Roosevelt was the obvious choice, she wisely preferred to keep as low a profile as possible in the days leading up to the concert. She recommended her close friend Caroline O'Day, congresswoman-at-large from New York, who, deeply committed to social reform and progressive causes, was one of the most active women in Democratic politics. Mrs. O'Day turned the facilities of her office over to sending out more than 500 telegrams to members of the Cabinet, Congress, and the Supreme Court, and editors, artists, and civic leaders. By Easter Sunday more than 300 had responded, including Chief Justice Charles Evans Hughes, Justices Black and Reed, Secretary of the Treasury Henry Morgenthau, Attorney General Frank Murphy; Senators

Borrah, Wagner, La Follette, Taft, and Cappen; Mary Bethune, Tallulah Bankhead, Frederic March, and Katharine Hepburn.

In all of the fury of activity in those last days before the concert, White never forgot the symbolic significance of the site and its historical attachment to the long years of struggle for black Americans. "We have drafted a program," he wrote to Anderson, "that we think is going to become a historic document."[85] He wanted the program, with its lines from the Gettysburg Address, distributed by boy scouts, "white and colored." He suggested to Goode that "'America' should be sung instead of 'The Star Spangled Banner' not only for the ironic implications but because more people know the words and it is more singable."[86]

Easter Sunday morning in Washington was unusually cold and overcast. In spite of the weather, the Knights Templar sunrise service at Arlington and the rites at the Washington Cathedral were expected to draw the earliest of the 200,000 tourists in town for the annual Easter celebrations. Estimates of the throng that would converge at the Lincoln Memorial at five o'clock in the afternoon for Anderson's concert ranged from 70,000 to 100,000. To handle the huge crowds at the Memorial, the Park Service had enlisted the help of 500 building guards and special details of Metropolitan police. The streets around the Memorial were closed off and parking was allowed on Constitution Avenue and behind the Navy and Munitions buildings, but no traffic would be allowed to enter the Memorial Circle. The crowd began to assemble several hours before the start of the concert, the earliest arrivals trying to find places as close to the steps of the Memorial as possible. By five o'clock the crowd was spread out the length of the pool, and people were standing as far as the base of the Washington Monument. There were baby carriages parked under the trees, and many women in the crowd carried babies in their arms. Because of the estimated size of the crowd there had been some concern expressed for Anderson's safety. Mordecai Johnson, Howard University's president, was worried that some organization like the Ku Klux Klan might do something to disrupt the concert. The huge crowd, however, which the Park Service estimated at 75,000, remained attentive and patient. Just before the start of the program the clouds moved off to the north as the sun came out and only the brisk wind that whipped in off the Potomac caused the crowd to stir.[87]

Anderson spent a fitful and sleepless Saturday night before Easter Sunday. Around midnight she telephoned Hurok, in an actual state of fright, wanting to know if she really had to go through with the concert.

On Sunday she gained much of her composure, realizing that there really was no turning back. "I could not run away from this situation. If I had anything to offer, I would have to do so now. It would be misleading, however, to say that once the decision was made I was without doubts."[88] Before noon, Anderson, accompanied by her mother and sisters, left Philadelphia for Washington's Union Station, where they arrived about one-thirty. There had been some concern about where the Andersons would stay in Washington, since no hotel would take them, but the problem was resolved when the former governor of Pennsylvania, Gifford Pinchot, and his wife, opened their house to them. From the Pinchots', Anderson and her accompanist, Kosti Vehanen, were driven to the Lincoln Memorial. It was still early in the afternoon and the crowd had not yet begun to assemble. Kosti tried out the piano and Anderson looked over the music (she was to perform, in addition to "America," "O mio Fernando," and Schubert's "Ave Maria" before a short intermission, then a group of spirituals including "Gospel Train," "Trampin,'" and "My Soul's Been Anchored in de Lord,"), and both tried out the amplification system, a battery of six microphones that would broadcast the half-hour concert nationwide over NBC's Blue Network.

Later in the afternoon a huge black limousine with motorcycle escort brought Anderson to the Memorial, accompanied by Hurok and her lawyer, Hubert Delany. "When we returned that afternoon I had sensations unlike any I had experienced before. . . . The murmur of the vast assemblage quickened my pulse beat. There were policemen waiting at the car, and they led us through a passageway that other officers kept open in the throng. We entered the Monument and were taken to a small room. We were introduced to Mr. Ickes, whom we had not met before. He outlined the program. Then came the signal to go out before the public."[89] Just before the concert was to begin, accompanied by Assistant Secretary Chapman and Congresswoman O'Day, Anderson made her way onto the platform of the Memorial.

Most of the sponsors who had planned to attend were already in their seats at the Monument, filling the 200 places that had been reserved. Newsmen and photographers paid attention mostly to the politicians and government leaders—indeed, several senators from northern states had contrived to get seats at the front of the platform, making sure that photographers could not miss their presence. Supreme Court Justices Black and Reed were there, and Morgenthau, Ickes, and Chapman from Roosevelt's Cabinet. From the Senate were Clark of Missouri, Cappen of Kansas, Guggey of Pennsylvania, and Wagner of New York. A number of southern politicians had requested tickets for the sponsors' platform, but changed their minds when they learned that seating on the platform, as in the open spaces in front of the Monument, would not be segregated.[90]

Secretary Ickes spoke briefly before the concert began. Enthusiastic applause greeted his very first sentences. "In this great auditorium under the sky," he began, "all of us are free. When God gave us this wonderful outdoors and the sun, the moon, and the stars, He made no distinction of race, or creed, or color." He spoke of Washington, of Jefferson, and of Lincoln. "Facing us down the Mall beyond the Washington Monument . . . there is rising a memorial to that other great Democrat in our short history, Thomas Jefferson, who proclaimed that principle of equality of opportunity which Abraham Lincoln believed in so implicitly and took so seriously." Then he introduced Anderson. "Genius, like justice, is blind. For genius has touched with the tip of her wing this woman, who, if it had not been for the great mind of Jefferson, if it had not been for the great heart of Lincoln, would not be able to stand among us a free individual today in a free land. Genius draws no color line. She has endowed Marian Anderson with such voice as lifts any individual above his fellows, as is a matter of exultant pride to any race. And so it is fitting that Marian Anderson should raise her voice in tribute to the noble Lincoln, whom mankind will ever honor. We are grateful to Miss Anderson for coming here to sing to us today."[91]

The sun had finally broken through the clouds but the air remained brisk and Anderson clutched her fur coat closely around her as she made her way along the green-carpeted platform to the bank of microphones, the figure of Lincoln looking down on her from between the two massive columns which frame his image. As Anderson later wrote, "I had a feeling that a great wave of goodwill poured out from these people, almost engulfing me. And when I stood up to sing our National Anthem I felt for a moment as if I were choking. For a desperate second I thought that the words, well as I know them, would not come. I sang, I don't know how. There must have been the help of professionalism I had accumulated over the years. Without it I could not have gone through the program."[92] Not all of the concert was preserved in the newsreel footage that was filmed that day, but the parts that were have an emotional impact that has not dimmed through the years. Those moments of hushed expectancy before Anderson began to sing are there on film, moments in which Anderson seems so vulnerable and alone, so nearly terrified of the awesomeness of the occasion, that those around her must have wondered if she would be able to sing at all. The music transforms her almost immediately. With her eyes closed and her head raised proudly, a look of determination takes over. And, as she sings "America," she does not use the word "I." "Of thee I sing" becomes, whether by design or not, "to thee we sing."[93]

Anderson sang with great control and with a kind of weighty expressiveness in the short program that followed the National Anthem, but with the same sequence of near panic followed by determined concentration once the music began. In the "Ave Maria," she did not allow herself to open her eyes during the long piano interludes between verses, as if afraid to confront directly the enormous throng before her. At its end she did not bow or acknowledge the audience at all, but walked quickly to her seat, clearly seeking the people around her on the stage for strength and support. She was more herself during the spirituals on the second half of the program, her eyes open and her face mimicking the humor or sadness of the words. As an encore she sang the spiritual, fittingly enough, "Nobody Knows the Trouble I've Seen." She then said a few words to the audience, expressing the sense of gratitude that she felt for the huge numbers of people who had come to hear her sing. "I am so overwhelmed, I just can't talk. I can't tell you what you have done for me today. I thank you from the bottom of my heart."[94] As the *Washington Post* reported the next day, "When the concert was finished the crowd, in attempting to congratulate Miss Anderson, threatened to mob her and police had to rush her back inside the memorial where the heroic statue of Lincoln towers. Even there, well-wishers threatened to overwhelm her, and the prompt action of Walter White of the American Association for the Advancement of Colored People, who stepped to a microphone and appealed to the crowd, probably averted a serious incident."[95]

Walter White, the true architect of the Lincoln Memorial concert, remembered those moments of near panic years later, when he wrote about the events he had witnessed.

As the last notes of "Nobody Knows the Trouble I've Seen" faded away the spell was broken by the rush of the audience toward Miss Anderson, which almost threatened tragedy. Oscar Chapman ploughed through the crowd and directed me to the microphone to plead with them not to create a panic. As I did so, but with indifferent success, a single figure caught my eye in the mass of people below which seemed one of the most important and touching symbols of the occasion. It was a slender black girl dressed in somewhat too garishly hued Easter finery. Hers was not the face of one who had been the beneficiary of much education or opportunity. Her hands were particularly noticeable as she thrust them forward and upward, trying desperately, though she was some distance away from Miss Anderson, to touch the singer. They were hands that despite their youth had known only the dreary work of manual labor. Tears streamed down the girl's dark face. Her hat was askew, but in her eyes flamed hope bordering on ecstasy. Life which had been none too easy for her held out greater hope because one who was also colored and who, like herself, had known poverty, privation, and prejudice, had, by her genius, gone a long way toward conquering bigotry. If Marian Anderson could do it, the girl's eyes seemed to say, then I can, too.[96]

In the weeks and months that followed the concert, the old disparity, in which the Washington alliance worked tirelessly behind the scenes while Anderson was either ignorant of what was going on or took comfort in keeping at a safe distance what she did know, was replaced by a different and more ironic disparity. For the alliance it was business as usual, while Anderson, no longer hounded for reactions by the news media, was greeted with the same wild excitement and curiosity that was normally reserved for film stars. Houston, White, and other members of the MACC, in fact, had lost none of their resolve to continue the fight on the Washington front. Houston and Lovell took advantage of the presence in Washington of D.A.R. delegates to the Continental Congress to appeal to Mrs. Robert, whom they hoped would be forced to respond more mildly to the MACC when not so isolated from national representation. They wrote to her on April 13. Reviewing the events of the previous months, they requested that no individual or organization be barred from Constitution Hall on account of race.[97] At the end of May, when delegates were long gone from the scene, Mrs. Robert met with members of the MACC committee. There was to be no change of policy.

In the meantime, White put his prestige and influence behind an exciting proposal to memorialize Anderson's appearance at the Lincoln Memorial with a mural painting that would be installed in the Department of the Interior. The idea came from Edward Bruce, chief of the section on fine arts in the Treasury Department, who had attended the concert and was so moved, as he explained, by Anderson's singing of "America," that he wanted "to capture for posterity, the solemnity, grandeur and challenge of that moment."[98] A Marian Anderson Mural Fund Committee was formed, with Bruce as chairman and a distinguished list of cosponsors, to raise money for the project. Their appeal was made primarily to the youth of America, "because Miss Anderson both as an artist and as a person represents what can be done in this country despite discrimination and other handicaps."[99] The mural was to be executed by the winner of a national anonymous competition open to all American artists.

For Anderson, full understanding of her appearance at the Lincoln Memorial would come only later, when the events in Washington gradually forced her to assume a role of social and historical importance that she felt unequal to. For the moment, she experienced only the heightened excitement and enthusiasm that greeted her as she finished her season of concerts. She had, in fact, become a celebrity. The mood in the black press especially was one of euphoria. To the *New York Amsterdam News* she became "la belle Anderson," and "a fashion plate."[100] At her Carnegie Hall concert a week after her appearance at the Lincoln Memorial, near hysteria reigned as people sitting on the floor rushed to the stage at the end of the concert to get a better look at the singer and to call out encores.[101] Anderson was guest of honor at a reception and supper after the concert given by the Theater Arts Committee at Essex House. Mayor La Guardia, already a devoted admirer, toasted her to the 300 guests as "one of America's greatest artists."[102] It was an evening in which distinguished blacks—the poet Countee Cullen, the actress and singer Ethel Waters, Elie Lescot, the Haitian minister to the United States— were among those present, mingling with devoted New Dealers to share in the sense of victory they all felt. La Guardia remained lighthearted and jovial as he celebrated the recent victory of democratic ideals and tolerance over pettiness and racial prejudice. "I've been in public life for fifty-five years and haven't been invited by the DAR," he quipped. Walter White, in a more sober mood, paying tribute to La Guardia's endorsement and presence at the reception, said of the mayor that "America's answer to racial hatred and racial bigotry was just another star in the crown of the little flower."[103]

Anderson's new fame quickly reached as far west as Hollywood. Twentieth Century Fox lost no time in taking advantage of the newly created association between Anderson and the hero of their new film, John Ford's *Young Mr. Lincoln,* starring Henry Fonda. On May 30, in Springfield, Illinois, where the world premiere occurred among celebrities, film moguls, newspapermen, and excited citizens of Lincoln's birthplace, Anderson was invited to sing as part of the festivities. Three days later, at the Fox Wiltshire Theatre in Los Angeles, she was cheered alongside Cesar Romero, Alice Brady, and Eddie Collins.[104]

If Anderson felt any sense of personal resolution to the controversy that had waged for months over her appearance in Washington, it was when she finally saw the first lady again. Mrs. Roosevelt honored the first of her promises to Walter White on June 8, when Anderson performed in the White House on the occasion of the visit of King George VI and Queen Elizabeth. It was a stately and elaborate affair in which Anderson joined Lawrence Tibbett and Kate Smith in a long and elaborate program designed to impress the British monarch and his wife with the musical diversity of sharply contrasting segments of American life. There were Negro spirituals arranged by Nell Hunter and sung by the North Carolina Spiritual Singers, a community activity group sponsored by the WPA; folk dances by the Soco Gap Square Dance Team, from Ashville, North Carolina; and a group of four folk singers from Cook Creek, Kentucky. Anderson sang "Ave Maria" and two spirituals.[105] It was not until after the concert that she and the other guests were introduced to the royal couple and she was finally able to exchange a few words of greeting with Mrs. Roosevelt. For Anderson, the exchange was spoiled briefly by her introduction to the queen a moment before. In talking with Mrs. Roosevelt, Anderson, as she liked to relate in later years, was still preoccupied and embarrassed by the curtsy that she had risked when introduced to Queen Elizabeth. As she came out of the curtsy, which she had practiced diligently beforehand, she was no longer facing in the direction of the queen.[106]

On July 2, in Richmond, Virginia, at the annual conference of the NAACP, an audience of more than 5,000 watched Mrs. Roosevelt present the Spingarn Medal to Anderson. The formal statement of the committee, in honoring her, declared that "Marian Anderson has been chosen for her special achievement in the field of music. Equally with that achievement, which has won her world-wide fame as one of the greatest singers of our time, is her magnificent dignity as a human being. Her unassuming manner, which has not been changed by her phenomenal success, has added to the esteem not only of Marian Anderson as an individual, but of the race to which she belongs."[107]

Mrs. Roosevelt told the crowd that Anderson "had the courage to meet many difficulties" and that "her modesty and her great gifts are well known." In a brief address before the ceremony, referring indirectly to the Washington controversy, she asserted that "people cannot grow up good citizens unless we provide good environment for all the people. In the end, the price we pay for people not fit to be citizens is far greater than the sacrifice we must make to provide decent environment." Again it was Mrs. Roosevelt's presence that made the ceremony as much personal as ideological. Indeed, Anderson expressed as much in her brief remarks in accepting the award, noting "the significance it carries," and the honor to have received it "from the hands of our First Lady, who is not only a first lady in name, but in every deed."[108]

Many years later, in responding to a young girl who had written to her inquiring about what had happened during the time of the concert at the Lincoln Memorial, Anderson explained that a concert she was scheduled to give had to be postponed, and that Mrs. Roosevelt then invited her to sing at the Lincoln Memorial. She was not merely simplifying the complex and troubling events of a period in her past for a young person who might not yet be ready to understand their full meaning. She was, in fact, indulging herself in a memory of the events as she wished them to be.[109]

CHAPTER ELEVEN

Marriage and Career
(1939–1943)

During the fall and winter of 1939, Marian and Orpheus were spending more and more time together. Aware that Orpheus had become her steady and apparently exclusive escort, the press inevitably drew its conclusions, in the case of the black press often in headlines whose size was normally reserved for impending world crises. "Although no official announcement has been given," reported the *Chicago Defender*, "sources confirm rumors that Miss Marian Anderson will marry Razel [a childhood name for Orpheus] Fisher, prominent New York architect."[1] Friends too noticed the change in Marian's feelings toward Orpheus. "Why is it you have so much time to give him and so little to give me," Billy King wrote to Marian, slipping easily into his role of spurned and jealous suitor: "why is it that I had to invite myself to accompany you home from the concert the last time I was in New York? None of these questions do you offer any solution to when we are talking together, I cannot forget how he remained at your apartment in New York when he hangs around there most every night, does he not think another fellow needs a break sometime? I think I might come over to the next recital in New York and please don't have him around, I cannot get a chance to talk music or nothing else when he is there, then to top it all off to tell me that you were going to marry him, do you know I cannot get over that."[2] Like others who were close to Marian during her years of professional struggle, Billy feared that she might now devote too large a part of her life to pursuits that would exclude him, that might even jeopordize what she had worked so hard for.

But Marian had never resigned herself to a life without marriage. It was only a matter of timing. She was now one of America's most sought-after singers. The Lincoln Memorial concert had helped to make her a national celebrity. Now in her forties, anxious for the comforts of a home of her own, steady and enduring companionship, even occasional domesticity, she was ready for marriage. What may have seemed to the outside world a drastically uncharacteristic alteration in a life so far devoted exclusively to singing and to family was for her the well-considered decision not to put off Orpheus any longer. In fact, Marian had made up her mind to marry him years ago. In spite of the periods of separation and even estrangement, misunderstandings, and reconciliations, their relationship had endured since they were in high school. In November 1939, when Marian left for the start of the new season, there were still many things about her marriage to Orpheus that had to be decided. In turn, desperate, loving, entreating, scolding, tender, and splenetic, Orpheus confided his feelings to her in a steady stream of letters that remain virtually the only record of their relationship during the long months that Marian was away on tour.

For Orpheus, the biggest obstacle to marriage remained Marian's career. Orpheus was enthusiastic and imaginative about his work—he always had architectural schemes in his head, small and large projects alike—but his career was not, as Marian's was for her, the central fact of his existence. He needed a woman's love and companionship in his life, and the long periods of separation caused him considerable anguish. Indeed, separation was one of the refrains of his letters: "Marian, my dearest I miss you so much," he wrote one evening after a phone call from her, "I am absolutely no good when you are away from me. It usually takes me about 6 weeks to get back to normal and by that time you are on your way back to me, and the same thing takes place over and over again."[3] Often the leave-taking was bitter and unpleasant. To his recriminations Marian would sometimes respond in ways that to Orpheus seemed annoyingly placid and unsympathetic. "You spoke of my next move," he wrote to her in a moment of particular exasperation. "What is my next move, I am waiting for you to come back to me so that we can be married, is there some other move for me to make?"[4]

Orpheus's reputation as a lady's man was still a problem for Marian. For years Orpheus was used to a bachelor's existence. He was gregarious, dashing and still handsome, and light-skinned enough to move back and forth across the color line whenever he chose. Living in New York, Orpheus saw opportunity all around him. Marian was trusting, often too trusting, but she knew his reputation as a lady's man as well as anyone.[5]

His promises to her "to be a good boy" are fervent,[6] but some are not hard to read as implicit reproaches that the warmth and love that he so misses when she is away are not sufficient when they are together: "My darling I miss you so much. You must know it takes a lot of will power to keep away from the desire to see other women while you are away. It is only my love and hope and knowledge that you are coming back soon that makes me be a good boy. So my dearest when you do return I don't want you to be alarmed when I exhibit my love for you. I shall need lots and lots of loving when you come back so get ready and set to go."[7] Were there not times when the strain of such conditions made their time together as difficult as separation?

Distrustful, needy, impatient, Orpheus saw enemies everywhere opposed to their marriage, especially the people who were involved in Marian's career. Kosti and the Enwalls were particular targets of his suspicion: "The letter that Kosti wrote Mr. Delany is only a blind and his friendly actions toward him at your party were only intrigue. . . . Concerning the Enwalls I really don't think much of Therese [Enwall's wife]. I am quite sure that she is a phony that is the way she impresses me, as for him I am sure that the only thing he is interested in is his fee, and nothing else so I am sure that Kosti has asked his help in convincing you that you shouldn't marry. Please don't listen to them my dear."[8] Certainly there were those—Kosti, Enwall, and Hurok, particularly—who were wary of Orpheus, for he made no bones about how much he looked forward to the day when Marian would retire. Often he was merely indulging playfully in wishful thinking: "I exposed myself to the weather too much. Please don't worry as I shall be all right within a few days, if not you must cancel the balance of your concerts and come home and nurse me."[9] On other occasions, however, he was sober and reflective about it: "I want you to think of the time when you shall not sing and when you should have a home and family and quiet."[10]

Orpheus's suspicious harangues were alarming enough to elicit from Marian more frequent replies. She wrote to him from Chicago in January, counseling restraint:

> Without calling names I do know that the three people to whom you referred would be quite affected by any <u>great</u> change in my life, and while they might be selfish, I'd hate to think that none of the interest they show is genuine. I don't mean to overestimate their <u>affection</u> but feel on the other hand that you <u>might</u> be prone to underestimate it. Our middle way would be best perhaps, all the while keeping ears, eyes and mouth open.[11]

When she wrote to him from San Francisco in March the machinations of friends, especially Kosti, who liked gossip and who was not above meddling, were still troubling them:

> If any of the interested parties depended on K working on me, their hopes are dead. I must admit that there may be those who would be highly pleased to find there <u>could</u> be some differences between you and so-and-so, and altho I have no intention of trying to change your mind, I still don't see why one should play right into their hands. I may be considered many things, but I am not altogether blind to what's trying to be brot about. That is why I would like you to have a little more consideration (faith) when I speak on that subject. And now that you see the object of all this, it <u>need not</u> present any serious trouble. So much for that, my sweet."[12]

Orpheus himself, when given the chance, could be irresistibly charming and did much to smooth the way with friends:

> Mr. Enwall called me and asked me to have supper with them and Mr. Delany which of course you know I refused, but joined the Enwalls at 10 o'clock at their hotel and I took them to a night club and the Mrs got properly tight. I took her some flowers and when I took them back to the hotel she kissed me putting both arms around my neck and said she changed her mind and now she liked me very much and hoped that you and I would marry as soon as possible. Well my dear that's enough of that don't you think so.[13]

Their common bond was the home that they would one day share. Orpheus sounded the theme in letter after letter during those winter months of 1939 and 1940. The burden of finding a house fell naturally to him, and he hoped that his enthusiasm and eventual success would drive away whatever misunderstandings continued to exist. In truth, Orpheus felt constantly in need of proving his love and his worth to Marian, who was rarely emotionally demonstrative or passionate enough for him. For Orpheus, the search became a way to renew his love for her, to confirm that she could depend on him alone for what she wanted: "My darling I think from the houses which I have shown you, you and I can pick one from this list. I would prefer for no one to help us in picking one of these homes. I want you to have faith in me."[14]

Looking for a home had become the promise of a life together. Orpheus never lost his enthusiasm, sending Marian photographs and lovingly hand-drawn plans for her comments, but the search was a struggle both physically and emotionally. Orpheus said at one point that he travelled more than 10,000 miles in New York, New Hampshire, and Connecticut in search of a property that would keep them close to New York City, one that they could afford yet would have the comforts they wanted. Many times on the verge of success, a property would be suddenly taken off the market when the owners discovered they were black: "Marian I am so sorry about the Gidden house, but my dear one must expect these things in a country so full of hate and prejudice."[15] It was not simply the color line between white and black that formed a barrier to success; in the end, the more delicate and personal one that separated Marian from Orpheus caused more anguish, and a heavy burden of guilt that Marian was only too ready to assume. As she explained to Emily Kimbrough some years later, "If King [Orpheus was known as King to family and close friends] were not married to me, or to someone else with as dark a skin as mine, he could live anywhere he chose and hold any job he's qualified for. The minute I come into the picture everything changes. . . ."[16] When a real estate agent was encouraged by a mutual friend to show Orpheus a particular property, the agent was appalled. "You must be crazy," the agent told the friend. "Why, the Smiths' house isn't far from the places of [two well-known families]. Don't you know King is married to Marian Anderson? She can't live near those people."[17] As Marian went on, "To this day I don't know whether that mutual friend thinks King is not a Negro. The point is that my very existence, whatever kind of person I am, set up a boundary line for King as well as for me."[18]

Orpheus had to struggle not only with the vicissitudes of an exhausting search, he had to conform to Marian's schedule, one which kept her away except for a week or so at a time. By the spring of 1940, during the last months of her tour, Marian was unable to hide her frustration and anxiety: "My dear, and if you are feeling up to it, would you try to see what Miss Donahue has, so that we'll have more to choose from when I come back. I think it is imperative that either one place or another be decided upon during the week I have at home in March so that by the end of May it would be ready for occupancy. Don't you agree?"[19] But March came and went without success. When Marian left the States in mid-June to fulfill an engagement of six concerts in Hawaii that would keep her on the islands until the first week of July, they had still not found an appropriate house that anyone was willing to sell them.

There was also the fact of Orpheus's previous marriage to Ida Gould, from whom he was still not divorced. The letters between Marian and

Orpheus during the closing months of 1939 and into the new year make not the slightest mention of the divorce but the problem could hardly have been very far from their thoughts. Only in February, when Marian expressed a new degree of certainty about wanting a home to live in that spring, did Orpheus's divorce proceedings begin. In fact, it was Ida, who lived with her and Orpheus's six-year-old son, James, in Hazleton, a small town not far from Phildelphia, who filed for divorce.[20] Perhaps she was angry enough with all of the publicity about Orpheus's impending marriage to Marian to want to put a legal end to their long separation, an end that was now bound to come one way or another. Perhaps it was Orpheus, facing up finally to the emotional strain of confronting Ida and the son whom he had abandoned to his mother and grandmother, who urged Ida to seek a divorce. However it came about, once set in motion, it was not to be granted until December. In the meantime, the search for a home went on, absorbing their energies, acting as a refuge from the emotional difficulties that the divorce process was bound to bring.

For both Marian and Orpheus, the last weeks of June were the most anxious time in a search that had gone on for nearly a year. In the midst of a series of concerts in Hawaii, Marian found herself suddenly facing the prospect of doing without Kosti for the last three of her concerts. Generally discreet and intensely private about his personal life, Kosti had become embroiled in a sexual indiscretion the precise nature of which remains unclear but was apparently homosexual in nature. In order to deflect any scandal, Hurok advised that Kosti return immediately to Finland on some prospect or other.[21] Distracted by difficulties of having to perform with a new accompanist on less than a full day's notice, Marian felt more than ever cut off from King's troubles on the other side of the world.

As for King, apparently the prospect of the approaching summer without a house was too much: "Finally I got so disgusted I bought our house without Miss Anderson seeing it. The owner tried to stop the sale later, but it was too late."[22] King, in fact, had found a hundred-acre property at the western end of Danbury, Connecticut, about an hour and a half drive from New York. On half the property, on one side of Joe's Hill Road, there was a twelve-room, three-story Victorian farm house, and on the other side of the road, an old barn and fields that had not been worked in some time. Considering the size of the property—Marian confessed later that they had had to buy twice as much acreage as they needed "so we wouldn't contaminate the neighborhood"[23]—and the beauty and relative seclusion of the countryside, the price agreed on, $18,000, was a bargain, less than many of the properties that had been snatched away at the last minute. But the excitement and satisfaction over the purchase of the property was dampened for King by the necessity of having to see Delany more regularly than he would have wished. Delany still aroused in him, in fact, the old jealousy and anger: "I really and truthfully believe that your lawyer would like for you to not have a home, because a home would put you in a frame of mind to marry."[24] But the agreement she had with King—that she would purchase the property while he would, as far as his money allowed, pay for the work and furnishings in the house, and material and equipment needed at the start for the farm—made it necessary for Delany to act on Marian's behalf in order to arrange for the settlement of the property.[25]

The transfer of property took place on July 7, with Marian still not back from Hawaii. By the time she got her first look at the farm later that summer, King had already purchased some furniture and started repairs on the house. With King able to work on the farm only on weekends, Marian's nervous anticipation of the moment when they would actually be able to spend time together on the farm gave way more than once to impatience and disappointment: "Whenever I had as much as twelve free hours I took a train to Brewster, New York, and he met me at the station and took me to the house. I remember walking into the front door once and seeing that the steps had been torn out; the place looked a wreck. To get to the second floor you had to climb up a ladder. I was appalled by the mess. 'You've ruined my house,' I said to King. Nothing he could say by way of reassurance consoled me."[26] In fact it was many months before the house was actually habitable, and many more months before some of the plans for decorating and furnishing the house could be realized.

For Marian, nervous impatience with progress on the house and farm gave way over the summer to her concerns about the coming season. Because of the staggering amount of publicity that she received following her Washington appearance and the increased demand for concerts from nearly all parts of the country, she thought the time had come to approach Hurok for a better contract. Indeed, the physical toll that longer and more strenuous seasons were taking made it imperative to confront Hurok. In her last year with Kosti, which ended in the summer of 1940, Anderson gave nearly eighty concerts in the States alone. Her last concert, a Carnegie Hall benefit for a group of organizations that included the NAACP, YMCA, National Urban League, and the International Committee on African Affairs, drew some of the harshest words yet from the critics. Writing in *The Nation* about the benefit concert, Bernard Haggin reported later in the year that Anderson's "voice was threadbare and had a strong vibrato. This was due partly to the fatigue of the season's ninety or a hundred concerts, which represented her manager's lack of conscience and her own lack of good sense."[27]

By the end of the summer they reached an agreement. How Hurok felt about the outcome is not known, but Anderson was satisfied enough with the results to boast with uncharacteristic bravado to King: "You know darling this contract business is always unpleasant and from the very beginning I was not pleased with the terms. The fact that the show down came now instead of earlier was simply because I appreciated what 'the office' did for me and wished them to benefit well therefrom. This accomplished, and the recent tremendous publicity made this moment the most propitious. It is only natural that a fellow disliked having his income cut down a bit altho he has had more than his proper share previously."[28] What they agreed to was that Anderson would sing no more than fifty or sixty concerts in the States a year, and that she would receive two-thirds of the gross for each concert rather than a fixed fee, the kind of arrangement, in fact, that Hurok reserved for his most important artists. In the first years under the new contract she received on the average about $1,600 per concert in comparison with her previous fee, which ranged from $1,250 to $1,500. If the increase was less than she might have wanted at the start, there was still the psychological advantage of earning more when local managers earned more, an advantage particularly appealing during a year of such "tremendous publicity" and acclaim.[28]

The contract business settled, there was still the problem of accompanist to deal with, for everyone thought it best that Kosti not return to America. As it turned out, the solution lay near at hand. The previous April, during the week before the Lincoln Memorial concert, Kosti had become ill and had to be hospitalized for a few days. Franz Rupp, the eminent émigré German pianist and chamber musician, was then under contract to Hurok, who quickly engaged him to replace Kosti. Rupp agreed to take over for Vehanen, first in St. Louis, then Birmingham and Atlanta. Anderson and Rupp got on well together. Except for spirituals, Rupp had played most of Anderson's repertory many times with other singers, and he was able to adapt to the special requirements of a new artist with extraordinary efficiency. When the need arose during that summer of 1940 for a permanent accompanist for Anderson, Rupp, one of three candidates, was chosen quickly.

Rupp was one of a number of German musicians who fled from Germany to the United States during the 1930s. He was born in 1901 in Schöngau and moved to Munich with his family when he was still a boy. He studied piano at the Royal Academy, hoping for a solo career, but his skill as an accompanist provided him with a steadier income than he could hope to achieve as a soloist in inflation-ridden postwar Germany. In 1924, he formed a partnership with the baritone Heinrich Schlusnus, one of the most important lieder singers of the interwar period. His success with Schlusnus brought him into contact with Kreisler, with whom he began to play in 1930, a partnership that established Rupp as one of the leading chamber musicians and accompanists in Germany.[30] A strong and outspoken critic of Hitler and the Nazis, Rupp's fortunes began to deteriorate once Hitler came to power in 1933. It was Rupp's break with Schlusnus, in 1934, that led eventually to his departure from Germany. As Rupp later recounted the story: "We were very close friends until Hitler came to power and Mr. Schlusnus became a Nazi. From then on we had many arguments on the question until he sent me the 1st letter stating definitely that he cannot work further with a State's enemy. Soon after, I made him my farewell letter—after which he denounced me at the Reichs Culture Chamber (Reichsmusikherrschaft) in Berlin, stating that I am an enemy of the German government."[31] Only the intervention of an adjutant to Goebbels prevented his being sent to a labor camp. After the break with Schlusnus he found it increasingly difficult to remain in Germany, particularly since his wife, Steffanie, was Jewish. In September 1938, with a few dollars in his pocket and the promise that Steinway would send his piano on to the States, Rupp and his wife, with the help of friends in the government, left Germany for America.

When the offer to accompany Anderson came from Hurok in the summer of 1940, Rupp was not immediately persuaded. He had continued his partnership with Emanuel Feuermann when the cellist emigrated to America in 1938 and, soon after his own arrival, began to play with other musicians, Erica Morini and William Primrose among them. Hoping to build a solid career, with solo engagements as well as accompanying, he was at first reluctant to accept a contract that would require as many as sixty concerts a year, leaving him little time for much else professionally. Hurok was persuasive, offering him a three-year contract and his assurance, as Rupp liked to tell it in later years, that Anderson could not possibly last more than a few years. For the time being it was an opportunity that promised Rupp stability and a far better income than he was used to in America. In the end he accepted. Anderson and Rupp worked together in the months before the start of the season, setting off in October 1940 for their first concert in Harrisburg, Pennsylvania. They gave fifty-two concerts that year during a season that took them from New York to San Francisco, from Vancouver to Abilene, Kansas.

Anderson took some time to adjust to the new partnership. Rupp was used to playing for singers with different ranges, repertories and stylistic inclinations and could adapt easily. Anderson had had the same accompanist for a decade; moreover, she did not like the anxiety that came from performing with someone she was not accustomed to. Rupp, in fact, was a very different kind of musician from Kosti and the change took some getting used to. As an accompanist, Kosti was somewhat retiring and self-effacing, Rupp more direct and assertive. Kosti's rhythm tended toward the limp and weakly articulated—Bernard Haggin, an immensely astute critic, found Kosti "increasingly anemic and rhythmically invertebrate"[32]—while Rupp was rhythmically bracing and dynamic. With Rupp all the lines of the musical texture stood out with great clarity, each individually incised. In Vehanen's playing the texture was often muddy. "In the beginning," Anderson later recalled, "Franz played, for my taste, much more as a pianist than as accompanist. He is a thorough and excellent musician, but I found myself hampered. In German songs, for instance, the tempos suddenly became different from those I had been taught and grown accustomed to." Nonetheless, even during their first year or two together, critics noticed the superiority of Rupp and the influence he was having on Anderson's performances. At the start, New York critics commented little on Rupp's contributions, having already become accustomed to his abilities. Critics elsewhere, however, took note with surprise and enthusiasm. "This season she has a new accompanist," wrote the critic of the *Toronto Globe and Mail,* "the brilliant young pianist, Franz Rupp, and (perhaps under his inspiration) her touch is lighter than in the past and her program was less sombre."[33] After a concert in Minneapolis, the resident critic was even more assertive: "His work Tuesday night was a vital and brilliant contribution—half the recital, as far as I was concerned."[34]

Like Vehanen before him, Rupp had a distinct influence on Anderson's repertory. Without Vehanen, Anderson gave up learning the Scandinavian literature, preferring in the years ahead to sing only a small number of Sibelius and Kilpinen songs with which she felt comfortable. With Rupp, on the other hand, she found a guide steeped in the repertory of German lieder, the literature closest to her heart. In time he encouraged her to sing more Brahms and Handel, composers to whom he thought her particularly well suited. In her own way Rupp's wife, Steffi, proved to be as important a guide to German lieder as her husband. Before marrying Franz, as Steffanie Schwarz, she had had a successful career of her own as an opera singer. She was a regular member of the theaters of Dortmund and Braunschweig, where her roles included the lighter Wagnerian soprano parts as well as Butterfly, Nedda, Santuzza, Donna Anna, Salome, and Carmen. She was especially admired for her Madama Butterfly and Sieglinde, roles which she was invited to sing in Munich and Vienna. She gave up her operatic career when she married Franz—she was eighteen years his senior and nearly forty when they married—but she liked teaching and in America found opportunities to coach young singers. In time, Steffi became a valuable and trusted coach for Marian too, watching over her German, exchanging ideas about interpretation, even demonstrating on occasion how a song or aria should go.[35]

Anderson's American recording career began in earnest with Rupp. In Europe, during the 1930s, the constant travel, the often impromptu changes of schedule, and Kosti's preference for returning to Finland during vacations, made recording difficult. Hurok understood the value of recordings and goaded his artists relentlessly to make them, but he was content in his first years with Anderson to concentrate on reviving her career in America after a long absence. Rupp's presence and the security of Anderson's career now made recording far more easy. As Hurok liked to point out, Rupp lived in New York, a few hours away from Danbury, his vacations fell naturally together with Anderson's, and he enjoyed the atmosphere of the recording studio. Why not use some of the time in which they were now working together on programs—the early summer, or the fall before the start of the new season—to make records? The success of some of her European recordings with Kosti, and Hurok's frequent badgering, helped persuade Anderson that the time was right, but she never became entirely comfortable in the studio. "To tell the truth I never liked the idea of singing into a microphone. I like to see faces before me. I like to sense a reaction. Singing into a microphone in a studio is like performing into dead space; there are engineers and technicians around, but even them I cannot see."[36]

Their first season over, Anderson and Rupp made preparations for their first recording sessions in late June and early July, and again in September 1941. In the ten sessions that summer, reluctant to record pieces that were new to her repertoire, Anderson preferred to record songs she knew well and had sung for years, a pattern from which she hardly ever strayed. Among her choices in those first sessions were spirituals, Schubert's "Die Forelle," "Der Doppelgänger," "Auf dem Wasser zu singen," and "Der Tod und das Mädchen," and the Brahms "Die Schnur, Die Perl an Perle." The Brahms she thought one of her very best recordings but she was unhappy with the Schubert songs and accepted, after many takes, only "Der Tod und das Mädchen." She did consent to record one novelty, however. Rupp convinced her to learn and record the two

Brahms songs for contralto, viola, and piano, no doubt thinking of how eloquent a partner the violist, William Primrose, would make. The three recorded the two songs at the very first session in June.

During her first season with Rupp, a number of honors and awards began to come her way, testimony to her new prestige and popularity on the national scene. Even earlier, in February 1940, she had been recognized in a nationwide poll conducted by the Schomburg Collections of the New York Public Library and the Association for the Study of Negro Life and History for her distinguished achievement in the improvement of race relations. Mrs. Roosevelt and Secretary Ickes shared the recognition with Anderson—the three old comrades now; among the others honored were Benny Goodman, Richard Wright, Joe Louis, and George Washington Carver.[37] Later in the year came the membership medal from the NAACP, an honorary doctorate from Temple University, and, in the spring of 1941, the Bok Award.

Edward W. Bok founded "the Philadelphia Award," the name he gave to it in 1921, for presentation annually "to a Philadelphian who had done some service that redounds to the credit of the city." At the ceremony at the Philadephia Academy of Music, Anderson told the audience that the money—recipients received $10,000—"shall enable some poor, unfortunate but nevertheless very talented people to do something for which they have dreamed all of their young lives."[38] With her award, Anderson established the Marian Anderson Scholarship Fund, an annual competition for vocalists between the ages of sixteen and thirty, with awards ranging from several hundred to a thousand dollars.

From the start it was a competition like few others. Anderson was well aware that "contests, which do not fit all people, are [not] always the best way of finding people with talent. No one need tell me that there are imponderables, that one youngster may be calm as a contestant and another too nervous to do himself justice."[39] Her solution, simple as it was novel, was to keep the competition close to home, in the hands of friends and associates—even family—who knew her well and understood her purpose.[40] For the first competition, which took place at the Ethical Society in Philadelphia in October 1942, Rupp and Mary Saunders Patterson, her first teacher, were two of the judges. A young singer from Atlanta, Georgia, Alvaretta Britten, was the first scholarship winner. In the scholarship fund's first decade, recipients would include Camilla Williams, the first black singer to appear with the New York City Opera, Mattiwilda Dobbs, among the first black singers to appear at the Metropolitan Opera, William Smith, Betty Allen, Judith Raskin, Sara Mae Endich, and Gloria Davy.[41]

To describe the Marian Anderson Scholarship Fund as a family affair is not to diminish its seriousness of purpose or the high standard of performance to which the contestants were held, but to recognize the service that Ethel DePreist and Alyse Anderson provided through the long years of the Fund's existence. Marian thought it best to stay out of the way, but Ethel and Alyse were two of its guiding spirits. Ethel, along with Hubert Delany, was made a trustee and acted on occasion as one of the judges. If a contestant arrived in town needing a hot meal or a place to stay the night, they could depend on the Andersons for help. When a young and talented contestant, not yet ready for a career, made a poor showing during the competition, he or she would be advised about the proper path to follow in the friendliest and most sympathetic way. In later years Leontyne Price and Jessye Norman entered the competition while still young and virtually unknown. Neither was a winner but both profited from the encouragement to continue their studies. Once the competition got off the ground, Marian asked Alyse to act as secretary to the Fund, no easy job almost from the beginning. The number of applications rose quickly from 28 the first year to more than 600 a decade later, when the work of processing applications, notifying contestants and arranging for auditions took from July to October, when the auditions were normally held. After the the war ended and applications increased further, Marian paid Alyse a yearly salary for her work, adding immeasurably to her self-esteem and enabling her to enjoy the gratitude and friendship of contestants and award winners.

Although the years following America's entrance into the war, in December 1941, did not alter in significant ways the rhythm of Anderson's career, they did for a time put a stop to her recording activity. In October 1942, James Petrillo, president of the American Federation of Musicians, succeeded in passing a resolution banning the production of records except for the war effort and for use in the home. Petrillo's war on mechanical recordings, together with the War Production Board's restriction on the use of shellac, which went into effect almost immediately after America entered the war, caused a nearly complete cessation of recording activity for more than two years. Anderson did not make records again until December 1944, when the Victor Company signed a royalty agreement with the AFM that allowed musicians back into the studio.[42]

Petrillo's stranglehold on the recording industry was at least in part counterbalanced by a more benign, even sympathetic, attitude toward radio. He tried, for example, to get radio stations to use a greater number of staff musicians and to increase radio employment for them. Foreign artists were prohibited from radio employment, which opened up opportunities for American-born musicians, who in the classical field still felt the burden of America's preference for European and European-trained artists. Petrillo's generous attitude toward radio, and the greater importance that radio came to hold in the everyday lives of people all across America during the war, brought artists like Anderson into homes with ever greater regularity, creating audiences that would not have a chance to hear such artists on a regular basis in the concert hall. The Bell Telephone Hour, which was broadcast weekly on Monday evenings over the NBC network, was one of the most popular classical programs, featuring singers and instrumental soloists performing together with Donald Voorhees and the Bell Telephone Orchestra. The half-hour program, whose general format remained fixed from week to week, included several, usually light, orchestral pieces interspersed with solo numbers by a weekly guest artist accompanied by Voorhees and the Orchestra.

Anderson made her first appearance on the Bell Telephone Hour on November 2, 1942, singing Bizet's "Agnus Dei," two spirituals, and the aria "Adieu, forêts." She became immensely popular with radio audiences, making three or four appearances each season with Voorhees during the next decade. The format of the Telephone Hour suited Anderson perfectly; she enjoyed the small and enthusiastic studio audience that often held family or friends (each artist received ten tickets for each broadcast) and the opportunity to perform with a conductor and orchestra on a regular basis. She had only to travel up to New York in the afternoon of the day of a broadcast in time for a rehearsal at 5:30, before the broadcast two hours later. Lieder and chansons played only a small role in the programs because there were so few appropriate orchestral arrangements—more dramatic lieder such as "Der Erlkönig," "Sappische Ode," and "Von ewiger Liebe" were among the few exceptions. As a result, Anderson almost always sang an operatic aria which, together with spriituals and music of Bach and Handel, complemented her recital appearances by creating a musical atmosphere that was more popular to audiences.[43]

The Telephone Hour broadcasts did not disrupt the schedule of Anderson's annual tours, which was much as it was before the war, beginning in early October and ending in early May, with trips to the midwest states in the early winter, and northwest in January or February. Each season Anderson gave as many as four concerts in Carnegie Hall—at the start of the season, in early January when the tour resumed, and in the spring—many of which were benefits. Since 1935 she had performed in 178 cities across the country, singing in all but seven states.

Soon after Anderson's return to America in 1935, Hurok had hired Isaac Jofe to act as her traveling manager, to arrange schedules and accommodations and to shield her from the hostility, insult, and humiliation she might meet from hotel staff, from local managers, and in restaurants. Jofe was born in Russia and had trained there for a time for a career as a tenor, but the revolution set him on a different course that took him across Europe and finally to America. Since his contract with Hurok—his wife had died many years before—Jofe lived in a small apartment across from Carnegie Hall when he was not traveling. He loved music passionately, especially opera, and claimed to know every song in Anderson's repertoire, all in the original languages. Indeed, he was not above demonstrating to her how a song should go at the least encouragement.[44]

As émigrés, each driven from the land of his birth, Rupp and Jofe shared a common past that enabled them to identify with Anderson's own experiences and to be sympathetic and understanding of her needs. For all three, there was nothing so important as music, and this helped to unite them as companions. In many ways, of course, they were as different as could be, but the differences, in personality and inclination, somehow only served to bring them closer together, for they admired and trusted each other immensely. Jofe was easily indignant and could be hot-tempered, his temperature rising and his arms flailing as he related a recent offense; Rupp was quietly persistent, gently ironic, on occasion slightly pompous. As for Anderson, feeling protected and understood, amused by their squabbling and in awe of their wide learning and heated discussions, she relaxed her guard, revealing more of her natural warmth and earthy humor.

On the road for as many as six or seven months of the year, with only a day or two of rest between concerts, Rupp and Jofe became for much of the year Marian's family, her "two grenadiers," as she liked to call them. It was Jofe who suffered most the trials of departure from one place to another, for Marian packed away at one time or another in her twenty or so bags, in addition to gowns and clothes for vast changes of weather—they could be in Montana one month and the deep South the next—an iron, ironing board, sewing machine, radio and recording machine, the sleeping bag that Enwall had given her, a hot plate, and assorted dishes. Some of the things that went along made it possible for her to avoid confrontation—she could boil some eggs or soup in her room, for example, when she was not welcome in a hotel dining room. Other items served the kinds of projects that she planned for the long months away from home—sewing curtains or clothes for the summer.

Much of their traveling was done by train, which was in those years more practical and comfortable than flying. When the journeys were long, the men often talked politics and Marian listened. "To kill time on some trips," she later recalled, "we took to playing cards. It would be no understatement to say that I am no card shark. To be honest, I have no card sense at all, and I am hopeless when it comes to games. But I agreed to try when Jofe and Franz urged me. After a while I noticed that before every game there was something of a tussle between the two men. I could not understand why. I would not say that tempers flared, but there is no doubt that the ironic comments were meant to be cutting. I finally figured out that they were sparring over position; each wanted desperately to sit where I would be discarding. How wise they were!"[45]

Even the summers often saw the three together. Anderson and Rupp worked together on programs during the summer, Rupp coming down from New York to Connecticut, very often with Steffi, with whom Marian had formed a warm friendship. Rupp and his wife often vacationed with Marian, Orpheus sometimes joining the group. Jofe, who considered himself the guardian of artistic quality, liked to be present when Anderson and Rupp discussed programs, defending good taste when he thought it imperiled. As Anderson liked to relate, "'No good,' Jofe will say about a number. 'The song does not make much of a point, and it isn't anything you should do.' Then he turns to Franz. 'And you should know better than to let her sing it,' he says. 'What's wrong with it,' he replies. 'Everything.' 'We need some good music,' Franz protests. 'Who says it's good music,' Jofe demands."[46] And so it went.

If the rhythm of touring changed little during the war, the texture was imbued with the impromptu audiences of servicemen that Anderson sang for in hospitals and military establishments across the country. Paul Robeson used such occasions not only to sing for the troops but to bring the message of the war in Europe closer to home, by universalizing the struggle against oppression. In Kansas City, he sang a group of Russian songs as well as the "Jim Crow" song; at the Uline Auditorium, in Washington, in a concert for the Chinese war relief, he sang the Chinese Communist "Cheelai" ("March of the Volunteers").[47] For Anderson, concerts for the troops were occasions to lighten the mood and to recall the pleasures of home and family for young men who were about to go to war. She sang spirituals for them, and "Danny Boy" and "Songs My Mother Taught Me." The informal and unrehearsed atmosphere that usually reigned, the chance to talk to servicemen and the unrestrained demonstrations of gratitude from the troops brought out her natural warmth, humor, and unaffected directness, qualities that were less apparent in the more formal setting of the recital hall.

In Topeka, Anderson sang for wounded men who found it difficult to sit for very long but who would not let her leave—"that performance," she later remembered, "lasted forty-five minutes, and I was more touched than the audience."[48] At a camp for black soldiers near Seattle, she sang for the men as they stood in formation. In Sausalito, California, a free concert was arranged at the Marin Shipyards, attended by a few hundred soldiers who sat and listened as they ate their lunch. One of the most memorable concerts was at Shephard Field, in Texas. Anderson and Jofe—Rupp had already left by car—were to be flown there together with the wife of the colonel who had made the arrangements and the pilot, in a tiny plane that could barely hold the four of them. After refueling in Waco and taking off, one of the engines became engulfed in smoke and they had to return to Waco—"the plane took a turn as if it were spinning on a dime"—before starting out again. They reached Shephard Field with only minutes to spare, where thousands of men stood waiting on the field.[49]

In late September 1942, a few days before the start of her annual tour, Anderson received an invitation from the D.A.R. to appear in Constitution Hall. Since the Lincoln Memorial concert, Houston and the MACC had continued to put pressure on the D.A.R. to reverse its policy with respect to black performers. Hurok too had asked for the use of Constitution Hall each year so that he could include Washington in Anderson's annual tours. But the D.A.R. held firm to its exclusionary policy and Anderson had not sung in Washington since 1939. During the summer of 1942, in considering plans to offer Constitution Hall for a series of benefit performances to aid the war relief, the D.A.R. invited Anderson to give the first concert. As the *New York Times* reported on September 30, Anderson's selection "reflected no change in the standing policy of the organization which about 1927 adopted a rule against the leasing of Constitution Hall for performances by Negroes."[50] In an effort to broaden support for legitimate war relief organizations, however, the D.A.R. was apparently prepared to consider at least ideologically acceptable blacks in its plans.

It was a risky undertaking for the D.A.R. One of the members, refusing to be named, said that " the society's decision on the matter is sure to create dissension among the members. However, I don't think it important enough to cause a flurry outside the ranks."[51] If D.A.R. leadership was looking for an opportunity to heal the breach with Anderson without being dictated to by Hurok or the MACC, why not an invitation that had patriotism and good will behind it? Indeed, the *Washington Post* hailed the D.A.R.'s invitation as a significant gesture in creating good relations with the singer.[52] The last thing the D.A.R. expected was more controversy. It was supplied nonetheless, and in short order, by Walter White. Having seen the press reports that the invitation to Anderson did not reflect any change in the D.A.R.'s policy, he fired off a barrage of telegrams. To Hurok he wrote that "acceptance under such humiliating conditions would be most unfair to Miss Anderson."[53] His advice to Anderson, whom he had not bothered to consult before writing to Hurok, was to "urge you refuse invitation. The overwhelming majority of the public would support you in such a stand, I believe."[54] He did not spare the D.A.R., demanding to know whether they "expect any self-respecting artist of Miss Anderson's character to accept such a proposal."[55]

On October 3, two days after receiving his telegram, Hurok wrote to Fred Hand: "Miss Anderson will give this concert subject to the specific agreement by the Executive Committee that no segregation in the seating arrangements be exercised," and that "her appearance in Constitution Hall is to be construed as a precedent that hereafter Constitution Hall will be open to her in the normal course of her annual tours."[56] No doubt Hurok and Anderson felt compelled, at least at the outset, to stand united with White, but their feelings had moved away from his since the Lincoln Memorial concert. Hurok surely was shrewd enough to realize that to stage a showdown on the issue of precedence in the face of an invitation from the D.A.R. to help the war relief would bring much adverse criticism, undoing some of what was gained from the Lincoln Memorial concert. The truth is that, for Hurok, the D.A.R.'s refusal to lift its ban on black performers had ceased to be a matter of practical relevance. Since the Lincoln Memorial concert, in fact, Hurok had almost given up on Washington as a viable city to include in Anderson's annual tours.

On the question of segregation in general, neither Hurok nor Anderson saw eye to eye with White. White kept his sharp eyes and ears open for any report about the segregation of audiences in the South, urging artists to refuse to perform under such conditions. Some, like Robeson and the pianist Hazel Scott, were already doing this on their own. Hurok and Anderson, however, were unwilling to risk losing southern audiences by taking so strong a position. A test case came only a month later, in fact, when negotiations were still going on with the D.A.R. White's attention was drawn to a case in which a local manager in Louisville, Kentucky, had arranged for segregated seating at an Anderson concert. White urged Anderson not to appear; his answer came not from Anderson herself, but from Gerald Goode, Hurok's representative, with Anderson apparently in agreement: "Public relations strategy requires that issue of segregation concentrated for the present in Washington where moral victory is in sight. To bring up segregation issue in another city would deflect public interest with possible danger of confusion. We are heartily in favor of striking down segregation wherever it rears its head but having gained a beach head in Washington we do not wish to scatter our forces in the current battle for public opinion."[57] What could have appeared more confusing than to take one position about segregation in Washington and another in Louisville at virtually the same time? The high moral tone of Goode's response was meant as much to bolster a decision not to take a strong position against segregated audiences in the South than to achieve a moral victory in Washington. What would eventually transpire in Washington, at least for Hurok and Goode, was of little consequence.

If Hurok could afford to be cavalier about the outcome of the D.A.R.'s invitation, Anderson was inclined to treat it in a more personal way. She was always saddened by any occasion that denied her the opportunity to appear before an audience that wanted to hear her sing, never more so than when large numbers of blacks would be deprived of her singing. Moreover, she did not believe in forcing the issue of segregation from the outside. To her, refusing to sing before any form of segregated audience was neither a positive nor a constructive act. Where segregation was, in fact, unavoidable, her solution was to insist on vertical seating, in which an imaginary line is drawn from back to front that allows both races to have equal seating opportunities. For her this policy of "enlightened segregation" provided an acceptable compromise, one allowing both races to come together in at least some form of equality. Under such circumstances it was her hope that she could bring them closer together still by communicating with them what she loved most. So why, then, did she concede to White's demand for no segregation? Did she feel that she owed him her support, at least in Washington, where he had worked so hard on her behalf?

Whatever the reasons, her need to act quickly at the beginning of October came at a difficult time emotionally. Since the middle of September, James DePreist, Ethel's husband, lay gravely ill in Jefferson Hospital of acute heart disease. He had suffered intermittently from hypertension, but his heart attack in early September was unexpected, the family utterly unprepared for so serious an illness. While still in the hospital, having contracted pneumonia, DePreist died on October 7, only forty-eight years old. Ethel was inconsolable, so devasted during the funeral services that she had to be helped out of the chapel before the conclusion.[58]

It was, in fact, only days before DePreist's death that the D.A.R.

required an answer, a time when Anderson could not have given the matter much careful thought. In going along with White, Anderson was making the most expedient decision for the moment. As it turned out, neither the president-general nor Hand could give any immediate answer of their own to her condition that there be no segregation of any kind, since it would have to be turned over to the Executive Committee, which was not scheduled to meet before October 30. The answer came during the first days of November. Hand wrote to Hurok: "I am instructed to advise you that the invitation sent you under date of September 28, 1942, was the same as that thus far extended to other artists for War Benefit Concerts. It is regretted that Miss Anderson, through you, her manager, has not accepted the invitation as extended. No appearance of any artist, attraction or event can ever be considered as a precedent insofar as future engagements in Constitution Hall are concerned."[59]

The press did what it could to stir up the old controversy. "D.A.R. Again Bars Marian Anderson from Its Hall," proclaimed the *Washington Post,* for example.[60] Yet the old feeling of indignation and collective protest had given way to the image of two squabbling parties, the one "seizing a chance to get even with the society that once had barred her from its stately and privately owned hall,"[61] the other "refusing to be dictated to."[62] In the polarizing atmosphere that absorbed the media during November, Anderson herself was viewed more often than not as the unreasonable party. In the South particularly she lost favor, often roundly criticized for the conditions that she and her "clique" imposed on the D.A.R.: "Here is deliberate trouble-making, no doubt inspired by the clique that seeks to break down the racial barriers. What is the ultimate aim of this clique, to which the President's wife has given such valiant support? Does it wish to absorb the negroes into the white race? The clique will not answer the question, and until it is answered, the Marian Anderson type of incident will become more frequent, more irksome and more dangerous to our domestic peace."[63]

This time around Anderson drew the line. By the first week in November, having had time to reflect, she decided that she would not allow the D.A.R.'s refusal to lift its ban on black artists to prevent her from contributing her part to the war effort. If Hurok thought of the concert as an affordable loss, Anderson saw it as an opportunity to repay one genuine gesture of goodwill with another. How far she might have gone on the matter of segregation is hard to say, for the D.A.R., in a genuine spirit of compromise, accepted the demand that the concert be unsegregated, the first time in its history that it permitted such a concert to be held in the hall. On December 2, the agreement was announced to the press, and Hand turned over the sale of tickets and publicity to Hurok's office. When the date for the concert, January 7, was announced and tickets went on sale in the Woodward Building in downtown Washington, there was concern and nervousness, especially among blacks, who were used to being restricted to the balcony. Two weeks before the concert, White went so far as to try to determine on his own whether only gallery tickets were being sold to blacks.[64] He was assured that "there is no evidence of discrimination or segregation."[65]

At the last minute Anderson decided to donate the proceeds of the concert not to the Army Emergency Relief Fund, as she had originally intended, but to United China Relief. Was it to remind the D.A.R. of their recent refusal to allow Paul Robeson to give a benefit concert in the hall for the China Relief? A coincidence, perhaps. Less likely a coincidence, surely, was Interior Secretary Harold Ickes's announcement, exactly one week before Anderson's concert, that a special ceremony would be held in the auditorium of the South Interior Building on January 6, one day before Anderson's concert in Constitution Hall, to dedicate the mural that Mitchell Jamieson had executed commemorating the concert at the Lincoln Memorial. Hardly anyone failed to note the significance of the timing, or the connection that was being drawn between the two events. Twenty-four hours before Anderson's concert at Constitution Hall, many of the key figures of the Washington coalition that had brought about the Lincoln Memorial concert gathered together in the Interior Building. Charles Houston presented Jamieson's mural, which portrays the crowd reacting to the emotional impact of Anderson's singing. In the foreground is a view of the mixed crowd that thronged the Mall; in the distance, Anderson is seen standing on the topmost steps of the Memorial, the brooding statue of Lincoln between towering white columns looming behind her. Ickes addressed the audience before Anderson sang, his message leaving no doubt of the connection that he wished to draw with the concert that would take place the next evening: "It takes more strength of character to admit a change of conviction than to adhere tenaciously to it, and so I say that nothing that the Daughters of the American Revolution could do would give them greater credit or be in more seemly keeping with their tradition than to open this series of concerts with Marian Anderson."[66]

The following evening Constitution Hall was sold out. Among the 4,000 that filled the hall, more than half of them black, old comrades in arms once again gathered, the ranks filled out from the previous evening. To a huge outburst of applause, Mrs. Roosevelt entered her box at eight-thirty with a party of guests that included Mrs. Henry Morgenthau, Jr.,

Admiral Sir Percy Nobel and Lady Nobel, and Lieutenant Richard Miles. Members of Roosevelt's government were more prominent than they had been three years earlier on the platform of the Lincoln Memorial. They included Justices Black and Douglas, Attorney General Biddle, Ickes and Chapman, Claude Wickard, secretary of Agriculture, the undersecretary of War, Robert Patterson, the Chinese ambassador, Wei Tao-Ming, and Senators Caraway, Hill, Reynolds, and Smathers. Anderson sang a characteristic program that included songs of Scarlatti and Haydn; Schubert lieder; the aria "Pleurez, mes yeux" from Massenet's *Le Cid*; songs by Griffes, Quilter, and Sadero; and a group of Negro spirituals. She allowed herself one oblique remark to underscore the symbolic significance of the evening, not a reference to the D.A.R.—that would have been for her uncharitable—but a proud acknowledgment of the accomplishment of one of her own people. To the Schubert group she added the "Ave Maria," dedicating it "to the memory of the great Negro scientist, George Washington Carver," who had died only weeks before.[67]

It was during the war years that the full promise of Marianna Farm came into being. Marian and King did not share a great many interests, nor could they react with much more than admiration and pleasure to the other's professional achievements. About Marianna Farm, however—the beauty and serenity that it promised, the gardens, the pets and farm animals they envisioned growing and thriving on the land—they were as one. Marianna Farm was their most intense and satisfying collaboration. Marian was the visionary, seeing in her mind's eye a refuge of splendor and luxury from work and travel, and from the insensitive and hurtful impact of prejudice and rejection that was never far away. King was the executor, the great designer and planner, working in some capacity on every nook and cranny of the house and the farm. He helped dig the trench for the pipe that would carry water from the well to the house, he designed and built furniture, worked on the guest quarters in the back of the house, rebuilt the old cow barn, and gave in to Marian's desire for a flat roof on her studio that could be used as a sundeck. It was enough for Marian to envision for King to execute. He was also the more practical of the two, worrying almost from the beginning about the huge expenses that the house and farm would require, concerns that Marian was for years loath to take very seriously.[68]

By the end of the first year the animals began to arrive, taking up residence on the farm on both sides of Joe's Hill Road. Never very far from the big house, and more often than not in the house, were the family pets—cats and dogs of various breeds and temperaments. The cats came and went, but the dogs—Fargo the airdale, Rex the German shepherd, Fenon and Fala, the Kerry blues (the latter named for FDR's Fala)—were treated as family. They were pampered, spoiled, and loved in the intense way often evidenced by owners who, whether by preference or circumstance without children of their own, lavish all of their parental affection on pets. By the spring of 1943, there were cows and chickens on the farm. In early May, when Marian was in Mexico for a series of concerts, the sheep arrived one weekend in a driving storm so miserable that King had trouble getting them off the boxcar. At the end of the month the pigs arrived and King could write to Marian, who was still on tour, that "the children are well and the farm looks perfectly wonderful."[69]

Orpheus was finding it more and more difficult to divide his time between New York and Marianna. After the purchase of the farm he had kept both his apartment in New York and his connection to the architectural firm where he had worked for a number of years. Weekends and holidays found him at Marianna—Thurston and Ida, who stayed on permanently, kept things going throughout the year—but the travel back and forth was exhausting and the demands of the farm on his time constantly escalating. In March 1943, King gave up his job in New York to settle permanently on the farm, taking a position in Danbury as a draftsman with the Barden Corporation. Barden had been established the previous year for the purpose of supplying the precision ball bearings for the famous Norden bombsight. By the summer of 1943, the Norden bombsight would become indispensable to the precision bombing that made possible the shift in air power in Europe from German to Allied hands. There was a spirit of camaraderie and pride at the Barden Corporation that appealed to King, and enough time now that he was living at Marianna for him to revive an old interest in the restoration of country homes.[70]

In spite of the work over several years on Marianna Farm, and King's move from New York to Danbury, marriage was a long time in coming. Speculation and reports about a "secret marriage" between Marian and King went on in the press for several years.[71] Indeed, the idea of a "secret marriage" seemed to many the most plausible explanation for the fact that King and Marian had apparently been living together at Marianna, when Marian was not away on tour, even before King settled permanently on the farm. That they were seen together in and around Danbury, that the farm required the contracting of outside work in which both King and Marian were engaged, that there were gatherings during the summer months bringing family and guests to the farm—these things could hardly go unnoticed in Danbury.

As early as the spring of 1941—King had obtained his divorce from Ida Gould the previous December—the *Pittsburgh Courier* had reported that "at least two individuals who assertedly journeyed from Philadelphia to Danbury to be present last week at a 'reception party,' declared emphatically that Fisher was officially introduced at the reception as Miss Anderson's husband."[72] Did Marian and Orpheus find some amusement at the confusion they were causing about the true nature of their relationship? The note that Marian wrote to King a few months later certainly suggests as much. "Dear Mr. Fisher," the letter went, "Please find enclosed a check covering the second six months and completing the one year's return agreement for your services as architect and supervisor of work and other alterations at Marianna Farms, Conn. The work has been highly satisfactory and I desire to confer with you later, relative to renewing the expired agreement. Yours truly, (Miss) Marian Anderson."[73] The coy formality of the note does suggest that at least Marian could, on occasion, find amusement in their double life.

However comfortable their life together had grown at Marianna, there were apparently concerns that kept the timing of their marriage problematic. Family loyalties always took precedence for Marian; the death of Ethel's husband, and the burden she now carried of raising a son who was then only six years old, intensified Marian's caretaking instincts and required planning and emotional adjustment. Once King settled permanently on the farm, there were emotional adjustments of a different order, for the move brought King's private life closer in view than it had ever been while he lived in New York. How much Marian could trust King to stay clear of other women during the long months that she was on tour could hardly have been far from her thoughts.

That she often thought the worst is evident from the nearly hysterical tirade that filled the pages of one of her letters to King during the early months of 1943:

So now my darling I must go to the auditorium to do that job which brot me here. But don't go away, there is something else I want to talk to you about. I'll take another minute and tell you it's about having strange people (strange to me) in the home when I am not there. Please, please Freibe [Marian's pet name for King] <u>don't</u> do it. It is not a strange request for almost any woman resents having people, any people, especially those whom she doesn't know or knows only slightly, in her home when she is not there. The question of how fine the person is, has nothing to do with it, for I wouldn't want even the President or the "Little flower" to come there during my absence. You can understand this, can't you, baby?[74]

In the end, however, it was no doubt the issue of color that determined the delicate decision of when to marry. The complicated months of searching for a home had introduced a new wave of prejudice into their lives. Nothing could have been more damaging emotionally to their new life together than to encourage speculation about King's color, to the possibility that King and Marian were, in fact, an interracial couple, inevitable in a new community where they were not yet well known and accepted. And nothing could have been more difficult than finding the most appropriate means for eliminating such speculation. King's divorce had freed him legally and emotionally from a past life, but those facts, should they become known, would have only fueled more gossip and considerable censure. The course they settled on apparently was to wait until the press lost interest in the subject of their marriage, to put enough time behind speculation and curiosity until they could be married quietly and inconspicuously. On July 17, 1943, two and a half years after King's divorce, three years after Marian had purchased Marianna Farms, they were married in a quiet ceremony in the Bethel Methodist Church, not far from Danbury. No official announcement was given to the press at the time. Only later in the year, in mid-November—Marian was already on tour, in the Midwest—did Hurok inform the media. A short, routine announcement was carried by the *New York Times* on the nineteenth: "Marian Anderson, the Negro contralto, was married on July 17 to Orpheus H. Fisher, New York architect, it was announced yesterday by her manager S. Hurok. The ceremony took place in Bethel, Conn. Neither the singer nor her husband had been married before. Her age was given as 38, his as 43. The couple will make their home in Mill Plane, just outside Danbury."[75]

CHAPTER TWELVE

*Postwar Years
(1943–1952)*

M arian and King were approaching fifty as the war drew to a close.
Marianna had become a haven to them. As the farm grew, however, so did the costs required to maintain it, far beyond what either had
anticipated. King especially became more and more alarmed at the escalating expenses. "When we purchased this property," he wrote to Marian
while she was on tour, "I didn't think it was going to cost this much to
maintain it. I think we should do something about it before all our
money is gone. I don't think that you and I should live in a style far above
our income do you? Well we certainly are doing that just now. I know
that you don't like me to write like this but I want you to think about it
before it is too late."[1]

King was by nature more temperate about money matters than Marian. His solution was to sell off part of the farm in order to reduce
expenses significantly. Of course he saw other advantages to such a solution. It was Marian's earnings and not his that went into maintaining
Marianna. To reduce expenses in such a way would mean that Marian
could cut back professionally and spend more time at home. For King,
Marian was still away far too much of the year, and not, therefore, the
kind of wife and companion that he still hoped for. If the idea of working
less appealed to Marian, her responsibilities to her family—she was supporting her mother and two sisters as well as Ethel's son, Jimmy—and
her passion for the concert stage inevitably interfered. However much
she resolved to sing less and spend more time at home, these intentions
were swept away in the opportunities that presented themselves as the
war came to an end.

One such situation came at the end of 1944, when Petrillo's war on the recording industry ended. In the last weeks of December, Anderson returned to the studio after more than two years. She began modestly at that first session, limiting herself to Schubert's "Der Tod und das Mädchen," a contemporary song by Christopher Thomas, and the spiritual "Sometimes I Feel Like a Motherless Child." She was not pleased with any of them. Again the following spring there were sessions, which produced Schumann's "Stille Tränen" and "Der Nussbaum," and two Haydn songs, "My mother bids me bind my hair" and "She never told her love." From then until the end of 1947, there were regular sessions in the spring and early summer months, and often late in the year.

An opportunity of a different sort came about as the result of a letter Anderson received from William Dickinson, a Chicago voice coach. Dickinson wrote that he had attended her concerts and felt that he could help her technically. She knew nothing about the man whatsoever, and the people to whom she spoke about him were honest enough to admit that he sounded like a "crackpot." But Anderson was intrigued nonetheless. Boghetti had died a few years back, and although Rupp and his wife were immensely important to her artistically, she wanted a voice coach with whom she could study whenever she felt the need. As always, she was drawn to one who held out the promise of teaching her new repertoire or, even though she balked instinctively at any technical instruction that came into conflict with her sense of the natural basis of her singing, a teacher who claimed to have an original technical method.[2]

Dickinson must have been persuasive beyond his own imaginings, for Anderson invited him to spend some of the summer in Danbury so that she could judge him for herself. King found a room for him with Virginia Wren, a Danbury friend, and Marian went to work with him. He had wanted a singing career of his own, dealing with his disappointment by devising his own method of teaching other aspiring singers. Anderson later remembered little more than that he played his own exercises, sang them first himself, cupping his hand to his ear to hear himself better, and then tried to get her to imitate what he had done. Some no doubt thought her naive or insecure to invite him in the first place. The fact is that Dickinson's offer came at a particularly vulnerable time for Anderson. It was not only Boghetti's death that had left her feeling deprived of the kind of teacher she could trust. Critics had begun to notice vocal problems—an occasional flatness of pitch, a less opulent sound in the lower register, unevenness—that worried her.

Dickinson, of course, was not the answer, but Edyth Walker was. Walker was born in New York in 1867 and, like every American singer of her generation, went to Europe to study. Her operatic debut came in

1894, when she appeared as Fidès in Meyerbeer's *Le Prophète* in Berlin. Later she sang in Vienna and at London's Covent Garden, establishing herself as one of the most important Wagnerian mezzo-sopranos. In 1903, she made her debut with the Metropolitan Opera, where, for the next three years, she began to sing soprano as well as mezzo roles. Brünnhilde as well as Amneris were among her roles there. She continued to sing, mostly in Germany, until after the First World War, when she retired, devoting the last decades of her life to teaching, first in the American Conservatory at Fontainebleau, and then in New York. It was Madame Cahier who encouraged Anderson to go to Walker for study, and during the late forties they formed a warm friendship as teacher and pupil. Walker, like Anderson, had an enormous range, and she understood Anderson's voice and the concerns that she brought with her to her lessons as few teachers had. "She kept me there sometimes one or two hours or more," Anderson remembered, "until it was felt that something was really accomplished. I needed the security that she gave that I hadn't had before. That is the way I would like to teach."[3]

During the decade after her return to America in 1935, orchestral appearances had played only a marginal role in Anderson's annual tours. Monteux, Mitropoulos, and Ormandy remained loyal to her, inviting her to perform regularly; otherwise there were occasional appearances with less than front-rank orchestras. The fact is that the number and variety of orchestral invitations had been considerably less than for white singers of Anderson's accomplishment and renown. The discriminatory barrier that prevented black singers from appearing on the operatic stage extended to the performance of such works as the Bach Passions, the Beethoven Ninth Symphony and *Missa Solemnis,* Handel's *Messiah,* and the Verdi *Requiem,* works in which a group of soloists was required.

In the years immediately after the war, however, the number of orchestral invitations for Anderson to appear as soloist did increase. During the late forties there were invitations from Rodzinski and the New York Philharmonic (she had appeared with the Philharmonic often at Lewisohn Stadium during the summer but never during the orchestra's regular season), Thomas Sherman and the Little Orchestra Society, and Dorati in Dallas, among many others. These invitations in turn encouraged her to expand her repertoire, which had always been limited to a small number of operatic arias and lieder, mostly those of Brahms, for which orchestral accompaniments existed. Monteux suggested she learn the Liszt scena, "Jeanne d'Arc au bûcher," which she sang with great success. Successful too were "Schlage doch" (Cantata no. 53) of Bach and Mozart's concert aria for alto, "Ombra felice." For her first appearance with Rodzinski, she set her sights high, attempting the Mahler *Lieder eines Fahrenden Gesellen,* trying it out first with Monteux in a pair of concerts in February 1946, and then with the New York Philharmonic in April.

Anderson had studied the *Lieder eines Fahrenden Gesellen* as well as the *Kindertotenlieder* with Cahier, but found it difficult to find the right mood for the former, preferring instead the more intensely dramatic *Kindertotenlieder.* Monteux was no help. He disliked Mahler and conducted few of his compositions during his long career. Rodzinski was a better guide, but Anderson needed a longer period of study when it came to so challenging a work. Olin Downes, who reviewed her performance in the *New York Times,* had few positive words about her interpretation: "No one would accuse her of musical misrepresentation, but the conviction as well as the mastery of nuance which is hers when she is accompanied by a piano was rather lost in the orchestral shuffle."[4]

Anderson never sang the Mahler *Lieder eines Fahrenden Gesellen* again, but her disappointment over so singular a failure must have been short-lived, coming as it did during a period in which critics and audiences noticed a new warmth and intensity, a fuller maturity to her singing as well as a warmer, less reserved manner on the concert platform. Some actually speculated that she must be in love, others pointed to her recent marriage, once it became known. In this simple wisdom they were not wrong. Marriage was broadening her emotional experience, teaching her ways of accommodation and understanding that were often difficult and hurtful, but could only affect in a positive way her interpretation of music that called for subtle psychological and dramatic insight. There were new depths now to be heard in her singing. In one of her New York recitals that season, Anderson sang the aria "Ne me refuse pas," from Massenet's *Hérodiade,* from the scene in which Herodias implores her husband, Herod, to avenge the insult that she has just received from John the Baptist. In the aria, the scorn and anger that begins her confrontation with Herod fall away as she attempts, tender and supplicating, to persuade Herod to help her. "Despite the masterly and sensitive work accomplished by the singer in general, the climax of the recital was reached in the aria 'Ne me refuse pas,' from Massenet's *Hérodiade,*" wrote Noel Straus in the *New York Times.* "Never before has this reviewer heard Miss Anderson arrive at the dramatic heights scaled in the splendid interpretation of this operatic excerpt. The lengthy recitative was thrilling in its fierce ardor, while the altered mood of tenderness in the aria itself was strikingly maintained to the powerful terminating phrases."[5]

In a period of such artistic and personal satisfaction, a period in which the whole country began to shake off the long years of war and to breathe the air of hopefulness, retirement must have been the last thing on Anderson's mind. The possibility was brought home to her nevertheless by the unsettling news that doctors had discovered a small cyst on her esophagus. Apparently there was no immediate danger but the growth would have to be removed and a considerable period of convalescence would be required. The news came soon after the holiday season, during the first weeks of 1946. King urged Marian to have the operation immediately so that she could be well by spring. No one was prepared to say whether or not she would be able to sing after such an operation.[6] Overriding King's and others' protests, ignoring the possible consequences of not acting quickly, fearful of ill-health and possibly even retirement, Anderson concentrated on the commitments of a long season of concerts that lay just ahead. The year ended triumphantly with a cover story in *Time* magazine.

Only during the spring of 1947, during a tour of the West Indies, did her health begin to suffer. "It was so hot in Jamaica and Havana that electric fans had to be used on the stage. I returned home completely exhausted and with a sore throat. I was glad that my concert season had ended. I treated the sore throat with the usual remedies. A month passed and it grew worse instead of better."[7] She visited Dr. Gustav Bucky in New York, who thought she had a throat infection, perhaps from a tropical germ she had picked up on tour. During the summer she had little appetite and lost twenty pounds. Through the autumn of 1947 and the spring of 1948 she kept her concert engagements, as she later recalled, "with the utmost effort."[8] That season was one of the most demanding in years, with three Carnegie Hall concerts on the schedule. There was a particularly exhausting stretch toward the end of November when concerts in Nashville, Chicago, Richmond, Montreal, and Boston allowed her only a single day's rest between appearances. The whole of February and the first part of March were taken up with a tour of the West Coast that took her from Los Angeles to Vancouver.

In the summer of 1948 Anderson felt unable to face the grueling prospect of another season of concerts. Dr. Bucky called in a specialist and surgeon, Dr. Rudolph Nissen, who took another series of X-rays of her throat. Both were concerned more than ever about the growth that showed up on the plates. On June 29, Anderson entered the Jewish Hospital in Brooklyn and was operated on the following day. "A cyst was removed from the food pipe near the base of my lungs—top of solar plexus, I guess you call it. The operation was very intricate and had to be performed through my neck. Tubes were inserted in my throat so I could breathe. This, I understand, was an extremely delicate matter. The least deviation might permanently injure my vocal chords."[9] Anderson was in the hospital for twelve days. When she left the hospital she was cautioned by the doctors not to use her voice to sing. Not until August did the doctors feel she was ready to test her voice. She sent for Rupp, who came at the end of the month, and together they talked about the coming season, set to begin in Ann Arbor, on October 13. As they walked to the studio they decided they would choose only familiar numbers, that Rupp would be prepared to fill in with piano pieces should she be unable to sing an entire concert. "My studio is removed from the house. A brook runs by it. It is very quiet. An occasional wind in the trees is the only sound. Suddenly, I knew in my heart that I would sing again." She suggested that they try a little French song she had never done before. "I sang it straight through from beginning to end without the slightest difficulty. After that I wasn't afraid."[10]

On October 13, Anderson sang before an audience of 6,000 people in Ann Arbor's Hill Auditorium. "I did not feel at any time that I wouldn't be able to go on to the end."[11] She sang *arie antiche,* Schubert lieder, songs by American composers, Negro spirituals, and, for good measure, the extraordinarily demanding "Suicidio," from Ponchielli's *La Gioconda.*[12] A month later, at her first Carnegie Hall concert of the season, her three doctors and her nurse, Betty Unkeles, came to hear her. "I was happy, and so were they."[13]

The experience of the operation and convalescence did not shake Anderson's resolve to continue to perform as much as she had before. If anything it increased her determination. She was philosophical about how long her career and the good health it required would last. She was, as always, prepared to trust in God. On the practical side, if she couldn't alter what God held in store for her, she could at least influence what Hurok was willing to pay her for her work in the years that remained. Before the year's end she instructed her lawyer to inform Hurok that, "in light of experiences of the current season and other relevant considerations," she wanted a new contract.[14] Hurok agreed to an increase from two-thirds to 70 percent of the income of her concerts. They wrangled only over plans for a tour of Europe the following summer. There had been talk since the war's end about a return to Europe. Anderson had not sung there in almost fifteen years, and her recent illness added to her resolve to sing there again. Hurok explained that, in view of the depressed economic conditions still reigning in much of Europe in the postwar period, she could not hope to earn fees comparable to those in the States. Somehow an agreement was reached. On April 28, four days after her last concert of the season, at Carnegie Hall, Anderson sailed on the *Queen Elizabeth* for a two-month tour of Europe that would take her to Paris and London, Scandinavia, Switzerland, Belgium, and the Netherlands.

The excitement and hospitality that greeted Anderson and Rupp throughout the tour—throngs of reporters and photographers, lavish receptions, sold-out concerts with stage seating at virtually every concert—was far greater than Marian had dared expect. The first concert of the tour, at the Palais de Chaillot, in Paris, on May 7, set the pattern for the months that followed. "There was an excitement in the air that one could not miss. The performance began about ten after 9 and the ovation was magnificent, the audience inspiring, the result being that we gave one of our best concerts in some time. Aside from the applause, women shrieked, men yelled out bravo bravo bravo and there was the stamping all over the house. Certain numbers on the program had to be repeated before one dared continue and toward the end I lost count of the number of times we had to bow."[15]

In keeping with the unique rapport that existed between Anderson and the Scandinavian people, nearly half of the twenty-three concerts of the tour were scheduled in the Scandinavian capitals. On May 6, en route to Stockholm from Paris for a concert the following evening, Anderson and Rupp arrived in Copenhagen. More than twenty photographers formed part of a huge reception that gathered in a special room at the airfield, where drinks were served to the photographers and press people. The warmth and enthusiasm of the reception were diminished only by the long shadow of Paul Robeson, who had just weeks before given concerts in Copenhagen and Oslo as part of a four-months-long concert tour of Europe.[16] After concerts in Britain, Robeson went to Paris, joining 2,000 delegates from fifty countries, to attend the Congress of the World Partisans of Peace. It was a particularly heated and tense period in Cold War politics, and in the burgeoning struggle at home over civil rights. Robeson sang at the conference and made some casual remarks. He spoke first on behalf of colonial peoples and their struggle for civil rights, then turned to the plight of blacks back home. The prosperity enjoyed by Americans in the postwar period, he said, had been brought about by European immigrants and millions of black workers who, he proclaimed, were not prepared to fight in any war against anyone, including the Soviet Union. His speech, made even more provocative by misquotation in the American press, made him new enemies and embroiled him in escalating controversy.[17]

By the time Robeson arrived in Copenhagen for two concerts, at the end of April, he was exhausted and demoralized about the reaction back home to his Paris speech, yet no less outspoken in his beliefs. When he learned that the liberal newspaper, *Politiken,* which was sponsoring his concerts, supported Denmark's joining the North Atlantic Treaty Organization, he obtained release from his contract and sang under the sponsorship of the communist paper, *Land og Folk.*[18] By the time Anderson arrived in Copenhagen, reporters were already prepared to draw her out over Robeson's appearances in Scandinavia. An article had already appeared near the end of April, in a Swedish newspaper, claiming Anderson was as radical as Robeson, although not as aggressive as he over the question of blacks and their treatment in the States.[19] She was growing used to the comparisons made between her and Robeson in America, which had grown more frequent in the years since the end of the war. But in Copenhagen, amidst so enthusiastic a reception, the reporters took her by surprise when they asked her about Robeson's ideas and what he had done in Scandinavia. She felt unprepared—she had not, in fact, learned anything about his appearance in Paris or his recent concerts in Scandinavia—and because she knew little of what was happening, could not defend her own position. She pleaded ignorance to reporters but felt rattled, preparing herself for another round of questions in Stockholm.[20]

In Stockholm, mercifully, she was spared more questions about Robeson. Enwall met her at the airport, escorting her to her room in the Grand Hotel, where another press reception was held. The concerts in Stockholm—on the seventh, tenth and again the fourteenth, with another in Göteborg squeezed in on the twelfth—did not go well. The cold weather and delays they had experienced at Cherbourg were beginning to have their effect. Anderson was in the throes of a cold, without enough time between concerts to feel properly rested. On the sixteenth she left for Helsinki for a single concert the following evening at the Messuhalli. "Kosti was at the airport and grabbed me before I had time to say anything. He does look older but not as much as I had expected since Therese [Enwall's wife] said I wouldn't recognize him. We were photographed together many times and he was so pleased."[21] Kosti, nervous about their meeting again after the awkward and embarrassing circumstances of their parting nearly a decade before, had written to her a few days before her arrival, awkwardly yet touchingly personal, trying hard to reestablish their old closeness. "I am very curious to see you. Eight years is a long time. Are you very elegant? Do you have a really beautiful concert gown? Do you have many new rings and diamonds? Do you have new pearls and jewelry? Have you gotten slender or fat? I know that you still have your beautiful eyes. Those have not changed. I will be very happy to see you again."[22]

The mood of excitement and celebration was heightened the following afternoon when Avra Warren, the American ambassador to Finland, with many Finnish and American dignitaries present, presented Anderson with the Order of the White Rose during a ceremony at the American legation. The Order of the White Rose, Finland's highest civilian honor in recognition of service to Finnish art and culture, was presented to Anderson for her long years of dedication to the music of Sibelius and Kilpinen. Kosti accompanied Anderson that evening for the largest concert of the entire tour. Seven thousand people thronged the Great Hall, with many turned away.

> Wherever one could stand there was someone. People were packed solid up and down the stairway and their enthusiasm was exhilarating. When the concert was over they would not let us go and that was the most difficult part of all. Kosti was so happy, so very happy. . . . And true to form he had ordered extra police but not ten as long ago, but forty. Can you imagine? Well when we finally started to the car, we had to have the help of the police and the street for ever so far was lined so thick that the 'cops' had a terrific time clearing a lane large enough for our car to pass thru. The people cheered, yelled and beat upon the car windows, doors and fenders. It was a demonstration the likes of which is seldom seen.[23]

The critics were hardly less enthusiastic. Some noted that time had taken its toll on Anderson's voice. Her singing requires more work, one said; her *forte* is not as free and unbroken in her upper range as it once was; there is some flat singing on occasion. But all agreed that "as an interpreter Marian Anderson has grown even more profound than before. Her performances are now of the highest artistic standard and it would be difficult to find their equal."[24] The program included two rarely performed songs of Kilpinen, "Die Fusswaschung" and "Siehe, auch ich liebe." Her performance of Sibelius's "War es ein Traum?" (this time in German) had to be repeated. Finally, as if to compensate Kosti for her reluctance to sing in Finnish after so many years, she sang his arrangement of the folk song "Tuku-tuku lampaitani" in Finnish, which she had to repeat.

On June 3, Anderson arrived in Zurich from Copenhagen for the second part of the tour, surprised to see that "things here are quite different to those in Scandinavia."[25] There, she wrote home, "sugar, soap, tea, coffee and many other things are rationed and in Denmark you had to get a coupon for every meal," while in Zurich "it's possible to get anything you want if you have the money." With the concert in Zurich on the eighth, the busiest weeks of the tour began, with appearances nearly every other day. If the concerts in Scandinavia were the high point of the tour, a depressingly low point was reached by the time Anderson arrived in Belgium, for concerts on the fifteenth in Brussels and seventeenth in Liège. In Brussels, the critic of *La Lanterne* found her to be, both technically and interpretively, only a stand-in for the artist they once knew: "For if you ask me then where the genuine Marian Anderson is, because this one [who appeared here two days ago] would be merely her double and a mere reflection of her, I would say to you that the real, the great Marian Anderson survives in our memories."[26] The concert in Liège did not go much better: "Marian Anderson has returned to us after an absence of eleven years. We listened to her with a curiosity mingled with a little fear. Would she make the same impression on us as before? Yes, but only in the Negro spirituals."[27]

The truth is that, for the first time, Anderson was finding the demands of a European tour, coming as it did immediately upon the heels of a strenuous American season, far more exhausting a challenge than she was prepared for. She was finding, in fact, that she needed more rest between concerts and greater stamina than in the past to stave off the technical problems that had begun to assert themselves. Anderson's singing was now less uniform from one appearance to another, an entirely satisfying concert less predictable than it had been. And it was harder now to be away from home. Anderson had desperately wanted to sing again in Europe, but she had not counted on how much she would miss King and the quiet peacefulness of the early summer months that they had grown used to. They had planned a vacation in Europe for July and August, which they both hoped would ease the strain over Marian's refusal to be more the kind of traditional wife that King wanted. As the time for King's arrival neared—they had decided to meet in Paris before the final concert in Deauville—Marian became more and more preoccupied with how best to ensure that King would enjoy himself. "Would like to see the midnight sun in Scandinavia," she wrote to him while still in Copenhagen. "The best time is between the 1st and 17th July I believe and there is the possibility that I could take a concert in Sweden and thus lighten our way."[28] Their time together, first in France and then in Sweden with the Enwalls, did little to achieve a lasting solution. At best it was a postponement.

Anderson's fifteenth annual American tour, the first leg of a series of concerts that would take her from the States to Europe, and then to South America before its conclusion ten months later, began in New York with a recital in Carnegie Hall on November 30. During the months of a season that straddled the end of one decade and the start of a new one, Marian and King began to face more honestly than before the conflicts that had clouded their marriage from the beginning. Indeed, they had already taken one positive step, agreeing on a proposal that King had been making for some time. Before Anderson left for Europe, they had put the house and the fifty acres on which it stood up for sale. King was already busy with plans for a new house that he would design and help to build across the road, on a small knoll not far from Marian's studio and the pool—a house, he liked to say, where he would make it more difficult for the Andersons to visit so easily. While the new house was being built, they would divide their time between the small guest house and an apartment in New York—they had found one to their liking at 730 Riverside Drive—which King especially had wanted for a long time. Practical decisions that skirted the deeper problems of King's loneliness and injured self-esteem, or Marian's feelings of guilt and remorse for too often putting work and family before King's needs. Yet plans that exhilarated them and helped to improve their relationship.

By the time Marian left for Europe, on the second leg of a tour that would include Paris, London, Berlin, Munich, Zurich, and Geneva—a dozen European concerts in all by the end of June—she and King had gone so far as to seek the advice and help, as Marian put it, "of those who should be fitted by experience to give the right answers which was my grounds for asking in the first place."[29] Writing to him on board the *Queen Elizabeth* on route to Paris, on May 25 (1950), she found the distance and composure to give him her version of where they then stood, after a parting in which "you leave a bit sad and I full of remorse." She was solicitous, as always, and apologetic, writing that "this time it's my indecision and what hurts is, there is some truth in what you say." Yet she stood her ground as well, encouraging King to find satisfaction in his own strengths: "You have been disappointed, I know, for that I am sorry, but maybe all the blame should not be put at my door, because you, more than any other person I know, being unique as you are, have had opportunities that would not present themselves to other men, and success and failure for either of us should not have to hinge on the last seven years, important as they are." Sensitive to King's feelings of inadequacy, both financially and professionally, she encouraged him to take the lead. "The way you expressed yourself about a home and the right kind of living made so much sense, happily it's not too late to do something about it. 'I can make a living for both of us,' you said, 'so let's try to do something about it.' I'll remember that." Unrealistic perhaps but practical, outwardly confident that there were solutions just around the corner, she put her hope in the future: "Let's not look backwards nor brood over what we cannot alter but rather take stock of what we have, agree on a plan of action and proceed from there. Do you realize that <u>we've never</u> planned our future? Shame on two nice people. . . . We should be able to work out a plan which would give me the time to take care of 'my little boy.' I'd just love being a housewife."[30]

Aided by her emotional truce with King, not to mention a much shorter and more leisurely tour than that of the previous year, the concerts in Europe were a series of triumphs. Because the prices of tickets "are not to imagine," the audiences were often smaller than they had been before the war, yet the enthusiasm of the audiences and the critics alike made for rhapsodic receptions. The concerts in Germany (Berlin on the fourth and Munich on the sixth) were the most gratifying for Rupp as well as Anderson. Until then, neither had performed together before German-speaking audiences, and both were returning to the earlier days of their musical studies, Anderson in Berlin and Rupp at the Munich Conservatory. In Berlin a mixed Allied and German audience filled the Titania Palast, with half of the tickets given to students. Major General Maxwell Taylor, the U.S. commandant in Berlin, flew in from Frankfurt to attend the performance. There was tumultuous applause throughout the program, no more so than after the last spiritual, "O What a Beautiful City!"[31]

"In Munich," Marian wrote to King a week later, "the success was fantastic and Franz was not only in his seventh heaven but in the eighth. He told me that he has never lived thru such a great success in all his life."[32] The critic of the *Neue Zeitung* epitomized the press reception at both concerts, dwelling particularly on the "astonishing empathy and adaptability with which Anderson made the specifially German emotional world of the Schubert lied her own."[33] Anderson had not sung in Germany since the day that she stood before a small circle of friends and well-wishers in the Psychological Institute in Berlin, nearly twenty years before, trying out for the first time in public the Brahms *Vier ernste Gesänge*. Now a German audience was welcoming her home artistically. As the *Neue Zeitung* critic wrote, ". . . in critical places one is surprised by a wonderfully accomplished phrase or even a single tone in which her soul seems to open. From such moments the whole song achieves a new illumination. Her natural expressiveness imparts to songs like 'Der

Erlkönig' and 'Der Tod und das Mädchen' a deeply moving dramatic power, while in others, like 'Liebesbotschaft,' the charm of her delivery is spellbinding."[34] The European tour ended in Genoa on the twenty-first. From there, Anderson sailed for South America for a tour of twenty concerts that would extend into the second week of September. As during the previous summer, King joined Marian for part of the South American tour, meeting up with her in Rio, prepared to fly home should he receive news that their property had been sold.

The annual American tour in the fall and winter months, concerts in Central America in the spring, a European and then South American tour in the summer—this now was the extended season that continued throughout most of the decade with only occasional variation. Only the growing criticism of her unyielding middle-of-the-road position on segregated audiences in the South marred the enthusiastic acclaim that greeted her on both continents. In the postwar period many blacks were taking a more aggressive stance against segregation, in the South as well as the North. Blacks had put their lives on the line during the war; now they wanted a fair and equal share of opportunity and prosperity. For years now, Robeson had refused to sing before segregated audiences. More recently, the singer Hazel Scott refused to sing to a segregated audience in the Gregory Gym in Austin, Texas, where Anderson was scheduled to appear during her next American season.

Newsweek, in a cover story on Anderson in April 1949, had drawn attention to her concert in Montgomery, Alabama, the previous January, praised "her way of touring the South—demanding her vertical seating, yet bowing to regional custom by avoiding hotels exclusively patronized by whites."[35] Yet only a few weeks before the *Newsweek* cover story, after her concert in Columbia, South Carolina, Mrs. Andrew W. Simkins, a resident of Columbia, had written to her:

> I sorely regret that the rank segregation that your local sponsors have imposed upon South Carolina Negroes prevents my hearing you tonight. . . . I think you must have definite feelings on segregation as imposed on our people, for the Constitution Hall incident must have etched those impressions deeply. But I know that you cannot possibly realize the indignity one suffers when he must face self (Negro) imposed segregation. Our local music festival, organized years ago, never brought you here, although often requested to do so. The officials, no doubt, felt that you would not tolerate the very embarrassment you must face tonight. However, the citi-

zens of both races who appreciate art and beauty would not quibble about who sat next to them. . . .[36]

As the decade of the 1950s got underway, local NAACP officials in the South, with Walter White and the National Association behind them, along with other black community leaders, began to act in a more organized way, using boycotts to try to deter prominent performers from singing before segregated audiences. Richmond, Virginia, was the scene of one of the first such organized boycotts. On January 5, 1951, the Richmond branch of the NAACP, at an overflowing meeting at the Ebeneezer Baptist Church, announced its campaign to abolish segregation in places of public assembly. Included in its boycott efforts were Sarah Vaughn, Fred Waring, and the Ballets Russes de Monte Carlo, events scheduled to appear the following month at the Mosque theater. More immediate action was planned for Anderson's concert, scheduled for January 16 in the Mosque, and, later that month, an appearance by Duke Ellington.[37] On the sixth, Dr. J. M. Tinsley, local president of the NAACP, wrote to Anderson, explaining their position and informing her that they planned "to urge all of our members and other freedom-loving citizens to refrain from attending your concert or any other similar affair unless such segregated conditions are not to prevail."[38] Anderson may have discussed the matter with Hurok; publicly, she remained silent.

White lent his support to the Richmond branch, urging Hurok to take some kind of action in accord with Tinsley's efforts. On January 12, White received word of Hurok's, and presumably Anderson's, position:

> We feel very strongly that under the circumstances it would be unwise to make an issue of the segregation at the time, and, indeed, unfair to Miss Anderson. We feel, and many people share our view, that Miss Anderson's policy in the years past has resulted in a vast improvement in the relations between Negro and white in the Southern states and has brought the problem of segregation closer to a real solution than would have been the case if she had followed more militant tactics.[39]

As far as the Richmond concert was concerned, Hurok argued that "the lateness of his protest made it impossible for us or Miss Anderson to alter the terms of our legal contract with the local auspices of the concert, or to cancel the concert without undue hardship and embarrassment for all concerned."[40] It was precisely the local managers who would be most reluctant to agree to any arrangement involving nonsegregation that went against statute or local mores. For the Richmond appearance, taking a stand meant canceling the concert, which neither Hurok nor Anderson was willing to do. The local NAACP picketed Anderson's appearance, urging the black community to boycott the event. Many did. Although it had been sold out long in advance, enough black patrons turned in their tickets so that an anticipated audience of 4,000 was reduced to 1,400, with most of the more costly sections set aside for blacks conspicuously empty on the night of the concert.[41]

In preparation for a meeting later in the month with Hurok, who claimed that he was willing not to allow concerts in the South if that was what the NAACP wanted, White prepared the ground by writing to a number of black leaders in the region, asking for their candid views about whether they agreed "that it would be valuable for Miss Anderson to announce that she will hereafter sing to no segregated audience."[42] Those whose confidential views were sought included Mary McLeod Bethune; local NAACP officials in Birmingham, New Orleans, Dallas, Fort Worth; publishers of black newspapers; and other prominent blacks in academic life and the law. Only one of the sixteen who responded, George Flemmings, president of the Fort Worth, Texas, branch of the NAACP, advised against persuading Anderson to no longer sing to segregated audiences. So long as the form of segregation can be tolerated, he argued, "then there is no doubt in my mind but that Negroes in the South will be inspired to take pride in their own people, even though they must accept a segregated method of doing so. It inclines toward giving a greater sense of appreciation for the worth of Negroes to the white group to attend such concerts set up by them on a segregated pattern."[43]

The others who responded had already crossed over the line onto the side of those who had had enough, who could no longer suffer indignity and second-class citizenship, part of a small army of crusaders in the vanguard fighting against segregation. The arguments that were presented to White could hardly have come as a surprise. Mrs. Bethune stated them more simply and directly than the others:

> I feel that we have been tolerant and patient in our approach to this whole question all these years, and I believe that the time has come when people like Marian Anderson and others who believe in the complete annihilation of segregation and discrimination should make the public announcement that they would not appear before any segregated audience. Marian Anderson has come a long way up

the ladder with her marvelous voice and her economic security is such that it could be done without any loss to her. If she cannot do it today, I am sure I do not know when she or anyone else in her position can do it.[44]

What may very well have taken White by surprise was the depth of irritation and even resentment that more than one harbored against Anderson and her refusal to act more courageously in the South. Daniel Byrd, NAACP field secretary from New Orleans, for example, wrote to White that "the people of the South are proud of Marian Anderson but have often criticized her for appearing before a segregated audience. Their comments of disapproval have been softly spoken but they definitely object. Miss Anderson is the best known, best loved lady of our group and stands as a criteria for Negro Youth. She should not surrender to segregation lest she destroy some of the love these young people have for her."[45] Another responder, Frank Stanley, president of the *Louisville Defender,* was still rankled over the Louisville concert of a decade earlier, back in November 1942: "At this performance I refer to there was no segregation. However, it was not through the efforts of Anderson or Hurok. We were waging an all-out fight to sit anywhere in our auditorium. Prior to the Anderson performance, we had persuaded Catherine [*sic*] Dunham to protest segregated seating. As a follow-up, we wired Anderson and Hurok to cancel if necessary. They refused to cooperate at all, and only after Wilson Wyatt (then Mayor) ruled that there would be no segregation were Negroes sold first-class tickets. Negroes turned out in large number."[46]

Apparently neither Hurok nor Anderson were persuaded sufficiently by what White had learned to take a stand. Meetings continued. On May 16, having invited Marshall and Wilkins among other NAACP officials to join them, White met with King.[47] The meeting focused on Anderson's proposed concerts in Texas the next season. This time White sent out a letter to civic leaders and attorneys throughout Texas, asking: "Is it possible under Texas law to have unsegregated public assemblies? If so, are there leading white citizens willing to make a public statement pointing out the feasibility of non-segregation for the Marian Anderson concerts scheduled for your city next season?"[48] The responses were again positive and encouraging. Houston, Dallas, and Galveston, it turned out, had no local or state segregation ordinances for theater or public assemblies. All those who responded felt that Anderson, regardless of existing statutes, could be presented to nonsegregated audiences without significant negative reaction, that her singing before mixed audiences would improve community relations and have important educational value.[49]

Anderson listened to the voices of the South, and by the beginning of the new year had taken her first stand against segregated audiences at her concerts. In the last weeks of January 1952, she sang before unsegregated audiences in Jacksonville and Miami, Florida, for the first time in the history of the state. In Jacksonville several hundred dissatisfied whites demanded a refund when Colonel Edward Henry, recorder for the Duval County Armory (where the concert was scheduled), after first refusing to allow an unsegregated seating arrangement, changed his mind and allowed the mixed concert to go on.[50] When Anderson arrived in Miami two days later she was afforded a hero's welcome.

> I was not prepared for what awaited me. Luckily I had put on one of the new dresses I got from Milgrim's and when we alighted from the train there was a slew of people waiting, including a newsreel camera man, two women from the daily papers, a representative from the Negro Press, photographers, club delegates and so on. . . . I was taken to a car, the last word in a convertible and it was draped in red white and blue bunting and on the sides were 3 big sheets with "Welcome to Marian Anderson". . . . We had a motor cycle escort and before I reached my destination the manager turned to me saying, "Miss Anderson, the parade will begin at 4:30 and we will start from there." Well you could have knocked me over with a feather."[51]

At the concert, although fifty plainclothes officers, including FBI agents, the largest police protection ever given an artist in Miami, circulated constantly through the audience and backstage, there were no incidents.[52]

Cautiously and at her own pace, Anderson was changing with the times, and the times were changing because of her. The previous April 1951, Harold Maynard, the new manager of Constitution Hall, had urged the D.A.R. management to allow Dorothy Maynor, the black soprano, to sing with the National Symphony Orchestra. He was "trying very hard," he said, "to change the situation that resulted from the Anderson incident in 1939."[53] The following April, a few months after her concerts in Florida, Anderson sang once again at the Lincoln Memorial, this time at the memorial services for Harold Ickes, closing a circle begun thirteen years earlier. A year later, on March 14, 1953, as part of the American University concert series, Anderson sang to an unsegregated audience in Constitution Hall. "May I say that when I finally walked into Constitution Hall and sang from its stage I had no feeling different from what I have in other halls. There was no sense of triumph. I felt that it was a beautiful concert hall, and I was happy to sing in it." And as she added, "the essential point about wanting to appear in the hall was that I wanted to do so because I felt I had that right as an artist."[54]

CHAPTER THIRTEEN

On the World Stage
(1952–1958)

Early in 1953, Anderson and Rupp were invited to give a series of concerts in Japan by NHK, the Japanese Broadcasting Corporation. The tour was to begin at the end of April and continue until the beginning of June.[1] They would be among the first Western artists to appear in Japan in the postwar period, at the beginning of Japan's extraordinary musical development which, in the years to come, would make Tokyo one of the most cosmopolitan musical centers in the world. It would be Anderson's introduction to the people of Asia, a part of the world that would become more and more the center of America's foreign policy interests throughout the decade.

Unfortunately, plans for the tour came at a time when Anderson was preoccupied both with the changes going on at Marianna and with Alyse's poor health. After the sale of the farmhouse and half the property, King had designed and helped build a new house across the road, a ranch-style, three-bedroom house completed only a few months earlier. For two years now, Marian and King had divided their life between the small guest house at Marianna and the small apartment they had found on Riverside Drive in New York. Marian was full of plans to decorate and furnish a home that she felt would take some getting used to after the gracious, old world luxury of the farmhouse, plans that she would now have to put off until the early summer.[2]

Only weeks before the start of the tour, Alyse's health had deteriorated to the point where she had to be hospitalized because of a drinking problem. The problem had worsened since the death of William Runner—Uncle Bill, as he was known to the Anderson family—who for some years had been living with Alyse and her mother on Martin Street as a boarder, taking the furnished room in the basement in return for doing the cooking and other chores. He was a gentle and considerate man who, estranged from his wife, had found a home for himself with the Andersons and remained devoted to them until his death. He and Alyse grew to love each other and their relationship, quiet and discreet, was the emotional center of both their lives as they grew older. His death the previous October was devastating for her. For most of her life Alyse had felt unloved, always striving to be loved and more often than not feeling unworthy of it. With Bill she found a relationship that was both loving and supportive. As he lay in the hospital she had tried to convey to Marian how emotionally stunned she felt: "To see Bill just deteriorate before my eyes. Then when I mustered strength even beyond my strength and went to see him to find him that way I believe was my greatest shock and when I left him he was crying for me. Then when it was over the finality of it was something that I could never explain."[3]After his death she struggled against loneliness and the feeling of loss, but the going was hard and her drinking increased. That fall her health was sufficiently threatened to require several months of hospital care.

Only Anderson's emotional discipline in regard to her work, the ruthlessly steady focus her work required, and the complete and unquestioning devotion of family enabled her to leave for Japan. With the American part of her tour over, Anderson, Rupp, and Jofe left for California, from where they would fly first to Wake Island and then to Tokyo. It was only during the short flight to Tokyo, when she saw rice paddies far below shining like small sheets of glass in the glare of the sun, that Anderson began to feel a nervous excitement about visiting Japan, apprehensive of the difficult scenes and embarassing questions she expected to face, yet wanting very much to experience traditional Japanese culture. When they landed in Tokyo they were greeted by two little Japanese girls—by appearances, no more than five years old—dressed in doll-like kimonos, each one carrying two huge bouquets of flowers which they presented to Anderson and Rupp. Tetsuro Furukaki, the president of NHK, and some of his representatives, with a huge crowd of people looking on, greeted them, taking them first to their hotel and then to a press conference. That evening, at a traditional Japanese dinner arranged for them by Furikaki, Anderson had her first taste of the exquisitely ceremonial character of Japan. "As our car drove up there were servants waiting to sprinkle water before us. Then at the steps there were cloth slippers to wear in place of our shoes."[4] When they were seated on the floor, "several girls brought in tables and pillows. Then came the food, and presently more girls whose business seemed to be to attend to the guests—principally, I would say, the men."[5] After the dinner there was entertainment, "with dancing and singing girls performing their ancient art."[6]

At the first concert a few days later, in Tokyo's Hibiya Hall, whatever lingering uneasiness she felt about singing to an audience whose language and musical tradition were so far removed from any in her experience disappeared as she felt the intense concentration, the absolute quietness of their listening. Indeed, she was startled at first by the "deep silence and immobility" of the audience. "They were not upsetting in any way, but they made me feel that a similar intensity was expected of me."[7] Japanese music lovers were already among the most enthusiastic buyers of classical recordings and many who came to hear her sing knew her recordings. Indeed, those at NHK who had arranged Anderson's tour with Hurok had written to him asking expressly for Bach and Handel, Schubert and Brahms lieder, "Deep River," and "Ave Maria." The deepest impression on the audience that night came from Schubert's "Der Erlkönig" and "Abschied," some of the English folksongs arranged by Britten, and the spirituals, "O What a Beautiful City!" and "He's Got the Whole World in His Hands." About Schubert's "Der Erlkönig," one critic wrote: "She is at home in every style, and gives to each selection its intrinsic quality with a versatility that is little short of miraculous. This was especially true of the group of Schubert lieder—and more particularly Der Erlkoenig. In her dramatic rendition of this song, Marian Anderson succeeded perfectly in creating the illusion that four different persons—the father, the child, Erlkoenig, and the narrator—were present on the stage."[8]

There were ten concerts in the tour, including a broadcast and one appearance with the Tokyo Symphony Orchestra. In addition to the four recitals in Tokyo, there were concerts in Osaka, Nagoya, and Hiroshima. "The Japanese are indefatigable planners. My schedule was as rigid as a railroad timetable. Days were laid out in units of three—one for sightseeing, and this was planned down to the minute; one for a concert; and one, praise be, for rest."[9] The NHK officials who traveled with Anderson and her party were careful to guard Anderson from any embarrassment or awkwardness caused by onlookers or the press. Only in Nagoya did she have a moment of discomfort. After a rehearsal at the NHK Studio, the women there asked her to record her answers to questions they had prepared. One asked her what changes she thought Japanese women should adopt. Caught off guard, she did the best she could with "since I did not know them personally I could not intelligently suggest changes."[10] In between concerts there were days set aside for sightseeing: a boat trip in the evening at Gifu, accompanied by fireworks; a visit to the holy city of Kyoto, a meeting with Count Olani, the head of the Buddhist community, and his wife, the sister of the empress. She reserved the greatest praise for the stylized theatrics of the Noh actors and the wonderful costumes of the Kabuki theater. Everywhere, there were gifts expressing welcome and gratitude—medallions from the students at an opera school in Tokyo, a white leather-bound Bible from the Gideons of Japan.

Unforgettable—for Anderson, the highlight of the tour—was her audience with Empress Nagako and two of her children, Prince Yoshi and Princess Suga. At the imperial palace, Anderson and Rupp were specially entertained by the court orchestra before the arrival of the empress. For their audience, Anderson and Rupp "were brought into another room, which had rising tiers of seats. There was a stairway at the center of this arrangement, leading to the topmost seats, where the Empress sat with her children, the men and women of the court below them."[11] Anderson sang some German lieder, including "Ave Maria," an aria, and a group of spirituals, the first time in its 2,600 year history that a Negro guest had performed for the imperial court. Afterward, the empress greeted them in a small adjoining chamber and presented Anderson with a hand-carved figure, made of camphor wood, of a Noh performer, and to Rupp, a beautifully decorated lacquer box.

Anderson's first Asian tour was orginally planned to end with her concert in Tokyo on May 25, but officials at the American Embassy in Japan asked if she would agree to sing for the troops in Korea. On the morning of May 27, Anderson, Rupp, and Jofe, dressed in full army fatigues, left from the Army air base in Tokyo for Tague in an Army transport ("flying boxcar," as she carefully noted in the diary she kept of her trip to Japan and Korea) together with a hundred soldiers, and from there boarded a train to Pusan.[12] There was to be an open-air concert the following evening. A huge crowd that had come from long distances had already gathered in the pouring rain. Anderson wanted the concert postponed until the following day because of the weather. During the next few days she sang on improvised stages, in hospital corridors, often outdoors to standing audiences who huddled together, swaying back and forth. The twenty-ninth was the grimmest day. "The depressing sight," she wrote to Alyse, "of destitute refugees and a town which needs everything is not easily forgotten."[13] She sang in the ROK Army Hospital in the early afternoon and later was taken by helicopter aboard the *Jutlandia,* a Danish hospital ship on United Nations service. On the way to the landing deck she saw close-range swathes of bombed and burnt Korean homes and buildings. Aboard ship, wounded soldiers listened to Anderson singing as they received blood transfusions. Among the patients she comforted were a group of wounded Turks who had just arrived and were being cared for. At the Twenty-First Evacuation Hospital later that day one soldier told her: "I have been here for ten months, Miss Anderson, and after what I have heard I can last another ten months."[14]

On the eve of her departure from Korea, Anderson told a newspaper interviewer that this part of her tour had given her tremendous satisfaction.[15] Back home, she had taken a difficult step on the issue of segregated audiences, and although the victories in Florida were encouraging, she was growing defensive and unhappy about the criticism she was receiving for not doing more in the growing civil rights struggle. In Japan she had been kept away from unpleasantness, but her four days in Korea, with the fighting still going on, brought her face to face with the grim realities of war. She had been shaken by what she saw, but the experience had given her a sense of fulfillment that she sorely needed.

On the first of June, Anderson, Rupp, and Jofe returned to Tokyo in preparation for the trip home, which brought them first to Hawaii, for three concerts in Honolulu, before the flight back to the States. With only three months of vacation before the start of a ten-week tour of England and Scotland, Anderson threw herself into getting the new house comfortable and properly furnished. Cozily functional rather than spacious in the style of the farmhouse, the L-shaped, eight-room, one-story house sat atop a small knoll that commanded a sweeping view of the Berkshire Valley. The ranch-style house tolerated guests less easily than the old farmhouse, but the small, two-story frame guest house was now only a few hundred yards from the new home, and the small, rustic swimming pool even closer.

By summer's end Marian and King's small circle of close friends, often joined by the Anderson clan, King's sister, Pauline, and various Fisher nephews, could be found on weekends sitting around the pool or preparing an outdoor barbecue. Rex Stout, the novelist and creator of the Nero Wolf novels, and his wife, Pola, who lived a few miles away, in Brewster, were among the most frequent visitors. Marian adored them both, forming a friendship with Pola, and often looking to Rex for advice about professional matters. Most often the Stouts were joined by other close friends—Jimmy and Josephine Owens, who lived on Lake Canosha, which Marian loved visiting; Sylvester Carter, a noted black surgeon and his wife Gwen, who lived in New York and often rented the small guest house for part of the summer; and E. Sims Campbell, the artist. On occasion other neighbors—Dorothy Fields, or Fredric March and his wife, Florence Eldridge among them—would join the regulars.[16]

For a time the new home represented a resolution of sorts to the strains of marriage. For several years, in long hours of manual labor, often eliminating a contractor, King had labored alongside the workmen in the construction of the house. His design and engineering ingenuities were everywhere apparent, from the circulating hot water heating system designed especially for the house to the innovative lighting system, in which all the lights were controlled by four master switches. The creation of his "dream house" provided King with a sorely needed feeling of pride and a new sense of ownership. For her part, although not willing to make any plans toward retirement—indeed the decade of the 1950s saw her at home less than ever before—Anderson, at least during the summer months, made efforts to become the homemaker King had always yearned for. If the old problems reemerged, they did so more gently. Some of those close to Marian and King found them more patiently sollicitous than ever to each other. Others thought the old world gentility and courtly manners that now characterized their marriage, the elaborate ceremony at meals and other occasions, signs of a new respect for each other.[17]

The year ahead—ten weeks in Europe, the yearly tour of the States, concerts in South America in the spring—brought the usual assortment of critical disappointments, honors and awards, and traditional policies of segregated seating. Even before the start of the season, in Baltimore, when the Hurok agency's attempt to book a concert for Anderson there on behalf of Baltimore Fellowship, Inc., the local branch of an interracial and interfaith organization with which Anderson was associated in Philadelphia was thwarted by the management of the Lyric Theatre. Hurok proposed four open dates for the January benefit concert and was told that none of them was open. The theater's manager, Frederick Huber, refused to discuss its long-standing segregation policy, which applied to the stage but not in this case to the audience.[18] The governor's interracial commission, in fact, had been trying for almost two years to force the theater to modify its policy. The issue intensified in the press, bringing enough negative response from the theater's patrons to force the board of the Lyric, a few weeks later, to reverse itself. Anderson, because of her "artistic standing," and "the earnest requests from the stockholders and patrons,"[19] would be allowed to sing in the theater in January, although its rule on segregation would stand. As a private business corporation, the management argued, it was "not subject to any compulsion or restraint under the provisions of the Federal Constitution."[20] The board's position was a compromise that Anderson was no longer willing to make, and the plans for the concert were abandoned.

In mid-year, Anderson faced a new kind of unpleasantness. *Jet* magazine published a scathingly critical article on the state of Anderson's voice that included a survey of recent concert reviews from critics around the country.[21] The survey was neither representative nor fair. The list of critics was headed by Claudia Cassidy, of the *Chicago Tribune,* who was quoted as saying that "Miss Anderson is now in the pitiful dusk of a glorious career and her once-noble voice is now a ravaged ghost, rusted, unsteady, often (painfully) out of tune."[22] Cassidy's heavy-handed and well-known extremism apart, a certain consensus was forming that Anderson's voice had lost some of the bloom and tonal beauty of former years, that problems of pitch as well as breathing were becoming noticeable. But there was at the same time a consensus that her interpretive art had grown more subtle and more profound, and that her command of a wide range of styles and periods was as striking as ever. About her January concert in New York, the *Times* was quoted: "She is unable to achieve the sort of tonal glory that seemed to come easy to her in earlier days."[23] But the same critic also said, after a concert that included Schubert's "Der Wanderer," "Erstarrung," "Nacht und Träume," and "Der Erlkönig"; Strauss's "Befreit" and "Cäcilie;" "Les berceaux," "Aurore," and "Fleur jetée," of Fauré; music of Bach and Saint-Saëns, and a group of spirituals: "She brings such sincerity, such imaginative insight, and such comprehending musicianship to everything she does that she always makes a deep impression. Each of her selections, too, emerges as a small, self-contained drama, which is freshly conceived and tellingly projected."[24]

The honors that came Anderson's way that year included the Swedish government's "Litteris et Artibus" award, presented to Anderson by King Gustav of Sweden during her tour of Scandinavia, and an honorary degree from Dickinson University. None meant more to her than the opening of the Marian Anderson Recreation Center, a $700,000 facility featuring the latest in recreation equipment and furnishings, on Seventeenth and Fitzwater in South Philadelphia, only two blocks from the house on Martin Street where she had spent much of her early life. At the dedication ceremonies in July, the mayor of Philadelphia, Joseph S. Clark, Jr., spoke of the center as the embodiment of a principle "aimed at ending the erosion of human resources which is such a disturbingly prominent feature of present-day big city life."[25]

In September 1954, at a supper party hosted by Hurok after the New York premiere of the Old Vic's performance of *A Midsummer Night's*

Dream—Hurok had brought the production to America from England—Rudolph Bing, the general manager of the Metropolitan Opera, in a conversation with Anderson, asked her casually if she would like to sing at the Met. Hardly thinking anymore about appearing in opera, the offer took Anderson by surprise. She was struggling to learn the *Poema do Itabira,* a difficult work both rhythmically and melodically, for solo voice and orchestra by Villa-Lobos, which she was scheduled to perform at a pair of concerts with Paul Paray and the Detroit Symphony in December. Set to a Portuguese text by Carlos Drummond de Andrade, the *Poema* portrays the emotionally desperate feelings of de Andrade's characters, orchestrated so as to conjure up the starkness of the desert of Itabira. Anderson had met Villa-Lobos during the war while on a tour of South America. It was with Anderson's voice in mind that Villa-Lobos had composed the *Poema* several years later, dedicating the work to Anderson. Never having sung it before, she wanted badly to satisfy the composer.[26]

Also distracting her were Hurok's urgings that she agree to the publication of an autobiography.[27] Hurok had raised the issue at least a year before, perhaps to counteract the critical response to the state of her voice and the effect the critics might have on the box office. Simon and Schuster had shown interest and proposed someone to work with Anderson on the book but she found the whole idea threatening. That her privacy would be invaded on the broadest scale, that she might be judged beyond the safely confined world of music, were things that she was unwilling to face. The talks with Simon and Schuster came to nothing.[28] In the following months the possibility of an autobiography was raised again by Doubleday, who proposed three authors with whom Anderson might find it congenial to work, among them Ruth Goode, who worked with Hurok on *Impresario,* his own story. She found none of them acceptable.[29] Then someone thought of Vincent Sheean, who more than any of the others understood the nature of Anderson's art. In many ways that was the crux of the matter for Anderson, and she not surprisingly accepted the idea, but this time Sheean was unwilling: "It was an enormous grief to me . . . when I had to refuse to write the book. . . . I wrote to my agent and asked him to tell Mr. McCormick that I might revere and esteem you beyond measure but I could not ever possibly <u>be</u> you. . . . I felt that there was nobody in the world to whom I could more willingly give my small gift of writing, if it could be on the basis of truth and nothing but the truth. If I should pretend to be you, this would negate the greatest truth of all, which is your singing. . . ."[30]

In a casual way Bing had offered Anderson the opportunity not only to sing in opera—that, in fact, had happened many times before—but to become the first black singer in the Metropolitan Opera's history. That supper party conversation may have been informal, but the road leading up to Bing's proposal went back nearly half a decade.[31] Not long after Bing came to the Met in 1950, he began to talk about ending the policy of not hiring black singers. His first move occurred in 1951, when he hired the black dancer Janet Collins as a prima ballerina. Whether or not he chose to avoid bringing a black singer to the Met before he tested the waters more modestly is hard to know. He earned a great deal of praise for this appointment in the face of a basically recalcitrant board, whom he had not consulted. When the board expressed its disapproval, he responded, or so the story goes: "Well I didn't know I couldn't."[32] Max Rudolph, who began to conduct at the Met in 1946 and was later appointed assistant manager in charge of artistic administration, was as eager as Bing to bring black singers to the Met.

After the war, the Met's exclusionary policy came more and more under heavy fire, and both men were keenly aware that the policy had persisted for far too long. Even before the war black singers could be heard from time to time on the New York operatic stage, not only in Mrs. Dawson's Negro Opera Company but in smaller companies, the opera group of the National Orchestral Association and the Salmaggi Opera, for example, in which blacks occasionally sang alongside whites. In 1944 László Halász founded the New York City Opera and began almost immediately to invite black singers to perform. In 1945 Todd Duncan sang Tonio in *I Pagliacci,* and a year later Camilla Williams made her operatic debut there in *Madama Butterfly.* The baritone Lawrence Winters sang there as well, making his operatic debut in 1948 as Amonasro in *Aïda.* Ironically, Anderson herself was instrumental in helping to form Halász's determination to break the color barrier at the New York City Opera. They had gotten to know each other in 1931, when Halász was hired to accompany Anderson in three concerts in Czechoslovakia. They spent many hours together talking as well as rehearsing, dining together in restaurants and traveling from Prague to the provinces for two of the concerts. Anderson told Halász about conditions in the States, about how impossible it would be for them to dine and travel together so easily there. Halász, as he recalled, was surprised and repelled by what he heard, enough so that, when he founded the New York City Opera, he was determined to seek out talented black singers and invite them to perform.[33] Indeed, he talked to Hurok about Anderson coming to the City

Opera—he was thinking, in fact, of the roles of Ortrud (*Lohengrin*) or Santuzza (*Cavalleria rusticana*) for her—but Hurok wanted to hold out for the Met, where he thought she properly belonged.

In April 1950, in an interview broadcast during the intermission of a concert by the New York Philharmonic, Bing said that "as far as the Metropolitan Opera is concerned I can only repeat that I shall be happy to engage Negro singers if I can find the right voice for the right part."[34] Bing's statement was widely quoted, setting off excited speculation in the black press. Feeling that his statement had been misinterpreted, he told a reporter later that "I will not exclude anyone because he is colored. Nor will I engage anyone because he is colored. It is not my job to further the Negroes' cause, however sympathetic I may be. It is my job to run the Met. I intend to do this on the basis of quality alone. I am not straining every muscle to find Negro singers. I am looking for the best, regardless of race or creed."[35] He did try to find them. A number of black singers were given auditions in Bing's early years with the Met. Muriel Rahn auditioned for the Met four times between 1948 and 1956. The mezzo Carol Brice was given a stage audition in March 1950. Both were found wanting technically.[36] In 1953, the baritone Robert McFerrin won the Metropolitan Auditions of the Air, and although there was at that time no absolute promise of a contract, there was considerable enthusiasm for McFerrin to sing at the Met.

At the supper party, when Bing first asked Anderson if she would like to sing at the Met, he told her he was thinking of her for the role of the sorceress, Ulrica, in Verdi's *Un Ballo in maschera*. Max Rudolph had also been thinking that Ulrica would be an appropriate role for a black singer's first appearance at the house; it was, in fact, the role he had in mind for Carol Brice a few years back.[37] Ulrica appears in only a single scene, in Act I of the opera, but her prophecy foretells much of the subsequent action. Not only does she have a splendid aria at the start of the scene, but she also interacts in important ways with the other singers. Although Bing was considering Anderson for the role of Ulrica, she was not an easy or obvious choice. Among those at the Met who wanted to engage a black singer, Anderson was not taken all that seriously. Sylvia Olden, a black pianist and protégée of Max Rudolph, who came to the Met as a rehearsal coach in 1950, did not even think to mention Anderson to Rudolph when she was asked about what blacks she thought should sing at the Met. Olden felt that Anderson was too old then, that the time for such a debut had long passed.[38] Indeed, in a letter that was prompted by his announcement during the New York Philharmonic intermission, in which he was urged to invite Anderson, Bing expressed reservations about Anderson's dramatic ability to sing in opera: "Nobody can admire Marian Anderson more than I do, but I am unaware that she has any operatic experience and it is indeed difficult for a concert singer even of Miss Anderson's high level just to step onto an opera stage. However, as I said, I do not feel any kind of discrimination against Negro singers and if I have any opportunity to engage one or more of them, I shall be glad to do so."[39]

What then lay behind Bing's invitation to Anderson? Bing was genuinely committed to inviting black singers to the Met from the time he became general manager, and Rudolph supported the idea. Furthermore, he was perfectly capable of defying a resistant board if necessary when the time came. He also meant what he said about his refusal to hire singers for any other than artistic reasons, and when artistic principles were in his view compromised, he could just as easily fire singers summarily, refusing to submit to public sentiment and critical judgment. Hurok too was a powerful and determined man, capable of putting pressure on Bing. He had wanted Anderson to sing at the Met for years. When he heard of the Met's more sustained interest in black singers and the possibility that one or more would undoubtedly be invited before long, he may very well have pressured Bing to find a role for Anderson. Brice, Rahn and others had failed to make a successful impression with their auditions, but McFerrin had already won the Metropolitan Auditions of the Air, making a Met debut almost certain. Some have suggested that McFerrin's debut was, in fact, held up until the barrier against blacks could be broken with as little controversy and as much universal acclaim as possible.[40] In spite of his and others' reservations, with most of the season already planned, Bing decided to engage Anderson. No other black singer had the universal appeal, both artistically and personally, of Anderson; no other black singer would serve the Met as well in preparing the way for others. The weight of history and of conscience went into Bing's decision.

Anderson's own feelings about singing in opera had always been ambivalent. She often said, at least in the early days of her career, that to sing in opera had been a dream of hers, yet she pursued the opportunities that came her way with a surprising lack of determination. She was never drawn to opera, at least to the purely musical side, with the same urgency as she was to the world of song. When asked if she knew *Un Ballo in maschera,* she was forthright enough to say that she didn't know a single opera from start to finish.[41] Indeed, the idea of singing in opera was always more a romanticized fantasy for her—raising visions of herself extravagantly costumed and trying her hand at acting—than a realistic musical goal. She realized as a mature artist that the consistency and artistic security she felt with an accompanist who shared her musical ideals was not a part of the opera singer's experience. She may have wished for the glamour of the world of opera, but it was not a world that served her musical values.

No wonder that when the opportunity to sing Ulrica was presented, her first thoughts went to the technical demands of the role. At the start she did not feel certain about her ability to sing the part at all. "I glanced through the part of Ulrica. My first impression was that it lay too high for my voice. But by this time I had agreed to spend some time working on the part. The understanding was that after I had studied it a bit I would have an audition with Dimitri Mitropoulos, who was to be the conductor, and then we would give our opinions as to whether I would do the role."[42] The first weeks of study were discouraging. She found that she was facing difficulties in learning the role that she would not have faced "if she had applied herself all along the way."[43] Nervous about the heavy burden she was being asked to bear in altering a long-standing policy at the Met as well as accepting a new kind of musical challenge, she was as hard as ever on herself, imagining all sorts of inadequacies. Nearing sixty, facing the realities of opera for the first time, and once more asked to carry the burden of altering history, she had good reason to be apprehensive. As it turned out, Jofe was a big help. He was a fanatic about opera, knowing its ins and outs and many of the people who worked in and around the Met. He suggested that she go to Paul Meyer for coaching, "a very sensitive person who knows every role in the opera and could probably sing them all in several languages."[44]

When she felt ready, she went to Mitropoulos with Paul Meyer, who played the piano for her. "There is a high A in Ulrica's aria, and I must confess that I was not too happy about it. By then I was no longer going out of my way to sing notes above the staff. Furthermore, it was morning, and I don't like reaching for top notes that early. I got to the A and squeezed it out. As I sang it I glanced at Mr. Mitropoulos. His head remained bent over the score, and he gave no sign, which was wonderful of him."[45] Mitropoulos was encouraging. "You haven't worked on it enough yet and you don't know it thoroughly," he said. "When you know it, it will go."[46] Anderson was still not convinced and asked for more time with the piece before she made up her mind. But before she reached home Mitropoulos had already made up his mind. He had called Bing and given his approval, and Bing had called Hurok and fixed the terms—$1,000 for each appearance, the highest fee for a singer for a single performance then being paid at the Met. A press announcement was prepared, and on October 7, Anderson was issued a contract for three performances of *Un Ballo in maschera* during January 1955, the first performance to occur on January 7, with Mitropoulos conducting and a cast that would include Richard Tucker, Zinka Milanov, Leonard Warren, and Roberta Peters.

Although rehearsals at the Met were not scheduled until December 20, Anderson took every opportunity she could find when not on tour to study her role. She worked with Steffi Rupp on the vocal demands of her part as well as with Meyer. When rehearsals at the Met began, she was advised to study with Victor Trucco, a member of the conducting staff, who made sure that she knew the tempi and the phrasing that Mitropoulos wanted. Trucco went over the Italian text with her, encouraging her to write it out in full with English equivalents. A long chain of support and guidance was being put in place for Anderson, each member not only helping her with various aspects of her role but preparing her for her next coach. Trucco started her thinking about the gestures and movement associated with the role in preparation for her work with Herbert Graf, the stage director. As Anderson later recalled: "Each day brought a new step in the collective enterprise that is opera. We had sessions with piano in which singing and acting were fused. Then came the rehearsals of the duet with the soprano, Zinka Milanov, who was doing the principal female role. Next the tenor, Richard Tucker, joined us for the trio. The entire act was assembled, and then I met the chorus and later the orchestra."[47] Roberta Peters, who sang the role of Oscar, remembered how Anderson, although she came to rehearsals very shy and self-effacing, became transformed the moment she began to sing, singing out in full voice and with fierce concentration. Mitropoulos, sensitive to her nervousness, encouraged her throughout the rehearsals, giving her special time, constantly sensitive to her needs.[48]

In spite of her nervousness and lack of experience, Anderson found the whole experience of preparing and rehearsing exhilarating.

Some people know how to order their lives so that they do things on schedule. I do not have that gift, but I had to adapt myself to the way the Metropolitan did things. I had become so saturated with my concert life that I found I scarcely had time for anything but getting my work done. At the Metropolitan I had to stretch my hours to crowd more activity into them, and somehow all this caused the blood to race through me with new meaning. I felt incredibly alive, able to do any amount of extra tasks. I even managed to get some of my letters answered, and that's really something.

On January 7, 1955, Anderson made her debut at the Metropolitan Opera as Ulrica, the first black singer to perform there in its seventy-one-year history. The house had sold out within days of the first announcement of her appearance. The black press was represented from as far away as the West Indies. Anderson's role called for her to appear only in the second scene of Act I, which takes place in Ulrica's cave, a crowd watching in the background, eager for the first words of Ulrica's incantation, "Re dell'abisso, affrettati" ("King of the depths, make haste"). But on opening night the curtain refused to go up and the music of the short orchestral introduction had to be halted. That minor mechanical problem took only minutes to correct, but it injected an extraordinary degree of nervous expectation, even momentary alarm, into the vast spaces of the Met. When the curtain finally rose to reveal Anderson sitting before the cauldron in the darkness of the cavern, the audience erupted into an ovation that lasted nearly five minutes.

> I trembled, and when the audience applauded and applauded before I could sing a note I felt myself tightening into a knot. I had always assured people that I was not nervous about singing, but at that moment I was as nervous as a kitten. I was terribly anxious that this of all things should go well, but there were things that happened to my voice that should not have happened. With all the experience I had behind me, I should have been firm and secure, but my emotions were too strong.[49]

When the curtain came down at the end of the scene there was relative silence, the audience waiting for the singers to come before the curtain. There was outburst after outburst as Anderson appeared with the other singers. Bing had put a stop to solo bows, but when Anderson appeared alone with Milanov, the soprano throwing her arms around her and kissing her on the cheek, a tremendous demonstration welled up from all parts of the house. Olin Downes, the distinguished music critic of the *Times,* wrote in his column the next day: "As the act proceeded and the voice warmed it gained in sonority and concentrated resonance. The first aria lies more comfortably for the voice in its middle register than the second one, the 'E lui,' which asked more of range and dramatic delivery than the first. Indeed, the two passages, the first in the dark tonality of C minor, the second in the brighter and more militant major key, significantly supplement each other. Miss Anderson drove the contrast home, at the same time that her voice took on its normal resonance and emotional appeal. . . . There was no moment in which Miss Anderson's interpretation was commonplace or repetitive in effect. In Ulrica's one-half act, by her native sensibility, intelligence, and vocal art, Miss Anderson stamped herself in the memory and the lasting esteem of those who listened."[50]

Not all the critics were as kind as Downes. Many chose to be more frank about the technical limitations of Anderson's singing, musing ruefully about how long she had to wait before coming to the Met. There were even some grumblings from patrons and subscribers who opposed Bing's now obvious commitment to engage black singers. Of course, such criticsms were beside the point. Together Anderson and Bing, in a single evening of joyful purpose, were changing the face of opera for black singers. Because of the exigencies of her schedule, Anderson sang in only two performances of *Un Ballo in maschera* that season, the second performance coming four days after her debut when the Met traveled to Philadelphia. A week later, Robert McFerrin, who had been kept in the wings for the right moment, made his debut in the house as Amonasro in Verdi's *Aida.* Anderson was engaged the next season for six more performances of Ulrica, the first four in New York, the last two in Cleveland and Boston, for the Met's spring tour. There was some talk at the Met for a while about other roles for her, more out of kindness perhaps than actual intent. Bing was counting no doubt on Anderson's temperate judgment that her career at the Met could not continue. True to his word, however, Bing lost no time in engaging who he judged to be qualified black singers. During Anderson's second season at the Met, in fact, he engaged the young lyric coloratura soprano, Mattiwilda Dobbs, a Marian Anderson Scholarship winner in 1947, to sing the role of Gilda in Verdi's *Rigoletto.*

For a time after her performances at the Met, Anderson's mood alternated between euphoric confidence and sober reflection. Loath to put behind her the fairy tale–like atmosphere that had been patiently created for her, an atmosphere in which she found a new degree of self-discipline, she imagined herself—one wonders with how much seriousness—in other roles that she might sing. She even talked for a while about learning the role of Azucena, in Verdi's *Il Trovatore,* one of the roles that she had dreamed of singing years before.[51] But these were daydreams, comforting for a time but unrealistic. In the end Anderson knew this. An unremitting sense of pride is what remained—in her accomplishment in portraying the one operatic character she was granted to sing, and more lastingly in the sense of purpose she inspired in black singers and the possibilities she helped to open for them.

A sense of sobriety about her singing also took over. Given the national attention paid to her debut, she felt the limitations of her singing glaringly exposed. For years, since the death of Edyth Walker in 1950, she had been without a teacher. Walker had done wonders for her vocally. On her own, she had to fight against her lack of self-discipline. She was, in fact, prone to laziness when it came to regular work on technical problems. It was Camilla Williams who came to her aid with the suggestion of a new teacher. Williams had been one of the first Marian Anderson Scholarship winners, and one of the first black singers to sing at the New York City Opera. Anderson trusted Williams enough to take her advice to go to Marion Freschl for study. Hungarian-trained, Freschl came to the United States already an experienced teacher. She had heard Anderson in Europe, and was not only taken with her singing but with the unique qualities which she felt inhabited the voices of black singers. Once in America, she taught at the Curtis Institute and the Juilliard School, eager to train black singers; Shirley Verrett was another of her students. It was a felicitous choice. Freschl was an enormously dedicated teacher, with considerable insight into the technical problems of singers. Indeed, as Anderson's work with Freschl progressed, many found her voice more secure, freer, and younger sounding.[52]

Only months after her Met debut, near the end of March, Anderson boarded a plane for Rome on her way to Israel for a series of concerts that would extend throughout April. Since her early successes in Europe, Anderson had wanted to sing there, to visit the land that provided the source and the inspiration for many of the spirituals she sang. Another of her dreams was coming true. There had been plans for her to sing in Palestine, in 1935, but nothing had come of them. Now she was anticipating particularly her appearances with the Israel Philharmonic. Paul Kletzki was to be the conductor, with Anderson contributing the Brahms *Alto Rhapsody* and several operatic arias, including "Re dell'abisso" from *Ballo*. The tour was one of the most grueling that Hurok had ever arranged. Because of the small size of Tel Aviv's Edison Hall, where the orchestra regularly performed, ten appearances were required for each subscription concert in order to accommodate the public. In addition, there were recitals planned for Tel Aviv, Jerusalem, and Haifa during the latter part of April, when Anderson would be joined by Rupp.

In Rome, Anderson felt the beginnings of a virus. She worried about the possible cancellation of concerts, but the flight from Rome to Israel took her mind off how badly she was feeling. "Flying over the coast line," she noted in her diary, "I had a strange and exhilarating feeling. Keen excitement ran thru the plane's capacity load of those coming to spend Passover in the new land."[53] There was a big turnout at Lidda airport, with representatives from the American Embassy and the Philharmonic and an unexpected and happy visit with Mrs. Roosevelt who, hearing that Anderson was arriving for a series of concerts, wanted very much to see her before her own departure a few hours later. By the time Anderson saw a doctor the next morning, the virus was more firmly entrenched, and the first rehearsal and concert with the orchestra had to be postponed. The following day the doctor examined her again, finding her vocal chords discolored, but agreed that she might try to sing so long as she did not talk or remain in any room that was smoky. She rehearsed the *Alto Rhapsody* with the chorus and "Mon coeur" from *Samson et Dalila*—"very strenuous and not wise what I'm doing," she noted in her diary.[54] After the rehearsal, she went to see a specialist, who found that there was congestion in the trachea, and recommended inhalations of streptomycin and penicillin.

On April 2, after a second cancellation, Anderson made her first appearance with the Israel Philharmonic. She was far from satisfied, noting in her diary, "performance not as good as I would have it, but we got thru with it substituting "Mon Coeur," for the 2 programmed arias. Gave no encore."[55] What she failed to note was the sensation she created with her performance of the *Alto Rhapsody*. German was for the most part boycotted then as a language, the chorus singing its part in Hebrew. Anderson could easily have sung in German—on each of her recitals, in fact, she sang a group of German lieder—but she chose to learn the entire text of her part in Hebrew. As always, she accomplished this linguistic feat with extraordinary precision and naturalness. The audience was moved by her desire to communicate with them more directly, the critics noting with some astonishment that, as one of them put it, "we should mention as well with appreciation Brahms's Rhapsody, which was sung in perfect and articulate Hebrew. Because the translation was difficult to grasp, the complex words rang out from the great singer more naturally than their content was understood by the audience."[56]

In the weeks ahead, the ten scheduled appearances with the orchestra were increased to thirteen, with two recitals in Tel Aviv and one in Haifa—sixteen appearances in less than three weeks. By the end of the month Anderson's voice had recovered, but her initial indisposition only heightened the feeling of expectancy. The critics, even when duly noting that her technical resources were diminished, were enraptured, praising her artistry and command of style. There was not a single dissenting voice, from *Al-Hamishmar* ("There was sensuality and primal temperament in the Spanish songs; 'The Burial of King Nago' will remain engraved in our memory, particularly the intense expressive quality of the death scene")[57] and *Ha Arez* ("Miss Anderson has a uniquely warm-hearted talent for expressing Schubert songs, their melodic line, and she beautifully suits the appropriate tonal color to them, ... achieving unsurpassed vocal perfection in songs like "Wohin," "Tod und das Mädchen," and "Erlkönig")[58] to *Jedioth Hayom* (". . . she revealed an art which, in its elevation, depth, and devotion, could hardly be surpassed").[59] The *Jerusalem Post,* commenting on one of her performances of the *Alto Rhapsody,* said of Anderson: "Recovered from her indisposition she had not only perfect control in all registers of her wonderful voice, but the deepest penetration into the spirit of this masterpiece. One could scarcely imagine a more moving rendition. . . ."[60]

In the end it was not so much the enthusiasm of the audiences nor the critical acclaim that moved Anderson, but the pioneering spirit she saw among the Israelis, their dedication and hard work. She saw much of the history of her own people—their struggle against oppression—mirrored in the lives of those who had come to hear her. "The audiences in Israel," she later explained, "were something special. They were made up of young people who had found a refuge and a home there, and their hunger for music was exceptional. But no audience was more remarkable than those we had when we performed at two kibbutzim, those pioneering agricultural communities created by dedicated men and women who had the faith and energy to cause a desert to bloom."[61]

Whether helping to celebrate Passover in the kibbutz Givat Brener, singing to the thousands who gathered at the base of a small hill not far from the mountains of Syria, at the kibbutz Ein Gev, near the Sea of Galilee, or visiting the Dead Sea or the River Jordan, Anderson experienced the biblical and historic sites she visited as a kind of pilgrimage to a land she had sung about all her life. As she visited the River Jordan, the walls of Jericho—the one not nearly so wide, nor the other so high as the spirituals she sang had led her to believe—she could see in Israel "the geographic places that represented the reality" of her background and traditions, and they stirred her deeply.

For the Israelis, who had great sympathy with the plight of blacks in America, Anderson's visit had a special appeal that was not shared by any of the great artists who came to Israel to perform. She was inspirational to all segments of Israeli society. To members of the older generation, many of whom belonged to left-wing political groups and were interested in the latest socialist ideas, Anderson was seen as an important champion of civil rights. Toni Halle, a German Jew who had been educated in the great liberal German Jewish tradition, invited Anderson to speak about civil rights to the students of Tichon Hadash, a small social-ist, Russian-oriented high school in Jerusalem which he had helped to found. Uncomfortable with the invitation, she nevertheless accepted, telling the students how important it was to love their country and how impressed she was with the Israeli spirit of creativity and idealism. Young people responded to her with equal enthusiasm, inspired by her courage and her own struggle for equality. The younger generation particularly was drawn to the exoticism of a black performer and to the spirituals, the first black music of any kind heard in Israel. A few years later, when *Porgy and Bess* was brought there by its original troop, the performances cre-ated a sensation. [62]

At the end of her stay in Israel, impressed by the musical talent of the young people (many young aspiring singers found their way to Ander-son, to sing for her and to discuss their problems), and wanting to create a bond with the people of Israel, especially its youth, that would last beyond her brief visit, Anderson contributed part of her fee to setting up an annual scholarship to be given each year to several gifted singers. In a final interview, dressed in an Israeli-made blouse, she told reporters: "You make it easy for one of my race to feel very, very much at home here from the first moment. To stand on the banks of the Jordan, or to see Jerusalem and those other places so tied up with one's religious back-ground and our spirituals, makes a profound impression. One knows that later, when there has been time to absorb these great happenings, their impact will be even greater."[63]

Once back home, the dilemma of what to do about the proposed autobi-ography still weighed on Anderson. Hurok proposed various collabora-tors. Anderson rejected them all. Finally Hurok thought of Howard Taubman, a music writer for the *New York Times*. It was Taubman who had written the enthusiastic and appreciative review of Anderson's first concert under Hurok, two decades earlier. He, like Sheean, had extraor-dinary respect for and understanding of her art. Moreover, he and his wife lived in Danbury, only a few miles from Marianna, making him, so Hurok hoped, less of a stranger to Anderson than others. Having gradu-ally warmed to the idea of an autobiography, Anderson found Taubman acceptable, but Taubman felt overly pressured with his newspaper job, and so was reluctant to accept. With pressure from both Anderson and Hurok, Taubman, who said he needed the money, gave in. In the agree-ment Anderson signed with him, Anderson agreed to turn over to Taub-man, for the duration of his work, all available material, including letters, diaries, and notes pertinent to the book. Taubman was to do all of the research for the book, and to "create it in written form."[64] Both planned to find a trade publisher after the manuscript was completed.

In spite of her decision to go ahead with the project, Anderson was frightened by the prospect of opening up her life and her thoughts to someone she really didn't know. Indeed, she refused to give Taubman access to a single document, although he was able to have conversations with family members and with Hurok and his assistants. In the end, Taubman had to make do with a tape recorder, preparing in advance a list of topics and questions for Anderson. Beginning in the fall of 1955, they worked together at Marianna over the course of several months. Taubman found her unable to be frank about the difficulties of her childhood, or to talk easily about the prejudice and discrimination she faced. Whenever a subject arose that gave her any discomfort—the music school that turned her away, the need to criticize others, the Lincoln Memorial incident—she more often than not turned the tape recorder off before she was willing to go on. More than once, this inability to be frank caused Taubman to threaten to abandon the project. He urged her a number of times not to hold anything back, and although Anderson made an effort to give Taubman what he wanted, she was really not able. The effort that the work caused both of them is captured in the taped material. At times school masterish and dour, trying to push Anderson as gently as possible, Taubman cannot always hide his frustration. Anderson in turn often sounds intimidated and uncertain, happy as a schoolgirl when she elicits real satisfaction from Taubman.[65]

The disagreements did not end once Taubman completed the book. Anderson read a draft of the manuscript and disliked it. She particularly disliked Taubman's title, *My Lord, What a Morning.* Presumably it emphasized the importance of spirituals too much and, by implication, assigned her the status of black singer. Anderson also wanted all mention of the Lincoln Memorial concert removed. Uncertain about how to proceed, she asked Rex Stout to read the draft. He told her she was being unreasonable, that Taubman had done a brilliant job. For Anderson, Stout was a voice of wisdom and authority, and he convinced her to allow the book to be published. Picked up by the Viking Press, *My Lord, What a Morning* came out the following summer and was greeted warmly by reviewers.[66] The whole experience had been a trial for Anderson but the success of the book encouraged her, in the coming years, at least when the circumstances were not too inhibiting, to be more frank with interviewers about her feelings, to be more open with them about the painful aspects of her life.

★ ★ ★

During the 1950s, Anderson was becoming one of the most admired and dependable black celebrities in government circles, a black woman of extraordinary accomplishment who was also loyal, patriotic, and reluctant to criticize publicly the treatment of blacks. Official Washington recognition of Anderson came during the first month of the new year, when she performed at the inaugural ceremonies for Eisenhower's second term. The president had been criticized by blacks during his first term because of his cautious attitude toward civil rights, especially his unwillingness to act against state-imposed segregation after the landmark *Brown* v. *Board of Education* decision of the Supreme Court. Indeed, a 1955 Gallup poll revealed that Eisenhower's popularity among black voters had declined considerably during his first term.[67]

Since one of the most dramatic and symbolically important breakthroughs for blacks during that first term was Anderson's Metropolitan Opera debut, the Eisenhower administration wanted to keep her accomplishment before the public. Already underway, in fact, were State Department plans for her to act as a goodwill ambassador as part of its gradually expanding program of international cultural exchange. The death of Stalin in 1953 and, two years later, the Geneva Summit in July 1955, had opened the way to increased cultural exchanges between the United States and Russia. A few months after the meetings in Geneva, Carlton Smith, director of the American National Arts Foundation, traveled to Moscow to begin discussions about American-Soviet cultural exchange. American policy on this subject was still confused, without broad public support or government consensus. Nonetheless, anxious to combat Soviet propaganda that democratic ideals in the United States counted for little when it came to minorities, State Department officials were eager to include significant black artists in their plans. In addition to the enthusiastically received production of *Porgy and Bess,* Smith proposed sending a group of artists to the Soviet Union, including Anderson and Leontyne Price.[68]

Neither Anderson nor Price was among the few Americans that actually went. For their part, the Soviet Union sent to the United States Emil Gilels and David Oistrakh, whose debuts in the fall of 1955 were among the most sensational musical and political events of the decade. It was not Hurok, but Columbia Artists Management, working with the State Department and the Soviet Ministry of Culture, that presented them to the American public. When Hurok was ready the next year to engage in his own cultural exchange mission with the Soviet Union, he gave no thought to Anderson. The Soviet Union had set the terms of cultural exchange, in a dramatically competitive spirit, by sending two of its greatest instrumentalists, both artists in the prime of their careers. Canny as ever, Hurok sent Isaac Stern and Jan Peerce, two of his most popular artists, to the Soviet Union in the spring of 1956. Like Gilels and Oistrakh, they were both relatively young and artistically in their prime. Although born and trained in the United States, they also happened to be of Russian parentage. For Hurok, Anderson, now in the last decade of her career, was no longer a useful player in the high-stakes cultural competition the Soviet Union had initiated.

The State Department thought differently. Moreover, it had recently been presented with new funding to expand cultural exchange. In August 1954, as part of a $5 million appropriation for American participation in foreign trade fairs and cultural events, Congress set aside half for a new program in which the American National Theater and Academy, a private organization that had been sending artists abroad since the 1940s, would act as a contractor and advisor to the State Department's U.S. Information Agency (USIA), to help organize cultural exchange. In the years to come, ANTA would help the State Department expand considerably its cultural exchange activities to Asia and Africa, spheres of influence where it was becoming increasingly important for the United States to engage in propaganda.[69]

For several years now the State Department had been aware of the impact that Anderson's Met debut was having abroad. The most intense interest came from Asian countries.[70] Shackled with their own histories of subjugation by white colonial powers, the Asian countries were particularly sensitive to civil rights issues in the United States. While Hurok was planning carefully for the day when he could bring the Moiseyev dancers and the Bolshoi Ballet to America, the State Department's Information Agency, in connection with ANTA, was putting together its plans to send Anderson on the most ambitious and extended tour of Southeast Asian countries ever undertaken by an American artist.

ANTA arranged for Anderson to give twenty-six concerts in twelve countries beginning in the last week of September, and lasting until November 30. Seoul and Pusan would be the first stops. Formosa, Hong Kong, and Manila would follow in early October, with concerts in Saigon, Phnom-Penh (Cambodia), Rangoon, Bangkok, Singapore, and Kuala Lumpur during the remaining weeks of October. In November, Anderson would travel to Ceylon (Colombo and Kandy) and then India (Madras, Bombay, New Delhi, and Calcutta). Engagements in Pakistan (Dacca, Lahore, and Karachi) would bring the tour to an end. For some years Anderson had refused to sing more than fifty concerts a season. Having turned sixty early that year, her voice no longer as technically secure as it was in previous decades, she was being asked to sing nearly thirty concerts in two months' time.[71]

She was being sent to Asia not simply as a concert singer. The arrangements for the tour were not in the hands of the Hurok office but ANTA and the USIA. In addition to the schedule of concerts that ANTA had arranged with local musical organizations, the USIA was free to arrange impromptu visits to local schools, churches, and charity organizations, and to encourage exchanges between Anderson and government officials, local civic leaders, and the news media. Adding to the strain she felt at having to face so much public exposure unconnected to her performances was the knowledge that she would be a spokeswoman for her country, seen and judged by the American public. Planning a "See It Now" television program about her tour, to be narrated by Edward R. Murrow, CBS sent along a crew of technicians prepared to follow Anderson as much as their 1,500 pounds of equipment would permit.

In that curious way in which events conspire, the weeks before Anderson was set to leave for Korea were burdened by events that would plague her throughout the tour. On September 4, the issue of school desegregation erupted in the South with ugly force when Governor Orval Faubus of Arkansas ordered the national guard to prevent nine black students from attending Little Rock's Central High School. For nearly three weeks the crisis mounted. When Faubus withdrew the national guardsmen on the twenty-third, leaving the students to face an angry mob of several thousand that surrounded the school, Eisenhower was forced to act. The next morning he authorized sending federal troops to Little Rock. That evening, in Seoul, Anderson and Rupp were scheduled to give the first concert of the tour.

From the beginning of the tour, in interviews and press conferences in nearly every city, Anderson was questioned about the racial dissension in Little Rock, the reporters and interviewers trying hard to bait her. Little record survives of what she told interviewers in Asia about those events, although she did recall some of what she had said in Asia to an interviewer in the States a few months after the tour. "We told them that it [the trouble at Little Rock] was a very unfortunate thing," she said, "and that we were sorry it had happened. We felt very grieved about it. We didn't go into any long discussion. This was neither the time nor the place for it and we were not sufficiently acquainted with the developments. We felt that personal opinions would be fine only if they could be of any help. We were there because we believe in America and if you don't believe in a thing you shouldn't try to represent it."[72] Unfortunately, the only comment preserved in the "See It Now" broadcast was taken from a press conference in Rangoon. When one of the reporters there asked her, "Would you like to sing for Governor Faubus in Little Rock," she answered without hesitation: "If it could help at all I should be very delighted to. If Governor Faubus would be in the frame of mind to accept it for what it is, for what he could get from it, I should be very delighted to do it." What she wanted to convey was that her singing, as a gift not altogether of her own doing, was bound up inextricably with her love for others and her faith. Like one's faith, she was unwilling to deny the gift of her singing to anyone ready to benefit from it. That response came back to haunt her during the 1960s, portraying her as someone too ready to appease.

Away from the stage, it was not all politics. In Bangkok, Anderson visited a class of young girls who were studying English; in Rangoon, she shared her views about religion with Domiya Seyn, a Buddhist scholar; in New Delhi, at the All India Radio Station, she talked with a woman about the plight of the "little people" around the world who aspired to do great things. Often she used the words of spirituals to convey how she felt. To the girls in the school in Bangkok she talked about the meaning of "Trampin'." For Domiya Seyn it was "O What a Beautiful City!," and in New Delhi, "I open my mouth to the Lord and I never will turn back." With these words—on occasion she would sing part of a spiritual—she described her feelings and her philosophy, finding in them a universal language. She found that the people she spoke to shared with her a deep faith and a belief in a better world, and that they all yearned for a sense of belonging. She often talked to them about what she had learned from her mother, about the sin of pride in feeling too complete, and the peace of mind that faith brings.

Although, as Anderson herself came to realize, "this non-musical or extra-musical part of the tour, its general or larger significance . . . overshadowed the concerts in many places," the events themselves were invariably sold out, the audiences attentive and enthusiastic.[73] To reduce the strain of so difficult a tour, Anderson and Rupp had prepared only two programs, both consisting of pieces long a part of her recital programs. In the first program, there was a group of Handel arias and a group of Schubert lieder (the ever present "Der Erlkönig" and "Der Tod und das Mädchen," filled out with "Ständchen," "Aufenthalt," and "Wohin"), the *Samson et Dalila* aria "Mon coeur," an American group, including Barber's "Nocturne" and Howard Swanson's "The Negro Speaks of Rivers," and a group of spirituals. On the second program were songs of Purcell, Scarlatti, and Haydn; a group of German lieder (Brahms and Schubert, this time "Auf dem Wasser zu singen," "An die Musik," and "Ungeduld"); and Ulrica's aria from *Un Ballo in maschera,* followed by the usual English songs (Griffes and folk song arrangements by Britten and Quilter) and spirituals. Even more than usual, it was the spirituals that had the profoundest effect on the audiences. "In every case these old songs, so full of sorrow for a present life and hope for a future one, touched the hearts of the listeners," she explained. "When I try to think of why the spirituals have this power to erase all barriers and all boundaries, it seems to me most probable that it arises from this religious origin and their expression of a religious hope."[74]

The familiarity of the programs sometimes contrasted with the often inappropriate and makeshift conditions of the theaters. "There are no regular concert halls to be found in the Asian cities. . . . In a good many halls, and some of the biggest ones, big screens had been built in for movies, thus filling all the space on stage: in these it was necessary for the singer to enter from the front, go up some steps and stand in front of the screen. . . . some would accommodate an audience of six hundred, others larger numbers. . . . In Hong Kong we sang in a football stadium (with amplifiers, of course) which held eight thousand people, and many others filled the windows and balconies of the high modern buildings behind it."[75]

In some cases—in Delhi, for example—the audiences were made up of a small and educated elite who had a great hunger for Western music and artists. At many concerts, important dignitaries and heads of state were prominent. At Assumption College in Bangkok, King Phumiphol Adulyadej, the king of Thailand, who sat on a specially raised platform in a roped-off area of the theater, came down from the royal dais to shake hands with Anderson and to exchange a few words of greeting, one of only several times in Thailand's history that the king rose to greet a visitor. Taken by complete surprise, the audience watched in awe and amazement as the king extended his hand and expressed his delight in Anderson's appearance in Thailand. Nehru and his daughter, Indira Gandhi, sat as part of the audience in New Delhi; after the concert, Anderson was entertained by Nehru in his home, where they discussed the great problems facing his country. In Rangoon, Premier U Nu came personally to greet her backstage after her concert at Engineering College Hall: "Your performance tonight is a rare combination of good voice, good technique and very good dramatic acting," he told her. "The beauty and charm of your music are manifested in your dazzling eyes and childlike lips."[76]

In many cases Anderson was able to reach diverse audiences, especially when local USIA officials were able to travel around to schools and universities, discreetly depositing material about Anderson and the recognition her own country afforded her. Students were often the target of USIA propaganda. In New Delhi, for example, Chris Rosenfeld, the wife of the chief information officer of USIA, traveled to campuses showing a movie about Anderson in the days before the concert. In every city, ANTA made sure that the tickets, often no more than a dollar or two, were affordable to ordinary workers and students.

The most moving experiences of the tour, those which had the profoundest effect on Anderson and the people of Asia, were those informal occasions in which she could communicate in song, in settings less formal than concert halls. In Kuala Lumpur, on the very day on which the Malaysian flag was raised in the United Nations to celebrate the new nation, Anderson, holding fast to the Malay words in her hands lest she forget them, sang the national anthem in the language of her audience before her concert. In New Delhi she broke precedent again. Although no visiting dignitary from any foreign nation had ever been invited to speak at the Gandhi memorial, she was granted permission to lay a wreath there. Leading a throng of several thousand people, she was introduced by the mayor of Old Delhi. Anderson spoke very little, preferring to sing "Lead Kindly Light," which she knew to be a favorite of Gandhi.

On occasion, away from the CBS crew and the endless reporters and interviews, Marian and King, happy to be traveling together for the entire tour, caught glimpses of another Asia. "I felt it first and strongest at Pusan, in Korea," Anderson later recalled, "poverty and suffering on a scale unknown to us in the west. It is less constantly visible in Formosa and Hong Kong, but at the refugee camps outside Saigon we felt it strongly again. There is hardly anywhere you can go, as far as I can tell, in any of these countries, without feeling that privation, under-nourishment, all the effects of poverty, have gone as far as they can go."[77] There were moments of surprise and humor as well, especially when Marian and King could snatch some time away from official duties to walk in the bazaars, to see, as they liked to say, "those who don't come to concerts." One of those moments occurred in a shop in Singapore, whose Indian proprietor seemed to have been expecting them: "I've been waiting for you for three days, Miss Anderson," he told them. There were beautiful brocades and silks which the proprietor tried to sell them, all the time keeping up a running commentary in fluent English and seeming to know a great deal about them. Worried about the problem of air transport, they decided not to buy anything. When the proprietor realized this was the case, he said to them, cheerfully: "Well, what are you going to do with your money, Miss Anderson? Take it to heaven with you?"[78]

On December 30, the one-hour "See It Now" television record of Anderson's trip to Asia was broadcast on CBS. Edward R. Murrow narrated the program, titled "The Lady from Philadelphia." As the documentary statement of Anderson's efforts on behalf of the State Department in Southeast Asia, it remains the only published record of her tour. In the 1960s, during the darkest days of the civil rights struggle, the unsubtle and heavy-handed propaganda of the program, and Anderson's unswerving willingness to extol the virtues of American liberty and freedom, became easy targets of criticism. Yet Anderson's sincerity, the quiet modesty with which she spoke, and the pride she conveyed in the accomplishments of black people, brought a positive response from television viewers when the program first aired. Of course there was criticism, mostly from the South. Some stations there refused to carry the program, and angry viewers let their feelings be known to CBS. One viewer in Tampa, Florida, found the program and Anderson's comments about blacks in her own country demeaning—why was there mention of Little Rock and the Lincoln Memorial, yet not enough about "the many of our race who are on top."[79] Another from Augusta, Georgia, found the entire filmed record a carefully rehearsed propaganda effort by the NAACP and Washington officials "to maliciously coerce and mislead the American people by depicting the South as the unpardonable offender."[80] There were editorials denouncing the program, one editor claiming that "the film was so dishonest as a picturization of southeast Asia as to be disgusting."[81]

As far as the State Department and the majority of the American public were concerned, Anderson's Asian tour was an unqualified triumph. Only after she returned to the States did she unburden herself of the frustration and indignities that she had had to endure. "If in your long experience you've given your utmost for an ideal," she wrote Hurok a few months after she had returned from Asia, "and then only to find that this has not been enough, then you may know something of the feeling I had. . . ."[82] Although Jofe had asked for a contract for the tour, she went on to explain, none was ever provided. Furthermore, USIA officials insisted, against her better judgment, that every concert be taped for later broadcast, admitting at the same time that this was not generally the rule with other artists. Then there was the concert in Hong Kong: "I accepted Hong Kong against my better judgment and the manager there, Mr. Odell, said quite frankly and openly that he had been opposed to it, but had been persuaded to go along. It went very well, but could have gone otherwise. It was in a football stadium, and was more a spectacle than artistic. . . ."[83]

Pride and loyalty kept Anderson from informing State Department officials how she felt. She had agreed to represent her country in Asia; she was not about to complain to them that things had not always gone well. Hurok, on the other hand, was someone in whom she could confide. He better than most would understand the real issue: "I was told beforehand that this tour would be strenuous but I do not believe that anyone realized how strenuous. For there were things, the world situation being what it is, required of me as a Negro that would not be required of someone else."[84]

The world saw nothing of the emotional cost of the tour on Anderson. The recognition it gained her brought a new round of honors that continued throughout the year. In May she received the Einstein Award for citizenship, and Lord and Taylor, at its twenty-first award luncheon, honored her as an "unofficial ambassador," along with Mrs. Roosevelt and Senator Fulbright. During commencement season, she received honorary degrees from Mount Holyoke College, New York University, and the University of Pennsylvania. In October, the New York branch of the American Association of University Women named her woman of the year. More honors, from the Distinguished Daughters of Pennsylvania, Oberlin College, and the National Institute of Social Sciences, followed in the months ahead.

In mid-July, it was reported in the *New York Times* that Lester Holzman, Democratic representative from Queens, had asked Eisenhower to appoint Anderson, on the basis of her extraordinarily successful tour of Asia, assistant secretary of State in charge of African affairs.[85] Holzman was unaware that the administration, thinking along similar lines since at least March, was ready to submit to the president a list of proposed delegates to the thirteenth session of the United Nations, with Anderson as one of five alternate delegates. By training and experience, Anderson was an unusual appointee for government service, but in attempting to demonstrate that theirs was a government of merit and equal opportunity, the Eisenhower administration was learning "the symbolic value of selective minority appointments to visible (though not challenging or controversial) administration positions."[86] The administration's record with regard to United Nations appointees was spotty. The appointments to previous delegations of Charles H. Mahoney, a Detroit lawyer, and Archibald. J. Carey, a minister and lawyer from Chicago, had not quelled the outcry from black leaders over the selection, in July 1953, of Governor James F. Byrnes of South Carolina.[87] Worldwide sentiment over Anderson's Asian tour had been so positive that the administration wanted to keep Anderson before the public eye.

When first approached by the State Department early in the spring, government service must have been the last thing on Anderson's mind, and she refused to serve. Without any experience that she thought appropriate for such a position, feeling inadequate by temperament and knowledge to assume a role so at odds with the world of singing, she was hesitant to think seriously about the invitation. Her experiences in Asia forced her to reconsider. In India, where poverty and undernourishment were greatest, she had begun to ask herself what more she could do to help the people of Asia. "Although we may know what we want," she had said at the time of her Asian tour, "this does not constitute a guide to what others want. Our whole problem, therefore, is one of insight and imagination: it is the problem of <u>how</u> to help, rather than of when, where or how much. Much money has been spent and will be spent on assistance in the struggle for people's welfare in India and nearby countries. It is going to be spent anyhow; we can only hope that it will be spent for the best possible results. If it were reasonable to hope so, we might hope that it would be spent with love."[88]

Finally she turned to Mrs. Roosevelt for advice about what to do. By the time Secretary of State Dulles phoned her, in early May, she had changed her mind. On July 23, her name, together with the names of nine other appointees, were sent to the Senate for confirmation.[89] A few days later the official announcement came that Anderson would be a part of the thirteenth United Nations delegation. Having accepted the appointment, she was prepared to face whatever she would be asked to do with undivided seriousness. She canceled all of her concert dates and lecture appearances until the new year, planning to stay in her apartment in New York with King for the duration of the session. In view of the success of her Asian tour, and her desire to work in an area dealing with human rights and race relations, she was assigned to the Trusteeship Council, the committee that dealt with all matters relating to the status and well-being of the trust territories. Most of the eleven territories administered by the Trusteeship Council (more than half in Central Africa; the others, island territories in the southwestern Pacific) had been held under League of Nations mandate until the end of World War II. Many were in the last stages of achieving self-governance. Few of the delegates appointed by nonadministering members were experts in territorial administration.

Often delegates acquired a familiarity with territorial issues when they participated in missions to the trust territories. Anderson would be asked simply to carry out the instructions of her government.[90]

One can imagine Anderson's impressions during those hectic opening days in September as the United Nations prepared for the work of its opening session. The swearing-in ceremony of the delegates, the atmosphere of excitement and curiosity among visitors and tourists queuing up in the General Assembly's public lobby as delegates arrived for the opening session on the thirteenth, would have provided little reminder of the grave events of the past summer and the debates they would occasion in later months. A more serious note took over when Dulles addressed the General Assembly on the eighteenth, giving prominence to the Chinese Communist bombardment of the Quemoy Islands, the second time in two years, at the same time managing to put a positive face on the presence of American troops in Lebanon.[91]

When Anderson arrived in her office at 2 Park Avenue during the session's opening week, her thoughts were on people rather than issues. "There are great areas," she told reporters on her first day of work, "where people overseas need to know and meet equivalent people in America. There are so many misconceptions." Again she stressed understanding. "The main feeling is that America has a lot of money and is attempting to buy what it likes. A lot of people don't want to be bought. They resent it. Especially since we give people what we think they ought to have, not what they should have. One mustn't give people things because we happen to think they need them. The important thing is to find out what they really need."[92]

Although there were daily meetings of the Trusteeship Council in the weeks and months ahead, Anderson played little role in debate or discussion. The State Department counted on the symbolic significance of her presence, her grace and modesty as a representative of her people, and her ability to reach out to others in friendly and compassionate concern. She was especially interested in the peoples of Africa. Although some interest had been expressed in her visiting Kenya, she had had no opportunity to give concerts in the African countries. Now she valued the opportunity to make friends among the delegations and to learn as much as possible from committee discussions about African customs and history. Living in New York gave her the opportunity to plan receptions both in the city—Marian and King had found a more comfortable apartment on Fifth Avenue (at 1200, near 101st Street, overlooking Central Park) a few years before— and at the United Nations, using those occasions to welcome delegates from the Council and to talk with representatives of countries where she had performed. In mid-October, as the American delegation and five others prepared to introduce the resolution that would call for approval of independence for Togoland, Anderson and King hosted a formal reception in their home for delegates from twenty-two countries. A month later, Anderson gave a small and more intimate luncheon at the United Nations, for delegates as well as friends—Mrs. Roosevelt, Pola Stout, and Emily Kimbrough were among them—using it as an opportunity to become better acquainted with Prime Ministers Olympio of Togoland and Ahidjo of the French Cameroons, whose efforts toward achieving independence were the subject of discussions during those weeks in the Council.[93]

On November 25, with less than a month left in the winter session, Anderson made her presence known in the Trusteeship Council in a way that no one would have anticipated.[94] Until then she had not experienced for herself the passion and sense of urgency the African peoples brought to the question of independence and self-government. Her own involvement began with two resolutions proposed by Ghana, Haiti, India, the Philippines, and Yugoslavia concerning the future independence of the French Cameroons, resolutions asking for a special session of the General Assembly for February 20, when the Council would make a report on the mission that had been sent to the Cameroons in order to prepare the way for discussions about the future of both the French and English Cameroons. Anderson was instructed to move to adjourn discussions that would lead to a special session of the General Assembly in February. The motion to adjourn debate was defeated, twenty-nine in favor and thirty-four against, with nine abstentions, the United States's vote to adjourn supported by France and England, the administering countries.

In the ensuing discussion, when countries were asked for explanations of their votes, Anderson read a prepared statement outlining the position of the United States. General Assembly sessions, she explained, should be devoted to questions of international peace and security. The question of the Cameroons' independence was of great importance and deserved careful consideration. In light of the fact that the Council had not yet heard the report of the special mission to the Cameroons, however, it would be premature to decide on the desirability of a special session. Anderson's statement brought an immediate outbreak of disappointment and anger from a number of African and Asian delegates. More than one delegate rose to express disappointment with Anderson. How could she, of all people, they wanted to know, speak out against calling a special session to consider the pleas of the African people? Angie Brookes, the delegate from Liberia, with whom Anderson had become friends in the preceding months, spoke out with special force against her.

Visibly shaken, Anderson asked for the floor. "There is no one in the room," she said, "who is more interested in the people whose fate we are trying to determine than I. Like many of the representatives, I am a member of an instructed delegation and we are here to carry out what is wanted, otherwise we would not be here."[95] If Anderson had been a more seasoned delegate, more aware of the realities of government service, she might have held back her feelings. But for that moment she did not consider American policy or established protocol; she simply spoke honestly about how she felt. "I didn't think about it beforehand," she said later, "I just did it."[96] Even though some delegates thought the whole affair "a tempest in a teapot,"[97] there was for the moment considerable confusion within the American delegation. Anderson's impromptu remarks were diplomatic, almost inscrutably indirect, but no one could be sure to what degree the incident would be blown up in the interest of propaganda. For the moment, officers rushed over to Anderson in an attempt to guard her from reporters, who wanted to question her about her break with policy. The next morning reporters awaited the arrival of delegates, hoping for more news, but were told that Anderson would have no more to say.

The controversy did not last long. Ironically, it was only the special regard in which Anderson was held by the African and Asian delegates, the reason for her appointment in the first place, that kept the issue alive at all. In general, the press found her courageous. *Pravda,* on the other hand, whose November 20 issue arrived by airmail in New York in the midst of the controversy, added its share of irony. The edition—"A good singer but a poor diplomat," was the headline—carried a story criticizing her silence on colonial issues in the face of American imperialist designs.[98] In the black press, however, she was proclaimed a hero. "Marian Gags on UN Africa Speech," ran the headlines in the various editions of the *Afro-American.*[99] In the end, it was Anderson's prestige that forced the United States delegation to find what face-saving solution it could. The day after the vote, it was agreed unanimously that the current session of the General Assembly would be "extended" to February 20, to discuss "exclusively" matters relating to the future of the Cameroons.

CHAPTER FOURTEEN

Retirement
(1959–1993)

The UN session ended December 13, in time for Marian and King to spend the holidays at Marianna. For both, the four months in New York had been rewarding, at times exhilarating. Anderson believed she had done some good at the UN. Her personal integrity, her warmth and sincerity, made her many friends there. King had enjoyed the social side of Marian's work—rubbing elbows with diplomats, foreign visitors, and state department officials. Indeed, his charm and congeniality had been a great comfort to Marian. But he missed the farm and his building projects in and around Danbury, and Marian was anxious to begin preparations for the coming season.

They had several weeks more together following the holidays. In mid-January Marian began her twenty-fourth season under Hurok's management. She was already on the road when King found himself facing an emotional reunion neither he nor Marian could have anticipated. Only a few days after Marian's departure, King received a phone call, as he wrote to her a few weeks later, "from a person who said that he was Jimmy my son, and that he was in this area and would like to see me."[1] King had not seen his son since his separation from his first wife nearly thirty years before.

Jimmy was only five when King had left his family; for a long time he felt only anger and resentment toward his father. Now a man of thirty-five, having recently married and hoping for children of his own, he wanted to see his father again, ready to form a more satisfying relationship with him and with Marian, whose career he had followed closely for years. The summer before, in fact, Jimmy, then in the area because of his work, had tried to see his father. "He told me that last summer while he

293

was here," King wrote to Marian, "he came up here to see us but got cold feet and did not drive into our driveway because he did not know how I would or you would receive him. He said that he followed you to Danbury and went to the Safeway Store and asked you for an autograph and he thanked you, he said he thought you were everything that he has heard about you."[2] When the phone call finally came, King arranged a meeting with Jimmy and his wife. They came to the farm, and in the succeeding weeks King saw them quite a few times.

In pouring out his feelings to Marian about his son, King came back again and again to the pride he felt in seeing him after so many years. "Not because he is my son," he wrote to Marian, "but he is quite good looking and about my height or a little taller and weighs about 170. His wife is charming and on the young side . . . I am very happy that he has become a fine young man and he seems to have both of his feet on the ground and a good head on his shoulders."[3] But King was apprehensive about the inevitable questions that were bound to arise: "I don't know what to do about this as I know his wife must think that he is white so I am just letting him make all of the moves."[4] In the midwest when King's letter arrived, Marian needed a few days before she felt ready to answer:

> I am glad that <u>you</u> told me about Jimmy being in the neighborhood and I am sorry I did not recognize him when he asked for an autograph. Considering that you told me about him <u>before</u> he was <u>born,</u> I am curious to meet him, after all these years. You spoke of not knowing "just what to do about" etc. And you are "just letting him make all the moves." This to me seems very wise because you are not well enough acquainted with Jimmy to know just what he would consider a problem. And if there is one and if he is like his father, he'd want to work it out himself. But be ready if he should ask your advice.[5]

Aware of how much support and reassurance King needed, she held back from him her disappointment with the bad reviews she was getting all along the tour. For her Carnegie Hall appearance, in March, for example, an event which Anderson always considered the artistic measuring rod of each season, she assembled a program more demanding and varied than those of recent years. In addition to the infrequently performed Masonic cantata of Mozart, "Die Ihr des unermesslichen Weltals," she sang lieder of Sibelius, Schubert, and Rachmaninoff. Ross Parmenter, of the *Times,* felt that "as an interpreter, as a mistress of dramatic projection and as a compassionate human being of moving sincerity, the contralto was as impressive as ever." He felt with equal conviction that "the years have taken the toll of her vocal resources. For all the early part of her program last night, her voice was thin, reedy and shaky. And later, when she was able to summon up more volume, it was not always under the surest control."[6] Kolodin too found the technical side of her singing that evening distressing: "Having been listening to Marian Anderson since her Town Hall debut on December 30, 1935, it is no part of pleasure to report that her latest appearance in Carnegie Hall found the once noble instrument only a vague suggestion of its former self."

The following spring, *Ebony* magazine, as part of its preparation for the article, "Should Marian Anderson Retire?," decided to approach Anderson directly.[7] A reporter from the magazine, in an interview in Mason City, Iowa, where Anderson was giving a concert, asked her how she felt about what the critics had been saying about her voice. "The critics," she answered, with unruffled calm, "as in all professions must be honest about their feelings whatever they may be—flattering or not. One should always write the truth as one sees it and no one else should influence one." As for retirement, she would decide when the time came to retire, not the critics: "We have thought about retirement, yes, and in that same direction we shall make our decision on retirement on the strength of our own thinking."[8]

As the *Ebony* article made all too clear, critics were not only hammering away at the deteriorating state of Anderson's voice, they had been debating the question of whether she should retire for some time. Some approached the question with polite indirection: "I have the feeling that Miss Anderson has done what she has to do. She was a great singer. She has a big enough name to go on for some time. She has been disappointing recently. However I would certainly not suggest that she retire."[9] Others opted for frontal attack: "Some artists should know when to make a graceful exit. Certain artists ought to quit before they disgrace their reputations, before they are washed up."[10] In spite of their unanimity of judgment about Anderson's declining vocal powers, most—at least those surveyed in the *Ebony* article—were torn between what their ears told them and their belief in the moral and humanitarian significance of Anderson's presence before the public. Indeed, more than one suggested that, given the recent success of her trip to the Far East and her work as a delegate to the United Nations, she could continue as an effective and inspiring symbol of achievement in any number of ways away from the concert platform.

Anderson was proud of what she had accomplished in the Far East and the United Nations, but she was no more politically or socially activist now than she had ever been. Government service or teaching were not attractive alternatives. The issue was principally one of artistic integrity. Later, when the time for retirement inevitably came, Anderson expressed, in her direct and eloquent way, the artistic dilemma that all serious artists face as they ponder the question of retirement: "It is impossible to make music like a faucet. It is something of the heart and soul. As long as they move, the music is there. Whether you can bring it forward is something else."[11]

Of course, there were financial concerns too. Anderson enjoyed teasing Rupp about the control he exercised over the minutiae of his income and investments. The truth is she envied Rupp's lifelong concern with a financially secure retirement. Neither she nor King was systematic about investments. They had for years complained to each other how erratic they had always been about planning carefully for the future. Although selling part of Marianna years ago had helped to reduce expenses, Anderson was still supporting her mother and two sisters. Their needs, in fact, could extend well into the years when she and King were themselves retired. If thoughts of this kind were on Anderson's mind when the *Ebony* article appeared, in the early days of June 1960, they must have seemed more relevant than ever, for it was then that she learned of her mother's illness. Mrs. Anderson had always enjoyed relatively good health. She was now eighty-six years old, somewhat frail yet far from bedridden, and suffering intermittently from loss of appetite and fluctuations of blood pressure, symptoms that, during the spring, had grown serious enough to require both a day and a night nurse, over a period of many weeks. Of course, she was well cared for at home, but Marian was worried enough to spend a good part of the summer in Philadelphia, taking her old room on Martin Street so that she could look after her mother.[12]

"It was a real joy," she wrote to the Rupps in August, back at Marianna, "to wait on mother."[13] Well before then the nurses had become unnecessary, Mrs. Anderson's appetite had returned, and she was able to sleep without medication, but Marian stayed on nevertheless. By the end of the summer, her mother's health restored, Anderson once again enjoyed the serene beauty of the farm, and she felt ready for the start of the new season. Her mother's swift recovery had done wonders for her spirits. So did the zeal with which Anderson's European agents beckoned. Plans for a European tour the following season were nearly concluded and, after repeated disappointments, the possibility of an Australian tour now seemed more than likely for the summer of 1962.

During the remaining weeks of the summer, Anderson went over the new season's programs with Rupp. For years the process had been a joint effort of selecting new songs as well as including often-performed ones. But the process had evolved into something different. Nervous about bad reviews, she preferred to arrange programs around a diminishing repertory of songs with which she felt most comfortable. These included works of Handel and Haydn, Schubert's "Der Doppelgänger" and "Der Erlkönig," the *Samson et Dalila* aria, "Mon coeur," some American songs (for example, Barber's "Nocturne" and Swanson's "The Negro Speaks of Rivers") and a group of spirituals. If Anderson saw this lack of diversity as an opportunity to focus on works that were important to her, Rupp complained to those close to him about the sense of routine that he felt. As far as he was concerned, Anderson had become lazy about learning new repertory.

The tour ran its course through a counterpoint of concerts, awards, and public appearances. The awards had begun back in the summer, when first Syracuse, then Boston University and Brandeis University, presented Anderson with honorary degrees. In July she was in New York to take part in a ceremony at City Hall in which the City of New York took title to Carnegie Hall, saving it from demolition. In November she was again in New York, this time at the Waldorf-Astoria, where she was presented with an illuminated scroll by the National Women's Division of the American Friends of the Hebrew University, who named her Woman of the Year.[14] And so it went into the new year. On January 20, 1961, a few minutes past noon, in weather that old-time political observers said was the worst of any Inauguration Day ceremony for any president since Taft, Anderson sang the "Star-Bangled Banner" at the inauguration of John F. Kennedy. A few days later, at New York's Waldorf-Astoria, she joined fellow artists in a tribute to Hurok, who was being honored by the American–Israel Cultural Foundation for distinguished service in the cause of cultural exchange.[15]

At the end of January, Anderson found a different reason for satisfaction, this time in a younger colleague's success. Leontyne Price had heard Anderson sing in Jackson, Mississippi, when she was nine, an experience that made an indelible impression on her. In 1947, only twenty years old and in her second year of college, she entered the Marian Anderson Competition, traveling from her home in Mississippi to Philadelphia for the auditions along with Lenora Lafayette, another scholarship applicant. Arriving the night before the auditions, exhausted and hungry, with nowhere to go and little money between them, the two young women called Alyse Anderson, who arranged for them to spend the night at the home of some friends, a young black organist, Kenneth

Goodman, and his mother, where they enjoyed a meal of collard greens and smothered chicken.[16] Feeling that Price showed promise but was not as far along as some of the other contestants, the judges did not award her a scholarship. Two years later, she entered the Juilliard School of Music. From the time she was invited to sing the role of Bess in the 1952 New York revival of Gershwin's opera, her success was assured.

On January 27, having already sung at the San Francisco Opera and the Vienna Staatsoper, Leontyne Price made her Metropolitan debut as Leonora in Verdi's *Il Trovatore,* earning an ovation that lasted over forty minutes, the longest such demonstration ever given in the house.[17] There had been other black singers at the Met after Anderson and McFerrin. During Anderson's second season there, the lyric coloratura soprano, Mattiwilda Dobbs, who had been awarded a Marian Anderson scholarship in 1947, made a highly successful debut as Gilda in Verdi's *Rigoletto.* But it was Price who, with an extraordinary voice and temperament, galvanized the public's attention, thus completing a process of change initiated by Anderson five years earlier. Soon after Price's debut an extraordinary succession of black singers made their way to the stage of the Met, Shirley Verrett, Grace Bumbry, and Martina Arroyo among them. "Now I write to thank you from the bottom of my heart," Price wrote to Anderson some weeks after her Met debut. "Your name belongs with my Mama and Daddy in spirit and what it contributed to my peace of mind and sense of direction on the night of my debut. God bless you and keep you. You were and still are my Beacon Light. Straight ahead!!"[18]

The season ended in April, with concerts at Dartmouth College and in Concord, New Hampshire. Anderson wanted to stay close to home during the summer, to be near her mother, whose health had worsened, and to work with Rupp on the coming season, which included a European tour in October. But she had agreed to participate in a conference on international peace in the Soviet Union in May, and later in the summer to sing at the Casals Festival in San Juan.

In 1959, Norman Cousins, editor of the *Saturday Review,* had visited the Soviet Union under the State Department's cultural exchange program. His experiences with the Soviet Union of Writers, private citizens, and government officials convinced him that it might prove useful to arrange a Soviet-American conference of private citizens—scientists, scholars, and artists—rather than government officials, to discuss problems of disarmament, world law, and economic development. Both governments approved of Cousins's idea. The conference was held at Dartmouth College in October 1960, with ten Russians and sixteen Americans attending. In addition to Cousins, the American group included George Kennan, Senator William Benton, Russel Crouse, and Agnes De Mille. There were a number of areas of agreement between the two sides, but, as Cousins later reported, more important was the fact that "lines of effective communication were opened up and human relationships were established."[19]

All the participants in the "first Dartmouth conference" were eager to continue the dialogue, the Russians extending an invitation to their American colleagues for a second conference. In May 1961, the members of this "second Dartmouth conference"—sixteen Americans and seventeen Russians—gathered around a green baize table in a former Crimean palace, then a sanitarium, overlooking the Black Sea, to discuss questions that had arisen at Dartmouth. On the American side were many graduates of the original conference and, in addition, Erwin Griswold, dean of the Harvard University Law School, and Margaret Mead. Among the Russians were writers, scientists, an economist, a film director, and a legal expert. In comparison with the conference at Dartmouth, the discussions were less informal, the questions treated more technically.[20]

No doubt Anderson was asked to participate in the second conference on the basis of her contributions to world understanding and her ability to build bridges between people of different cultures. Having little technical expertise in the subjects discussed in Nizhnaya Oreanda, Anderson treated the occasion as an opportunity to learn from the others. Indeed, she kept a detailed record of the issues discussed, very much as if she were attending a seminar in the problems of international peace. Peter Juviler, one of the staff participants, recalled that Anderson did not make her presence felt very strongly during the formal discussion; she seemed to him often tired and preoccupied.[21] During one of the afternoon sessions, in fact, she excused herself early in order to spend some time alone, walking along the harbor, before joining the others that evening for a concert of Ukrainian singers and dancers. At other times, however, especially during informal meetings and exchanges, when she felt more at ease, she made her presence strongly felt.

Griswold, too, kept a record of the conference proceedings, as well as of his personal experiences, during the two weeks he spent in the Soviet Union. More than once during the conference, Griswold was struck by Anderson's powerful and moving effect on those around her. One occasion came when the participants first arrived in the Soviet Union. "After the reception," Griswold recorded, "there was a big dinner for all the delegates, including other Russians who will not be going to the Crimea. There were at least fifteen toasts, by both Russians and Americans, all translated sentence by sentence as they were given. One was by Marian Anderson which was most eloquent. It had a Gettysburg Address–like quality. I wish it had been taken down or recorded, but I am afraid it is lost in time and space."[22]

Both the Americans and Russians had done considerable preparation for the conference, arming themselves with historical as well as technical information. The extensive preparation behind the conference reports made it difficult for Anderson to feel at ease about participating, but on the last day, when the topic turned to "education of the coming generation in the spirit of peace and friendship among nations," Anderson felt compelled to speak. She believed deeply in the importance of education for young people as a key factor in promoting understanding, and she could not let the occasion pass without sharing her feelings. In her record of the conference she noted down: "I made first speech, on education." But Griswold was struck by her spontaneous remarks enough to record them. "My voice will be weak," she began. "Education should begin in infancy. You must realize at what an early age a child shows his intention. This is the period to set a pattern by which the child lives his life. The toys I have in mind do not embrace the pistols, the guns, the all kinds of things that could bring sorrow and pain to a playmate. Whatever you teach your child will eventually come out in his makeup . . ."[23]

Less than two weeks after her return from the Soviet Union, Anderson left for San Juan, where she was scheduled to make two appearances at the Casals Festival, on June 14 and 16. Unlike the Crimea conference, where mutual understanding had to be established quickly by participants from different cultures and with different ideologies, the Casals Festival was an annual gathering of musicians who shared a common artistic philosophy. The first Casals Festival had taken place in Prades, in 1950, when Casals was persuaded by fellow musicians to play for the first time in public since the end of the Second World War. The festival continued each summer, without interruption, first in Perpignan, and, beginning in 1957, in San Juan, where Casals settled after his marriage to a young student, Marta Montanez. Some of the musicians of the original Prades festival returned each year to perform with Casals, in an atmosphere where the ideals of chamber music performance and a dedication to the music of Bach and the great Viennese masters were adhered to.

The musicians who assembled in San Juan in the summer of 1961 included Claudio Arrau, Alexander Schneider, Rudolf Serkin, and Isaac Stern. Anderson's appearance in San Juan was, for her, significant in several ways. Since her concerts at the Salzburg Festival, in 1935, where so much effort was expended by authorities to isolate her from the actual festival events, Anderson had had few opportunities to take part in the summer music festivals of Europe and America. Moreover, invited to sing only German lieder—Schubert on one program, Brahms on another—Anderson was invited as a specialist in the music of the central European tradition. For her, the invitation from Casals was a deeply gratifying recognition of her accomplishments as a lieder singer as well as a challenge that she did not take lightly.

Anderson chose difficult and emotionally wide-ranging programs for both evenings. On the fourteenth, framed by works of Handel and Bach, the two Schubert groups included "Suleika I," "Auf dem Wasser zu singen," "Im Freien," "Der Doppelgänger," and "Der Erlkönig"; then "Liebesbotschaft," "Abschied," the second Harper song (from *Wilhelm Meisters Lehrjahre*), "Der Jüngling und der Tod," and "Ungeduld." Two nights later, with Juan Castro, a guest artist, conducting works of Brahms and Mozart, Anderson sang Brahms's "Sind es Schmerzen, sind es Freuden," "Botschaft," "Von ewiger Liebe," the two songs with viola, with Alexander Schneider as viola soloist, and the *Four Serious Songs*. Acknowledging that the festival's invitation came far too late in her career, the critics paid Anderson's contribution little notice. The audience, however, sat in rapt concentration, enormously moved, especially by Anderson's interpretations of "Der Doppelgänger, "Der Erlkönig," and "Ungeduld," which brought forth huge outbursts of applause and cries of bravo. In the Brahms program there was a similar response, particularly for "Botschaft" and the *Four Serious Songs*. [24]

Anderson brought her nephew, Jimmy, to San Juan with her, as a graduation present, and to share with him the unique atmosphere surrounding Casals and the festival musicians. That summer marked the end of Jimmy's college years. He had attended the Wharton School of the University of Pennsylvania, where he majored in economics, graduating in 1958. He had at first intended to become a lawyer, but by the end of his four years at Wharton he had given up the idea, turning to music as a possible profession. Those who knew him well must have thought he had finally come to his senses, for he had been passionately drawn to music from a young age. His interests had so far been mostly in the jazz field. During his high school years, he had played the drums, and later he had had his own band. While at Wharton he organized a jazz ensemble with musicians from other schools in the area, winning an intercollegiate jazz competition, and he conducted the Pennsylvania Guild Orchestra, writing and arranging vocal solos for the group. [25]

After graduating from Wharton, Jimmy entered Pennsylvania's Annenberg School for Communication, thinking he would write music for movies. While at the Annenberg School, he took courses in theory, harmony, and orchestration at the Philadelphia Conservatory of Music, studying composition with Vincent Persichetti. In the summer of 1960, his formal education at an end, he was becoming more seriously drawn to the classical repertory, music his "Aunt Marian" had always shared with him. The friendly and intense atmosphere of music making made a strong impression on Jimmy, although in later years he remembered particularly the affection and esteem which the musicians, especially Casals, showed his Aunt Marian.

In October of 1961, Anderson left for a two month long tour of Europe, with concerts in London, Paris, and the major capitals of Scandinavia, the beginning leg of a long season that would include her first tour of Australia and New Zealand, in May and June, after concerts in America. In Scandinavia, although there was warm appreciation for her singing of Sibelius and Kilpinen, and good notices, the absence of Kosti—he had died a few years earlier—saddened her. His affection for her, and their long hours of reminiscing while Anderson shopped for presents, had become a regular accompaniment to her visits to Scandinavia. London was, as usual, cool, emphasizing her vocal problems with more gusto than her musical insights. Paris proved the high point of the tour, with the kind of response that for Anderson was the highest form of praise. Wrote one Paris critic: "The great surprise of the evening was her interpretation (in French) of Debussy [she sang "La chevelure" and Lia's aria from *L'Enfant prodigue*]: it would be hard to say which of the two is made for the other."[26]

Before she returned home, in early December, there were plans already afoot that would take her back to Europe for Christmas. The West Berlin Sender Freies TV Station was preparing a Christmas program aimed specifically at an East Berlin audience, for which a number of countries, including the United States, were being asked to contribute their talent. As Edward R. Murrow, then USIA chief, explained to Hurok, "the United States government is greatly concerned about the welfare of the German population on both sides of 'the Wall' and an interdepartmental decision at the highest level has been made to contribute to the success of this program."[27] In the immediate aftermath of the building of the Wall—the East German party secretary, Walter Ulbricht, had ordered its construction in early August, four months earlier—the USIA was hoping to use the film as a propaganda vehicle, already negotiating to provide a worldwide audience for it. The Berlin TV station had specifically asked for the services of Anderson, stating that she was recognized the world over not only as an outstanding singer "but as a person of great dignity, human compassion and sincerity which blends perfectly with the overall theme of the program . . ."[28]

Hurok and Anderson were informed that the rehearsal and filming of the program were scheduled for December 25. Although this meant that Anderson would not be able to spend Christmas with her family, she was eager to participate. For Hurok the invitation was a satisfying coup. In 1956, when Anderson sang in West Berlin, Hurok had urged the State Department to allow her to include a visit to East Berlin. The State Department did not accept the idea, preferring instead "to have East Berliners come to West Berlin to hear her sing."[29] Now that East Berlin was closed off, this would be the only chance Anderson was likely to have of singing to an East Berlin audience. For her, the invitation had larger connotations. It was a way of aligning herself with the new administration's policy of bringing about greater world understanding and peace. In November she had had her first such opportunity under the new administration, when she became a founding member of the Freedom from Hunger Foundation formed by President Kennedy to attract public support and private contributions to aid projects combating hunger in the third world.[30] As a member of the foundation, she felt she was fulfilling a promise she had made to herself since her work in the United Nations. Moreover, she was as much a fan of the new president as anyone. Drawn to his youth and his charm, inspired by his sense of mission, she wanted to do her part.

Anderson arrived in West Berlin with Rupp on the morning of December 23. Dr. Lungh, director of the radio and TV station, greeted her warmly, but expressed surprise that they had chosen to arrive on the day of the performance. They were both stunned, not to mention exhausted by the long trip. There were apologies for the mix-up—the film was to be shown on Christmas day, but taped two days earlier—and forty-five minutes of rest for Anderson before she had to tape her share of the program. The film was shown in West Berlin and much of Western Europe, Anderson's part consisting of two spirituals and the Lord's Prayer. Anderson thought the whole affair mismanaged; nevertheless, she was unhappy when she learned that her view had reached the State Department.[31]

For both Marian and King, the new year, 1962, began badly and grew steadily worse. On January 31, King was admitted to Danbury Hospital, where tests showed he had diabetes. Although for the present he was required to take insulin, the doctors were encouraging, assuring him that in time he could control the disease with diet and exercise alone. Nevertheless, the news hit King hard. Although for years he had suffered from sinus problems and mild high blood pressure, King had always enjoyed relatively good health. Now in his early sixties, he was remarkably vigorous and active, working outdoors on the farm, doing carpentry work, and riding and swimming regularly. Thoughts of advancing age and of becoming less active began to affect his spirits. By the first week in February, after less than a week in the hospital, King was back at Marianna, depressed not only about his health but about the start of Marian's new season and the resulting separation. Marian's first concert was scheduled for the following week. Appearances in Canada and on the West Coast would keep her away from Marianna for most of February and March.

A concert in the State Department Auditorium in Washington, on March 22, part of a series sponsored by the president's cabinet, with Mrs. Kennedy as honorary chairperson, brought Anderson back home, her schedule finally allowing her some weeks to be with King. In early April, King's health was again cause for concern when he suffered a slight stroke and had to be hospitalized. Fortunately the damage was minimal, the weakness in the right hand and slurring of speech disappearing within a few days. The doctors were encouraged by King's rapid progress, and on the seventeenth he was released from the hospital, overjoyed at his rapid recovery but once again dreading the moment, in early May, when Marian would have to leave for concerts abroad.[32]

Anderson's tour of Australia and New Zealand was the fulfillment of a promise made fifteen years before, when plans for an Australian tour had had to be abandoned because of Anderson's throat illness and surgery. Her growing prestige internationally in the intervening years added to the excitement and anticipation felt among concert managers in Australia and New Zealand, encouraging Hurok to arrange a long and demanding tour that would last well over a month, from the last week in May until the end of June. Fifteen concerts were scheduled, with concerts in Sydney, Brisbane, Melbourne, and Adelaide, the New Zealand part of the tour including appearances in Auckland and Wellington. The four concerts in Sydney, within a single week, required that Anderson and Rupp prepare four different programs, adding to the strain of the tour.

To the public and press alike Anderson's tour was akin to a royal visit. "An interview with Marian Anderson," said one Melbourne writer in the *Daily Telegraph*, "is like an audience with a Crowned Head—in fact it'd be easy to imagine her as Empress of America, if there were such an appointment."[33] All the concerts were sold out, with huge crowds after each waiting to catch a glimpse of her as she left the theater. The critics were more ambivalent. Prepared to hear a singer of legendary status rather than one already sixty-five years old and nearing retirement, they could not hide their disappointment.[34]

The first group of concerts, during the end of May, went well enough, one critic in Brisbane praising Anderson, in songs of Handel, Schubert, Vaughn Williams, and Britten, for her "unerring sense of style and an instinctive feeling for drama."[35] Then during the first week of June, traveling from Brisbane to Melbourne, Anderson developed a cold that grew progressively worse. The next day, unable to sing a note at a morning rehearsal, she saw a doctor in the afternoon, who proscribed antibiotic capsules. The concert that night, in the Melbourne Town Hall, proved "a terrible strain."[36] So did the news from home. Full of news about the farm and the animals, King could not hide his loneliness and depression, trying to hide the full extent of the effort working outdoors now cost him. "I am not much help to them this year," he wrote to Marian, "as I am still not able to do much manual labor, you see I am too heavy for light work and too light for heavy work so I find it hard to find just the right job for me." Otherwise he let the animals express some of how he felt, not hiding much of what was really on his mind. "Dear Mommie," he wrote for Jasmin, one of the dogs, "I am going to close now as Daddy is coming to take both of us for a walk in the woods and you know how much I like to go in the woods and run away from Daddy but I always come back sooner or later."[37]

By the time she reached New Zealand, during the last week in June, Anderson felt much better, pronouncing the concert in Wellington on the twenty-fifth "the best concert of the tour."[38] But the New Zealand critics felt differently. Indeed, they were so harsh in their criticism as to cause one interviewer in New Zealand to ask Anderson whether she felt any resentment at having received such criticisms after so distinguished a career. "No, I don't at all," she answered, "I think anyone who wished to write is there because someone feels he is in a position to write. And the person writes very often his personal feelings about it. As long as he is sincere about his personal feelings he's at liberty to write it for the paper. You can't go around and say 'Don't write that,' or 'I don't like that,' or 'I do like it,' or whatever."[39]

Marian arrived home in mid-July, having looked forward for months to spending the rest of the summer with King. Less than a month later, the calm of Marianna was shattered by the news that Jimmy, who had spent most of that year in the Far East as an American specialist for the State Department, had contracted polio while in Thailand, only a few weeks before his scheduled return to the States. Jimmy had arrived in Thailand in February, having been invited by the State Department to work with musicians, play his own compositions, and lecture on American jazz. A month later, attending the rehearsal of a local symphony orchestra in Bangkok, he was offered a baton and invited to conduct, then and there, Schubert's Ninth Symphony. What followed was something close to an epiphany for Jimmy. As he later described the experience: "I got up on the podium, and it was as close to a revelation as anything that has ever happened to me. I was totally at one with the orchestra and the score. Everything was natural. Automatic. I felt like I had been conducting all my life."[40] Professionally, that was the turning point for Jimmy. He took every opportunity offered him to conduct in the succeeding months. On one of those occasions, while conducting Tchaikovsky's Fifth Symphony, the first symptoms of Jimmy's illness appeared.

Six days after being taken by ambulance to the Bangkok Nursing Home, Jimmy was able to write to his mother to tell her "as much as I know," he said. "Your fat, dumb son was conducting and rehearsing during 3 days of polio and a 102 degree fever. Now how was I supposed to know I had polio. Anyway last Wed. night it was unbearable so Thursday morning I called USIA [and] told Don Nuecterline . . . that I felt like death's playmate and would he send over a doctor. In 15 minutes the doctor came. I couldn't walk so he sent for the ambulance. And here I am."[41] Jimmy had been conducting the Bangkok Orchestra. "While rising on the ball of my right foot," Jimmy told an interviewer a few months later, "I felt a spasm in my calf. The night was hot and I was perspiring a great deal. After the concert I attended a dinner given by the U. S. ambassador in an air-conditioned restaurant. That was the beginning of it."[42]

Hospital tests confirmed that Jimmy had polio. As he told his mother, "My arms and body are fine; part of my back and my legs are not functioning but it will just be a matter of time says the doctor. I'm receiving electric shock stimulation to my muscles and this will keep them active. The Dr. wants me to be transported home on a stretcher and begin treatment in the U.S.A. for about 3 to 6 months."[43] The months of treatment would be a time to "A. Keep me out of the army," he told his mother, "B. Give me more time to build up a wider conducting repertoire by heart, C. Enable me to reduce, and D. Give me something constructive to do for a change."[44] Jimmy was not merely attempting to allay his mother's fears, but expressing the unshakable optimism of a man who saw opportunity and challenge where others saw reasons for self-pity and demoralization.

For the moment all Jimmy wanted was to get home. "Somebody

please get me home," he telegraphed his mother at the end of August.[45] Anderson contacted Edward R. Murrow, then head of the USIA, asking him to do what he could to get Jimmy back to the States as quickly as possible.[46] On September 4, Jimmy was loaded by stretcher onto a military cargo plane headed for Clark Air Force Base in the Philippines. Flying through thunder and rain storms while lying on a stretcher, for twelve hours, among seriously wounded medical evacuees from Viet Nam, Jimmy found the journey to be a nightmare.[47] In the States, he was admitted to Magee Memorial Hospital in Philadelphia where, between physical therapy treatments, he studied scores, and began composing a ballet, *A Sprig of Lilac.* He later said, "I am not grandstanding to say that contracting polio only intensified my desire to become a conductor. I was never more focused in my life. The personal discovery that I wanted to become a conductor was much more significant than the temporary disruption of polio."[48] Nevertheless, Jimmy worried about the physical challenges he would have to meet as a conductor. Polio had left him paralyzed from the waist down and, without braces and crutches, he would not be able to walk. "Now that I know what I want to do," he told Leonard Bernstein, "I can't do it."[49] Assuring Jimmy he would surmount his physical limitations if conducting was what he really wanted, Bernstein advised him to enter the Mitropoulos conducting competition. Bernstein's advice, and the belief and encouragement he showed the younger musician, proved the foundation of Jimmy's career.

Anderson's first contact with President Kennedy had been in January 1961, when she sang the "Star-Spangled Banner" at his Inaugural ceremonies. Later that year, during a brief ceremony at the White House, she joined other founding members of Kennedy's Freedom For Hunger Foundation. The following March, in connection with the concert she presented in the State Department Auditorium, she looked forward to the chance of talking with the president. He was unable to attend the concert, however, and, disappointed, she asked for a private meeting with him.[50]

Ordinarily Anderson's natural modesty would have held her back from such a request, but her admiration for the president, for his idealism and sense of commitment, encouraged her to act. At a time when she feared her moderation and respect for compromise would be interpreted as passivity, especially by the younger generation, she was looking for an appropriate occasion to express to Kennedy her commitment to the civil rights struggle. More than anything, she dreaded being thought of as no longer relevant to it. Although Kennedy did not as a rule meet with the artists sponsored by the president's cabinet, he agreed to talk with Anderson during the afternoon before her concert. She gave the president her latest recording of spirituals and received from him a reproduction of the Inauguration emblem.[51]

For nearly fifteen years, except for an occasional isolated concert, Anderson had remained in self-imposed exile from southern concert halls. That she was rarely able to sing to her own people in the South had brought her immense sorrow. In February 1963, she was at long last presented with the opportunity to demonstrate that an integrated concert tour of the South—in Texas, at least—could succeed without discord.

The idea for an integrated tour of Texas cities originated with C. T. Johnson, an Austin businessman, who spent four years working with Hurok organizing a series of concerts that would take Anderson to San Antonio, Dallas, Austin, and Houston during the last week of February 1963.[52] The time seemed propitious for such a tour. In the years following 1960, Texas had made extraordinary progress in integration, much of it, especially in Houston, accomplished quickly and smoothly, albeit with the aid of media blackouts during periods of sit-ins and strikes in order to deter violence.[53] City officials, concert managers, and the media now felt confident that an Anderson tour would be greeted enthusiastically. Indeed, a veritable media frenzy greeted Anderson throughout the tour. Johnson described this reaction for the USIA's chief, Edward R. Murrow, who had asked to be kept informed of the details of Anderson's tour: "The Associated Press and United Press used three pictures and three different stories of Miss Anderson. I was informed that this was the first time they had used the picture of an artist . . . At every airport she was met by all the newspapers, television, and radio media. Her press conferences . . . at the hotels, I am told were among the largest that have ever taken place."[54]

At the airport in San Antonio, the start of the tour, she was greeted by over a thousand people. In spite of the heavy rain, the list of dignitaries waiting for her as she arrived from New York at 10:30 in the evening included San Antonio's mayor, the president of the Chamber of Commerce, the city manager and postmaster, the president of the Negro Chamber of Commerce, as well as other prominent civic and church leaders and arts patrons.[55] A few days later, on the morning of her concert in Austin, at a ceremony at the State Capitol, Anderson was made an honorary Texas citizen by Lieutenant-Governor Preston Smith, acting on behalf of Governor John Connally, who was recuperating from an illness. That evening, in the Municipal Auditorium, 3,500 people, including Vice-President Johnson and his wife, who delayed their departure to

Washington in order to entertain Anderson at their ranch a few days later, gathered to hear her sing.[56]

Although the critics thought Anderson's concerts, all of them sold out, a triumph, it was not her interpretations of Handel or Schubert that the newspapers chose to emphasize. By the time the last concert, in Houston, was over, her tour was being hailed in the media as a milestone in race relations. Johnson may have been exaggerating when he wrote to Murrow that, in the words of the city editor of one of the largest newspapers in Texas, "the bringing of Miss Anderson to our state has done more to help solve our racial problem than any other thing in Texas history."[57] Yet Johnson was prepared to back up this opinion with facts. In Johnson's own city of Austin, for example, as he later told Murrow, Anderson was given the Jim Hogg suite at the Driskill Hotel, although only a few weeks before Anderson's arrival a statewide Negro association of ministers had not been able to find a single hotel or motel that would accept any of their members.[58]

"Like peace," Anderson told an interviewer in San Antonio anxious for her views on racial questions, "[integration] is everyone's business . . . We hope to do our part in furthering it . . ."[59] For her, doing one's part meant the readiness to act when the right moment arrived. For Anderson's tour of Texas and triumphal return to the South after nearly fifteen years of waiting, the right moment had come.

During the summer of 1963, in the wake of the violence in Birmingham, Anderson found other opportunities to feel relevant. At the end of July, she hosted an afternoon affair at Marianna, sponsored by the Danbury chapter of the NAACP, to raise money for the Freedom Fund. In ninety-degree heat, more than 200 people enjoyed Anderson's hospitality and listened to the NAACP's executive director, Roy Wilkins.[60] As one of the organizers of the March on Washington for Jobs and Freedom, set for August 28, Wilkins was using every opportunity to urge people to take part in what was being planned as the largest peaceful demonstration for economic freedom and civil rights in the country's history.[61]

A week later, Anderson was informed by telegram of the part she was to play in the march. "The entire committee," Wilkins informed her, "unanimously decided that invitation to sing Star Spangled Banner be extended to you for this historic occasion. Committee will consider it great honor if you will agree to do this."[62] To mark her symbolic association with the Lincoln Memorial, where the afternoon events of the march would take place, Anderson was scheduled to sing the National Anthem at the start of the afternoon rally that would end with the appearance of Martin Luther King, Jr. Sadly, because of the huge crowds, Anderson did not arrive at the platform in time to sing the National Anthem. Roy Wilkins, who noticed Camilla Williams standing at the front of the huge crowd, motioned her to come up to the platform to stand in for Anderson.[63]

Anderson had wanted desperately to appear at the Washington March. Not only did she feel she had earned the right to gather with all of the other participants at the site where, a quarter of a century before, she had lent her name and accomplishments to a significant moment of history, she wanted to feel a part of a new generation's aspirations. Once on the platform, she recovered her composure quickly and, with her eyes closed, her voice carrying easily to the farthest reaches of the Reflecting Pool, she sang "He's Got the Whole World in His Hands." The huge throng on that late August afternoon, the majority of whom were young people who more than likely had never heard Anderson sing, listened politely, reserving their enthusiasm for Mahalia Jackson, whose rendition of "I Been 'Buked and I Been Scorned" drove the crowd into a near frenzy.[64]

Anderson's disappointment with the way things turned out in Washington came at a difficult time as she was struggling with the realization that she could not postpone her retirement much longer. However much "her heart and soul were still working," as she had expressed her feelings about retirement a few years earlier, she now had to accept the fact that her declining and unpredictable vocal powers were becoming too much of a threat to her artistic integrity. By the fall, she was ready to meet with Hurok to discuss concrete plans for a final tour. On her mind was not so much the artistic details of the tour, for which she was prepared to let Hurok take the lead, but her fear that she would not have enough savings to live on after her retirement. His education over, Jimmy was now making great strides as a young conductor, but there were still Ethel and Alyse to care for as well as Mrs. Anderson, who, now nearly eighty-nine years old, was growing frail and would need considerable looking after. For his part, Hurok did not want Anderson's career to simply dwindle to a close in a way that would not draw the kind of publicity and sense of celebration he believed appropriate.[65]

Discussions during the fall centered around the idea of a world tour and the strategies necessary for securing the best dates and the largest fees. Anderson was prepared to announce her retirement during those months, but Hurok wanted to hold out for the right opportunity, one that would focus media attention on the announcement. In July, Anderson was chosen as one of thirty-one recipients of the Presidential Medal of Freedom, an honor that might provide the kind of opportunity Hurok was looking for. Although the medal had been awarded sporadically since 1945, President Kennedy had decided that it should be awarded annually to a distinguished group of citizens. President and Mrs. Kennedy had redesigned the medal and Kennedy had appointed a committee to recommend the awards.[66]

The awards ceremony was held in the State Dining Room of the White House on December 6. President Kennedy had been assassinated two weeks earlier. President Johnson conducted the ceremony, during which thirty-one distinguished citizens in the fields of government, the arts, the sciences, education, labor, social work, and the law, many of them selected by President Kennedy, were awarded the country's highest civilian award. The entire ceremony was haunted by the tragic death of the young president. Before the presentation of the medal, President Johnson spoke of the "moments of utmost sorrow, of anguish and shame" felt by the entire country.[67] As the *New York Times* reported, "Mrs. Kennedy was not in the room for the ceremony. When her husband's posthumous citation was read, however, and his medal received by Attorney General Robert F. Kennedy, she could be seen standing in a small anteroom. Most of those in the State Dining Room were not aware of her presence."[68]

Others in the arts receiving the Medal of Freedom besides Anderson were Pablo Casals and Rudolf Serkin in music; the writers E. B. White, Thornton Wilder, Edmund Wilson, and Mark S. Watson; the painter Andrew Wyeth; architect Ludwig Mies van der Rohe; and the photographer Edward Steichen. Anderson's citation read: "Artist and citizen, she has ennobled her race and her country, while her voice has enthralled the world."[69] In the *Times* report the following day, the sole photograph of the ceremony captured a radiantly smiling Anderson together with President Johnson.[70]

For Hurok, timing was everything. Spurred into action by the White House ceremony and the prominence awarded Anderson in the *Times,* Hurok planned a press conference for December 12 to announce her retirement. Hoping to take advantage of the warm relations Anderson had established with the Johnsons, Hurok wrote to the president requesting a message from him that could be read during the press conference. In this instance Hurok's timing, as he was eventually informed by Frederick Holborn, a special assistant in the White House Office, was ill-advised. The president felt that the promotional event planned by

Hurok would not be an appropriate time for recognizing Anderson, all the more since "the 30-day period of mourning for President Kennedy was still being observed."[71]

During the morning of the twelfth, Anderson and Hurok faced a bank of newsmen and reporters at the St. Regis Hotel in New York to announce Anderson's plans to retire from the concert stage after a world tour that would begin the following fall, 1964. For both Anderson and Hurok the conference was an emotional experience anchored in a relationship that stretched back nearly thirty years. Hurok, in introducing Anderson, recalled some of the incidents that marked the beginning of the singer's career, when hotels and restaurants refused her service because of her color. There were the inevitable questions from the press about Anderson's feelings toward the D.A.R. "I forgave the DAR many years ago. You lose a lot of time hating people," she told the reporters.[72] Although plans for Anderson's world tour were not yet concluded, Hurok announced, the itinerary so far included Japan and the Far East in February; Europe, Israel, and the African countries in May and June; and North and South America, as well. Anderson's farewell appearance in the United States was scheduled for Easter Sunday, April 18, 1965, at Carnegie Hall.[73] Asked about her plans for retirement, Anderson said they included becoming more active in the civil rights struggle. "The position of the Negro artist was good today," she told reporters, "study opportunities were better and the concert field was open."[74]

Hurok's ambitious plans for a final world tour softened somewhat the sadness and the inevitable sense of impending loss that Anderson felt once the decision about retirement had been made. There was also the coming holiday season, but the distraction and support she might have counted on from family and friends who gathered each year in Danbury for Christmas and New Year's were replaced now by concern and worry over the increasing seriousness of Mrs. Anderson's health. Ethel and Alyse had decided to remain on Martin Street this holiday season, as Mrs. Anderson was far too frail to travel to Danbury. Shortly after the new year began, during the early morning of January tenth, Anna Anderson died of heart failure, at the age of eighty-nine.

On the morning of the thirteenth, amid snow, sleet, and freezing temperatures—"a veritable blizzard," Marian noted on her calendar—family and friends made their way into Tindley Temple, the large and imposing Methodist Church at Fifteenth and Broad Street, to pay their respects to Anna Anderson.[75] Since her marriage more than seventy years before, she had quietly held to her Methodist upbringing.

Few people at Anna Anderson's funeral knew the story of her parents' decision to become Methodists—the story of how there were no churches in Boonsboro for the Ruckers, Anna's parents, to attend on Sundays, and of how the preacher was able to make his way to Boonsboro only once a month. Rather than rely on the preacher, Robert Rucker and his family made the trip to Lynchburg each Sunday, and, although the greater part of Lynchburg was Baptist, the most prestigious church there, attended by many of the educated and professional people in the city, was the Union Methodist Church, at Ninth and Jackson Street. That was the church Robert Rucker chose for his family.[76] After her marriage, Anna had worshipped at the old Bainbridge Street Methodist Church, which had through the years grown into the Tindley Temple.

Through her dedication and dignity, Anna Anderson had endeared herself to many generations of Tindley Temple's congregation. Over the years, as Marian achieved greater success and prominence, first in Europe and then in the United States, Anna Anderson had emerged as a celebrity in her own right, often asked to serve on the church's social committees and invited to talk to the ladies auxiliary and to other church groups about her daughter's achievements.

By eleven o'clock, a large crowd had gathered for the funeral service in the vast interior of the Tindley Temple. There were selections by the choir, and several people spoke, among them the pastor of Union Baptist Church, whom Marian had asked to perform the eulogy. John King, Queenie's eldest son, had assembled the other Anderson men to act as pallbearers. In the early afternoon, in the driving snow and sleet, family and friends made their way to Eden Cemetery, where Anna Anderson was laid to rest.[77]

In the weeks and months after her mother's death, Anderson coped, as always, by throwing herself into her work. In February, she began work on an album of popular songs—"Believe Me If All Those Endearing Young Charms," "Comin' Thro' the Rye," "Loch Lomond," and "Love's Old Sweet Song" were among those to be included—as part of a project in collaboration with the composer Robert Russell Bennett, who had agreed to arrange the songs for string quintet, flute, oboe, recorders, and harpsichord. The Bennett arrangements were one of a series of four long-playing recordings Anderson had agreed to record for RCA during the months leading up to the beginning of her farewell tour. Hurok, as always, was counting on the publication of new recordings to attract attention and provide publicity. Anderson wanted to leave a final legacy of recordings that would reflect a wide-ranging repertoire and variety of styles. In addition to the Bennett arrangements, Anderson had committed herself to an album of Schubert lieder and another of Brahms lieder, as well as a new recording of spirituals.[78]

For Anderson to undertake so ambitious a schedule of recordings so late in her career took great courage. She was under no illusions about how much stamina, not to mention plain good fortune, would be required to fulfill even a part of the schedule. During the sessions a few years back for an album of Christmas carols, Anderson had had to make dozens of takes for many of the songs. During the 1950s, Anderson had worked tirelessly in the recording studio in an effort to produce a successful album of Brahms lieder as well as another collection of songs with English texts, but except for an album of spirituals released in 1952, and a second collection of spirituals completed at the end of August 1961, the latter in response to the advent of stereophonic recording, all of Anderson's efforts remained unreleased. Among the projects during the decade of the 1950s that Anderson did not approve were three different attempts at a recording of the Brahms *Four Serious Songs,* a work that had been in her repertoire for three decades.[79]

Even before the final sessions for the Bennett arrangements, in late May 1964, Anderson embarked on still another album of spirituals, one unlike any she had worked on before. Joseph Habig, producer for RCA, initiated the idea of commissioning an entirely new collection of arrangements for what would undoubtedly be Anderson's final recording of spirituals. He brought the idea to the composer Hall Johnson, whose spiritual arrangements Anderson had been singing for decades and whom she admired and respected. Drawing on his vast repertoire of materials, Johnson produced a collection of twelve new arrangements for Anderson. In keeping with his philosophy that the performance of spirituals should preserve something of the original style of performance, when the songs were actually composed and transmitted as part of an oral tradition, Johnson created a cycle of twelve arrangements for Anderson that were more "involved inspirationally," more sermon-like in their intensity and rhythmic insistence, than the arrangements of spirituals conceived in the art song tradition inaugurated by Burleigh. The theme of Johnson's cycle—that whatever the hardships and misfortunes of life, Jesus instills hope and the promise of a better life—is taken from the penultimate song, "Just Keep on Singin'."[80]

Johnson was not sparing in asking Anderson to enter into an emotional world she was not used to, an artistic accommodation she had never found sympathetic. The Introduction to the cycle, for example, begins with a low drawn-out moan, then the spoken words, "I done come a long way, and I got a long way to go." Here, and similarly at the outset of other songs in the cycle, Anderson had to act out in the most direct and uninhibited way, sometimes with the sound of heavy footsteps or the lash in the background, the sorrow and pain of the Negro. To judge from the final recordings of his arrangements, which gradually emerged through the fall, Anderson entered into Johnson's world with utter conviction. It was partly her respect for Johnson, bordering on awe, that helped her to set aside any scruples she might have felt. By the time the project was completed, Anderson had learned to sing with a raw directness and gospel-like fervor that sounds like second nature to her.[81]

Habig's project not only provided Anderson with a sense of excitement and artistic challenge during a period of self-imposed limitations in her concert repertoire, it also helped solidify an important friendship. The friendship, with John Motley, a young black choral conductor and pianist, had begun the previous November when she took part in a Lincoln Center tribute honoring Eleanor Roosevelt, who had died in November 1962. The Eleanor Roosevelt Memorial Foundation, the group sponsoring the concert, had chosen Motley as the musical director for the concert. Already a protégé of Hall Johnson, Motley was then enjoying a great success in New York conducting his All City Junior High School Chorus. He had studied music at New York University and then Westminster Choir College after World War II, specializing at Westminster in choral conducting. After agreeing to perform in the memorial concert for Mrs. Roosevelt, Anderson had told Jerry Parker, the administrative coordinator of music for the New York Board of Education and a close friend of Motley, that she wanted to meet him, since he would be playing for her for the first time. Motley and Parker went to see Anderson in her apartment on Fifth Avenue. When Anderson asked to hear Motley play, he sat down at the piano and played "He's Got the Whole World in His Hands." Anderson was immediately drawn to him, not only to his playing, but to his modesty and easygoing authority.[82]

Naturally enough, Hall Johnson wanted Motley to accompany Anderson in the cycle of spirituals he was creating. In early 1964, Motley and Anderson began to rehearse regularly. During one of their first sessions, in going over "Oh, Heaven Is One Beautiful Place, I Know," the first spiritual of the cycle, Motley could see the difficulties Anderson was having in staying on pitch, especially in a short phrase early in the song consisting of a tricky downward series of intervals. Motley thought he could help Anderson technically, especially with her pitch problems, and told her so, in the most forthright way. By then, with their concert at

Lincoln Center behind them, Anderson had grown to trust Motley, who, she could see, was a teacher and coach of conviction and sympathy. On her own, Anderson had always found it difficult to work on technique and to vocalize regularly when she was not seeing a teacher. Since her lessons with Madame Freschl, she had done without one. Motley's quiet authority and patience inspired her. During the summer and early fall, Anderson and Motley worked together relentlessly, sometimes for as long as seven hours a day. There were sessions with Hall Johnson in the early fall, but for months leading up to them, she and Motley worked together not only on the Johnson spirituals, but on technique. With a variety of vocal exercises, many of his own devising, Motley worked on instilling in Anderson an intensified perceptual awareness of her own sense of pitch as well as improving support for the voice, especially in the lower register.[83]

Anderson's farewell American tour began on October 24, 1964, in Washington's Constitution Hall. Most likely it was Hurok's idea, and not hers, to link the opening of the tour to the historic and symbolic significance Constitution Hall had played in her career. To heighten the significance, it had been decided—here again one can imagine Hurok's influence—that the opening concert would be recorded and issued by RCA as soon as possible. The recording took place, although not without some concern and angry frustration along the way. A month before the concert, Harold Maynard, the manager of Constitution Hall, met with Patrick Hayes, who, as the head of the Hayes Concert Bureau, was the local manager for Anderson's concert, informing him that the D.A.R. was willing to allow the recording with the stipulation, on the advice of counsel, that there be "no language anywhere in the recording and in the written text of the jacket and liner pertaining to past recitals and experiences."[84] When informed by Hayes of the D.A.R.'s stipulation, RCA replied that "we were more than reluctant to grant to any outside organization any jurisdiction whatsoever in editorial and/or publishing rights which were ours, and ours alone; and that we saw no necessity for such a stipulation."[85]

Ten days before the concert, the D.A.R. had not relented. Indeed, they now insisted, with more direct language, on the stipulation that "there would be no reference made in publicity, liner or newspaper releases dealing with the unfortunate incident that resulted in Miss Anderson's historic Lincoln Memorial concert."[86] RCA was prepared to refuse, but Anderson, who felt that a refusal might create an unfortunate situation and unnecessary publicity that would serve no useful purpose, asked RCA to comply.[87]

The program Anderson presented in Constitution Hall remained unvaried during the entire tour. With its skillful blend of musical and dramatic contrasts, it was a program that Anderson had gradually fashioned during the sixties:

I

Tutta raccolta ancor	Handel
Ch'io mai vi possa	Handel
The Spirit's Song	Haydn
My Mother Bids Me Bind My Hair	Haydn

II

Suleika I	Schubert
Liebesbotschaft	Schubert
Der Doppelgänger	Schubert
Der Erlkönig	Schubert

III

Nocturne	Samuel Barber
The Negro Speaks of Rivers	Howard Swanson
The Ploughboy	arr. by Benjamin Britten
Blow, Blow Thou Winter Wind	arr. by Roger Quilter

IV

Let Us Break Bread Together	arr. by William Lawrence
O What a Beautiful City!	arr. by Edward Boatner
Hear de Lam's A-Cryin'	arr. by Lawrence Brown
Ride On King Jesus	arr. by H. T. Burleigh

V

Done Found' my Los' Sheep	arr. by Rosamund Johnson
Lord I Can't Stay Away	arr.by Roland Hayes
Let's Have a Union	arr. by Hall Johnson
He's Got the Whole World in His Hands	arr. by Hamilton Forrest

By the end of the tour the following April, Anderson had sung in nearly fifty American cities. Sadly enough, she gave only four concerts in the South: on November 2, at Stillman College, in Birmingham; two days later in Charlotte, North Carolina; and later on in Florida. Local managers in the South may have felt cautious about booking Anderson, and Hurok was, perhaps, not sufficiently persistent in trying to convince them that times had changed. The last concert of the tour came on April 18, 1965, Easter Sunday afternoon, in Carnegie Hall, where Anderson had given more than fifty concerts since her return to America thirty years before. She was greeted by a huge, cheering, sold-out house overflowing onto the stage. There were many celebrities in the audience, as well as 200 friends and family members seated in the specially reserved boxes Anderson had arranged for them.[88]

To Rupp and others, Anderson seemed unusually relaxed before the concert. "That's the right thing," Anderson murmured softly to Rupp, "that's the way to be."[89] To Joan Barthel, a *Times* interviewer, on the other hand, Anderson had earlier in the day seemed anything but relaxed. As Barthel wrote, "she is not easily interviewed. Her replies are often general to the point of vagueness, her reticence underlined by her consistent use of the plural, or the third person . . . The method is disconcerting, but an inevitable result, apparently, of her concept of the shared self."[90] At the end of the concert, after the last encore—Saint-Saëns's "Mon coeur s'ouvre à ta voix"—with the audience still refusing to leave, Anderson seemed pensive. Hurok urged her to sing again, to which she replied merely, "No. It's finished."[91]

Whatever confluence of emotions Anderson was feeling at the end of the tour, it was her sister Alyse who was most on her mind, and in the succeeding weeks the gradual worsening of Alyse's health absorbed her attention. For years Alyse had suffered from anemia, and more recently she had waged a quietly courageous battle with leukemia. By the end of the first week of May, Marian and Ethel were alarmed enough about her health to send for Alyse's physician, Dr. Ramsey. He talked with Alyse for a while, trying not to alarm her too much but suggesting she be hospitalized, and a few days later Marian took her to the hospital. On the ninth, a heart specialist was called in, and a blood transfusion was ordered. Alyse's condition weakened in the days to come and, although she rallied briefly, the doctors advised against too much optimism. On May 21, Alyse died of heart failure.[92]

The funeral mass was held three days later at St. Charles, the neighborhood Roman Catholic church where Alyse had worshipped. Rarely feeling sufficiently loved or realizing a sense of purpose as satisfyingly complete as Marian's devotion to singing or Ethel's desire to raise a family, Alyse had spent a large part of her life searching. After her hospitalization at Eagleville, in 1953, she had found a haven in the Roman Catholic Church and had converted to Roman Catholicism. The church brought her companionship and a sense of individual purpose. After her conversion, church activities gradually absorbed more and more of her time and over the years she had inspired affection not only at St. Charles, but at St. Theresa's, where she frequently attended lectures, and at St. Patrick's, a large and prominent Catholic church near Rittenhouse Square. Among the letters of condolence the family received was one from James Tate, the mayor of Philadelphia, who learned of Alyse's illness through the clergy at St. Patrick's.[93]

Although Anderson had formally announced her "retirement," the reality was that she had committed herself to several additional concerts. At the end of June, she sang for the first time with her nephew, James De Preist, who had been asked to conduct the Philadelphia Orchestra at Robin Hood Dell, Philadelphia's outdoor amphitheater. Although De Preist had never conducted the Philadelphia Orchestra, or any other major American orchestra for that matter, more than one conductor had put his faith in the twenty-eight-year-old conductor. After winning the Mitropoulos competition the previous December, De Preist had been chosen by Leonard Bernstein, the conductor of the New York Philharmonic, to be one of his assistants.

Coming so soon after Alyse's death, the concert was a great strain on Anderson, but she never considered withdrawing. Thinking that the Dell concert would be his only opportunity to perform with Anderson, DePreist wanted her to sing, as he later recalled, "absolutely everything that he had admired about Aunt Marian's art."[94] More than generous in accommodating her nephew's unrestrained enthusiasm, Anderson and DePreist performed the Brahms *Four Serious Songs,* arias from *Un Ballo in maschera* and *Samson et Dalila,* Schubert's "Ave Maria" and a group of spirituals DePreist himself arranged for orchestra. Max de Schauensee, the critic of the *Philadelphia Evening Bulletin,* who had been attending concerts in the Dell for twenty-five years, wrote the next day that he had never seen as large a crowd "struggling into the summer auditorium."[95]

Anderson had dreamed of visiting Africa since she had served as a delegate to the United Nations. She was, therefore, only too happy to agree to serve as a member of the United States Committee for the First World African Festival of the Arts, planned for April 1966, in Dakar. The idea of the festival, conceived by Léopold Sédar Senghor, the president of Senegal, was to bring together leading black figures from around the world, scholars as well as artists, to showcase the great achievements, both traditional and modern, of the African people.[96]

One of the problems confronting the various international committees organizing the festival was the difficulty in raising sufficient funds to finance so complicated an undertaking. As one of a series of fund-raising events planned by the French committee and supported by Georges Pompidou, the French premier, Anderson was invited to sing a program of spirituals in the Sainte-Chapelle, in Paris. The series was to include a showing of the film, *Carmen Jones.* Although the film had been barred from release in France by legal action taken by the heirs of Georges Bizet, the composer of *Carmen,* permission for a single, nonprofit showing had been granted.[97] In September 1965, Anderson and John Motley, whom she wanted as her accompanist for the concert, flew to Paris for several days. They rehearsed the program on the twenty-seventh. The concert the next evening attracted a glamorous audience of French celebrities and African diplomats—President Senghor was present—all willing to pay $100 to attend the recital and the showing of *Carmen Jones* the next evening. The French committee believed in Anderson's drawing power enough to offer her a fee of $10,000. According to the *Times,* Maria Callas was the only artist to have received a higher fee in France for a single appearance. For the half-hour program, Anderson and Motley performed sixteen spirituals, ending with "He's Got the Whole World in His Hands."[98]

In the end, Anderson did not join the other American artists—these included Armenta Adams, Martina Arroyo, Duke Ellington, Leonard DePaur and his chorus, and the Marion Williams Gospel Singers—in Senegal. Writing to the State Department in March, she was as uncomfortably indirect as she could be:

> Since our last communication with you on February 2, 1966, regarding the First World Festival of Negro Arts, in Dakar, Senegal, there has been a little condition that has put one a wee bit below par, necessitating a slowing down of activities. Although it is not the result of the flu, our physician strongly opposes the necessity of receiving the immunization shots, as well as undertaking the African visit. One has hesitated to say that she was forced to forego this commitment, but we have now been convinced that it is imperative to let you know that we will be unable to attend the First World Festival of Negro Arts. We feel that you will understand and appreciate this disappointment.[99]

A few months later, on July 9 and 10, in a concert at Grant Park, Illinois, with the Chicago Symphony Orchestra conducted by DePreist, Anderson sang for the last time in public. She narrated Copland's *Preamble For a Solemn Occasion* and, at the end of the program, offered a group of spirituals. In addition, DePreist conducted Dvorak's Seventh Symphony and the Suite from Ravel's *Daphnis et Chloé*. For half a century, since Anderson's performance that summer afternoon in 1915 when she sang with the other students of Mary Saunders Patterson, music had been her deepest passion and sacred responsibility. It was left to her nephew, Jimmy, now to embody those ideals.

The unrestrained enthusiasm of the sell-out audiences throughout the United States during Anderson's farewell tour was the kind of incentive that always stimulated Hurok's imagination. "She doesn't have to sing," he had told reporters after Anderson's farewell concert in Carnegie Hall. "She can do some readings of Lincoln and Jefferson and then maybe sing a few spirituals. It'll go like a house on fire."[100] Anderson had thought the idea appealing enough to try it out in the summer of 1965. At a concert at Lewisohn Stadium with Arthur Fiedler and the Metropolitan Opera Orchestra on the eve of Independence Day, as part of a program featuring the music of American composers, Anderson narrated Copland's *A Lincoln Portrait* for the first time and sang a group of spirituals Hall Johnson had arranged for her for the recording of *Just Keep On Singin'*.[101]

Copland's *A Lincoln Portrait* was commissioned in 1942 by the conductor André Kostelanetz as one of a group of four musical portraits of great American figures. The country had been drawn only months before into the Second World War, and Kostelanetz envisioned a series of works that would embody uplifting characteristics of the national spirit and stand in harmony with the upsurge of patriotic fervor felt by most Americans. Copland's *A Lincoln Portrait* is a thirteen-minute work organized into three sections. The first two sections are for orchestra alone. As Copland later wrote, "In the opening, I hoped to suggest something of the mysterious sense of fatality that surrounds Lincoln's personality, and near the end of the first section, something of his gentleness and simplicity of spirit."[102] The second section, in which Copland makes use of several tunes of the period, is an "attempt to sketch in the background of the colorful times in which Lincoln lived."[103] Only in the last section does the narrator appear, quoting from Lincoln's writings and framing the excerpts with simple narrative passages against the orchestral backdrop.[104]

A Lincoln Portrait, in which Anderson appeared as narrator for more than a decade, held tremendous appeal for her. While for the younger, more outspoken, more militant generation of the 1960s, Lincoln's image lost a great deal of its significance, Anderson, like most blacks of her generation, felt deeply the force of his words and his deeds, and she was able to communicate this feeling to her audiences. Because she made no commercial recording of the work, she is little associated with the interpretive history of the piece. Fortunately, however, live recordings of her narration do exist. She spoke Lincoln's words with directness and fervor, differentiating, without any trace of exaggeration, Lincoln's voice from that of the narrator. In the famous concluding lines, "the government of the people, by the people, for the people shall not perish from the earth," Anderson achieved a level of intensity audiences found extraordinarily moving.[105]

Anderson's performances of *A Lincoln Portrait* generated considerable excitement, not only because of her interpretive abilities but also because of the historic association stemming from the events surrounding the Lincoln Memorial concert, events that many who came to hear her no doubt remembered. The narrating of Copland's work was a fortunate choice for Anderson at this time of her life. She was able to receive artistic satisfaction from a relatively brief work, one that did not depend on her singing voice. Her performances also brought in regular income. Maintaining Marianna was costly, more so than ever. Marian and King continued to talk about cutting costs, but they found it difficult to change their style of living in any dramatic way. They remained generous, to others as well as to themselves. Eventually they gave up their New York apartment, but that is as far as their cost-cutting went.

Anderson's passion still lay in performing. To reporters during her farewell tour, she had spoken earnestly of becoming "a housewife with a vengeance" and of doing more for civil rights and adopted children. But no one who knew her well could have believed that she would be satisfied with full-time domesticity. As for political and social causes, it was far easier for her to respond to calls for help than to vigorously initiate action. The governor of Connecticut, John N. Dempsey, appointed her one of twenty-five founding members of the State Commission on the Arts, and a year later, in December 1966, President Johnson appointed her as one of eight new members to the National Council on the Arts, but in both cases her participation was more honorary than actual. Anderson's most significant support, financial and advisory, went to Young Audiences, a national organization with many local chapters throughout the country that brought musicians and dancers into the classroom as a way of introducing music to young people, and to other organizations that helped create educational opportunities for students.

In the end, retirement for Anderson was a gradual process. While far from becoming the housewife she had imagined, she spent more time together with King, going to horse shows, to the theater, and to others' performances—Tony Bennett was a particular favorite of Marian's. On her own, Anderson liked nothing more than to spend the day in New

York shopping and having lunch or dinner with a friend, often with Pola Stout or Gwendolyn Carter.[106]

Professionally, during the 1960s and most of the 1970s, Anderson remained a Hurok artist and was assigned to the lecture bureau that Hurok managed as part of his agency. As lecturer, she spoke at colleges and music conservatories and at various commemorative occasions, her speeches prepared mostly by writers attached to Hurok's lecture bureau. As narrator, she was limited for the most part to the Copland work, but other such opportunities came along on occasion. In January 1967, for example, as part of a concert celebrating the memory of Toscanini, she was asked to appear as narrator in the first performance of *Joseph and His Brothers,* a work for narrator, soloists, chorus and orchestra by the American composer Robert Starer. The concert was presented by the American–Israeli Cultural Foundation and brought together many musicians who had made significant contributions to the musical life of Israel, including the conductor, William Steinberg, who had been instrumental in the training of the Palestine Symphony Orchestra after the Second World War and, of course, Anderson, who had established a vocal competition for young Israeli singers after her tour of Israel a decade earlier.[107]

For more than a decade, Anderson appeared as narrator in the Copland work more regularly than anyone else in its long history. Indeed, over the years, Anderson appeared in the work as many as thirty or forty times, traveling one season from Detroit to St. Louis to Hollywood, another season, from Orlando to Buffalo to Los Angeles. She thus came to know a whole generation of young conductors, among them Seiji Ozawa, Henry Lewis, and Lawrence Foster. She also got to perform with older conductors with whom she had never sung, including Sixten Ehrling and Stanislav Skrowaczewski. Particularly memorable were those occasions on which she performed with Copland himself and with her nephew, Jimmy.[108]

Anderson's desire to remain in the public eye, as well as to bring in regular income, motivated her to continue working, but she began to feel the strain of performing and lecturing. During her concert tours, Hurok had always provided her with a traveling manager. Stuart Warkow and then Michael Sweeley took over from Jofe after his retirement to arrange travel and accommodations and to ease the difficulties of travel. Now in her seventies, Anderson would often have to travel to an engagement on her own, carrying her own luggage and fighting the crowds at Grand Central Station in New York. Her health remained remarkably robust, but she began to suffer from high blood pressure, sometimes arriving back at Marianna more than usually strained.[109]

Marian was also facing the illness and passing of old friends and colleagues. Billy King and Marian had led separate lives from the time of their rupture during the mid-1930s. Over the years, Marian spoke about Billy only infrequently, with gratitude and admiration but also with a degree of coolness that was unusual for her. She was never far from his thoughts, however. Judging from the recollections of many of his friends, he spoke admiringly of Marian, recalling with pride how instrumental he had been in the early years of her career. On occasion, however, his old bitterness returned as he confided how he had been eliminated once Marian's career had blossomed.[110] After his first stroke, in 1973, Marian visited him in the nursing home in Lawrenceville, New Jersey, where he was convalescing. They had not seen each other in more than a quarter of a century. Marian brought him a small gift and sat with him, but he was unable to recognize her until she stood up to leave.[111] Marian's visit had stirred up his old feelings for her enough that, the following year, again in Lawrenceville after a second stroke, he tried to reach Marian by phone a number of times, always without success. It was the Christmas season of 1974, and particularly his recollection of Marian singing "O Holy Night" and "Crucifixion" with the Union Baptist Choir, that finally prompted him to write again. Apparently confused about how much time had passed in both their lives, he wrote her that "it is not my purpose to ask you to sing when you visit me, but they have heard so much about you, they feel that I can do wonders with you in asking you to sing. But I told them, such was not the case, that you indeed had commitments that you had to fill."[112] Billy died a few months later in a Trenton hospital.

Hurok, of course, had been a guiding presence in Marian's life for nearly forty years. His death in 1974 at the age of eighty-five came as a shock to her as it did to everyone. Up to the time of his death, Hurok was full of plans and new ideas. That very season, in fact, he had managed the comeback tour of Maria Callas and Giuseppe di Stefano. On March 5, after having lunch with Andrés Segovia, Hurok left for a meeting at the Chase Manhattan Bank with David Rockefeller, the bank's president. He was planning to discuss with Rockefeller the possibility of using Radio City Music Hall for a new attraction he was preparing featuring Nureyev. A few blocks away from the bank, Hurok fell to the ground, unconscious. He was taken to Beekman Downtown Hospital and, after several failed attempts to revive him, died of a massive heart attack. When two New York synagogues Hurok had occasionally visited refused, on the grounds that he had never been a member of their congregations, to handle his funeral, the Hurok office got in touch with Jan Peerce. Peerce proposed that the funeral take place in Carnegie Hall, where, on March 9, more than 2,600 people bid farewell to the impresario. Anderson joined Peerce and Isaac Stern, both long associated with Hurok, on the stage for the short service. Stern played a Bach Partita; Peerce, asking the audience to rise, sang a Jewish hymn made up of psalms.[113] Anderson delivered the eulogy. "He launched hundreds of careers," Anderson said, "he magnified thousands of others, and in the process he brought joy and a larger life to millions. He made not ripples, but waves, even beyond his own shores, and what is one to say of the man who guided one's life for nigh on to forty years? He was more than the supreme impresario. He was teacher, counsel, friend and even more than that, he was the 'we' in all of us."[114]

A few days after New Year's Day 1975, Marian and King were having dinner at home, together with Pauline, who had come up from Wilmington for the Christmas holiday. During the meal, as King was speaking, his speech changed in mid-sentence. He left the table and went immediately to bed. He was in no pain and, for the moment, only his speech seemed to be affected. He and Marian knew that it had to be a stroke. King's physician, Dr. Robert Miller, who had been called in the previous year as a consultant, had found transient signs of an impending stroke, especially numbness and arterosclerotic changes in circulation. Now, King's condition worsened and, after three days of decline, he was taken by ambulance to Danbury Hospital, where he was placed in the post-operative unit. The next day he suffered a second, more serious stroke which left him with paralysis on his right side, mostly in his leg, and a halting, moaning kind of speech.[115]

King's condition improved gradually and in a few weeks he was transferred to the Rusk Institute of Rehabilitation on Thirty-fourth Street in Manhattan. King found the staff caring and dedicated, and after several weeks of therapy his speech improved dramatically. After a few weeks back home, he had regained some mobility and was able to walk, although sometimes with difficulty and not without help. Marian often found the strain of caring for King at home arduous. For the first few years Marian employed part-time nurse's aides, and she eventually hired a regular, part-time housekeeper, Ruth Ingaren, but in the evenings Marian took care of King herself. He was a large man—his illnesses had done relatively little to discourage his hearty appetite—and it was no small matter for Marian to help him in and out of bed and around the house. After a while, King was able to walk more easily, but his unsteadiness sometimes caused him to fall, and Marian would have to try to lift him up and get him into bed.

Marian and King had not planned for the expense of full-time home care. King's illness convinced her that only by selling Marianna could she acquire sufficient capital for the years ahead. The farm was put into the hands of an agent, and eventually Marianna and its forty-six acres were bought by a developer, who agreed to a plan allowing Marian and King to remain there as rent-paying tenants for as long as they liked.

For a few years after King's strokes, Anderson continued to make appearances, both as narrator and speaker, but the physical effort of travel began to take a greater and greater toll on her health. After a performance as narrator with the Dance Theater of Harlem, in Dallas in 1976, Anderson arrived home physically exhausted, exhibiting a rise in blood pressure and slurred speech. With medication to bring down her blood pressure, she recovered quickly from what Dr. Miller, who had begun to treat Marian as well, assumed was hypertension and a vascular spasm. A few months later, after a performance of *A Lincoln Portrait,* there was a similar incident, this time a little worse.[116]

Around the time of the Dallas episode, plans for a Carnegie Hall gala celebration of Anderson's seventy-fifth birthday had just gotten underway. For a while there was some concern about whether she would be able to attend, but Dr. Miller was able to assure the management that in view of how well she was responding to medication, he saw no reason why plans for the concert could not go ahead. On February 27, 1977, with an audience that was, in the words of the *Times* story the next day, "pure Marian Anderson—some luminaries, some family members, children, adults, black and white,"[117] Anderson, a little frail and not quite herself, celebrated what was publically thought to be her seventy-fifth birthday but what was, in reality, her eightieth. The Carnegie Hall concert, the proceeds of which were to go, at Anderson's request, to Young Audiences, had been planned as an occasion for bringing together performers with a strong personal connection to Anderson—the singers Leontyne Price and Shirley Verrett as well as members of the Dance Theater of Harlem, an organization for which Anderson felt strong sympathy because of the importance it placed on providing young students with the best training for the lowest possible tuition.

In the end, the concert became the setting for an extended series of tributes celebrating far more than Anderson's status as an artist. Henry Labouisse, executive director of the United Nations Children's Fund, recalling Anderson's service as a United Nations delegate, presented her with the United Nations Peace Prize. Mayor Beame presented her with the Handel Medallion for her cultural contributions "to the city, the country and the world." Rosalynn Carter, with whom Anderson and some of her family were sharing a box, presented her with President Carter's birthday wishes and informed her—and the vast audience in the hall—of the congressional resolution that had been passed the previous Friday authorizing the Treasury Department to strike a gold medal in Anderson's honor for her "untiring and unselfish devotion to the promotion of the arts in this country during a distinguished and impressive career of more than half a century."[118]

The actual presentation of the Congressional Medal took place much later, in August 1978, in a small ceremony at the White House. To coincide with that presentation and as part of the worldwide commemoration of the 150th anniversary of Schubert's death, RCA Records released a long-playing album of Schubert and Brahms lieder recorded by Anderson in 1966, only months before her seventieth birthday. The album seems to have produced little critical comment one way or another, yet Anderson's voice exhibited a surprising freshness and bloom in comparison with the Constitution Hall farewell recital released the previous year. From the conversational ease and humor of Brahms's "Vergebliches Ständchen," to the deep simplicity and perfectly controlled line of Schubert's "An die Musik," or the hypnotic, trance-like inwardness of "Gretchen am Spinnrade," Anderson produced a series of interpretations in which each song was inhabited with the wisdom and truthfulness of a lifetime's experience of lieder singing. Still, it was a curious release. Since the issuing of the series of recordings around the time of Anderson's farewell tour, in 1964–65, which had included the reappearance of some of Anderson's important lieder recordings of the 1930s and 1940s, there had not been a single re-release of any of Anderson's earlier records. There were any number of recordings in RCA's vaults—Schubert and Brahms lieder, the series of Sibelius songs, Schumann's *Frauenliebe und -leben*—that had been denied the public for more than thirty years and that would have done more honor to her unique qualities as a singer. Indeed, the legend of Anderson, already written so deeply into the social consciousness of the country, was beginning to obscure the memory of Anderson the artist, the record of her singing now kept alive more by individual memory and official tribute than by any consistent effort to keep her most important and representative recordings before the public.[119]

★ ★ ★

The demands on Anderson's time—whether to accept awards or honorary degrees, to talk to young people in colleges or conservatories, or to devote time to arts organizations—hardly abated during her eighties. Bouts of unsteadiness, or episodes of acute hypertension that would sometimes bring on temporary vascular spasms affecting her speech, would make her wary of traveling. Otherwise, it was not in her nature to say no. A month before her eighty-fifth birthday, for example, Anderson attended the gala concert in her honor at Carnegie Hall, where she heard arias and duets sung by Grace Bumbry and Shirley Verrett and greetings from Mayor Koch, and President Reagan read by Isaac Stern.[120] A few years later, in July 1984, at a ceremony at City Hall in New York, she accepted the first Eleanor Roosevelt Human Rights Award. Mayor Koch had to help her up from her wheelchair, but once on her feet, Anderson stood on her own at the podium and told those present, "I have thanked my good Lord for her many times. I am only sorry the youngsters of today shall not have seen her in the flesh." At the end of the ceremony, when the roomful of guests sang "He's Got the Whole World in His Hands," Anderson wept.[121]

In many ways, Marian and King were still able to enjoy their time together at Marianna just as they had planned to do for years, taking a short walk out of doors when the weather was pleasant and King felt steady enough to manage with the help of a nurse, seeing family and friends, and sitting together in the library watching television or talking. Dr. Miller, who had retired in 1983, came to the house at lunchtime once a week to visit. After the onset of King's illness, Marian had written to King's son, James, who had not visited his father for some time, urging him to come to the farm. In spite of James's reconciliation with his father some years earlier, he still felt enough bitterness to keep him away from his father for long periods. Finally, his own son urged him to patch things up again. James never forgot how, at his first visit to the farm in years, King "cried like a baby."[122]

Marian had pastimes that kept her occupied on her own. She liked to work on sewing projects or spend time in her darkroom developing pictures. Most important, however, for King as well as Marian, now that they were both more sedentary than either had been used to, were those occasions when there was company, whether visits arranged carefully in advance or impromptu social calls. Ruth, who had eventually become a full-time caregiver and housekeeper, sometimes kept Anderson in more isolation from the outside world than she would have preferred. At one time a Salvation Army volunteer, Ruth was consumed by an almost evangelical zeal to protect Anderson's comfort. There usually came a time, however, when, with the same quiet authority with which Benjamin Anderson had stood up to Isabella, Marian stood her ground. Marian took special pleasure in the visits of children. Whenever anyone brought a child to see her, the child would immediately gain center stage. Jeannette De Fazio, who came to work for Marian as a part-time secretary in 1982, later recalled that Marian "could care less if she got any work done on Thursdays" when she brought her granddaughter Nicole with her to work; Marian "wanted to watch the baby and to hold her."[123]

Anderson was also visited by both younger as well as more established black singers—"my girls," Marian always called them, and these visitors joined the same inner circle as a neighbor's children or grandchildren. Jessye Norman and Kathleen Battle came to Marianna to meet Anderson and to tell her of their successes in the world of opera. John Motley was a frequent visitor and the only one of Marian's friends or family who could get her to sing. He would sit down at the piano and play one or two spirituals they had worked on together. By the time Motley got to "This Little Light of Mine"—the trick never failed—Marian was relaxed enough to hum along and, on occasion, to sing.[124] Marian stayed in touch with Franz Rupp, but she did not see him very often. Franz was now in his eighties too and, after Steffi's death in 1976, had happily remarried, this time to a much younger woman, Sylvia Stone, who no less than Steffi indulged his every wish.

Gradually King's health worsened. He could no longer walk on his own, even with help, and became more and more confined to a wheelchair. Round the clock nurse attendants in eight-hour shifts were required to take care of him at home. King's doctor as well as family and friends tried to convince Marian that it would be far easier on everyone if King were in a nursing home. After a while she gave in to the idea and King did go to a nursing home, but after a few weeks Marian could not stand how miserable he felt away from home. He longed to be back at Marianna, where he could sit in the dining room or library and look out at the trees and the flowers. After a few weeks, Marian brought him home. Whenever the idea of a nursing home came up again, Marian refused to consider it. "I want to be able to put my head on the pillow at night and sleep peacefully," she said.[125]

In the middle of March 1986, King contracted pneumonia and was taken to Danbury Hospital. After a week or so he appeared to be out of danger and was expected to come home, but early in the morning of March 26, at the age of eighty-five, he died suddenly of cardio-pulmonary arrest. Marian arranged a small memorial service for him at the

New Hope Baptist Church in Danbury, which King had designed and where he had been a member for many years. Among those who gathered in the chapel were King's son James, his sister Pauline, and Robert O'Neill, a nephew.

For a while after King's death, Marian thought of moving back to Philadelphia to live with Ethel on Martin Street. The idea had come up a number of times through the years. For a while there had been talk of finding a house in another Philadelphia neighborhood, or a house halfway between Philadelphia and Danbury that both Ethel and Marian would find comfortable and convenient should the time arrive for such a change. No one who knew Marian well, however, put much stock in the possibility. Marian, like King, wanted to be able to see the trees and the flowers blossom around Marianna in the spring, and to enjoy summers in the country. Marianna had been Marian's home for over forty years and she was not able to think seriously of pulling up roots now that she was approaching ninety.

Ethel was now more than ever a comfort to Marian. They had established a bond of communication over the years that continued to serve them well. Every evening Marian called Martin Street, as she had done since she had begun touring half a century before. For the holidays—Easter, Thanksgiving, and Christmas—Ethel came to Marianna, at Christmas remaining until after the new year, and during the summers Ethel spent several weeks at Marianna. Although it was becoming more difficult for Marian to travel, she rarely complained about being lonely. The round-the-clock nurses that cared for her, especially those she grew particularly fond of, were as much companions as active caretakers. Some who had come to work for her in order to take care of King now took care of her. Marian also had frequent visitors. One was June Goodman, an old Danbury friend. They had known each other for more than forty years but had become much closer since June had enlisted Marian's aid in laying the groundwork and raising money for the Charles Ives Performing Arts Center, a Danbury cultural center that had been established in 1980 to serve as the site of a summer music festival. Another frequent visitor was Sandra Grymes, a cousin of Marian's whom she always referred to lovingly as her niece. Sandra came down from New York whenever she could to see Marian and tell her about the latest happenings on the musical scene.

June and Sandra shared Jimmy's missionary zeal about the importance of keeping alive the record of Marian's greatness as a singer, which all three felt should remain at the center of Marian's legacy. Anderson was never a willing ally when plans to focus publicly on her life and achievements came up. Having lived her life and contributed what she could, she never pondered over her legacy. "Aunt Marian had no expectation," Jimmy later recalled, "that people would or should remember what she had accomplished, and was always surprised when it happened."[126] Nevertheless, others pressed on. June wanted Anderson to be honored by her "hometown" of Danbury in the form of an annual award established in her name that would be given to promising young American singers. In this way, June thought, the award Anderson had herself established in the 1940s could be reborn, rendering permanent tribute to Anderson's work in promoting the careers of young singers. June helped convince the Charles Ives Center to establish a Marian Anderson Celebration Committee to raise money to finance the endowment for the award. With June as the chairwoman and Isaac Stern as honorary chairman, the committee began two years of work to reach its goal of raising $500,000.[127]

As part of the fund raising, the Ives Center suggested a gala concert in Anderson's honor. At first Anderson was loath to agree, simply thinking no one would come. But on August 13, 1989, in spite of the threat of thunderstorms, 2,500 people gathered in the pavilion of the Ives Center to hear Jessye Norman, Isaac Stern, and Julius Rudel and the Ives Symphony Orchestra. "I know enough not to speak after Isaac Stern," Anderson told the audience. "So I shall say to you from the bottom of my heart, I thank you; I love you."[128] A year later, Sylvia McNair became the first recipient of the Marian Anderson Award.

Early in 1989, WETA, the public radio and television station in Washington, as part of its cultural affairs programming, approached Jimmy with the idea of developing a television documentary about Anderson's life. Anderson objected to the idea but, in the end, Jimmy talked her into it. In order to coax her into becoming more at ease with the idea, and to enlist her help in the difficult project of establishing the factual background for the documentary, Jimmy took advantage of one of Ethel's visits to Marianna to encourage his mother and Marian to reminisce about their early years in South Philadelphia and the beginnings of Marian's career. One morning during breakfast, Jimmy set up a small tape recorder in the dining room and urged the two to start from the beginning, prompting them with questions and urging them to be accurate about when things happened. Ethel enjoyed the experience, providing details about growing up, recalling her favorite stories, and scolding Jimmy for becoming impatient with the leisurely pace she adopted. Marian rarely entered into the spirit of casual fun around the table, weighing what she said more soberly and deliberately than Ethel.[129]

When the WETA film crew came up to Marianna in the summer of 1989 to begin filming Anderson's portion of the documentary, it was Jimmy who asked the questions and encouraged her to talk, and that helped considerably to relax her.

In many ways, Ethel, with her prodigious memory of events that had taken place more than half a century before, proved to be the family historian for the project. Sadly, she did not live to see the completed documentary. She came up from Philadelphia around Christmas time, as she did each year. Having planned to stay for a week or two into the new year, she complained of not feeling well and decided to return home early. A few weeks later, she suffered a brain aneurysm and was taken to Jefferson Hospital. Although she had just turned eighty-eight on January 14, she had been in surprisingly good health and the doctors were pleased at her rapid progress. Yet on February 1, 1990, with hardly any warning, Ethel died of complications brought on by the aneurysm.[130]

Marian rarely revealed a great deal of how she felt, but there was no mistaking how shattered she was by Ethel's death. Dr. Miller, who had remained a loyal friend, had gotten word of Marian's unusually apathetic condition and came over to Marianna to see her. When he came into the dining room he found her sitting mutely at the table, unable to talk. He held her hand for a while and just sat with her at the table. Finally, kissing her on the forehead, he quietly left the room.[131] Gradually, in the weeks and months following, Marian pulled herself together and went on. Having agreed to participate in the WETA documentary, she made no objection to a second series of interviews in June. The following May 1991, two months after celebrating her ninety-fourth birthday, she traveled to the Kennedy Center for a private showing of the film, "Marian Anderson," narrated by Avery Brooks. Early in the day, before the film showing that evening, Anderson, accompanied by Jimmy and Sharon Percy Rockefeller, the president of WETA, went to the White House for tea with Mrs. Bush and a photo session with President Bush. A few nights later, the film was shown on public television. Its reception was mixed. One critic found the accounts of Anderson by friends and associates—they included Franz Rupp, Patrick Hayes, members of Union Baptist Church, and opera singers Jessye Norman and Mattiwilda Dobbs—"wearyingly worshipful," yet at the same time, like most viewers, was struck by the immense dignity of her every appearance throughout the film.[132]

Later that summer, at a routine examination Anderson underwent at Danbury Hospital, doctors discovered the early signs of bowel cancer.

Anderson found the doctors there too aggressive, and she made it clear that she did not want surgery or the intervention of machines. She wished only to remain at home and to be made as comfortable as possible. One of Anderson's friends suggested that she be seen by Dr. Micheline Williams, a Danbury physician. Although usually too busy to make house calls, Dr. Willliams agreed to see Anderson at Marianna. "I don't want to be treated for anything they find," she told Dr. Williams, who found Anderson delightful and fascinating to listen to, although obviously lonely.[133] Before long, Dr. Williams noticed how much Anderson was anticipating her visits, and often they were as much social calls as examinations. Marian would have been content to live out the remainder of her life at Marianna, but Jimmy and his wife, Ginette, wanted Marian to be with them in Portland.[134] They were worried about her welfare and wanted to look after her themselves. For the short time left to Marian, Jimmy wanted her to be with family. Jimmy talked the idea over with Dr. Williams, and both agreed it was a good idea. Marian gradually came to accept the idea as God's will, agreeing, with mixed emotions, to move to Portland.

During the months of packing, Anderson gradually became more comfortable with the idea. June, Sandra, and Jeannette De Fazio took charge of most of the work, helping Marian sort through a lifetime of accumulations. The fact that Wilhelmina Fortnos, one of Anderson's nurse attendants whom she especially liked, would be able to remain with Marian in Portland for as long as it proved necessary, added immeasurably to her sense of comfort. Mush, Marian's cat, would also be making the trip with her, providing another comforting link between Marianna and Portland. On July 6, 1992, a few days before Anderson was scheduled to fly to Portland, she suffered another vascular spasm. She refused to go to the hospital and by the next day had recovered well. On the morning of the ninth, Jimmy and Ginette, who had flown to Connecticut to accompany Marian on the trip, flew with her to Portland, along with Wilhelmina. Mush went along in a cat carrier.[135]

There was some concern among Marian's closest friends and family that, at her age, she would not easily adjust to her new surroundings. But those who traveled to Portland to visit her invariably found her content and looking healthier than during her last months at Marianna. Ginette doted on her even more than Jimmy. June Goodman, having carefully packed in dry ice Marian's favorite chocolate raspberry ice cream, made the trip in the fall, and, at Thanksgiving, Eleanor Peters, one of Marian's oldest friends, came up from Los Angeles to be with her.[136]

On February 27, 1993, Marian celebrated her ninety-sixth birthday.

She was feeling more tired than usual and not eating as well as she had, but she talked on the phone throughout the day with friends offering birthday wishes. During the next month her health declined considerably, and in March Marian suffered an epileptic seizure. Her physician, Dr. Ruth Medac, prescribed dilantin, a seizure drug, and tried to make her as comfortable as possible. Ginette, who was with Jimmy in Sweden, where he was giving concerts, came home as soon as they got word of Marian's illness. Marian rallied a bit over the next few weeks, but near the end of March another seizure occurred, and Marian, having by then lost her speech, began to slip in and out of a coma. Jimmy canceled his remaining concerts and arrived home around the first of April. During the weeks before Jimmy's return, Ginette had slept in Marian's room so that she would not be alone. Once home, Jimmy took up the vigil. On Wednesday evening, April 7, Jimmy had a concert in Salem with the Oregon Symphony Orchestra. Somehow, when he got home, he had a premonition that Marian would not survive the night. He had been studying the score of Mahler's Tenth Symphony at the time. Perhaps it was his preoccupation with Mahler's last work, which the composer left unfinished, that heightened his awareness. He spent the rest of the night in Marian's room, sitting at the desk. Around 4:30 in the morning of the eighth, Marian died.

On a warm and bright Sunday morning in June 1993, more than 200 people made their way into Union Baptist Church, in South Philadelphia, to attend a memorial service for Marian Anderson.[137] Inside the church, there was a relaxed and genial atmosphere as family members who had not seen one another for a long time greeted each other, old friends embraced, and older members of the congregation shared with each other and their children their feeling of pride in how much Union Baptist had done to nurture the extraordinary talent of "our Marian." The Reverend Gregory L. Wallace, the church's pastor, told all of those present: "Back in the first decade of this century, the members of this church saw in Marian Anderson the gifts of God. They saw in her what others had seen in Beethoven and Shakespeare and perhaps even Michelangelo. We all have been blessed by her music of the soul, music that transcends time. The members of this church heard in that voice the grace and benediction that only God can give."

Sandra Grymes spoke at the service about how Marian and her sisters were "trained to cast a stoic face upon gratuitous insults." She spoke also about Marian's inner faith "that made her stronger than all of us," and about how Marian's "trips into the world and her returns to us enlarged our vision of our individual possibilities." The last to share his memories of Marian was Jimmy. He was mindful of Marian's admonition about the way she wished to be remembered. She had said to him, "No fuss." So now Jimmy spoke without fuss, telling stories of what it was like growing up on Martin Street in a family defined by the love and faith and strength of determined women, Aunt Marian among them. Jimmy told the gathering about the importance of Union Baptist Church on his family's life. "They had wonderful times in this church," he said, "and this is essentially why we are here today. This church is central to our lives, central to our faith, central to everything we did." Finally Jimmy spoke of Marian's voice. "No one could pay tribute to Marian Anderson better than my Aunt Marian herself," he said, "with that extraordinary voice that seems to come from the center of each of us." As he walked slowly away from the podium, Marian's voice rose up, filling Union Baptist Church with the words of the spirituals she loved—"Deep River," "Crucifixion," and, finally, "He's Got the Whole World in His Hands." For those gathered there, she accomplished what she had always accomplished. With her voice, she lifted their spirits.

Appendix 1: Repertory

Vocal and Choral

AHLE, JOHANN GEORG (1651–1706)
Ardent Longing (Brünstiges Verlangen)

ALMAN, SAMUEL (1878–1947)
I shall not die

ALVAREZ, FERMIN MARIA (1833–1898)
La partida

BACH, JOHANN SEBASTIAN (1685–1750)
Die Art verruchter Sünden, from Cantata 54
Bereite dich Zion, from *Christmas Oratorio*
Bist du bei mir, BWV 508
Du Herr, du kronst allein das Jahr mit deinem Gut, from Cantata 187
Du machst, o Tod, mir nun nicht ferner bange, from Cantata 114
Erbarme dich, from *St. Matthew Passion*
Es ist vollbracht, from *St. John Passion*
Jesu deine Liebeswunden, from *Die geistlichen Lieder und Arien*
Jesus macht mich geistlich reich, from Cantata 75
Jesus schläft, was soll ich hoffen?, from Cantata 81
Komm' süsser Tod, from *Die geistlichen Lieder und Arien*
Kreuz und Krone sind verbunden, from Cantata 12
Mein Wandel auf der Welt, from Cantata 56
Murre nicht, lieber Christ, from Cantata 144
My Heart Ever Faithful (Mein gläubiges Herze), from Cantata 68
Schlage doch, gewünschte Stunde, Cantata 53 (attributed to Bach but thought to be by Melchior Hoffmann, 1685–1715)
Wer Sünde tut, der ist von Teufel, from Cantata 54

Widerstehe doch der Sünde, from Cantata 54
Zum reinen Wasser er mich weist, from Cantata 112

BACHELET, ALFRED (1864–1944)
Chère nuit

BANTOCK, GRANVILLE (1868–1946)
A Feast of Lanterns
The Simurgh, from *Songs of Persia*

BARBER, SAMUEL (1910–1981)
The Daisies, Op. 2
I hear an army, Op. 10/3
Nocturne, Op. 13/4

BASSA, JOSÉ (1670–1730)
Menuet chanté

BASSANI, GIOVANNI BATTISTA (ca. 1657–1716)
Dormi bella, dormi tu

BEACH, AMY MARCY CHENEY (1867–1944)
Ah, love, but a day!

BECKER, REINHOLD (1842–1924)
Frühlingszeit

BEDFORD, HERBERT (1867–1945)
The Coming of Love
Homecoming

BEETHOVEN, LUDWIG VAN (1770–1827)
Busslied, Op. 48/6
Die Ehre Gottes aus der Natur, Op. 48/4
Freudvoll und leidvoll, Op. 84/4
In questa tomba oscura, WoO 133
Mit einem gemalten Band, Op. 83/32
Neue Liebe, neues Leben, Op. 75/2
Vom Tode, Op. 48/3
Wonne der Wehmut, Op. 83/1

Appendix 1: Repertory

BEERS, JACQUES (1902–1947)
African Rhythms (dedicated to Marian
    Anderson):
Anchor line
Frogs, where are you going?
Oh, boat come back to me

BELLINI, VINCENZO (1801–1835)
Odiò la pastorella

BEMBERG, HERMANN-EMMANUEL
    (HENRI) (1859–1931)
A toi
Aime-moi!
Chant hindou

BENCINI, PIETRO PAOLO (c. 1670–1755)
Tanto sospirerò

BENEDICT, JULIUS (1804–1885)
The Gypsy and the Bird

BERNHEIM, MARCEL (DATES UNKNOWN)
Le sommeil des faucons, from *Cinq
    poèmes arabes*

BIANCHINI, GUIDO (1885–1971)
Obstination
Paysage triste

BIZET, GEORGES (1838–1875)
Agnus Dei, from *L'Arlésienne*
Ouvre ton coeur

BLAND, JAMES (1854–1911)
Carry me back to old Virginny

BOND, CARRIE JACOBS (1862–1946)
A Perfect Day

BORODIN, ALEXANDER (1833–1887)
Aus fremden Land (Dlia beregov
    otchizny dalnoi)

BRAHMS, JOHANNES (1833–1897)
Alto Rhapsody, Op. 53
Am Sonntag Morgen, zierlich angetan,
    Op. 49/1

An die Nachtigall, Op. 46/4
An die Tauben, Op. 63/4
Auf dem Kirchhofe, Op. 105/4
Auf dem See, Op. 59/2
Bei dir sind meine Gedanken, Op. 95/2
Botschaft, Op. 47/1
Dein blaues Auge hält so still, Op. 59/8
Ein Wanderer, Op. 106/5
Feldeinsamkeit, Op. 86/2
Frühlingstrost, Op. 63/1
Der Gang zum Liebchen, Op. 48/1
Heimweh II, Op. 63/8
Immer leiser wird mein Schlummer,
    Op. 105/2
Die Kränze ,Op. 46/1
Liebestreu, Op. 3/1
Das Mädchen spricht, Op. 107/3
Mädchenfluch, Op. 69/9
Mädchenlied, Op. 107/5
Die Mainacht, Op. 43/2
Meine Liebe ist grün wie der Flieder-
    busch, Op. 63/5
Nicht mehr zu Dir zu gehen, beschloss
    ich, Op. 32/2
O komme, holde Sommernacht, Op.
    58/4
O kühler Wald! Wo rauschest du, Op.
    72/3
O liebliche Wangen, ihr macht mir Ver-
    langen, Op. 47/4
O Nachtigall, dein süsser Schall, Op.
    97/1
Ruhe, Süssliebchen, im Schatten, Op.
    33/9
Sapphische Ode, Op. 94/4
Der Schmied, Op. 19/4
Die Schnur, die Perl an Perle, Op. 57/7
Schwesterlein, Schwesterlein (*Deutsche
    Volkslieder,* vol. III)
Sehnsucht (Volkslied), Op. 14/8
Sind es Schmerzen, sind es Freuden,
    from *Die Schöne Magelone,* Op. 33/3
Ständchen, Op. 106/1
Der Tod, das ist die kuhle Nacht, Op.
    96/1
Two Songs for Alto, Viola, and Piano,
    Op. 91
Unbewegte, laue Luft, Op. 57/8

Vergebliches Ständchen, Op. 84/4
Verzweiflung, Op. 33/10
Vier ernste Gesänge, Op. 121
Von ewiger Liebe, Op. 43/1
Wiegenlied, Op. 49/4
Wir wandelten, wir zwei zusammen,
    Op. 96/2
Zigeunerlieder, Op. 103

BRIDGE, FRANK (1879–1941)
Oh that it were so

BROWNELL, LEILA M. (dates unknown)
Four Leaf Clover

BUCKY, FRIDA SARSEN (1883 or
    1884–1974)
Angel's Song
Gabriel's Song
Hallelujah
Hear the wind whispering
Three Wise Men

BURLEIGH, HENRY THACKER (1866–1949)
The Grey Wolf
In the Wood of Finvara

CACCINI, GIULIO (c. 1545–1618)
Amarilli mia bella, from *Le nuove musiche*
Tanto sospirerò

CADMAN, CHARLES WAKEFIELD
    (1881–1946)
Call me no more

CALDARA, ANTONIO (c. 1670–1736)
Come raggio di sol
Infelice usignuolo
Sebben, crudele

CAMPBELL-TIPTON, LOUIS (1877–1921)
Le cri des eaux

CAPUA, ANTONIO (1623–1669)
Dal sen del caro sposa

CARISSIMI, GIACOMO (1605–1674)
A bruno vestiti

No, no mio core

CARPENTER, JOHN ALDEN (1876–1951)
The Pools of Peace

CESTI, MARC' ANTONIO (1623–1669)
Tu manca vi a tormentari

CHADWICK, GEORGE WHITEFIELD
    (1854–1931)
La danza, from Six Songs, Op. 14

CHAMINADE, CÉCILE (1857–1944)
L'anneau d'argent
L'été

CHAUSSON, ERNEST (1855–1899)
Le colibri, Op. 2/7
Le temps des lilas, from *Poème de l'amour
    et de la mer*

CIMARA, PIETRO (1887–1967)
Cante di primavera

COHEN, CECIL (1894–1967)
Eros
Rivets!

COLERIDGE-TAYLOR, SAMUEL
    (1875–1912)
Big Lady Moon
Island of Gardens
You may lay so still, from *Songs of Sun
    and Shade*

COOLS, EUGÈNE (1877–1936)
Down in Lover's Lane
Mammy
Wid de Moon, Moon, Moon

DAVIS, GEORGE GIBSON (dates unknown)
A Peasant Mother's Lullaby

DEBUSSY, CLAUDE ACHILLE (1862–1918)
Beau soir
La chevelure, from *Chansons de Bilitis*
En sourdine, from *Fêtes galantes*
Fantoches, from *Fêtes galantes*

Fleur des blés

Il pleure dans mon coeur, from *Ariettes oubliées*

La mer est plus belle, from *Trois mélodies de Paul Verlaine*

Les cloches, from *Deux romances*

DELAFOSSE, LÉON (b. 1874–?)
La fleur que je désire

DEL RIEGO, TERESA (1876–1968)
Homing

DELIBES, LÉO (1836–1891)
The Maids of Cadiz

DONAUDY, STEFANO (1879–1925)
O del mio amato ben
Spirate pur spirate

DONIZETTI, GAETANO (1797–1848)
La zingara

DOUGHERTY, CELIUS (1902–1986)
Portrait
Song for Autumn
Weathers

DOUTY, NICHOLAS (1870–1955)
The Lotus

DUNHILL, THOMAS (1877–1946)
To the Queen of Heaven

DUPARC, HENRI (1848–1933)
Chanson triste
L'invitation au voyage
La vie antérieure

DURANTE, FRANCESCO (1684–1755)
Danza, danza fanciulla gentile
Vergin tutt' amor

DVORÁK, ANTONIN (1841–1904)
Songs My Mother Taught Me (Cigánské melodié), Op. 55

ESTEVE Y GRIMAU, PABLO (birthdate unknown–1794)
El luto de garrido

DE FALLA, MANUEL (1876–1946)
Canción, from *Siete canciones populares españolas*
Jota, from *Siete canciones populares españolas*
El paño moruno, from *Siete canciones populares españolas*

FAURÉ, GABRIEL (1845–1924)
Adieu, from *Poème d'un jour,* Op. 21/3
Après un rêve, Op. 7/1
Au bord de l'eau, Op. 8/1
Aurore, Op. 39/1
Automne, Op. 18/3
Les berceaux, Op. 23/1
Clair de lune, Op. 46/2
Dans les ruines d'une abbaye, Op. 2/1
Fleur jetée, Op. 39/2
L'hiver a cessé, from *La bonne chanson,* Op. 61/9
Nell, Op. 18/1
Rencontre, from *Poème d'un jour,* Op. 21/1
Le secret, Op. 23/3
Sylvie, Op. 6/3
Toujours!, from *Poème d'un jour,* Op. 21/2
Tristesse, Op. 6/2
Le voyageur, Op. 18/2

FISKE, DWIGHT (1892–1959)
The Bird

FOSTER, STEPHEN COLLINS (1826–1864)
My Old Kentucky Home
Old Folks at Home

FOURDRAIN, FÉLIX (1880–1923)
Chanson norvégienne
L'oasis

FRANCK, CÉSAR (1822–1890)
Air de l'Archange, from *Rédemption*

Lied
La procession
Nocturne
S'il est un charmant gazon
Le vase brisé

FRESCOBALDI, GIROLAMO (1583–1643)
Se l'aura spira, from *Primo libro d'arie musicali per cantarsi*

GAGLIANO, MARCO DA (c. 1575–1642)
Dormi, amore

GIBBS, CECIL ARMSTRONG (1889–1960)
Summer Night

GINASTERA, ALBERTO (1916–1983)
Canción del árbol del olvido

GIORDANI, GIUSEPPE (1744–1798)
Caro mio ben

GRANADOS, ENRIQUE (1867–1916)
Andalucia
Elegia eterna
La Maja dolorosa

GRETCHANINOV, ALEXANDER (1864–1956)
Berceuse (Kolybel'naia), Op. 1
The Captive (Uznik), Op. 20/4
The Death (Smert'), Op. 15

GRIEG, EDVARD (1843–1907)
En svane, Op. 25/2
Fra Monte Pincio, Op. 39/1
Jeg elsker dig, Op. 5/3
Zur Johannisnacht (Og jeg vil ha mig en Hjertenskjaer), Op. 60/5

GRIFFES, CHARLES TOMLINSON (1884–1920)
Auf geheimnem Waldespfade
Evening Song
The Half-Ring Moon
If I could go with you
Night on ways unknown has fallen
Upon their grave

We'll to the woods, and gather May, Op. 3/3

GUASTAVINO, CARLOS (b. 1914)
Apegado a mi
Cita
Rocio
La rosa y el sauce

HAGEMAN, RICHARD (1882–1966)
Music I heard with you

HAHN, REYNALDO (1875–1947)
D'une prison
Si mes vers avaient des ailes

HANDEL, GEORG FRIDERIC (1685–1759)
Dank sei Dir, Herr (spurious; forgery by Siegfried Ochs)
Daughter of Sion, from *Brockes Passion*
Dignare domine (Vouchsafe, O Lord), from *Te Deum for the Victims of Dettingen*
Figli del mesto cor
Die Flöte weich gefühl (The soft complaining flute), from *Ode for Saint Cecilia's Day*
He shall feed His flock, from *Messiah*[1]
He was despised, from *Messiah*
Lass mich wandern (Let me wander not unseen) (Siciliana), from *L'Allegro, il Penseroso ed il Moderato*
O Numi eterni, from *La Lucrezia*
So wie die Taube (As when the dove), from *Acis and Galatea*
Begrüssung (Tears such as tender fathers shed), from *Deborah*

HAYDN, FRANZ JOSEPH (1732–1809)
The Mermaid's Song
My mother bids me bind my hair (Pastoral Song)
Piercing Eyes
She never told her love
The Spirit's Song
La vie
The Wanderer

Appendix 1: Repertory

HINDEMITH, PAUL (1895–1963)
  Sing on there in the swamp, from Nine
    English Songs

HOOK, JAMES (1746–1827)
  Bright Phoebus
  Softly waft, ye southern breezes

HÜE, GEORGES-ADOLPHE (1858–1948)
  J'ai pleuré en rêve

HUMMEL, FERDINAND (1855–1928)
  Halleluja

IRELAND, JOHN (1879–1962)
  Hope the Hornblower
  When lights go rolling round the sky

JACOBSEN, MYRON (1884–1934)
  Last Love

JOHNSON, JOHN ROSAMOND (1873–1954)
  Since you went away
  Song of My Heart

KILPINEN, YRJÖ (1892–1959)
  Benediction
  Det var i v årens ljusa tid, Op. 45/2
  Die Fusswaschung, Op. 59/1
  Med strömmen, Op. 29
  Och tröskorna tego, Op. 41/4
  Siehe, auch ich liebe, Op. 59/5
  Von zwei Rosen, Op. 59/3

KORNGOLD, ERICH WOLFGANG
  (1897–1957)
  A Little Love Letter

LA FORGE, FRANK (1879–1953)
  Hills
  Song of the Open

LALO, EDOUARD (1823–1892)
  L'esclave

LEHMANN, LIZA (1862–1918)
  The Cuckoo
  Daddy's Sweetheart

LIEURANCE, THURLOW (1878–1963)
  By the Waters of Minnetonka
  Love Song

LISZT, FRANZ (1811–1886)
  Die drei Zigeuner
  In Liebeslust
  Jeanne d'Arc au bûcher
  Loreley

LOTTI, ANTONIO (c. 1667–1740)
  Pur dicesti, o bocca bella

LUND, SIGNE (1868–1950)
  Night

MACGIMSEY, ROBERT (1898–1979)
  If he change my name

MAHLER, GUSTAV (1860–1911)
  Kindertotenlieder
  Liebst du um Schönheit, from *Rückert
    Lieder*
  Lieder eines fahrenden Gesellen
  Rheinlegendchen, from *Des Knaben
    Wunderhorn*
  Der Schildwache Nachtlied, from *Des
    Knaben Wunderhorn*
  Urlicht, from *Des Knaben Wunderhorn*

MALOTTE, ALBERT HAY (1895–1964)
  The Lord's Prayer

MARCELLO, BENEDETTO (1686–1739)
  Il mio bel foco

MARTINI (SCHWARZENDORF), JEAN PAUL
  EGIDE (1741–1816)
  Plaisir d'amour

MARX, JOSEPH (1882–1964)
  Blissful Night (Selige Nacht)
  Nocturne
  Wanderers Nachtlied

MASCAGNI, PIETRO (1863–1945)
  Pique dame

MASSENET, JULES (1842–1912)
Crépuscule
Elégie

MCDONALD, HARL (1899–1955)
Come, thou spirit of the night

MELARTIN, ERKKI GUSTAF (1875–1937)
Give me thy heart

MENDELSSOHN, FELIX (1809–1847)
Auf Flügel des Gesanges, Op. 34/2
But the Lord is mindful of His own,
from *St. Paul,* Op. 36
Jagdlied, Op. 84/3
Nachtlied, Op. 71/6
O rest in the Lord, from *Elijah,* Op. 70[2]

MERIKANTO, OSKAR (FRANS) (1868–1924)
Oi, muistatko viela sen virren

MITTLER, FRANZ (1893–1970)
Evensong
The Goose Girl

MORRIS, RAYMOND AUGUSTUS
(1907–1944)
The Song

MOZART, WOLFGANG AMADEUS
(1756–1791)
Alleluja, from *Exsultate Jubilate,* K. 165
Als Luise die Briefe ihres ungetreuen
Liebhabers verbrannte, K. 520
Die Alte, K. 517
An Chloe, K. 524
Ch'io mi scordo di te, K. 505
Dans un bois solitaire, K. 308 (259b)
Die ihr des unermesslichen Weltalls
Schöpfer ehrt *(Kleine deutsche Kantate),*
K. 619
Das Kinderspiel, K. 598
Das Lied der Trennung, K. 519
Ombra felice, K. 255
Parto inerme, e non pavento, from *La
Betulia liberata,* K. 118 (74c)
Ridente la calma, K. 152 (210a)
Das Veilchen, K. 476

NEVIN, ETHELBERT (1862–1901)
The Rosary

NIN, JOAQUÍN (1879–1949)
Alma sintanos
Jota tortosina
Minué cantado
Tonada de la niña perdida

NORDOFF, PAUL (1909–1977)
There shall be more joy

NORDQVIST, GUSTAF (1886–1949)
Schwalben fliehen

OBRADORS, FERNANDO J. (1897–1945)
Del cabello más sutil

PAGE, NATHANIEL CLIFFORD (1866–1956)
Believe me if all those endearing young
charms

PAISIELLO, GIOVANNI (1740–1816)
Chi vuol la zingarella

PARKER, HORATIO (1863–1919)
The South Wind

PERGAMENT, MOSES (1893–1977)
Vision

PERGOLESI, GIOVANNI BATTISTA
(1710–1736)
Se tu m'ami (attributed to Pergolesi, but
written by Alessandro Parisotti,
1835–1913)
Tre giorni son que Nina (attributed to
Pergolesi, but thought to be perhaps
by Vincenzo Legrenzio Ciampi,
1719–1762)

POULENC, FRANCIS (1899–1963)
Air champêtre
Air romantique
Le tombeau

PRICE, FLORENCE B. (1888–1953)
Songs to the Dark Virgin

PURCELL, HENRY (1658 OR 1659–1695)
Ah, how sweet it is to love, from *Tyran-nic Love or The Royal Martyr*
I Attempt from love's sickness to fly, from *The Indian Queen*
Fairest Isle, from *King Arthur, or the British Worthy*
Hark, how all things in one sound rejoice, from *The Fairy Queen*
Not all my torments can your pity move
Nymphs and Shepherds, from *The Libertine*
There's not a swain on the plain

QUILTER, ROGER (1877–1953)
Blow, blow thou winter wind
Daybreak
Dream Valley
The Golden Sunlight's Glory
I got a robe
It was a lover and his lass
A Land of Silence
Love's Philosophy
Music, when soft voices die
My Life's Delight
O mistress mine
Take, o take those lips away

RACHMANINOFF, SERGEI (1873–1943)
As fair is she as noon day light (Ona, kak polden' khorosha), Op. 14/9
Before my window (U moyevo okna), Op. 26/10
The Christ is risen (Khristos voskres), Op. 26/6
Ecstasy of Spring (Vesenniye vodï), Op. 14/11
In the silence of the secret night (V molchan'i nochi taynoy), Op. 4/3
O thou billowy harvest field (Uzh tï miva moya), Op. 4/5
Soldier's Bride (Polyrabila ya na pechal' svoyu), Op. 8/4
The Tryst (Siren'), Op. 21/5

RASBACH, OSCAR (1888–1975)
Trees

RAVEL, MAURICE (1875–1937)
Chanson italienne, from *Chants populaires*
Vocalise en forme de habanera

RESPIGHI, OTTORINO (1879–1936)
Pioggia
Sopra un aria antica

RIMSKY-KORSAKOV, NICOLAI (1844–1908)
The Nightingale and the Rose (Pleninshis rozoy solney), Op. 2/2

RODGERS, RICHARD (1902–1979)
You have to be carefully taught, from *South Pacific*

ROGERS, JAMES HOTCHKISS (1857–1940)
The Star: A Fragment from Plato

ROSS, GERTRUDE (1889–1957)
Dawn in the Desert

RUMMEL, WALTER MORSE (1887–1953)
Ecstacy

RUSSOTTO, LEO (1896–1978)
Sometime

SAAR, LOUIS (1868–1937)
At the Spinning-Wheel

SADERO, GENI (1886–1961)
Amuri, amuri
E quanna tu canta
Era la vo
Tarantella

SAINT-SAËNS, CHARLES CAMILLE (1835–1921)
La cloche
La solitaire

SARTII, GIUSEPPE (1729–1802)
Lungi dal caro bene

SCARLATTI, ALESSANDRO (1649–1725)
Chi vuole innamorarsi

Già il sole del Gange
Rosignuolo che volando
Rugiadose, odorose
Se Florindo è fedele

SCHINDLER, KURT (1882–1935)
La colomba (Tuscan folk song), from
    Folk-song Paraphrases, Op. 12

SCHUBERT, FRANZ PETER (1797–1828)
Abschied
Die Allmacht
Am Grabe Anselmo
An die Leier
An die Musik
An den Mond
An mein Herz
Auf dem Wasser zu singen
Auf der Brücke
Auf der Donau
Aufenthalt, from *Schwanengesang*
Auflösung
Aus Heliopolis I
Ave Maria (Ellens Gesang III)
Blumenschmerz
Dass sie hier gewesen
Dem Unendlichen
Der Doppelgänger, from *Schwanengesang*
Du bist die Ruh
Du liebst mich nicht
Der Erlkönig
Erstarrung, from *Winterreise*
Fischerweise
Die Forelle
Fragment aus dem Aeschylus
Frühlingstraum, from *Winterreise*
Gretchen am Spinnrade
Gruppe aus dem Tartarus
Gute Nacht, from *Winterreise*
Heidenröslein
Die Hoffnung
Im Abendroth
Im Freien
Im Frühling
In der Ferne, from *Schwanengesang*
Die junge Nonne
Der Jüngling am Bache
Der Jüngling und der Tod

Die Krähe, from *Winterreise*
Lachen und weinen
Lieb Minna
Liebesbotschaft, from *Schwanengesang*
Lied der Mignon (Heiss mich nicht
    reden)
Das Lied im Grünen
Der Lindenbaum, from *Winterreise*
Die Männer sind mechant, from *Vier
    Refrainlieder*
Meeres Stille
Memnon
Der Musensohn
Nacht und Träume
Nachtstück
Nähe des Geliebten
Pflicht und Liebe
Die Post, from *Winterreise*
Rastlose Liebe
Romanze
Die Rose
Seligkeit
Ständchen (Horch, horch, die Lerch')
Stimme der Liebe
Suleika I
Thekla
Der Tod und das Mädchen
Ungeduld, from *Die schöne Müllerin*
Verklärung
Die Vögel
Vom mitleiden Maria
Der Wanderer
Der Wanderer an den Mond
Wehmuth
Der Wegweiser, from *Winterreise*
Wer nie sein Brot mit Tränen ass
    (Harfners Gesang II)
Wiegenlied (D498)
Wohin? from *Die schöne Müllerin*
Der Zwerg

SCHUMAN, WILLIAM (1910–1992)
Orpheus with His Lute

SCHUMANN, ROBERT (1810–1856)
Der arme Peter, Op. 53/3
Aufträge, Op. 77/5
Dichterliebe, Op. 48

Appendix 1: Repertory

Aus alten Märchen winkt es
Hör' ich das Liedchen klingen
Ich grolle nicht
Ich will meine Seele tauchen
Im Rhein, im heiligen Strome
Ein Jüngling liebt ein Mädchen
Und wüsstens die Blumen, die
    kleinen
Wenn ich in deine Augen seh'
Frauenliebe und -leben, Op. 42
Frühlingsnacht, from *Liederkreis,* Op. 39
In der Fremde, from *Liederkreis,* Op. 39
Der Nussbaum, from *Myrthen,* Op. 25
Stille Tränen, from *Zwölf Gedichte,* Op. 35
Waldesgespräch, from *Liederkreis,* Op. 39
Wanderlied, from *Zwölf Gedichte,* Op. 35
Widmung, from *Myrthen,* Op. 25

SCOTT, CYRIL (1879–1970)
    Blackbird's Song
    Cherry Ripe
    Lullaby
    A Serenade
    A Song of London

SERLY, TIBOR (1900–1978)
    Flower Song

SHALIT, HEINRICH (dates unknown)
    May

SIBELIUS, JEAN (1865–1957)
    Aus banger Brust, Op. 50/4
    Black Roses (Svarta rosor), Op. 36/1
    Come away, death (Kom nu hit, död),
        Op. 60/1
    De begga rosorna, Op. 88/2
    En slända, Op. 17/5
    Fåf äng önskan, Op. 61/7
    Flickan kom ifrån sin älsklings möte,
        Op. 37/5
    Im Feld ein Mädchen singt, Op. 50/3
    Långsamt som kvällskyn, op. 61/1
    Men min fågel märks dock icke, Op.
        36/2
    Norden, Op. 90/1
    På verandan vid havet, Op. 38/2

Säv, säv, susa, Op. 36/4
Solitude (dedicated to Marian Ander-
    son)[3]
Sommarnatten, Op. 90/5
Die stille Stadt, Op. 50/5
Vattenplask, Op. 61/2
War es ein Traum? (Var det en dröm?),
    Op. 37/4

SIGMANDE, HERMINE (dates unknown)
    Spring and Love

SINDING, CHRISTIAN (1856–1941)
    Dér skrek en fågel

SJOGREN, EMIL (1853–1918)
    I dödens tysta tempelgårdar

SPEAKS, OLEY (1874–1948)
    Sylvia

SPROSS, CHARLES GILBERT (1874–1961)
    Fulfillment
    Will o' the wisp

STRADELLA, ALESSANDRO (1642–1682)
    Pietà signore

STRAUSS, RICHARD (1864–1949)
    Befreit, Op. 39/4
    Breit' über mein Haupt dein schwarzes
        Haar, Op. 19/2
    Cäcilie, Op. 27/2
    Du meines Herzens Kronelein, Op.
        21/2
    Freundliche Vision, Op. 48/1
    Geduld, Op. 10/5
    Die Georgine, Op. 10/14
    Morgen, Op. 27/4
    Die Nacht, Op. 10/3
    Ruhe, meine Seele, Op. 27/1
    Schlechtes Wetter, Op. 69/5
    Ständchen (Serenade), Op. 17/2
    Von dunklen Schleier umsponnen, Op.
        17/4
    Zueignung, Op. 10/1

Appendix 1: Repertory

STRICKLAND, LILY TERESA (1887–1958)
Mah Lindy Lou

STROZZI, BARBARA (1619–c. 1664)
Amor dormiglione

SULLIVAN, ARTHUR (1842–1900)
The Lost Chord

SWANSON, HOWARD (1909–1978)
Joy
The Negro Speaks of Rivers

TAVARES, HEKEL (1896–1969)
Funeral d'un rei Nago

TCHAIKOVSKY, PIOTR ILYICH (1840–1893)
He truly loved me so (On tak menya
   lyubil), Op. 28/4
If I had only known (Kabï znala ya),
   Op. 47/1
None but the lonely heart (Net, tolko
   tot, kto znal), Op. 6/6
Only thou alone (Lish tï odin), Op. 57/6
Disappointment (Déception), Op. 65/2
Whether day dawns? (Den li tsart?), Op.
   47/6
Whither goest thou? (Où vas-tu?), Op.
   65/1
Why? (Otchevo?), Op. 6/5

TCHEREPNIN, NIKOLAI (1873–1945)
A Kiss (Ia b'tiebia potsielovala), Op. 21/4

TERRY, WOODMAN
The Answer

THAYER, WILLIAM ARMOUR (1874–1933)
My Laddie

THOMAS, CHRISTOPHER (1894–?)
A Maiden
O men from the fields
O my heart is weary

THOMPSON, RANDALL (1899–1984)
Velvet Shoes

TORELLI, GIUSEPPE (1658–1709)
Tu lo sai

TOSTI, PAOLO (1846–1916)
La serenata

VARONA, LOUIS FELIPE (dates unknown)
Punto guajiro

VAUGHAN WILLIAMS, RALPH (1872–1958)
The Roadside Fire, from *Songs of Travel*
Silent Noon

VEHANEN, KOSTI (1887–1957)
Aboard Ship
Cantilena
Deserted Street
Evening Song
Finnish Humoresque: The Girl the
   Boys all Love
Finnish Sailor's Song: When the Wind
   Blows from the South
Four Liebeslieder
Little Finnish Folksong: The Little
   Shepherd Calls to his Herd
Pastorale
Pour l'amour
Thine Image
The White Horse

VERACINI, FRANCESCO MARIA
(1690–1768)
Pastoral

VILLA-LOBOS, HEITOR (1887–1959)
Nhapopé, from *Modinhas e Canções,*
   Album no. 1
Poema do Itabira
Redondilha, from *Serestas*

WAGNER, RICHARD (1813–1883)
Schmerzen, from *Wesendonk Lieder*
Träume, from *Wesendonk Lieder*

WARLOCK, PETER, PSEUD. (PHILIP HESEL-
TINE) (1894–1930)
Yarmouth Fair

Appendix 1: Repertory

WECKERLIN, JEAN-BAPTISTE-THÉODORE
(1821–1910)
L'amour est un enfant timide
L'amour s'envole
Berger et bergère
La chanson de Jean de Nivelle

WELDON, JOHN (1676–1736)
Prithee, Celia

WELLS, JOHN BARNES (1880–1935)
The Owl

WOLF, HUGO (1860–1903)
Anacreons Grab, from *Goethe Lieder*
Auch kleine Dinge, from *Italienisches Liederbuch*
Auf ein altes Bild, from *Mörike Lieder*
Er ist's, from *Mörike Lieder*
Fussreise, from *Mörike Lieder*
Gebet, from *Mörike Lieder*
Gesang Weylas, from *Mörike Lieder*
In dem Schatten meiner Locken, from *Spanisches Liederbuch*
Nachtzauber, from *Eichendorff Lieder*
Neue Liebe, from *Mörike Lieder*
Nun lass uns Frieden schliessen, from *Italienisches Liederbuch*
Das verlassene Mägdlein, from *Mörike Lieder*
Wer sein holdes Lieb verloren, from *Spanisches Liederbuch*
Zur Ruh, from *Sechs Gedichte*

WOLFF, ERICH (1874–1913)
Faden

WOODMAN, RAYMOND HUNTINGTON
(1861–1943)
Love's in my heart
Love's on a high road

WYBLE, JOHN MELVIN (dates unknown)
Aureole

ZIMBALIST, SAMUEL A. (1897–1956)
Folksong of Little Russia
O take me to your breathing heart

Operatic Roles

VERDI, GIUSEPPE (1813–1901)
Un Ballo in maschera: Ulrica

GLUCK, CHRISTOPH WILIBALD VON
(1714–1787)
Orfeo ed Euridice: Orfeo[4]

Operatic Arias

BANTOCK, GRANVILLE (1868–1946)
Sappho: Evening Song

BELLINI, VINCENZO (1801–1835)
Norma: Casta diva

BIZET, GEORGES (1838–1875)
Carmen: En vain pour éviter (Card Scene)

BONONCINI, GIOVANNI MARIA
(1670–1747)
Griselda: Per la gloria d'adorarvi
Astarto: Pietà, mio cara bene

CESTI, MARC' ANTONIO (1623–1669)
Orontea: Intorno all' idol mio

DEBUSSY, CLAUDE ACHILLE
(1862–1918)
L'Enfant prodigue: Azaël! Pourquoi m'as-tu quitté? (Air de Lia)

DONIZETTI, GAETANO (1797–1848)
La Favorita: O mio Fernando

GALUPPI, BALDASSARE (1706–1785)
Adriana in Siria: E ingrate, le reggie

GLUCK, CHRISTOPH WILIBALD VON
(1714–1787)
Alceste: Divinités du Styx
Armide: Chant de la Naïade
Paride ed Elena: O del mio dolce ardor
Seminamide Reconossciuta: Vieni, che poi sereno

348

Appendix 1: Repertory

GOUNOD, CHARLES FRANÇOIS (1818–1893)
Cinq Mars: Nuit resplendissante
La Reine de Saba: Plus grand dans son
obscurité

HALÉVY, JACQUES (1799–1862)
Charles VI: Humble fille des Champs

HANDEL, GEORG FRIDERIC (1685–1759)
Alcina: Verdi prati
Amadigi di Gaula: Ah! Spietato
Sento la gioia
Atalanta: Care selve
Ezio: Nasce al bosco
Il Floridante: The trumpet is calling (Un
ombra di pace)
Oh what pleasure (Vanne, segu'il mio
desio)
Giulio Cesare in Egitto: Empio dirò tu sei
Piangerò la sorte mia
Ottone, Re di Germania: Come to me,
soothing sleep (Io sperai trovar riposo)
Vieni o figlio!
Partenope: Furibondo, spira il vento
Radamisto: Sommi Dei
Rinaldo: Il Tricerbero humiliato
Scipione: Tutta raccolta ancor
Semele: O sleep, why dost thou leave
me?
Serse: Ombra mai fu
Speranze mie fermate
Siroe, re di Persia: Ch'io mai vi possa

HUMPERDINCK, ENGELBERT (1854–1921)
Hänsel und Gretel: Evening Prayer
(Abends will ich schlaffen gehn)

LEGRENZI, GIOVANNI (1626–1690)
Eteocle e Polinice: Che fiero costume

MASSENET, JULES (1842–1912)
Hériodiade: Ne me refuse pas
Le Cid: Pleurez, mes yeux
Werther: Va! laisse couler mes larmes

MEYERBEER, GIACOMO (1791–1864)
Le Prophète: Ah, mon fils
O prêtres de Baal

MONTEVERDI, CLAUDIO (1567–1643)
Il Lamento di Arianna (arr. Respighi)

MOZART, WOLFGANG AMADEUS
(1756–1791)
La Clemenza di Tito: Parto, parto
Le Nozze di Figaro: Dove sono

PICCINNI, NICCOLÒ (1728–1800)
Alessandro nelle Indie: Se il ciel mi divide

PONCHIELLI, AMILCARE (1834–1886)
La Gioconda: Suicidio

PURCELL, HENRY (1658 OR 1659–1695)
Dido and Aeneas: When I am laid in earth

RINALDO DI CAPUA (c. 1705–c. 1780)
Vologeso re de' Parti: Dal sen del care sposo

ROSSINI, GIOACCHINO (1792–1868)
Il barbiere di Siviglia: Una voce poco fa

ROSSI, LUIGI (1597–1653)
Mitrane: Ah' rendimi

SAINT-SAËNS, CHARLES CAMILLE
(1835–1921)
Samson et Dalila: Tonight seeking hither
my presence . . . O love, from thy
power (Samson, recherchant ma
présence . . . Amour! viens aider ma
faiblesse)
Softly awakes my heart (Mon coeur
s'ouvre à ta voix)

SCARLATTI, ALESSANDRO (1649–1725)
Digrone: Sento nel core

TCHAIKOVSKY, PIOTR ILYICH (1840–1893)
The Maid of Orleans: Adieu, forêts
The Queen of Spades: Dear friends, in
sportive lack of care (Podrugi milyye,
V bespechnosti igrivoi)

THOMAS, AMBROISE (1811–1896)
Mignon: Oh my heart is weary (Me voilà
seule, hélas!)

VERDI, GIUSEPPE (1813–1901)
Don Carlo: O Don fatale
La Forza del destino: Madre, pietosa
Vergine
Pace, pace mio Dio
Un Ballo in maschera: Re dell'abisso

WAGNER, RICHARD (1813–1883)
Rienzi: Gerechte Gott
Tannhäuser: Allmächt'ge Jungfrau

Negro Spirituals[5]

All God's Chillun Got Shoes (William
Grant Still)
At the Feet of Jesus (Hall Johnson)
The Awakening (J. Rosamond Johnson)
Behold That Star (Henry Thacker
Burleigh)
By an' By (Henry Thacker Burleigh)
Cert'ny Lord (Hall Johnson)
City Called Heaven (Hall Johnson)
Crucifixion (John C. Payne)
Deep River (Henry Thacker Burleigh)
Dere's No Hidin' Place Down Dere
(Lawrence Brown)
Didn't My Lord Deliver Daniel?
(Lawrence Brown)
Done Foun' My Los' Sheep (J. Rosamund
Johnson)
Don't You Weep When I'm Gone (Henry
Thacker Burleigh)
Early One Morning (William Tarrasch)
Everytime I Feel de Spirit (Lawrence
Brown)
Fix Me, Jesus (Hall Johnson)
Follow Me (Robert Nathaniel Dett)
Glory in-a Mah Soul (Raymond
McFeeters)
Go Down Moses (Henry Thacker
Burleigh)
Goin' to Ride up in de Chariot (Lawrence
Brown)
Gospel Train (Henry Thacker Burleigh)
Great Gittin' Up Mornin' (Lawrence
Brown)
Hard Trials (Henry Thacker Burleigh)

Hear de Lam's a-Cryin' (Lawrence
Brown)
Heav'n, Heav'n (Henry Thacker
Burleigh)
He's Got the Whole World in His Hands
(Hamilton Forrest)
Hold On! (Hall Johnson)
Honor, Honor (Hall Johnson)
Hush! Hush! Somebody's Calling My
Name (Edward Boatner)
I Am Bound for de Kingdom (Florence B.
Price)
I Been in de Storm So Long (Hall John-
son)
I Don't Feel Noways Tired (Henry
Thacker Burleigh)
If He Change My Name (Robert
MacGimsey)
I Got a Home in-a Dat Rock (Lawrence
Brown)
I Know the Lord Laid His Hands on Me
(Lawrence Brown)
I Stood on de Ribber ob Jerdon (Henry
Thacker Burleigh)
I'm a Poor Pilgrim
I'm Going to Tell God (Lawrence Brown)
I'm So Glad (Robert Nathaniel Dett)
I'm Troubled in Mind (Will Marion Cook)
I Want Jesus to Walk with Me (Edward
Boatner)
I Was There When They Crucified My
Lord (Robert MacGimsey)
Jesus Walked This Lonesome Valley
(William L. Dawson)
Joshua Fit de Battle ob Jericho (Lawrence
Brown)
Lead Me to de Watah (William Lawrence)
Le's Have a Union (Hall Johnson)
Let Us Break Bread Together (William
Lawrence)
Little David, Play on Your Harp (Henry
Thacker Burleigh)
Lord, I Can't Stay Away (Roland Hayes)
My Good Lord Done Been Here (Hall
Johnson)
My Lord, What a Mornin' (Henry
Thacker Burleigh)

Appendix 1: Repertory

My Soul's Been Anchored in de Lord (Florence B. Price)
My Way's Cloudy (Henry Thacker Burleigh)
New Born Again
Nobody Knows the Trouble I See (Lawrence Brown)
Nobody Knows the Trouble I See (J. Rosamund Johnson)
O What a Beautiful City! (Edward Boatner)
O Zion Hallelujah (Robert Nathaniel Dett)
Oh, Didn't It Rain? (Henry Thacker Burleigh)
Oh, Glory! (Hall Johnson)
Oh, Lord, Have Mercy on Me (Edward Boatner)
Oh Peter Go Ring-a Dem Bells (Henry Thacker Burleigh)
Oh Rock Me Julie (Henry Thacker Burleigh)
Oh, The Land I Am Bound For (Robert Nathaniel Dett)
Oh, Wasn't Dat a Wide Ribber? (Henry Thacker Burleigh)
On Ma Journey (Edward Boatner)
Plenty Good Room (Edward Boatner)
Poor Me (Robert Nathaniel Dett)
Poor Mourner's Got a Home at Last (Gustav Klemm)
Ride On, King Jesus! (Henry Thacker Burleigh)
Rise and Shine (Edward Boatner)
Roll, Jord'n Roll! (Hall Johnson)
Scandalize My Name (Henry Thacker Burleigh)
Sinner Please Doan Let Dis Harves' Pass (Henry Thacker Burleigh)
Some for Paul and Some for Silas (Edward Boatner)
Somebody's Knocking at Your Door (Robert Nathaniel Dett)
Sometimes I Feel Like a Motherless Child (Lawrence Brown)
Soon-a Will Be Done (Edward Boatner)
Spirit o the Lord (Eva Alberta Jessye)

Steal Away (Henry Thacker Burleigh)
Swing Low, Sweet Chariot (Henry Thacker Burleigh)
Talk About a Child (William L. Dawson)
Trampin' (Edward Boatner)
Tryin' to Make Heaven My Home
Wade in de Water (Edward Boatner)
Wake Up, Jacob! (Clarence C. White)
Wash Me, O Lord! (Donald Tweedy)
Watercarrier (Avery Robinson)
Way Up in Heaven (Hall Johnson)
Weepin' Mary (Henry Thacker Burleigh)
Were You There? (Henry Thacker Burleigh)
Where Does the Road Lead? (Delmar Molarsky)
Who is Dat Yondah? (Henry Thacker Burleigh)

Folk Song Arrangements[6]

Ack värmeland (Josef Jonsson)
All through the night
Allt under himmelens fäste (Josef Jonsson)
L'angélus
The Ash Grove (Benjamin Britten)
Barbara Allen (Roger Quilter)
Bergerette (Kosti Vehanen)
Coming through the Rye
Danny Boy (Fred E. Weatherly)
Det gingo två flickor (Karl Ekman)
The Dusty Miller (Herman Hans Wetzler)
Early One Morning (William Tarrasch)
Eli, Eli
Eppie MacNab (Herman Hans Wetzler)
Glädjens blomster (Josef Jonsson)
Home, Sweet Home
Kristallen den fina (Josef Jonsson)
Läksin minä kesäyönä käymään (Selim Palmgren)
Little David (Hall Johnson)
Nuit d'été (Selim Palmgren)
O Waly, Waly (Benjamin Britten)
Oliver Cromwell (Benjamin Britten)

Appendix 1: Repertory

Over the Mountains (Roger Quilter)
Paka, paka
Perché non duorme
The Plough Boy (Benjamin Britten)
Quando jurse la nuvella
The Sally Gardens (Benjamin Britten)
Sweet Nightingale (Franz Rupp)
The Truth About a Child (William L. Dawson)
Tuku-tuku lampaitani (Kosti Vehanen)

Uti vaar hage (Josef Jonsson)
When Love Is Kind

Works with Narrator

COPLAND, AARON (1900–1990)
A Lincoln Portrait
Preamble for a Solemn Occasion

STARER, ROBERT (B. 1924)
Joseph and His Brothers

Appendix 2: Discography

Part 1: Commercial Recordings

For each entry, the recording date, place, and matrix number are indicated immediately following the title and composer or arranger.

When known, the take number appears immediately after the matrix number, separated by a hyphen.

Example: B-29072-2 = matrix B-29072, take 2.

Catalog numbers are listed by format: 78, 45, LP, or CD. For 78 or 45 sets, the catalog number of the set is given first, followed in parentheses by the catalog number of the specific record in the set which contains the particular selection listed.

Example: M-882-1 (18507-A) = 78 set M-882-1, 78 number 18507 (= part of the set M-882-1), side A.

Unless otherwise noted, accompanist is Kosti Vehanen, piano, 1935–1940; Franz Rupp, piano, 1941–1966.

I. Victor Talking Machine—Acoustical 78s, 1923-24

Deep River (arr. Burleigh)
12/10/23 (Camden, New Jersey)
  B-29072-2
with orchestra, cond. by Rosario Bourdon
78: 19227-A

My Way's Cloudy (arr. Burleigh)
12/10/23 (Camden, New Jersey) B-
  29073-3
with orchestra, cond. by Rosario Bourdon
78: 19227-B

My Lord What a Mornin' (arr. Burleigh)
3/24/24 (Camden, New Jersey) B-29689
with orchestra, cond. by Rosario Bourdon
unissued

Heav'n, Heav'n (arr. Burleigh)
3/24/24 (Camden, New Jersey) B-29690
with orchestra, cond. by Rosario Bourdon
unissued

Go Down Moses (arr. Burleigh)
3/24/24 (Camden, New Jersey) B-29691

with orchestra, cond. by Rosario Bourdon
unissued

Heav'n, Heav'n (arr. Burleigh)
4/18/24 (Camden, New Jersey) B-29895
with orchestra, cond. by Rosario Bourdon
unissued

Go Down Moses (arr. Burleigh)
4/18/24 (Camden, New Jersey) B-29896
with orchestra, cond. by Rosario Bourdon
unissued

Go Down Moses (arr. Burleigh)
5/20/24 (Camden, New Jersey) B-29896
with orchestra, cond. by Mr. Prince
unissued

Heav'n, Heav'n (arr. Burleigh)
5/20/24 (Camden, New Jersey)
  B-29895-5
with orchestra, cond. by Mr. Prince
78: 19370-B
CD: Eklipse EKR CD 26

Go Down Moses (arr. Burleigh)
5/29/24 (Camden, New Jersey) B-29896-9

with orchestra, cond. by Mr. Prince
78: 19370-A
CD: Eklipse EKR CD 26; RCA CD 7911-2-RG

Nobody Knows the Trouble I See (arr. Brown)
11/21/24 (Camden, New Jersey) B-31346
with orchestra, cond. by Josef Pasternack
unissued

My Lord, What a Mornin' (arr. Burleigh)
11/21/24 (Camden, New Jersey) B-31347
with orchestra, cond. by Josef Pasternack
unissued

My Lord, What a Mornin' (arr. Burleigh)
12/12/24 (Camden, New Jersey) B-31347
with orchestra, cond. by Josef Pasternack
unissued

Nobody Knows the Trouble I See (arr. Brown)
12/12/24 (Camden, New Jersey) B-31346
with orchestra, cond. by Josef Pasternack
unissued

My Lord, What a Mornin' (arr. Burleigh)
12/23/24 (Camden, New Jersey)
B-31347-10
with orchestra, cond. by Josef Pasternack
78: 19560-B
CD: Eklipse EKR CD 26

Nobody Knows the Trouble I See (arr. Brown)
12/30/24 (Camden, New Jersey)
B-31346-12
with orchestra, cond. by Josef Pasternack
78: 19560-A
CD: Eklipse EKR CD 26

II. HMV—1928, 1930 Electrical 78s

Deep River (arr. Burleigh)
8/28/28 ("C" Studio, Small Queen's Hall) BB-14284
with Lawrence Brown
78: B-2828-A; Victor 22015-A

CD: Magnum Music MCCD 017; Pearl GEMM CD 9318

Heav'n Heav'n (arr. Quilter)
8/28/28 ("C" Studio, Small Queen's Hall) BB-14285
with Lawrence Brown
78: B-2828-B; Victor 22015-B
CD: Pearl GEMM CD 9318

Tonight seeking hither my presence . . . O love, from thy power (Samson, recherchant ma présence . . . Amour! viens aider ma faiblesse), from *Samson et Dalila* (Saint-Saëns)
9/17/28 ("C" Studio, Small Queen's Hall) CC-14363
with orchestra, cond. by L. Collingwood
unissued

O Don fatale, from *Don Carlo* (Verdi)
9/17/28 ("C" Studio, Small Queen's Hall) CC-14364
with orchestra, cond. by L. Collingwood
unissued

Tonight seeking hither my presence . . . O love, from thy power (Samson, recherchant ma présence . . . Amour! viens aider ma faiblesse), from *Samson et Dalila* (Saint-Saëns)
9/4/30 (Kingsway Hall) CC-14363
with orchestra, cond. by L. Collingwood
78: C-2047; Victor 18008
CD: Eklipse EKR CD 26; Memoir Classics CDMOIR 432; Pearl GEMM CD 9318

Softly awakes my heart (Mon coeur s'ouvre à ta voix), from *Samson et Dalila* (Saint-Saëns)
9/4/30 (Kingsway Hall) CC-19717
with orchestra, cond. by L. Collingwood
78: C-2047; Victor 18008
CD: Eklipse EKR CD 26; Fanfare CDD3447; Magnum Music MCCD 017; Memoir Classics CDMOIR 432; Pearl GEMM CD 9318

Appendix 2: Discography

O Don fatale, from *Don Carlo* (Verdi)
9/4/30 (Kingsway Hall) CC-14364
with orchestra, cond. by L. Collingwood
78: C-2065
CD: Fanfare CDD3447; Memoir Classics
  CDMOIR 432; Pearl GEMM CD 9318

Plaisir d'amour (Martini)
9/11/30 (Kingsway Hall) CC-19724
with orchestra, cond. by L. Collingwood
78: C-2065
CD: Fanfare CDD3447; Flapper PAST
  CD 7073; Magnum Music MCCD 017;
  Memoir Classics CDMOIR 432; Pearl
  GEMM CD 9318

Caro mio bien (Giordani)
9/11/30 (Kingsway Hall) CC-19725
with orchestra, cond. by L. Collingwood
78: C-2066
CD: Flapper PAST CD 7073; Memoir
  Classics CDMOIR 432; Pearl GEMM
  CD 9318

He was despised, from *Messiah* (Handel)
9/11/30 (Kingsway Hall) CC-19726
with orchestra, cond. by L. Collingwood
78: C-2066
CD: Pearl GEMM CD 9318

Trampin' (arr. Boatner)
9/15/30 ("C" Studio, Small Queen's Hall)
  BB-20204
78: B-4253-A
CD: Pearl GEMM CD 9318

Oh, Wasn't Dat a Wide Ribber? (arr.
  Burleigh)
9/15/30 ("C" Studio, Small Queen's Hall)
  BB-20205
78: B-4253-B
CD: Flapper PAST CD 7073; Pearl
  GEMM CD 9318

III. Artiphon—1930[1]

Heav'n, Heav'n (arr. Burleigh)
with William King, piano
78: D-11749
CD: Flapper PAST CD 7073

Sometimes I Feel Like a Motherless Child
  (arr. Brown)
with William King, piano
78: D-11750
CD: Flapper PAST CD 7073

Azaël! Pourquoi m'as-tu quitté?, from
  L'Enfant prodigue (Debussy)
with orchestra
78: D-11767
CD: Magnum Music MCCD 017

Adieu, forêts, from *Jeanne D'Arc*
  (Tchaikovsky)
with orchestra
78: D-11768
CD: Magnum Music MCCD 017; Pearl
  GEMM CD 9405

O mio Fernando, from *La Favorita*
  (Donizetti)
with orchestra
78: D-11769/70
CD: Magnum Music MCCD 017; Pearl
  GEMM CD 9405

Tonight seeking hither my presence . . . O
  love, from thy power (Samson, recherchant ma présence . . . Amour! viens
  aider ma faiblesse), from *Samson et
  Dalila* (Saint-Saëns)
with orchestra
78: D-11771
CD: Pearl GEMM CD 9405

*IV. Gramplastrest (Soviet Grammophone
  Company)—1935[2]*

The Cuckoo (Lehmann)
5/23/35 (October Hall, Moscow)

Summer (L'été) (Chaminade)
5/23/35 (October Hall, Moscow)

Watercarrier (arr. Robinson)
5/23/35? (October Hall, Moscow)

Trampin' (arr. Boatner)
5/23/35? (October Hall, Moscow)

Appendix 2: Discography

V. HMV—1935–1937

Ave Maria (Ellens Gesang III) (Schubert)
10/29/35 (Copenhagen) 2CS.224
unissued

Die Allmacht (Schubert)
10/29/35 (Copenhagen) 2CS.225
unissued

The Cuckoo (Lehmann)
10/29/35 (Copenhagen) 0CS.226
unissued

Tuku-tuku lampaitani (arr. Vehanen)
10/29/35 (Copenhagen) 0CS.226
unissued

Flickan kom ifrån sin älsklings möte, Op.
  37/5 (Sibelius)
10/29/35 (Copenhagen) 0CS.227
unissued

Dignare domine (Vouchsafe, O Lord),
  from *Te Deum for the Victims of Dettingen*
  (Handel)
4/4/36 (Studio Albert, Paris) 0LA.1015-2
78: DA-1480; Victor 1767
CD:Eklipse EKR CD 26; Memoir Classics CDMOIR 432; Nimbus NI 7895;
  Pearl GEMM CD 9318

Lass mich wandern (Let me wander not
  unseen) (Siciliana), from *L'Allegro, il
  Penseroso ed il Moderato* (Handel)
4/4/36 (Studio Albert, Paris) 0LA.1016
unissued

Die Mainacht, Op. 43/2 (Brahms)
4/4/36 (Studio Albert, Paris) 2LA.1017-1
78: DB-2951; Victor 14610
CD: Memoir Classics CDMOIR 432;
  Nimbus NI 7895; Pearl GEMM CD
  9318

Der Nussbaum, from *Myrthen,* Op. 25
  (Schumann)
4/4/36 (Studio Albert, Paris) 2LA.1018
unissued

Der Tod und das Mädchen (Schubert)
4/7/36 (Studio Albert, Paris) 0LA.1025
unissued

Die Forelle (Schubert)
4/7/36 (Studio Albert, Paris) 0LA.1026
unissued

Come away, death (Kom nu hit, död), Op.
  60/1 (Sibelius)
4/7/36 (Studio Albert, Paris) 0LA.1027
unissued

Finnish Folksongs
  1. Läksin minä kesäyönä käymään (arr.
     Palmgren)
  2. Tuku-tuku lampaitani (arr. Vehanen)
4/7/36 (Studio Albert, Paris) 0LA.1028-1
78: DA-1523; Victor 1809
CD: Memoir Classics CDMOIR 432;
  Nimbus NI 7895; Pearl GEMM CD
  9318

Ch'io mai vi possa, from *Siroe, re di Persia*
  (Handel)
4/7/36 (Studio Albert, Paris) 0LA.1029-1
78: DA-1480; Victor 1767
CD: Eklipse EKR CD 26; Memoir Classics CDMOIR 432; Nimbus NI 7895;
  Pearl GEMM CD 9318

Aus banger Brust, Op. 50/4 (Sibelius)
6/29/36 (Studio Albert, Paris) 0LA.1153-1
78: DA-1580-A; Victor 2146-A
CD: Nimbus NI 7895; Pearl GEMM CD
  9405

Im Feld ein Mädchen singt, Op. 50/3
  (Sibelius)
6/29/36 (Studio Albert, Paris) 0LA.1154
originally unissued
CD: VAI Audio VAIA 1168 (take 1)

Die stille Stadt, Op. 50/5 (Sibelius)
6/29/36 (Studio Albert, Paris) 0LA.1155
unissued

Långsamt som kvällskyn, Op. 61/1
  (Sibelius)

6/29/36 (Studio Albert, Paris) 0LA.1156-1
78: DA-1580-B; Victor 2146-B
CD: Nimbus NI 7895; Pearl GEMM CD 9405

Komm' süsser Tod, BWV 478, from *Die
geistlichen Lieder und Arien* (Bach)
6/30/36 (Studio Albert, Paris) 0LA.1161-1
78: DA-1529; Victor 1939
CD: Eklipse EKR CD 26; Nimbus NI
7895; Pearl GEMM CD 9318

Come away, death (Kom nu hit, död), Op.
60/1 (Sibelius)
6/30/36 (Studio Albert, Paris) 0LA.1027-3
78: DA-1523; Victor 1809
CD: Nimbus NI 7895; Pearl GEMM CD
9405

Der Tod und das Mädchen (Schubert)
6/30/36 (Studio Albert, Paris) 0LA.1025
unissued

En slända, Op. 17/5 (Sibelius)
7/3/36 (Studio Albert, Paris) 2LA.1164
unissued

Der Nussbaum, from *Myrthen,* Op. 25
(Schumann)
7/3/36 (Studio Albert, Paris) 2LA.1018-3
78: DB-2951; Victor 14610
CD: Fanfare CDD3447; Memoir Classics
CDMOIR 432; Nimbus NI 7895; Pearl
GEMM CD 9318

Lass mich wandern (Let me wander not
unseen) (Siciliana), from *L'Allegro, il
Penseroso ed il Moderato* (Handel)
7/3/36 (Studio Albert, Paris) 0LA.1016-2
78: DA-1529; Victor 1939
CD: Eklipse EKR CD 26; Nimbus NI
7895; Pearl GEMM CD 9318

De begga rosorna, Op. 88/2 (Sibelius)
7/3/36 (Studio Albert, Paris) 2LA.1165
unissued

Var det en dröm?, Op. 37/4 (Sibelius)
7/3/36 (Studio Albert, Paris) 2LA.1165

originally unissued
CD: VAI Audio VAIA 1168 (take 1)

Aufenthalt, from *Schwanengesang* (Schubert)
7/7/36 (Studio Albert, Paris) 2LA.1182
78: DB-3025; Victor 14210
CD: Eklipse EKR CD 26

Ave Maria (Ellens Gesang III) (Schubert)
7/7/36 (Studio Albert, Paris) 2LA.1183-1
78: DB-3025; Victor 14210
CD: Eklipse EKR CD 26; Memoir Clas
sics CDMOIR 432; Nimbus NI 7895;
Pearl GEMM CD 9318

Der Tod und das Mädchen (Schubert)
11/13/36 (Studio Albert, Paris) 0LA.1025-
6
78: DA-1025; DA-1550; Victor 1862
CD: Eklipse EKR CD 26; Memoir Clas
sics CDMOIR 432; Pearl GEMM CD
9318

Die Forelle (Schubert)
11/13/36 (Studio Albert, Paris)
OLA.1026-1
78: DA-1550; Victor 1862
CD: Eklipse EKR CD 26; Fanfare
CDD3447; Memoir Classics CDMOIR
432; Nimbus NI 7895; Pearl GEMM
CD 9318

Sometimes I Feel Like a Motherless Child
(arr. Brown)
11/2/37 (Studio Albert, Paris) 0LA.2187-1
78: DA-1597; Victor 1982
CD: Fanfare CDD3447; Magnum Music
MCCD 017; Nimbus NI 7882

Dere's No Hidin' Place Down Dere (arr.
Brown)
11/2/37 (Studio Albert, Paris) 0LA.2190-1
78: DA-1597; Victor 2032
CD: Fanfare CDD3447

Everytime I Feel de Spirit (arr. Brown)
11/2/37 (Studio Albert, Paris) 0LA.2190-1

78: DA-1597; Victor 2032
CD: Fanfare CDD3447

Lord, I Can't Stay Away (arr. Hayes)
11/2/37 (Studio Albert, Paris) 0LA.2188-1
78: DA-1670; Victor 1966

Trampin' (arr. Boatner)
11/2/37 (Studio Albert, Paris) 0LA.2302-1
78: DA-1669; Victor 1896
CD: Eklipse EKR CD 26; Flapper PAST
CD 7073; Nimbus NI 7882

Were You There? (arr. Burleigh)
12/16/37 (Studio Albert, Paris) 0LA.2189-1
78: DA-1670; Victor 1966
CD: Flapper PAST CD 7073; Nimbus NI
7882

I Know the Lord Laid His Hands on Me
(arr. Brown)
12/16/37 (Studio Albert, Paris) 0LA.2303-1
78: DA-1669; Victor 1896
CD: Eklipse EKR CD 26; Flapper PAST
CD 7073

Deep River (arr. Burleigh)
11/38 (Studio Albert, Paris) OLA.2829-1
78: DA-1676; Victor 2032
CD: Nimbus NI 7882

I Don't Feel Noways Tired (arr. Burleigh)
11/38 (Studio Albert, Paris) OLA.2830-1
78: DA-1676; Victor 1982
CD: Nimbus NI 7882

VI. RCA Victor—1936–1966

City Called Heaven (arr. Johnson)
1/14/36 (New York Studio No. 3) CS-
98636-1
78: 8958-A
CD: Eklipse EKR CD 26; Flapper PAST
CD 7073; Nimbus NI 7882; RCA
09026-63306-2

Lord, I Can't Stay Away (arr. Hayes)
1/14/36 (New York Studio No. 3) CS-
98637-1

78: 8958-B
CD: Eklipse EKR CD 26; Fanfare
CDD3447; Flapper PAST CD 7073;
Memoir Classics CDMOIR 432; Nim-
bus NI 7882; RCA 09026-63306-2

Heavn', Heavn' (arr. Burleigh)
1/14/36 (New York Studio No. 3) CS-
98637-1
78: 8958-B
CD: Eklipse EKR CD 26; Fanfare
CDD3447; Memoir Classics CDMOIR
432; Nimbus NI 7882; RCA 09026-
63306-2

Ave Maria (Ellens Gesang III) (Schubert)
1/14/36 (New York Studio No. 3) CS-
98638
unissued

Aufenthalt, from *Schwanengesang* (Schubert)
1/14/36 (New York Studio No. 3) CS-
98639-1
78: 14210-B
CD: Nimbus NI 7895; Pearl GEMM CD
9318

Ave Maria (Ellens Gesang III) (Schubert)
2/4/36 (New York Studio No. 3) CS-
98638-2
78: 14210-A
CD: Fanfare CDD3447; Magnum Music
MCCD 017; RCA CD 7911-2-RG

Go Down Moses (arr. Burleigh)
2/4/36 (New York Studio No. 3) CS-
99537-2
78: 1799-A
CD: Fanfare CDD3447; Flapper PAST
CD 7073; Memoir Classics CDMOIR
432; Nimbus NI 7882; Pearl GEMM
CD 9405

My Soul's Been Anchored in de Lord (arr.
Price)
2/4/36 (New York Studio No. 3) CS-
99538-2

78: 1799-B
CD: Flapper PAST CD 7073; Nimbus NI 7882; Pearl GEMM CD 9405

Säv, säv, susa, Op. 36/4 (Sibelius)
2/5/36 (New York Studio No. 3) BS-99539-2
78: 1766-A
CD: Nimbus NI 7895; Pearl GEMM CD 9405

Flickan kom ifrån sin älsklings möte, Op. 37/5 (Sibelius)
2/5/36 (New York Studio No. 3) BS-99540-2
78: 1766-B
CD: Memoir Classics CDMOIR 432; Nimbus NI 7895; Pearl GEMM CD 9405

Crucifixion (arr. Payne)
6/1/38 (New York Studio No. 3) CS-023462
unissued

Oh Rock Me Julie (Burleigh)
6/1/38 (New York Studio No. 3) CS-023463
unissued

I Don't Feel Noways Tired (Burleigh)
6/1/38 (New York Studio No. 3) CS-023463
unissued

Frühlingstraum, from *Winterreise* (Schubert)
6/1/38 (New York Studio No. 3) CS-023464
unissued

Der Doppelgänger, from *Schwanengesang* (Schubert)
6/1/38 (New York Studio No. 3) CS-023465
unissued

Alto Rhapsody, Op. 53 (Brahms)
1/8/39 (Academy of Music, Philadelphia)

with the Philadelphia Orchestra and the University of Pennsylvania Men's Glee Club, cond. by Eugene Ormandy
Part 1; CS-030914-3
78: 15408-A
CD: Biddulph LAB 150; Fanfare CDD3447; Pearl GEMM CD 9405
Part 2; CS-030915-1
78: 15408-B
CD: Biddulph LAB 150; Fanfare CDD3447; Pearl GEMM CD 9405
Part 3; CS-030916-1
78: 1919-A
CD: Biddulph LAB 150; Fanfare CDD3447; Pearl GEMM CD 9405
Part 4; CS-030917-2
78: 1919-B
CD: Biddulph LAB 150; Fanfare CDD3447; Pearl GEMM CD 9405

Dein blaues Auge hält so still, Op. 59/8 (Brahms)
1/8/39 (Academy of Music, Philadelphia) CS-030918-1
with the Philadelphia Orchestra, cond. by Eugene Ormandy
78: 15409-A
LP: LM-2712
CD: Biddulph LAB 150; Memoir Classics CDMOIR 432; Pearl GEMM CD 9405

Der Schmied, Op. 19/4 (Brahms)
1/8/39 (Academy of Music, Philadelphia) CS-030918-1
with the Philadelphia Orchestra, cond. by Eugene Ormandy
78: 15409-A
LP: LM-2712
CD: Biddulph LAB 150; Memoir Classics CDMOIR 432; Pearl GEMM CD 9405

Immer leiser wird mein Schlummer, Op. 105/2 (Brahms)
1/8/39 (Academy of Music, Philadelphia) CS-030919-9
with the Philadelphia Orchestra, cond. by Eugene Ormandy
78: 15409-B

LP: LM-2712
CD: Biddulph LAB 150; Memoir Classics
CDMOIR 432; Pearl GEMM CD 9405;
RCA CD 7911-2-RG (take 1)

Von ewiger Liebe, Op. 43/1 (Brahms)
1/8/39 (Academy of Music, Philadelphia)
with the Philadelphia Orchestra, cond. by
Eugene Ormandy
Part 1; CS-030920
unissued
Part 2; CS-030921.
unissued

When I am laid in Earth, from *Dido and
Aeneas* (Purcell)
6/26/39 (New York Studio No. 3) CS-
037760-1
78: 17257-A
CD: Pearl GEMM CD 9069; VAI Audio
VAIA 1168

Se Florindo è fedele (Scarlatti)
6/26/39 (New York Studio No. 3) CS-
037761-2
78: 17257-B
CD: Nimbus NI 7895; Pearl GEMM CD
9069; VAI Audio VAIA 1168

Die Flöte weich gefühl (The soft complaining flute), from *Ode for Saint
Cecilia's Day* (Handel)
6/26/39 (New York Studio No. 3) BS-
037762
originally unissued
CD: VAI Audio VAIA 1168 (take 1)

Begrüssung (Tears such as tender fathers
shed), from *Deborah* (Handel)
6/26/39 (New York Studio No. 3) BS-
037763
originally unissued
CD: VAI Audio VAIA 1168 (take 2)

Sinner Please Doan Let Dis Harves' Pass
(arr. Burleigh)
6/26/39 (New York Studio No. 3) BS-
037764

originally unissued
CD: VAI Audio VAIA 1168 (take 1)

Honor, Honor (arr. Johnson)
6/26/39 (New York Studio No. 3) BS-
037764
originally unissued
CD: VAI Audio VAIA 1168 (take 1)

Were You There? (arr. Burleigh)
6/27/39 (New York Studio No. 3) BS-
037766
unissued

Agnus Dei, from *L'Arlésienne* (Bizet)
6/27/39 (New York Studio No. 3) BS-
037767
unissued

Deserted Street (Vehanen)
6/27/39 (New York Studio No. 3) BS-
037768
unissued

Mr. President and Mrs. Roosevelt
3/27/40 (New York Studio No. 3) BS-
048618-1
unissued; private issue 10770-A

Your Majesties
3/27/40 (New York Studio No. 3) BS-
048619-1
unissued; private issue 10770-A

Two Songs for Alto, Viola, and Piano, Op.
91 (Brahms)
6/30/41 (New York Lotos Club, 6th
Floor)
with William Primrose, viola, and Franz
Rupp, piano

1. Gestillte Sehnsucht
Part 1; CS-066342-4
78: DM-18509-A; M-882-1 (18507-A)
LP: LM-2712
CD: Biddulph LAB 150; Pearl GEMM
CD 9069
Part 2; CS-066343-3
78: DM-18510-A; M-882-2 (18507-B)

LP: LM-2712
CD: Biddulph LAB 150; Pearl GEMM
CD 9069

2. Geistliches Wiegenlied
Part 1; CS-066344-3
78: DM-18510-B; M-882-3 (18508-A)
LP: LM-2712
CD: Biddulph LAB 150; Pearl GEMM
CD 9069
Part 2; CS-066345-3
78: DM-18509-B; M-882-4 (18508-B)
LP: LM-2712
CD: Biddulph LAB 150; Pearl GEMM
CD 9069

In the silence of the secret night, Op. 4/3
(Rachmaninoff)
7/1/41 (New York Lotos Club, 6th Floor)
CS-066351-2
with William Primrose, viola, and Franz
Rupp, piano
78: 10-1122-B
CD: Nimbus NI 7895; Pearl GEMM CD
9069; RCA CD 7911-2-RG; VAI Audio
VAIA 1168

Elégie (Massenet)
7/1/41 (New York Lotos Club, 6th Floor)
CS-066352-2
with William Primrose, viola, and Franz
Rupp, piano
78: 10-1122-A
CD: Pearl GEMM CD 9069; VAI Audio
VAIA 1168

Crucifixion (arr. Payne)
7/1/41 (New York Lotos Club, 6th Floor)
CS-066353
originally unissued
CD: RCA CD 7911-2-RG (take 2)

O What a Beautiful City! (arr. Boatner)
7/1/41 (New York Lotos Club, 6th Floor)
CS-066354-1
78: 10-1040-B
CD: Eklipse EKR CD 26; Fanfare
CDD3447; Flapper PAST CD 7073;
Magnum Music MCCD 017; Memoir

Classics CDMOIR 432; Nimbus NI
7882

Sind es Schmerzen, sind es Freuden, from
Die Schöne Magelone, Op. 33/3 (Brahms)
7/2/41 (New York Lotos Club, 6th Floor)
CS-066364
unissued

Die Schnur, die Perl an Perle, Op. 57/7
(Brahms)
7/2/41 (New York Lotos Club, 6th Floor)
CS-066365
LP: LM-2712
CD: Nimbus NI 7895

Die Forelle (Schubert)
7/2/41 (New York Lotos Club, 6th floor)
CS-066366
originally unissued
CD: VAI Audio VAIA 1168 (take 3)

Der Doppelgänger, from *Schwanengesang*
(Schubert)
7/2/41 (New York Lotos Club, 6th Floor)
CS-066367
unissued

Der Jüngling und der Tod (Schubert)
7/2/41 (New York Lotos Club, 6th Floor)
CS-066368
unissued

Auf dem Wasser zu singen (Schubert)
7/2/41 (New York Lotos Club, 6th Floor)
CS-066369
unissued

Trampin' (arr. Boatner)
7/3/41 (New York Lotos Club, 6th Floor)
CS-066376
originally unissued
CD: RCA 09026-63306-2 (take 1); VAI
Audio VAIA 1168 (take 2)

My Soul's Been Anchored in de Lord (arr.
Price)
7/3/41 (New York Lotos Club, 6th Floor)
CS-066377-2

78: 10-1124-A
CD: RCA 09026-63306-2; VAI Audio
  VAIA 1168

Let Us Break Bread Together (arr.
  Lawrence)
7/3/41 (New York Lotos Club, 6th Floor)
  CS-066378
originally unissued
CD: VAI Audio VAIA 1168 (take 3)

Der Tod und das Mädchen (Schubert)
9/8/41 (New York Lotos Club, 6th Floor)
  BS-066755
unissued

Let Us Break Bread Together (arr.
  Lawrence)
9/8/41 (New York Lotos Club, 6th Floor)
  CS-066378-1
78: 10-1040-A
CD: Eklipse EKR CD 26; Flapper PAST
  CD 7073; Magnum Music MCCD 017

Poor Me (arr. Dett)
9/8/41 (New York Lotos Club, 6th Floor)
  BS-066754
unissued

Coming through the Rye
9/9/41 (New York Lotos Club, 6th Floor)
  BS-066756-2
78: 10-1125-A

Will o' the wisp (Spross)
9/9/41 (New York Lotos Club, 6th Floor)
  BS-066757-3
78: 10-1123-B
CD: VAI Audio VAIA 1168

The Cuckoo (Lehmann)
9/9/41 (New York Lotos Club, 6th Floor)
  BS-066758-3
78: 10-1125-B
CD: VAI Audio VAIA 1168

Hard Trials (arr. Burleigh)
9/9/41 (New York Lotos Club, 6th Floor)

BS-066759-2
78: 10-1124-B
CD: Flapper PAST CD 7073; RCA
  09026-63306-2

Dere's No Hidin' Place Down Dere (arr.
  Brown)
9/9/41 (New York Lotos Club, 6th Floor)
  BS-066759-2
78: 10-1124-B
CD: Flapper PAST CD 7073; RCA
  09026-63306-2

Der Tod und das Mädchen (Schubert)
9/9/41 (New York Lotos Club, 6th Floor)
  BS-066755
unissued

Great Songs of Faith
9/24-9/25/41 (Academy of Music,
  Philadelphia)
with the Victor Symphony Orchestra,
  cond. by C. O'Connell

O rest in the Lord, from *Elijah,* Op. 70
  (Mendelssohn)
9/24/41; CS-071000-2
78: M-850 (18325-B)
45: WCT-1111 (449-0042-B)
LP: LCT-1111-B
CD: Eklipse EKR CD 26; Pearl GEMM
  CD 9069

But the Lord is mindful of His own,
  from *St. Paul,* Op. 36 (Mendelssohn)
9/24/41; CS-071001-2
78: M-850 (18325-A)
45: WCT-1111 (449-0044-B)
LP: LCT-1111-B
CD: Eklipse EKR CD 26; Pearl GEMM
  CD 9069

He shall feed His flock, from *Messiah*
  (Handel)
9/24/41; CS-071002-1
78: M-850 (18324-A)
45: WCT-1111 (449-0044-B)
LP: LCT-1111-B

CD: Nimbus NI 7882; Pearl GEMM
CD 9069; RCA CD 7911-2-RG

Es ist vollbracht, from *St. John Passion,*
BWV 245 (Bach)
9/25/41
Part 1; CS-071003-3
78: M-850 (18326-A)
45: WCT-1111 (449-0041-A)
LP: LCT-1111-B
CD: Nimbus NI 7882; Pearl GEMM
CD 9069
Part 2; CS-071004-3
78: M-850 (18326-B)
45: WCT-1111 (449-0041-B)
LP: LCT-1111-B
CD: Nimbus NI 7882; Pearl GEMM
CD 9069

He was despised, from *Messiah* (Handel)
9/25/4; CS-071007-3
78: M-850 (18324-B)
45: WCT-1111 (449-0043-B)
LP: LCT-1111-B
CD: Pearl GEMM CD 9069

Carry me back to old Virginny (Bland)
9/25/41 (Academy of Music, Philadelphia)
CS-071005-1
with the Victor Symphony Orchestra,
cond. by C. O'Connell
78: 18314-A
45: 49-0555-A
CD: Fanfare CDD3447; Flapper PAST
CD 7073; Magnum Music MCCD 017

My Old Kentucky Home (Foster)
9/25/41 (Academy of Music, Philadelphia)
CS-071006-1
with the Victor Symphony Orchestra,
cond. by C. O'Connell
78: 18314-B
45: 49-0555-B
CD: Fanfare CDD3447; Flapper PAST
CD 7073; Magnum Music MCCD 017

Sometimes I Feel Like a Motherless Child
(arr. Brown)

12/13/44 (New York Studio No. 2) D4-
RB-507
unissued

O men from the fields (Thomas)
12/13/44 (New York Studio No. 2) D4-
RB-508
unissued

Der Tod und das Mädchen (Schubert)
12/13/44 (New York Studio No. 2) D4-
RB-509
unissued

Alto Rhapsody, Op. 53 (Brahms)
3/3/45 (San Francisco War Memorial
Opera House)
with the San Francisco Symphony and the
Municipal Chorus of San Francisco,
cond. by Pierre Monteux
78: M-1111 (Part 1: D5-RC-1056-2; Part
2: D5-RC-1057-4; Part 3: D5-RC-
1058-5; Part 4: D5-RC-1059-1)
CD: RCA CD 7911-2-RG

My mother bids me bind my hair (Pastoral Song) (Haydn)
4/10/45 (New York Studio No. 2) D5-
RB-196
78: 10-1199-A
LP: LM-2712

She never told her love (Haydn)
4/10/45 (New York Studio No. 2) D5-
RB-197-1
78: 10-1199-B
LP: LM-2712

O men from the fields (Thomas)
4/10/45 (New York Studio No. 2) D5-
RB-198
unissued

Bright Phoebus (Hook)
4/10/45 (New York Studio No. 2) D5-
RB-199-1
78: 10-1300-B

Lullaby, Op. 57/2 (Scott)
4/10/45 (New York Studio No. 2) D5-
  RB-200
unissued

Befreit, Op. 39/4 (Strauss)
4/11/45 (New York Studio No. 2) D5-
  RC-243
unissued

Morgen, Op. 27/4 (Strauss)
4/11/45 (New York Studio No. 2) D5-
  RC-244
unissued

Stille Tränen, from *Zwölf Gedichte,* Op. 35
  (Schumann)
4/11/45 (New York Studio No. 2) D5-
  RC-245-2
78: 11-9173-B
LP: LM-2712
CD: Eklipse EKR CD 26; Nimbus NI
  7895; RCA CD 7911-2-RG (take 1)

Der Nussbaum, from *Myrthen,* Op. 25
  (Schumann)
4/11/45 (New York Studio No. 2) D5-
  RC-246-2
78: 11-9173-A
LP: LM-2712
CD: Eklipse EKR CD 26; RCA CD 7911-
  2-RG (take 1)

Hear the wind whispering (Bucky)
4/12/45 (New York Studio No. 2) D5-
  RB-201-2
78: 10-1260-B

Hold On! (arr. Johnson)
4/12/45 (New York Studio No. 2) D5-
  RB-202-2
78: 10-1278-B
CD: Eklipse EKR CD 26; RCA 09026-
  63306-2

Der Tod und das Mädchen (Schubert)
4/12/45 (New York Studio No. 2) D5-
  RB-203
unissued

Wohin?, from *Die schöne Müllerin*
  (Schubert)
4/12/45 (New York Studio No. 2) D5-
  RB-204-2
78: 10-1327-B
CD: Nimbus NI 7895

Lullaby, Op. 57/2 (Scott)
4/12/45 (New York Studio No. 2) D5-
  RB-200
unissued

Ave Maria (Ellens Gesang III)
  (Schubert)
5/9/46 (New York Studio No. 1 or 2) D6-
  RC-5847-2
78: 11-9836-A
45: 49-0136-A; ERA-19-A; WDM-1530
  (49-3313-B)
LP: LM-98; LM-6074 (*60 Years of Music
  America Loves Best*)

Aufenthalt, from *Schwanengesang*
  (Schubert)
5/9/46 (New York Studio No. 1 or 2) D6-
  RC-5846-2
78: 11-9836-B
45: 49-0136-B
LP: LM-6074 (60 Years of "Music America Loves Best")

Poor Me (arr. Dett)
5/10/46 (New York Studio No. 1 or 2)
  D6-RB-1780-2
78: 10-1278-A
CD: Eklipse EKR CD 26; RCA 09026-
  63306-2

O men from the fields (Thomas)
5/10/46 (New York Studio No. 1 or 2)
  D5-RB-198-3
78: 10-1300-A
CD: VAI Audio VAIA 1168

Lullaby, Op. 57/2 (Scott)
5/10/46 (New York Studio No. 1 or 2)
  D5-RB-200-4
78: 10-1260-A

Appendix 2: Discography

Der Tod und das Mädchen (Schubert)
5/10/46 (New York Studio No. 1 or 2)
  D5-RB-203-2
78: 10-1327-A
45: WDM-1530 (49-3314-B)
LP: LM-98
CD: Nimbus NI 7895; RCA CD 7911-2-
  RG

Great Songs of Faith
6/11-6/12/46 (New York Lotos Club)
with the Victor Sinfonietta, cond. by
  Robert Shaw

Jesus schläft, was soll ich hoffen?, from
  Cantata 81 (Bach)
6/11/46; D6-RC-5967-1
78: M-1087 (11-9378-B)
45: WCT-1111 (449-0041-A or 449-
  0042-A)
LP: LCT-1111-A
CD: Eklipse EKR CD 26; Nimbus NI
  7882

Zum reinen Wasser er mich weist, from
  Cantata 112 (Bach)
6/11/46; D6-RC-5968-1
78: M-1087 (11-9379-A)
45: WCT-1111 (449-0042-A)
LP: LCT-1111-A
CD: Eklipse EKR CD 26; Nimbus NI
  7882

Bereite dich, Zion, from *Christmas Oratorio,* (Bach)
6/11/46; D6-RC-5969-2
78: M-1087 (11-9379-B)
45: WCT-1111 (449-0043-A)
LP: LCT-1111-A
CD: Eklipse EKR CD 26; Nimbus NI
  7882

Kreuz und Krone sind verbunden, from
  Cantata.12 (Bach)
6/12/46; D6-RC-5970-2
78: M-1087 (11-9378-A)
45: WCT-1111 (449-0041-A)
LP: LCT-1111-A

CD: Eklipse EKR CD 26; Nimbus NI
  7882

Erbarme dich, from *St. Matthew Passion,*
  244 (Bach)
6/12/46
Part 1; D6-RC-5971-2
78: M-1087 (11-9380-A)
45: WCT-1111 (449-0044-A)
LP: LCT-1111-A
CD: Eklipse EKR CD 26; Nimbus NI
  7882; RCA CD 7911-2-RG
Part 2; D6-RC-5972-2
78: M-1087 (11-9380-B)
45: WCT-1111 (449-0044-A)
LP: LCT-1111-A
CD: Eklipse EKR CD 26; Nimbus NI
  7882; RCA CD 7911-2-RG

Nobody Knows the Trouble I See (arr.
  Johnson)
5/5/47 (New York Studio No. 2) D7-RB-
  814-2
78: 10-1428-A
45: ERA-62-A; WDM-1238 (49-0787-A)
LP: LM-110; LM-2032 (=AVMI-1735)
CD: RCA 09026-63306-2

Ride On, King Jesus! (arr. Burleigh)
5/5/47 (New York Studio No. 2) D7-RB-
  815-2
78: 10-1428-B
45: WDM-1238 (49-0787-B)
LP: LM-110; LM-2032 (=AVMI-1735)
CD: RCA 09026-63306-2

Hear de Lam's a-Cryin' (arr. Brown)
5/6/47 (New York Studio No. 2) D7-RB-
  816-2
78: 10-1429-A
45: WDM-1238 (49-0788-A)
LP: LM-110; ERA-62-A; LM-2032
  (=AVMI-1735)
CD: RCA 09026-63306-2

Sinner Please Doan Let Dis Harves' Pass
  (arr. Burleigh)
5/6/47 (New York Studio No. 2) D7-RB-
  817-1

78: 10-1429-B
45: WDM-1238 (49-0788)
LP: LM-110; LM-2032 (=AVMI-1735)
CD: RCA 09026-63306-2

Honor, Honor (arr. Johnson)
5/6/47 (New York Studio No. 2) D7-RB-
   817-1
78: 10-1429-B
45: WDM-1238 (49-0788)
LP: LM-110; LM-2032 (=AVMI-1735)
CD: RCA 09026-63306-2

My Lord, What a Mornin' (arr. Burleigh)
5/6/47 (New York Studio No. 2) D7-RB-
   818
unissued

Were You There? (arr. Burleigh)
5/7/47 (New York Studio No. 2) D7-RB-
   819-2
78: 10-1431-A
45: ERA-62-B; WDM-1238 (49-0790-A)
LP: LM-110; LM-2032 (=AVMI-1735)
CD: RCA 09026-63306-2

Soon-a Will Be Done (arr. Boatner)
5/7/47 (New York Studio No. 2) D7-RB-
   820-1
78: 10-1430-B
45: ERA-62-B; WDM-1238 (49-0789-B)
LP: LM-110; LM-2032 (=AVMI-1735)
CD: RCA 09026-63306-2

On Ma Journey (arr. Boatner)
5/7/47 (New York Studio No. 2) D7-RB-
   821-1
78: 10-1431-B
45: WDM-1238 (49-0790-B)
LP: LM-110; LM-2032 (=AVMI-1735)
CD: RCA 09026-63306-2

The Gospel Train (arr. Burleigh)
5/7/47 (New York Studio No. 2) D7-RB-
   821-1
78: 10-1431-B
45: WDM-1238 (49-0790-B)

LP: LM-110; LM-2032 (=AVMI-1735)
CD: RCA 09026-63306-2

My Lord, What a Mornin' (arr. Burleigh)
5/7/47 (New York Studio No. 2) D7-RB-
   818-3
78: 10-1430-A
45: WDM-1238 (49-0789-A)
LP: LM-110; LM-2032 (AVMI-1735)
CD: RCA 09026-63306-2

Morgen, Op. 27/4 (Strauss)
12/16/47 (New York Studio No. 2) D7-
   RC-8234-2
78: 12-0734-A
45: 49-0675-A
LP: LM-2712
CD: RCA CD 7911-2-RG

Der Jüngling und der Tod (Schubert)
12/16/47 (New York Studio No. 2) D7-
   RC-8235-2
78: 12-0580-B
45: 49-1040-B
LP: LM-2712
CD: Nimbus NI 7895; VAI Audio VAIA
   1168

Befreit, Op. 39/4 (Strauss)
12/16/47 (New York Studio No. 2) D7-
   RC-8236-2
78: 12-0734-B
45: 49-0675-B
CD: VAI Audio VAIA 1168

Der Doppelgänger, from *Schwanengesang*
   (Schubert)
12/16/47 (New York Studio No. 2) D7-
   RC-8237-2
78: 12-0580-A
45: 49-1040-A
LP: LM-2712
CD: Nimbus NI 7895; VAI Audio VAIA
   1168 (take 1)

Come to me, soothing sleep (Lo sperai
   trovar riposo), from *Ottone, re di Germania* (Handel)

1/3/50 (New York Studio No. 2) E0-RC-
15-2
45: 49-3157-A

Oh what pleasure (Vanne, segu'il mio
desio), from *Floridante* (Handel)
1/3/50 (New York Studio No. 2) E0-RC-
16-1
45: 49-3157-B

The trumpet is calling (Un ombra di
pace), from *Floridante (Handel)*
1/3/50 (New York Studio No. 2) E0-RC-
16-1
45: 49-3157-B

Liebesbotschaft, from *Schwanengesang*
(Schubert)
1/3/50 (New York Studio No. 2) E0-RB-
3020-1
45: 49-3158-A; WDM-1530 (49-3313-A)
LP: LM-98
CD: Eklipse EKR CD 26; RCA CD 7911-
2-RG (take 2)

Dem Unendlichen (Schubert)
1/4/50 (New York Studio No. 2) E0-RC-
17-1
78: 12-1250-B
45: 49-1278-B

Thekla (Schubert)
1/4/50 (New York Studio No. 2) E0-RC-
18-2
78: 12-1250-A
45: 49-1278-A

Gretchen am Spinnrade (Schubert)
1/4/50 (New York Studio No. 2) E0-RB-
3027-2
45: 49-3158-B; WDM-1530 (49-3315-B)
LP: LM-98
CD: Eklipse EKR CD 26

Kindertotenlieder (Mahler)
2/26/50 (San Francisco War Memorial
Opera House)

with the San Francisco Symphony, cond.
by Pierre Monteux
1. Nun will die Sonn' so hell aufgeh'n!;
E0-RC-400-2
45: WDM-1531 (49-3316-A)
LP: LM-1146-B
CD: RCA 09026-61891-2
2. Nun seh' ich wohl, warum so dunkle
Flammen; E0-RC-401-1
45: WDM-1531 (49-3317-A)
LP: LM-1146-B
CD: RCA 09026-61891-2
3. Wenn dein Mütterlein; E0-RC-402-2
45: WDM-1531 (49-3318-A)
LP: LM-1146-B
CD: RCA 09026-61891-2
4. Oft denk' ich, sie sind nur ausgegan-
gen; E0-RC-403-2
45: WDM-1531 (49-3318-B)
LP: LM-1146-B
CD: RCA 09026-61891-2
5. In diesem Wetter! (Part 1); E0-RC-
404-2
45: WDM-1531 (49-3317-B)
LP: LM-1146-B
CD: RCA 09026-61891-2
6. In diesem Wetter! (Part 2); E0-RC-
405-2
45: WDM-1531 (49-3316-B)
LP: LM-1146-B
CD: RCA 09026-61891-2

Frauenliebe und -leben, Op. 42 (Schumann)
3/29/50 (New York Studio No. 2)
1. Seit ich ihn gesehen; E0-RC-841-2
78: 12-3040-A
45: WDM-1458 (49-3040-A)
2. Er, der Herrlichste von allen; E0-RC-
841-2
78: 12-3040-A
45: WDM-1458 (49-3040-A)
3. Ich kann's nicht fassen, nicht glauben;
E0-RC-842-2
78: 12-3041-A
45: WDM-1458 (49-3041-A)
4. Du Ring an meinem Finger; E0-RC-
842-2

78: 12-3041-A
45: WDM-1458 (49-3041-A)
3/30/50 (New York Studio No. 2)
5. Helft mir, ihr Schwestern; E0-RC-
847-1
78: 12-3041-B
45: WDM-1458 (49-3041-B)
6. Süsser Freund, du blickest mich ver-
wundert an; E0-RC-847-1
78: 12-3041-B
45: WDM-1458 (49-3041-B)
7. An meinem Herzen, an meiner Brust;
E0-RC-848-2
78: 12-3040-B
45: WDM-1458 (49-3040-B)
8. Nun hast du mir den ersten Schmerz
getan; E0-RC-848-2
78: 12-3040-B
45: WDM-1458 (49-3040-B)

Alto Rhapsody, Op. 53 (Brahms)
10/20/50 (Manhattan Center)
with the Victor Symphony Orchestra and
the Robert Shaw Chorale of Men's
Voices, cond. by Fritz Reiner
Part 1; E0-RC-1887-2
45: WDM-1532 (49-3319-A)
LP: LM-1146-A
Part 2; E0-RC-1888-2
45: WDM-1532 (49-3320-A)
LP: LM-1146-A
Part 3; E0-RC-1889-2
45: WDM-1532 (49-3320-B)
LP: LM-1146-A
Part 4; E0-RC-1890-1
45: WDM-1532 (49-3319-B)
LP: LM-1146-A

Ai nostri monti, from *Il Trovatore* (Verdi)
12/19/50 (New York) E0-RC-1977
with Jan Peerce and the RCA Victor
Orchestra, cond. by Erich Leinsdorf
unissued

Ständchen, (Horch, horch, die Lerch')
(Schubert)
1/18/51 (New York Studio No. 2) E1-RC-
2143-1

45: WDM-1530 (49-3315-A)
LP: LM-98

Wohin?, from *Die schöne Müllerin*
(Schubert)
1/18/51 (New York Studio No. 2) E1-RC-
2144-1
45: ERA-19; WDM-1530 (49-3315-B)
CD: RCA CD 7911-2-RG; VAI Audio
VAIA 1168

Die Forelle (Schubert)
1/18/51 (New York Studio No. 2) E1-RC-
2145-2
45: WDM-1530 (49-3314-B)
LP: LM-98

Der Erlkönig (Schubert)
1/18/51 (New York Studio No. 2) E1-RC-
2146-3
45: ERA-19; WDM-1530 (49-3314-A)
LP: LM-98
CD: VAI Audio VAIA 1168

O little town of Bethlehem (Redner)
1/19/51 (New York Studio No. 2) E1-RB-
0118-1
45: WDM-7008 (49-3832-A)
LP: LM-7008-A
CD: BMG Special Products 44574-2

Silent Night (Grüber)
1/19/51 (New York Studio No. 2) E1-RB-
0119
45: WDM-7008 (49-3832-A)
LP: LM-7008-A

The First Noël
1/19/51 (New York Studio No. 2) E1-RB-
0120-2
45: WDM-7008 (49-3834-A)
LP: LM-7008-A

Adeste fideles
1/19/51 (New York Studio No. 2) E1-RB-
0121-1
45: ERA-116-A; WDM-7008 (49-3833-A)
LP: LM-7008-A
CD: BMG Special Products 44574-2

Hark! The herald angels sing
(Mendelssohn)
1/19/51 (New York Studio No. 2) E1-RB-
0122
unissued

Carry me back to old Virginny (Bland)
2/1/51 (New York Studio No. 2) E1-RC-
1984-2
45: WDM-1703 (49-3805-A)
LP: LM-1703

My Old Kentucky Home (Foster)
2/1/51 (New York Studio No. 2) E1-RC-
1985-2
45: WDM-1703 (49-3805-B)
LP: LM-1703

Hark! The herald angels sing
(Mendelssohn)
4/10/51 (New York Studio No. 2) E1-RB-
0122-2
45: ERA-116-A; WDM-7008 (49-3834-B)
LP: LM-7008-B
CD: BMG Special Products 44574-2

Cantique de Noël (Adam)
4/10/51 (New York Studio No. 2) E1-RB-
1736-1
45: ERA-116-B; WDM-7008 (49-3833-B)
LP: LM-7008-B

Angel's Song (Bucky)
4/10/51 (New York Studio No. 2) E1-RB-
1737-2
45: WDM-7008 (49-3832-B)
LP: LM-7008-B

Hallelujah (Bucky)
4/10/51 (New York Studio No. 2) E1-RB-
1738-1
45: WDM-7008 (49-3832-B)
LP: LM-7008-B

Vier ernste Gesänge, Op. 121 (Brahms)
5/13/52 (New York Studio No. 2)
  1. Denn es geht dem Menschen; E2-
   RC-0819-1

  2. Ich wandte mich und sahe; E2-RC-
   0820-1
  3. O Tod, wie bitter bist du; E2-RC-
   0821-1
  4. Wenn ich mit Menschen; E2-RC-
   0822-1
originally unissued
CD: VAI Audio VAIA 1168

Deep River (arr. Burleigh)
5/14/52 (New York Studio No. 2) E2-RB-
0811-1
45: ERB-7006 (549-0011-A)
LP: LRM-7006-A; LM-2032 (=AVMI-
1735); LPM-1765 *(Best Loved Sacred
Songs Volume 1)*
CD: RCA 09026-63306-2

He's Got the Whole World in His Hands
(arr. Forrest)
5/14/52 (New York Studio No. 2) E2-RB-
0812-1
45: ERA-287; ERB-7006 (549-0011-A)
LP: LRM-7006-A; LM-2032 (=AVMI-
1735); LM-2071
CD: RCA 09026-63306-2

Plenty Good Room (arr. Boatner)
5/14/52 (New York Studio No. 2) E2-RB-
0813-1
45: ERB-7006 (549-0012-B)
LP: LRM-7006-B; LM-2032 (=AVMI-
1735)
CD: RCA 09026-63306-2

Everytime I Feel de Spirit (arr. Brown)
5/14/52 (New York Studio No. 2) E2-RB-
0823-1
45: ERB-7006 (549-0011-B)
LP: LRM-7006-B; LM-2032 (=AVMI-
1735); LM-2361
CD: RCA 09026-63306-2

O What a Beautiful City! (arr. Boatner)
5/14/52 (New York Studio No. 2) E2-RB-
0824-1
45: ERB-7006 (549-0011-B)
LP: LRM-7006-B
CD: RCA 09026-63306-2

If He Change My Name (arr. MacGimsey)
5/14/52 (New York Studio No. 2) E2-RB-0825-1
45: ERB-7006 (549-0011-B)
LP: LRM-7006-B; LM-2032 (=AVMI-1735)
CD: RCA 09026-63306-2

Go Down Moses (arr. Burleigh)
5/14/52 (New York Studio No. 2) E2-RC-0814-1
45: ERB-7006 (549-0012-A)
LP: LRM-7006-A; LM-2032 (=AVMI-1735); LM-2574 *(60 Years of Music America Loves Best)*
CD: RCA 09026-63306-2

Crucifixion (arr. Payne)
5/14/52 (New York Studio No. 2) E2-RC-0815-1
45: ERB-7006 (549-0012-A)
LP: LRM-7006-A; LM-2032 (=AVMI-1735)
CD: RCA 09026-63306-2

Sometimes I Feel Like a Motherless Child (arr. Brown)
5/14/52 (New York Studio No. 2) E2-RC-0816-1
45: ERB-7006 (549-0012-B)
LP: LRM-7006-B; LM-2032 (=AVMI-1735)
CD: RCA 09026-63306-2

Let Us Break Bread Together (arr. Lawrence)
5/14/52 (New York Studio No. 2) E2-RC-0817-1
45: ERB-7006 (549-0012-B)
LP: LRM-7006-B; LM-2032 (=AVMI-1735)
CD: RCA 09026-63306-2

Roll, Jord'n Roll! (arr. Johnson)
5/14/52 (New York Studio No. 2) E2-RC-0813-1
45: ERB-7006 (549-0011-A)

LP: LRM-7006-A; LM-2032 (=AVMI-1735)
CD: RCA 09026-63306-2

Frauenliebe und -leben, Op. 42 (Schumann)
6/17/52 (New York Studio No. 2)
    1. Seit ich ihn gesehen; E2-RC-0860
unissued

O little town of Bethlehem (Redner)
9/24/52 (New York Studio No. 2) E2-RB-0119-1
45: ERA-116-B

Re dell'abisso, from *Un Ballo in maschera* (Verdi)
1/9/55 (Manhattan Center, New York)
with the Metropolitan Opera Orchestra, cond. by Dmitri Mitropoulos
LP: LM-1911 (Highlights from A Masked Ball)

Brahms Songs
11/8-12/1/55 (New York Studio No. 2)
all songs unissued
    Vier ernste Gesänge, Op. 121
    11/8/55
        1. Denn es gehet dem Menschen; F2-RB-7758
        2. Ich wandte mich und sahe; F2-RB-7759

Botschaft, Op. 47/1
11/9/55; F2-RB-7750

Vier ernste Gesänge, Op. 121
11/9/55
        1. Denn es geht dem Menschen; F2-RB-7758
        2. Ich wandte mich und sahe; F2-RB-7759
        3. O Tod, wie bitter bist du; F2-RB-7760
        4. Wenn ich mit Menschen; F2-RB-7761

Dein blaues Auge hält so still, Op. 59/8
11/10/55; F2-RB-7746

Appendix 2: Discography

Der Schmied, Op. 19/4
11/10/55; F2-RB-7749

Vergebliches Ständchen, Op. 84/4
11/10/55; F2-RB-7753

Immer leiser wird mein Schlummer,
Op. 105/2
11/10/55; F2-RB-7756

Die Meinacht, Op. 43/2
11/15/55; F2-RB-7744

O kühler Wald! Wo rauschest du, Op.
72/3
11/15/55; F2-RB-7748

Vergebliches Ständchen, Op. 84/4
11/15/55; F2-RB-7753

Von ewiger Liebe, Op. 43/1
11/17/55; F2-RB-7745

Sehnsucht (Volkslied), Op. 14/8
11/17/55; F2-RB-7747

Wir wandelten, wir zwei zusammen,
Op. 96/2
11/17/55; F2-RB-7755

An die Nachtigall, Op. 46/4
11/17/55; F2-RB-7757

O liebliche Wangen, ihr macht mir Verlangen, Op. 47/4
11/30/55; F2-RB-7751

Wiegenlied, Op. 49/4
11/30/55; F2-RB-7752

Feldeinsamkeit, Op. 86/2
11/30/55; F2-RB-7754

O kühler Wald, wo rauschest du, Op. 72/3
12/1/55; F2-RB-7748

O liebliche Wangen, ihr macht mir Verlangen, Op. 47/4
12/1/55; F2-RB-7751

Wiegenlied, Op. 49/4
12/1/55; F2-RB-7752

Feldeinsamkeit, Op. 86/2
12/1/55; F2-RB-7754

Songs to English Texts
12/2/55-1/5/56 (New York Studio No. 2)
all songs unissued
The Plough Boy (arr. Britten)
12/2/55; F2-RB-8173

The Sally Gardens (arr. Britten)
12/2/55; F2-RB-8174

Songs My Mother Taught Me (Cigánské
melodié), Op. 55 (Dvorák)
12/2/55; F2-RB-8177

None but the lonely heart (Net, tolko tot,
kto znal), Op. 6/6 (Tchaikovsky)
12/2/55; F2-RB-8178

Over the Mountains (arr. Quilter)
12/20/55; F2-RB-8175

Coming through the Rye
12/20/55; F2-RB-8176

Blow, blow thou winter wind (Quilter)
12/20/55; F2-RB-8179

Lullaby, Op. 57/2 (Scott)
12/20/55; F2-RB-8180

Lullaby, Op. 57/2 (Scott)
1/3/56; G2-RB-701

Songs My Mother Taught Me (Cigánské
melodie), Op. 55 (Dvorák)
1/3/56; G2-RB-702

Believe me if all those endearing young
charms (Page)
1/3/56; G2-RB-703

Trees (Rasbach)
1/3/56; G2-RB-704

A Perfect Day (Bond)
1/4/56; G2-RB-741

Danny Boy (arr. Weatherly)
1/4/56; G2-RB-705

The Lost Chord (Sullivan)
1/4/56; G2-RB-706

When love is kind (Traditional)
1/4/56; G2-RB-707

Four Leaf Clover (Brownell)
1/4/56; G2-RB-708

The Lord's Prayer (Malotte)
1/5/56; G2-RB-758

By the Waters of Minnetonka (Lieurance)
1/5/56; G2-RB-759

The Lost Chord (Sullivan)
1/5/56; G2-RB-706

A Perfect Day (Bond)
1/5/56; G2-RB-741

Brahms Songs
5/20-5/22/58 (New York Studio B)
all songs unissued
Vier ernste Gesänge, Op. 121
5/20/58
  1. Denn es geht dem Menschen; J2-RB-3903
  2. Ich wandte mich und sahe; J2-RB-3904
  3. O Tod, wie bitter bist du; J2-RB-3905

Der Schmied, Op. 19/4
5/21/58; J2-RB-3909

Wiegenlied, Op. 49/4
5/21/58; J2-RB-3914

Von ewiger Liebe, Op. 43/1
5/21/58; J2-RB-3954

Vergebliches Ständchen, Op. 84/4
5/21/58; J2-RB-3955

Sehnsucht (Volkslied), Op. 14/8
5/21/58; J2-RB-3956

Die Meinacht, Op. 43/2
5/22/58; J2-RB-3912

He's Got the Whole World in His Hands and
  18 Other Spirituals
8/28–8/31/61 (New York Webster Hall)
LP: LM/LSC-2592
CD: RCA 09026-61960-2
Behold That Star (arr. Burleigh)
8/28/61; M2-RB-3456-5

Heav'n, Heav'n (arr. Burleigh)
8/28/61; M2-RB-3457-8

Oh, Wan't Dat a Wide Ribber? (arr.
  Burleigh)
8/28/61; M2-RB-3458-4

Oh Peter Go Ring-a Dem Bells (arr.
  Burleigh)
8/28/61; M2-RB-3459-16

He's Got the Whole World in His Hands
  (arr. Forrest)
8/28/61; M2-RB-3476-6

I Stood on de Ribber ob Jerdon (arr.
  Burleigh)
8/30/61; M2-RB-3463-11

Trampin' (arr. Boatner)
8/28/61; M2-RB-3465-5

Dere's No Hidin' Place Down Dere (arr.
  Brown)
8/29/61; M2-RB-3478-5

Done Foun' My Los' Sheep (arr. J. R.
  Johnson)
8/29 and 8/30/61; M2-RB-3466-6

Lord, I Can't Stay Away (arr. Hayes)
8/29/61; M2-RB-3469-10

Oh, Didn't It Rain? (arr. Burleigh)
8/30/61; M2-RB-3460-6

Hard Trials (arr. Burleigh)
8/30/61; M2-RB-3461-5

My Soul's Been Anchored in de Lord (arr.
  Price)
8/30/61; M2-RB-3468-6

Hold On! (arr. Johnson)
8/30/61; M2-RB-3471-8

Great Gittin' Up Mornin' (arr. Brown)
8/30/61; M2-RB-3472-1

Sometimes I Feel Like a Motherless Child
  (arr. Brown)
8/30 and 8/31/61; M2-RB-3477-6

I Am Bound for de Kingdom (arr. Price)
8/31/61; M2-RB-3482-1

I Want Jesus to Walk with Me (arr. Boatner)
8/30/61; M2-RB-3482-4

Scandalize My Name (arr. Burleigh)
8/31/61; M2-RB-3482-3

Poor Me (arr. Dett)
8/28/61; M2-RB-3464
unissued

Steal Away (arr. Burleigh)
8/29/61; M2-RB-3482
unissued

Poor Mourner's Got a Home at Last (arr.
  Klemm)
8/30/61; M2-RB-3480
unissued

Christmas Carols
9/18–10/20/61 (New York Webster Hall)

all songs unissued
Deck the Halls
9/18 and 10/20/61; M2-RB-3500

The First Noël
9/18/61; M2-RB-3501

God rest you merry gentlemen
9/18/61; M2-RB-3502

Hark! The herald angels sing
  (Mendelssohn)
9/18/61; M2-RB-3503

O little town of Bethlehem (Redner)
9/18/61; M2-RB-3504

Joy to the world (Handel)
9/21/61; M2-RB-3505

Angels we have heard on high
9/21 and 10/20/61; M2-RB-3506

O come, all ye faithful
9/21 and 10/20/61; M2-RB-3507

Good Christian men, rejoice
9/21 and 10/20/61; M2-RB-3508

O Sanctissima
9/21 and 10/20/61; M2-RB-3509

Gabriel's Song (Bucky)
9/21 and 10/20/61; M2-RB-3510

Angel's Song (Bucky)
9/22/61; M2-RB-3511

It came upon a midnight clear (Willis)
9/22 and 10/3/61; M2-RB-3512

Cantique de Noël (Adam)
9/22 and 10/3/61; M2-RB-3513

Silent Night (Grüber)
9/22, 10/2, and 10/20/61; M2-RB-3514

Angels we have heard on high (Smart)
10/2/61; M2-RB-3515

Shepherds! Shake off your drowsy sleep
10/2/61; M2-RB-3516

While shepherds watched their flocks
(Handel)
10/2/61; M2-RB-3517

Beautiful Savior
10/2 and 10/20/61; M2-RB-3518

Away in a Manger (Spilman)
10/2/61; M2-RB-3519

Jingle Bells (Pierpont)
10/3/61; M2-RB-3520

The Twelve Days of Christmas (Niles)
10/3 and 10/20/61; M2-RB-3521

Marian Anderson Christmas Carols
4/25–5/12/62 (New York Webster Hall)
with Franz Rupp, Orchestra, and Chorus,
cond. by Robert Russell Bennett[3]
all carols arranged for orchestra by Robert
Russell Bennett
LP: LM/LSC-2613; FTC-2118
The First Noël
4/25/62; N2-RB-2783-7
CD: BMG Special Products 44574-2

Deck the Halls
5/3 and 5/12/62; N2-RB-2784-12
CD: BMG Special Products 44574-2

O Sanctissima
4/25/62; N2-RB-2785-13

Joy to the World! (Handel)
4/26/62; N2-RB-2786-26
CD: BMG Special Products 44574-2

Away in a Manger (Spilman)
4/27/62; N2-RB-2787-11
CD: BMG Special Products 44574-2

Silent Night (Grüber)
5/3 and 5/12/62; N2-RB-2788-19
CDBMG Special Products 44574-2

God rest you merry gentlemen
4/25/62; N2-RB-2789-12
CD: BMG Special Products 44574-2

Jingle Bells (Pierpont)
5/2/62; N2-RB-2790-13

It came upon a midnight clear (Willis)
4/26/62; N2-RB-2791-6
CD: BMG Special Products 44574-2

Angel's Song (Bucky)
4/27 and 5/3/62; N2-RB-2792-14

The Twelve Days of Christmas (Niles)
5/4/62; N2-RB-2793-14

We wish you a merry Christmas
4/26 and 5/12/62; N2-RB-2794-12

Ave Maria (Ellens Gesang III) (Schubert)
5/4 and 5/12/62; N2-RB-2795-29

Songs at Eventide
2/21–5/28/64 (New York Webster Hall)
with Franz Rupp, harpsichord; and
orchestra, cond. by Robert Russell Bennett[4]
all songs arranged for orchestra by Robert
Russell Bennett
LP: LM/LSC-2769
Songs My Mother Taught Me *(Cigánské
melodie),* Op. 55 (Dvorák)
2/21, 4/15, 4/20, and 5/25/64; RR-A1-
0864, RR-A1-3560

Believe me if all those endearing young
charms (Page)
4/13, 5/26, and 5/28/64; RR-A1-0877, RR-
A1-3570

All Through the Night (Old Welsh Air)
4/14, 4/15, and 5/26/64; RR-A1-0874, RR-
A1-3567

Last Night (Kjerulf)
4/14, 4/23, and 5/25/64; RR-A1-0873, RR-A1-3566

Flow Gently, Sweet Afton (Burns, Spilman)
2/22, 4/15, and 5/27/64; RR-A1-0867, RR-A1-3563

Evening Prayer (Abends will ich schlaffen gehn), from *Hänsel und Gretel* (Humperdinck)
2/22, 4/14, and 5/28/64; RR-A1-0865, RR-A1-3561

Coming through the Rye
4/30 and 5/26/64; RR-A1-0875, RR-A1-3568

Drink to Me Only with Thine Eyes (Mellish)
4/13, 4/14, and 5/28/64; RR-A1-0876, RR-A1-3569

Loch Lomond (Kreisler)
2/22, 4/30, and 5/27/64; RR-A1-0866, RR-A1-3562

Love's Old Sweet Song (Bingham, Molloy)
2/22, 4/23, and 5/25/64; RR-A1-0868, RR-A1-3564

Annie Laurie (Douglass, Scott)
4/20 and 5/27/64; RR-A1-0872, RR-A1-3565

Cradle Song (Brahms)
2/22, 4/14, and 5/28/64; RR-A1-0865, RR-A1-3559

Jus' Keep on Singin'
9/24–10/6/64 (New York Webster Hall)
with John Motley, piano
all songs traditional, arranged by Hall Johnson
LP: LM/LSC-2796

CD: RCA 09026-61960-2 (includes all songs except "Oh, Glory!")

Oh, Heaven Is One Beautiful Place, I Know
9/24 and 9/26/64; RR-A1-4837

Lord, How Come Me Here?
9/28/64; RR-A1-4838

Prayer Is de Key
9/28/64; RR-A1-4839

He'll Bring It to Pass
9/29 and 9/30/64; RR-A1-4843

You Go!
9/28/64; RR-A1-4841

Jus' Keep on Singin'
9/28/64; RR-A1-4842

Ain't Got Time to Die
9/28/64; RR-A1-4840

I Been in de Storm So Long
9/29/64; RR-A1-4844

I've Been 'Buked
9/29/64; RR-A1-4845

Le's Have a Union
9/30/64; RR-A1-4846

Oh, Glory!
10/6/64; RR-A1-4849

Jus' Keep On Singin'
9/30, 10/6/64; RR-A1-4847

Ride On, King Jesus!
9/30, 10/6/64; RR-A1-4848

Farewell Recital
10/24/64 (Washington DC Constitution Hall) RR A5 4874
recorded live
LP: LM/LSC-2781

Ch'io mai vi posa, from *Siroe, re di Persia*
(Handel)
The Spirit's Song (Haydn)
My mother bids me bind my hair (Pastoral Song) (Haydn)
Suleika I (Schubert)
Liebesbotschaft, from *Schwanengesang*
(Schubert)
Der Doppelgänger, from *Schwanengesang*
(Schubert)
Der Erlkönig (Schubert)
Blow, blow thou winter wind (Quilter)
The Plough Boy (arr. Britten)
Let Us Break Bread Together (arr.
Lawrence)
O What a Beautiful City! (arr. Boatner)
Ride On, King Jesus! (arr. Burleigh)
Done Foun' My Los' Sheep (arr. J. R.
Johnson)
Lord, I Can't Stay Away (arr. Hayes)
He's Got the Whole World in His Hands
(arr. Forrest)
Ungeduld, from *Die schöne Müllerin*
(Schubert)

Schubert and Brahms Lieder
1966 (New York Webster Hall) TRRS-
2343 (songs 1–8); TRRS-2344 (songs 9–15)[5]
LP: ARL1-3022

Liebesbotschaft, from *Schwanengesang*
(Schubert)
Ungeduld, from *Die schöne Müllerin*
(Schubert)
Der Tod und das Mädchen (Schubert)
Die Forelle (Schubert)
An die Musik (Schubert)

Suleika I (Schubert)
Gretchen am Spinnrade (Schubert)
Wiegenlied ("Schlafe, schlafe")
(Schubert)
Der Erlkönig (Schubert)
Heidenröslein (Schubert)
Von ewiger Liebe, Op. 43/1 (Brahms)
Botschaft, Op. 47/1 (Brahms)
Vergebliches Ständchen, Op. 84/4
(Brahms)
Der Schmied, Op. 19/4 (Brahms)
Dein blaues Auge hält so still, Op. 59/8
(Brahms)

VII. Folkways—1963

*Snoopycat: The Adventures of Marian
Anderson's Cat "Snoopy"*
1/1963 (New York)
LP: SC 7770
All songs by Frida Sarsen Bucky

A Little Black Kitten
The Motherly Dark of the Night
Such an Inquisitive Kitty
Snoopy's Music Box
Snoopy's Lullaby
Follow the Moon Barrels and Boxes
Listen to the Clatter
Poor Forgotten Snoopy
The Looking Glass
The Frog
The Turtle
The Owl Fire-Flies
Dance of the Kittens
A Princess Fair
Nightsong

Appendix 2: Discography

Part 2: Noncommercial Recordings

In the listings under live material, only works of which no commercial recordings exist, and occasionally other works which are of unusual interest or importance, are included. All of the libraries and archives listed below have complete records of their holdings of Anderson material. CD releases of this material are also included.

The University of Pennsylvania collection of test pressings includes recordings made for both HMV and RCA. The home recordings in the University of Pennsylvania archives are of variable quality. They were made in Anderson's studio during the 1940s and 1950s at Marianna. Some of the performances are recorded faintly and are difficult to hear. Others contain frequent interruptions or are not complete. Nevertheless, these home recordings contain material that is worthy of serious study, containing as they do performances of works of which there are no other examples. Among these latter, for example, are five songs from Schumann's *Dichterliebe,* Arianna's Lament by Monteverdi, seventeenth-century songs and arias, and a few songs in Spanish and Portuguese.

I. Live Material

Institut Audio-Visuelle: French Radio Broadcasts
Christoph von Gluck, "Divinités du Styx" from *Alceste.* With the Orchestre National de France, cond. by Jascha Horenstein, 11/22/56 (CD: Music and Arts CD-784(2))

Library of Congress: Broadcasting Collections of the Motion Picture, Broadcasting, and Recorded Sound Division. Collection includes Lincoln Memorial concert (CD: Legendary Recordings LRCD 1031), Bell Telephone Hour Broadcasts, Magic Key of RCA Broadcasts, Ford Sunday Evening Hour Broadcasts, Voices of America Broadcasts, Concert Hall Broadcasts.
Giuseppe Verdi, *Un Ballo in maschera.* With the Metropolitan Opera, 10/12/55 (CD: Myto Records 2 MCD 942.100; additional CD release of "Re dell'abisso" only: Legendary Recordings LRCD 1031)
Georges Bizet, "Agnus Dei" from *L'Arlésienne.* With the NBC Symphony Orchestra, cond. by Frank Black, 10/15/44

From Bell Telephone Hour Broadcasts:
Ludwig van Beethoven, "Die Ehre Gottes aus der Natur," Op. 48/4, 7/19/43
Gabriel Fauré, "Après un rêve," Op. 7/1, 4/12/48
Gabriel Fauré, "Nell," Op. 18/1, 12/5/49
Christoph von Gluck, "Divinités du Styx" from *Alceste,* 9/11/44 (CD: Eklipse EKRCD 19)
Charles Gounod, "Plus grand dans son obscurité" from *La Reine de Saba,* 12/13/43 (CD: Eklipse EKRCD 19; Legendary Recordings LRCD 1031)
Charles Griffes, "Evening Song," 12/13/43
Hall Johnson (arr.), "Fix Me, Jesus," 4/12/48
Frank La Forge, "Hills," 3/29/43 (CD: Eklipse EKRCD 19)
Thurlow Lieurance, "By the Waters of Minnetonka," 9/11/44
Robert MacGimsey (arr.), "I Was There When They Crucified My Lord," 3/29/43
Jules Massenet, "Pleurez, mes yeux" from *Le Cid,* 6/17/46 (CD: Legendary Recordings LRCD 1031)
Ethelbert Nevin, "The Rosary," 7/19/43

Appendix 2: Discography

Sergei Rachmaninoff, "O thou billowy harvest field," Op. 4/5, 9/11/44
Jean Sibelius, "Black Roses" ("Svarta rosor"), Op. 36/1, 8/6/45
Piotr Ilyich Tchaikovsky, "None but the lonely heart" ("Net, tolko tot, kto znal"), Op. 6/6, 6/17/46
Clarence C. White (arr.), Wake Up, Jacob!, 4/9/45

Museo Pablo Casals
1961 Casals Festival, Puerto Rico:
  6/14/61: Franz Schubert:
  "Abschied"
  "Auf dem Wasser zu singen"
  "Im Freien"
  "Wer nie sein Brot mit Tränen ass" (Harfners Gesang II)
  6/16/61: Johannes Brahms:
  "Sind es Schmerzen, sind es Freuden" (from *Die schöne Magelone*), Op. 33/3
  Vier ernste Gesänge, Op. 121

New York Public Library: Rogers and Hammerstein Archives of Recorded Sound Collection includes Bell Telephone Hour broadcasts (Bell Telephone Hour Collection), Little Orchestra Society concerts (Little Orchestra Society Concert Recordings Collection), NBC Symphony Orchestra program of 15 October 1944 (Armed Forces Radio Service Collection).

From Bell Telephone Hour Broadcasts (with the Bell Telephone Hour Orchestra, cond. by Donald Vorhees):
Johann Sebastian Bach, "My Heart Ever Faithful" (Mein gläubiges Herze) from Cantata 68, 11/5/51
Vincenzo Bellini, "Casta diva" from *Norma,* 10/11/43 (CD: Eklipse EKRCD 19; Legendary Recordings LRCD 1031)
Vincenzo Bellini, "Odiò la pastorella," 1/10/49
Georges Bizet, "Agnus Dei" from *L'Arlésienne,* 4/24/44
Johannes Brahms, "Sapphische Ode," Op. 94/4, 1/6/47
Gabriel Fauré, "Après un rêve," Op. 7/1, 4/12/48
Gabriel Fauré, "Nell," Op. 18/1, 12/5/49
César Franck, "Air de L'Archange" from *Rédemption,* 11/22/48
Christoph von Gluck, "Divinités du Styx" from *Alceste,* 9/11/44 (CD: Eklipse EKRCD 19); 9/23/46
Charles Gounod, "Plus grand dans son obscurité" from *La Reine de Saba,* 12/13/43 (CD: Eklipse EKRCD 19; Legendary Recordings LRCD 1031)
Georg Frideric Handel, "Ombra mai fu" from *Serse,* 1/18/43 (CD: Legendary Recordings LRCD 1031)
Georg Frideric Handel, "Speranze mie fermate" from *Serse,* 12/5/49
Ferdinand Hummel, "Halleluja," 9/14/42
Thurlow Lieurance, "By the Waters of Minnetonka," 9/11/44
Jules Massenet, "Ne me refuse pas" from *Hériodiade,* 1/6/47 (CD: Legendary Recordings LRCD 1031)
Jules Massenet, "Pleurez, mes yeux" from *Le Cid,* 6/17/46 (CD: Legendary Recordings LRCD 1031); 4/16/51
Wolfgang Amadeus Mozart, "Alleluja" from *Exsultate Jubilate,* 6/26/44, 9/23/46

Appendix 2: Discography

Sergei Rachmaninoff, "O thou billowy harvest field," Op. 4/5, 9/11/44

Franz Schubert, "Die Allmacht," 12/2/46

Jean Sibelius, "Black Roses" ("Svarta rosor"), Op. 36/1, 8/6/45

Jean Sibelius, "Solitude" from *Belshazzar's Feast,* Op. 51, 3/13/50

Piotr Ilyich Tchaikovsky, "None but the lonely heart" ("Net, tolko tot, kto znal"), Op. 6/6, 6/17/46

Giuseppe Verdi, "Pace, pace mio Dio" from *La Forza del destino,* 12/10/45 (CD: Eklipse EKRCD 19); 3/18/46

Spirituals:

"Cert'ny Lord" (arr. Hall Johnson), 3/31/47

"Fix Me, Jesus" (arr. Hall Johnson), 4/12/48

"I'm Going to Tell God" (arr. Lawrence Brown), 1/19/53, 5/3/43

"Steal Away" (arr. Henry Thacker Burleigh), 10/22/45

"Wake Up, Jacob!" (arr. Clarence C. White), 4/9/45

"Where Does This Road Lead" (arr. Delmar Molarsky), 12/2/46

Little Orchestra Society Concerts:

Johann Sebastian Bach, "Schlage doch, gewünschte Stunde," from Cantata 53, 11/29/48

Franz Liszt, "Jeanne d'Arc au bûcher," 11/29/48

Wolfgang Amadeus Mozart, "Ombra felice," 11/29/48

Philadelphia Orchestra Archives

Aaron Copland, *A Lincoln Portrait.* With the Philadelphia Orchestra, cond. by Aaron Copland, 8/6/76

Private Collection

Bach Aria Group Concert, 12/5/51:

"Die Art verruchter "Sünden" from Cantata 54

"Du Herr, du kronst allein das Jahr mit deinem Gut" from Cantata 187

"Du machst, o Tod, mir nun nicht ferner bange" from Cantata 114

"Jesus macht mich geistlich reich" from Cantata 75

"Murre nicht, lieber Christ" from Cantata 144

"Wer Sünde tut, der is von Teufel" from Cantata 54

"Wiederstehe doch der Sünde" from Cantata 54

Stanford University Archives

San Francisco Symphony Broadcasts (cond. by Pierre Monteux):

Georges Bizet, "Agnus Dei" from *L'Arlésienne,* 3/13/49 (CD: Eklipse EKR 49)

Franz Liszt, "Jeanne d'Arc au bûcher," 3/13/49 (CD: Eklipse EKR 49)

Swedish Radio Archives

University of Pennsylvania: Rare Book and Manuscript Library
Marian Anderson Collection of Miscellaneous Sound Recordings (Ms. Coll. 208)

II. Test Pressings and Home Recordings

University of Pennsylvania: Rare Book and Manuscript Library
Marian Anderson Collection of Test Pressings, 1936–1966 (Ms. Coll. 207)
Marian Anderson Collection of Home Studio Recordings, ca. 1935–1950 (Ms. Coll. 206)

References

Notes on Sources

The research on this biography is based primarily on a small number of significant sources. By far the most important are the Marian Anderson Papers (MAP). The MAP are housed in the Rare Book and Manuscipt Library of the University of Pennsylvania and consist of diaries, scrapbooks, newspaper clippings, autobiographical material, promotional material, awards, memorabilia, personal and general correspondence, music, books, phonograph recordings, and tapes. The Westlake and Albrecht catalog (see Bibliography) covers Marian Anderson's initial gift of papers to the University of Pennsylvania, made in 1977, but not the additional gifts made in 1987 and 1991. The entire MAP holdings are now recatalogued, making the Westlake and Albrecht citations no longer valid.

Another important source is the autobiography of Marian Anderson, *My Lord, What a Morning* (ML). ML was organized and written by Howard Taubman from a series of interviews, taped over the course of several months in 1955 and 1956, in Anderson's studio at Marianna Farm, in Danbury, Connecticut. Taubman was given access to only a very few documents, none dealing with MA's private life, although he did meet briefly with members of MA's family and with some representatives of Sol Hurok, MA's manager. The tape recordings of all of the sessions are catalogued as Interviews Conducted by Howard Taubman, 1955–56 (henceforth MA/Taubman tapes), Ms. Coll. 201, in the Rare Book and Manuscript Library, University of Pennsylvania. There is, in addition, a complete transcript of the tapes in MAP. The tapes contain material that Taubman did not include in ML. I have also made use of a tape of Marian Anderson and Ethel DePreist reminiscing informally about family history (henceforth MA/ED tape). The origins of the tape are discussed in chapter 14.

Of considerable importance is the newspaper coverage of MA's life and career, especially in the black press, where it is generally more extensive than in the white press, especially for the period 1915 to 1925. In addition to the *Philadelphia Tribune,* the *New York Age, Amsterdam News, Pittsburgh Courier, Chicago Defender, Norfolk Journal and Guide,* and the *Baltimore Afro-American* are the most consistently useful black newspapers.

Finally, interviews with a great many individuals connected to MA in a variety of ways have proved invaluable.

References

People Interviewed

Betty Allen

Marian Anderson

Brenda Anderson

Martina Arroyo

Miriam Axelrod

Anne Baccari

Lillian Bass

Robert Bass

Karin C. Bivins

Max Brownstein

Rabbi Campbell

Ann Chapman

Jeanette DeFazio

Ginette DePreist

James DePreist

Tracy DePreist

Lilly Venning Dickerson

Dr. Harry M. Delany

Mattiwilda Dobbs

Gladys Duckett

Todd Duncan

Martin Feinstein

James Fischer

George Fisher

Judy Fisher

Sarah Fisher

June Goodman

Kenneth Goodman

Raymond Green

Sandra Grymes

László Halász

Afrika Hayes

Patrick Hayes

Jehoash Hirshberg

John Hopkins

Rochelle Horowitz

Dr. J. Edward Hoy

Reverend David Johnson

Lowell Johnston

Alice E. Jones

Peter Juviler

Abraham Kaplan

Catherine King

John King

Edith Klain

Hilde Kolb

Sylvia Olden Lee

Thomas Logan

Annis Lynch

James Rudolph Lynch

Khalil Mahmud

Cornelius McDougall

Robert McFerrin, Sr.

Reed Maroc

Mrs. V. D. Johnston Maxwell

Dr. Ruth Medac

Dr. Robert Miller

John Motley

Robert O'Neal

Virginia Nicoll

Mildred Oser

Jerry Parker

Eleanor Peters

Roberta Peters

Malcolm Poindexter

Alma Poindexter

Pastor Ralph Reavis

Sally Rose

Sylvia Rupp

Florence May Santiago

Luther Saxon

Karl Ulrich Schnabel

William A. Smith

Comfort Sparks

Robert Starer

Gladys Strickland

Howard Taubman

Thomas Thornley

Shirley Verrett

Stuart Warkow

Mrs. John A. Welsh

Margaret Wettlin

Camilla Williams

Dr. Micheline Williams

Virginia Wren

References

A number of people have kindly given me access to privately held material:
Betty Allen (material on MA's connection with the Harlem School of Music)
James DePreist (letters, programs and private papers of MA, now in MAP)
Tracy De Preist (tape of reminiscences by MA and Ethel DePreist)
George Fisher (material on Orpheus Fisher's family history)
Sarah Fisher (material on history of Union Baptist Church)
June Goodman (material on the Marian Anderson Award, administered by the
    Charles Ives Center in Danbury, Connecticut)
László Halász (programs of concerts in Czechoslovakia, 1931)
Afrika Hayes (tape and material about Roland Hayes)
Patrick Hayes (material on Lincoln Memorial Concert and D.A.R.)
Edith Klain (documents on Dr. Lucy Wilson and South Philadelphia High School)
Ward Marston (test pressings and tapes of MA)
Eleanor Peters (photographs and recordings of MA)
Malcolm Poindexter (material on Lisa Roma and Azalia Hackley)
Bonnie Rowen (film of Lincoln Memorial concert)
Sylvia Rupp (tapes, programs, test pressings, letters, and private papers relating to
    Franz Rupp)

Manuscript Sources

Dwight D. Eisenhower Library: White House Central Files
FDR Library, Hyde Park: Eleanor Roosevelt Papers
Fisk University, Special Collections: Julius Rosenwald Fund Records
Historical Society of Pennsylvania: Program Collection of the Academy of Music
John F. Kennedy Library: White House Name Files
Library of Congress: NAACP Papers
Lyndon B. Johnson Library and Museum: White House Central Files
Metropolitan Opera Archives
Moorland-Spingarn Research Center, Howard University: Marian Anderson Papers
National Archives at College Park, MD: General Records of the Department of
    State
National Archives Building, Washington, DC: Records of the Secretary of the Inte-
    rior
Smith College, Sophia Smith Collection, Women's History Archive: Marian Ander-
    son File
University of Pennsylvania, Rare Book and Manuscript Library: Marian Anderson
    Papers; Musical Fund Society of Philadelphia Records

Bibliography

Anderson, James. D. *The Education of Blacks in the South, 1860–1935.* Chapel Hill: University of North Carolina Press, 1988.

Anderson, Marian. *My Lord, What a Morning: An Autobiography.* New York: Viking Press, 1956.

Anderson, Peggy. *The Daughters: An Unconstitutional Look at America's Fan Club—The D.A.R.* New York: St. Martin's Press, 1974.

Bailie, Helen Tufts. *Our Threatened Heritage: A Letter to the Daughters of the American Revolution.* Cambridge, MA: D. A. R. Committee of Protest, 1928.

Benedetti, Jean. *Stanislavski.* New York: Routledge, 1988.

Berger, Graenum. *Black Jews in America: A Documentary with Commentary.* New York: Commission on Synagogue Relations, Federation of Jewish Philanthropies of New York, 1978.

Bing, Sir Rudolf. *5000 Nights at the Opera.* Mattituck, NY: Ameron House, 1972.

Black, Allida M. *Casting Her Own Shadow: Eleanor Roosevelt and the Shaping of Postwar Liberalism.* New York: Columbia University Press, 1996.

———. "Championing a Champion: Eleanor Roosevelt and the Marian Anderson 'Freedom Concert'." *Presidential Studies Quarterly* 20, no. 4 (1990): 719–736.

———. "A Reluctant but Persistent Warrior: Eleanor Roosevelt and the Early Civil Rights Movement." In *Women in the Civil Rights Movement: Trailblazers and Torchbearers,* edited by Vicki L. Crawford, Jacqueline Anne Rouse, and Barbara Woods, 233–249. *Black Women in United States History,* vol. 16. Brooklyn, NY: Carlson Publishing, 1990.

Blakely, Allison. *Russia and the Negro: Blacks in Russian History and Thought.* Washington, DC: Howard University Press, 1986.

Branch, Taylor. *Parting the Waters: America in the King Years, 1954–63.* New York: Simon and Schuster, 1988.

Brosseau, Grace Lincoln Hall. "The Completion of a Great Project." *Daughters of the American Revolution Magazine* 64, no. 4 (1930): 197–210.

Brown, Jesse E. "Prophet William Saunders Crowdy and the Church of God and Saints of Christ: The Implications of His Life and Thought for the Mission of the Church." Doctor of Ministry diss., Colgate Rochester Divinity School, 1986.

Burk, Robert Fredrick. *The Eisenhower Administration and Black Civil Rights.* Knoxville: The University of Tennessee Press, 1984.

Butterworth, Neil. *The Music of Aaron Copland.* New York: Toccata Press, 1985.

Carter, Marva Griffin. "Hall Johnson: Preserver of the Old Negro Spiritual, 1888–1970." Master's thesis, New England Conservatory, 1975.

Chambers, S. Allen Jr. *Lynchburg: An Architectural History.* Charlottesville: University Press of Virginia, 1981.

Cheatham, Wallace McClain. "Black Male Singers at the Metropolitan Opera." *The Black Perspective in Music* 16:1 (Spring 1988): 3–20.

Christian, W. Asbury. *Lynchburg and Its People.* Lynchburg, VA: J. P. Bell Company, 1900.

Clarke, Jeanne Nienaber. *Roosevelt's Warrior: Harold L. Ickes and the New Deal.* Baltimore: Johns Hopkins University Press, 1996.

Cole, Thomas R. *No Color Is My Kind: The Life of Eldrewey Stearns and the Integration of Houston.* Austin: University of Texas Press, 1997.

Bibliography

Cook, Blanche Wiesen. *Eleanor Roosevelt. Vol. 1, 1884–1933.* New York: Penguin Books, 1992.

Copland, Aaron and Vivian Perlis. *Copland: 1900 Through 1942.* New York: St. Martin's Press, 1984.

Cousins, Norman. "Dialogue with the Russians." *Saturday Review* XLIV:25 (1961): 8–10, 46.

Cuney-Hare, Maud. *Negro Musicians and Their Music.* New York: Da Capo Press, 1974.

Daly, Victor R. "Washington's Minority Problem." *Crisis* 46 (1939): 170–171.

Dannett, Sylvia G. L. *Profiles in Negro Womanhood.* 2 vols. New York: M. W. Lads, 1964.

Dargan, William. "Congregational Gospels." Ph.D. diss., Wesleyan University, 1983.

Davenport, M. Marguerite. *Azalia: The Life of Madame E. Azalia Hackley.* Boston: Chapman and Grimes, 1947.

Duberman, Martin Bauml. *Paul Robeson: A Biography.* New York: Ballantine Books, 1989.

Dubin, Murray. *South Philadelphia: Mummers, Memories, and the Melrose Diner.* Philadelphia: Temple University Press, 1996.

Du Bois, W. E. B. *The Philadelphia Negro: A Social Study.* Philadelphia: University of Pennsylvania, 1899.

Ellis, Edward Robb. *A Nation in Torment: The Great American Depression, 1929–1939.* New York: Kodansha International, 1970.

Embree, Edwin R. *Thirteen Against the Odds.* New York: The Viking Press, 1944.

Epstein, Dena J. *Sinful Tunes and Sprituals: Black Folk Music to the Civil War.* Urbana: University of Illinois Press, 1977.

Samuel A. Floyd, Samuel A., Jr., ed. *Black Music in the Harlem Renaissance: A Collection of Essays.* New York: Greenwood Press, 1990.

Foner, Philip S. *Paul Robeson Speaks: Writings, Speeches, Interviews, 1918–1974.* Secaucus, NJ: Citadel Press, 1978.

Franklin, Vincent P. *The Education of Black Philadelphia: The Social and Educational History of a Minority Community, 1900–1950.* Philadelphia: University of Pennsylvania Press, 1979.

Fryer, Peter. *Black People in the British Empire.* London: Pluto Classic, 1988.

Gallup, Stephen. *History of the Salzburg Festival.* London: Weidenfeld and Nicolson, 1987.

Gelatt, Roland. *The Fabulous Phonograph, 1877–1977.* 2d ed. New York: Collier Books, 1977.

Gentile, Thomas. *March on Washington, August 28, 1963.* Washington, DC: New Day Publications, 1983.

Gerhardt, Elena. *Recital.* London: Methuen, 1953.

Gerson, Robert A. *Music in Philadelphia.* Westport, CT: Greenwood Press, 1940.

Gill, Anton. *A Dance Between Flames: Berlin Between the Wars.* London: Abacus, 1993.

Gilliam, Dorothy Butler. *Paul Robeson: All-American.* Washington, DC: The New Republic Book Company, 1976.

Goldin, Milton. *The Music Merchants.* New York: Macmillan, 1969.

Green, Constance McLaughlin. *The Secret City: A History of Race Relations in the Nation's Capital.* Princeton, NJ: Princeton University Press, 1967.

Green, Jeffrey P. "Conversation with . . . Leslie Thompson: 'Trumpet Player from the West Indies'." *The Black Perspective in Music* 12, no. 1 (1984): 98–127.

———. "Roland Hayes in London, 1921." *The Black Perspective in Music* 10, no. 1 (1982): 29–42.

Bibliography

Hayden, Robert C. *Singing for All People: Roland Hayes, a Biography.* Boston: Select Publications, 1989.

Hayes, Patrick. "White Artists Only." *The Washingtonian* (April 1989): 95–103.

Helm, MacKinley. *Angel Mo' and her Son, Roland Hayes.* Boston: Little, Brown and Company, 1942.

Houghton, Norris. *Moscow Rehearsals: An Account of Methods of Production in the Soviet Theatre.* New York: Harcourt, Brace and Company, 1936.

Hurok, Sol, with Ruthe Goode. *Impressario: A Memoir.* New York: Random House, 1946.

Jay, David, ed. *Growing Up Black: From the Slave Days to the Present—25 African-Americans Reveal the Trials and Triumphs of their Childhoods.* New York: Avon Books, 1968.

Kaplan, Barbara Beigun. *Land and Heritage in the Virginia Tidewater: A History of King and Queen County.* Richmond, VA: King and Queen County Historical Society, 1993.

Kaut, Josef. *Festspiele in Salzburg.* Munich: Deutscher Taschenbuch Verlag, 1970.

Kessler, Harry, Graf. *In the Twenties: The Diaries of Harry Kessler.* Translated by Charles Kessler. New York: Holt, Rinehart and Winston, 1971.

Kimbrough, Emily. "My Life in a White World." *Ladies' Home Journal* 77 (1960): 54, 173–174, 176.

Kirby, John B. *Black Americans in the Roosevelt Era: Liberalism and Race.* Knoxville: University of Tennessee Press, 1980.

Kirk, Elise K. *Musical Highlights from the White House.* Malabar, FL: Krieger Publishing Company, 1992.

Klaw, Barbara. "'A Voice One Hears Once in a Hundred Years': An Interview with Marian Anderson." *American Heritage* 28, no. 2 (1977): 50–57.

Klemperer, Otto. *Klemperer on Music: Shavings from a Musician's Workbench.* London: Toccata Press, 1986.

La Forge, Frank, and Laura La Forge Webb. *Among the Pleiades and Other Stars During the Golden Age of Music: Musical Memoirs of Frank La Forge.* Pittsburgh: Dorrance Publishing Company, 1993.

La Ganke, Lucile Evelyn. "The National Society of the Daughters of the American Revolution: Its History, Policies, and Influence, 1890–1945." Ph.D. diss., Western Reserve University, 1951.

Lane, Roger. *Roots of Violence in Black Philadelphia 1900–1960.* Cambridge, MA: Harvard University Press, 1986.

Lash, Joseph P. *Eleanor and Franklin: The Story of Their Relationship Based on Eleanor Roosevelt's Private Papers.* New York: W. W. Norton and Company, 1971.

Lebrecht, Norman. *Who Killed Classical Music? Maestros, Managers and Corporate Politics.* Secaucus, NJ: Birch Lane Press, 1996.

Leider, Frida. *Playing My Part.* Translated by Charles Osborne. New York: Meredith Press, 1966.

Leitner, Robert D. *The Musicians and Petrillo.* New York: Bookman Associates, 1953.

Lemons, J, Stanley. *The Woman Citizen: Social Feminism in the 1920s.* Urbana: University of Illinois Press, 1973.

Levine, Lawrence W. *Black Culture and Black Consciousness.* New York: Oxford University Press, 1977.

LeVine, Victor T. *The Cameroons, from Mandate to Independence.* Berkeley: University of California Press, 1964.

Bibliography

Lincoln, Natalie Sumner. "Constitution Hall Consecrated." *Daughters of the American Revolution Magazine* 63, no. 11 (1929): 645–650.

Lotz, Rainer and Ian Pegg, eds. *Under the Imperial Carpet: Essays in Black History, 1780–1950*. Crawley, England: Rabbit Press, 1986.

Lovell, John Jr. *Black Song: The Forge and the Flame: The Story of How the Afro-American Spiritual Was Hammered Out*. New York: Paragon House, 1972.

———. "Washington Fights." *Crisis* 46 (1939): 276–277.

Magna, Edith Scott. "Constitution Hall." *Daughters of the American Revolution Magazine* 63, no. 9 (1929): 517–522.

Mandel, William M. *Soviet but Not Russian: The "Other" Peoples of the Soviet Union*. Edmonton, Canada: University of Alberta Press, 1985.

Marshall, Herbert, and Mildred Stock. *Ira Aldridge, the Negro Tragedian*. London: Feffer and Simons, 1958.

McAleer, John J. *Rex Stout: A Biography*. Boston: Little, Brown and Company, 1977.

McNeil, Genna Rae. *Groundwork: Charles Hamilton Houston and the Struggle for Civil Rights*. Philadelphia: University of Pennsylvania Press, 1983.

Mezerik, A. G. ed. *Colonialism and the United Nations*. New York: International Review Service, 1964.

Morrison, Allan. "Who Will Be the First to Crack Met Opera?" *Negro Digest* (Sept. 1950): 52–56.

Murray, John N., Jr. *The United Nations Trusteeship System*. Urbana: University of Illinois Press, 1957.

NAACP Papers. Part 2: Personal Correspondence of Selected NAACP Officials. Microfilm Edition.

NAACP Papers. Part 15: Segregation and Discrimination: Complaints and Responses, 1940–1955. Series B: Administrative Files. Microfilm Edition.

Noble, Jeanne L. *Beautiful, Also, Are the Souls of My Black Sisters: A History of the Black Woman in America*. Englewood Cliffs, NJ: Prentice-Hall, 1978.

Potter, Dorothy T., and Clifton W. Potter, Jr. *Lynchburg: "The Most Interesting Spot."* 2d ed. Lynchburg, VA: Beric Press, 1985.

Poyurovskii, B. "Immanuel Kaminka." *Mastera Khuozestvennovo Slova*. Moscow: Iskusstvo, 1983.

Read, Anthony and David Fisher. *Berlin Rising: Biography of a City*. New York: W. W. Norton and Company, 1994.

Reagon, Bernice Johnson, ed. *We'll Understand It Better By and By*. Washington, DC and London: Smithsonian Institution Press, 1992.

Reavis, Ralph. *Virginia Seminary: A Journey of Black Independence*. Bedford, VA: The Print Shop, 1989.

Robinson, Harlow. *The Last Impressario: The Life, Times, and Legacy of Sol Hurok*. New York: The Viking Press, 1994.

Robinson, Robert. *Black on Red: My 44 Years Inside the Soviet Union*. Washington, DC: Acropolis Books, 1988.

Rogers, J. A. *World's Great Men of Color*. 2 vols. New York: J. A. Rogers, 1947.

Sady, Emil L. *The United Nations and Dependent Peoples*. Westport, CT: Greenwood Press, 1974.

Saerchinger, Cesar. *Artur Schnabel: A Biography*. Westport, CT: Greenwood Press, 1957.

Sandage, Scott A. "A Marble House Divided: The Lincoln Memorial, the Civil Rights

Movement, and the Politics of Memory, 1939–1963." *Journal of American History* 80, no. 1 (1993): 135–167.

Schnabel, Artur. *My Life and Music.* New York: St. Martin's Press, 1963.

Scobie, Edward. *Black Britannia: A History of Blacks in Britain.* Chicago: Johnson Publishing Company, 1972.

Scruggs, Philip Lightfoot. *The History of Lynchburg, Virginia 1786–1946.* Lynchburg, VA: J. P. Bell Company, 1968.

Sheean, Vincent. *Between the Thunder and the Sun.* New York: Random House, 1943.

Shirakawa, Sam H. *The Devil's Music Master: The Controversial Life and Career of Wilhelm Furtwängler.* New York: Oxford University Press, 1992.

Shultz, Gladys Denny. *Jenny Lind: The Swedish Nightingale.* Philadelphia: J. B. Lippincott Company, 1962.

Simpson, Anne Key. *Hard Trials: The Life and Music of Harry T. Burleigh.* Metuchen, NJ: Scarecrow Press, 1990.

Sims, Janet L. *Marian Anderson: An Annotated Bibliography and Discography.* Westport, CT: Greenwood Press, 1981.

Smith, Carleton. "Roulades and Cadenzas." *Esquire* 18 (July 1939): 79, 167–169.

Smith, Homer. *Black Man in Red Russia: A Memoir.* Chicago: Johnson Publishing Company, 1964.

Somerville, Mollie D. *Eleanor Roosevelt as I Knew Her.* Charlottesville, VA: Howell Press, 1996.

Southern, Eileen. *Biographical Dictionary of Afro-American and African Musicians.* Westport, CT: Greenwood Press, 1982.

———. *The Music of Black Americans: A History,* 2d ed. New York: W. W. Norton and Company, 1983.

Spender, Stephen. *World Within World: The Autobiography of Stephen Spender.* London: Hamilton, 1951

Steane, J. B. *The Grand Tradition: Seventy Years of Singing on Record.* London: Duckworth, 1974.

Stokes, Anson Phelps. *Art and the Color Line: An Appeal Made May 31, 1939 to the President of the Daughters of the American Revolution to Modify Their Rules So as to Permit Distinguished Artists Such as Miss Marian Anderson to Be Heard in Constitution Hall.* Washington, DC, 1939.

Story, Rosalyn M. *And So I Sing: African-American Divas of Opera and Concert.* New York: Warner Books, 1990.

Stovall, Tyler. *Paris noir: African Americans in the City of Light.* Boston: Houghton Mifflin, 1996.

Taubman, Howard. *The Pleasure of Their Company: A Reminiscence.* Portland, OR: Amadeus, 1994.

Traubel, Helen. *St. Louis Woman.* New York: Duell, Sloan and Pearce, 1959.

Turner, Patricia. *Dictionary of Afro-American Performers, 78 RPM and Cylinder Recordings of Opera, Choral Music, and Song, c. 1900–1949.* New York: Garland, 1990.

Tuttle, William M. Jr. *Race Riot: Chicago in the Red Summer of 1919.* New York: Atheneum, 1970.

Vehanen, Kosti. *Marian Anderson: A Portrait.* New York and London: Whittlesey House, 1941.

Villard, Oswald Garrison. "What the Blue Menace Means." *Harpers Magazine* 157 (October 1928): 529–540.

Bibliography

Von Eckardt, Wolf von, and Sander L. Gilman. *Bertolt Brecht's Berlin: A Scrapbook of the Twenties.* Garden City, NY: Anchor Press, 1975.

Vriend, Sharon R. "The Controversy Before the Concert: The Dialogue in the European American Press Regarding the Discrimination Against Marian Anderson, 6 January 1939 through 8 April 1939." Master's thesis, Bowling Green State University, 1994.

Walker, Beersheba Crowdy. *The Life and Works of William Saunders Crowdy.* Philadelphia: Elfreth Walker, 1955.

Walter, Bruno. *Theme and Variations: An Autobiography.* Translated by James A. Galston. New York: Alfred A. Knopf, 1946.

Ware, W. Porter, and Thaddeus C. Lockard, Jr. *P. T. Barnum Presents Jenny Lind: The American Tour of the Swedish Nightingale.* Baton Rouge: Louisiana State University Press, 1980.

Washington Landmark: A View from the D. A. R.—The Headquarters, History, and Activities. Washington, DC: National Society, Daughters of the American Revolution, 1975.

Watkins, T. H. *The Great Depression: America in the 1930s.* Boston: Little, Brown and Company, 1993.

———. *Righteous Pilgrim: The Life and Times of Harold L. Ickes, 1874–1952.* New York: Henry Holt and Company, 1990.

Weiss, Nancy J. *Farewell to the Party of Lincoln: Black Politics in the Age of FDR.* Princeton, NJ: Princeton University Press, 1983.

Westlake, Neda M., and Otto W. Albrecht. *Marian Anderson: A Catalog of the Collection at the University of Pennsylvania Library.* Philadelphia: University of Pennsylvania Press, 1981.

White, Walter Francis. *A Man Called White: The Autobiography of Walter White.* Athens, Georgia and London: University of Georgia Press, 1948.

William Allen White. *Forty Years on Main Street.* New York: Farrar and Rinehart, Inc., 1937.

Williams, Patricia J. *The Rooster's Egg.* Cambridge, MA: Harvard University Press, 1995.

Wolters, Raymond. *Negroes and the Great Depression: The Problem of Economic Recovery.* Westport, CT: Greenwood Publishing Corporation, 1970.

Wynia, Elly M. *The Church of God and Saints of Christ: The Rise of Black Jews.* New York: Garland Publishing, 1994.

Zangrando, Joanna Schneider and Robert L. Zangrando. "ER and Black Civil Rights." *Without Precedent. The Life and Career of Eleanor Roosevelt.* Joan Hoff-Wilson and Marjorie Lightfoot, eds. Bloomington: Indiana University Press, 1984, pp. 88–107.

$\mathcal{N}otes$

CHAPTER 1

1. I have followed closely the version of the story that appears in ML, pp.13–14.
2. Because birth records for King and Queen County, Virginia, do not exist before 1853, Benjamin Anderson's birth date cannot be established with absolute certainty. His marriage certificate, filed on December 30, 1869, and on file in the King William County Courthouse, King William, Virginia, indicates that he was born in 1848, a more likely birth date than the one indicated on his death certificate (1858), or the one given in the 1900 census (September 1853). The King and Queen County birth records are on microfilm in the Library of Virginia, Richmond, Virginia: *King and Queen County Birth Register of the Bureau of Vital Statistics, 1853–1896*).
3. Only the 1900 census documents the fact the Benjamin and Isabella Anderson gave birth to eight children. In the birth records of King and Queen County, Virginia, of which some entries from the 1870s and 1880s no longer exist, only four Anderson children's birth entries can be found: Miniva (b. August 14, 1873), Mary B. (b. October 2, 1877), James R. (b. December 17, 1879), and Walter T. (b. October 15, 1885). Miniva and James did not survive infancy. The surviving children, in addition to Mary and Walter, included John Berkley, Robert William, and Richard. I am grateful to Brenda Anderson for sharing copies of family documents with me, including the marriage certificate of Benjamin and Isabella Anderson.
4. For a useful history of King and Queen County, Virginia, see Kaplan (1993).
5. On the history of South Philadelphia neighborhoods, see especially Dubin (1996). The author was kind enough to discuss his work with me before the publication of his book. Also important, from a sociological vantage point, is DuBois's classic *The Philadelphia Negro* (1899). I also learned a great deal about early twentieth-century South Philadelphia from interviews with Gladys Duckett, who, doing the late 1930s and early 1940s, lived at 772 South Martin Street, only five doors away from the Andersons.
6. On Rucker family history, interviews with James Rudolph Lynch (March 1, 1994) and Annis Lynch (March 1, 1994), and the MA/ED tape. Records of Robert Rucker's business ventures are in the Lynchburg Musem and the Jones Memorial Library, Lynchburg. I am grateful to Lynchburg historians Dorothy and Clifton Potter for helpful suggestions and information about Lynchburg's history. The most useful histories of Lynchburg are Dorothy and Cliffton Potter (1985), Scruggs (1968), and Christian (1900).
7. The single handwritten page is in MAP.
8. ML, p. 3
9. In the catalogues of the Virginia Seminary, which regularly included lists of alumni, there is no record—between the years 1892, when she was nineteen, and 1896, when she left Lynchburg for Philadelphia—of Anna Anderson having graduated. I am grateful to Pastor Ralph Reavis for searching through the school catalogues for me and for discussions about the history of the Virginia Seminary. For its history, see Reavis (1989).
10. Either because the information was for some reason not conveyed in time, or because the Andersons had not yet decided on a name, there are no first or middle

names on Marian Anderson's birth certificate. On all existing documents, however, "Marian" is the spelling used by the family, and is the form MA always used, although "Marion" occurs frequently on concert programs before and during the 1920s. As for MA's middle name, the initial "E" does occur on occason on early concert programs. On only a single existing document—the certificate presented to MA as a newly elected fellow of the American Academy of Arts and Sciences, May 8, 1957—does a middle name, Elina-Blanche, occur.

11. ML, pp. 4–5.
12. ML, p. 5.
13. Ibid.
14. ML, p. 3.
15. ML, p. 7.
16. From a typed document [n.d.], the contents prepared by Anna Anderson, about her daughter's childhood, in MAP.
17. Barbara Klaw (1977), p. 52.
18. Sylvia G. L. Dannett (1966), p.161.
19. ML, p. 11.
20. On the Stanton School and its curriculum, many interviews with Malcolm Poindexter, who attended the school a few years after Anderson had graduated and who later joined the faculty, and Gladys Duckett, who also attended the school during the same period as Poindexter. As for primary school, without the help of school records (see note 36), one can likely assume that Anderson attended either Pollock, a black primary school at Sixteenth and Fitzwater, only a half block from her grandparents' home, where the Andersons were then living, or Chester A. Arthur, at Twentieth and Catharine, a mixed school that many black families living in the neighborhood would have preferred.
21. Anna Anderson to Bishop Jones, January 28, 1941, in MAP.
22. See DuBois (1899), pp. 213–216; for the history of Union Baptist Church, here and in later sections, I also drew on *Union Baptist Church,* a monograph published by the church in 1992, on the occasion of its 160th anniversary. For the latter, and other material on the church's history and Anderson's involvement with it, I am grateful to Sarah Fisher, a member of the church for more than sixty years; also interviews with Anne Baccari and Alice E. Jones, both longtime members of Union Baptist.
23. ML, p.8.
24. MA/ED tape.
25. On Hackley's career and accomplishments in Philadelphia, see Davenport (1947), pp. 111–120. I am grateful to Malcolm Poindexter for drawing my attention to Davenport's book and for presenting his copy of it to me as a gift.
26. Davenport (1947), p. 115.
27. ML, p.14.
28. MA/ED tape.
29. ML, p.19.
30. ML, p.18.
31. Interview with Marian Anderson, December 9, 1992.
32. ML, p.16.
33. On the footwashers' storefront church, interviews with Malcom Poindexter, Gladys Duckett, Lily Venning Dickerson, Marian Anderson, and Lillian Bass; also, discussions with Rabbi Campbell, the spiritual leader of the present congregation,

whose church, now on Broad Street near Fifteenth, is the descendant of Bishop Crowdy's church (see note 34).

34. On Bishop Crowdy's career and his teachings, see Walker (1955), Brown (1986), and Wynia (1994).

35. MA/ED tape.

36. Unfortunately, I have had to do without the benefit of Anderson's public school records with which to establish an exact chronology of her education. After a lengthy search, Paul Hanson, director of the Office of Communications of the School District of Philadelphia, was unable to locate any records for any of the Anderson children. Marian Anderson's certificate for having completed the course in cooking, dated June 13, 1910, issued, in accordance with interviews with Malcolm Poindexter and Gladys Duckett, after the sixth grade of the Stanton School's curriculum, would indicate that Anderson graduated from Stanton in June, 1912. A brief article in Crisis (October 1916), which began to document Anderson's career the preceding year, records that she was then in her second year at the William Penn High School.

37. ML, p. 26.

38. ML, pp. 27–28. The "Inflammatus," for soprano and chorus, from the Stabat Mater of Rossini, has only a single, climactic high C. Anderson's accomplishment must have been significant enough for her to add several more high C's through the years as she retold the story.

39. MA/ED tape.

40. ML, p. 29.

41. ML, p. 30.

42. *Philadelphia Tribune,* April 4, 1914.

CHAPTER 2

1. The exodus of black teachers from Philadelphia and its effect on the teaching of music there formed the basis of the article, "Do We Appreciate the Efforts of Our Classical Musicians?," which appeared in the *Philadelphia Tribune,* Oct. 16, 1915; later that year (December 14), the *Philadelphia Tribune* reprinted an article that Carl Diton, who was then teaching at Talladega College, in Alabama, had published earlier in the November issue of the *Musician,* "The Present Status of Negro-American Musical Endeavor." Diton's article praised the musical achievements of black musicians and teachers and emphasized the importance of the role of the music teacher in improving the status of black musicians. While he did not have Philadelphia alone in mind, his own departure from Philadelphia in 1929, after a decade of teaching there, deprived students of one of its most active and imaginative musicians.

2. Interviews with Malcolm Poindexter (April 23, 1993; June 11, 1993; July 23, 1993).

3. Interview with Poindexter (July 1, 1993), when he spoke vividly of Anderson telling him about her attempts to find a teacher, how resentful she was and how disappointing and difficult it was to make any progress.

4. Kimbrough (1950), p. 77.

5. Kimbrough (1950), p. 77. This incident has become the emblematic story of racial intolerance in MA's early years, repeated in nearly every biographical sketch and article. It is recounted in ML, chapter 4, "Shock"; the version on the MA/Taubman tapes (#20) is much briefer (the details must have been told to Howard Taubman

with the tape recorder turned off, which MA tended to do when she felt that a topic was too personal to be discussed in the book). It adds only several details to the story—that the suggestion of the music school did not come from a Negro but from a white person, and that he would not have expected the response that she received. The version in the interview with Emily Kimbrough is more detailed; MA was much more open with Kimbrough than she was with Howard Taubman. Of course, much of the impact of the story over the years, unintentionally to be sure, comes from MA's refusal to give the name of the school. She did not like to criticize or to lay blame except in the most circumspect and indirect ways.

The identity of the school will no doubt remain speculative, but there is evidence that is worth presenting. The incident must have happened a year or so before MA began to study with Patterson, perhaps sometime in early 1914. Some of the concrete details of the story are suggestive. In most versions MA recalled that the school was not far away from where the family was then living (which would have been 2011 Carpenter or 751 S. Martin Street). In those years the only music schools of some consequence in that neighborhood were the Combs Conservatory of Music, at 1327–31 S. Broad St., and the Philadelphia Musical Academy, at 1617 Spruce. Both schools offered vocal instruction. There is also MA's insistence that the school no longer existed (i.e., in 1955, at the time of the preparation of ML). Both schools did, however, exist then, the Combs School as late as several years ago. On other occasions, however, MA insisted that the school was not the prestigious Curtis Institute, without insisting at the same time that the school no longer existed. Taken together, these statements seem very much like understandable attempts to prevent people from wrongly speculating about the school's identity. Perhaps we should not take MA's insistence so literally, but only as a way of saying that the name doesn't matter. Although MA accepted an honorary degree from the Combs School in 1976, it seems reasonable to argue that she would not have refused such an honor if it had been the Combs School that had, in fact, turned her away. She would have seen the gesture as welcome progress, and been happy to accept.

I raised the question of the identity of the school with Malcolm Poindexter in two interviews (July 1, 1993; July 16, 1993) and his recollections bear consideration for several reasons. He was nearly the same age as MA when they came to know each other and saw one another frequently, and he was raised in South Philadelphia and well-known and respected within the black musical community. He was a gentle and soft-spoken man, full of quiet charm, very well educated, a private teacher of voice and a teacher in the public schools of Philadelphia for decades. More important, however, is that his recollections, chronologically and factually, have been repeatedly confirmed in a variety of ways. I found him to be resolute, however, in refusing to commit himself on anything about which he did not feel a good measure of certainty. His efforts and commitment in all of my interviews with him (there were eight in all) always took on a nearly moral tone of seriousness.

Poindexter remembered conversations with Joseph Lockett, a pianist of some distinction, who held a number of positions as organist in Chicago churches after leaving Philadelphia. Lockett told him that he had been turned away from the head of the same music school as MA, with the words: "You ought to find people of your own color to support you." How Lockett knew that it was the very same school was not made as clear as it might have been by Poindexter; the implication of the inter-

views was that these were the kinds of things that were talked about in the community, as similar experiences of great hurtfulness were shared. Poindexter himself was
less clear about the name of the school and would not commit himself to a defini-
tive answer, mentioning as possibilities the Philadelphia Conservatory and the
Combs School. He did seem certain the school no longer existed and that it was on
Spruce Street. The Philadelphia Conservatory of Music at that time was at 822 N.
Broad Street, but the Philadelphia Musical Academy, which was often confused
with the Philadelphia Conservatory in interviews (with Kenneth Goodman, for
example, July 14, 1993, and apparently Poindexter, July 1, 1993, who thought that
the conservatory was on Spruce Street) was located at the time at 1617 Spruce
Street.

6. ML, p. 35; see also MA/Taubman tapes (#1) for an account of Butler's help in
bringing MA to Patterson, omitted in ML.

7. ML, p. 36; on the Pattersons, interviews with Poindexter, who knew them well, and
Lily Venning Dickerson, who played for Patterson's students and whose sister, Mat-
tie Venning, studied singing with her.

8. ML, pp. 46 ff.

9. May 22, 1915.

10. See the *Philadelphia Tribune,* April 13, 1918, for the beginning of the newspaper's
recognition of his accomplishments as a promoter in Philadelphia.

11. *Philadelphia Tribune,* "A Worthy Cause," May 29, 1915.

12. A review appeared in the *Philadelphia Tribune,* July 3, 1915; the reviewer took the
occasion to encourage the black community to help "bring to her artistic training
the benefits of a well balanced and cultured mentality."

13. In spite of Reifsnyder's importance as a teacher in Philadelphia, in the first three
decades of the century, among both the black and white communities, she is
remembered now only in biographical articles about MA. Her singing career can be
traced in part in the program collection of the Academy of Music, now in the Historical Society of Pennsylvania, and in the program collection of the Musical Fund
Society of Philadelphia Records, at the University of Pennsylvania. She appeared in
recital at the Witherspoon Hall, as contralto soloist in *Messiah* with the Choral Society of Philadelphia, as accompanist for Marguerite Sibley, and in joint recital with
her, all between 1919 and 1924.

14. ML, p. 48.

15. *Philadelphia Tribune,* June 9, 1917.

16. Lester A. Walton, in the *Pittsburgh Courier,* July 25, 1925.

17. ML p. 21.

18. On the career of Roland Hayes, see Hayden (1989), Helm (1942), Rogers (1946),
Daniel Lyman Ridout, "Singing a Race Upward," *The Epworth Herald,* May 18,
1929; on Hayes's activity in Philadelphia, *Philadelphia Tribune,* February 3, 1916.

19. The other singers were the soprano, Lydia McClane and Noah Ryder, a young bass
from Nashville.

20. *Philadelphia Tribune,* April 15, 1916.

21. *Crisis,* May 1916.

22. *Crisis,* April 1917.

23. ML, p. 40.

24. There are more details of Marian's first trip to the South on the MA/Taubman tapes
(#25) than in ML, pp. 40–41.

25. ML, p. 40.
26. During MA's youth, the Austrian-born singer Ernestine Schumann-Heink (1861–1936) was the most famous and beloved contralto in the world. Because of her extraordinary technique—like MA she had an enormous range, from low D to high B-flat—her remarkable interpretive gifts, and the enormous affection with which she was held in Europe and America, Schumann-Heink was, and for many still is, the universal point of reference for the contralto voice.
27. *Savannah Morning News,* December 29, 1917; the reviews were altogether unanimous: *Savannah Press,* December 29, 1917 ("Her voice is exquisitely rich and full and mellow. Her control is marvelous, the music just seeming to come without any effort from the singer"); *Savannah Tribune,* January 5, 1918 ("She has the most melodious and richest contralto voice heard here in many years. Its range is little short of wonderful and the ease with which she made her most difficult notes was indeed charming").
28. Interview with Lillian Bass (January 9, 1993).
29. *Philadelphia Tribune,* May 4, 1918; the review there, April 27, 1918, was not a serious consideration of MA's performance, but a tribute to her talent and her popuarity among the black community of Philadelphia.
30. *New York Age,* April 27, 1918.
31. I am grateful to a number of people for providing me with information and newspaper and other articles about Dr. Wilson: Bill Esher, president of the South Philadelphia High School Alumni Association; Herbert Jung, the present principal of the school; interview with Lily Venning Dickerson, who graduated from the school, as did MA, in 1921; interviews with Edith Klain, Anne Baccari, Mildred Oser, Miriam Axelrod, all graduates of the class of 1924 and, therefore, freshmen when MA was a senior; and interview with Margaret Wettlin. Particularly useful was the article prepared by Roslyn Sacks Serota in June, 1922 , "Lucy Langdon Wilson—a Woman for All Time." Dr. Wilson's achievements in Philadelphia were honored in 1934 when she received the Bok Award, founded in 1921 by Edward W. Bok and given each year in recognition of distinguished service rendered to Philadelphia.
 2. Interview with Lily Venning Dickerson (January 30, 1993).
33. Communication from Virginia Nicoll, whose mother, Jessie Fleming Vose, was Hubbard's accompanist in Boston when MA auditioned for Hubbard.
34. ML, p. 29.
35. Course information for Saenger's summer program is in MAP.
36. I have made use of the following in discussing the formation of the NANM in Chicago: Patterson (1993), Johnson (1956); the account of the first national meeting that appeared in the *Chicago Defender,* August 9, 1919, written by its first secretary and one of its principal supporters, Nora Douglas Holt, and Carl Diton's account of its first four years, in *Crisis,* May, 1923. Also useful is the review of its first decade, in the *Chicago Defender,* by Maude Roberts George, September 1, 1928.
37. Details of the Chicago rioting and strike from reports in the *Chicago Defender, The Broad Ax,* and the *Chicago Daily News.*
38. *Chicago Defender,* August 9, 1919.
39. Taken from the minutes of the first meeting, and cited in Patterson (1993), p. 41.
40. ML, pp. 60–61; the account in ML of the NANM scholarship and the choice of the Yale School of Music differs somewhat from the version in the MA/Taubman tapes

(#31); only the choice of Yale is clearly confirmed by published accounts of NANM activities: see Patterson (1993), pp. 88–94, the *Columbus Dispatch,* July 28, 1922. According to Patterson (p. 281), MA was awarded a first prize scholarship in 1927 as well.

41. MA's recollections are given in ML, pp. 48 ff. and the MA/Taubman tapes (#1, 3, 9, 22). Boghetti's recollections are in the *Philadelphia Record,* December 25, 1938, and in the *Evening Public Ledger,* March 14, 1935; for Boghetti's career and teaching, interviews with Marian Anderson and Raymond Green; see also Traubel (1959), pp. 79 ff.

42. *Philadelphia Tribune,* May 1, 1916.

43. The incident is described in ML, p. 51, and slightly differently in the MA/Taubman tapes (#22).

44. See Traubel (1959), pp. 79 ff.

CHAPTER 3

1. ML, p. 80.

2. ML, p. 81.

3. On Orpheus Fisher's family background, interviews with George Fisher, Judy Fisher, James Fischer, and Robert O'Neal. James Fischer is Orpheus Fisher's son by his first marriage (see chapter 3); George Fisher is the son of George Fisher, one of Orpheus Fisher's brothers, and Judy, his wife; Robert O'Neal is the grandson of Anne Fisher Maybry, one of Orpheus's two sisters.

4. I am most grateful to Khalil Mahmud, the archivist at the Langston Hughes Memorial Library, Lincoln University, for the information on George Fischer's education.

5. On Orpheus Fisher's early years, interviews with James Fisher and George Fischer; also publicity document about Orpheus Fisher prepared in early 1946 for the publicity department of Hurok attractions, in MAP.

6. MA/Taubman tapes (#1).

7. ML, pp. 63–64. For information on William King, interviews with Malcolm and Alda Poindexter, Luther Saxon, Comfort Sparks, William A. Smith, Thomas Logan, Thomas Thornley, J. Edward Hoy, and Reverend David Johnson.

8. ML, p. 63.

9. Interview with Malcolm Poindexter (August 6, 1993); in this and other interviews Poindexter spoke more than once about how lazy and unambitious Marian often seemed to Billy King.

10. *Philadelphia Ledger,* May 19, 1922.

11. *New York Age,* June 3, 1922.

12. I am grateful to Bernadette Moore, formerly archivist for BMG, for providing me with the recording sheets of MA's recording sessions with the Victor Talking Machine Co., HMV, and RCA, and to Claudia J. Depkin, Senior Archivist for BMG, for generous help with BMG's recording materials.

13. Sol Graulnick, librarian in the music division of the Free Library of Philadelphia, was kind enough to provide information on the Philharmonic Society of Philadelphia, and on its treasurer, Dr. Hirsch.

14. The *Ledger*'s comments were quoted in the *Philadelphia Tribune,* December 22, 1923, as were those of the *Evening Bulletin,* in which the critic noted that MA's singing of the two spirituals "swept the audience into a fervor of enthusiasm. . . ." and of the

Inquirer ("She is possessed of a contralto of great beauty and power, and her use of her gift showed that she has been well schooled").

15. One of these students was apparently Henrietta Waddy (communication from Tony Heilbut), the Philadelphia-born gospel singer who was for many years a member of the Clara Ward Singers; another student, Wallace Newsome, highly self-critical to judge from his letter, wrote to MA, December 14, 1925: "Just a line to inform you, that after a thorough consideration of my ability, possibilities and various activities, I have reached the decision to discontinue my music lessons as an act of expediency. Thanking you for all you have done for me and wishing you continued success in your career." Another, Mrs. Mae Hunt, who traveled to MA's home in Philadelphia by boat in the early 1920s for lessons, was recalled in a letter, February 6, 1979, to MA from Dr. Brenda Flowers Savage, a member of the English department of Lincoln University. Both letters are in MAP. Poindexter (interview July 1, 1993) mentioned another student, a contralto, Alva Retta Britton. Poindexter spoke about how little Marian's heart was in teaching; "she wanted to sing," he said.

16. Marian's relationship with her Harlem promoter and manager is described in ML, p. 70, MA/Taubman tapes (#3).

17. On the musical life of Harlem, see Southern (1983), pp. 434 ff.; Samuel A. Floyd, Jr., "Music in the Harlem Renaissance: An Overview," and Ron Spearman, "Vocal Concert Music in the Harlem Renaissance," both in Floyd (1990). In an interview with George Nathaniel Redd, Betty Leonard recalled MA's appearance, in 1921, at one of the Harlem casinos, during the intermission of a Kappa Alpha Psi dance, when she performed for a large number of people (see Floyd [1990], pp. 20–21).

18. ML, pp. 76–77.

19. ML, p. 77.

20. Orpheus to MA, January 29, 1923, in MAP.

21. According to James Fischer, Orpheus dropped the "c" from the original spelling of the family name sometime during World War II. James Fischer believes that Orpheus was advised, because of anti-German sentiment, to adopt the less Germanic spelling. All of Orpheus's siblings and their descendants, as far as I could determine, use the "Fisher" form as well.

22. On Orpheus Fisher's student days and marriage to Ida Gould, interviews with James Fischer. MA never spoke of Orpheus Fisher's first marriage or of his son in any interview.

23. All three citations from the *Sun*, April 26, 1924. The criticisms of MA's interpretive ability, especially in lieder, were equally harsh in other reviews: *Herald Tribune*, April 26, 1924 (". . . the expressive possibilities of her German lieder, Strauss, Brahms and Schubert, seemed far from fully fathomed."), *New York Age*, April 25, 1924 ("She seems to lack the power to project her personality into her singing, and the result is that her performance is stilted and constrained.") The most positive review appeared in *Musical America*, May 3, 1924, but a note of reservation about interpretation was not absent ("When she learns to infuse more fire and abandon into her interpretations, her art will gain immensely in human appeal").

24. *New York Age*, April 25, 1924.

25. MA's reactions to the concert are in ML, pp. 72 ff.

26. See White (1948), pp. 180–181.

27. MA's experiences in the stadium contest are described in ML, chapter 9, "Contest."

Notes

28. ML, pp. 102–103.
29. An interview with Boghetti after the winners were announced appeared in the *Philadelphia Tribune,* July 25, 1925. Catherine Richardson (later Mrs. Catherine Richardson Boor), Boghetti's rehearsal pianist who played for MA and Reba Patton during the contest (not "Miss Johnson," as in ML, p. 101), recalled details of the contest in a letter to MA, August 27, 1958, in MAP.
30. *Philadelphia Tribune,* July 4, 1925.
31. *New York Herald Tribune,* August 27, 1925. Olin Downes, one of the most respected of New York music critics, took positive notice of MA'a singing for the first time in the pages of the *New York Times,* August 26, 1925 ("The beauty and expressive capacities of her voice and the native interpretive ability of the artist made an immediate and excellent impression. It is a voice and a talent of unusual possibilities").
32. *Philadelphia Tribune,* October 24, 1925.
33. Dayton concert: April 11, 1926, reviews in the *Dayton Journal* (April 12, 1926) and the *Dayton Herald* (April 12, 1926); Greensboro concert: December 1, 1925, reviews in the *Greensboro Daily News* (December 2, 1925) and the *Norfolk Journal and Guide* (December 12, 1925); concert in Norfolk: April 2, 1926, review in *Norfolk Journal and Guide* (April 10, 1926).
34. Concert in Winston-Salem: January 13, 1927, reviews in the *Evening Star* (January 14, 1927), and the *Winston-Salem Journal* (January 14, 1927); concert in Greensboro, at the A. and T. College of North Carolina: January 14, 1927; concert in Charlotte: January 18, 1927, review in the *Charlotte News* (January 19, 1927); concerts at Gorrell's warehouse: May 24, 25, 1923), review of the second concert in the *Winston-Salem Journal* (May 26, 1923).
35. In interviews, Malcolm Poindexter and Luther Saxton spoke about Billy's affairs with women as well as his homosexuality. During the years in which Billy and MA regularly toured, there are many letters to MA from Orpheus, all in MAP, in which he expresses his concern about Billy's intentions toward MA: for example, January 29, 1923 (". . . is that Billy King staying in his place? do you understand me?"); undated, but the same period ("How is Billy King? tell him that a rival asked for him and wishes to be remembered.") During the 1930s, when Billy and MA were separated for long periods during MA's extended European tours, Billy's letters to MA frequently contain sexual innuendos, reflecting the various roles Billy felt compelled to express toward MA when their relationship was undergoing a great deal of stress. This difficult period in their relationship is discussed in Chapter 8. Several letters in MAP refer to MA's desire to have a chaperon provided by local managers: November 1, 1925 (Marian Anderson Management to the Reverend A. Myron Cochran), November 28, 1925 (J. M. Marquess to MA). There are two letters in MAP that indicate there was gossip and speculation about MA's relationship with Billy King among local managers: A. Myron Cochran, who was making plans for MA's comfort and entertainment related to a concert in Nashville, to Katherine Brock, of the Judson Agency, February 28, 1931 (". . . the question has arisen as to whether or not they are husband and wife. It happens to be known to some of us that at one time they were lovers and we have wondered whether or not that estate has consummated in marriage"); Hattie Clark, of the Judson Agency, to MA, March 10, 1931 ("You will also find a most amusing letter that we received from Nashville, which we answered very vaguely. May we ask that you write a line to Mr. Cochran, as we believe he should have the necessary information from the highest authority.

We told him that 'to the best of our knowledge the relationship existing between Miss Anderson and Mr. King is nothing more than a friendly one, held steadfast by their common artistic interest'").

36. ML, p. 91.
37. ML, p. 118.

CHAPTER 4

1. See Scobie (1972), especially chapters 9–ll, and Fryer (1988), especially pp. 440 ff., on the history of blacks in Britain between the wars; on popular entertainers in the British capital, see Jeffrey P. Green (1984). A number of black American newspapers included regular columns on the activities of blacks in England. Ivan H. Browning's column, "Across the Pond," in the *Chicago Defender,* is particularly helpful.

2. MA's recollections of her year in London are in ML, chapter 18 ("First Trip to Europe") and, with different details emphasized, in MA/Taubman tapes (#5, 6); see also the interview with MA by Bernice Dutrieuille, in the *Philadelphia Tribune,* October 4, 1928, just after MA's return from London.

3. ML, p. 121.
4. ML, p. 124.
5. Daniel Kelly to MA, June 25, 1949, in MAP.
6. On the matinee at the pavilion for the benefit of the flood victims, see *West Africa,* February 4, 1928, and for Alberta Hunter's role in the matinee, see Taylor (1987), pp. 97 ff.
7. Taylor (1987), chapter 4, discusses Hunter's performances in London and her friendship with MA.
8. Anna Anderson to MA, December, 25, 1927, in MAP.
9. Orpheus Fisher to MA, February 21, 1928, in MAP.
10. Raphael is remembered now for the most part only in connection with his friendship with Roger Quilter and the role he played in performances of Quilter's songs. He recorded a number of Quilter's songs and some lieder of Wolf, one of which ("Nun wandre, Maria," from the *Spanisches Liederbuch*) is described with much affection by J. B. Steane (1993), pp. 608 ff. Raphael's appreciation of Quilter's songs is discussed in his "Roger Quilter: 1877–1953: The Man and His Songs," in *Tempo* (Winter, 1953–54), p. 20.
11. Marshall and Stock (1958), p. 308. A letter and brochure in MAP that Amanda Aldrich sent to MA, July 27, 1932, includes a list of her students and her compositions. As a composer Aldrich used the name Montague Ring.
12. I am following the brief biography of Louis Drysdale by Ben Marcato, "In the World of Music," in a London journal, *The Country House and Estate, a High-Class Review of Modern Progress for all Interested in Country Life,* reprinted in *New York Age* (December 18, 1926), and the short biographical statement in *Chicago Defender* (February 22, 1930). By the time MA arrived in London, Drysdale was successful enough as a voice teacher to have the largest and most detailed advertisement among the voice and instrumental teachers in the *London Musical Courier.*
13. Mills's letter appeared in the *New York Age,* December 18, 1926. Nell Hunter talked about her studies with Drysdale in the *New York Age,* June 4, 1930. Ethel Waters's success with Drysdale is mentioned in the *Chicago Defender,* March 15, 1930. American readers could learn of Drysdale's career from an article about him in the *Chicago Defender,* February 22, 1930. There is a letter from Drysdale to MA, August

29, 1930, in MAP, in which he congratulated MA for her performance at the Proms earlier that month.

14. See *Philadelphia Tribune,* October, 4, 1928.

15. Gerhardt, p. 170

16. See Gerhardt (1953) on the singer's career.

17. MA talked about Schumann-Heink and Onegin in ML, pp. 56, ff. and about Onegin in a letter to Billy, August 7, 1929 (MAP); about Matzenauer, in ML, pp. 114 ff.

18. See note 1. The London success of Will Marion Cook's Southern Syncopated Orchestra is described in *Crisis* 19:3 (January 1920), pp. 140–141. There is a short biography of John Payne, together with a list of his recordings, in Turner (1990), pp. 282 ff. A short appreciation of Payne's career appeared in the *Baltimore Afro-American,* October 26, 1946.

19. See *New York Age,* April 7, 1923.

20. Ibid, where a report from London on the "invasion of colored players" was included, describing the controversy surrounding the opening of the new cabaret.

21. A report of the concert of Lawrence Brown and John Payne appeared in the *New York Age,* November 10, 1923, and included a communication from Lady Cook to the writer, Lucien H. White, about the success and the importance of the concert for English audiences. The report included excerpts from the notices of the concert from the English press, all praising the singer for his simplicity and eloquence.

22. See Jeffrey P. Green (1982) for a review of Hayes's career in London for the year 1921, and Hayden (1995), pp. 29 ff., on Hayes's concerts in London and Berlin.

23. Letter from Alyse Anderson, April 15, 1928, in MAP.

24. Letter to Alyse Anderson, March 13, 1928, in MAP.

25. *London Times,* June 16, 1928.

26. Unidentified London newspaper, [n.d.], in MAP.

27. See note 26.

28. See note 25; a short review appeared as well in the *Observer,* June 17, 1928 ("Miss Marian Anderson's voice is of an undeniably beautiful quality, especially its soft tone. Her attack is often loose. She has a good command of languages, but her English needs tidying").

29. On the Robesons' stay in London in 1928, see Duberman (1989), pp. 113–124. I am grateful to Paul Robeson, Jr. for searching through his mother's diary and copying out the entry for me about MA's concert: "Marian Anderson, with her glorious contralto voice, sings a concert at Wigmore Hall; her program the formal type, with Sir Roger Quilter himself accompanying her in a group of his songs. A most enthusiastic audience and favorable press notices—due justice to her lovely voice." Essie Robeson's diary is part of the Robeson Family Archives, Moorland-Spingarn Research Center, Howard University. Among the other events that month for "our folks" (the phrase is Essie Robeson's) was a party in Maida Vale, with the Robesons and MA among the guests, along with Turner Layton, Tandy Johnstone, Ella and Leslie Hutchinson, Johnny and Mildred Hudgins, John Payne and Lawrence Brown. See Duberman (1989), p. 116.

30. *London Times,* August 17, 1928 ("The singing of Verdi's 'O don fatale' by Miss Marian Anderson deserves a word. Hers is a voice of fine quality through its entire range, and she delivered the big phrases with an understanding of their style."); *Daily Mail,* August 17, 1928 ("A success was scored in Verdi's 'O don fatale,' by Miss Marian Anderson, a coloured contralto with a voice of beautifully smooth quality.

The volume was not great; but the singer had been well trained, every note was musical, and her Italian was good."); *Daily Chronicle,* August, 17, 1928 ("Miss Anderson has a contralto voice of exceptionally fine quality and big compass. Her first solo was the famous Verdi aria, 'O don fatale' ('Don Carlo'), which on account of its unusual range, usually is transposed for most contraltos. But Miss Anderson sang it in the original key, with fine beauty of tone and dignity of style. In the second part of the programme the young artist gave some of those exquisite 'spirituals,' with charming effect."). Similarly in the *Daily News and Westminster Gazette,* August 17, 1928, *Morning Post,* August 17, 1928, and *Daily Telegraph,* August 17, 1928.

31. MA to Mrs. Anderson, August 21, 1928, in MAP.
32. I am grateful to Ray Gillespie, the archive assistant at EMI Music Archives, for providing me with the HMV recording sheets of MA's recordings. The spirituals recorded were "Deep River" and the Roger Quilter arrangement, "I Got a Robe," both accompanied by Lawrence Brown. For details of recording sessions see Appendix II.
33. Interviews with MA in the *Philadelphia Tribune,* October 4, 1928; *Baltimore Afro-American,* October 6, 1928; MA's farewell party is covered in the *Chicago Defender,* by Ivan H. Browning, October 13, 1928.
34. See the *Baltimore Afro-American,* October 6, 1928.

CHAPTER 5

1. Lebrecht (1996), especially pp. 93 ff., was particularly helpful on Judson's role in American musical life.
2. MA's relationship with the Judson management is discussed in ML, pp. 108, ff.
3. One such opportunity was offered by Leopold Stokowski, conductor of the Philadelphia Orchestra. In October 1928 (Stokowski's first letters to MA are not in MAP, but MA's response to one of them, dated October 23, is), Stokowski wrote to Anderson expressing interest in having her perform with the orchestra and asked her for suggestions about music she might sing. MA sent Stokowski a list of operatic numbers and "my best selection of Negro Spirituals" (October 23). Stokowski responded on October 28, expressing interest in all the spirituals, as well as Schubert's "Der Erlkönig" and Debussy's Air de Lia (from *L'enfant prodigue*). On November 1, MA was informed by Colledge that Judson's view was that "nothing further can be done at the moment." Anderson pursued the matter with Stokowski, informing Colledge on November 23 that, having had two interviews with Stokowski "this week," the conductor had chosen some spirituals for MA to perform and had "fixed the first or third week in April as the time when I shall appear with the Orchestra." No such concert was arranged, however. In March 1929, the possibility was taken up again. MA wrote to Judson on March 13 expressing how anxious she was to appear with Stokowski. The last surviving letter dealing with MA's appearance with Stokowski is dated April 9, in which MA informed Stokowski of her interest in performing one of Leo Ornstein's works with him. No concert ever took place. Judson, who was then the manager of the Philadelphia Orchestra, could easily have facilitated such a concert, but the evidence suggests that, for some reason (perhaps he thought MA was not ready for such an appearance, or that the orchestra was not ready for a black singer) he opposed it.
4. October 12, 1928.
5. *Evening Bulletin,* October 13, 1928.

Notes

6. *Herald Tribune,* December 31, 1928 ("The opening group of arias and songs by Pur-cell, Scarlatti, Martini, Debussy and the ensuing lieder of Schubert, Strauss, and Schumann did not disclose her talents to best advantage, proving rather outside her interpretive grasp and presenting problems of diction . . ."); *New York Times,* December 31, 1928 ("She did not appear as much at home in German as in English text, and some of the German songs, such as Schubert's 'Allmacht,' could have had more intimate understanding.")

7. Several pages of MA's four-part harmony exercises survive, and are in MAP.

8. MA's letter to Gerhardt does not survive, but its contents are clear from Gerhardt's response, June 30, 1929, in MAP.

9. There are only four letters to MA from Eric Simon, who was working at the time for the Berlin concert management of Hermann Wolff and Jules Sachs, all from the period of April and May 1929, and all concerned with suggestions about how MA might find a way to study with Elena Gerhardt.

10. Plans for the summer festival are described in the *Seattle Daily Times,* June 6, 1929.

11. Reviews of the first concert (June 9): *Seattle Daily Times,* June 10, 1929, *Seattle Post-Intelligencer,* June 10, 1929.

12. MA sang two more concerts in Seattle, August 4 and 11; both were reviewed in the *Seattle Daily Times* on the day following the concert. The black press took special notice of MA's success in Seattle, with articles in the *New York Age,* September 21, 1929, and the *Philadelphia Tribune,* September 12, 1928.

13. The itineraries for MA's first two seasons with Judson have been established from 1) reviews and articles, especially in the black press, of MA's concerts, too numerous to include; 2) letters to Colledge from MA during the period, all in MAP; 3) a pub-licity brochure from the Recital Management Arthur Judson, 1929–1930; and 4) two handwritten lists by MA, containing most of the concerts for the 1929–1930 season, with fees, both in MAP. MA to Colledge, October 8, 1928 (MAP), mentions many concerts planned for the season; it also contains many suggestions for fees, revealing how much of a struggle was required for MA to raise her fees from previ-ous seasons.

14. *Philadelphia Tribune,* October 17, 1929.

15. *Evening American,* November 19, 1929. MA's previous concerts in Chicago were recalled by Maude Roberts George, in her review of the concert in the *Chicago Defender,* November 23, 1929.

16. The meeting of Rosenwald officials and MA is discussed in ML, pp. 131 ff. The Rosenwald Fund Papers, in Fisk University, contain the record of MA's relationship with the Rosenwald Fund committee, including application, letters and telegrams, letters of recommendation for MA requested by the committee, and reports on her progress from teachers in Germany.

17. Soon after graduating from high school, in fact, MA had begun to use (February 27) 1903 as her official date of birth. This is the birth date given in many reference books, although 1902 and 1900, even 1908, are sometimes given. And on occasion, February 17 instead of 27 occurs. In later years, MA's official version of her age gave rise to amusing responses by family and friends. Franz Rupp, who was born several years after MA, liked to ask, in mock perplexity, how he had gotten to be older than MA. And Ethel Anderson, when she was asked her age (she was born in 1902), would often respond that she would have to consult with Marian.

18. *New York Telegram,* March 3, 1930; also the *New York Sun,* March 3, 1930 ("Schu-

bert's 'Die Krähe,' for instance, displayed well the unusual fine quality of her lower register, but here and in Brahms's 'Von ewiger Liebe,' her delivery, while artistic, was hardly imbued with deepest expressiveness"). The most positive review appeared in the *New York American,* March 3.

19. MA to George R. Arthur, March 6, 1929, Rosenwald Fund Papers.
20. MA to George R. Arthur, May 29, 1930, and telegram responses from Athur, all in Rosenwald Fund Papers.

CHAPTER 6

1. See the letter from Max Walter to MA, March 14, 1930, in MAP, in which he urges her to trust he will make all the necessary arrangements once she is in Berlin.
2. ML, p. 136.
3. Ibid.
4. There are letters throughout August 1930 from Mrs. Anderson to MA in MAP with news about Ethel and Alyse.
5. Orpheus Fisher to MA, August 27, 1930, in MAP.
6. Mrs. Anderson to MA, August 28, 1930, in MAP.
7. Gertrud von Erdberg to MA, August 29, 1930, in MAP.
8. The detail's about MA's concerts in Czechoslovakia are in MA to Mrs. Anderson, October 13, 1930, in MAP.
9. Before MA left for Berlin, Judson had communicated with European managers to find out what coaches would be available in Berlin. He suggested she contact the contralto Sophie Breslau, who was prepared to hear MA. Nothing came of the suggestion. See Judson to MA, March 18, 1930, in MAP.
10. Max Walter to MA, May 14, 1930, in MAP.
11. Arnold Meckel to MA, April 10, 1930. In addition to the proposal that Anderson make her debut at the Paris Opera, Meckel indicated his willingness to manage all of her concerts in Europe, even if she had already made commitments to managers in England and Germany. MA responded the same day, only too eager to agree to Meckler's terms. Apparently nothing came of Meckler's proposals. Both letters are in MAP.
12. ML, p. 137.
13. In MA to Mrs. Anderson, October 13, 1930, MA explained to her mother how the differing views of the two coaches "made it a bit difficult for me." In MAP.
14. MA to Mrs. Anderson, October 13, 1930, in MAP.
15. Karl Ulrich Schnabel, in an interview (November 6, 1994), remembered attending MA's Berlin debut with his parents.
16. *Vossiche Zeitung,* Berlin, October 11, 1930.
17. MA to Mrs. Anderson, October 13, 1930.
18. *Berliner Tageblatt,* November 4, 1930; *Signale für die Musikalische Welt,* Berlin, October 15, 1930. Other reviews appeared in the *Morgenpost,* October 12 ("But this remarkable woman even sings German songs with a natural superiority in her mastery of style, her diction is skillfully accentuated and her musicality is impressive."), *Deutsche Allegmeine Zeitung,* October 17 ("All these German songs, especially those by Beethoven, she sings with profound understanding, inspired and thoroughly musical as one does not hear them but quite rarely.") and the *Allegmeine Musikzeitung,* October 17 ("The whole manner of her interpretation is at all times artistic, she avoids exaggerations, she know how to develop a song and she shows

warmth without sentimentality.") All the Berlin reviews, in translation, can be found in MAP. The black press reported on MA's success in Berlin widely: see, for example, *Chicago Defender,* November 8, 1930; *Philadelphia Tribune,* October 20, 1930; *Tuskegee Messenger* (undated newpaper clipping in MAP).

19. The tea arranged by Madame Cahier was reported in the *Berliner Zeitung am Mittag,* October 31, 1930, *Grünwald Echo,* November 2, 1930, and *Tempo,* October 31, 1930.

20. MA to Ida Brown [n.d. and only in draft], in MAP.

21. See note 20.

22. See ML, pp. 136–137, and Vehanen, pp. 15 ff.

23. Kessler, p. 396

24. Spender, pp. 110–111.

25. Draft of a letter, no date, perhaps to Ida Brown, in MAP.

26. MA to Max Walter [n.d. and in draft only], in MAP.

27. For an enthusiastic review and MA's first newspaper interview in Scandinavia, see the *Bergen Aftenblad,* November 7, 1930.

28. ML, p.144.

29. MA to Mr. J. Mango-Plange, a London friend, about her successes in her first Norwegian concerts.

30. ML, p. 142.

31. From an undated and identified newspaper interview, in Norwegian, in MAP.

32. Reviews appeared in, among others, *Suomenmaa* and *Helsingin Sanomat,* both November 25, 1930.

33. see note 26.

34. *Suomenmaa,* November 27, 1930.

35. Max Walter to MA, November 22, 1930, in MAP.

36. ML, p. 145.

37. There is a lenghthy correspondence betwen Billy King and Colledge about plans for the coming American season, and letters from Billy King to MA keeping her informed of the progress made by the Judson agency in arranging the coming season; see, for example, MA to Mrs. Anderson, August 5, 1930, and Billy King to MA, November 21, 1930. All in MAP.

38. See, for example, Colledge to MA, August 5, 1931; Teresa Cloud to a Mr. Clements, December 14, 1930, in reference to a possible concert in Pasadena ("People are frankly too poor this year to spend money on concerts by any but the most famous artists and even for them it is a bit of a struggle"); M. Morrow, of the Judson agency, to MA, February 5, 1931, in reference to a concert in Washington DC ("... it is necessary to postpone your concert in that city from February 8 to somtime in April owing to such poor Box Office returns"); M. Morrow to MA, March 24, 1931 ("We wish you to know that inasmuch as Mr. Hackney is not able to guarantee the Minneapolis and St. Louis fees, it is very probable that these cities will be cancelled"). The difficulties Judson was having in finding enough dates caused MA to insist on guarantees, which put considerable strain on their relationship: Judson to MA, April 28, 1931 ("I have devoted more time to the contract with you than with any artist who has ever been with this Management. I do not intend to waste any more time. If you wish to sign the contract as last arranged, please do so and let me have it. If not, I regret very much that we can no longer continue representing you"). All in MAP.

39. Claude Barnett to MA, February 17, 1931. MA, it must be said, was generally reluc-

tant to spend large sums on publicity, or to respond to requests for human interest material that could be used for press books, although she was urged repeatedly by Billy King and the Judson agency to do so. See, for example, Dole Jarmel, the Judson press representative, to Billy King, May 27, 1931, who complains to him that he has never received from MA an answer to his request for biographical data and other impressions and opinions that could be used for a press book.

40. Relevant correspondence in the Rosenwald Fund file for MA.
41. Orpheus to MA [May 15, 1931], from Atlantic City, in MAP.
42. See note 40.
43. Johnen to George Arthur, October 30, 1931. Johnen, as well as Raucheisen and Amanda Aldrich, were asked to submitt letters to the Rosenwald Fund about Anderson's progress. Johnen's is the only letter in the Rosenwald Fund file on MA..
44. *Deutsche Allgemeine Zeitung,* August 7, 1931.
45. Interview with Halász, December 10, 1992.
46. From an undated and unidentified newspaper interview, in Swedish, in MAP.
47. From an undated, unidentified Stockholm newspaper review, in MAP.
48. On Vehanen and MA's meeting with Sibelius, see Vehanen, pp. 25 ff.; ML, pp. 148–149.
49. ML, p. 148.
50. Vehanen, p. 29.
51. *Helsingin Sanomat,* November 13, 1931.
52. Vehanen, pp. 29–30.
53. *Suomenmaa,* November 17, 1931.
54. ML, p. 140.

CHAPTER 7

1. There is considerable correspondence from the Judson agency in MAP laying out itineraries for the years covered in this chapter, as well as handwritten itineraries by MA for most of the seasons, on occasion with detailed earnings and expenses.
2. *Columbus Citizen,* February 13, 1932.
3. MA to Hattie Clark, April 14, 1932, in MAP.
4. *Boston Evening Transcript,* April 12, 1932.
5. I have followed the short biography of Hall Johnson in Southern (1982).
6. See chapter 14 for the recording of the cycle of spirituals "Just Keep On Singin'," with John Motley as accompanist.
7. About the scholarship from La Forge, see MA to Judson, April 15, 1932, in MAP.
8. Orpheus Fisher to MA, in MAP. Although undated, the letter clearly falls within this period.
9. On Ethel Anderson's relationship with and marriage to James DePreist, interviews with William A. Smith, Kenneth Goodman, James DePreist.
10. ML, p. 114.
11. MA's handwritten account of the period, with earnings and expenses, is in MAP.
12. Ada Cooper to Billy King, September 15, 1932, in MAP.
13. Ada Cooper to Billy King, September 15, 1932, in MAP.
14. Ada Cooper to Billy King, December 1, 1932.
15. La Forge, p. 143. I am grateful to Ward Marston for kindly providing me with a tape copy of MA's test pressing.
16. See the *Philadelphia Tribune* article, April 13, 1933.

17. Enwall to MA, July 4, 1933, in MAP.
18. *Hufvudstadsbladet,* October 2, 1933.
19. Several Swedish-language reviews of the concert are in MAP, although the newspapers are not identified. One reviewer, for example, pointed out that MA failed for the most part to grasp the temperament of the Gypsy singer embodied in the Brahms songs.
20. Considerable correspondence from Enwall exists in MAP detailing MA's itineraries from the fall, 1932 to December 1935. More valuable still is MA's handwritten notebook of every concert for this period of more than two years, with the full contents of programs provided for every concert.
21. MA to Mrs. Anderson, October 29, 1933, in MAP.
22. I have constructed the following account of MA's experience in Denmark from material in MAP: an article by Thyra Edwards, for the Associated Negro Press, [n.d.], "Nordics rave over Marian Anderson but Denmark bank says she makes too much money and ban is placed on her;" an article by Roy De Coverley, "Marian Anderson in Denmark," [.n.d.], for an unidentified journal or magazine; an interview with Vehanen for *Helsingin Sanomat,* [n.d.]; article in *Dagens Nyheder,* December 3, 1933, "Marian Anderson Is Not Allowed to Give Anymore Performances Here."
23. *Dagens Nyheder,* December 3, 1933.
24. Vehanen interview in *Helsingin Sanomat,* [n.d.].
25. Ibid.
26. *Dagens Nyheder,* December 3, 1933.
27. *Politiken,* December 4, 1933.
28. MA's handwritten copy of her speech, with many changes incorporated, is in MAP.
29. See Vehanen, pp. 161 ff.
30. Vehanen, pp. 164–65.
31. MA to Maunie (Alyse), December 10, 1933.
32. Ibid.
33. Helmer Enwall to MA, February 7, 1934, in MAP.
34. MA to Helmer Enwall, February 9, 1934, in MAP.
35. See MA to Billy King, February 17, 1934, in MAP.
36. *Berlingske Tedende,* February 19, 1934.
37. See, for example, the review in *Politken,* February 19, 1934, a translation of which, prepared for Anderson to use as publicity material, is in MAP. There are many translations of reviews of Anderson's European concerts during the early 1930s in MAP.
38. Handwritten text of telegram, February 24, 1934, in MAP.
39. Mrs. Anderson to MA, March 15, 1934, in MAP.
40. Alyse to MA, March 25, 1934, in MAP.
41. MA to Alyse, April 11, 1934, in MAP.
42. MA to Billy King, April 5, 1934, in MAP.
43. I follow, in the following paragraphs, the account of Lind's American tour in Porter and Lockhard, Jr.

CHAPTER 8

1. ML, p. 152.
2. *Le Jour,* May 4, 1934. By the end of the month, reviews in *Action Française* (May 5), *Excelsior* (May 7), *Le Ménéstrel* (May 11), *Le Journal* (May 17), and *Paris-Midi* (May 22) had appeared.
3. *The Morning Post,* May 10, 1934.
4. *The Sunday Referee,* May 13, 1934.
5. *New York Herald Tribune,* January 7, 1951.
6. ML, p. 154.
7. Ibid.
8. Ibid.
9. ML, p. 155
10. *The Daily Mail,* June 19, 1934
11. ML, p. 150.
12. MA to Arthur Judson, June 20, 1934, in MAP.
13. Calvin W. Franklin, of the Judson agency, to MA, July 17, 1934, in MAP.
14. MA to Arthur Judson, August 3, 1934, in MAP.
15. Billy King to MA, July 2, 1934, in MAP.
16. Ibid.
17. MA to Mrs. Anderson, August 6, 1934, in MAP.
18. Ibid.
19. Ibid.
20. Ibid.
21. Vehanen, p. 40.
22. MA to Mrs. Anderson, October 7, 1934, in MAP.
23. Helsinki newspaper review, undated and unidentified, in MAP.
24. MA to Mrs. Anderson, October 10, 1934, in MAP.
25. ML, p.148.
26. Billy King to MA, October 11, 1934, in MAP.
27. Billy King to MA, January 28, 1934, in MAP.
28. Ibid.
29. Vehanen, pp. 65–66.
30. Vehanen, p.70.
31. Vehanen, p. 69.
32. Ibid.
33. Vehanen, p. 71.
34. Vehanen, p. 72.
35. Vehanen, p. 75.
36. On black Americans in the Soviet Union during the Stalin years, Rudd is particularly useful.
37. ML, p. 176.
38. Quoted in Duberman, p. 186.
39. For Robeson's visit to Russia in 1935, I follow Duberman, pp. 182 ff.
40. Vehanen, p. 81.
41. Ibid.
42. ML, p. 176.
43. On Stanislavsky's 1935 production of *Carmen,* see Benedetti, pp. 330 ff.

44. ML, p. 177.
45. MA's contract with the Soviet Gramophone Company, dated May 22, 1935, for the Lehmann and Chaminade songs, is in MAP. The Robinson and Boatner spirituals were apparently recorded at or about the same time, since a review of them appeared in *Izvestye,* July 30, 1935. In his review in *Izvestye,* Gregory Polanovsky wrote: "Exceptional mastery in the way she handles the songs, and also phenomenal control of voice make the records especially valuable for those schools where the Soviet youth is being taught the art of singing."
46. Vehanen, p. 86.
47. Vehanen, p. 93.
48. Vehanen, pp. 98–99.
49. Vehanen, p. 103.
50. Vehanen, p. 110.
51. ML, p. 179.
52. Vehanen, p. 111.
53. I have used the information in Poyurovskii (1983) in discussing Kaminka's career.
54. Kaminka's letters to MA are all in MAP.
55. The Salzburg authorities' response, in MAP, is quoted in Wilhelm Stein to Helmer Enwall, May 18, 1935.
56. Helmer Enwall to Wilhelm Stein, May 21, 1935. On the same day, Enwall wrote to MA, explaining the situation and enclosing a copy of Stein's letter. Both letters are in MAP.
57. *New York Times,* July 9, 1935.
58. Ibid.
59. In Josef Kaut's *Festspiele in Salzburg,* for example, an exhaustive documentary performance history of the festival for the years 1920 to 1969, there is not a single mention of MA's appearance at the Mozarteum in 1935.
60. *Salzburger Volksblatt,* August 29, 1935.
61. Vehanen, p. 130. Vehanen, one of those who actually heard what Toscanini said about MA, is the only one to have recorded Toscanini's words. I have let his version stand although the more common one—"Yours is a voice such as one hears only once in a hundred years"—has stood for decades as Toscanini's famous encomium of MA. MA herself, in ML, p. 158, gives the latter version, although she says that it was Madame Cahier who "heard and told me of Maestro's words. . . ."
62. Sheean, p. 25.
63. There are nearly forty letters from Billy King to MA for the years 1934 and 1935, the whole sequence a valuable record of Billy's changing emotional attitudes.
64. Billy King to MA, August 23, 1935, in MAP.
65. Ibid.
66. Mrs. Anderson to MA, October 31, 1935; Alyse to MA, Sunday PM [October, 1935], among others, in MAP.
67. MA to Harry T. Burleigh, September 21, 1935, draft of letter and copy of letter in MAP.
68. Harry T. Burleigh to MA, October 16, 1935, in MAP.

CHAPTER 9

1. Hurok, p. 24. My principal source on Hurok's life and career is Robinson.
2. From *Norfolk Journal and Guide* clipping in MAP, undated.

3. ML, pp. 167–168.
4. *New York Times,* December 31, 1935.
5. ML, p. 168.
6. *Philadelphia Tribune,* January 17, 1936.
7. *Philadelphia Tribune,* January 23, 1936.
8. Ibid.
9. Although he is not mentioned in any of the standard reference works in architecture devoted to biography, Orpheus seems to have had a varied career as an architect by the mid-1930s. According to a biographical statement about Fisher prepared for or submitted to the publicity department of Hurok Attractions by a close family member during the 1940s, among other projects, he worked for the Department of Public Education in Philadelphia helping to design school buildings; worked on additions to Yale and Princeton university buildings; and went to South America twice as a member of a firm that designed buildings in Buenos Aires. The biographical statement is in MAP.
10. Orpheus Fisher to MA, Tuesday night at 6:30 [January 21, 1936], in MAP.
11. Ibid.
12. On music in the White House during these years, see Kirk, chapter 6, the most useful source for me.
13. See Kirk, p. 114.
14. Vehanen, p. 223.
15. ML, p. 194.
16. *Washington Daily News,* February 21, 1936.
17. Vehanen, p. 223.
18. Quoted in Kirk, p. 111.
19. ML, pp. 169–170.
20. ML, p. 170.
21. MA's own handwritten record of fees and expenses is in MAP.
22. *Philadelphia Afro-American,* December 20, 1935.
23. Vehanen, p.177.
24. Vehanen, p.180.
25. Vehanen, p. 182.
26. *New York Times,* July 19, 1936.
27. My source on Furtwängler and the Nazis is Shirakawa, chapter 11.
28. Walter, p. 320.
29. Ibid.
30. Ibid.
31. *New York Times,* July 19, 1936.
32. Quoted in the *New York Times,* July 19, 1936.
33. Ibid.
34. Vehanen, p. 37.
35. Mrs. Anderson to MA, October 22, 1936, in MAP.
36. Mrs. Anderson to MA, June 14, 1936, in MAP.
37. Draft of letter from MA to John Payne [n.d.], in MAP.
38. *Baltimore Afro-American,* January 21, 1939.
39. MA to Sol Hurok, January 28, 1939, in MAP.
40. Sol Hurok to MA, March 26, 1937, in MAP.

41. Elsie Illingworth (of the Hurok agency) to Don A. Davis (of the Hampton Institute), March 31, 1939, in MAP.
42. Mark Levine (manager of Hurok's concert department) to Don A. Davis, April 5, 1939, in MAP.
43. Don A. Davis to MA, April 7, 1939, in MAP.
44. Telegram from Mr. and Mrs. James Weldon Johnson, March 21, 1937, in MAP.
45. Hurok, p. 244.
46. *New York Times,* January 7, 1939, in MAP.
47. *New York Times,* April 17, 1939.
48. *Buffalo Courier-Express,* January 27, 1937.
49. Milwaukee newspaper clipping, unidentified, undated, of February 14, 1937 concert, in MAP.
50. *Washington Herald,* May 10, 1938.

CHAPTER 10

1. Magna, p. 517.
2. Lincoln, p. 648.
3. On the repressive policies of the D.A.R., see Peggy Anderson, chapter 1; Lemons, pp. 223–224; Cook, p. 243; La Ganke, chapter 11. La Ganke's dissertation is one of the most important works on the history of the D.A.R., and I have made considerable use of it in this chapter.
4. Lemons, pp. 223–224, La Ganke, chapter 11; Villard, pp. 529 ff.; and Bailie, pp. 12 ff.; all discuss the blacklisting policies of the D.A.R. My discussion of the D.A.R.'s policies during this period is based on the works cited here and in note 3.
5. *New York Times,* May 3, 1928.
6. The phrase, referring to the members of the Anne Adams-Tufts chapter of Cambridge, Massachusetts, that formed a D.A.R. Committee of Protest in 1928, is Villard's, p. 529.
7. Mrs. Brousseau's comments to the press are quoted in Villard, p. 529.
8. William Allen White, p. 135.
9. See Voris, pp. 192 ff., my principal source for the work of Carrie Chapman Catt.
10. *New York Times,* May 16, 1930.
11. *New York Times,* March 13, 1931.
12. *New York Times,* January 25, 1938.
13. Magna, p. 522.
14. Peggy Anderson, p. 125.
15. On the early history of Constitution Hall and its use by black performers, I am indebted to Peggy Anderson, pp. 125, ff., Patrick Hayes's article in *The Washingtonian,* and interviews with Patrick Hayes. Peggy Anderson made use of a document, "Facts Concerning the Management of Constitution Hall Dating from 1929 to 1940," prepared by Fred Hand, in her book on the D.A.R., and included a number of quotations from it. Unfortunately, I have had to depend on those quotations alone. Mrs. Charles Keil Kemper, president-general of the D.A.R., who kindly provided me with useful material, was unable to find any copy of Hand's statement.
16. Quoted in Peggy Anderson, p. 125.
17. Quoted in Peggy Anderson, p. 126.
18. Patrick Hayes, pp. 96–97.

19. Quoted in Peggy Anderson, p. 126.
20. Ibid.
21. See Peggy Anderson, p. 127.
22. From Hand's "Statement," quoted in Peggy Anderson, p. 127.
23. On appearances by blacks in Washington theaters, I am indebted to Peggy Anderson, pp. 127–128, 344–345, and Stokes, pp. 7 ff.
24. See Peggy Anderson, p. 112.
25. Details of Howard University's application to the Washington school board, for the use of the Armstrong High School auditorium for MA's 1936 and 1937 concerts, are summarized in the "Statement" prepared by Superintendent Frank W. Ballou, described in note 52.
26. Hurok, p. 255.
27. The relevant chronology and events related to securing Constitution Hall, and eventually Washington's Central High School, have been set out and discussed, in various degrees, a number of times in the literature. I mention those sources I have made use of: Peggy Anderson, chapter 5; Patrick's Hayes's article in *The Washingtonian*; Carleton Smith's article in *Esquire*; Vriend's dissertation; Weiss, pp. 257 ff.; Black (1996), and articles by Sandage, and Black (1990). There is also a chronology of events, including quotations from letters and other documents (from June 3, 1938 to February 26, 1939), prepared by Gerald Goode for Hurok, entitled "The D.A.R. versus Marian Anderson," in MAP.
28. On Eleanor Roosevelt and civil rights, see, for example, Black (1996, 1990) and Zangrando and Zangrando.
29. On segregation in Washington, see Constance Green, Stokes, Daly, and Lovell.
30. On the career of Charles Houston, a key player in the Anderson controversy, see McNeil.
31. McNeil, p. 76.
32. *Washington Times-Herald,* January 12, 1939.
33. *Washington Times-Herald,* January 15, 1939.
34. Hurok to Fred Hand, January 23, 1939. A copy of the letter is in MAP.
35. Quoted in Carleton Smith (1939), p.79, and Vriend, p. 22.
36. Quoted in Anderson, p. 114.
37. Harlow Robinson (1994), p. 232.
38. See the *New York Times,* March 16, 1933.
39. Early evidence of White's interest in Anderson's career appears in an interesting letter of White to Roland Hayes, June 13, 1924. At the time he wrote to Hayes that "she has a marvelous voice but she sings too mechanically and without any great depth of feeling." Nor did he approve of her choice of the encores "My Lindy Lou" and "The Cuckoo." In NAACP Papers, Part II, Personal Correspondence of Selected NAACP Officials, reel 7.
40. *Washington Post,* February 21, 1939.
41. A copy of the telegram is in MAP.
42. A copy of the Flagstad telegram, as well as some of the other responses, are in MAP.
43. Quoted in Peggy Anderson, p. 113.
44. Quoted in Peggy Anderson, pp. 113–114.
45. Walter White to Mary Johnson, January 21, 1939, in NAACP Papers, Groups II, Marian Anderson General 1938–39, box L2.
46. *Washington Post,* February 20, 1939.

47. Walter White to the Board of Management, Daughters of the American Revolution, January 21, 1939, in NAACP Papers, Groups II, Marian Anderson General 1938–39, box L2.

48. Mrs. Henry M. Robert, Jr. to Harold L. Ickes, February 3, 1939, in National Archives, Washington DC, Records of the Secretary of the Interior, RG 48, Central Classified Files 1937–1953, Marian Anderson Subfile, entry 1-280, box 2967.

49. Included in the materials sent to me by Mrs. Charles Keil Kemper.

50. Hurok, pp. 256–257.

51. Quoted in Peggy Anderson, p. 116.

52. In "Statement on the Application for the Use of the Central High School Auditorium for a Recital by Miss Marian Anderson," prepared by Superintendent Frank W. Ballou, February 28, 1939, p. 3. The "Statement" is in the NAACP Papers, Group II, Anderson, Marion, Central High School Conflict, (D.C.) 1939, box L1 (Addendum). As an explanation of School Board policy, some of the history of its application, and a review of the 1936 and 1937 applications to the School Board for the use of Armstrong High School for a recital by Anderson, the document is important. I have made use of it in the following sections.

53. "Statement," p. 9. See note 51.

54. "Statement," p. 10. See note 51.

55. Quoted in "Report of the Committee of the Board of Education on Community Use of Buildings, March 3, 1939," in NAACP Papers, Group II, Anderson, Marion, Central High School Conflict (D.C.)1939, box L1.

56. The formation and the work of the MACC is discussed in some detail in Black, "Championing a Champion" (1990), also Vriend, pp. 30 ff.

57. Lovell, p. 277.

58. There is a copy of the handbill in MAP.

59. Eleanor Roosevelt to V.D. Johnston, February 9, 1939, in FDR Library, Anna Eleanor Roosevelt Papers, box 1505–07.

60. Eleanor Roosevelt to Mrs. Henry M. Robert, Jr., February 26, 1939, in FDR Library, Anna Eleanor Roosevelt Papers, box 1521-22.

61. "My Day," February 26, 1939, in FDR Library, Anna Eleanor Roosevelt Papers, My Day, box 3073.

62. *Washington Post,* March 19, 1939.

63. ML, p. 185.

64. Telegram from Hurok to Anderson, February 27, 1939, in MAP.

65. Ibid.

66. Ibid.

67. Walter White to MA, January 21, 1939, in MAP. See also, for example, Alyse Anderson to MA, March 3, 1939 (". . . Oh gee, I just started to tell you something else but I'm so excited, they just gave a news flash that the board of education in D.C. has just reversed itself and are inviting you there. There goes the telephone oh the activity has started. Girl, you are just too bad, there it goes again . . ."); Alyse Anderson to MA, March 14, 1939; Alyse Anderson to MA, March 21, 1939, all in MAP.

68. ML, p. 187.

69. ML, pp. 187–188.

70. Houston's words are quoted in the *Washington Post* article of March 2, 1939, an account of the meeting at the Franklin School that I follow here.

71. Quoted in the *Washington Post,* March 2, 1939.

72. Memorandum to Walter White and Hubert Delany from Charles Houston, March 4, 1939, in NAACP Papers, Group II, Anderson, Marion, Central High School Conflict (D.C.) 1939, box L1. My description of the March 3 meeting is based on Houston's "Memorandum."

73. Ibid.

74. On Cohen's acceptance and Ballou's withdrawal of the offer, see the *Washington Post,* March 18, 1939.

75. Hurok is quoted in a press release of the NAACP, February 24, 1939, in NAACP Papers, Group II, Marian Anderson Press Releases 1939, box L2.

76. *Washington Post,* February 18, 1939.

77. *Washington Times-Herald,* January 15, 1939.

78. Walter White to Charlie [Charles Houston], March 21, 1939, in NAACP Papers, Group I, General Correspondence March 17–23, 1939, box C-59.

79. Walter White to Charlie [Charles Houston], March 6, 1939, in NAACP Papers, Group II, Anderson, Marion, Central High School Conflict (D.C.), 1939, box L1.

80. Memorandum dated March 22, 1939, ibid.

81. Walter White to Hurok, March 13, 1939, ibid.

82. Walter White to MA, March 24, 1939, in MAP.

83. Walter White to MA, April 4, 1939, in MAP.

84. White, p. 182.

85. Walter White to MA, April 4, 1939, in MAP.

86. Walter White to Charles Houston and V.D. Johnston, March 31, 1939, in NAACP Papers, Group II, Anderson, Marion, Central High School Conflict (D.C.), 1939, box L1.

87. See the account of the concert in the *Washington Post,* April 10, 1939.

88. ML, p. 189.

89. ML, p. 190.

90. See Ernest K. Lindley's column in the *Washington Post,* April 12, 1939.

91. Text of Icke's speech at the Lincoln Memorial, in MAP.

92. ML, p. 191.

93. Scott A. Sandage, in his 1993 article (see Bibliography), pp. 135–136, made me aware of MA's change of "Of thee I sing" to "To thee we sing."

94. ML, p. 192.

95. *Washington Post,* April 10, 1939.

96. White, pp. 184–185.

97. Charles Houston and John Lovell, Jr., to Mrs. Henry M. Robert, Jr., April 13, 1939, in NAACP Papers, Group II, Marian Anderson General 1938–39, box L2.

98. Marian Anderson Mural Fund Committee press release, in MAP.

99. Ibid.

100. *New York Amsterdam News,* June 3, 1939.

101. *New York Times,* April 17, 1939.

102. Ibid.

103. Ibid.

104. *New York Times,* May 31, 1939.

105. See the *New York Times,* June 9, 1939.

106. ML, p. 195.

107. *New York Times,* January 26, 1939.

108. *New York Times,* July 3, 1939.
109. The young girl's letter to MA is in MAP.

CHAPTER 11

1. *Chicago Defender,* June 10, 1939. See also *New York Amsterdam News,* April 22, 1939 ("What's that! Miss Anderson plans marriage?"), *Baltimore Afro-American,* October 5, 1940 ("Reports say Marian Anderson will wed"), *Pittsburgh Courier,* May 3, 1941 ("Marian denies marriage").
2. Billy King to MA, April 8, 1940, in MAP.
3. Orpheus Fisher to MA, [n.d.], in MAP. There are a large number of letters from Orpheus to MA for the period 1939–1944. Many of them are undated, but it is clear from their contents that they belong to this period and, in many cases, in which year they fall.
4. Orpheus Fisher to MA, Thursday, February 1, 1940, in MAP.
5. See, for example, Orpheus Fisher to MA, March 1940: "You must know it takes a lot of will power to keep away from the desire to see other women while you are away. It is only my love and hope and knowledge that you are coming back soon that makes me be a good boy." Also Wednesday at Midnight [n.d.]: "Marian I am trying to be good until you return and I am trying very hard." Both in MAP.
6. See note 5.
7. Ibid.
8. Orpheus Fisher to MA, [n.d.], in MAP.
9. Orpheus Fisher to MA, Tuesday at noon [March 1940], in MAP.
10. Orpheus Fisher to MA, [n.d.], in MAP.
11. MA to Orpheus Fisher, January 27, 1940, in MAP.
12. MA to Orpheus Fisher, March 6, 1940, in MAP.
13. Orpheus Fisher to MA, Thursday, February 1, 1940, in MAP.
14. Orpheus Fisher to MA, [n.d.], in MAP.
15. Orpheus Fisher to MA, Thursday, February 1, 1940, in MAP.
16. Kimbrough, p. 176.
17. Ibid.
18. Ibid.
19. MA to Orpheus Fisher, March 6, 1940, in MAP.
20. Surviving details of the divorce proceedings can be found in the continuous docket book, #425 (case #733) for March term 1940, in the Prothonotary Office of the Luzerne County Court House, PA. The divorce was initiated on February 5, 1940, and granted on December 10, 1940. The divorce file was destroyed in a flood in 1972. I am grateful to David Roberts, the file clerk in the Prothonotary Office, for his help.
21. About Kosti, interviews with Sylvia Rupp and James DePreist.
22. *Hartford Courant,* August 6, 1989, p. 12.
23. Kimbrough, p. 176.
24. Orpheus Fisher to MA, [n.d.], in MAP.
25. Orpheus Fisher to MA, undated but clearly a day or two before July 7, 1940. In MAP.
26. ML, pp. 284–85.
27. *The Nation,* Sept 14, 1940, p. 225.

28. MA to Orpheus Fisher, January 27, 1940, in MAP.

29. There is a reasonably complete series of Statement of Accounts, with MA's fees and amounts paid to her, prepared by the Hurok office for the 1940s and 1950s in MAP.

30. I am grateful to Sylvia Rupp for providing me with copies of newspaper clippings and of articles dealing with Franz Rupp's life and career, as well as German newspaper clippings about the operatic career of his first wife, Steffi Rupp.

31. Franz Rupp to a Mr. Eric Adler, March 6, 1946. In the letter, Rupp recounts the story of the end of his relationship with Schlusnus. A copy of the letter was given to me by Sylvia Rupp.

32. See note 27.

33. *Globe and Mail, Toronto,* March 29, 1941.

34. Minneapoplis newspaper clipping, November 25, 1942, in MAP.

35. See note 30; also interviews with Sylvia Rupp.

36. ML, p. 280.

37. *New York Times,* February 14, 1940.

38. *New York Times,* March 18, 1941.

39. Ibid.

40. Interviews with James DePreist.

41. A complete list of scholarship winners, and many applications, are in MAP.

42. On Petrillo and the recording industry, see Gelatt, pp. 278 ff.

43. Most of MA's appearances on the Bell Telephone Hour are preserved. See the Discography for details.

44. Most of the information about Jofe comes from ML, pp. 228 ff.

45. ML, pp. 237–238.

46. ML, p. 242.

47. See Duberman, pp. 251 ff.

48. ML, p. 271.

49. ML, pp. 272–273.

50. *New York Times,* September 30, 1942.

51. Quoted anonymously in the *Washington Post,* September 30, 1942.

52. Ibid.

53. Telegram from Walter White to Sol Hurok, October 1, 1942, in NAACP Papers, Part 15, Series B, Microfilm Edition, reel 2.

54. Telegram from Walter White to MA, October 1, 1942, in NAACP Papers, Part 15, Series B, Microfilm Edition, reel 2.

55. Telegram from Walter White to President General, D.A.R., October 1, 1942, in NAACP Papers, Part 15, Series B, Microfilm Edition, reel 2.

56. Sol Hurok to Fred Hand, [October 3, 1942], copy in MAP.

57. Telegram from Gerald Goode to Walter White, November 9, 1942, in NAACP Papers, Part 15, Series B, Microfilm Edition, reel 2.

58. Interviews with Kenneth Goodman, who was a friend of the Andersons for many years and who, as a pianist, accompanied Ethel Anderson whenever she sang publicly.

59. Quoted in a Hurok Attractions press release, "D.A.R. rejects Marian Anderson," [n.d.], in MAP.

60. *Washington Post,* November 5, 1942.

61. Ibid.

62. Ibid.

63. *Charleston News and Courier* editorial, November 6, 1942.
64. Telegram from Walter White to Leslie Perry, December 19, 1942, in NAACP Papers, Part 15, Series B, Microfilm Edition, reel 2.
65. Telegram from Walter White to Leslie Perry, December 19, 1942; telegram from Leslie Perry to Walter White, December 19, 1942. Both in NAACP Papers, Part 15, Series B, Microfilm Edition, reel 2.
66. *Norfolk Journal and Guide,* January 16, 1943.
67. *New York Times,* January 8, 1943.
68. See note 3. King's letters to MA during the period provide a valuable record of the progress of renovations at Marianna, and of King's involvement with every facet of them.
69. Orpheus Fisher to MA, May 23, 1943, in MAP.
70. I am grateful to Lila Shaker, the office service manager of the Barden Corporation, for information about the Barden Corporation and for making available to me information on Orpheus Fisher's employee card.
71. See note 1.
72. *Pittsburgh Courier,* May 3, 1941.
73. (Miss) Marian Anderson to Mr. Fisher, July 8, 1941, in MAP.
74. MA to Orpheus Fisher, April 2, 1943, in MAP.
75. *New York Times,* November 19, 1943.

CHAPTER 12

1. Orpheus Fisher to MA [late 1944], in MAP.
2. Information on Dickinson and his relation to MA comes from the MA/Taubman tapes (# 30); interviews with Virginia Wren, a long-time Danbury resident; and Wren's article, "Recollections of Marian Anderson and the Village of Mill Plain," in the *Citizen News,* May 12, 1993, a copy of which the author kindly sent me.
3. ML, p. 209.
4. *New York Times,* April 5, 1946.
5. *New York Times,* November 11, 1946.
6. See Orpheus Fisher to MA, Feb 13, 1946, and Orpheus Fisher to MA, February 14, 1946, both in MAP.
7. From an unidentified newspaper interview, the first page missing, [n.d], in MAP.
8. Ibid.
9. See note 8.
10. Ibid.
11. Ibid.
12. During the 1940s, less frequently in the 1950s, MA liked to occasionally program an aria from the soprano's operatic repertory. These included, in addition to "Suicidio," arias from Verdi's *Forza del destino,* Bellini's *Norma,* Mozart's *Marriage of Figaro,* and Wagner's *Tannhäuser.* She sang them all, of course, transposed down. Several performances from this repertory, from the Bell Telephone Hour, have been issued, without the consent of MA, on records and on CD. On the evidence of these issues—I have made allowances for possible inaccuracies of pitch—MA sang "Pace, pace, mio dio" transposed down a step, to A-flat, and "Casta diva" down a step as well, from the F of many published editions to E-flat. Giuseppe Boghetti has left an account of the circumstances surrounding MA's interest in "Allmächt'ge Jungfrau" (Elizabeth's Prayer) from *Tannhäuser:* ". . . take it from Joe Boghetti, Mar-

ian has the voice, musical pulse and intuition to sing anything. Listen—the other day she came in for practice and I had her sing 'Elizabeth's Prayer' from *Tannhäuser*. She had never seen it before, but she sang it at sight. And I want to tell you that after a few repeats she sang it better than I've ever heard it sung—and I've heard 'em all." Boghetti's recollections are from the *Philadelphia Record,* December 25, 1938.

13. Ibid.
14. Quoted in Sol Hurok to MA, January 7, 1949, in MAP. From the time MA began to pay King $10,000 a year to act as her business manager (as early as 1946), King began to encourage MA to improve her contract with Hurok. See, for example, Orpheus Fisher to MA, February 13, 1946, where he refers to "Hurok and his scheming mind." In MAP.
15. MA to Orpheus Fisher, May 15, 1949, in MAP.
16. Ibid.
17. See Duberman, pp. 341 ff.
18. See Duberman, p. 349.
19. Unidentified Swedish newspaper clipping, April 28, 1949, in MAP.
20. See MA to Orpheus Fisher, May 15, 1949, for MA's account of her arrival in Scandinavia and her treatment by the press.
21. MA to Orpheus Fisher, May 24, 1949, in MAP.
22. Kosti Vehanen to MA, May 11, 1949, in MAP.
23. Ibid.
24. Unidentified Swedish newspaper clipping, May 18, 1949, in MAP.
25. MA to Orpheus Fisher, June 5, 1949, in MAP.
26. *La Lanterne,* June 17, 1949.
27. *Le Soir,* June 19, 1949.
28. MA to Orpheus Fisher, May 29, 1949, in MAP.
29. MA to Orpheus Fisher, May 21, 1950, in MAP.
30. All from MA to Orpheus Fisher, May 21, 1950, in MAP.
31. Details of MA's concerts in Berlin and Munich in MA to Orpheus Fisher, June 20, 1950, in MAP.
32. Ibid.
33. *Neue Zeitung* (Munich), June 7, 1950.
34. Ibid.
35. *Newsweek,* April 25, 1949, p.85.
36. Mrs. Andrew W. Simkins to MA, April 4, 1949, in MAP.
37. Documents detailing plans of the NAACP Richmond Branch to boycott Ellington's concert are in NAACP Papers, Part 15, Series B, Microfilm Edition, reel 2.
38. Dr. J.M. Tinsley to MA, January 6, 1951, in NAACP Papers, Part 15, Series B, Microfilm Edition, reel 2.
39. Mae Frohman to Walter White, January 12, 1951, in NAACP Papers, Part 15, Series B, Microfilm Edition, reel 2.
40. Ibid.
41. Details on the picketing of MA's concert from a NAACP Richmond Branch document, February 13, 1951, in NAACP Papers, Part 15, Series B, Microfilm Edition, reel 2; also, the *New York Times,* January 10, 1951.
42. From a copy of the letter that went to Mary McLeod Bethune from Walter White, January 26, 1951, which includes the information: "Mr. Hurok stated that he is totally in agreement with the NAACP's fight against segregation. He further stated

that if the NAACP advised him that it was the best thing to do, he would refuse to schedule Miss Anderson for any more concerts in the South." In NAACP Papers, Part 15, Series B, Microfilm Edition, reel 2.

43. All of the responses to White's letter are in the NAACP Papers, Part 15, Series B, Microfilm Edition, reel 2.

44. Ibid.

45. Ibid.

46. Ibid.

47. Memo from Walter White to Mssrs. Current, Marshall, Moon, Wilkins, May 11, 1951, in NAACP Papers, Part 15, Series B, Microfilm Edition, reel 2.

48. Telegram from Walter White, May 18, 1951, in NAACP Papers, Part 15, Series B, Microfilm Edition, reel 2.

49. The responses from Texas civic leaders and attorneys are in NAACP Papers, Part 15, Series B, Microfilm Edition, reel 2.

50. *New York Times,* January 25, 1952.

51. MA to Orpheus Fisher, February 10, 1952, in MAP.

52. *Jet,* February 7, 1952.

53. *New York Times,* April 22, 1952.

54. ML, p. 193.

CHAPTER 13

1. In addition to the information MA provided about her tour of Japan in ML, pp. 255 ff., there is also her diary for the period April 26–May 29, 1953 in MAP, in which MA gives what is for her an unusually detailed record of her trip.

2. During the fall of 1952, King wrote to MA often about the progress on the new house. On October 2, 1952, for example, King wrote to MA: The walls of the foundation are in and finished, and to-day we have put in the septic tank . . . all of this must be done before Mr. Kovacs can back-fill, tomorrow I hope to be able to get in the oil storage tank and after that is completed we can start with the steel work." And a week later: "I find it difficult to leave the work on the new house, as to-day we were busy setting the steel which we didn't finish until 5:30 to-day, things are going along rather well with the new house, Monday the carpenters report for work to start the framing of the super-structure."

3. Alyse Anderson to MA, October 12 and 13, 1952, in MAP. I am grateful to James DePreist for the frank discussions during interviews about Alyse's struggle with health problems. About Alyse's relationship with William Runner, interviews with James DePreist, Kenneth Goodman, and Sandra Grymes. To judge from Ethel's letters to her, in MAP, Alyse spent nearly three months—from sometime in March to the middle of June 1953—in Eagleville Hospital, in Eagleville, Pennsylvania.

4. ML, p. 256.

5. Ibid.

6. Ibid.

7. ML, p. 257.

8. From an English language newspaper clipping, unidentified and undated, of a review by Hans E. Pringsheim, in MAP.

9. ML, p. 256.

10. Diary entry for May 16, 1953, in MAP.

11. ML, p. 258.

12. Diary entry for May 27, 1953, in MAP.
13. MA to Alyse Anderson, June 3, 1953, in MAP.
14. Quoted in an interview article in *Pacific Stars and Stripes,* June 21, 1953
15. The article cited in note 14 remains the best source of information on MA's experiences in Korea, and of her feelings about what she witnessed and accomplished there.
16. About "the regulars" and their friendships with MA and King, interviews with James DePreist and Max Brownstein.
17. I found the interviews with Robert O'Neal, who, of all of King's nephews, was the closest to King and MA, particularly illuminating on the subject of King and MA's marriage. Interviews as well with James DePreist.
18. *New York Times,* September 24, 1953.
19. *Variety,* November 18, 1953.
20. Ibid.
21. *Jet,* April 22, 1954.
22. Ibid.
23. Ibid.
24. *New York Times,* January 25, 1954.
25. *New York Times,* July 31, 1954.
26. Although the work was dedicated to MA, Asdrubal Lima sang in the premiere of the work on December 30, 1946, in Rio de Janeiro, with the composer conducting the Orquestra do Teatro Municipal. The handwritten text, over which MA wrote in all of the note values of the vocal part, is in MAP. MA's performance of *Poema* took place on December 8, 1954, when, in addition to the Villa-Lobos work, MA sang Bach's "All Is Fulfilled," from the *St. John Passion,* and "Prepare Thyself, Zion," from the *Christmas Oratorio.*
27. From Taubman, chapter 20, and interviews with him (December 4 and 14, 1992), it is clear that Hurok put considerable pressure on MA to produce an autobiography.
28. In Henry W. Simon to MA, October 19, 1953, in MAP, Simon proposes that a colleague of his, Jerome Bohm, work with MA to produce an autobiography, but the suggestion was apparently not taken up.
28. Ken McCormick (editor in chief of Doubleday) to Rex Stout (who was acting as an intermediary for MA with potential writers and publishers), October 21, 1954, in MAP.
29. Vincent Sheean to MA, October 9, 1954, in MAP.
30. For information on Rudolph Bing's and Max Rudolph's attempts to bring black singers to the Met, I am grateful to conversations with and correspondence from John Pennino, assistant archivist at the Met, as well as to Sylvia Olden Lee (interview, January 24, 1996), a black vocal coach who came to work at the Met in the summer of 1950. See also Allan Morrison's article in the *Negro Digest.*
32. Bing, p. 184: "I never had the slightest question about engaging Miss Collins, and I told the board about it after the contract was signed."
33. Interview with László Halász, December 10, 1992.
34. Bing's intermission statement is quoted in Allan Morrison's article in the *Negro Digest,* p. 53.
35. Bing's statement is quoted in Allan Morrison's article, p. 53.
36. Information on auditions of black singers at the Met, from a letter to the author from John Pennino, January 27, 1998.

37. On Rudolph's interest in bringing black singers to the Met, and his interest in Carol Brice, interview with Sylvia Olden Lee, January 24, 1996.

38. Interview with Sylvia Olden Lee, January 24, 1996.

39. Letter from Rudolph Bing, April 20, 1950, Metropolitan Opera Archives. The correspondent's name was withheld by the archives.

40. Robert McFerrin, Sr., in an interview on June 17, 1993, did not remember any discussion with the Met about the relationship between the date of his Met debut and that of MA. One important black singer, who asked not to be named, in an interview on November 14, 1992, suggested that McFerrin's debut may have been postponed so that MA would be the first black singer at the Met. She felt that the pressure came from Sol Hurok. When I posed the question to John Pennino, assistant archivist of the Metropolitan Opera, his response (in a letter to the author, March 17, 1995) was: "Whether the administration felt that Anderson, in deference to her reputation, should be given pride of place by being the first singer to break the color barrier or that her entry would make it easier for lesser known African-Americans to be engaged, is open to question. [MA's] agent, Sol Hurok, was a very powerful and influencial person, how much he may have had to do with all of this is open to speculation." Wallace McClain Cheatham, in his article "Black Male Singers at the Metropolitan Opera," pp. 5–6, makes the case that McFerrin's Met debut had to wait until a singer of Anderson's reputation and stature could be engaged.

    There is some evidence that Bing had made some attempt in previous years to engage MA. That is what MA herself says, with no details, in ML, p. 96. According to Howard Taubman, a music critic for the *New York Times:* "Mr. Hurok . . . had been proposing [MA's] name to the Metropolitan on and off for fifteen years. [Hurok] added that Mr. Bing had made the first serious inquiry last year, but Miss Anderson's concert schedule had been too full." *New York Times,* October 8, 1954.

41. ML, p. 296.

42. ML, p. 297.

43. MA/Taubman tapes (# 21).

44. ML, p. 297.

45. ML, p. 298.

46. Ibid.

47. ML, p. 300.

48. Interview with Roberta Peters, March 25, 1995.

49. ML, p. 302.

50. *New York Times,* January 8, 1955.

51. MA/Taubman tapes (# 21).

52. Michael Sweeley, an assistant to Hurok and MA's traveling manager at the time, felt that MA was singing much better after her work with Freschl. He also remembers MA herself saying as much. From an interview with Sweeley, April 14, 1998.

53. From MA's diary entry for March 27, 1955. MA's diary record of her trip to Israel extends from March 27 to April 7, 1955, in MAP.

54. Diary entry, March 29, 1955.

55. Diary entry, April 2, 1955.

56. *Davar,* April 29, 1955.

57. *Al-Hamishmar,* May 2, 1955.

58. *Ha Arez,* April 22, 1955.

59. *Jedioth Hayom,* April 22, 1955.

60. *Jerusalem Post,* April 20, 1955.

61. ML, p. 259.

62. I am grateful to Jehoash Hirshberg (interview, April 3, 1994) for information on MA's visit to Tichon Hadash. Now a professor of music at the University of Jerusalem, Hirshberg was a high school student when MA visited Israel. He told me how vividly he remembers MA singing the *Alto Rhapsody* in Hebrew (he went to one of MA's concerts with his parents) and of the extraordinary effect it had on the audience.

63. *Jerusalem Post,* April 22, 1955.

64. The "Memorandum of Agreement" between MA and Howard Taubman is dated August 1, 1955, in MAP.

65. In relating his experiences of working with MA, Taubman held back a great deal of information which he was willing to convey to me in interviews (see note 27). All of the tapes of the sessions, which became the basis for Taubman's writing the autobiography, as well as a typescript of the tapes, are in MAP.

66. An annotated list of reviews is included in Sims, pp.102–103.

67. I am indebted to Burk, pp. 68 ff., on Eisenhower's attitudes toward civil rights and his appointment of blacks to executive positions..

68. For the discussion of Soviet-American cultural exchange, here and in what follows, I have made use of Robinson, pp. 342 ff.

69. See the article in *Time,* "Culture for Export," (June 6, 1955, p. 78) and in the *New York Times* ("U.S. Lifts Curtain on Culture Drive"), February 28, 1955.

70. In a Foreign Service dispatch from Madras, for example, Henry G. Ramsey, a principal officer in the American consulate, informed the State Department, January 10, 1955: "As an indication of the prominence accorded by the South Indian press to all evidence of discrimination or non-discrimination toward Negroes in the United States, there is transmitted an article by F. BALARIAN, The Hindu's New York correspondent, on the recent appearance of Miss Marian Anderson at the New York Metropolitan Opera House." In RG 59, decimal file 991.61/1-1055, National Archives at College Park, Maryland. In fact, the State Department had received regular dispatches from foreign consulates in the West Indies and South America of MA's reception there since the late 1940s. The dispatches are in RG 59, decimal file 032 Anderson, Marian, National Archives at College Park, Maryland.

71. Schedules and itineraries of MA's Far East tour exist in many forms in MAP. I am grateful to Sylvia Rupp for giving me access to Franz Rupp's diaries, in which he carefully noted all of his appearances with MA. The main published sources of MA's Far East trip are the "See It Now" film, "The Lady from Philadelphia," and the recording (see Discography) derived from the film. In MAP there are numerous newspaper clippings of reviews and some interviews from many of the cities in which MA appeared. The *Times* article cited in note 72 is also useful. See also note 73.

72. *New York Times,* December 29, 1957.

73. From "We Remember Asia," by MA, a typed report of her trip to the Far East, with changes and corrections, in MAP. The report apparently was never published, although it may have served as the basis for speeches.

74. Ibid.

75. Ibid.

76. Premier U Nu's comment to MA is included in the film "The Lady from Philadel-phia."

77. See note 73.

78. Ibid.

79. Mrs. Frances Frese to Edward R. Morrow, December 31, 1957. A copy is in MAP.

80. Fred F. Powers to Edward R. Morrow, January 3, 1958. A copy is in MAP.

81. The editorial, a clipping of which is in MAP, appeared in the *Hutchinson* (Kansas) *News,* a copy of which was sent to MA.

82. From an undated letter draft to Hurok, in MAP.

83. Ibid.

84. Ibid.

85. *New York Times,* July 15, 1958.

86. Burk, p.69.

87. See Burk, p. 69. On Walter White's opposition to the appointment of Byrnes, see the *New York Times,* July 28, 1953.

88. See note 73.

89. In a White House memorandum for Governor Sherman Adams from Robert Gray, a White House assistant, March 13, 1958, MA is included in a list of proposed United Nations delegates that represents the State Department's "current think-ing." In Dwight D. Eisenhower Library, White House Central Files, 85-B. In the letter from John Foster Dulles to MA, May 2, 1958, Dulles confirms that MA had agreed to serve a few days before, in a telephone conversation with her.Dulles's let-ter is in MAP. In a White House memorandum for Governor Adams from Robert Gray, May 9, 1958, the governor is informed that "Marian Anderson and Barry Bingham, both Democrats, have 'regretted'." In Dwight D. Eisenhower Library, White House Central Files, 85-B. In a White House memorandum for Governor Adams from Gray, May 23, 1958, the governor is informed that MA "has changed her mind." In Dwight D. Eisenhower Library, White House Central Files, 85-B.

90. On the functions of the Trusteeship Council and the history of the Cameroons, I have found the following works very useful: Mezerik, Murray (especially pp. 221 ff.), LeVine (chapter 7), and Sady (especially chapter 4).

91. See the *New York Times,* September 13, 1958, about Dulles's address to the General Assembly, a complete text of which is in MAP.

92. *New York Times,* September 18, 1958.

93. See the *New York Times,* October 20, 1958.

94. The sequence of events of November 25 and 26 is reported in detail in the *New York Times,* November 26 and 27, 1958. See also the *Washington Post,* November 27, 1958 and *Christian Science Monitor,* November 28, 1958 for additional details.

95. MA's remarks were carried in the *New York Times,* November 26, 1958, and in vir-tually all of the newspaper coverage over the next two weeks.

96. *St. Louis Post-Dispatch,* November 28, 1958.

97. *Washington Post,* November 27, 1958.

98. See the *St. Louis Post-Dispatch,* November 28, 1958.

99. *Baltimore Afro-American,* December 6, 1958. See also *Pittsburgh Courier,* December 6, 1958 ("U.N. listens as Marian takes stand opposite to U.S. motion"); *Philadelphia Tribune,* December 2, 1958 ("Marian opposes stand of U.S. on Africa issue).

Notes

CHAPTER 14

1. Orpheus Fisher to MA, January 30, 1959, in MAP.
2. Ibid.
3. Ibid.
4. Ibid.
5. MA to Orpheus Fisher, February 23, 1959, in MAP.
6. *New York Times,* March 30, 1959.
7. Marc Crawford, "Should Marian Anderson Retire?," in *Ebony* 15 (June, 1960), 77–81.
8. Ibid, p. 81.
9. Winthrop Sargeant, quoted in *Ebony* article, p. 78.
10. Quoted anonymously in *Ebony* article, p. 78.
11. *New York Times,* September 29, 1965.
12. Details of Mrs. Anderson's illness in MA to Franz Rupp, August 18, 1960. Letter in author's possession.
13. Ibid.
14. *New York Times,* July 1, 1960 and November 11, 1960.
15. *New York Times,* January 20, 1961 and January 25, 1961.
16. Interviews with Kenneth Goodman; Price's application is in MAP.
17. See, for example, *New York Amsterdam News,* February 4, 1961.
18. Leontyne Price to MA, March 12, 1961, in MAP.
19. Cousins, p. 9. Cousins's article provides the most useful account of the background to the "second Dartmouth conference."
20. In addition to the Cousins article, I have made use of the following material in discussing the "second Dartmouth conference": "Diary and Report of a Trip to Russia: May 13–31, 1961," a confidential and private document written and circulated by Erwin N, Griswold; a list of delegates, with biographical information, sent to MA by the organizers of the conference; and MA's detailed diary of reports and speeches of the conference, all in MAP. See also articles in the *New York Times,* June 1, 1961, and *Bridgeport Sunday Post* (Connecticut), July 2, 1961, by Stuart Chase, one of the participants in the conference.
21. Interview with Peter Juviler, June 29, 1995.
22. Griswold, p. 12; see note 20.
23. Griswold, p. 115; see note 20.
24. I am grateful to Maria Fernandez and Anibal Ramirez for helping to make available to me the tapes of MA's Casals Festival performances.
25. Information on James DePreist's career from interviews as well as from the following articles: Noel Hynd, "The Compass of His Soul," in the *Pennsylvania Gazette,* March 1993, pp. 18–24; Charles Passy, "Heart and Mind: The Musical Ascent of James DePreist," in *Symphony Magazine* (Portland, Oregon), January/February 1989, pp. 52–56.
26. From unidentified, undated French newspaper clipping about Anderson's concert in the Salle Pleyel, in MAP; see also review in *Le Figaro,* March 14, 1961.
27. Wire from Edward R. Morrow to Sol Hurok, November 30, 1961, in MAP.
28. Ibid.
29. From a State Department memorandum, June 5, 1956, of a conversation between Robert O. Burke, a State Department official, and Sol Hurok, who had asked

whether there would be any objections to MA visiting East Berlin and Budapest while on tour in Europe. In RG 59, decimal file 032 Anderson, Marian, National Archives at College Park, Maryland.

30. *New York Times,* November 23, 1961.
31. Memo from Sol Hurok to Edward R. Murrow, January 13, 1962, and MA to Sol Hurok, July 31, 1962, both in MAP.
32. Interviews with James DePreist and Dr. Robert Miller, Sept 22, 1998.
33. *Daily Telegraph* (Melbourne), May 22, 1962.
34. There are a number of Australian newspaper clippings in MAP, unidentified and undated, that provide an account of MA's Australian concerts.
35. *The Sunday Mail* (Brisbane), June 3, 1962.
36. From MA's calendar for June 6, 1962, in MAP.
37. Orpheus Fisher to MA, May 30, 1962, in MAP.
38. On MA's calendar for Monday, June 25, 1962, in MAP.
39. *New Zealand Listener,* July 13, 1962.
40. Quoted in Hynd article (see note 25), p. 20.
41. James DePreist to Ethel DePreist, August 22, 1962, in MAP.
42. *Philadelphia Daily News,* October 31, 1962.
43. See note 41.
44. Ibid.
45. Telegram from James DePreist to Ethel DePreist, August 31, 1962, in MAP.
46. See the letters from Edward R. Murrow to MA, November 6, 1962, and MA to Edward R. Murrow, [n.d.], both in MAP.
47. James DePreist to Ethel DePreist, Wednesday 5th [September 5, 1962], in MAP.
48. Quoted in Hynd article (see note 25), p. 21.
49. Ibid.
50. MA's request for a meeting is alluded to in a memorandum from Kenneth O'Donnell (special assistant to the president) to Jon Newman, April 28, 1962. Newman, apparently, had written to President Kennedy asking him to meet with Thornton Wilder. The request was not granted because, "To my knowledge, it is not standard procedure for the guest artist to meet with the President, but was only done once in the case of Marian Anderson. The reason for this being that Miss Anderson is a friend of the Attorney General's and Mrs. Ethel Kennedy's. This call was handled on more of a personal and social basis, rather than recognition of Miss Anderson as an artist." In White House Name Files, JFK Library.
51. See note 50 and the *New York Times,* March 23, 1962.
52. See articles in the *Dallas Times Herald,* February 3, 1963, the *American-Statesman* (Austin), February 10, 1963 and the *Houston Post,* February 24, 1963, on MA's tour of Texas cities.
53. On the history of desegregation during the 1960s in Texas, and especially Houston, see Cole, which I have found extremely useful.
54. C.T. Johnson to Edward R. Murrow, March 14, 1963, in MAP.
55. From San Antonio newspaper clipping, unidentified and undated (but with February 20, 1963 indicated in pencil), in MAP.
56. *Austin American,* February 24, 1963 and February 26, 1963.
57. See note 54.
58. Ibid.
59. See note 55.

Notes

60. *Danbury News-Times,* July 29, 1963, the *New York Times,* July 29, 1963.
61. On the history of the March, see Branch, chapter 22, and Gentile.
62. Telegram to MA from Roy Wilkins, August 21, 1963, in MAP.
63. Interview with Rochelle Horowitz, the transportation coordinator for the March.
64. See Gentile, pp. 216–217
65. Interview with Michael Sweeley (an assistant to Hurok and MA's traveling manager during the last part of her career), April 14, 1998.
66. *New York Times,* December 7, 1963.
67. Ibid.
68. Ibid.
69. From a press release from the Office of the White House Press Secretary, with texts of citations of those receiving the Medal of Freedom, in MAP.
70. See note 66.
71. Frederick L. Holborn to Mr. Alex Rose (president, United Hatters, Cap and Military Workers International Union), December 17, 1963. Mr. Rose had telegrammed his endorsement of the request by Hurok. In Marian Anderson Name File, Box 162, White House Central Files, LBJ Library.
72. *New York Times,* December 13, 1963.
73. In the end, MA's farewell tour was limited to the United States and Canada. Apparently concerts abroad were still being discussed as late as April, 1965. See, for example, *New York World-Telegram and Sun,* April 17, 1965.
74. *New York Times,* December 13, 1963.
75. On her calendar for January 10, 1965, MA wrote in: "Mother passed. Thirteenth service at 11 A.M. Tindley Temple. Burial at Eden. Veritable blizzard." In MAP.
76. Information about the Ruckers from interview with James Rudolph Lynch, March 1, 1994. James Rudolph Lynch is the son of Ada McDaniel Lynch and Abner Lynch, whose first wife was Elnora Rucker Lynch, Anna Anderson's sister.
77. Obituaries in the *New York Times,* January 10, 1964 and *Philadelphia Tribune,* January 14, 1964; also interview with John King, Queenie Anderson King's son (January 11, 1999), who attended the funeral.
78. The contract for the series of recordings is dated May 8, 1964; the "signed and fully executed copy" was sent to MA by Patricia Goerke, Joseph Habig's secretary, October 2, 1964. Both in MAP.
79. See the Discography for recording sessions during the 1950s devoted to the Brahms *Four Serious Songs.*
80. On background to and preparation for the recording, interviews with John Motley.
81. MA was nominated for a Grammy Award by The National Academy of Recording Arts and Sciences in 1965 in the category of Best Gospel or Other Religious Recording.
82. Interviews with John Motley, and interview with Jerry Parker, April 14, 1998.
83. Interviews with John Motley; the rehearsal tape with MA, Motley, and Hall Johnson, is in Ms. Coll. 204, Rare Book and Manuscript Library, University of Pennsylvania.
84. Quoted in Roger G. Hall, manager, Red Seal Artists and Repertoire, to Harold Maynard, October 15, 1964, in MAP.
85. Ibid.
86. Ibid.
87. Ibid.

88. *New York Times,* April 19, 1965. There are numerous newspaper clippings of reviews of MA's farewell tour in MAP. Some are not reviews of a particular concert at all, but tributes to MA's career. Others emphasize the technical decline of MA's voice. Most strike a middle ground and point out technical problems as well as praise MA's artistry.

89. In article on MA by Bernard Weintraub, the *New York Times,* April 19, 1965.

90. *New York Times,* April 18, 1965.

91. Article on MA by Jimmy Breslin, *New York Herald Tribune,* April 19, 1965.

92. Details about Alyse's final illness written by MA on her calendar, May 1965, in MAP.

93. James H. J. Tate to MA, May 26, 1965, in MAP.

94. Interview with James DePreist, August 27, 1997.

95. *Philadelphia Evening Bulletin,* June 29, 1965.

96. MA was invited to serve on the United States committee in the fall of 1964. The official invitation to MA to serve as a member of the United States delegation to the festival in Dakar is dated July 30, 1965 (David L. Osborn, deputy assistant secretary, United States Department of State, to MA), but her participation as a member of the delegation had been discussed as early as the preceding December. In the minutes of the meeting of the Unites States committee, December 11, 1964, the possibility that MA might sing at the Festival was being left for her to decide. Minutes and other documents in MAP.

97. *New York Times,* September 15, 1965.

98. Ibid.

99. MA to David L. Osborn, March 15, 1966, in MAP.

100. See note 89.

101. *New York Times,* July 3, 1965.

102. In Copland and Perlis, p. 342.

103. Ibid, p. 343.

104. On the compositional history of *A Lincoln Portrait,* I have found Copland and Perlis, and Butterworth useful.

105. I have had the benefit of a tape of MA's narration in a performance with Copland conducting the Philadelphia Orchestra at Saratoga, New York, August 5, 1976.

106. On MA's post-retirement years, multiple interviews with James DePreist, Max Brownstein (a friend of MA's and Orpheus Fisher's for many years), June Goodman, Sandra Grymes, Robert Bass, John Motley, and Jeanette DeFazio.

107. *New York Times,* January 23, 1967, and interviews with Robert Starer, January 12, 1999, and Abraham Kaplan, who directed the Starer work, January 16, 1999.

108. MA narrated *A Lincoln Portrait* with DePreist as conductor, April 27, 1969, with the Symphony of the New World, at New York's Lincoln Center, and February 7 and 8, 1975, with the Indianapolis Symphony Orchestra, in Indianapolis, Indiana; with Copland as conductor, on June 28, 1969, with the Zagreb Philharmonic Orchestra at the Temple University Music Festival, and on August 5, 1976, with the Philadelphia Orchestra at Saratoga, New York.

109. Interviews with Dr. Robert Miller.

110. Interview with Comfort Sparks, a second cousin to Billy King, October 15, 1993.

111. Billy King to MA, July 5, 1973, in MAP.

112. Billy King to MA, December 4, 1974, in MAP.

113. I am following Robinson's account of Hurok's last illness and funeral, pp. 458 ff.

114. Quoted in Robinson, p. 460.
115. Details of King's initial stroke and hospitalization on MA's calendar, in MAP; on the immediate aftermath of King's strokes, interviews with Dr. Robert Miller, and with Robert Bass, January 20, 1999.
116. Interviews with Dr. Robert Miller.
117. *New York Times,* February 28, 1977.
118. Ibid.
119. See, for example, my essay, "The Many Voices of Marian Anderson," included in the compact disc issued by VAI, in 1998, of "rare and unpublished recordings, 1936–1952."
120. *New York Times,* February 1, 1982.
121. *New York Times,* July 26, 1984.
122. Interviews with James Fischer.
123. Interview with Jeanette DeFazio, June 26, 1993.
124. Interviews with John Motley and with Robert Bass, January 20, 1999.
125. Interview with Robert Bass, January 20, 1999.
126. Interview with James DePreist, January 25, 1999.
127. *New York Times,* June 25, 1989, and interviews with June Goodman.
128. *New York Times,* August 15, 1989.
129. I am grateful to James DePreist and his daughter, Tracy DePreist, for providing me with a copy of the tape discussed here.
130. About Ethel DePreist's final illness, interview with James DePreist, January 25, 1999.
131. Interview with Dr. Robert Miller, September 22, 1998.
132. *New York Times,* May 8, 1991.
133. Interview with Dr. Micheline Williams, who was MA's physician in Danbury from June 1991 to July 1992, July 2, 1997.
134. In 1980, DePreist was appointed music director of the Oregon Symphony Orchestra, gradually settling in Portland, the home of the orchestra, with his second wife, Ginette, whom he met in Quebec during his tenure as music director of the Orchestre Symphonique de Québec, a position he held until 1983. DePreist's first marriage to Betty Childress, with whom he had two daughters, Tracy and Jennifer, ended in divorce in 1980.
135. On MA's last weeks in Danbury before flying to Portland, interview with Dr. Williams, June 30, 1997, and interviews with James DePreist and Jeanette DeFazio.
136. About MA during this period, interviews with Marian Anderson and James and Ginette DePreist, December 8 and 9, 1992, interviews with James and Ginette DePreist, June Goodman, and Sandra Grymes.
137. *Philadelphia Inquirer,* June 7, 1993; interviews with James DePreist and Ginette DePreist, and with Sandra Grymes, who kindly provided me with a copy of her speech.

REPERTORY

1. MA was the alto soloist in *Messiah* in April 1916, with the People's Choral Society of Philadelphia, and on January 24, 1921, at Union Baptist Church, in Philadelphia.
2. MA was the alto soloist in *Elijah* in April 1917, with the Elijah Club of Boston.
3. Sibelius's song, "Solitude," for voice and piano, with a Swedish text, is a reworking of "The Jewish Girl's Song," for strings and mezzo-soprano, the third movement

of the composer's *Belshazzar's Feast,* Op. 51 (written in 1906 and published the next year), his incidental music to Hjalmar Procopé's play. Silbelius intended the new work for MA, as a way of recognizing her devotion to his music, and dedicated it to her in 1935. "Solitude" remains unpublished; the manuscript is in MAP.

4. Anderson performed the role of Orfeo in a concert performance of Act II at the Caramoor Music Festival, Katonah, NY, June 21, 1958, with Alfred Wallenstein conducting the Caramoor Festival Orchestra.

5. In a few cases, the arrangement that Anderson used is unknown.

6. The folk song arranger is not indicated when the arranger is unknown or when it is not clear which arrangement Anderson used.

DISCOGRAPHY

1. All Artiphon recordings were made in Berlin during the second half of 1930, when Anderson was studying there on a Rosenwald Fellowship. For the original Artiphon recordings, matrix numbers and catalog numbers are identical. Successive catalog/matrix numbers refer to two sides of a single 78 RPM record. All of the original Artiphon recordings were then rereleased both on 78 RPM and on long-playing records. Some of these rereleases were made directly from the original masters (released by Ultraphone, Sonata, and Phonycord), and others are dubbings (released by Davis, Bellvox, Royale, and Allegro Royale). I am grateful to Ward Marston for this information.

2. According to Niels Høirup, the metal parts and documentation of Anderson's Soviet recordings apparently have not survived.

3. All pieces were recorded first with Franz Rupp, piano. Orchestra and chorus were dubbed in at a later date.

4. All pieces were recorded first with Franz Rupp, harpsichord. Orchestra was dubbed in at a later date.

5. Although most of Anderson's recordings were released within a year after their recording, this album of Schubert and Brahms lieder was not released until 1978, in conjunction with the 150th anniversary of Schubert's death and Anderson's being awarded the Congressional Medal of Freedom.

Index

Index

Anderson, Ethel May, *see* DePreist, Ethel
  May Anderson
Anderson, Grace (cousin), 23, 24, 26
Anderson, John Berkley (father), 21
  death of, 22–23
  fatherhood of, 18–19
  marriage of, 16–17
  religious life of, 17
Anderson, Marian:
  academic education of, 20, 25–26, 27,
    28, 33, 34, 35, 40–41, 45, 48–49, 90
  accompanists for, 37, 52–54, 88, 89, 97,
    103, 110, 121, 141–42, 157–58,
    168–69, 211, 223, 225–29, 269, 320
  on air travel, 140
  on arts commissions, 322
  Asian concert appearances of, 261,
    262–65, 282–88
  on audience responses, 99, 106, 126,
    146, 212, 263
  as aunt, 174–75, 301, 302, 307, 319
  author's conversations with, 7
  autobiography of, 268, 279–80
  birth of, 17, 90
  career dedication of, 21, 27, 52, 92, 122,
    153–54, 164, 219, 243, 247, 248, 318,
    321
  celebrity of, 15, 127, 215, 219, 281
  childhood of, 15, 17–28, 280, 335
  children enjoyed by, 329
  in church choir, 21, 26–27, 36–37, 324
  community support received by,
    27–28, 30, 33–34, 46, 54, 63, 85, 163,
    180
  conductors' relationships with, 143,
    148–49, 173, 177, 245, 246, 315–16,
    323
  contemporary composers' works sung
    by, 89
  contest won by, 61–63
  critical response to, 28, 33, 36–37, 38,
    39–40, 44–45, 54–55, 57, 60–61, 63,
    79–80, 85–86, 87, 90, 91–92, 98–99,
    105, 109, 113, 114, 123, 129, 133–34,
    136–37, 141, 161, 179, 224–25, 227,
    246, 251, 252, 254–55, 263, 267,
    274–75, 277–78, 294–95, 302, 304–5
  cultural exchange activities of, 281–89,
    298–300

D.A.R. refusal in booking of, 180,
    189–204, 207, 312, 316
  death of, 333–35
  dignity of, 180, 332
  discomfort over public controversy felt
    by, 155, 203–4, 210–11, 217
  documentary films on career of, 283,
    287, 331–32
  dogs and cats enjoyed by, 239–40, 305,
    333
  early musical talent of, 19–22
  earnings of, 22, 64–65, 84, 89, 105–7,
    110–11, 116, 120, 124–25, 129, 136,
    137, 168, 175, 176, 178–79, 225, 243,
    248, 272, 296, 310, 320, 322, 323
  European concerts performed by, 76,
    78–81, 96–99, 101, 103–6, 108,
    109–11, 113–14, 122–37, 139–41, 143,
    148–49, 154–57, 169–74, 248–52, 253,
    254–55, 302
  expressiveness of, 32, 54–55, 91–92,
    106, 109, 121, 246, 254–55, 278,
    294–95, 327
  family background of, 15–17, 37
  family responsibility felt by, 26, 34–35,
    66, 138–39, 241, 243, 253, 296, 310,
    330
  farewell concert tour of, 310, 312,
    316–18, 321, 322, 327
  first European sojourn of, 66–82
  in Germany, 90–91, 92–103, 108–11,
    114, 254–55, 302–3
  health problems of, 62, 161, 247–48,
    250, 276, 277, 304, 305, 320, 323, 326,
    328, 330, 332–34
  homes of, 18, 23, 25, 58–59, 221–22,
    223–24, 239–42, 243, 248, 253, 261,
    265, 290, 309, 322, 326, 328, 330, 333
  honors awarded to, 180, 194, 201, 204,
    216–17, 229, 251, 267, 288, 297, 311,
    326–27, 328, 331
  Lincoln Memorial concerts of, 207–15,
    217, 219, 259, 280, 309–10, 316, 322
  linguistic skills of, 32–33, 54, 70, 71, 86,
    94–95, 96, 99, 106, 110, 113, 120, 121,
    135, 141, 153, 174, 251, 277, 286
  managers for career of, 57–58, 65–66,
    83–84, 89, 96–97, 103, 104, 106, 107,
    110–11, 115, 117–18, 120–22, 126–27,

Index

Index

Index